CANADIAN
aDVERTISING →in action

SEVENTH EDITION

CANADIAN
aDVERTISING →in action

SEVENTH EDITION

Keith J. Tuckwell St. Lawrence College

PEARSON

Prentice
Hall

Toronto

Library and Archives Canada Cataloguing in Publication

Tuckwell, Keith J. (Keith John), 1950–
    Canadian advertising in action / Keith J. Tuckwell. — 7th ed.

Includes index.
ISBN 0-13-147769-2

1. Advertising—Textbooks. 2. Advertising—Canada—Textbooks. I. Title.

HF5823.T82 2006659.1   C2005-900642-0

0-13-147769-2

Vice-President, Editorial Director: Michael J. Young
Acquisitions Editor: Laura Paterson Forbes
Director of Marketing, Business and Economics: Bill Todd
Developmental Editor: Pam Voves
Production Editor: Cheryl Jackson
Copy Editor: Ann McInnis
Proofreader: Claudia Forgas
Production Coordinator: Patricia Ciardullo
Page Layout: Joan M. Wilson
Permissions Manager: Susan Wallace-Cox
Permissions Research: Lisa Brant
Art Director: Mary Opper
Cover Image: Sid Tabak

1 2 3 4 5   10 09 08 07 06

Printed and bound in the United States of America.

To Esther . . . and our children,
Marnie, Graham, and Gordon

Brief Contents

Contents

PART 5   COMMUNICATING THE MESSAGE: Integrated Media Choices   347

Preface

The sixth edition of *Canadian Advertising in Action* has been revised according to feedback from current and potential adopters. Input from reviewers was sought at various stages of development of this edition. Five key requests were made by reviewers. They wanted some new cases that would be suitable for preparing advertising plans or projects; they wanted to ensure there would be a good balance between theory and practice; they wanted an emphasis on strategic planning in order to show the relationship between advertising and other components of marketing communications; they wanted local market examples; and of course they wanted the most up-to-date material that is humanly possible presented in a clear, concise format.

Rest assured that I have done everything possible to satisfy these requests. Most competing advertising textbooks do not include cases. Cases were added to the sixth edition of *Canadian Advertising in Action*, but going into the seventh edition it was clear that new cases were needed. Three new cases involving well-known companies and brands are included. You will find them ideal if you use the traditional case study approach or if you require solutions in an advertising plan format.

A key strength of *Canadian Advertising in Action* has always been its balance between theory and practice. This edition retains such a balance and actually provides many new illustrations that demonstrate current advertising practices in action. In addition to the new examples embedded in paragraphs, 24 of the 30 vignettes are new, and four of the five "Practice of Advertising" features that appear at the end of each section of the book are new. Further, a complete marketing communications plan based on the planning models that appear in the textbook appears in Appendix II.

Strategic planning remains a key topic in this edition. Chapter 4: Strategic Planning Concepts for Marketing Communications presents an overview of planning and shows the relationships between objectives, strategies, and execution. Several planning models are included in the chapter. Chapter 5: Creative Planning Essentials and Chapter 7: Media Planning Essentials include strategic planning discussion and several planning models. These models will prove useful for the case studies. The marketing communications plan in Appendix II clearly shows planning relationships between media advertising and other forms of marketing communications.

Some local market examples have been included, but the master strategy regarding examples for this book remains national in scope. In order to please as many readers as possible, a good national example (about a company or brand that is known all across Canada) is always a good illustration. Such examples make it easier to draw relationships between theory and practice.

Once you look at this book you will realize it is the most up-to-date book on the subject. All current hot buttons are included: direct segmentation and customer relationship management, branded content, the latest on client–agency relations, media convergence, audience fragmentation, and advertising's relationship with other integrated marketing communications activities are just some examples. All statistical information has been updated and as indicated earlier an overwhelming majority of the vignettes and Practice of Advertising features are new.

Finally, this is the first time that *Canadian Advertising in Action* has been published in a four-colour format. The addition of full colour brings all of the advertisements and photographs to life and adds a completely new dimension to the book. I can now say that the book is clear, concise, and colourful, a potent combination that should have an impact on you and your students.

Kindly examine the content of this book carefully. I am confident you will find it to be a unique and contemporary presentation of advertising and marketing communications practice, and worthy of consideration for use in your classroom.

Critical Issues

This edition focuses on essential issues that are shaping contemporary communications practice. Among these issues are relationship marketing and the need for direct-response communications to help build relationships, the impact of technology and how it has changed the way that organizations communicate, and the rising demands among client organizations for integrated marketing communications programs to resolve their business problems.

These issues have an impact on communications planning. The seventh edition retains its primary focus on advertising and its strong emphasis on strategic planning. The goal was to present planning strategies in the context of how plans fit together. For example, what are the connections between marketing plans, marketing communications plans, and advertising plans? What are the links between advertising plans, sales promotion plans, and public relations plans? In keeping with past editions, all material is presented with a Canadian perspective. The concepts developed here are relevant to business, marketing, and advertising students, as well as to future managers who are embarking on a career in marketing communications.

Features

Input provided by reviewers has resulted in several key changes to the seventh edition. Among the more important and exciting changes and additions are the following:

- In the sections titled **The Practice of Advertising**, which follow each major section of the text, four new illustrations have been added. Each of these illustrations demonstrates the application of advertising or planning concepts relevant to that part of the text. For example, the illustration at the end of Part 1: Advertising and Marketing Communications Today speaks to the ever-changing dimensions of client–agency relationships and how they affect the development of ad campaigns. The illustration that follows Part 3: Creating the Message includes a creative brief, rough ads, and final ads for a public-service campaign dealing with issues associated with depression. The illustration at the end of Part 5: Communicating the Messages: Integrated Media Choices shows how other components of marketing communications are added to the mix in order to have an integrated plan to resolve marketing problems. Appendix II includes a marketing communications plan for the Schick Quattro razor. It neatly shows how various components of marketing communications are integrated together. Advertising plays a key role in this plan.

- Of the 30 **Advertising in Action** vignettes, 24 are new. Those that remain from the last edition have been updated. These vignettes reflect newsworthy stories about advertisers or agencies and embrace a cross-section of companies and industries. Among the featured organizations and brands are Rethink, Bud Light, Harvey's, Absolut, Lexus, Fairmont Hotels, Harley-Davidson, Volkswagen, Pepsi-Cola, General Motors, Ford, Kraft, Labatt, Axe, and Off!

- Advertising remains the primary focus of the book but, since companies are looking for "total communications solutions," how advertising interacts with the various components of the integrated marketing communications mix must also remain an important aspect of the book. The traditional mass media alternatives are discussed in Chapters 7 through 10. Integrated media alternatives are discussed in Chapters 11 through 14. The integrated media chapters include direct-response media, internet communications, sales promotion, public relations, and event marketing and sponsorships.

- The chapter that formerly discussed media research (Chapter 8 in the sixth edition) has been eliminated in this edition. Essential media research content has been retained but in a different manner. Appropriate research information has been added to each of the media chapters so it can be discussed at the appropriate time. This provides a more thorough presentation of material in the media chapters. Reviewers liked this approach!

- Three case studies are included in a separate section following the last chapter of the text. These cases will challenge the students to demonstrate their understanding of how to develop a plan to resolve a specific problem. At the discretion of the teacher, students can provide solutions in a case study format or in an advertising/marketing communications plan format. Each case has been designed so that a complete solution or part solution can be the expectation. For example, if the case calls for a complete advertising plan, but time does not permit that, then only a creative plan or media plan could be the expectation for the assignment. The cases involve well-known companies and brands that students will readily identify with: Holiday Inn, Molson Canadian, and Dairy Queen.

- One of my personal goals was to ensure clarity of presentation and better flow from chapter to chapter and section to section. Therefore, wherever possible, an attempt was made to streamline material. As indicated above, media research material was integrated into the various media chapters. Some integrated marketing communications content was streamlined with the blessing of the reviewers. For example, the topic of personal selling was eliminated since most adopters do not cover that topic in an advertising course. The former edition had six distinct parts, but with the elimination of the research chapter the new edition is divided into five distinct parts. Finally, some chapter material was re-sequenced where necessary. Without a doubt these changes have produced a better flow to the material. Reviewers were quite satisfied with these changes.

- The direction for this book clearly remains on communications process and strategic planning principles that should apply to any and all industries. The examples and plans that are included in this book embrace business-to-consumer situations, business-to-business situations, product situations, and service situations. The principles of advertising planning and marketing communications planning are adaptable to any business or marketing problem.

- Countless new visual illustrations have been added to give the text a fresh, new look. New ads from Gillette, Sony, Kraft, Ontario Dairy Farmers, Mitsubishi, State Farm Insurance, Infiniti, Porsche, Harvey's, Colgate-Palmolive, Procter & Gamble,

Shell Oil, Audi, General Mills, and many others aptly demonstrate important advertising and marketing communications concepts. Presented in colour for the first time, all of the figures are more visually striking!

The new edition retains important elements of the previous editions. The text is presented in a practical, student-oriented style and provides good balance between theory and practice. It is written from a Canadian perspective while considering the influences on communications from all over the world. All media information and data are Canadian—an important consideration for students who someday could be employed in the Canadian communications industry.

Pedagogy

- **Learning objectives** Each chapter starts with a list of learning objectives directly related to the key concepts presented in the chapter.

- **Advertisements, figures, charts, and graphs** Throughout each chapter, key concepts and applications are illustrated with strong visual material. Sample advertisements augment the Canadian perspective and demonstrate key aspects of communications strategy and execution.

- **Key terms** Key terms are highlighted within the text and defined in the glossary at the end of the text.

- **Weblinks** Helpful internet sites are identified throughout the text and are easily identifiable by the Weblinks icon shown here in the margin.

- **Review questions and discussion questions** Both sets of questions allow students to review material and apply concepts learned in the chapter.

- **Appendix I: Case Studies** A unique set of three case studies for some well-known companies and brands will challenge the students' abilities to develop appropriate plans and solutions for specific marketing problems.

- **Appendix II: Marketing Communications Plan—Schick Quattro** An extremely useful model for reviewing the format of marketing communications plans. It shows how the various models presented in the text are adapted to a real planning situation.

- **Appendix III: Advertising Regulations and Legislation** A useful reference tool for students.

- **Appendix IV: Glossary** A lexicon of key terms and definitions appears at the end of the textbook.

Supplements

A comprehensive supplements package accompanies the seventh edition.

INSTRUCTOR'S RESOURCE CD-ROM WITH TESTGEN, INSTRUCTOR'S RESOURCE MANUAL, POWERPOINT PRESENTATIONS, IMAGE GALLERY, AND TRANSPARENCY MASTERS

Pearson TestGen is a special computerized test item file that enables instructors to view and edit the existing questions, add questions, generate tests, and print the tests in a variety of formats. Powerful search and sort functions make it easy to locate questions and arrange them in any order desired. TestGen also enables instructors to administer tests on a local area network, have the tests graded electronically, and have the results prepared in electronic or printed reports. The Pearson TestGen is compatible with IBM or Macintosh systems.

The ***Instructor's Resource Manual*** contains Learning Objectives, Chapter Highlights, Additional Illustrations of Key Concepts, Answers to End-of-Chapter Questions, Discussions Questions, and a Video Guide.

PowerPoint Presentations include up to 25 slides per chapter with Weblinks and images and figures used in the text. They are also available for downloading from the Companion Website.

An ***Image Gallery*** provides selected full-colour ads published in the text.

Transparency Masters of selected PowerPoint slides illustrating key figures and concepts are also available electronically on the CD-ROM.

CBC/PEARSON EDUCATION CANADA VIDEO LIBRARY

A new video series that includes recent segments from *Undercurrents, Venture,* and *Marketplace,* all CBC shows, is available with the seventh edition. The video cases and details of how to include the videos in class discussion are included in the Instructor's Resource Manual. Each video portrays visually an important element of marketing communications discussed in the textbook. Each case is described briefly and a short series of questions is included to stimulate discussion.

COMPANION WEBSITE

The Companion Website at **www.pearsoned.ca/tuckwell** is a handy reference for students. The site includes practice questions, experiential exercises, Weblinks to related sites, CBC videos, and more. Visit the site for a learning experience!

TELEVISION BUREAU OF CANADA BESSIES

A reel of award-winning commercials from the Bessies Awards 2003 and 2004 is available to instructors using this edition of *Canadian Advertising in Action.*

The Television Bureau of Canada annually recognizes excellence in Canadian television advertising with the Bessies Awards program. The commercials that are included with *Canadian Advertising in Action* feature the best in recent advertising for Canadian companies. Please contact your Pearson Education Canada sales representative for details. These videos are subject to availability. For further information about The Bessies or to inquire about the Television Bureau of Canada's library of over 30 000 commercials, please contact The Television Bureau of Canada, 160 Bloor Street East, Suite 1005, Toronto, Ontario, M4W 1B9; telephone (416) 923-8813; or visit their website at www.tvb.ca.

Organization

This book is organized into five sections:

PART 1: ADVERTISING AND MARKETING COMMUNICATIONS TODAY

The initial section presents an overview of today's advertising industry and the organizations that comprise it. The relationships between agencies and clients are explored along with some of the controversial issues facing the industry. The relationship of advertising with other components of the integrated marketing communications mix is explored.

PART 2: MARKETING COMMUNICATIONS PLANNING

The initial chapter presents key topics related to consumer behaviour, market segmentation and identifying target markets, and market positioning strategies. Knowledge of these topics provides essential input for strategic planning. The second chapter examines the relationships between corporate planning, marketing planning, and advertising planning, illustrating how each type of plan contributes to achieving organizational objectives.

PART 3: CREATING THE MESSAGE

A detailed discussion of creative planning is presented in this section. The initial chapter focuses on the creative development process by examining the content of a creative brief. The roles of creative objectives and creative strategies are discussed in detail along with research techniques and creative evaluation processes. The next chapter focuses on creative execution and presents various alternatives regarding design, layout, and production of advertising.

PART 4: COMMUNICATING THE MESSAGE: PLANNING MESSAGE PLACEMENT IN TRADITIONAL MEDIA CHOICES

The initial chapter in this section (Chapter 7) is devoted to media planning and gives consideration to the development of media budgets, media objectives, strategies, and tactics. The next three chapters evaluate the use and effectiveness of the various traditional media alternatives. The strengths and weaknesses of television, radio, magazines, newspaper, and out-of-home media are presented along with media-buying practices for each medium.

PART 5: COMMUNICATING THE MESSAGE: INTEGRATED MEDIA CHOICES

This section focuses on media alternatives beyond the traditional mass media. In the quest to reach customers more efficiently, organizations are embracing direct-response advertising and internet communications. These topics are the focus of the first two chapters. The remaining two chapters introduce the role and effectiveness of other integrated marketing alternatives including sales promotion, public relations, and event marketing and sponsorships.

The format of chapters is consistent throughout the book. Chapters start with a list of learning objectives directly related to key concepts presented in the chapter. Chapter summaries are located at the end of each chapter, along with review questions and discussion questions, which serve two purposes: to reinforce key concepts presented in each chapter and to stimulate discussion on issues and problems confronting practitioners today. Following each major section of the text are detailed case illustrations entitled "The Practice of Advertising." Each case illustration reinforces key principles from the section of the text it represents. The Appendixes contain case studies, a sample marketing communications plan, a selection of laws and regulations that govern Canadian advertising, and a glossary that defines key terms.

Acknowledgments

Many organizations and individuals have contributed to the development of the seventh edition of this text. I would like to sincerely thank the following organizations for their special co-operation and contribution:

3M Canada
Audi
BBM Bureau of Measurement
Bell Canada
Bell Globemedia
BMW Canada
Bose Corporation
Cadbury Beverages Canada Inc.
Calloway Golf Company
Canadian Advertising Rates and Data
Canadian Business
Canadian Geographic
Cara Foods
Cardonline
CIBC
CKCO Television
Clorox Company of Canada Ltd.
Colgate-Palmolive Canada
Dairy Farmers of Ontario
Delta Hotels and Resorts
EPCOR
General Mills Inc.
IAB Canada
Infiniti
InterContinental Hotels Group
Jaguar Canada Inc.
Labatt Breweries of Canada
LensCrafters
LLunden & Associates Limited
Maytag Canada
Mazda Canada
Melitta Canada Inc.
Mitsubishi Canada
Molson Canada
NCH Promotional Services

Nestlé Canada
Nike Canada
Nissan Canada
Olympus America Inc.
Oral-B Laboratories
Pepperidge Farm
Pepsi-Cola Canada
Pfizer Canada Inc.
Porsche Cars North America Inc.
Procter & Gamble
Ralph Lauren
Remtulla Euro RSCG
Rethink
Rogers Media
Save.ca
Shell Oil
Sony
State Farm Life Insurance Company
Tetley Canada
The Bradford Exchange
The Gillette Company
The Globe and Mail
The Salvation Army
Tourism New Brunswick
Tourism Price Edward Island
Toyota Canada
Tropicana Products Inc.
Unilever Canada
United Way of Greater Toronto
Visa International
Volkswagen Canada Inc.
Welch Foods Inc.
Whitehall-Robins Inc.
Wrigley Canada
Yahoo! Inc.

For undertaking the task of reviewing the textbook at various stages of development, and for the time and energy they put into the review process, I would like to thank Brahm Canzer, CEGEP John Abbott College; Judith Nash, SAIT; Robert Stayner, Red River College; Janice M. Shearer, Mohawk College; Richard A. Appleby, Okanagan University College; Heather Stevens, George Brown College; Steve Janisse, St. Clair College; Barry Mills, College of the North Atlantic; Christina Clements, Humber College; and John Russell, Lethbridge Community College.

From Pearson Education Canada I would like to sincerely thank Laura Forbes, Acquisitions Editor; Pamela Voves, Developmental Editor; Cheryl Jackson, Production Editor; Patricia Ciardullo, Production Coordinator; Joan Wilson, Formatter; and Lisa Brant, Permissions Researcher.

I would sincerely like to thank David Sharpe, vice-president and creative director at Remtulla Euro RSCG, and his creative team for providing the story and illustrations for the Depression Awareness campaign. This campaign appears in the Practice of Advertising section for Part 3. I would also like to thank their client, the Centre for Addiction and Mental Health, for allowing the Depression Awareness campaign to be used in such an important way in the book.

Another book is complete and for supporting me along the way I must sincerely thank my family. To Marnie, Graham, and Gord. . . thank you! As always, a very special thank-you to my wife, Esther.

A Great Way to Learn and Instruct Online

The Pearson Education Canada Companion Website is easy to navigate and is organized to correspond to the chapters in this textbook. Whether you are a student in the classroom or a distance learner you will discover helpful resources for in-depth study and research that empower you in your quest for greater knowledge and maximize your potential for success in the course.

Companion
Website

[www.pearsoned.ca/tuckwell]

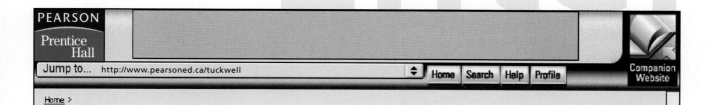

PEARSON
Prentice Hall

Jump to...   http://www.pearsoned.ca/tuckwell | Home | Search | Help | Profile |

Companion
Website

Home >

PH Companion Website

Canadian Advertising in Action, Seventh Edition, by Keith J. Tuckwell

Student Resources

The modules in this section provide students with tools for learning course material. These modules include:

- Learning Objectives
- Application Exercises
- Internet Exercises
- Web Destinations
- PowerPoint Presentations
- Quizzes
- Glossary

In the quiz modules students can send answers to the grader and receive instant feedback on their progress through the Results Reporter. Coaching comments and references to the textbook may be available to ensure that students take advantage of all available resources to enhance their learning experience.

General Resources

The modules in this section provide students with material for further research. These modules include:

- CBC video cases
- Video clips of the 2003 and 2004 Bessies
- Canadian advertising trends and strategies
- Career Resources

Instructor Resources

The modules in this section provide instructors with additional teaching tools. Downloadable PowerPoint Presentations, and an Instructor's Manual are just some of the materials that may be available in this section. Where appropriate, this section will be password protected.

Advertising and Marketing Communications Today

Part One focuses primarily on advertising and its role within the integrated marketing communications mix.

Chapter 1 examines the role of advertising and its relationship to other marketing and marketing communications activity, discussing the forms of advertising, the elements of integrated marketing communications, the factors conducive to investing in advertising, and the issues facing the advertising industry.

Chapter 2 introduces the key organizations comprising the marketing communications industry, describing the roles and responsibilities of client organizations and communications companies in planning and implementing marketing communications programs.

PART

1

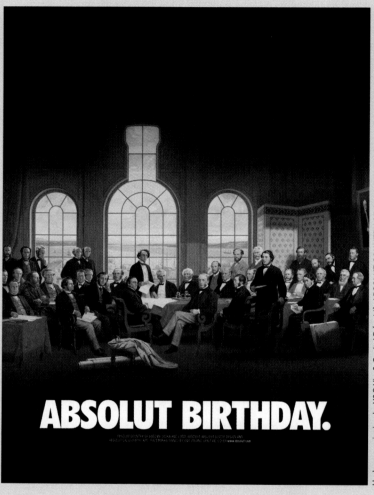

CHAPTER 1

1

Advertising in a Marketing Communications Environment

Learning Objectives

After studying this chapter, you will be able to

- Assess the role of advertising and its relationship to marketing and other elements of marketing communications

- Identify distinctions among the various forms of advertising

- Identify and define the seven components of integrated marketing communications

- Explain the conditions that are necessary for advertising to be effective

- Identify the basic social and business issues confronting the marketing communications industry in Canada

- Describe the role that laws and regulations play in guiding marketing communications programs in Canada

The Importance of Advertising

Advertising is undoubtedly the most visible form of marketing and marketing communications today, and it is an industry that is continuously evolving due to rapid changes in technology. It will continue to be an exciting and dynamic career field for students.

Advertising is all around us, and we as consumers underestimate the influence it has on us. Have you ever really thought about the influence that advertising has on you? Consciously or subconsciously, advertising messages reach us each day because we spend so much time with a wide variety of media. In fact, on a daily basis, television reaches 85 percent of adults 18 years plus. The corresponding figures for other primary media are radio 76 percent, newspapers 66 percent, internet 54 percent, and magazines 34 percent. Further, the time spent with each medium tells another tale about potential exposure to advertising messages. On an average day, adults 18 years plus spend 3 hours and 24 minutes watching television, 2 hours and 24 minutes listening to the radio, 36 minutes online, 30 minutes reading a newspaper, and 18 minutes reading a magazine.[1] Whether we realize it or not, these statistics indicate the media plays an important role in our lives.

Ads also appear on outdoor posters, shopping carts, in movie theatres, and in sports stadiums. The list could go on and on, but by now you can readily see the potential influence of advertising. Advertising in Canada is big business! In fact, in 2002 the amount spent on advertising was estimated to be C$10.9 billion, a 1.6 percent increase over 2001. Television advertising, with 24 percent of net advertising revenues ($2.6 billion), accounts for the largest portion of advertising among the mass media in Canada. Daily newspapers follow closely with $2.5 billion when all sources of ad revenue are considered (national, local, and classified).[2] For additional details refer to Figure 1.1.

The largest advertising categories in Canada include telecommunications companies and broadcasters, retail stores, and packaged goods companies. Among the largest advertisers are BCE, Procter & Gamble, General Motors, Hudson's Bay Company, and Philip Morris Companies.[3]

Advertising plays a major role in achieving brand and company business objectives by helping to attract new customers and by retaining current customers. The very nature of mass advertising as seen on television, heard on radio, or read in magazines and newspapers builds brand awareness and interest and helps form customers' opinions about a brand or company. The nature of contemporary advertising is now more

FIGURE
1.1

Net advertising revenues by medium (Canada—millions of dollars)

Medium	2002	% of Total
Television	2 612	23.9
Newspaper	2 510	22.9
Radio	1 094	10.0
General Magazines	558	5.1
Out-of-Home	273	2.6
Catalogue/Direct Mail	1 511	13.8
Internet	117	1.1
Yellow Pages	1 060	9.7
Miscellaneous	1 194	10.9
Total Net Advertising Revenue	10 929	100.0

Medium	Sub-Division	Dollars 2002
Television	National Spot	1 265
	Local Spot	377
	Network	444
	Specialty Channel	508
	Infomercial	18
Total Television		**2 612**
Newspaper	National	576
	Local	1 108
	Classified	826
Total Newspaper		**2 510**

Source: TVB Canada, **www.tvb.ca**.

targeted based on database management and interactive marketing techniques. New opportunities tend to be more micro-based (e.g., direct-response techniques and internet communications) than macro-based (mass advertising), but, nonetheless, the purpose is the same—to help a brand or company grow.

Ipsos-Reid
www.ipsos.ca

An Angus Reid (now Ipsos-Reid) research study helps substantiate the importance of advertising. The study shows that a positive corporate image is likely to help ensure a specific brand ends up on the consumer's list of products to consider. In fact, 85 percent of adults surveyed believed that a positive corporate image affects their purchase choices.[4] This data supports the maxim that "people do business with companies they like." Essentially, a company's advertising and other forms of marketing communications reflect everything that a company stands for and provides an umbrella from which all products and services carried by the company will benefit. It is designed to transform consumers' attitudes.

THE ROLE OF ADVERTISING

Advertising is best defined in terms of its purpose. It is a paid form of marketing communication through the media designed to influence the thought patterns and purchase behaviour of a target audience. While advertising can accomplish specific tasks, such as increasing the public's awareness of a product or service or inducing trial purchase through a promotion incentive, its primary role is to influence the behaviour of a target market (or target audience) in such a way that members of the target market view the product, service, or idea favourably. Once consumers develop a favourable attitude toward a specific service or brand of product, advertising attempts to motivate them to purchase that service or brand of product. Advertising can be both an informative and a persuasive form of communication.

Very often a company measures the success of an advertising campaign strictly in terms of product sales, but such measurement is very misleading. There is no direct relationship between advertising and sales. A major problem with linking sales directly to advertising is that other variables, not just advertising, influence the consumer's decision-making process. Advertising does not operate in a vacuum; it is simply one component of the process—a subset of marketing and a complementary element of other integrated marketing communications activity. Marketing decisions regarding matters such as product, price, distribution, sales promotion, personal selling, and event marketing, for example, all combine to have an effect on sales. Therefore, it is neither reasonable nor practical to isolate one variable, such as advertising, and hold it responsible when sales decline (or rise). All variables must be analyzed in relation to one another and to the specific goals that each was intended to achieve. Figure 1.2 reviews the position of advertising in the marketing and marketing communications process.

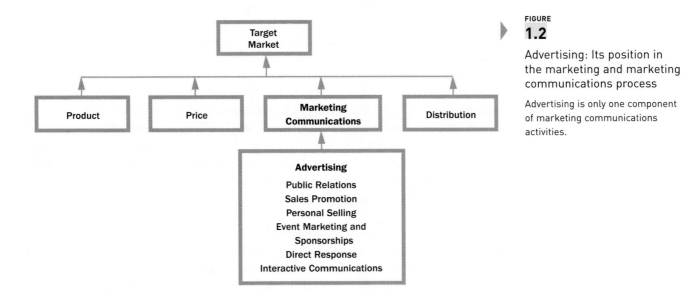

FIGURE
1.2

Advertising: Its position in the marketing and marketing communications process

Advertising is only one component of marketing communications activities.

ADVERTISING AND INTEGRATED MARKETING COMMUNICATIONS

The nature of communications generally, and advertising specifically, has changed considerably in the past decade. Previously, advertising was viewed as a separate entity and companies called upon advertising agencies to develop advertising campaigns that would help build brands. Over time, however, the marketplace has changed dramatically and organizations now evaluate and employ other forms of marketing communications along with advertising to achieve their business objectives.

Today, more and more companies are approaching communications as a complete package, and that package is referred to as integrated marketing communications. **Integrated marketing communications (IMC)** involves the coordination of all forms of marketing communications into a unified program that maximizes the impact on consumers and other types of customers. It embraces many unique yet complementary forms of communication: media advertising (the primary focus of this textbook), direct-response communications, online interactive communications, sales promotions, public relations, event marketing and sponsorships, and personal selling. The goal of integrated marketing communications is to coordinate the various components of the marketing communications mix so that all of the components work together to achieve common objectives.

The thrust toward integrated marketing communications has forced traditional advertising agencies to rethink their roles and relationships with clients. Whereas once they were solely responsible for advertising, they are now responsible for providing input into any or all aspects of the marketing communications mix. Many traditional advertising agencies have been transformed into marketing communications companies.

Because of advancing technology, companies now perceive communications differently. The traditional mass communications alternatives (television, radio, magazines, newspapers, outdoor advertising) still play a key role, but technological change has introduced more specialized media into the mix. A variety of direct-response techniques (direct-response television, direct mail, telemarketing) and the internet are now part of the total package. Their presence means that a more coordinated and consistent effort is required from marketing communications planners.

The first steps in developing an advertising and communications program have not changed. It all starts with a thorough analysis of the target market, market conditions, and competitors. With regard to the target market, essential information is gathered on media consumption patterns, the relevance of a company's message to customers, and when customers are most receptive to messages. The information is accumulated in a database that includes demographic and psychographic information. Armed with such information, the organization can reach customers effectively and efficiently.

Prior to examining advertising in detail, let's briefly explain the other components of the marketing communications mix. The marketing communications mix comprises seven distinct elements: advertising, public relations, sales promotion, personal selling, event marketing and sponsorships, direct-response communications, and interactive communications (see Figure 1.3).

PUBLIC RELATIONS **Public relations** includes a variety of activities that an organization undertakes to influence the attitudes, opinions, and behaviours of interest groups toward an organization. For example, a company might issue press releases announcing the launch of a new product. The release would include all of the virtues of the product and the way it will be advertised. The objective is to generate free publicity through the media (e.g., stories about the product will appear on newscasts or in newspapers). These positive news reports make the product or company credible in the eyes of the public.

SALES PROMOTION **Sales promotion** is an activity that encourages an immediate response from consumers and distributors of a product or service. On the consumer side, strategies such as coupons, cash refunds, and contests are offered by manufacturers to encourage buying activity. Among distributors, a company will offer a variety of price discounts to encourage volume buying or seasonal buying, or to encourage

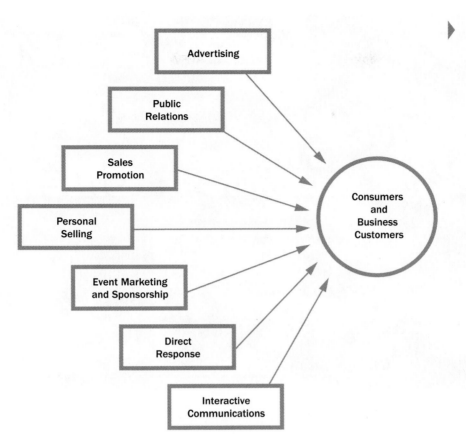

FIGURE
1.3
The concept of integrated marketing communications

"A chain is only as strong as its weakest link." This famous expression applies to integrated marketing communication. Integrated marketing communications programs are successful when all components of the communications mix are complementary to each other. Regardless of the medium used or activity undertaken the customer must receive a unified message.

merchandising activity in retail stores. Such strategies are frequently implemented in conjunction with an advertising campaign. Refer to Figure 1.4 for an illustration.

PERSONAL SELLING **Personal selling** is a personalized form of communication that involves a seller presenting the features and benefits of a product or service to a buyer for the purpose of making a sale. To illustrate the importance of personal selling, consider how a new product such as Crest Night Effects Whitener or the Crest SpinBrush Pro arrives on the shelf at your local Shoppers Drug Mart. The Procter & Gamble sales representative would have to present the merits of these brands to a buyer at Shoppers' head office. If the buyer doesn't accept the offer that is put forth (e.g., if the quality of the sales promotion and price discounts were unacceptable), these products will not be available in Shoppers Drug Mart. The job of personal selling is to secure widespread distribution of the product, one retail account at a time.

EVENT MARKETING AND SPONSORSHIP **Event marketing and sponsorship**—planning, organizing, and marketing an event or simply providing sponsorship money to support an event—is a growth area of marketing communications. Similar to public relations, participation in a major event (e.g., the Bell Canadian Open Golf Championship) often yields favourable news coverage and publicity for the sponsor. While the direct benefits of event participation are difficult to measure, potential customers may feel better about the sponsor knowing that it is participating in something the customer is interested in. Molson's association with rock music through its "Molson Canadian Rocks" concert series ultimately influences beer purchases in one way or another.

Molson
www.molson.com

FIGURE
1.4

Gillette combines a coupon offer and contest in one promotion to encourage immediate purchase

DIRECT-RESPONSE COMMUNICATIONS **Direct-response communications** is a form of advertising where messages are delivered directly to potential customers on an individual basis. Direct mail is the most common means of delivering these messages, but other forms of communication such as direct-response television, direct-response print, and telemarketing now play a more significant role. The advent of **database marketing** provides a means of reaching customers directly. Since the activity is immediate and one-on-one, as opposed to mass advertising on television, marketing and advertising organizations know immediately how effective their direct-response strategies are.

ONLINE INTERACTIVE COMMUNICATIONS The future of **online interactive communications** is the future of marketing. A bold statement, but it is very true. Given the rapid pace of advancing communications technology, the internet has the potential to become the biggest single-source generator of revenues among all direct-response communications alternatives. The internet is direct, and it is interactive. Database management techniques and an emphasis on customer relationship management programs are making marketers and advertisers move toward "information-driven communications." Though the development of the internet as a communications medium is still in the infancy stage, there is little doubt that the internet will be vital to the success of a company from now on. In terms of advertising, organizations are pursuing opportunities through banner advertising, sponsorship of websites of interest to specific target audiences, rich media messages (TV-style ads), and permission-based email.

For more insight into the role of advertising and how it works with other elements of marketing communications, see the Advertising in Action vignette **Yes Folks, Advertising (Good Advertising) Really Does Work**.

The Forms of Advertising

Advertising can be divided into two broad categories: consumer advertising and business-to-business advertising. Advertising can also be described as being product-oriented and promotional-oriented.

CONSUMER ADVERTISING

Consumer advertising refers to persuasive communications designed to elicit a purchase response from consumers. Advertising directed at consumers is subdivided into four types: national advertising, retail advertising, end-product advertising, direct-response advertising, and advocacy advertising.

National advertising is the advertising of a trademarked product or service wherever that product or service is available. In spite of its name, national advertising is non-geographic. National advertising messages communicate a brand name, the benefits offered, and the availability of the product or service. Advertising messages for branded products such as Colgate toothpaste, Rogers AT&T cellular communications, Honda automobiles, and Michelin tires are all classified as national advertising.

Rogers
www.rogers.com

As the name implies, **retail advertising** is the advertising used by a retail store to communicate store image, store sales, and the like. Usually, the retailer advertises the lines of merchandise it carries, which include generic brands, private-label brands, and national brands. The framework of retail advertising can thus be expanded to include the re-advertising of national brands. Retail advertising includes advertising by large department stores such as The Bay, Wal-Mart, and Zellers, as well as specialty chain stores such as The Gap, Tip Top, Old Navy, Bluenotes, and Sportchek.

End-product advertising is the advertising done by a firm that makes part of a finished product. Advertising of this nature encourages consumers to look for this particular component when buying a final product. In the computer market, Intel was very successful with its "Intel Inside" campaign. In this campaign, consumers were encouraged to look for the Intel chip—they were told through advertising that it was the most powerful chip available.

Intel Corporation
www.intel.com

Direct-response advertising involves advertising directly to consumers and bypassing traditional channels of distribution (wholesalers and retailers) in the delivery of the product. Such advertising includes infomercials that are shown on television (e.g., CD and DVD offers for music and movies), direct-mail offers, and email advertising on the internet. Ads such as these include information on how customers can order goods and services directly.

Advocacy advertising is any public communication paid for by an identified sponsor that presents information or a point of view on a publicly recognized, controversial issue. The purpose of advocacy advertising is to influence public opinion. The United Way's campaign about helping the homeless dramatically depicts the nature of the problem while encouraging the public to find a solution. See Figure 1.5 for an illustration.

United Way
www.unitedway.ca

BUSINESS-TO-BUSINESS ADVERTISING

Business-to-business advertising refers to advertising directed by business and industry at business and industry. Advertising to professional groups (such as doctors, lawyers, and accountants) is an example of this form of advertising. The major types of business-to-business advertising are trade advertising, industrial advertising, service-industry advertising, and corporate advertising.

FIGURE
1.5

An example of advocacy
advertising

When you give to United Way, you're helping homeless people overcome the obstacles in their lives by providing things like shelter, hot meals and training programs. With United Way-funded agencies helping so many in our community, making a difference is easier than you think. Visit www.unitedway.ca

WITHOUT YOU, THERE WOULD BE NO WAY

United Way

Trade advertising is advertising done by manufacturers, and it is directed at channel members. The objective of trade advertising is to communicate a convincing message that will encourage intermediaries to carry and resell the product. Messages usually stress that the product is a success (thereby suggesting that other intermediaries have accepted the product), that the manufacturer will offer promotions to help resell the product, and that profit margins are based on average selling prices. This type of advertising reaches customers by such industry-related publications as *Canadian Grocer*, *Hardware Merchandising*, and *Food in Canada*.

Industrial advertising is advertising by industrial suppliers to industrial buyers. The decision whether to purchase capital equipment, accessory equipment, fabricated parts, and raw materials may be influenced most by personal selling. However, advertising in industrial publications or direct-response advertising can stimulate initial awareness of a product and develop sales leads. Rogers Media provides numerous publications for industrial advertisers in various specialized industries (e.g., *Heavy Construction News*, *Canadian Packaging*, *Materials Management and Distribution*, and *Design Engineering*).

Yes Folks, Advertising (Good Advertising) Really Does Work

The success of an advertising campaign is, rightly or wrongly, measured by results: results such as sales and market-share growth, numbers of customers, and repeat business generated by existing customers. Labatt Breweries of Canada found success when it brought the Bud Light Institute into the hearts and minds of male beer drinkers. The Institute is dedicated to providing ingenious solutions to everyday chores and responsibilities so that men (25 to 35 years old) can spend more time with their buddies more often.

The Bud Light campaign demonstrates a good lesson in advertising. If something is working well, don't dare change it. Prior to accepting the Bud Light Institute campaign, Labatt had rejected about 20 different ideas, but when they saw the Institute concept they instantly knew it was a go! It's strange, and strangely reassuring, to hear that beer commercials get made for exactly the reasons you think they get made: some guys like the idea. In beer marketing there's a lot at stake so the usual routine is to test ads for brand recall, empathy, bonding, and persuasion. But research data is one thing and gut instinct is another. "If you have something that is right, you let it rip!"

The Institute campaign has run for four years and along the way there have been some interesting and offbeat advertisements and commercials. The most recent versions involve greeting cards for all kinds of excuse occasions (for those who wish to buy, they are available in Music World stores across Canada). One television spot shows an apologetic man returning from a golf match to be greeted by his formally dressed wife. He presents her with a card that says, "Sorry I missed your cousin's wedding." The couple embraces and all is forgiven.

An earlier television execution showed a Viking invasion ruining a family reunion. Of course it was all a plot of the husband who didn't want to attend. Another commercial shows a guy skipping out for an evening while his significant other is engrossed in the 24-hour figure skating channel. He is so thankful for such a channel. While such ads seem very stereotypical they have been very effective with the target audience. All commercials end with that familiar phrase "Now that calls for a Bud Light."

In related communications activities Bud Light distributed tens of thousands of its Ulterior Emotions CD, a spoof album full of hits like "You're Beautiful (Can I Go Up North This Weekend?)." There were also some media stunts along the way. Bud Light erected joke billboards at construction sites around Toronto announcing, "Coming soon! The Bud Light Institute." The website now plays a key role in extending and personalizing the campaign. A popular destination at the site (**www.budlightinstitute.ca**) is the Excuse Centre. Here men can learn fresh approaches for old excuses under categories such as "Get Out of the House" and "Get Out of the Doghouse."

Has it worked? Overwhelmingly yes! In the first year of the campaign, market share in Ontario increased 33 percent, the following year 44 percent. In the past three years, the brand has seen overall growth of 65 percent and there are no signs of the campaign dying down. Truly good advertising has helped grow the light beer segment!

Source: Adapted from Sara Minogue, "Institutional Savvy," *Strategy*, July 28, 2003, pp. 17, 25 and **www.budlightinstitute.com**.

Service-industry advertising raises awareness and communicates detailed information about products and services designed for companies in the service industry. Drug manufacturers, for example, address the medical profession through a number of publications including *The Medical Post* and *Canadian Family Physician*. The legal profession is reached through *Canadian Lawyer* and *The Lawyer's Weekly*. Other professions have similar publications.

Corporate advertising focuses on the broader services of a company and is designed to convey a favourable impression of the company among its various publics (e.g., shareholders, consumers, suppliers, and business customers). It may do so by showing the strength of the people employed by the firm or the resources a firm allocates to solving customers' problems, or it may simply promote goodwill. The ad for Pfizer in Figure 1.6 is an example of a corporate message. Very often the organization's public relations department is responsible for this type of advertising.

An example of corporate advertising

*I*magine the medical miracles these eyes will see

We're Pfizer.
We're developing the cures of the future.
We put heart and soul into our search for
the wonder drugs of the 21st century.
It is our greatest hope that someday soon,
the only place you'll find cancer
will be on a history exam,
or that Alzheimer's, the disease that
robs memories, will itself fade into the past.
At Pfizer, we look to the future
with the knowledge that the only thing
that is incurable is our passion.

©1999, Pfizer Canada Inc.
Kirkland, Quebec H9J 2M5

Canada's Research-Based
Pharmaceutical Companies

Pfizer
Life is our life's work

www.pfizer.ca

Courtesy: Pfizer Canada Inc.

PRODUCT AND PROMOTIONAL ADVERTISING

Product advertising is advertising that informs customers of the benefits of a particular brand. Most of the examples described in the previous section are product advertising. Essentially, an advertiser communicates a feature, an attribute, and a benefit. A *feature* is something about a product (e.g., the Teflon coating on a frying pan); an *attribute* is the functional result of the feature (e.g., the pan is easy to clean); and the *benefit* clarifies how it is important to the consumer (e.g., using the new pan will give them time to spend on other things). Features, attributes, and benefits are communicated in functional or emotional terms and consumers respond to them. See Figure 1.7 for an illustration.

**FIGURE
1.7**

A product-oriented advertisement stressing features and benefits. A strong visual reinforces the message.

Courtesy: Sony of Canada Ltd.

Promotional advertising is designed to accomplish a single task—to get consumers to take action immediately. Generally, promotional advertising communicates a distinct reason why buying now is better than buying later. Automobile manufacturers, for example, are known to advertise rebate programs and low-cost financing programs. Packaged-goods companies such as Kraft and Gillette use coupons, contests, and other incentives to encourage action by consumers (refer back to Figure 1.4 for an example).

Gillette
www.gillette.com

Conditions Necessary for Using Advertising Effectively

For advertising and other forms of marketing communications to be effective, certain conditions must be favourable. Managers and planners must analyze certain factors and judge whether the investment in advertising will contribute to the achievement of marketing objectives. Advertising is one of the most expensive forms of marketing communications, and it is not always the right solution. Sometimes it is better to go in a different direction with communications strategies, for example, in directions that are less costly. A number of conditions are evaluated prior to making the decision to advertise.

MARKET AND PRODUCT DEMAND

Assuming that customer needs have been properly identified, the first task of advertising is to stimulate demand for the product or product category. The introduction of a new product concept is quite challenging, since the marketing communications must first make customers recognize a need, then stimulate a purchase response based on that recognition.

If a market and product already exist, the manager will analyze the primary demand trends and selective demand trends. **Primary demand** refers to demand for the product category (product class). For example, the demand for automobile tires must be positive if brands within this category (e.g., Goodyear, Firestone, or Michelin) are to be advertised successfully. Positive demand obviously provides the best economic environment in which to advertise. Conversely, if primary demand is declining, investment in advertising should be reduced or even withdrawn.

Wine Council of Ontario
www.wineroute.com

The situation is somewhat more complex in mature markets. To illustrate, the Wine Council of Ontario (WCO), a trade group that represents 40 Ontario wineries, launched a $20 million ad campaign in 2002 to stimulate sales of Ontario wines. In rationalizing the campaign, which involved an equal financial contribution from the Ontario government and the wineries, Kevin Nullmeyer, vice-president of marketing with the WCO, says, "In every other region of the world, the home player would have between 75 percent and 80 percent of the market. In Ontario, local wines only have 40 percent." The goal of the campaign is to raise market share from 40 percent to 50 percent by 2007. In Ontario the wine industry sees a great opportunity, but they have to overcome consumers' perceptions regarding quality. In research conducted by the WCO, people would say, "I know Ontario makes good wine but I'm not sure I would buy it."[5]

Selective demand refers to demand for a specific product (brand) within a product category. When selective demand is positive, growing from year to year, the decision to advertise is relatively simple. Based on the wine example above, individual wineries in Ontario would advertise a selection of their more popular brands in order to create awareness and trial purchases. The wineries use the primary demand campaign as leverage to support their own brand campaigns. At some point, a company must eventually decide when it will reduce or eliminate advertising support. Does a firm support brands with profit potential, or does it attempt to protect brands for which selective demand has declined? An examination of the influence of the product life cycle on advertising activity will help to resolve this question.

PRODUCT LIFE CYCLE

The stage of a brand in its product life cycle also influences decisions on advertising. A **product life cycle** is defined as the movement of a product through a series of four stages, from its introduction to its eventual withdrawal from the market. Life cycle theory posits that a product starts out slowly in the introduction stage, experiences rapid sales increases in the growth stage, experiences marginal growth or decline each year as it matures, then enters the decline stage where sales drop off at a much faster rate each year. The conditions and characteristics that are present in each stage of the life cycle are quite different. Therefore, different strategies and tactics are used in each stage.

The critical stages for advertising are the introduction and growth stages. The **introduction stage** is a period of slow sales growth as a new product idea is introduced to the market. Losses are frequently incurred due to the high initial investment required to launch a product.

Advertising objectives focus on the creation of primary demand if it is a new product category, and creating awareness for the new brand name and package in the consumer's mind. Since trial purchase is another objective, an introductory campaign will likely include promotion incentives (e.g., the distribution of coupons or trial-size samples). Strategists believe that if these objectives are to be accomplished, the product must enter the market with a sizeable budget and powerful message—do it right the first time out. If so, a multimedia campaign is implemented—at very high cost. This short-term commitment to advertising enables the brand to grow before new and competing innovations occur. Profits will be generated at a later stage of the life cycle.

The product's **growth stage** is the period of rapid consumer acceptance. It is also a period in which profits rise significantly. Several competitive brands will enter the market to get a piece of the action, which means that the original product must continue to invest aggressively in advertising to build market share. Competition is intense. A company's commitment to advertising must continue as its product strives for growth or defends its position in the marketplace. Deciding how much to spend is often difficult. It is possible that competitors with less market share but with ambitious growth plans may force another company to spend more on marketing communications than it desires to spend.

In the growth stage, marketing communications performs a dual role. There is still ample opportunity to attract new users, so creating awareness remains a priority; and, since competitors have entered the market, objectives must also focus on brand preference. A brand must clearly distinguish itself from competing brands (e.g., give customers a valid reason why they should buy their brand over another brand). By now, the target market is more clearly defined and understood, so there is an opportunity to select media that will reach the target audience more efficiently.

In summary, the combination of awareness and preference objectives and competitive spending levels will tend to increase the size of a budget. The fact that more is known about the target market can provide more efficient use of media and lower advertising costs. Generally speaking, however, the desire to maintain high levels of growth requires a significant investment in marketing communications. Unlike the introduction stage however, sales are rising so rapidly that profits materialize.

The **mature stage** is characterized by a slowdown in sales growth (marginal growth and marginal decline); the product has been accepted by most of its potential buyers. Profits stabilize and begin to decline because of the expenses incurred in defending the brand's market-share position.

When a product is in the mature stage, advertising tends to give way to other forms of marketing communications. Assuming that new strategies are not implemented to rejuvenate the product, funds formerly allocated to advertising the product may be shifted into other areas such as sales promotion and price discounting. In the mature stage, the objective is to conserve money rather than spend it. There are exceptions to every rule, however, since this is a period where the only way to grow is to steal business from the competitor(s). In Canada's soft-drink market, for example, sales are relatively flat from year to year. Consumers are switching to other beverage alternatives such as juices and bottled waters. Both Coca-Cola and Pepsi are leading brands with similar spending patterns in advertising. If one company were to reduce its investment, what might happen to its market share? With so much at risk, it is the actions of the competition that will determine how much is spent on advertising.

In maturity, a brand faces a choice. Does it adopt a defensive strategy and try to maintain market share, or does it adopt an offensive strategy and try to rejuvenate the brand? Should a defensive strategy be adopted, budgets will be established at a level that will maintain the brand's market-share position. Since maintenance of current customers is a priority, there is often greater spending on sales promotion activity than on media advertising. Promotions that encourage brand loyalty are very popular at this stage (e.g., cash refunds, contests, and premium offers) since they are designed to encourage repeat purchases and multiple purchases.

Organizations that opt to rejuvenate a brand adopt a more aggressive attitude. Strategies will be implemented to extend the product life cycle. Strategic options available include modifying or improving the product, presenting new uses for the product (and thereby increasing frequency of use), or attracting new user segments to the product. Regardless of the strategic option selected, advertising will play a key role in communicating the new direction. In the coffee market, brands such as Maxwell House and Folgers focus on package improvements to breathe new life into their mature products. Maxwell House offers the EZ-Open Fresh Seal—their sealing process keeps unwanted air out so the product is fresher than ever before! Folgers counters with the Aroma Seal, a plastic lid that keeps coffee fresh when the product is stored. See Figure 1.8 for an illustration.

DECLINE STAGE The **decline stage** occurs when sales begin to drop rapidly and profits erode. Products become obsolete as many consumers shift to more innovative products entering the market. Price cuts are a common marketing strategy at this stage, as competing brands attempt to protect their share in a declining market.

Objectives involve planning and implementing withdrawal from the market, because the costs of maintaining a product in decline are quite high. General Motors recently withdrew the Pontiac Aztek from the market after four futile years of trying to convince enough buyers to take a chance and endure the stares and taunts of fellow drivers. The radically styled, not-quite-car, not-quite-truck "crossover utility vehicle" that featured a built-in cooler and fold-out tent was heavily advertised during its life cycle but never quite caught on with the public.[6]

In the decline stage there is little sense in providing advertising support. The budget should be cut so that profit is maximized and funds are generated that can be invested in new products or growth products with greater profit potential.

FIGURE
1.8

An ad campaign designed to rejuvenate a mature product: Folgers coffee

COMPETITIVE ADVANTAGE

Prior to investing in marketing communications, a brand must offer something unique and desirable to a market segment—a competitive advantage. A distinctive message must be planted in the consumer's mind.

The most common way to show advantage is to **demonstrate the superiority** of a given product by comparing it to a similar product or by simply making significant claims about what the product will do. The claims a product makes about itself must be meaningful to consumers. Consider the case of Alpine gum, a competitor of Hall's lozenges in the cold/cough remedy market. Hall's controls the market with a 75 percent share but Alpine has a significant benefit over the competition: its medicinal properties last 20 minutes, compared to only seven or eight minutes for a lozenge. Launching Alpine into a well-entrenched category in a new format was challenging. Initial ads used the words, "Menthex [an ingredient] won't cure the common cold, but it can knock the snot out of a sore throat." Taglines such as "chew your cold out" and "chew your cough

Alpine Gum
www.wrigley.com/wrigley/product/
products_alpine.asp

out" were also used. A print ad showed a piece of gum in a teaspoon with the statement "cool relief for sore throats." Hall's' share is now down to 66 percent, indicating the Alpine campaign has had an impact—the message was meaningful![7] Refer to Figure 1.9 for an illustration.

Another way of showing advantage is to communicate **product innovation**—that the product is on the cutting edge of technology or research and development. Innovation is extremely important in the oral care product category. When Procter & Gamble launched Crest White Strips it stimulated a teeth-whitening craze in North America. Consumers started searching for economically priced alternatives for having whiter teeth. Colgate-Palmolive quickly followed with a brand called Simply White, but it involved a completely different method of application. Not to be outdone on the innovation side of things, Pfizer/Adams launched Trident White, a gum product that extends the brand's basic healthy teeth benefit. Unlike competitors' gums that lack taste, Trident delivers whitening benefits along with a cool, fresh taste.[8]

A third opportunity to demonstrate advantage while differentiating one brand from another is to stress **hidden qualities**. A hidden quality refers to some unique feature that benefits consumers but that they cannot see, feel, or taste. The Trident gum example quoted above also meets the hidden-quality criteria. The chewing of the gum releases

Procter & Gamble
www.pg.com

FIGURE 1.9

Meaningful product claims have an impact on consumers' buying intentions

Courtesy: William Wrigley Jr. Company

the active ingredient that helps whiten a person's teeth. A natural product like milk offers all kinds of health benefits to consumers. In short, it makes things stronger—your bones, your teeth, and so on. Such a generic product is difficult to advertise, but milk producers across Canada do an excellent job of communicating the hidden qualities of milk. See Figure 1.10 for an illustration.

A more recent phenomenon in advertising is the progressive use of **lifestyle associations** to differentiate among products. Automobile manufacturers tend to be experts at targeting lifestyle aspirations by appealing to the emotional side of the purchase decision. Mitsubishi recently launched a campaign that resonated with young Canadian adults. Their ads show young buyers in situations they are most likely to be seen in: hanging out with their friends, listening to their music, and having a sense of community with themselves and, de facto, the car they drive in. Everyone is hip and having a blast as they drive through urban streets and well-lit tunnels. The commercials end with the phrase "Canada, meet Mitsubishi." And then, "Are you in?" The Mitsubishi marketing strategy is "spirited cars for

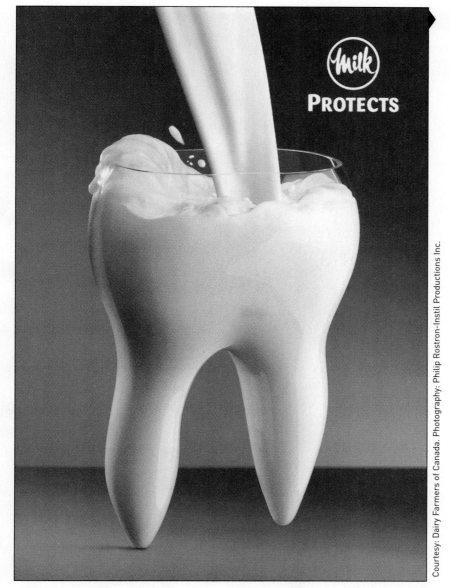

FIGURE 1.10

A strong visual image aptly communicates a hidden quality of milk

Courtesy: Dairy Farmers of Canada. Photography: Philip Rostron-Instil Productions Inc.

spirited people." The advertising makes an emotional connection with potential customers and shows how the car has a role in one's life.[9] Refer to Figure 1.11 for an illustration.

COMPETITIVE ENVIRONMENT

Keeping track of what competitors are doing and how much they are investing in marketing communications is important. If, for example, a brand finds itself in a product category where competitors invest heavily in advertising (e.g., when a toothpaste brand like Arm & Hammer has to compete with Colgate and Crest), that brand may want to evaluate activities that are less costly. The size of a brand in terms of market share and the financial resources that are available based on market share would suggest that less expensive alternatives, such as sales promotion or price discounting, would make more sense. Brand leaders tend to protect their turf by maintaining significant advertising budgets.

Conversely, if a company does decide to pursue advertising, it must do so at competitive levels if it is going to penetrate the clutter of messages issued by all brands in the

FIGURE
1.11

An advertising campaign that targets the lifestyle aspirations of young Canadians

marketplace. To quote Ronald Zarrella, North American marketing chief at General Motors Corporation, "In our business if you aren't spending at least $30 million [U.S.] on each brand every year, you are below sustaining levels of support. You are wasting money." To proceed on this basis requires a long-term commitment to advertising.[10]

PRODUCT QUALITY

Simply stated, a product must live up to the promise advertising makes. Advertising messages focus on the unique selling points of the product and the benefits the customer will derive from them. Getting the customer to try a product once, at great expense, only to be disappointed in the quality or whatever the primary benefit was to be (e.g., performance or durability) is a waste of money. It is imperative that the brand meet consumer expectations (deliver as promised) so that repeat purchases occur in the longer term. Inconsistent quality, for whatever reason, is inconsistent with customer relationship management programs that many companies are now implementing.

MANAGEMENT COMMITMENT

How management perceives the value of advertising is also important. A management group that possesses a short-term view (e.g., advertising is an expense item on a profit-and-loss statement) of how advertising will benefit the company will not be committed to a plan that requires a long period to achieve the desired results. When such a view persists, budget cuts are likely to occur during the course of a year and, since advertising spending is a highly visible item on the profit-and-loss statement, it is one of the first items reviewed in a profit-squeeze situation. Such action greatly disrupts an advertising plan, since stated objectives must be reassessed in the wake of reduced financial support. In the long term, cutbacks to the advertising budget have harmful effects on brand development in the marketplace.

Conversely, senior management who view advertising and other forms of marketing communications as a long-term investment are usually more willing to commit funds to a complete campaign. Obviously, such an attitude provides a preferable operating environment for managers responsible for developing advertising plans.

Issues of Contemporary Advertising

Advertising is an industry that is often under attack. It is also an industry that is grappling with change due to technological advancements. The issues confronting the industry right now are of both a social and a business nature.

SEX IN ADVERTISING: IS THERE TOO MUCH OF IT?

A common complaint about advertising revolves around the use of sex to sell something. As the old saying goes: "Sex sells!" So what's the beef among members of contemporary Canadian society? Critics charge that advertisers are using more and more sex with each passing year. Using sex appeals in an appropriate manner and for appropriate products seems natural, but gratuitous sex is something consumers shouldn't have to tolerate. Just recently, women objected to a risqué ad campaign for Terra work boots (Terra Footwear). Spearheaded by female members of the Canadian Autoworkers Union, the complaint mushroomed into a nationwide boycott of the boots. The outdoor advertising campaign featured scantily clad women in suggestive poses with air hoses, hammers, and tape measures as props. One headline read, "You probably can't keep your eyes off the waxed bootlaces."

Viewers of the ad were encouraged to visit **terrafootwear.com** for more details. At the website a video shows a woman wearing work boots ripping off her clothes in a strip bar. While she is dancing bare-breasted, a man in the front row mutters, "nice boots." Perhaps this element of the campaign does go too far! Terra said the ads weren't intended to offend, but to take a light-hearted approach to selling work boots. Women who have worked hard to gain acceptance in male-dominated workplaces disagreed, saying that "the campaign set women back by decades."[11] Terra eventually succumbed to union pressure and removed the billboards and video from its website.

For more insight into this controversial issue, see the Advertising in Action vignette **Heaven Forbid! Was There Sex in That Ad?**

SEX-ROLE STEREOTYPING

Advertising is constantly under attack for portraying women as objects—not necessarily as sex objects, but as objects that men desire. Advertisers have begun toning down more blatant examples of sexual stereotyping, but many are resorting to more subtle forms of sexism. More recently, reverse sexism has been a major subject of complaint. It seems that men are banding together to complain about how they are portrayed in television commercials. Men also object to how women are portrayed.

A recent poll from the United States shows both men and women react negatively to being stereotyped. Men dislike being portrayed as bumblers around the house, as incompetent, or as testosterone-driven idiots. Women dislike being portrayed as traditional homemakers, as being scatterbrained or stupid, but beautiful, or as sex objects.[12]

Men like ads where they are portrayed realistically, doing normal tasks such as working, driving, being with their family and being successful (e.g., a Chevy truck ad shows a dad working hard). Women like ads that depict the reality of balancing career and family, displaying real women with competence in a variety of roles and functions (e.g., State Farm insurance ads show that women don't have to be taken care of; they can do it). This type of information should be a wake-up call for ad agencies and advertisers. More attention must be paid to gender targeting. Ads must be more individualized and show less stereotyping—or advertisers will suffer the consequences. Refer to Figure 1.12 for an illustration.

MISLEADING ADVERTISING

Sometimes ads can mislead the public or simply misrepresent the brand. Sometimes the public misinterprets the advertiser's message and the campaign backfires. The control of misleading advertising is the responsibility of Advertising Standards Canada. (More information about their role in the advertising industry appears later in this chapter.) The most common complaints about misleading ads concern the accuracy and clarity of the message.

To illustrate, consider a few recent cases. An ad for Telus Mobility in Quebec offered customers of a specified competitor the opportunity, without charge, to exchange their cell phone for the advertiser's cell phone with the same package of features. When making the exchange consumers found they could not have the same features at the price charged by the current provider. ASC found the ads to contain inaccurate claims and statements and ruled accordingly.

Heaven Forbid! Was There Sex in That Ad?

What's all the fuss about? Sex in advertising is nothing new, but it seems as though there's much more of it. One can only hypothesize why advertisers are resorting to using sexual themes when trying to capture the imagination of their target audience. For certain the media is a primary culprit in fuelling the move to more sex. Television shows like *Sex and the City* feature female characters in all kinds of provocative scenes. Many plots in shows like *Will & Grace* are about sex, homosexuality, sexual prowess, and orgasms. *The Sopranos*, where characters use the *f*-word with abandon, is also creating a more liberal climate for advertisers. Look around—television programming is raunchier by the minute, and the internet delivers porn-for-payment by the carload.

Yes, sex is all over the media, but does that mean it should be used to sell products? For many advertisers and agencies the decision to use sex is based on relevancy. It should fit with the product category and the target market. Surprisingly, however, it works very well on the unlikeliest of categories, for it catches the audience by surprise.

Sex gets your attention while the lateral shift to the unexpected product leaves a lasting impression. A humorous spot for Hyundai that ran in Sweden provides a good illustration. Titled "Boytoy," the ad showed a woman driving with a much younger male passenger. As she pulled up to a traffic light, she reclined his seat so he was out of view, pulling up alongside a man who seems to be her husband. She then drives away laughing at her deception, as she pops the young male back into view with the touch of a button.

But the punchline comes when the husband, still idling at the light, pushes his button and up pops his date, a smiling young man decked out like the cowboy in the Village People. Sweden, it seems, is a country so liberated that they can advertise a car any way they want. Could Hyundai run this ad in Canada?

Sony Canada is the source of another interesting story about sex in advertising. The ad in question concerns a dog that licks its genitals and immediately afterwards licks the face of a young teenage girl (gross!!). When one thinks about Sony such traits as innovation, quality, and performance come to mind. You also think of integrity and leadership. Given these traits you would expect their advertising to express the same values while promoting the features and benefits of the various products being advertised.

Sony of Canada's general manager John McCarter admits, "We probably strayed too far from how Sony views the brand," for the ad did upset some corporate executives in their Japan headquarters. The ad agency responsible for the ad, McLaren McCann, defends the spot and claims it even burnishes Sony's reputation for leadership. "It marks Sony as a leader. Leaders push the boundaries and try new things." The agency also argued that the ad was created to run during youth-oriented programming, which is an environment overflowing with vulgarity and tastelessness, so it should be cut some slack. Sony of Canada, feeling pressure from corporate headquarters, eventually reviewed all of McLaren McCann's advertising efforts and fired the agency. The moral of the story: you never know who is really watching the ads and how they will react to them!

Sources: Patrick Allossery, "Sony spot crossed the line," *Financial Post*, February 5, 2001, p. C5, Trevor Shoenfeld, " When to say yes," *Marketing*, December 11, 2000, p. 15, and Paul Brent, "Sex certainly sells, but not the same everywhere," *Financial Post*, June 25, 1999, p. FP4.

Sony www.sony.ca

A radio commercial for Jetsgo was also judged to be misleading. The commercial stated that one-way flights for $59 were available to "anywhere Jetsgo flies" when booked through **Jetsgo.net**. When booking flights, consumers found extra fees and surcharges were added so that the ticket price was substantially higher than the advertised fare. The ad was deemed misleading because it did not disclose the fact that extra fees and surcharges applied.[13]

FIGURE 1.12

A State Farm Insurance ad portrays women in a desirable and contemporary manner

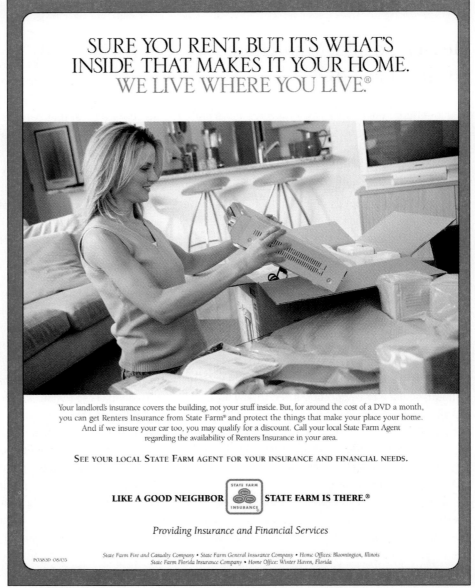

KEEPING PACE WITH TECHNOLOGY

Marketing and advertising managers must constantly monitor changes that influence advertising strategies. On the technology side, the increasing penetration of satellite dishes and the availability of so many stations have changed the way people view television. Further, the recent introduction of the PVR (personal video recorder) allows programs to be taped for viewing at a later time, commercial-free. Such technology puts the value of television advertising in question. As well, the rapid growth of the internet means that people are viewing television less, listening to radio less, and reading newspapers and magazines less. There are only so many hours available to be with the media each day.

While extremists are forecasting the end of the 30-second television commercial, there is still a frenzied demand for network television time. It is often the default medium for many advertisers simply because it is so visible. If the advertiser is seeking awareness, television is perceived to be the best solution! In the era of customer relationship management programs, however, such perceptions will have to change or much money will be wasted. Many advertisers have already moved to branded content, a strategy that involves placing products right in the TV program. Network hits such as *24* and *Alias* have gone as far as dedicating entire episodes to single wrap-around sponsors.[14] These particular shows have been attractive to high-tech advertisers.

CHANGING BUSINESS ENVIRONMENT

Other changes that must be addressed involve social and demographic trends. An aging population, smaller households, and ethnic diversity all represent new challenges for advertisers. Advertisers are obsessed with attracting young targets to their products when the reality is that older age groups have much more money to spend. The target-market priorities of many companies today are misguided. If they wish to survive, they must shift their focus so that a variety of different targets are given due consideration.

Many advertisers continue to portray Canadian households as traditional households (a white mother and father with two children) when households are anything but white and traditional. Critics of advertising claim that minority groups are not fairly represented, and they have a point. A sampling of recent Canadian magazines revealed the following: in *Canadian House & Home* only two of 37 ads with models included non-whites; in *Flare* only 10 of 86 ads featured people of colour, but in half of them they were among Caucasians; and in *National Post Business Magazine* only four of 22 ads represented minorities.[15] Such findings suggest that advertisers are not evolving with changes in Canadian society and, if they continue to follow the same path, will suffer the consequences when new groups of consumers reject them.

TRANSITION TO INTEGRATED MARKETING COMMUNICATIONS

Organizations today are searching for complete solutions for their communications needs. In the past it was common for various plans to be developed separately by distinct organizations that specialized in certain areas and operated independently. As indicated earlier, the environment has changed. Advertisers are looking at different ways of delivering messages, and they are experimenting with branded content.

Customer behaviour has also changed. Consumers today are less reliant on television and newspapers and more reliant on computers and telephones for receiving news and commercial messages. Such switches in allegiance force advertisers to evaluate different media choices. The goal of communications now is to deliver the same message through a variety of media in order to have a synergistic impact on the target. More traditional media, such as television and print, direct mail, and telephone, will continue to account for the lion's share of the media mix, while new media will continue to make inroads. No one media delivery channel will drive the marketing industry. Truly there is a merger going on between traditional media and information-based media that all organizations will eventually have to adapt to. Breaking through the clutter of advertising is increasingly more difficult and scary for advertisers. As well, advertisers must be mindful of consumers who want more detailed information about things that interest them. The internet will play a key role in shaping future marketing communications.

MEDIA CONVERGENCE

Convergence, defined as "coming together," is a trend in the media communications business in Canada. As in many other industries (such as technology, food manufacturing and processing, and automobiles), consolidation is occurring. When an industry consolidates there are mergers and acquisitions between very large companies to form even larger companies. The goal of such mergers is more market share and greater control within the industry.

The media in Canada is controlled by four very large companies: Bell Globemedia, CanWest Global Communications, Rogers Communications, and Quebecor. Bell Globemedia, for example, is a $4 billion company and a leading contender in practically every media platform—newspapers (*The Globe and Mail*), network television (CTV), specialty television (TSN and the Discovery Channel), and the internet (Sympatico-Lycos).[16] Bell and their competitors are now in the business of multi-platform media selling and cross-media advertising deals. In other words, they offer special deals to advertisers willing to advertise on all media outlets. Such a practice is very different from traditional media buying-selling models.

Multimedia deals with one media supplier suit large advertisers such as General Motors. Smaller advertisers simply do not have the resources or the need, for that matter, to be involved in multimedia programs—they would be wasting money. General Motors jumped on the convergence bandwagon with a campaign for Cadillac. A nine-month campaign called "Road to Success" was built around content devoted to three pillars: success in technology, business, and design. It featured print ads in *The Globe and Mail*, three 30-minute TV shows specifically created for the campaign and relating to each of the pillars, and a series of vignettes airing on broadcasts featuring content relevant to Cadillac customers. The campaign also utilized the Sympatico-Lycos and **globeandmail.com** websites to house a microsite that featured content relating directly to Cadillac. According to General Motors, "Bell Globemedia had a group of holdings and channels which were exactly appropriate for this program."[17] How many other advertisers will find such a good fit remains a key issue in the industry.

Should there be so much control by so few companies? Critics are concerned about the high degree of media concentration but acknowledge that the trend is occurring in other countries as well. From an advertising perspective there are some benefits and drawbacks. These media conglomerates are now in a position to offer advertisers complete solutions to achieve their marketing objectives. The bias in recommending one medium over another seems to be eliminated. With such control, however, it is conceivable that advertising rates (costs incurred by an advertiser when buying time or space in a medium) could rise. The true effect of these mergers and the impact they will have on the advertising community will not be known for a few years.

Laws and Regulations

The marketing communications industry in Canada is highly regulated. Regulation and control come from two primary sources: the Canadian Radio-television and Telecommunications Commission (CRTC), which governs all broadcasting laws including advertising; and Advertising Standards Canada, which administers regulations based on codes of practice that are voluntarily established.

CANADIAN RADIO-TELEVISION COMMUNICATIONS COMMISSION (CRTC)

The CRTC is an independent public authority in charge of regulating and supervising Canadian broadcasting and telecommunications. It serves the public interest and is governed by the *Broadcasting Act of 1991* and the *Telecommunications Act of 1993*. The

Broadcasting Act ensures that Canadians have access to a wide variety of high quality Canadian programming. The *Telecommunications Act* ensures access to reliable telephone and telecommunications services at affordable prices.

Canadian content is the cornerstone of the *Broadcasting Act*. It addresses several key issues:[18]

- The creation and production of Canadian programs and music
- Financial support for the broadcasting system for the creation of Canadian content
- Determining how much Canadian content must be aired on radio and television
- The ratio of Canadian and non-Canadian content distributed by Canadian cable companies and satellite providers
- Canadian ownership and control of the broadcasting system

In addressing these issues, the overall mandate of the CRTC is to enforce Parliament's intent that the national broadcasting system serve a national purpose. There are numerous broadcasting and telecommunications regulations that the CRTC is also responsible for. For a complete listing of these regulations and more information about the role of the CRTC, visit the CRTC website at **www.crtc.gc.ca**.

ADVERTISING STANDARDS CANADA

Advertising Standards Canada is the industry body committed to creating and maintaining community confidence in advertising. Its mission is to ensure the integrity and viability of advertising through industry self-regulation. ASC members include advertisers, agencies, media organizations, and suppliers to the advertising sector.

ASC operates two divisions. The Standards Division administers the industry's self-regulating code, the *Canadian Code of Advertising Standards*, handles complaints from consumers regarding advertising, and administers the industry's *Trade Dispute Procedure*. The Advertising Clearance Division previews advertisements in five categories, helping advertisers to adhere to applicable legislation, regulatory codes, and industry standards.[19]

The *Canadian Code of Advertising Standards* (Code) is the principal instrument of self-regulation. The Code was developed to promote the professional practice of advertising and forms the basis upon which advertising is evaluated in response to consumer complaints. The Code is supplemented by other codes and guidelines, including gender portrayal guidelines, which are intended to help advertising practitioners develop positive images of women and men in their commercial messages. The Code also addresses the following concerns about advertising:

- Accuracy and clarity of messages
- Disguised advertising techniques
- Price claims
- Bait and Switch
- Comparative advertising
- Testimonials
- Professional and scientific claims
- Safety

- Advertising to children and minors
- Unacceptable depictions and portrayals

For more complete details about the role of Advertising Standards Canada, see Appendix III of this textbook and visit the ASC website at **www.adstandards.com**.

It seems that Canadian consumers are complaining more about advertising than ever before! In 2003 there were 1133 complaints about 716 different advertisements. The council upheld 131 complaints about 57 advertisements. Retail advertising attracted the most complaints, followed by food and personal product categories. By medium, television advertising attracted the most complaints. Of the complaints received, more complaints were reviewed under Clause 14 (Unacceptable Depictions and Portrayals) than any other category. The second leading category involved complaints about misleading advertising.

To illustrate, one of the most complained about campaigns in recent memory was from K-ROCK 97.3, a radio station in Alberta. Billboard advertisements for the station's morning show showed three apparently nude men holding strategically placed nutshells in front of them. The complaint was based on the use of nudity in a public space advertisement that offended standards of public decency. In rendering a decision, the Council understood the intent of the ad—to show the off-base personalities of the morning show hosts—but felt nudity was being gratuitously exploited in the ad. They agreed that the ad did offend public decency.[20] Refer back the Misleading Advertising section in this chapter for additional examples of questionable advertising practice.

The advertising community gets upset over such decisions. More recently, a television spot for the Ford Focus was pulled because of complaints about a scene in which a female shopper pushes a male clerk into the hatchback of her car. Advertising Standards Canada ruled that the ad condoned violence and that it should be changed. Copywriters and art directors say it's no wonder Canada has a reputation for timid and boring advertising when agencies and clients are cautioned to stay away from the creative edge.[21]

SUMMARY

Advertising is any paid form of marketing communication designed to influence the thought patterns and purchase behaviour of a target audience. The specific role of advertising is to favourably influence potential customers' responses to a product by communicating relevant information about the product, such as how the product will satisfy a need.

The nature of communications has changed. Companies now plan and implement integrated marketing communications programs that embrace strategies beyond advertising. An integrated marketing communications strategy involves the coordination of advertising with other strategies such as sales promotion, public relations, personal selling, event marketing and sponsorships, direct-response advertising, and interactive communications. All of these elements combine to achieve common objectives.

Advertising is one element of marketing communications; granted, it is the most visible and probably most costly element. Advertising is divided into two broad categories: consumer advertising and business-to-business advertising. Advertising is also described as being product-oriented or promotional-oriented. Consumer advertising is used by companies that produce national brands and by retailers. It includes direct-response communications and advocacy advertising. Business-to-business advertising includes trade, industrial, service-industry, and corporate advertising. Corporate advertising is used to help create favourable images about a company or to promote a point of view held by a company. Product-oriented advertising communicates the unique benefits of a brand, whereas promotional advertising encourages customers to take action now (as opposed to later).

Before a company invests in advertising, a situation analysis should be conducted to determine if market conditions are favourable or unfavourable. If favourable, the investment in advertising should proceed. There must be market and product demand; the product must be at an appropriate stage in the product life cycle; the product should have a competitive advantage; the competitive environment must be conducive for investment; the product must be of adequate quality; and management must be committed to investing in communications in the long term. Finally, advertising must be integrated with other integrated marketing communications (IMC) elements to produce a coordinated and consistent message to customers.

Some of the major issues confronting the industry include the overuse of sex as an appeal technique, sex-role stereotyping, misleading advertising claims, the need to keep pace with changing technology, the changing business environment, the rapid movement toward integrated marketing communications, and media convergence.

Regulation and control of the advertising industry comes under the jurisdiction of the federal government through the Canadian Radio-Television and Telecommunications Commission, and under voluntary regulations administered by Advertising Standards Canada.

KEY TERMS

advertising   4

advocacy advertising   9

business-to-business
   advertising   9

consumer advertising   9

corporate advertising   12

database marketing   8

direct-response advertising   9

end-product advertising   9

event marketing and
   sponsorship   7

industrial advertising   10

integrated marketing
   communications (IMC)   6

national advertising   9

personal selling   7

product advertising   13

product life cycle   15

promotional advertising   13

public relations   6

retail advertising   9

sales promotion   6

service industry advertising   10

trade advertising   10

REVIEW QUESTIONS

1. What is the primary role of advertising? How is advertising related to marketing and marketing communications decisions?

2. What is integrated marketing communications and what role does it play in solving business problems today?

3. Identify and briefly explain the various components of integrated marketing communications.

4. Identify and briefly explain the various types of consumer advertising.

5. Identify and briefly explain the various types of business-to-business advertising.

6. What is the difference between product advertising and promotional advertising?

7. How do market demand and the product life cycle influence the decision to invest in or not invest in advertising?

8. How does a product communicate its competitive advantage? Identify the various options and provide a new example of each option.

9. How important is product quality when making the decision to invest in advertising? Briefly explain.

10. What roles do the Canadian Radio-Television and Telecommunications Commission (CRTC) and Advertising Standards Canada play in the advertising industry?

DISCUSSION QUESTIONS

1. Collect some print advertisements for a product that uses sex as its central means of appealing to its target market. Analyze the advertisements for applicability and potential impact. Do you agree or disagree with this type of advertising practice? Why or why not?

2. Reverse sexism and male stereotyping seem to be an issue in advertising today. From your perspective is it an issue or is it nothing more than a portrait of reality? Provide some examples to justify your opinion.

3. Will media convergence have a positive or negative effect on Canadian advertisers? For example, will it raise or lower the costs of advertising? What is your opinion on this or any related issues?

4. Is "stretching the truth" the same thing as "misleading advertising"? Is it okay to stretch the truth a little bit? What is your opinion? Review the section in the chapter about misleading advertising before formulating your thoughts.

5. Do Canadian advertisers accurately portray contemporary society or are they still portraying outdated images and lifestyles? Provide some examples to justify your opinion.

6. Read the Advertising in Action vignette **Heaven Forbid! Was There Sex in That Ad?** Is the use of sex and sexual innuendo in advertising acceptable, or should advertisers be more sensitive to the values of the viewing audience? For what kinds of products are sexual appeals appropriate? Provide examples to defend your position.

NOTES

1. ComQUEST Research 2000, TVB Canada, **www.tvb.ca/tvbresources.**

2. TVB Canada, **www.tvb.ca/tvbresources**.

3. Adbrands, **www.adbrands.net.ca**.

4. Jo Marney, "Image-building," *Marketing*, January 2/9, 1996, p. 15.

5. Susan Heinrich, "Ontario's grape expectations," *Financial Post*, May 27, 2002, p. FP7.

6. Paul Brent, "Farewell, old dog," *Financial Post*, June 7, 2003, p. FP6.

7. Lisa D'Innocenzo, "Gum 'knocks the snot' out of lozenge category," *Strategy*, April 8, 2002, p. 6.

8. Kristen Vinakmens, "The promise of pearly whites," *Strategy*, March 10, 2003, pp. 1, 6–7.

9. Laura Pratt, "TV ads aim for young hearts," *Toronto Star*, February 20, 2003, p. G8.

10. "Advertising Sage," *Report on Business Magazine*, September 1996, p. 25.

11. Sarah Sacheli, "CAW women's group objects to risqué ads," *Financial Post*, October 8, 2003, p. FP9.

12. Performance Improvement Pros Inc., *Advertising Survey*, 1993, **www.gendersell.com/advertising**.

13. Ad Complaints Report, 2004, First Quarter, **www.adstandards.com/en/standards/adComplaints**.

14. Anthony Crupi, "Will DVR really kill the 30-second ad," *Cable World*, September 29, 2003, **www.cableworld.com**.

15. Lisa D'Innocenzo, "The colour of marketing," *Strategy*, April 26, 2001, pp. 1, 6.

16. Jason Edmiston, "Putting it all together," *Marketing*, February 25, 2002, pp. 15–16.

17. Ibid., p. 16. **www.crtc.gc.ca/eng/BACKGROUND/Brochures**.

18. Advertising Standards Canada, **www.adstandards.com**.

19. Advertising Standards Canada, *2002 Ad Complaints Report*, p. 13.

20. Angela Kryhul, "Stifling nuisance or helpful guide," *Marketing*, March 11, 2002, p. 6.

CHAPTER

2

The Advertising Industry

Learning Objectives

After studying this chapter, you will be able to

- Identify the organizations that comprise the advertising industry

- Identify and describe the various advertising management systems used by clients

- Identify the roles and responsibilities of clients in the advertising development process

- Describe the roles and responsibilities of the agency in the advertising development process

- Discuss the nature of relationships between clients and agencies

- Distinguish among the various types of advertising agencies

- Outline the organizational structure of agencies and the functions of agency personnel

- Identify the key concepts associated with managing a client's business

- Identify the methods of compensating advertising agencies

This chapter focuses on the relationships between advertisers (the client) and advertising agencies. Once the primary groups that comprise the industry have been identified, discussion will focus on the relationships between clients and agencies as they develop and implement advertising campaigns.

The management of advertising does vary from company to company. Depending on the size and nature of the company, responsibility for communications programs could be with the advertising manager, marketing manager, or even the owner of a small business. Or, a product manager or brand manager may be entirely responsible for communications activities for his or her brands. While recognizing these title variations, this chapter will use the term "advertising manager."

Advertising agencies exist to help companies communicate with the public and to help market a company's product. The agency is a service company that provides an essential link between the client (advertiser) and the public. An agency provides expertise that a client itself does not possess. Specifically, the client company gains access to creative and media specialists who will be responsible for planning and implementing vital components of the overall marketing plan.

Composition of the Advertising Industry

The Canadian advertising industry comprises three primary groups: advertisers, advertising agencies, and the media. All advertising revenues generated in Canada result from

Association of Canadian Advertisers
www.aca-online.com

advertisers' print ads and broadcast commercials placed by advertising agencies in the media. Advertisers are the companies whose investment in advertising is largely responsible for keeping the other two component groups in business. Other organizations that support these primary groups include advertising production companies, audience measurement and media research companies, media support services, and regulation and control agencies.

ADVERTISERS (THE CLIENT)

Canadian advertisers include manufacturers, retailers, service firms, dot-com companies, governments, and non-profit organizations. Among the largest advertisers in Canada are BCE, General Motors, Procter & Gamble, and CanWest Global Communications (see Figure 2.1). The Association of Canadian Advertisers is a national association exclusively dedicated to serving the interests of companies that market and advertise their products and services in Canada. The ACA's mandate is "to exercise leadership in advancing the advertising interests and responsibilities of advertisers in Canada." Their objectives include the following: to identify and address issues that affect the interests of advertisers; to initiate, influence, and shape government and industry policy (a public relations role); to provide leadership to ensure advertising effectiveness; and to be a reliable and timely source of expertise and information for members.[1] By acting on such a wide variety of concerns and issues, the ACA protects and promotes advertisers' ability to advertise responsibly and cost-effectively.

ADVERTISING AGENCIES

Advertising agencies are service organizations responsible for creating, planning, producing, and placing advertising messages for clients. Most of the larger advertising agencies in Canada are subsidiaries of large American agencies. Mergers and acquisitions

FIGURE 2.1

Canada's top 10 advertisers

Rank	Advertiser	Media Spending ($ millions)
1	BCE	82.57
2	Procter & Gamble	77.34
3	General Motors	69.67
4	Hudson's Bay Company	64.63
5	CanWest Global Communications	54.08
6	Sears	53.14
7	Government of Canada	51.63
8	Toyota	49.6
9	Sony	41.25
10	Best Buy	38.73

Source: Reprinted with permission from the November 10, 2003 issue of Advertising Age. Copyright, Crain Communications Inc. 2003..

have been a popular trend in the agency business over the past decade, and this has affected agency structure and management all over the world. Essentially, four multinational marketing communications conglomerates—Omnicom Group (American), WPP (British), Interpublic Group (American), and Publicis Groupe (France)—control the advertising agency business worldwide. So extensive are their holdings that they cannot be listed in this textbook. Most large Canadian agencies are affiliated with these marketing communications companies.

Cossette Communication Group
www.cossette.com

In Canada the largest agencies include Cossette Communication Group (a Canadian-owned company) with domestic revenues of $140.4 million, Maxxcomm (a global company that owns a collection of Canadian agencies) with domestic revenues of $71.8 million, and Carlson Marketing Group (a collection of Canadian agencies) with revenues of $36.8 million.[2] The different types of agencies that exist include full-service agencies that provide a complete range of services to their clients, or specialists that offer only limited services in certain areas of expertise. For a listing of some of Canada's larger advertising agencies and their major clients see Figure 2.2.

There are all kinds of smaller, regional advertising agencies that serve the needs of local and regional clients. In Atlantic Canada, for example, Bristol Group and M5 are two agencies offering a complete range of marketing communications services. Among Bristol's clients are Ben's Bread and the Atlantic Lottery Corporation. M5's clients include Casino Nova Scotia and O'Regan's Automotive Group.

Institute of Communications and Advertising
www.ica-ad.com

The Institute of Communications and Advertising (ICA) is the national association representing full-service advertising agencies. The work of the ICA may be divided into two broad categories: external and internal. The external mission of the ICA is to act on behalf of the agency industry as spokesperson, negotiator, and defender of advertising. Its role is to discourage regulation, improve regulatory procedures, support self-regulation, and fight for the freedom to advertise. Its internal mission is to anticipate, serve, and promote the collective interests of ICA members with particular regard to defining, developing, and helping maintain the highest possible standards of professional practice.[3]

FIGURE
2.2

Canada's largest agencies and a selection of their clients

Agency	Gross Revenues ($ million)	Clients
Cossette Communication Group	140.2	Bell Canada, Coca-Cola, General Mills, General Motors, Home Depot, McDonald's, Shoppers Drug Mart
Maxxcomm	71.8	Client list not supplied for rankings
Carlson Marketing	36.8	Bank of Montreal, Canadian Tire, Ford Motor Company, Gillette, Kia Canada, Michelin
Marketel	20.5	Air Canada, Hydro Quebec, Johnson & Johnson, Nestlé, Rogers AT&T, Tourisme Quebec
Allard Johnson	19.3	Bombardier, Canadian Egg Marketing Agency, Dairy Farmers of Canada, GlaxoSmithKline, RBC Financial Group

Note: Several large American-owned agencies did not participate in the rankings for 2003. Such agency brands as MacLaren McCann, BBDO, and DDB are not included.

Source: "The Rankings," *Marketing*, June 23, 2003, p. 10.

THE MEDIA

The Canadian media are divided into numerous categories: *broadcast*, which includes radio and television; *print*, which includes newspapers and magazines; *out-of-home media*, which includes transit and outdoor advertising; *direct-response media*, which includes direct mail and direct-response television companies; and *internet advertising*, which includes portal sites such as **sympatico.ca, canoe.ca**, and **yahoo.com/ca**. In the 1990s the electronic media emerged as a viable and complementary alternative to traditional media such as broadcast and print. According to the latest revenue data available, net advertising revenue in Canada from all sources (the amount actually spent on media) totals $10.9 billion. The traditional mass media comprising television, daily newspaper, radio, magazines, and out-of-home generate $7.0 billion revenue. The remaining $3.9 billion comes from direct-response advertising, online advertising, yellow pages, and a variety of miscellaneous sources. Television is the largest single medium with advertising revenues of $2.6 billion.[4]

ADVERTISING SUPPORT COMPANIES

This group comprises research companies that measure and evaluate the effectiveness of advertising messages. Other support firms include photographers, radio and television commercial production houses, print production specialists, music and sound production and editing companies, and media representatives who sell time and space for particular media. These support service groups operate behind the scenes, and awareness of their existence, role, and function is low.

MEDIA SUPPORT SERVICES

All major media in Canada have a support group whose primary mandate is to educate potential advertisers about the merits of their particular medium. Acting as a resource centre of information, each organization attempts to increase its medium's share of advertising revenue in the marketplace. Where appropriate, these organizations also liaise with governments and the public on matters of interest. This group includes the Television Bureau of Canada (TVB), Radio Marketing Bureau, Newspaper Marketing Bureau, Magazines Canada, the Outdoor Advertising Association of Canada, and the Canadian Marketing Association.

RESEARCH AND AUDIENCE MEASUREMENT COMPANIES

Advertising planners working with limited budgets are constantly evaluating various media alternatives to develop the most effective and efficient media mix. To make sound media decisions requires a factual and objective information base. Media research, therefore, is concerned with quantitative measures of media exposure. In Canada, numerous independent organizations compile and publish reliable measurement data. Among these organizations are BBM Bureau of Measurement, Nielsen Media Research, Audit Bureau of Circulations, Canadian Circulations Audit Board, the Print Measurement Bureau, and Jupiter Media Metrix. The services provided by these organizations are discussed in appropriate media chapters later on.

Client-Side Advertising Management

Management of the advertising function usually falls under the jurisdiction of the marketing department in an organization. Thus, it is very common for numerous managers to be directly or indirectly involved with the task of advertising. The number of managers involved depends on the size and nature of the organization and on the relative importance that advertising plays in the marketing of the products. For example, in a large organization that uses the brand-management system, numerous managers may be involved in advertising. Junior-level managers are active in the day-to-day affairs of their brands, while senior-level managers are active in the approval process for advertising strategies of all company brands. In some organizations, approvals may be required from a brand manager, from all members of the marketing management ranks, and, finally, from the president of the company. Obviously, all managers are concerned about the quality and content of the messages communicated about the company and its products.

A **brand manager** (product manager) is an individual who is assigned responsibility for the development and implementation of marketing programs (including marketing communications) for a specific product or group of products. In the context of advertising and other forms of communications, the manager deals directly with the agencies on creative and media assignments, sales promotion programs, event marketing activities, and public relations. Internally, this system encourages friendly competition, as managers compete for the resources of the firm (people, time, and money) to ensure that their product receives the attention it deserves. Procter & Gamble, for example, would assign a brand manager to each of its laundry products: Tide, Downy, Gain, Cheer, Bounce, and Bold.

Typically, a brand manager reports to a category manager. A **category manager** is an individual who is assigned the responsibility for developing and implementing the marketing activity for all products grouped in the category. Category managers are common in large packaged-goods companies such as Procter & Gamble and Kraft. The category manager adopts a more generalized view of the business than would an individual brand manager. Consequently, trade-offs among brands are the decision of the category manager (i.e., determining which brands receive more or less advertising support, etc.). The brand managers mentioned above report to a category manager for laundry products in the Procter & Gamble management hierarchy.

Canada is a diverse country geographically and culturally. Therefore, there is a need for **regional campaigns** that reflect the nature and character of unique targets. Molson, for example, has a three-region structure that impacts on marketing communications: Western Canada, Ontario/Atlantic, and Quebec. A national marketing team manages a group of brands referred to as "strategic national brands." Canadian and Export are in this group. Each region has a staff of marketing, sales, and promotion personnel who develop marketing and communication strategies and implement plans for "strategic regional brands." According to Molson, such a system allows a company to build on its strengths and chip away at its weaknesses.[5] Regional managers can respond more quickly to changes in the marketplace.

Companies with growth aspirations now view the world as one market. And, to be as efficient as possible with marketing communications, they like to develop global campaigns. The often-used expression "Think globally and act locally" is now a common refrain among multi-national marketers. To illustrate, consider what McDonald's is attempting on a global scale. While not officially calling it a global advertising challenge, McDonald's convened a meeting of its 42 worldwide agencies to address how to improve the company's advertising. The corporate goal of McDonald's is to capture more meal occasions among young adults and families.[6] What emerged was a concept and theme from their German agency that was approved for use in all countries where McDonald's operates. The tagline for the new advertising is now well known: "I'm Lovin' It."

As indicated above, management structures can vary in organizations. For the purpose of presenting the roles and responsibilities of the client in a consistent manner, the term **advertising manager** will be used. The position of advertising manager is usually a mid-management position in the client organization. For such a position, the manager must possess analytical and planning skills, leadership skills, and knowledge and experience in the operation of the advertising industry. The advertising manager's position in the client organization is outlined in Figure 2.3. The figure also outlines the flow of communications between the advertising agency and the client at mid-management and senior management levels. For the sake of convenience, the diagram assumes the use of the brand-management system of advertising planning.

The advertising manager is responsible for coordinating advertising plans with plans for related marketing communications activity. The range of activity includes creative and media planning, sales promotion planning, event marketing planning, direct-response planning, and so on. In this capacity, the manager is responsible for developing the objectives and strategies for each plan. The following are the key areas of responsibility.

ADVERTISING PLANNING AND BUDGETING

Working with other marketing managers, the advertising manager will contribute to the marketing plan. At this stage, advertising would be recognized as one element in the marketing mix; hence, the role it will play in the achievement of objectives will be clearly identified. When the marketing plan is developed, general budget guidelines will be established that will aid in the development of a more comprehensive advertising plan at a later point. The expertise of the advertising manager will be called upon when budget requirements are being established in the marketing plan.

COORDINATING ADVERTISING WITH OTHER MARKETING COMMUNICATIONS

Other activities closely associated with advertising are sales promotion, event marketing, public relations, and marketing research. It is quite common for promotion activity to become part of the advertising communications process. Coupons and contests, for example, are often the focal point of an advertisement. Therefore, the advertising manager is responsible for integrating promotion activities and plans with advertising activities and plans. The internet must also be factored into the communications mix. Managers now evaluate alternatives such as banner advertising and website sponsorship opportunities (i.e., sponsoring sites that are popular with a target audience of interest to the advertiser).

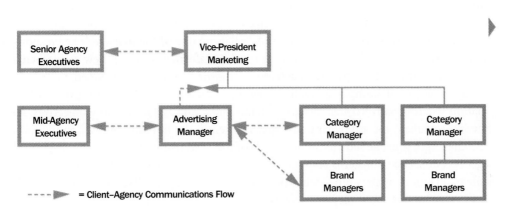

FIGURE
2.3

Position of the advertising manager in a client organization

The expression "a chain is only as strong as its weakest link" applies well to advertising and to its role in the marketing process. To be effective, advertising must work together with other marketing variables (product, price, distribution, and promotion) and, when appropriate, call upon the resources available in other marketing areas, particularly **marketing research**, so that better advertising plans can be developed. For example, potential messages can be tested at various stages of development or implementation to measure the impact they are having on the target audience.

Once advertising and other communications plans are finalized, the advertising manager must distribute plan details to sales management personnel. Communicating advertising details to the sales force is vital, since the information can be used to inform customers of programs that will help them resell company products.

MONITORING THE ADVERTISING PROGRAM

In this area, the advertising manager ensures that advertising execution is in accordance with the actual plan. For example, the manager may request a post-buy media analysis to ensure that desired reach levels were actually achieved. Also, the manager carefully reviews budgets and planned media expenditures throughout the year, making changes when necessary. A change in competitive activity might dictate an increase in spending, so the manager must know what options are available on short notice. Or, a company may be facing a profit-squeeze situation, and spending on advertising might have to be reduced. In this case, the manager must know what flexibility there is for cancellation of media.

EVALUATING THE ADVERTISING PROGRAM

The advertising manager is accountable for the success or failure of company advertising programs. Most advertising plans are based on quantifiable objectives, and whether these objectives are achieved can be determined through some form of **advertising research**. For example, a campaign may be designed to increase consumers' awareness of a product to a certain level, to generate sales leads, or to communicate a specific message. To measure the success of a commercial or print advertisement, the manager may conduct research at various stages (pre-test and post-test research). The evaluation process is critical, as the advertising manager must make recommendations for changes in advertising direction if research information so dictates. Also, research at carefully timed intervals, for any campaign, often helps in identifying potential trouble spots before they become problems.

LIAISON WITH ADVERTISING AGENCY

Advertising managers are the direct link with the advertising agency, and hence they are in constant contact with agency personnel, checking the status of assignments and projects that the agency may be working on. As a liaison, one of the manager's key responsibilities is providing the agency with appropriate information when new assignments occur. For example, if a new advertisement or commercial is to be developed, the advertising manager will compile a creative briefing document outlining appropriate information regarding advertising background and marketing and advertising objectives. As the intermediary, the advertising manager is often in the hot seat, because individuals and their egos must be satisfied at both ends of the advertising spectrum (client side and agency side). The manager is responsible for developing advertising that will be acceptable to all company personnel, who must approve the program (based on client input). Let's examine this situation more closely.

From the viewpoint of the agency, the advertising manager is the person it must satisfy first. If the manager does not like a particular creative or media recommendation, the chances that it will be seen, let alone approved, by others on the client side are minimal. As an experienced critic, and knowing client personnel and their expectations, the manager will provide the agency with feedback so that changes to the proposal can be made before the corporate approval stage.

On the client side, once the creative or media assignment meets the specifications outlined in the marketing plan or briefing document, the advertising manager must carry the agency proposal through the corporate approval network. At this stage, the idiosyncrasies of senior executives often come to the forefront. These executives offer opinions on how the advertisement or media proposal could be improved. The advertising manager must remain objective and use the required selling skills to combat unnecessary changes to agency proposals. The ongoing requests for changes to the proposal that result from the corporate approval system (and from attempting to satisfy each individual manager) often have a negative impact on client–agency relations. Client–agency relations are discussed later in this chapter.

Advertising Agency Roles and Responsibilities

Advertising agencies perform various functions, tailoring their services to meet the specific needs of individual clients. The actual degree of the agency's involvement and responsibility may vary among clients, depending on factors such as the size and expertise of the client company. For example, large advertisers such as Procter & Gamble, Kraft Canada, or Coca-Cola are typically staffed with marketing managers whose expertise is used for devising marketing strategies. In this case, the agency's role will likely be confined to advertising and other forms of marketing communications. A key role is to develop and implement creative and media plans that are effective and efficient. For small advertisers, many of whom may lack marketing skills, agencies can provide marketing planning assistance that will complement overall client operations, not just advertising.

Since the relationship between a client and an agency is essentially a partnership, each will contribute to the planning and decision-making process. The services that the advertising agency offers are experience and expertise in communications, planning assistance, and objectivity in the planning process.

PROVIDE EXPERIENCE AND EXPERTISE IN COMMUNICATIONS

Clients normally develop a comprehensive marketing plan that embraces all elements of the marketing mix (product, price, distribution, marketing communications, and public image). The agency will develop, in more detail, elements from the communications component of the plan. Specifically, the agency will use the guidelines and objectives established in the marketing plan to develop and execute an advertising plan that will contribute to the achievement of the client's objectives. Such a plan would include recommendations on creative (message) and media strategy that would embrace traditional print and broadcast media along with other options such as direct-response advertising, interactive media, event marketing, and sales promotion activities. The agency's responsibility is to recommend the most cost-effective solution to the client.

Pepsi-Cola
www.pepsi.ca

PROVIDE PLANNING ASSISTANCE

The agency, through its account group (account executives and account supervisors), provides assistance not only in advertising but also in other areas of marketing. Depending on the internal structure of the client, the account group might be used as an external planning group. Such external planning may be used in the areas of marketing research, sales promotion, and public relations. Account managers must look at the bigger picture, not just advertising, when it comes to solving a client's problems. If other elements of the marketing communications mix can play a vital role, then they too should be recommended as part of the solution.

PROVIDE OBJECTIVITY IN THE PLANNING PROCESS

Many advertisers tend to use advertising that suits the company's established style or image. Often, clients view a change in direction as a risk. The use of familiar-looking campaigns is a safe strategy, but it is not necessarily the most effective means of communicating with a target market. In advertising, safe usually means ineffective. The advertising agency is not directly associated with the internal environment and therefore can provide an objective perspective that might offer alternative directions and recommendations for communicating with target markets. This external position can result in the development of customer-oriented campaigns rather than company-oriented campaigns. For example, when Richard Burjaw, director of marketing at Pepsi-Cola Canada, first saw an outdoor ad for Diet Pepsi that depicted anthropomorphic ice cubes reaching up to their beloved soda, as though saying: "Pick me, pick me!" he couldn't help but be skeptical of the concept. BBDO, the advertising agency, didn't back down. They believed in the idea, and its uniqueness—it wasn't the typical style of soft drink advertising. After some tussling between the parties, Burjaw gave the approval to proceed.[7] The concept was successful and Burjaw now feels it is among Pepsi's best work ever. So you never know! Refer to the illustration in Figure 2.4.

FIGURE
2.4

An agency advertising concept initially questioned by Pepsi-Cola turned out to be a success

At first Burjaw thought this ad would look like an *Alien* outtake, but now he considers it among Pepsi's best work ever

PROMOTE ACTIVE LIAISON WITH CLIENTS

It is very important for agencies and clients to communicate regularly with each other. The account executive is the primary link between the agency and the client. An account executive channels vital information from the client into the agency and takes recommendations that are prepared by various agency departments back to the client for review. It is also appropriate for employees at similar management levels to be communicating with each other. For example, a director of account planning (agency) should keep in touch with the director of marketing (client) and the presidents of both organizations should meet periodically to discuss matters. Ongoing and open communications between the parties fosters an environment where both parties can prosper. It helps build a better partnership.

For a summary of the roles and responsibilities of clients and advertising agencies, refer to Figure 2.5.

Client–Agency Relationships

The quality of advertising produced is the outcome of a sound business/professional and personal relationship between a client and an agency. When the client–agency relationship is a partnership, the relationship is long term. If the relationship is one of buyer–vendor, the association is much more likely to be short term.

The connection between client and agency is often very delicate and can be broken for various reasons. Deteriorating relationships contribute significantly to the amount of account shifting that occurs in Canada each year. **Account shifting** refers to the movement of an advertising account from one agency to another. Clients are attracted to agencies that produce good creative and to agencies that develop campaigns that achieve business objectives.

There are a variety of reasons why clients shift their business to different advertising agencies. Most of these reasons have to do with the client–agency relationship—or lack of it. Following are some of the more common reasons for account shifting:

CLIENTS ARE RESPONSIBLE FOR:

- Providing appropriate background information and a budget for the advertising assignment
- Coordinating advertising strategies with other marketing communications strategies
- Monitoring the implementation of advertising programs
- Evaluating the effectiveness of advertising programs

AGENCIES ARE RESPONSIBLE FOR:

- Providing experience and expertise in specialized areas: mainly creative and media strategies and executions
- Offering planning assistance to solve clients' marketing problems
- Producing objective, customer-focused advertising strategies
- Conducting research when necessary to support advertising recommendations

FIGURE 2.5

A summary of the roles and responsibilities of clients and agencies

Regardless of the role and responsibility, if the client–agency partnership is to be a successful one there must be effective two-way communications between the partners. The partners must share a similar vision and agree to achievable objectives.

- Clients are dissatisfied with the quality of the advertising or any of the other services provided by the agency.

- There are new communications demands from clients that cannot be adequately served by existing agencies (e.g., all aspects of integrated marketing communications).

- There are philosophical differences between client and agency in terms of management style and approach, detected only after the association has begun. For example, the two parties might disagree on the direction the advertising should take.

- There is an absence of the team concept—the relationships between people do not develop, whether because of poor communications, differences in needs, or negative attitudes. Sometimes, the players on the teams change during the relationship, upsetting the chemistry that had existed.

- Clients decide to consolidate their business with fewer agencies (multi-product advertisers)—often, the reorganization of client management structures leads to changes in advertising assignments.

- Conflict situations may arise owing to account realignments in the United States (shifts at the U.S. parent agency often create shifts in Canadian subsidiaries). Also, agency mergers, in Canada or internationally, can bring competing accounts under one roof, which creates a need for one account to switch to another agency.

A client–agency partnership can dissolve quickly. Consider what happened between Wendy's Restaurants of Canada Inc. and its agency Bates Canada. Bates lost the Canadian business valued at $20 million annually because Wendy's in the United States decided to consolidate its Canadian and U.S. agencies under one roof; that roof was McCann Erickson of New York, parent company of MacLaren McCann of Toronto. Unexpectedly, MacLaren McCann Canada got the Wendy's advertising business in Canada. In rationalizing the decision, Wendy's said, "It gives tremendous synergies between the two countries. We are looking for efficiencies in how they spend our money."[8] The quality of work (good quality) provided by Bates Canada was not factored into this decision at all. Wendy's was a huge loss for Bates!

In 2003, Nike Canada announced its advertising account would be up for review (a surprise announcement for agency Cossette Communication Group). The potential loss of such a high profile account by Canada's largest ad agency could be a blow to Cossette's reputation and pocket book. Nike is the pinnacle of advertising success. It's one of the most successful market-driven brands in the past 20 years, and Cossette had a hand in the brand's development in Canada. While Cossette has been invited to participate in the review, along with several other agencies, Nike admits it is looking for new direction in its advertising—a warning sign for Cossette.[9]

To encourage the best possible relationship between clients and agencies, and to clearly review the expectations of parties, clients must conduct agency evaluations at planned intervals. Also, since the agency invests considerable resources in its client's business, it should have the opportunity to review the client's performance. A good working relationship depends on honest, open communication between the partners, an attitude of respect for each other, and the sharing of common goals so that both partners can be successful.

As indicated by the Nike example above, it is quite common for the agency to take the fall when its advertising does not meet the client's expectations. Among the shortcomings that a client might ascribe to its agency are a high degree of personnel turnover, understaffing, and lack of interest. A partnership, however, is a two-way street and agencies may see shortcomings with the client's role in the process. Among the problems that agencies have with their clients are poor communication of objectives and strategies, lack of senior management involvement, and indecision. Agencies also receive all kinds of praise from clients when their advertising strategies work. If the business results are good, rarely does a client complain.

In recent years there has been a trend toward **project assignments** and short-term relationships. Clients and agencies are not seeking commitment and nobody wants to get married. Many agencies report that it is the same kind of work, but it is handled on an "as-needed" basis. According to Terry Johnson's advertising agency, Allard Johnson Communications, "The project approach means you have to prove yourself over and over again, but that can work to your advantage. Most of our clients have been with us five or six years, even though we're working on a project basis."[10]

Project-based work offers flexibility for clients. If they don't like what the agency is doing, they can audition other agencies where the fit might be better, without going through a long review process. In these times, the pressure is squarely on the advertising agency; they must provide results or suffer the consequences.

For more insight into the dynamics between clients and agencies, see the Advertising in Action vignette **A Thing or Two About Client–Agency Relations**.

Types of Advertising Agencies

The type of agency a client chooses to work with can be a difficult decision. When choosing an agency, the client's goal is to find the one that will recommend and produce cost-efficient, effective advertising to achieve the desired results in a traditionally expensive area of communications. The client must consider factors such as agency size, the service mix the agency is capable of providing, and compatibility of personnel. Essentially there are four different types of agencies: full-service agencies, boutique agencies, media-buying service agencies, and specialist agencies. Let's examine the various types of advertising agencies operating in Canada.

FULL-SERVICE AGENCIES

Full-service agencies appeal strongly to larger advertisers that need the variety of services offered or require international connections for global advertising campaigns. Services most often provided by full-service agencies must embrace all of the possible demands a client may place on them. Therefore, the services list is diverse and may include product and marketing research, creative planning, creative development and execution, media planning and placement, sales promotion, public relations and direct response, and interactive communications. In other words, a full-service agency must offer integrated marketing communications solutions to its clients.

Many agencies are redefining what they do and are eliminating the advertising agency label in favour of a marketing communications label. As indicated earlier, Canada's largest agency recently changed its name to Cossette Communication Group partly to suggest the diversity of services it offers. Padulo Integrated Inc. is another agency whose name suggests "total-solution communications services."

Alternatively, full-service advertising agencies are acquiring or affiliating with specialists in other areas of marketing communications so they have access to the services their clients want. Cossette Communication Group either owns or is affiliated with

Padulo Integrated Inc.
www.padulo.ca/integration.html

ADVERTISING IN action

A Thing or Two About Client–Agency Relations

Clients and agencies share a common goal—to get the very best results for the client's business. On paper it sounds so simple, but the reality is that client–agency relationships can be very complicated. Establishing good working relationships that prevail over the long term to the mutual benefit of both parties is challenging.

Consider the following example of how quickly relationships can dissolve. A few years ago when the Holt Renfrew account was up for grabs, Roche Macaulay & Partners Advertising Inc. went after it. To do so, Roche had to resign its high-profile Harry Rosen account because the two clothing retailers were competitors (a conflict situation). The resignation was a surprise to Rosen, but the Holt Renfrew account was worth much more in terms of revenue for Roche. Holt Renfrew spent much more on advertising. Was the resignation motivated by money?

After holding the Holt Renfrew account for 16 months, Roche Macaulay was shown the door. The agency's irreverent ads were supposed to attract younger shoppers and refashion Holt as a hip place to shop. Evidently, Holt wasn't impressed with the work. The Holt account was then given to Zig Inc., a relatively new agency that ironically enough was started by Geoffrey Roche's former partner Andy Macaulay. The manner in which Roche was dismissed has created some resentment, but there's a saying that may apply here: "What goes around comes around." Perhaps the Roche Macaulay agency was just getting what it deserved. It might have been wiser to stay with Harry Rosen.

The reasons for dissolving a relationship are many; money and compensation disagreements, poor chemistry between the people on both sides, lack of constructive and meaningful communications, and failure to agree on creative or media direction are the reasons that lead the pack. All of these issues are within control of the two parties, however, and they can be corrected if the proper steps are taken. A framework for the relationship must be established when the relationship is in its infancy stages, and the client and agency must abide by it. The Institute of Communications and Advertising outlines a system, and more importantly an attitude, for building strong relationships. They identify 10 key points:

- Encourage genuine partnership, not lip service.
- Don't create a scorecard feeling.
- Relate everything to deliverables that are agreed upon initially.
- Don't obsess on negatives. Critique what needs fixing. Reinforce what is good.
- If something goes off the rails discuss the matter promptly. Don't wait for a review.
- Be candid with each other about risk. Understand the difference between "tried and true" and "out of the box and risky."
- Don't fall out over money.
- Be constructive and fair.
- As an agency, remember that you are providing a tool to do a job.
- As a client, remember that your attitude has an immense motivational effect.

As is the case in other kinds of relationships, things in advertising usually boil down to the quality of communications. Aldo Cundari, chairman and CEO of Cundari Integrated Advertising, says there should be clarity when first establishing the relationship. "Every client–agency situation is unique. Granted, process is needed to provide order. But being able to talk openly and constructively goes a long way in building a harmonious and effective relationship." He believes in regular "round table" sessions to discuss and analyze the business relationship.

Sources: Adapted from David Rutherford, "Starting with the right attitude," *Marketing*, January 28, 2002, p. 32; John Heinzl, "Holt dumps advertising agency," *The Globe and Mail*, September 11, 2001, p. B2; and Aldo Cundari, "Over-servicing is not the problem," *Marketing*, June 25, 2001, p. 41.

Cossette-Communication Marketing (a traditional advertising agency), Cossette B2B (an agency specializing in business-to-business communications), Impact Research (a company specializing in consumer research), Cossette Media (a media planning and buying specialist), Blitz Direct (a direct-marketing specialist), and Optimum Public Relations (a public-relations specialist), among others. MacLaren McCann is a full-service advertising agency, but it also owns MacLaren McCann Interactive (online communications), MacLaren McCann Momentum (an experiential marketing specialist—sports and entertainment product participation), M2 Universal (a media management and media planning company), and MacLaren McCann Healthcare (an agency specializing in pharmaceutical advertising and communications).

Traditional full-service agencies such as MacLaren McCann and Cossette-Communication Marketing are typically divided into three functional areas: account management (sometimes referred to as account services or client services), creative, and media. Figure 2.6 illustrates the internal structure of a typical full-service advertising agency.

Each primary functional area of a full-service agency plays a vital role in the development of advertising for clients. The account-management group works with the client to develop the advertising approach and objectives and oversees the whole process as it moves through the agency. The creative group develops copy and visuals for the various media that meet the advertising objectives. The media group develops the placement plan, determining where the advertising should be placed, for how long, in what media, and so forth.

CREATIVE BOUTIQUES

Creative boutiques are agencies specializing in the development of creative ideas and their execution for clients' advertising campaigns. In a world of specialization, it is now quite common for an advertiser to divide its advertising assignments among agency specialists, one of which is a creative boutique. Creative boutiques are usually formed and staffed by personnel previously employed by the creative departments of full-service agencies; their key personnel, due to past performance, have excellent credentials within the industry.

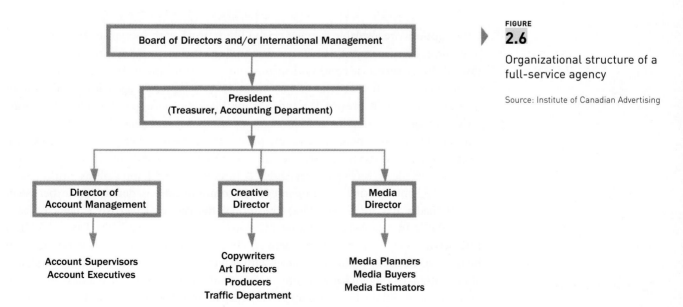

**FIGURE
2.6**

Organizational structure of a full-service agency

Source: Institute of Canadian Advertising

Using advertising and marketing objectives as a guideline, a creative boutique concentrates on producing the single most important component of a campaign—the sales message. Creative boutiques are quite successful in attracting clients from full-service agencies, especially if they are staffed with respected and successful creative people. Such was the case when Chris Staples, Tom Shepansky, and Ian Grais bolted from Palmer Jarvis DDB, a full-service agency based in Vancouver, to form a boutique named Rethink Communications. Three years later, Rethink has a full roster of clients that includes A&P, A&W, B.C. Lions football club, Bell Mobility West, Earls Restaurants, and the Canadian Cancer Society. Successful boutiques eventually blossom into much bigger agencies.

MEDIA-BUYING SERVICE

A **media-buying service** is a specialist agency responsible for planning and purchasing the most cost-efficient media for a client—that is to say, responsible for gaining maximum exposure to a target audience at minimum cost. In addition, a media-buying service often obtains government and other clearances for advertisements, ensures that each ad runs as scheduled, and generally takes care of administrative work associated with the media-buying transaction.

Since efficiency is important, the use of a media-buying service might generate cost savings that can be reinvested in the creative product. Very often a client will have creative matters handled by several different agencies but have the media planning coordinated and implemented by a media-buying service. Indeed, the use of creative boutiques and media-buying services together could provide the best of both worlds for advertisers. However, full-service agencies argue that they can handle both services equally well for their clients—and under one roof, too.

Among Canada's larger media-buying companies are M2 Universal, Zenith Optimedia, and Starcom. M2 Universal reported billings of $640 million in 2003. **Media billings** refer to the total dollar volume of advertising in terms of time and space handled by an agency in one year. Zenith Optimedia boasts a diversified client base of about 35 companies, covering almost every category. Key clients include General Mills, Nestlé, Hasbro, CIBC, and Hewlett-Packard.[11]

OTHER BOUTIQUES AND COMMUNICATIONS SPECIALISTS

Other options are available for clients who like to work with specialists. In today's cluttered media environment, clients are demanding efficiency and as a result are moving toward **direct-response communications** and away from the mass media. Such movement calls for a different kind of specialization. Consequently, agencies specializing in direct response are in greater demand. Carlson Marketing Group Canada Inc., the country's third largest marketing communications company, generates 55 percent of its revenues from direct-response advertising programs. Numerous full-service agencies have started separate direct-response agencies to meet the demands of their clients. Such agencies include FCB Direct, Grey Direct & Interactive, and Rapp Collins Worldwide.

With clients looking for more integrated communications, demand for expertise in digital media has increased. Most traditional full-service advertising agencies have diversified and established separate divisions for this task (e.g., MacLaren McCann Interactive and Grey Direct & Interactive). The range of what is available varies between high-powered multi-national agencies with interactive divisions to small, savvy, stand-alone **interactive agencies** with only a few years of experience. Rebellium Inc. is an example of an interactive start-up (1999) that has been very successful at integrating web-based advertising strategies with other forms of communications. Rebellium provides a range of digital solutions and a full complement of technology and creative services for websites, CD-ROM, kiosks, e-branding, design, e-commerce, and digital presentations. Its clients include Canon, Telus Mobility, AOL Canada, The Loyalty Group, and the Government of Ontario—some very big clients for a relatively new specialist.

Other specialists focus on **product categories** or niche market segments that are identified as profitable opportunities. Pharmaceutical marketing, for example, is a highly specialized product category where laws and regulations governing advertising are very different from other product categories. Consequently, it is an area that not many agencies get involved with. A few prominent agencies in this group include Remtulla Euro RSCG, MacLaren McCann Healthcare, and Integrated Healthcare Communications.

In the **niche market segment** area, there are agencies, or separate divisions of agencies, that specialize in targeting age groups such as youth and baby boomers. Padulo Integrated Inc. owns and operates six integrated business divisions, the newest division being BOOM Communications. BOOM focuses on the baby boomer market and helps advertisers understand that particular segment of the population. Boomers comprise a third of the adult population, a figure that caught the attention of Keith Hillmer, a veteran creative director and baby boomer who started BOOM. Says Hillmer, "The ad industry looks at the baby boomer market as some sleeping giant that it's afraid will wake up. But the boomers are awake, and you ignore them at your peril." Most advertisers focus on the 18-to-35 age group with youth-oriented advertising. BOOM is essentially an agency within an agency, with Hillmer accessing the resources of Padulo's much larger and more established firm while consulting with Padulo on how his clients can best reach boomers.[12] BOOM is a classic example of how a boutique-style agency gets started.

Clients tend to go in two different directions when selecting the type of agency they work with. Some migrate to the large multi-national agencies, while others prefer to work with boutique-style shops. The trend toward project assignments and shorter relationships is beneficial to the smaller agency where the costs of operations are lower. In contrast, larger agencies need a long-term relationship in order to operate cost-effectively. Boutiques offer clients a unique advantage. The highly experienced creative and media people who started the boutique usually work directly with the clients. Such is not the case in larger agencies. Ironically, these creative and media people honed their craft at much larger agencies.

For more insight into why clients are interested in the services provided by boutique-style agencies, refer to the Advertising in Action vignette **Rethink's Fresh Approach**.

Structure and Management of the Advertising Agency

We know that advertising agencies are divided into three primary functional areas: account management, creative, and media (see Figure 2.7). Large agencies may include additional departments, embracing functions such as marketing research, sales promotion, and public relations. The following sections summarize the roles and responsibilities of the primary functional areas of the agency: account planning and management, creative, and media.

Rethink's Fresh Approach

Rethink, Zig, Taxi, John St.—not exactly the usual names of advertising agencies, but names that suggest what these and similar agencies are about. These four boutique-style agencies just happen to be the hottest "creative" shops in Canada right now. Rethink was named *Marketing Magazine's* Agency of the Year in 2003, Zig won the award in 2002, and Taxi won it in 2001.

Rethink was nothing more than a creative start-up four years ago when partners and former award-winning Palmer Jarvis DDB employees Chris Staples, Ian Grais, and Tom Shepansky formed the company. Their vision was a no-frills operation that stressed creative at all costs. They were fed up with the bureaucracy that was associated with large full-service agencies. Rethink would be a boutique focused on finding creative solutions. In the span of four years, Rethink has won all kinds of advertising awards, has built an enviable client list, and certainly has acquired an enviable and formidable reputation in the industry.

Rethink's approach and attitude toward advertising is what attracts clients. Staples claims that research has knocked the stuffing out of advertising. Clients rely so much on focus groups and surveys that they forget their own instincts. He also complains about time. The average time between a client brief and a commercial going on air is 42 weeks in a big agency—that's longer than it takes to have a baby! Rethink works fast and loose. Creative meetings happen in hallways or doorways. Concepts are scribbled down on small notepads or a huge blackboard. Presentations are free of the usual jargon featuring catchphrases like "brand matrix," "key insights," and "consumer decision ladder." Staples believes big agencies are bound by and obligated to such jargon—it's all about process rather than ideas.

Just what is the attraction for clients? Its ideas! Darn good ideas! Rethink is responsible for A&P/Dominion's "Fresh Obsessed" campaign. The latest round of television spots features employees so obsessed with selling only the freshest fish that they had them flown in by helicopter. Other commercials show fresh-obsessed employees infiltrating the competition. At A&P Dominion, fresh is really an obsession! Dominion reports that their ads have hit all-time records in communications appeal. Consumer awareness of the Fresh Obsessed campaign is presently at 92 percent.

A campaign for Clover Leaf tuna increased sales by 35 percent. In Rethink's hands, something as mundane as tuna can develop hip cachet. So creative was the campaign that one of the ads, an ad showing a lemon on a fishhook, made the cover of *Applied Arts* magazine. Lorna Buchanan, vice-president of marketing for Clover Leaf, was thrilled with the campaign, saying, "You know that kind of sales increase doesn't come along every day." Campaigns like these build reputation and attract new clients. Other clients in the Rethink stable include Playland (an amusement park), Science World, and the B.C. Lions.

A defining moment in the life of Rethink occurred late in 2002. The president and CEO of A&P in the United States inquired if Rethink would like to pitch for their Farmer Jack business in Michigan. They would be competing against a few U.S. agencies. At the same time, another inquiry came from Brent Cuthbertson, the former head of marketing at Richmond Savings (a former client) and now director of marketing in Western Canada for Bell Mobility. Would Rethink consider developing some ideas for Bell in the West? At the time of the query, Bell Mobility was a client of Cossette Communication Group, Canada's largest full-service agency. Rethink now represents Farmer Jack and Bell Mobility in western Canada.

Rethink now finds itself at a crossroads. Do they remain a boutique agency or continue to expand? Says Staples, "This is a big moment of reflection for Rethink. We didn't think it would happen this fast. The initial plan was to be a small agency (40 employees maximum considering growth) and all of our efforts would be focused on the creative work." They have reached that point and have a layer of management and creative people below them. The three partners wonder if they will be able to give the personal touch to clients. After all, someone has to run the business. Rethink is a classic case of a company experiencing growing pains! For now the Rethink partners still answer their own phones and they remain active with the work. The goal, says Grais, is to hang onto the culture.

Rethink is not a full-service agency and they dislike comparisons to such operations. They are an alternative to what national and multi-national agencies offer. They don't do media or promotions. Chris Staples warns prospective clients that their model isn't for everyone.

Sources: Eve Lazarus, "Rethink's Fresh Obsession," *Marketing*, November 24, 2003, pp. 11–14; and Jennifer Hunter, "Shaking up the ad world," *Maclean's*, November 22, 1999, pp. 74–76.

ACCOUNT MANAGEMENT

As the name implies, **account management** staff are responsible for managing the affairs of the agency's clients. Account personnel perform a dual function: they are both consultants and coordinators. Account personnel must totally understand the client's business so that they can advise the client on a variety of strategic marketing issues, identify and motivate agency resources to build the client's business, and coordinate communications between the client and agency.

Account-management personnel must understand the major marketing issues facing the client and, using all available resources of the agency, recommend a course of action to the client. Thus, they are actively involved in the planning process and in presenting agency work to the client. They are expected to be experts on the consumer and to understand how the client's business relates to, and is perceived by, the consumer.

The account-management group includes an account executive, an account supervisor, and an account director.

ACCOUNT EXECUTIVE

Often viewed as occupying an entry-level position, the **account executive** is responsible for client contact, project planning, budget control, preparing annual advertising plans, and advising on strategic issues. The account executive liaises between the client and agency, and communicates frequently with the personnel in the client organization who are responsible for the advertising function (advertising manager, product manager). An account executive is usually responsible for one or several clients, depending on the size and resources of the agency. The working relationship between the agency account executive and the client product manager is close and frequent.

ACCOUNT SUPERVISOR

As a middle manager, the **account supervisor** manages a group of account executives and is therefore responsible for an expanded list of clients. Job functions include strategic planning, market analysis, competitive activity analysis, and analyzing and capitalizing on business-building opportunities. In such a position, the supervisor must look beyond the scope of current projects and assignments and assist in developing the future direction of a product or service.

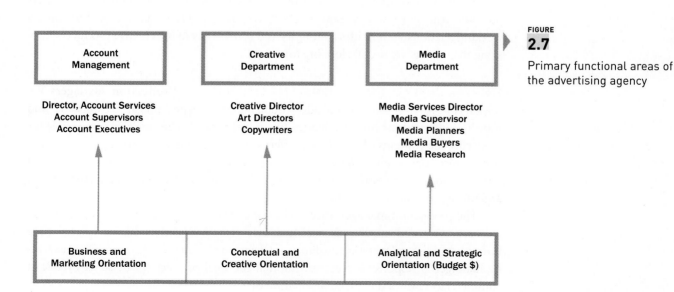

FIGURE
2.7
Primary functional areas of the advertising agency

ACCOUNT DIRECTOR   The **account director** deals directly with senior members of the client organization and is responsible for how the agency handles client accounts. Specific responsibilities include long-term planning, deployment of agency personnel, and overall account profitability. Also, the account director is responsible for working with senior agency executives from other functional areas in seeking new business for the agency.

CREATIVE DEPARTMENT

The **creative department** is responsible for developing the idea or concept for communications. Once the nature of the message (often referred to as the *creative concept*) has been established, members of the creative team must sell it to the client; once the client approves the concept, the creative team must execute the creative. Heading the creative department is the **creative director**, who oversees the development of all agency creative. The creative director is ultimately responsible for maintaining a high standard of creative quality on behalf of the agency. In such a position, the creative director must motivate the copywriters and art directors who work directly on client assignments.

COPYWRITER   The responsibility of the **copywriter** is to convert information provided by the client and account personnel (information concerning unique selling points, target-market profiles, purchase motivations, and so on) into an effective, persuasive sales message. The message must be presented in such a manner that it stands out and is relevant to potential customers. The copywriter develops the main idea of the advertisement in conjunction with an art director, then creates its various verbal components: the headline, sub-headlines, and body copy or text.

ART DIRECTOR   Using the same information resources as the copywriter, the **art director** is responsible for developing a visual communication that, combined with the copy, elicits a favourable reaction from the target market. Art direction requires knowledge in specialized areas such as graphic design, photography, and electronic publishing. An art director need not be an artist, but must understand the production process and be able to direct artists and technical production specialists.

While the jobs of copywriters and art directors are separate, individuals in these positions usually work as a team on client assignments. Over a period of time, such a working relationship provides continuity and consistency in the creative product, something that clients are usually looking for.

PRINT AND BROADCAST PRODUCTION MANAGER   **Production managers** are responsible for preparing print advertisements (newspaper, magazine, outdoor, and transit) and broadcast commercials (radio and television). They are also responsible for preparing the contents of direct-mail offers if direct-response advertising is part of the communications strategy. Since production is an activity that involves execution, it requires coordination with numerous external suppliers such as actors, directors of film and music, and camera operators.

The production manager offers technical advice about matters such as production cost estimates and ensures that all activities are completed within scheduled time frames—publishers' material deadlines or television air dates, for example. Often, a **traffic manager** is responsible for ensuring that the final product (print ad or broadcast commercial) reaches the media destination on time.

MEDIA DEPARTMENT

The media department is responsible for the planning and placement of advertising time and space. The proliferation of media forms, fragmentation within specific media (e.g., the large number of television channels available to viewers), the escalating cost of media, and the use of computers in the planning process have added to the complexity of the media responsibility. The functions of the media department are as follows:

- *Media planning* The plan that documents how the client's money will be spent to achieve advertising objectives is prepared and presented at this stage.

- *Media buying* Once approved, the elements necessary to execute the media plan are purchased. The objective when buying is to achieve the most at the least expense—that is, to achieve maximum impact and reach at the lowest possible cost to the client. Each purchase must be checked to see that it ran correctly. Sometimes, media buys must be upgraded midstream to compensate for audience loss (actual audience versus estimated audience). Media buying is a negotiated process between agencies or media-buying services and the media. Buying time and space in volume yields preferred rates for the advertiser.

- *Media research* Larger agencies have a media research department that provides up-to-date information regarding audiences and circulation. Such data are used frequently when alternative media forms (e.g., television, magazines, newspapers) are being compared, or when the respective abilities of specific media to reach a certain target market are being compared. With advancing computer technology, many agencies have online access to computer data banks containing media audience information. A number of independent research firms tap into these data banks to provide media analysis for agencies without online capabilities.

Position responsibilities in the media department are distributed among the media planner, media buyer, media supervisor, and media director.

MEDIA PLANNER   **Media planners** assess the strengths, weaknesses, cost efficiencies, and communications potentials of various media to develop a media plan. The ability to communicate is vital for planners, since they must sell the plan first within the agency and then to the client. Since the client's money is on the line at this stage, planners must be prepared to address all of the client's concerns. Media plans may go through many revisions before receiving client approval. One of the major challenges of a media planner today is to develop strategies and recommendations for integrating web-based advertising into more traditional advertising plans.

MEDIA BUYER   The **media buyer** is responsible for developing an intimate knowledge of the media marketplace and being aware of all developments affecting media buying. Buyers must evaluate and make decisions on the competitive claims of the various media in order to make the most efficient and effective buys for their clients. Good negotiating skills are vital if one is to be successful in a media-buying role.

MEDIA SUPERVISOR   The **media supervisor** is generally responsible for a team of media people and for coordinating the efforts of buyers and planners during the development and execution of the media plan.

MEDIA DIRECTOR   The responsibility of the **media director** depends on the size of the agency. In smaller agencies, the director is involved in planning and buying media. In a larger agency, the director is more of an administrator. As a senior manager, the director is ultimately responsible for the philosophy that governs the media planning function in the agency and is accountable to the client for media planning and placement. Working with other senior executives, the media director usually plays an active role in business presentations to new clients.

Managing the Client's Business

Several factors influence the professional relationship between the client and the agency.

AGENCY TEAMS

The amount of time an agency spends with a client and the personnel it allocates to serve the needs of the client affects the client–agency relationship. Agency management will form teams that will work together on a client's business. The employees who comprise a team vary among agencies, depending on factors such as the size of the agency and the various levels of personnel resources available. Generally, an **account group** includes the following:

- Account executive and account supervisor
- Art director and copywriter
- Media planner and media buyer

Keeping an account team together over a number of assignments benefits both the client and the agency. Familiarity with the products and the way the client operates are other obvious benefits. The agency team can draw upon past experiences with the client when considering new directions to pursue. Another benefit involves consistency in approach. The account team develops a strategy that will work over an extended period. Within that long-term strategy will be the flexibility to develop and execute new plans when needed. Clients who are subjected to changing personnel within an account group may question whether the agency values their business. Conversely, the agency may, by keeping an account team together, imply that a client's business is important and that it is trying to serve the client more effectively.

COMPETING ACCOUNTS

Agencies are exposed to extremely confidential client information when developing advertising plans. As a consequence, agencies will not, as a rule, accept assignments from an advertiser who is in direct competition with a current client. Numerous conflicts develop as an agency seeks new business. When agencies merge to form larger agencies, competing accounts are often brought together. In such a case, one of the clients (usually the smaller, in terms of media dollars) will take its business elsewhere, or the agency will resign the client's business.

AGENCY OF RECORD

Many large advertisers (companies with numerous divisions or multi-product lines) distribute their advertising assignments among several advertising agencies. Or the client may divide its assignments among agencies based on the nature of activity (e.g., advertising, public relations, sales promotion, direct response). From the client's perspective, dividing the business among several agencies is advantageous in that the different products or different services required will receive more attention and service than would be possible if all assignments were given to one agency. Since the agencies are competing with each other for new business, all of them seeking further assignments from the client, their performance on the products and services they handle will be of a high quality. Dividing the assignments, in other words, should positively affect the quality of the work.

On the media side of things, the client often appoints an **agency of record (AOR)**. This central agency is responsible for media negotiation and placement, and is often used by multiple-product advertisers that use more than one advertising agency. An AOR facilitates efficiency in the media-buying process, often making available greater discounts to the client by purchasing all media on a corporate (large-volume) basis. The AOR is responsible for corporate media contracts under which other agencies will issue their placement orders. Also, the AOR records all advertising placed, and is responsible for final allotment of time and space in a media schedule. As indicated earlier, some large advertisers have appointed a media-buying service as their AOR, leaving creative matters to traditional full-service agencies or other specialists. The AOR usually receives a slightly higher rate of commission if a commission-based compensation system is in place.

Agency Compensation

How an advertising agency is paid, and how much money it makes, is an issue frequently on the minds of both client marketing executives and agency managers. Marketing executives often argue that their agency is asking for too much money, or they feel they are paying for unnecessary services. Agency managers, on the other hand, believe that the profit margins on some of their accounts are too low in relation to the amount of resources allocated to the client. Needless to say, compensation is a primary area where clients and agencies are at odds.

There are three basic methods of compensating an advertising agency for the services it provides: a **commission** based on the dollar volume of media placed; a fee that considers the resources an agency allocates to servicing a client; and payment by results, a reduced-rate commission with incentives based on performance standards. A summary of the advantages and disadvantages of each system appears in Figure 2.8.

Clients are moving toward the payment-by-results method and away from the other methods. They are asking their agencies to be accountable for the strategies and executions being recommended. Agencies are asking clients to take more risks to prove to them that their ideas will produce the desired results.

THE COMMISSION SYSTEM

The commission system has been used in one form or another for more than 100 years. Until the early 1990s, the standard rate of commission had been 15 percent. If this system is used, the agency receives a 15-percent rebate from the media it is buying time or space from. The media allow accredited advertising agencies to buy advertising time and space at a 15-percent discount off quoted rates. This discount is granted to the agency for its work in analyzing client research, preparing the overall strategy, creating and producing the advertising material, media planning and buying, billing the client, and research in support of recommendations and discounts for prompt payment.[13]

The 15-percent commission applies only to the purchase of time and space. To illustrate the commission principle, let's assume that a total media purchase amounted to

FIGURE
2.8

The advantages and disadvantages of agency compensation methods

Clients are moving toward the payment by results method and away from the other methods. They are asking their agencies to be accountable for the strategies and executions being recommended. Agencies are asking clients to take more risks to prove to them that their ideas will produce the desired results.

COMMISSION SYSTEM

Pros:
- Simple to implement
- All services provided at no additional cost
- Pressure on agency to keep costs down

Cons:
- Profit on some brands (larger budgets); losses on others (smaller budgets)
- Agency recommendations for higher expenditures may be self-serving
- Payment based on media cost, not the work provided

FEE SYSTEM

Pros:
- Client pays only for services provided
- Promotes efficient client–agency relationship

Cons:
- High administration costs
- Difficult for agency to forecast workload

PAYMENT BY RESULTS SYSTEM (LOWER COMMISSION AND INCENTIVES)

Pros:
- Encourages neutral media recommendations involving a variety of media
- Additional revenue to agency for successful campaigns

Cons:
- Accountability; potential loss on account if results not achieved
- Influences beyond the control of agency could negatively impact advertising

$1 million. The agency commission would be $150 000, or 15 percent of $1 million. The client would pay the agency $1 million; the agency would retain $150 000 and forward the remaining $850 000 to the media.

Production costs involved with print advertising or television and radio commercials are paid by the client but at a different commission rate. Typically, a profit margin of 17.65 percent is added to the production costs incurred by the agency. For example, if the cost of producing a single 30-second television commercial is $200 000, the agency would receive $35 300 (200 000 plus 17.65 percent) for its services. The agency would bill the client $235 300 and from these funds the external suppliers who produced the commercial would be paid. Adding 17.65 percent to production costs works out to the same rate of pay as it does when deducting 15 percent from the total amount of media time and space the agency bills for its clients.

The commission system fell out of favour with clients because it fuelled a perception that agencies were making too much money from easy media-buying assignments. There was also a perception that it was contributing to an inherent bias within an agency to emphasize media that are more profitable for an agency to buy—television, for example, is a very easy medium for an agency to recommend.[14]

Clients using a media-buying service use different commission rates, as such a specialist performs only one basic function. For buying media the range is 2.5 to 3.0 percent; for buying television only the rate is 1.5 to 2.25 percent plus fees; for buying all media the rate is 2.25 percent plus fees. For planning and buying television the rate is 4 percent plus fees, and for planning and buying all media the rate is 5.0 percent.[15] Fees are typically added if the volume of the buy decreases or the target audience narrows from a demographic, psychographic, or geographic perspective.

THE FEE SYSTEM

In its truest form, the fee system avoids any form of commission and rewards an agency for the labour (time, effort, and energy) it puts into servicing the client. The advertiser and agency agree on an hourly, annual, or overall fee. The fee can vary according to the department or levels of salary within a department. In other cases, a flat hourly fee for all work is determined, no matter the salary level of the person doing the work. There has been a movement toward fees in recent years because so much of the work in advertising today is not traditional advertising—it has gone well beyond simply buying space in the mass media. Agencies are now making recommendations involving all aspects of integrated marketing communications. Commissions cannot be calculated on recommendations involving activities such as sales promotion, direct mail, and the internet. Fees are established by assigning costs of agency operations to a client. The agency then determines what hourly charge will recover these costs and provide the agency with a profit.

Some of the more common options are minimum guarantees, hourly rates, and costs plus profits. If a *minimum guarantee* is used, the client and agency establish a minimum income figure, including a profit, by making assumptions about the level of service required for a period of time, usually a year. If an *hourly rate* system is used, the agency assigns an hourly rate to those employees who have direct contact with the client. The rate is designed to recover agency costs and includes a profit margin. If a *cost-plus-profits* system is used, the amount paid to the agency includes the agency's direct costs (employee salaries), indirect costs (heat, light, and power), and profits. The costs associated with all of the people employed in the agency—including those who do not work directly on a client's business—are taken into account, along with other costs. In effect, indirect costs are added to direct costs, along with a provision for profit.

Fee systems tend to be cumbersome and require much administration and paperwork. The main drawback of the fee system is that it does not reflect the quality of the work by an agency or the impact it has on the client's business.

PAYMENT BY RESULTS (PBR)

One of the first advertisers to experiment with performance-based compensation was Procter & Gamble. Its rationale for moving away from the commission system was to encourage agencies to recommend a variety of media and to rely less on 30-second television ads, which are more expensive than other forms of media and thus garner larger commissions. As a result, agencies are paid a higher commission percentage for good business results and a lower percentage for poor results. According to Bob Wehling, global marketing officer for Procter & Gamble, "As we grow our agencies grow. It will keep us all focused on the end goal: increased brand sales."[16]

Moving to performance-based compensation will eliminate media bias (e.g., recommending media that generate fat commissions) and encourage holistic, media-neutral marketing. Many other companies now use this system, but an obvious drawback has been raised by agencies: linking the performance of a brand to advertising is tricky because sales can be affected by a host of factors, many of which are beyond the control of the advertising agency.

Molson is using an incentive system for its Canadian and Export brands. Molson bases its incentive agreements on three critical measures: brand share, advertising effectiveness, and advertising recall. The effectiveness of the now famous "Rant" commercial for Molson Canadian exceeded the company's benchmarks for persuasiveness, communication of brand message, and linkage between creative and brand.[17] In the commercial, a character named Joe stood in front of a screen showing stereotypical Canadian settings while he ranted about being a proud Canadian. Market share increased 2 percentage points, so the ad agency Bensimon Byrne D'Arcy received a healthy bonus.

There are three types of performance criteria used in PBR schemes to determine the remuneration paid to the agency: business performance, advertising performance, and agency performance. For more specific information about performance criteria refer to Figure 2.9.

It is difficult to determine which of these remuneration systems is best for the client and the agency. From the *Agency Remuneration Study 2002* conducted by the Association of Canadian Advertisers it was concluded that no single model can be deemed the best for all circumstances. Rather, the most effective model is the one designed to meet the needs of each client–agency relationship.[18] The compensation model should be designed to provide adequate professional service to the client, provide an incentive for both the client and the agency, fairly compensate the agency (e.g., offer reasonable profit levels), and be reviewed periodically for effectiveness.

FIGURE 2.9

Performance criteria included in a payment-by-results compensation model

Business Performance	Advertising Performance	Agency Performance
Sales volume	Advertising awareness	Agency service delivery
Volume growth	Brand image shifts	Relationship management
Relative brand performance	Attitude ratings	Functional competencies
Composite performance	Ad enjoyment	Contribution to "branding"
Market share	Brand personality	Project management
Customer loyalty	Predisposition to buy	Administration
Brand equity	Ad scores	Cost efficiency
Brand profitability	Persuasion index	Proactivity

The ICA 2000 Study on PBR shows the weighting emphasis was balanced as follows: Agency 41%, Advertising 30%, and Business results 29%. Further, 83% of Canadian PBR programs include business performance criteria, 65% include advertising performance criteria, and 78% include agency performance criteria.

Source: "Payment by Results 2, Advertising Agency Remuneration Best Practices," Institute of Communications and Advertising, **www.ica-ad.com**.

SUMMARY

The Canadian advertising industry comprises three primary groups and numerous support groups. The primary groups include the advertisers (client), advertising agencies, and the media. Support groups include the Institute of Canadian Advertising, the Association of Canadian Advertisers, and numerous media associations.

Advertising management usually comes under the jurisdiction of the marketing department. The size and marketing sophistication of the organization often dictate how advertising is managed. It could be the responsibility of a brand manager or category manager, or it could be the responsibility of many individuals. With marketing and communication strategy becoming more continental and global in scope (e.g., using strategies and executions that work elsewhere), managers are redefining targets and implementing campaigns on a North American or global scale.

In the advertising development process, the roles and responsibilities of the client include planning and budgeting, coordination of advertising with other marketing and marketing communications activity, monitoring the implementation of communications activities, liaising with the advertising agency, and securing executive approval to implement advertising plans. Once plans are implemented, the manager is responsible for evaluating advertising, for which he or she is held accountable.

Advertising agencies provide a variety of services to their clients, but their primary role is to provide experience and expertise in the communications process. In this area, the agency provides planning assistance and contributes an objective viewpoint to that planning process. Agency recommendations must be cost-effective and have impact on the intended target.

The goal of a client–agency relationship is to have a long-term partnership where both parties prosper. However, relationships between clients and agencies are often volatile and account shifting is a common occurrence in the industry. Such shifting occurs for reasons such as client dissatisfaction with the quality of work, philosophical differences in creative and media direction, and the absence of a team concept. For a client–agency relationship to be a lasting one there must be open and honest communication among the parties, mutual respect, and agreement on common goals. In recent years there has been a trend toward project assignments and short-term relationships. The nature of client–agency relationships is changing as the business environment changes. Short-term relationships place added pressure on agencies to perform.

Advertisers must evaluate the services provided by agencies and decide whether to use a full-service agency or hire a specialist that may or may not offer all of the services required. Specialists include creative boutiques, media-buying services, direct-response companies, and interactive communications companies. In recent years, product-category specialist agencies and niche-market specialist agencies have entered the picture, opting for work that is seen as unattractive or unprofitable by traditional agencies. In contrast, such boutique-style specialists see profitable opportunities.

Traditional, full-service agencies are managed in specific functional areas: account management, creative, and the media. Account management personnel consult with clients and coordinate activity within the agency. The creative department develops communication concepts, and the media department plans and places advertising time and space. The services that an agency provides to a client are usually handled by an account team, which includes an individual from each functional area.

Large multi-product advertisers often work with several agencies at the same time. In this situation the client designates one agency as their agency of record (AOR). The AOR is responsible for all media buying for all company brands regardless of which agency they are assigned to. The AOR may be a full-service agency or a media-buying service.

A major factor in client–agency relationships is the method by which the agency is paid. Two systems are used to compensate agencies: a commission system, under which the agency receives a percentage of the value of media purchased by an agency for a client; or a fee system, which is based on the services requested by the client. More recently, a payment-by-results system has become popular. In this system, agencies are compensated based on how well they meet predetermined performance criteria. Such a system usually involves a lower rate of commission and a bonus system.

KEY TERMS

account director   50
account executive   49
account shifting   41
account supervisor   49
advertising manager   37
advertising research   38
agency commission   53
agency of record (AOR)   53

art director   50
brand manager   36
category manager   36
copywriter   50
creative boutique   45
creative department   50
full-service agency   43
marketing research   38

media billings   46
media buyer   51
media director   51
media planner   51
media supervisor   51
media-buying service   46

REVIEW QUESTIONS

1. What are the three primary groups that constitute the advertising industry?

2. What are the alternative management systems used by clients to manage the advertising function? Briefly explain each system.

3. Identify and explain the roles and responsibilities of the client in the creation of advertising.

4. What are the key roles and responsibilities of advertising agencies in the advertising process?

5. What is meant by the phrase "client–agency relations"? What factors have a negative influence on the relationship? What factors have a positive influence on the relationship?

6. What does "account shifting" refer to? Why does account shifting occur?

7. How do a full-service agency, a creative boutique, and a media-buying service differ?

8. What are the primary functions of the following agency departments? Who are the key people in each area?

a) Account management
b) Creative department
c) Media department

9. Explain the concept of agency teams. Why is the team concept important to clients?

10. What is the agency of record (AOR)?

11. What are the three primary methods of compensating an advertising agency? Briefly describe each method.

12. A client spends $3 million on network television advertising, $450 000 on magazine advertising, and $250 000 on outdoor posters. The cost of producing two television commercials was $400 000 and the production charges for the magazines and outdoor posters were $60 000. How much commission does the client's advertising agency earn, given that the agency is compensated using the traditional rate of commission? What does the client pay in total? How much does the media receive in total?

DISCUSSION QUESTIONS

1. Assume you were the director of marketing for Pepsi-Cola Canada or the TDL Group Limited (parent company of Tim Hortons). Would you work with a full-service advertising agency or would you divide your work among various specialists such as creative boutiques, media-buying services, and other types of specialists? Justify your position. What factors determine the use of generalists or specialists?

2. Given that the client hires an agency to develop creative strategies, how involved in the creative development process should the client be? Where do the client's responsibilities end?

3. "The client–agency relationship is a partnership." Discuss the significance of this statement in the context of today's business environment. Is the statement true? What are the ingredients of a successful relationship?

4. Read the Advertising in Action vignette **Rethink's Fresh Approach**. The attitude and approach to creative development is much different at Rethink compared to traditional full-service agencies. What is your opinion of how they operate? Do you think their methods will continue to be popular with prospective clients or will they scare prospective clients off?

5. This chapter referenced a global campaign for McDonald's that uses the theme and slogan "I'm Lovin' It." The concept was developed by McDonald's agency in Germany. Is it possible for a company to take a concept like this and make it work on a global scale? Justify your position with appropriate rationale and provide a few examples of other successful or unsuccessful global concepts.

NOTES

1. Association of Canadian Advertisers, **www.aca-online.com**.

2. "The Rankings," *Marketing*, June 23, 2003, p. 10.

3. Institute of Communications and Advertising, **www.ica-ad.com/ factsheet**.

4. TVB Canada, **www.tvb.ca/tvbresources**.

5. Lara Mills, "Molson overhauls marketing team," *Marketing*, September 20, 1999, p. 17.

6. Kate MacArthur, "McD's talks tough with its agencies," *Advertising Age*, February 3, 2003, pp. 1, 33.

7. Kristen Vinakmens, "The idea belongs to everybody," *Strategy*, October 6, 2003, p. 3.

8. John Heinzl, "Wendy's switches $20-million ad account to MacLaren," *The Globe and Mail*, October 1, 2002, p. B6.

9. Susan Heinrich, "Rivals snap at Cossette's heels for Nike account," *Financial Post*, February 10, 2003, p. FP12.

10. Justin Smallbridge, "The short answer," *Financial Post*, August 12, 2002, p. FP12.

11. "Best media operations," *Strategy, The Canadian Marketing Report*, December 2003, pp. 57, 61.

12. John Gray, "Grumpy old ad men," *Canadian Business*, March 3, 2003, pp. 47, 48.

13. Institute of Communications and Advertising, **www.ica-ad.com/ remuneration**.

14. Joe Mandese, "Low margins? Agencies have created a monster," *Advertising Age*, February 22, 1999, pp. S12, S13.

15. Institute of Communications and Advertising, **www.ica-ad.com/ remuneration**.

16. John Heinzl, "P&G links ad agency payment to performance," *Globe and Mail*, September 16, 1999, p. B9.

17. Patrick Allossery, "Performance-based pay for agencies winning converts," *Financial Post*, May 8, 2000, p. C5.

18. "New study looks at how advertisers pay agencies," Association of Canadian Advertisers, March 12, 2003, **www.aca-online.com/news**.

THE practice OF ADVERTISING

Client–Agency Relations:
THESE ARE VERY DIFFERENT TIMES

There was a time when big advertisers worked with big agencies and small advertisers worked with small agencies. There were good, long-term relationships established between the two parties and a sense of loyalty to each other prevailed. Clients and agencies prospered.

Agencies grow by attracting new clients and new clients are attracted to agencies with track records of successful advertising campaigns. Even small agencies can become big agencies. When agencies grow they become bureaucratic and they wind up with layers of management much like their clients. Personalities on the client side have to deal with personalities on the agency side, and the next thing you know things aren't working out. Being big or dealing with the big agency isn't always best!

There are lots of reasons why clients fire their agencies: it could be a personality clash between key people; perhaps the level of service didn't meet expectations; there were philosophical differences on advertising direction; or not enough time was spent on the client's business. More recently, the issue of compensation—how much an agency should be paid for the services they provide—has surfaced as a sore spot between clients and agencies. Many clients feel they are paying their agencies too much and are not getting enough in return.

As in so many other business partnerships from the past, loyalty exists but the client–agency relationship is more short-term than long-term. Rather than committing to a marriage, other arrangements are now more popular. The relationship is more like an affair, or even an overnight fling, in some cases. For example, rather than have an agency on a retainer, why not simply hire the best agency available for specific projects as they crop up?

How Did It Happen?

Traditional advertising agencies that specialize in creating ads for mainstream media such as television, radio, magazines, and newspapers have fought off the challenges from upstart boutique-style agencies, but clients now have distinct choices regarding the type of agency they want to have manage their businesses. Will it be a generalist like the traditional agency, or will it be a specialist such as a creative boutique, a media planning and buying company, or any other type of specialist? Will it be a big agency or a small agency?

Client dissatisfaction with mainstream advertising agencies has played a key role in the development of boutique-style agencies. The issue was first raised by Hugo Powell, then CEO of Labatt Breweries of Canada, in 1993, in his now famous "Fire the Handlers" speech he delivered at a Canadian Congress of Advertising function. His speech featured the following phrases: "People handling clients. People handling creative people. People handling new business prospects. People handling New York. People and activities that cost millions of dollars. I don't want to pay for handlers. And I certainly don't want to pay for being handled."

His speech pointed to all kinds of pitfalls in the client–agency relationship. Putting words into action, his solution was to dismiss Labatt's big traditional agencies and hire a small shop just starting out. That shop was Ammirati & Puris. Powell's thinking was simple: a smaller shop would provide more hands-on service, would be able to react quicker to a fast-changing business environment, and would be less costly for Labatt.

Flash forward a bit and we find that, like lots of other small agencies, Ammirati grew into a bigger traditional agency as new clients came their way. Its destiny with Labatt was clear—it would be fired in favour of a small start-up operation created by Labatt to specifically serve its beer advertising needs. That agency's name was Grip Ltd. Labatt seems obsessed with being a big fish in a small pond, so much so that it created its own pond!

Have Agencies Compounded the Problem?

Labatt may be leading the charges in working with smaller agencies, but other events have happened to encourage the growth of boutique-style agencies. Many successful copywriters, art directors, creative directors, strategic planners, and media planners, fed up with the bureaucracy they faced working in traditional full-service agencies, had a desire to get back to basics. They didn't want to manage a client's business—they wanted to create the ads, they wanted to work more directly with clients to solve their problems, and they wanted to be front and centre in the relationship, not tucked away in an office somewhere.

When Geoffrey Roche launched what is now Roche Macaulay & Partners in 1991, he was on the cutting edge of change. His vision preceded the rant of Hugo Powell! Roche eliminated account executives on his team and placed greater responsibility in the hands of art directors and copywriters. They would have direct contact with clients to better understand their needs. Paul Lavoie, another successful creative director in the full-service environment, formed Taxi Advertising & Design. He called it "Taxi" to underscore his belief that large accounts could be managed by small teams of senior people—no more employees per account than could fit into a taxicab.

Today some of the most successful agencies are small agencies. Small for now, that is! *Strategy* magazine, a trade journal, devotes considerable time determining which ad agencies have the best creative. *Strategy* recently published a short list of seven agencies. With two notable exceptions, all agencies are small and free of ownership by conglomerate agencies. On the list are John St., Taxi, Zig, Rethink, and Bos. The other two are Palmer Jarvis DDB and Downtown Partners, both large agencies that are part of the Omnicom Group. Note how the names of the smaller shops are very different from those of the traditional agencies.

Where Did the Small Shops Get the Talent?

Fred Jaques, then president of Labatt Breweries North America, didn't score any points with ad agency executives when he stated publicly that the traditional agency model was "flawed." The comment offended just about everyone who works in the business. By flawed, his primary criticism was that agency compensation was based on the services provided rather than results. Wanting to be rid of such an archaic system, Jaques fired Ammirati & Puris. That was the start of a rapid downward spiral that Ammirati couldn't recover from. Within a year the agency was out of business in Canada.

Labatt's newest weapon in the beer wars was a stripped-down agency model comprising eight well-paid guys whose mission was to rewrite the advertising rulebook in Canada. Ironically, all members of Grip's new team were hired away from traditional advertising agencies. There was speculation that these writers and art directors were lured with pay packages in the $300 000 range—well above industry averages!

Labatt literally raided the industry for administrative and creative talent. Their roster of creatives read like a Who's Who at a Canadian advertising award show. The creative talent included Dave Chiavegato and Rich Pryce-Jones, both formerly of Palmer Jarvis DDB Toronto; David Crichton, co-founder of Crichton Kim-Kirkland Co.; Graham Lee, formerly creative director at Odiorne Wilde Narraway & Partners in San Francisco; Randy Stein, former creative director at Palmer Jarvis DDB Vancouver; and Scott Dube, former senior vice-president and creative director at BBDO Toronto.

Labatt's decision to form its own advertising agency and its hiring tactics were openly criticized by industry executives. Frank Palmer of Palmer Jarvis DDB Vancouver had reason to be upset, since Grip hired one of its top creative teams. The ultimate insult for him was that his agency works for Labatt on its Budweiser and Bud Light brands. "It's disrespectful," said Palmer. After learning of the hiring he asked Grip to "cease and desist in talking to any of his people."

Geoffrey Roche of Roche Macaulay & Partners wasn't pleased either. He lost his president to the new agency. "I don't think they [Labatt] have been necessarily honourable," said Roche.

"This agency will deliver on its promise of world-class advertising for less, said Bob Shanks, a Grip partner who was formerly president of Roche Macaulay & Partners. Grip's operating philosophy is clear: it will provide top-drawer advertising at lower cost thanks to a streamlined structure that avoids the layers of administration in a traditional agency.

Grip immediately assumed advertising responsibility for Labatt's flagship brands Blue and Blue Light, along with Labatt Classic, Kokanee, and Carlsberg. Grip is 100 percent owned by Labatt Breweries of Canada but it would operate independently from Labatt.

As an independent operating company, Grip can pursue other clients. Shortly after its formation Grip attracted Parmalat Canada Inc., a dairy products manufacturer.

Is the Grip Model the Right Model?

"If it ain't broke, don't fix it." Labatt has stirred up controversy about the effectiveness of the traditional client–agency model. In that model the client provides the required services and is paid a commission or a set fee for services rendered. Granted, the model might be a hundred years old, but for something to survive that long there can't be that much wrong with it.

"They have slighted the entire industry by criticizing the full-service model," said Frank Palmer, of Palmer Jarvis DDB, about Labatt's conduct.

Rupert Brendon, chairman of the Institute of Communications and Advertising, takes the argument a step further by saying, "While any advertiser is free to develop advertising in any way it suits them, and while we live in a society of free speech, it is disappointing and surprising to see Labatt denigrate and disparage a tried and true business model."

Allan Middleton, a former marketing executive and now a professor at York University, offers a different perspective. "From the outside the ad business always looks exciting, but, in fact, the way it runs itself, it is an intensely conservative business. They need to rethink the whole way they work with clients' needs in the modern era."

Paul Lavoie, president of Taxi, says Grip is a "good thing because it's a challenge to the industry. We're in the idea industry. Why would it be rejected so quickly? I think it's out of fear that it's a powerhouse of talent." Perhaps Lavoie understands the situation better. When he and a few partners formed Taxi they, too, were frustrated with the "flawed" traditional agency model. Lavoie does offer one gripe about Labatt, though. He didn't like the way Grip was launched. "Labatt had a bad experience with one agency and then they went out and dissed the entire industry. It was insulting."

Has Grip Lost Its Grip?

Fast forward to May 2004. Headlines in the business press tell of more changes in the industry. The biggest news involves Cossette Communications, one of Canada's largest ad agencies. Cossette has just lost the Bell Canada account, perhaps one of the largest accounts in Canada with annual media billings in the $50 million range. The account was lost to upstart agency Grip Ltd. The announcement has industry observers buzzing over how such a small agency managed to land such a high profile account.

Bell's decision to go with Grip reflects the growing trend of big companies opting to work with small upstart agencies. But critics and sources say Bell was fed up with the less-than-stellar creative Cossette was producing. "There were creative issues and Cossette was not able to rectify the problems."

Now that Bell is in Grip's hands, how important will the Labatt beer brands be in the whole scheme of things? All of a sudden that independently operated but 100-percent-owned subsidiary of Labatt is responsible for producing ads for one of Canada's largest advertisers. Will there be ample resources available to service the needs of Labatt brands? Will new people have to be hired, leading to those unnecessary layers of administration? Which account, Bell or Labatt, will have the best creative team working on its business? Will Grip become just another advertising agency caught between the desire to grow and its ability to serve clients in a personalized manner? Attracting accounts like Bell could be the undoing of Grip!

Questions

Much has been written in the business press about this story. You may wish to do some online research to uncover additional information. The relationship between clients and agencies is always a hot topic in the industry. What opinions do you have about the actions taken by Labatt Breweries? The following questions will provide some guidance to your thought process.

1. Is there such a thing as a perfect agency model?

2. Did Labatt slight the advertising industry when it attacked the traditional advertising agency model?

3. Is Labatt an exception or will other clients (large and small) pursue relationships with smaller agencies and specialized agencies?

4. What future do you see for Grip? Should Grip continue to pursue new clients? Could growth pose problems for Grip in terms of its relations with Labatt?

Adapted from Bertrand Marotte, "Cossette's loss of Bell to upstart Grip signals small is hot," *The Globe and Mail*, May 8, 2004, p. B5; Paul Brent, "Small shops shine through the gloom," *Financial Post*, September 29, 2003; Katherine Harding, "Getting a Grip," *Toronto Star*, January 27, 2002, pp. C1, C2; John Heinzl, "Labatt brews resentment," *The Globe and Mail*, January 11, 2002, p. E6; John Heinzl, "Labatt forms ad dream team in Grip agency," *The Globe and Mail*, January 9, 2002, p. B7; Patrick Allossery, "Traditional triumph," *Financial Post*, December 17, 2001, p. FP6.

Marketing Communications Planning

This section concentrates on the central theme of the text—planning the marketing communications effort.

Chapter 3 provides the foundation for marketing communications planning, presenting the important concepts of consumer behaviour, market segmentation and target marketing, and positioning.

Chapter 4 describes the elements of strategic planning and presents the content and structure of marketing plans and marketing communications plans. It establishes the relationships among these plans and provides an appreciation of the role and importance of planning in the development of all forms of marketing communications.

PART

2

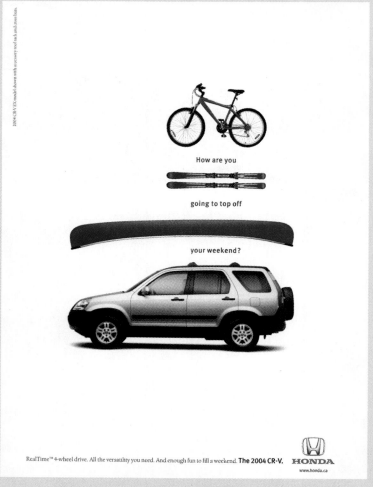

How are you

going to top off

your weekend?

RealTime™ 4-wheel drive. All the versatility you need. And enough fun to fill a weekend. **The 2004 CR-V.**

HONDA

www.honda.ca

2004 CR-V EX model shown with accessory roof rack and cross bars.

CHAPTER

3

Consumer Behaviour Concepts and Target Marketing

After studying this chapter, you will be able to

- Explain how consumer behaviour concepts influence the development of marketing communications strategies

- Assess the information needed to identify and select target markets

- Distinguish between demographic, psychographic, geographic, and behaviour-response segmentation variables

- Explain the influence of relationship marketing concepts on marketing communications strategy

- Explain the concept of positioning and its role in developing marketing communications strategies

This chapter discusses concepts that are important to the planning of advertising and marketing communications programs. For starters, the development of an effective advertising strategy relies heavily on an understanding of basic consumer behaviour. Uncovering what makes a particular customer group tick provides direction on what appeal techniques will grab an audience's attention. It may also provide insights into what media are best suited for reaching a group of customers. Organizations must identify profitable target markets by analyzing demographic trends, psychographic characteristics, and geographic or regional differences. The end result of such an analysis is a clear description of a target market that is worth pursuing. The chapter ends with a discussion of a variety of product-positioning strategies.

Consumer Behaviour

Consumer behaviour can be defined as the acts that individuals perform in obtaining and using goods and services, including the decision-making processes that precede and determine these acts.[1] A firm understanding of how behavioural tendencies apply to purchase decisions is of significant benefit to the marketing organization. Consequently, leading marketing organizations spend a considerable amount of money on marketing research in order to learn as much as they can about their customers, and perhaps get an edge on the competition in the process. Information is power, they say!

From a purely competitive perspective, marketers must have access to data concerning consumers' buying habits in order to develop more convincing communications programs that stimulate response by the target market. The purpose of most research boils down to obtaining answers to a few key questions:

- Who makes the buying decision?
- Who influences the buying decision?
- What motivates the buyers and influencers to take action?

Answers to the above questions will provide valuable input for developing a marketing strategy and marketing communications strategy. To illustrate, consider the behaviour of males when shopping for clothes. Men perceive shopping as a less-than-masculine endeavour and they are likely to bring along the opposite sex for reassurance when making decisions. Sharp men's wear retailers like Harry Rosen know this and consequently spend more time in the store selling the fashions to the females since their approval is essential. Many retailers have found that when they encourage both sexes to shop together, sales are higher.[2] Discussion of the key influences on consumer behaviour follows.

NEEDS AND MOTIVES

Needs suggest a state of deprivation—the absence of something useful. **Motives** are the conditions that prompt the action that is taken to satisfy the need (the action elicited by marketing and advertising activity). The relationship between needs and motives is direct with respect to marketing and advertising activity. Such activity must sufficiently develop the target market's need—through an appealing presentation of appropriate benefits—that the target is motivated to respond by purchasing the product or service.

Abraham Maslow
www.ship.edu/~cgboeree/maslow.html

Maslow's *hierarchy of needs* and *theory of motivation* have had a significant impact on marketing and advertising strategies. Maslow's need theory is based on the principle that needs can be classified from lower-level to higher-level, and it is based on two prevailing assumptions:[3]

1. When lower-level needs are satisfied, a person moves up to higher-level needs.
2. Satisfied needs do not motivate. Instead, behaviour will be influenced by needs yet to be satisfied.

Maslow states that individuals move through five levels (see Figure 3.1):

FIGURE 3.1

The Hierarchy of Needs

Source: Adapted from Maslow, Abraham H.; Frager, Robert D. (Editor); Fadiman, James (Editor), *Motivation and Personality*, 3rd Edition, © 1997. Adapted by permission of Pearson Education Canada Inc., Upper Saddle River, NJ.

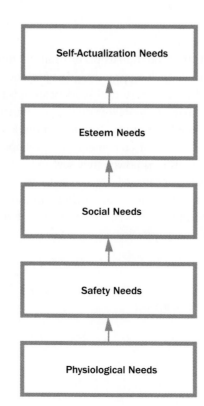

- **Physiological needs** hunger, thirst, sex, shelter

- **Safety needs** security, protection, comfort

- **Social needs** sense of belonging, love from family and friends

- **Esteem needs** recognition, achievement, status, need to excel

- **Self-actualization needs** fulfillment, to realize potential (achieve what you believe you can achieve)

Numerous advertising examples can be cited to demonstrate advertising applications of Maslow's need theory. Safety needs are used to motivate people to purchase automobile tires, life insurance, and retirement savings plans. State Farm Insurance delivers a message for life insurance that focuses on security and protection, a need that becomes a priority when adults become new parents. Refer to the ad in Figure 3.2 for a visual illustration.

FIGURE 3.2

An ad focused on safety and security needs

The desire to be accepted by peers (that is, the need for social satisfaction) is commonly appealed to in the advertising for personal-care products and clothing. Advertising for products in these markets tends to appeal to one's social consciousness. For example, the images presented by brands such as Guess and Calvin Klein have impact on style-conscious youth and people aged 20 to 29. Esteem needs are addressed in commercials that portray people in successful business roles and occupations; for example, an executive driving an automobile symbolic of success, such as a Cadillac, BMW, Porsche, or Jaguar.

PERSONALITY AND SELF-CONCEPT

Personality refers to a person's distinguishing psychological characteristics, those features that lead to relatively consistent and enduring responses to the environment in which that person lives. It is influenced by self-perceptions, which in turn are influenced by psychological needs, family, culture, and reference groups. Why do people buy designer-label clothing at high prices and in upscale boutiques when low-priced items performing the same functions are available? Such purchases are based on the images we desire to have of ourselves. To appreciate this principle, one must understand the self-concept theory.

Self-concept theory states that the self has four components: real self, self-image, looking-glass self, and ideal self.[4]

- *Real self* is an objective evaluation of the individual. It is you as you really are.
- *Self-image* is how you see yourself. You might, for example, see yourself as an aspiring athlete, musician, or writer, even though you may not be any of these. It's like a role you play.
- *Looking-glass self* is how you think others see you. A person's view of how others see them can be very different from how others actually see them.
- *Ideal self* is how you would like to be. It is what you aspire to.

Marketers know that, human nature being what it is, many important decisions are based on the looking-glass self and the ideal self. In other words, many goods and services are bought on the basis of emotion—goods that help us feel better, look better, and take us to the next level of fulfillment are very attractive to us. We may not achieve what we want but there is some psychological satisfaction in having something. For example, how does a busy executive who lives in an urban area justify purchasing a well-equipped luxury sports utility vehicle such as a Lincoln Aviator or an Infiniti FX45 when the vehicle will probably be used only for city and highway driving? The answer resides somewhere in the looking-glass self and ideal self—that automobile says something positive about the person to other people, at least in the mind of the person. The buyer is trying to tame the urban jungle. For an illustration refer to Figure 3.3. The reality of such a purchase is that the buyer may actually be perceived as foolish!

PERCEPTIONS

Perception refers to the manner in which individuals receive and interpret messages. From a marketing perspective, how individual consumers perceive the same product can vary considerably. Perceptual images are based on influences such as advertising, packaging, and pricing. It should be noted that consumers are not aware of all that goes on around them; they are quite selective about messages they receive. The messages they select to receive depend on their level of interest and need requirements. There are three levels of selectivity:

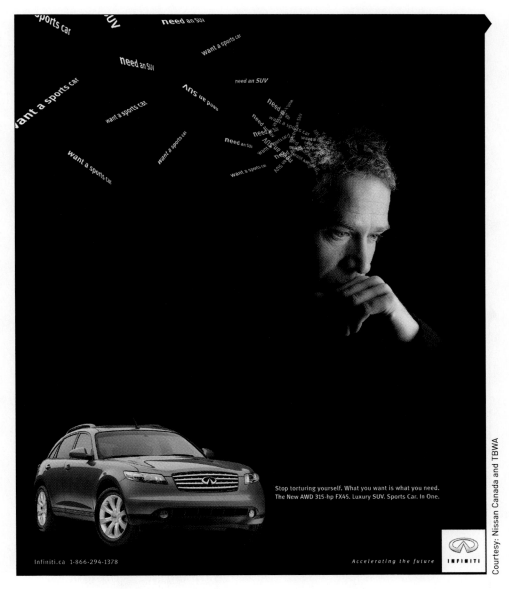

FIGURE
3.3

An ad that appeals to a person's looking-glass self or ideal self

- ■ *Selective exposure* Our eyes and minds notice only information that interests us.

- ■ *Selective perception* We screen out information and messages that conflict with previously learned attitudes and beliefs.

- ■ *Selective retention* We remember only what we want to remember.

Theories of perception help to explain why people respond differently to advertising messages. Quite simply, they do not notice them. For example, as a student you may be oblivious to automobile advertising because you are not ready to buy a car. Sure, you may see some ads for smart-looking cars and say, "Someday I will own one of those." But the message is quickly discarded. Like mother always said, "In one ear and out the other!" Things change at graduation, however. Your first job may necessitate new clothes and a new car, and suddenly you begin to absorb yourself in fashion and automobile advertising at the expense of all other messages. Companies like General Motors, Ford, and Toyota know that it's all a matter of timing—sooner or later you will tune in. No doubt there are automobile ads aimed at graduates posted somewhere in your school.

ATTITUDES

Attitudes are an individual's feelings, favourable or unfavourable, toward an idea or object (the advertised product). Generally speaking, organizations present their products to consumers so that they agree with the prevailing attitudes of their target audience. Product acceptance comes quicker. They have found that it is expensive to try to change attitudes. Sometimes, however, the public at large may take exception to your message and the way a company presents its product. Consider a situation like this: you are a marketing manager and you see an opportunity to target the gay community. Society seems to be more tolerant of gay relationships as such a lifestyle is now more out in the open. You conduct a cost–benefit analysis and are indecisive. You see a risk in alienating your core customers—they may leave for another brand with a mainstream image. The solution here lies in media strategy. By being able to target the gay community through special-interest publications, the mainstream target market will not see the message associating the brand with the gay lifestyle. At least that's the theory behind the media strategy. See Figure 3.4 for an illustration of this approach.

**FIGURE
3.4**

Social changes have produced new targets: Absolut appeals to the gay community

REFERENCE GROUPS

A **reference group**, or **peer group**, is a group, class, or category of people to which individuals believe they belong, whether or not they actually do. Their relationship to their reference group may influence their buying behaviour. Reference groups could include co-workers, sports teams, hobby clubs, fraternal organizations, and schoolmates. A member of a group experiences considerable pressure to conform to the standards of the group to "fit in." The desire to fit in influences the type of products a member will purchase.

With the right strategy, an advertiser need only associate their brand in a certain situation and the target will become interested in it. Mountain Dew, for example, transformed itself into a leading soft drink solely on the basis of an ad campaign that had lots of attitude. The "Do the Dew" campaign was aimed directly at hip teens who enjoy alternative sports like snowboarding and mountain biking. The ads were edgy and incorporated lots of action and loud music to grab the attention of teens. Just how successful was the campaign? Mountain Dew is about to surpass Diet Coke for third place in the United States, giving PepsiCo two of the top three brands in the market.[5] Teens obviously bought into the Mountain Dew image. An image of Mountain Dew advertising can be seen in Figure 3.5.

Mountain Dew
www.mountaindew.com

FIGURE
3.5

Lifestyle images and reference group associations have an influence on teens

Courtesy: Pepsi Cola Canada

The influence of reference groups is quite strong among young people. Ads such as those for Mountain Dew suggest that consumers can join certain groups or be part of a subculture by purchasing the product.

FAMILY

Members of a family influence buying decisions. The actual impact each member has on the decision depends on the type of product or service under consideration. Roles and responsibilities within families have changed with the times and the lines of responsibility are blurred between the male and female head of household. Children seem to have more influence than ever on what products their parents buy. Factors contributing to these role changes are the increasing numbers of two-income families and women working outside the home, as well as the growth of single-parent families.

To demonstrate how family responsibilities have changed, August shopping for the first day of school was once the domain of the mother. Moms carefully researched deals, bought each child a few nice outfits and school supplies, and they were off to school. Now, student shopping is a year-round social activity and advertisers talk directly to kids. According to Youth Culture, a marketing research company, the teen market spends about $1.7 billion on back-to-school needs, about $700 per teen. While parents make 60 percent of the purchases, 70 percent of teens come along to beg and plead, and it works![6] For more insight into how companies have adjusted their advertising strategies see the Advertising in Action vignette **Targeting the Real Buyers**.

At the parent level, much of the decision making is shared between partners, so many marketers are double targeting. **Double targeting** involves devising a single marketing strategy for both sexes. In its simplest form, a product would have one strategy for females and another for males—one brand with two unique messages. To illustrate, food and household-products companies have awakened to the fact that men are increasingly responsible for shopping, meal preparation, and general household cleanup. Products like Campbell's Soup and Tide detergent now feature males in leading roles in television commercials. Conversely, financial-services companies (investment dealers, insurance companies, and banks) and automobile manufacturers recognize the role and influence of women in matters of financial planning and major buying decisions and are tailoring their advertising strategies accordingly.

Identifying and Selecting Target Markets

The ability of a company to target specific customers is based on the concept of market segmentation. **Market segmentation** involves dividing a large market into smaller homogeneous markets (segments) based on common needs or similar lifestyles. Segmentation involves three steps: identifying market segments (e.g., describing the profile of the primary user), selecting the market segments that offer the most potential (e.g., typically targets that offer the greatest profit potential), and positioning the product so that it appeals to the target market.

When an organization identifies a target market, it develops a profile of the customer it wants to pursue. That profile becomes the first cornerstone of all marketing and marketing communications strategies for the product. The second cornerstone is a sound positioning strategy. Positioning strategy is discussed later in the chapter.

A target-market profile is the result of an organization's analysis of external variables that influence the direction of marketing strategy. These variables include

Targeting the Real Buyers

Shopping behaviour in Canada has changed dramatically in the past decade. Previously, mothers and fathers controlled the purse strings and actually did a lot of the shopping for their children. Not any more! Double-income, time-pressed families have reluctantly turned much of the buying for teens over to teens. Teen shopping is now a year-round social experience and big business for those retailers that pursue it.

On back-to-school shopping alone, the teen market spends $1.7 billion annually, an average of about $700 per teen in Canada. Add in tweens and you chalk up another $800 million. Surprisingly, or not surprisingly, marketers have been slow to react to the changes. They still approach back-to-school promotions as an August thing when the reality is anything but August. Teens are waiting to see what others are wearing before they go out and spend. Peer pressure and conforming to reference group norms are the priority for teens. What they buy just has to be right! Consequently, the buying season is much longer now. Since Zellers is a discount department store, the thought of teens buying clothes there may not seem that trendy. But Zellers is a step ahead of many competitors in how it approaches the teen market, and it is starting to pay dividends. Zellers established a goal for itself of extending its reach into a target group where it had no historic strength. Only recently did Zellers creative speak directly to teens. Zellers now advertises in key women's fashion magazines and they have a website that features an online change room where teens can interact with their Request brand, its most "trend right" clothes.

In the past year Zellers added television advertising. Different groups of teens are shown riding hip modes of transportation like Vespa scooters, and the new longer skateboards that are perfect for cruising. Then the groups all meet at a party. The idea is simple: no matter what you're into, there's a Zellers brand for you. Realizing that text messaging is all the rage with teens, Zellers also launched a contest via text messaging. The contest prizes included 10 shopping sprees valued at $500 and tickets to an exclusive movie night. To register, the teens had to visit the website.

Source: Adapted from Andrea Zoe Aster, "Back to school," *Marketing*, August 11/18, 2003, pp. 20, 21.

Zellers   www.hbc.com/zellers

demographic trends, social and lifestyle trends, and geographic (regional) trends. Behaviour-response variables also help form a target-market profile.

DEMOGRAPHIC SEGMENTATION

With **demographic segmentation**, target markets are identified and pursued on the basis of variables such as *age, gender, income, occupation, education, marital status, household formation,* and *cultural mix.* In Canada, certain demographic trends are having direct impact on the direction of marketing strategies and all forms of marketing communications. Discussion of these trends follows.

THE POPULATION IS GETTING OLDER Perhaps the most talked-about group in the past decade has been the **baby boomers**, or **boomers** as they are commonly referred to (those people born between 1946 and 1964), and the **grey market** (those born prior to 1946 and who just happen to be over the age of 50). These groups are and will continue to be a major buying influence for decades to come. Of course, the baby-boom generation spawned another blip in the age curve known as the **echo boom**. The children of boomers, often referred to as **Generation X** (born 1961 to 1981) and **Generation Y** (born

FIGURE
3.6

The over-50 market is an
attractive target

Source: Statistics Canada, "The Over-50
Market Is an Attractive Market," adapted
from Statistics Canada CANSIM
database, **http://cansim2.statcan.ca**
Table 052-0001.

Age Classification	MILLIONS OF PEOPLE		
	1996	2006	2016
0–9	3.968	3.941	3.125
10–19	4.024	4.384	4.301
20–34	6.896	6.837	7.402
35–49	7.217	7.977	7.610
50 plus	7.864	10.519	13.583

between 1976 and 1981) are causing headaches for goods and services that are aging with the population. Teens and tweens make up the remainder of the population and were born from 1982 onward.

The older age segments are wealthy segments. Canadians older than 50 years are free of financial obligations such as children and mortgages, so they should be seen as an attractive target. Many Canadians in this age group have developed a taste for the finer things in life. The sales growth of luxury items such as Belgian chocolates, imported and premium beer, and luxury automobiles all exceed growth of mainstream retail goods in the same categories. Imported and craft brews have grown 16 percent per annum over the last five years compared to an overall beer market growing only about 1 percent a year. The sales of BMW cars have risen 18 percent in the past five years while mid-range domestic automobiles have grown by only 4 percent.[7] Trends like these present opportunities for brands like BMW and Mercedes but pose problems for Ford and General Motors. For a summary of how the population is aging, refer to Figure 3.6.

Each generation has a different outlook, different values, and different needs, so the challenge facing many products is how to retain older customers while trying to attract new customers. To simply stay with an aging population does not make economic sense in the long term. No other company knows this better than Levi-Strauss. Boomers grew up with Levi's and are the customers that built the brand, but youth today see the brand as a relic from the past. Levi's has tried all kinds of advertising strategies to spark interest among teens but without success. As my own son says, "My dad wears them, I don't." That attitude represents an ominous challenge for Levi's. Eventually they will be out of business if they can't turn things around.

In a communications context the boomers and grey market represent the past while Generation X, Generation Y, and any group that follows represent the future (see Figure 3.7). The younger generations will be the foundation for the success of the internet as a means of communication and commerce. Eventually, the direct forms of communication such as the internet, cell phones, and PDAs (personal digital assistants) will take precedence over the traditional mass media.

THE ECONOMIC POWER OF WOMEN Gender has always been a primary means of distinguishing product categories—personal-care products, magazines, athletic equipment, and fashion are all categorized according to the gender of the buyer. Due to the increasing presence of women in the workforce outside the home (a significant change from earlier generations) and the changing roles of men and women in Canadian households, an organization will become increasingly "unisex" as both sexes buy and use similar products. Females have been fighting off stereotypical images and portrayals in advertising for years—the goal of which is to be represented as they are; not as they were.

GI GENERATION (1901–1924)

Depression survivors; they are conservative spenders and civic-minded.

SILENT GENERATION (1925–1945)

Lived the spectre of the Depression and war; they are conformists who are involved in civic life and extended families in a bid to recapture lost youth.

BABY BOOMERS (1946–1964)

Unapologetic consumers; they are newly liberated parents with high disposable income; they are value-driven despite indulgences; they fear words related to aging.

GENERATION X (1961–1981)

Cynical and media-savvy; they were once rebellious but are now an economic force; alienated, alternative, sexy.

GENERATION Y (1976–1981)

A subset of Generation X; they are edgy and focused on urban style; into retro style such as swing dancing, big bands, and outdoor life.

MILLENNIALS (1982–2002)

Tech-savvy and educated; they are multicultural; accustomed to sex and violence; they are growing up in an affluent society and have great spending power.

FIGURE
3.7

Characteristics of population generations

The combination of demographic and psychographic characteristics provides useful information to marketers, but it also presents challenges in terms of how to market a product to several different age groups at the same time.

Source: Reprinted with permission from the January 15, 2001 issue of Advertising Age. Copyright Crain Communications Inc. 2001.

Women currently represent 46.4 percent of Canada's labour force; 65 percent of Canadian mothers are employed (70 percent of them full-time); working women influence 95 percent of consumer purchases; women comprise 52.7 percent of professionals; and 34 percent of all Canadian businesses are owned by women. Statistics Canada reports that mothers do two-and-a-half hours more work per day than [employed] fathers.[8]

These women are multi-taskers. They go from the bank machine to the dry cleaners to the soccer pitch. Husbands, bosses, children, and friends all vie for their time. They are time-pressed and expect solutions when they buy. Insights like these spawned a new ad campaign for the newly redesigned Nissan Quest minivan. The campaign focuses on multi-faceted mothers. A TV commercial features various women loading their Quests, not with adorable tots, but with items signifying the non-motherly aspects of a woman's life: a surfboard, saddle, guitar, or golf clubs. The tagline for the campaign is: "Moms have changed. Shouldn't minivans?" Campaigns as intelligent as Nissan's are few and far between. Refer to the illustration in Figure 3.8.

THE FORMATION OF HOUSEHOLDS IS CHANGING   Trends such as the postponement of marriage to an older age, increased divorce rates, the desire to have fewer children, and same-sex partnerships are producing new household formations. That traditional family personified by the Cleavers in the television show *Leave It to Beaver*, with a working father, stay-at-home mother, and a couple of children, is now more of a myth than reality. Contemporary households are described by terms such as lone-parent

families (the result of divorce), blended families (the result of remarriage or common law arrangements), and same-sex families (the result of more openness and acceptance of gay lifestyles).

With families evolving so dramatically, other changes are also occurring. Between 1981 and 2001, smaller households represented the fastest growth in Canada. There are now as many one-person households as there are those with four or more people. Average household size decreased in the same period from 2.9 to 2.6 persons.[9]

And what about same-sex households? Some progressive-minded companies have started targeting the gay community with advertising messages. A recent print campaign by VanCity Credit Union features two gay men in an obviously affectionate pose and the tagline "I want to bank with people who value all relationships." According to Kari Grist, vice-president of marketing, "It was a bold move but the right move from a business perspective and from a values-alignment perspective."[10]

In the distilling industry, Absolut Vodka is targeting the gay community. A print ad for Absolut vodka uses the headline "Absolut Out" (aptly featuring a closet shaped like an Absolut bottle). Refer back to Figure 3.4 for an image of the Absolut ad.

ETHNIC DIVERSITY CONTINUES   Canada's ethnic diversity presents new opportunities for Canadian marketers. Canadian culture comprises numerous and diverse **subcultures** (subgroups of a larger population) with distinctive lifestyles based on characteristics such as religion, race, and location (region of country). As of 2001, Canada's visible minorities totalled 5.7 million or about 18 percent of the population. The largest minority groups are Chinese (23 percent of ethnic population), South Asian (21 percent), Black (19 percent), and West Asian/Arabs (13 percent). Canada's subcultures tend to be concentrated in three key regions: Ontario, Quebec, and British Columbia. Further, 75 percent of minorities live in four cities: Toronto (37 percent), Vancouver (15 percent), Montreal (14 percent), and Calgary/Edmonton (9 percent).[11]

Generally speaking, advertisers have been slow to capitalize on ethnic trends. How many ads actually feature minorities? Bud Light's Isaac, as in the black fellow at the end of the beer commercial who says "This calls for a Bud Light" comes to mind, but there aren't many others. Progressive companies see profit potential by tapping into ethnic niches, and those that take the time to prepare unique marketing and advertising programs are sure to be rewarded. Koo Creative (an Asian advertising division of Cossette Communications Group) recently produced a five-week multimedia campaign for Bell ExpressVu directed at the Chinese community. The campaign increased the Chinese subscriber base by 50 percent.

Tropicana Pure Premium juice has had success with the Chinese market. One of their coupon promotions featured a 68-cent coupon. In Chinese culture the numbers 6 and 8 combined mean "all roads lead to prosperity." The message was subtle but it had impact. The Chinese market fit closely with many of Tropicana's loyal consumers—high disposable income, well educated, and nutrition-conscious. An image of Tropicana's advertising appears in Figure 3.9.

Canada's Cultural Gateway
www.culture.ca

FIGURE 3.9

An ad targeting the Chinese community

Courtesy: QTG Canada Inc.

PSYCHOGRAPHIC SEGMENTATION

Contemporary marketing organizations have added a more sophisticated variable, referred to as *psychographics*, to their marketing arsenal. The combination of demographic and psychographic information provides the marketer with a more complete understanding of its target market. Marketers not only know who buys, but also why they buy. Therefore, the hot buttons they identify about their target are pressed when marketing communications are delivered.

Psychographic segmentation examines individual lifestyles in terms of *activities*, *interests*, and *opinions* (commonly referred to as AIOs). Therefore, when organizations target their products psychographically, advertising messages are associated with the lifestyle of the target market—the personality of the product matches the personality of the target.

Psychographic information shows how an individual's interest in a particular product depends on his or her lifestyle. Automakers produce and market a range of vehicles to satisfy the requirements of the various lifestyle groups. Trendy sports cars with European styling appeal to bold achievers (aggressive and confident individuals who are success and responsibility-oriented; they are motivated by status and prestige). Refer to Figure 3.10 for an illustration of **lifestyle advertising** directed at bold achievers.

**FIGURE
3.10**

An ad appealing to the bold achiever: An illustration of lifestyle advertising

Courtesy: Jaguar

Canada's beer and fashion industries use psychographic information when devising advertising campaigns. Leading brands such as Canadian and Blue (beer) and Guess and Calvin Klein (fashion) present images and lifestyles that are attractive to young adults. In the case of beer, the ads dwell on the idea that guys need to get together to do their thing—to enjoy good times together. Budweiser, for example, appeals directly to the blue-collar, rugged, outdoors type of male. Fashion brands Guess and Calvin Klein show young couples in provocative situations. It seems that a combination of sexual appeals and lifestyle appeals works well in this industry.

Numerous research studies have been conducted in an effort to classify consumers into psychographic cells. One such company, Millward Brown Goldfarb of Toronto, has classified Canadians into six psychographic cells within two broad segments: traditionalists and non-traditionalists. For a summary of these cells refer to Figure 3.11.

Segment	% of Population	Characteristics
TRADITIONALISTS		
Day-to-Day Watchers	24	The status quo; don't like change; motivated by familiarity and security; influenced by quality, brand name, and authority figures.
Old-Fashioned Puritans	18	Prefer simpler times; conservative values; motivated by price and quality; influenced by value messages and sales discounts.
Responsible Survivors	12	Frugal shoppers; have money but don't like parting with it; shop at low-end stores; heavy television viewers
NON-TRADITIONALISTS		
Joiner Activists	16	Idealists; liberal-minded; willing to spend; motivated by information; influenced by rational messages (quality, service, and price).
Bold Achievers	15	Aggressive and confident; success-oriented; innovators in terms of buying new items; influenced by messages stressing gratification.
Self-Indulgents	14	Resent authority; want easy road to success; motivated by self-gratification; buy impulsively; price not a factor; influenced by messages stressing gratification.

Source: Based on information compiled from studies conducted by Millward Brown Goldfarb.

FIGURE 3.11

Lifestyle segments in Canada

Psychographics allows a company to position its products better in the marketplace. Such intimate knowledge of consumers provides ammunition for compelling campaigns that focus on lifestyle associations. The combination of demographic and psychographic knowledge allows the marketing organization to better push the target's hot buttons. With sufficient motivation, the likelihood of purchase is stronger. The illustration in Figure 3.10 applies this principle.

GEOGRAPHIC SEGMENTATION

Geographic segmentation refers to the division of a geographically expansive market (Canada) into smaller geographic units (the Atlantic provinces, Quebec, Ontario, the Prairies, and British Columbia). The availability of psychographic information about target markets has complemented the use of geographic segmentation. Knowing more about targets in the various regions—their behaviour, attitudes, and interests—helps marketers and advertisers to develop marketing and advertising plans.

The region with the most obvious differences is Quebec, whose language and cultural characteristics necessitate the use of different marketing and advertising strategies. For example, a prominent Quebec entertainer or sports personality who endorses a brand will have much more influence there than a nationally known or foreign celebrity. Pepsi-Cola can claim the number-one position in Quebec (ahead of Coca-Cola) largely based on its understanding of French Quebec consumer behaviour and the influence that unique and innovative advertising has in that market. For years Pepsi has used famous French comedian Claude Meunier (a home-grown talent) in its advertising. Unlike other comedians, Claude can poke fun at Quebecers and get away with it. In the commercials he does his thing, the people respond to it, and Pepsi reaps the benefits. Coca-Cola could learn a lesson from this.

More Canadians than ever before are living in urban metropolitan areas. The latest census (2001) shows that 79.4 percent of Canadians live in an urban area with a population of 10 000 or more. As well, the population continues to concentrate in four broad urban regions: the extended Golden Horseshoe in Southern Ontario; Montreal and its adjacent region; the Lower Mainland of British Columbia and southern Vancouver Island; and the Calgary–Edmonton corridor. In 2001, 51 percent of the population lived in these regions.[12] It is not surprising, then, that successful marketing and advertising strategies have an urban orientation and reflect contemporary households dealing with contemporary issues.

Many Canadian organizations are moving away from "broadstroke" national marketing strategies and toward strategies based on regional considerations and opportunities. Other companies are proceeding in the opposite direction, developing universal strategies that are appropriate for all of North America, or even the global marketplace. The phrase "Thinking globally and acting locally" is a common theme among marketing organizations today.

BEHAVIOUR-RESPONSE SEGMENTATION

Behaviour-response segmentation involves dividing buyers into groups according to their occasions for using a product, the benefits they require in a product, the frequency with which they use it, and their degree of brand loyalty. Marketers using the **occasion for use** segmentation strategy show how the product can be used on various occasions. For example, products such as milk, orange juice, and eggs are often shown being consumed at times other than their traditional meal times. Reminding consumers that a product can be enjoyed at another time has an impact on sales volume.

Benefits sought segmentation is based on the premise that different consumers gratify different needs when they purchase a product. If a target market is rational in nature, the communications message will stress benefits such as quality, price, and dependability; if the target is influenced by emotions, the message plays on feelings such

Coca-Cola
www.cocacola.com

as sex, fear, love, and status. Consumers can be both rational and emotional and exhibit different shopping behaviours at the same time. For example, a recent trend shows Canadian consumers are trading down in some categories in order to trade up in other categories—they pamper themselves with the savings! Discount stores such as Wal-Mart, Payless Shoes, and Old Navy (rational behaviour) have reaped the benefits, as have brands such as Mercedes and BMW (emotional behaviour).

If **frequency of use** is considered, market research is undertaken to distinguish the characteristics of the heavy user from the average user. Very often an 80/20 rule applies (e.g., 80 percent of a brand's volume comes from 20 percent of its users). The profile of the heavy user, as characterized by demographic and psychographic variables, is used to determine the best way of presenting the product to attract potential users.

Loyalty response segmentation assesses the degree of brand loyalty held by consumers. Loyalty can vary considerably: a consumer could be very loyal, moderately loyal, or not loyal at all (e.g., they have a tendency to switch brands often). The characteristics of the most loyal group are identified and that information is used to develop messages that will attract similar users. A study from Grey Canada shows Canadian consumers to be promiscuous—in that they are willing to carry on affairs with multiple brands in a product category. A majority of Canadians revealed that price is the deciding factor when choosing brands in consumer goods categories.[13]

Companies analyze and evaluate the trends and characteristics described in these sections to identify the most profitable targets to pursue. The end result of the analysis is a profile of the prototype customer, who is described in terms of demographic, psychographic, geographic, and behaviour-response characteristics. For a summary of the various characteristics that may be included in a target-market description, refer to Figure 3.12.

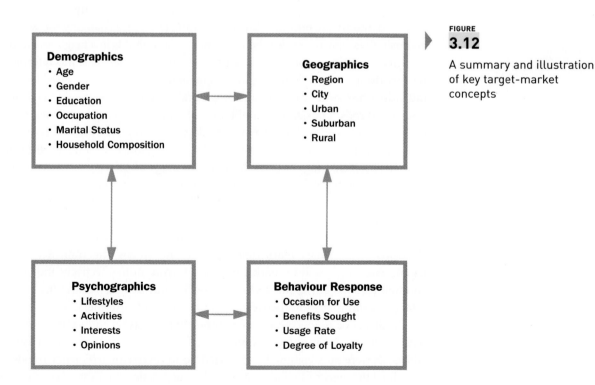

FIGURE
3.12

A summary and illustration of key target-market concepts

Demographics
- Age
- Gender
- Education
- Occupation
- Marital Status
- Household Composition

Geographics
- Region
- City
- Urban
- Suburban
- Rural

Psychographics
- Lifestyles
- Activities
- Interests
- Opinions

Behaviour Response
- Occasion for Use
- Benefits Sought
- Usage Rate
- Degree of Loyalty

DIRECT SEGMENTATION AND RELATIONSHIP MARKETING

Today, organizations have access to advanced information technology that involves the development and management of sophisticated computer and information processing systems. These systems allow for individual targeting and consumer-specific marketing programs. Such a thought is almost frightening!

Direct segmentation simply means that companies target customers individually. Companies are capable of differentiating products, prices, delivery strategies, and communications strategies for each customer. All of these actions are part of the customer relationship management (CRM) programs that most companies are implementing today. **Customer relationship management (CRM)** is a practice that is designed to attract, cultivate, and maximize the return from each customer the company does business with.

The backbone of a CRM program is an organization's database management system. A **database management system** involves compiling information about customers and their buying behaviour on a continuous basis. When this information is combined with demographic, psychographic, and geographic data, and information about media usage, there is sufficient ammunition available to design customized offers and advertising (creative and media) campaigns. Information is available from a variety of external sources including Statistics Canada, Canada Post, and marketing intelligence companies such as Nielsen Marketing Research and Millward Brown Goldfarb.

What has emerged is a concept called data mining. **Data mining** is the analysis of information that establishes relationships between pieces of information so that more effective marketing and communications strategies can be identified and implemented. Data-mining techniques attempt to locate informational patterns and nuggets within the database.[14] The goal is to identify prospects most likely to buy or buy in large volume, and to provide input on how to best communicate with that customer.

To demonstrate how new forms of segmentation are changing the ways companies do business, at one time it was believed that all households in a neighbourhood had similar characteristics—demographics, attitudes, and lifestyles. This was referred to as **cluster profiling** or geodemographic segmentation. Now it is possible to pinpoint individual houses by satellite and then obtain the name of the owner from property assessment rolls. The name is combined with other data described above, and voilà! The organization has enough information to devise a customized offer and communications program. Neighbours may receive different offers. Now that's direct (customized) marketing! This technology will result in greater usage of direct-response and online communications between organizations and their customers in the future.

Information about consumers is readily available; it seems that every time we buy something in a store (where the item is scanned into a database), or do something on the internet (where we agree to cookies being placed in our computers), we leave an electronic trail. Smart marketing organizations follow the trail, determine what it means, and then use it to market products to you more effectively and efficiently. In a communications sense, this technology will result in many more direct-response and internet communications between organizations and customers.

Kraft Foods is an example of a company that has taken to relationship marketing with a vengeance. Kraft saw all kinds of inefficiencies in their mass advertising programs (the costs were outweighing the benefits), so to reverse the efficiency trends it carefully examined the merits of relationship marketing practices in order to correct things. Kraft has experimented with a flurry of web promotions, direct-mail and database marketing programs, custom publishing, and television sponsorships. The company and many of its brands have internet sites, and the sites are a means of collecting data about customers. Simply put, the web provides an excellent opportunity to add "stickiness" to an existing relationship between Kraft and its customers.

Market Positioning Concepts

Positioning can be defined as the selling concept that motivates purchase, or the image that marketers desire a brand or a company to have in the minds of consumers. Positioning is a strategy based on competition. It involves designing and marketing a product to meet the needs of a target market, and creating the appropriate appeals to make the product stand out from the competition in the minds of the target market. Advertising plays a key role in positioning a product in the customer's mind.

Positioning involves an assessment of consumer needs and competitive marketing activity to determine new marketing opportunities. It involves a thorough understanding of the product in relation to competing products. The result is a clearly defined positioning strategy statement that provides guidance for all marketing and marketing communications strategies. The importance of positioning in the development of marketing strategy is presented in Figure 3.13.

A clearly worded positioning strategy statement provides guidance and direction for all marketing and marketing communications activities. All forms of communication should send out the same message about a brand or company.

It is very important that the positioning statement aptly describe a primary benefit and an image that is important to the target market. The statement should be clear, concise, and uncomplicated. Here is an example of an actual positioning strategy statement for Visa (credit card):

> To reinforce our leadership position in the credit card market, and to establish it as the preferred provider of all future products.

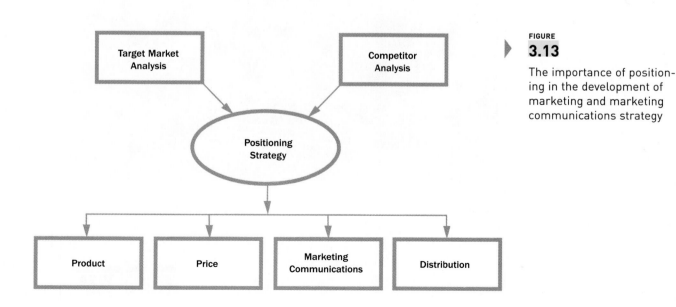

FIGURE
3.13

The importance of positioning in the development of marketing and marketing communications strategy

Visa portrays its positioning strategy in its marketing and advertising by focusing on transactions and acceptance virtually everywhere in the world. In many countries Visa uses the slogan "It's everywhere you want to be" to summarize its primary benefit. In Canada, Visa ads say, Visa is "All you need." See Figure 3.14 for an illustration of Visa's advertising.

POSITIONING AND MARKETING COMMUNICATIONS

The role of marketing communications, particularly the creative strategy (message), is to articulate the positioning strategy of a brand. Advertising will communicate the key selling point and influence the image of the product that the consumer retains. For example, who would have thought that Elastoplast bandages would use adult infidelity to show how fast the product heals superficial scrapes and cuts. In a TV spot called "Hide the Evidence" a man bids farewell to his lover but when looking in the mirror he discovers scratches on his back, inflicted during a passionate encounter. To hide the

FIGURE
3.14

An illustration of brand-leadership positioning

Courtesy: VISA Canada

ADVERTISING IN action

Harvey's: A Different Breed

Harvey's is the fourth or fifth ranked restaurant in the quick serve segment of the market, so doing battle with McDonald's, the undisputed leader, just doesn't make sense. What does make sense though is listening to your customers.

When Harvey's current ad agency, John St., was pitching the account, some consumer research they conducted revealed that Harvey's cooking process makes the best tasting burgers. What the agency realized was that Harvey's had always been run differently than its competitors. The burgers were cooked and dressed in front of the customers rather than built assembly-line fashion in the back of the store. The process has made the grill the star at Harvey's.

So, while the competitors are busy dressing their menus with healthier food choices and trying to be all things to all people, Harvey's would emphasize the heart and soul of the brand—Harvey's is about grilled burgers. Harvey's would be positioned as the place to go for grilled burgers. Unlike the competitors, Harvey's decided to concentrate on its core customer's needs, and that customer is a guy that just wants to chow down on a good burger.

Harvey's has gone in the opposite direction of conventional wisdom today—a direction that makes perfect sense to them. According to marketing manager Joanne Stewart, "A healthy push would have been all wrong, considering Harvey's has always promised a great-tasting burger perfected on the grill." Says Angus Tucker, co-creative director at John St., "Healthy is not really in Harvey's nature—a salad doesn't come out of a grill, so we've decided to focus on what built their business in the first place, which is a better hamburger prepared a better way."

Harvey's launched a campaign comprising television, print, and outdoor advertising with a tongue-in-cheek message: "A burger once in a while won't hurt you." One of the TV spots features a trio of guys attempting to light a barbecue, and causing an explosion in the process, while a second spot promotes the new six-ounce Big Harv, a man-sized burger for the true burger lover.

Sources: Adapted from Lisa D'Innocenzo, "Triumph of the underdog," *Strategy*, October 20, 2003, p. 1 and Paul Brent, "Harvey's sticks to its grilling," *Financial Post*, July 28, 2002, pp. FP1, FP4.

Harvey's   www.harveys.ca

evidence he applies an Elastoplast Fast Healing bandage. The man's wife then walks through the door and they embrace, whereupon the man discovers the same bandage on her shoulder.[15] Communication of main message accomplished!

Advertising can communicate the positioning strategy many different ways. Among some of the more common strategies and techniques are messages that compare one product to another, clearly differentiate one brand from competitors, portray leadership, show innovation, or present a lifestyle association.

HEAD-ON POSITIONING (COMPARATIVE POSITIONING) In head-on positioning, one brand is presented as equal to or better than another brand. This positioning is usually initiated by the number-two brand in a market as a means of challenging the leader. The strategy is to depict users of a competitive brand demonstrating preference for the advertised brand. Ads typically compare two brands on an attribute that is important to the target market. One brand is shown to be better. The "Pepsi Challenge" is now a classic example of such head-on positioning. In television commercials, non-believers were challenged in a taste test. Once they experienced the taste of Pepsi, their conclusion was rather obvious. The campaign did help build Pepsi's business by solidifying its number-two position in the soft-drink market.

A more subtle form of comparison involves one brand comparing itself to "other leading brands" in order to clearly point out it is better at what it does. A print ad for Cascade dish detergent shows two bowls that look clean with a headline saying, "Only one is clean." The body copy goes on to explain that other leading gels leave behind egg residue that you can't see. Cascade, however, breaks up egg residue. The ad ends with the tagline: "Cascade. No doubts."

Courtesy: Michael Kohn Studios/Harvey's Restaurants Canada

FIGURE 3.15

Harvey's positions itself as a destination for beef lovers

Head-on positioning strategies can be risky and expensive since the brand leader could respond to the challenge. What could result is a war of words through advertising, an expensive proposition that neither brand will benefit from.

BRAND-LEADERSHIP POSITIONING Established brands often use icons or signatures in their consumer communications that become highly recognized and synonymous with the brand. These devices then act as a simple and lasting reminder about the essence of the brand for consumers. Coca-Cola has successfully used this approach to build the world's most recognized brand. "Coke is it," "Can't beat the real thing," "Always Coca-Cola," and, more recently, "Real" are examples of universally recognizable signatures. The brand name, unique bottle, and popular slogan are a winning combination for Coca-Cola—they are instantly recognizable by consumers everywhere. The Visa illustration mentioned at the start of this section and Visa's slogan "All you need" (see Figure 3.14) is another example of brand leadership positioning.

PRODUCT-DIFFERENTIATION POSITIONING Product differentiation is a strategy that focuses on the unique attribute of a product—a feature that distinguishes it from all other products. It is a strategy that sells a product strictly on its own merit. Gillette's launch of the new Sensor 3 disposable razor is another good example of differentiation. The headline says it is "The Best Disposable Razor You Ever Threw Away." It's the only disposable razor with three spring-mounted blades, a non-slip handle, and a strip of aloe for extra lubrication—a multiple benefit product that keeps it well ahead of the competition. Not to be outdone, Schick launched the world's first four-blade razor in 2004. How many blades does a person need for a close shave?

In the fast food restaurant category, Harvey's has taken a bold step to differentiate itself from the other major chains. While a perception exists that all fast food is fattening, and competitors such as McDonald's and Wendy's are actively promoting healthier menus, Harvey's has chosen to emphasize its roots and promote great tasting grilled hamburgers and serving them with toppings that their customers want. Harvey's identifies itself with a guy that likes to barbecue beef. Harvey's slogan aptly portrays their positioning strategy: "Long live the grill." For an illustration of Harvey's advertising see Figure 3.15. For more insight into target marketing and positioning strategies, read the Marketing in Action vignette **Harvey's: A Different Breed**.

INNOVATION POSITIONING Innovation is sometimes more important for a company as a whole than for individual products. Companies seeking to establish their own image of continual technical leadership will use advertising to do so, positioning themselves on the leading edge of technology. Such positioning, if firmly established in the minds of customers, will benefit new products when they are introduced to the market. At the product level, innovation can create an advantage that will set one product apart from others and make it more appealing to the customer.

To illustrate, consider the challenge parents often face when trying to persuade their children to swallow cough medicine. Children always balk at the taste! According to the makers of Benylin, the struggles are over. Benylin is now available in a freezer pop format. Each freezer pop contains a teaspoon of Benylin DM. As the tagline says, "Made for kids. Easy for parents." Innovative thinking at Pfizer Inc. has provided a great solution to an age-old problem.

Procter & Gamble demonstrated innovation when it introduced Crest White Strips. Suddenly consumers became obsessed with the need to have whiter teeth. Not to be outdone, Colgate Palmolive quickly responded with their innovation—Colgate Simply White Night. Colgate claims their application process is much simpler—a coating of gel is applied to the teeth at nighttime. Colgate summarizes their positioning with the tagline: "Dramatically whiter teeth made even simpler." The battle between Crest and Colgate in this category is quite intense. See Figure 3.16.

LIFESTYLE POSITIONING In crowded markets, where product attributes are perceived as similar by the target market, firms must identify alternative ways of positioning their products. The use of psychographic information has allowed advertisers to develop campaigns that are based on the lifestyle of the target market. Essentially, the product is positioned to "fit in" or match the lifestyle of the user. The BMW advertisement that appears in Figure 3.10 is a good illustration of lifestyle positioning. The ad visually demonstrates how BMW is a natural part of the contemporary lifestyle of an upscale consumer.

Generally, lifestyle positioning through advertising uses emotional appeals such as love, fear, adventure, sex, and humour to elicit a response from the target. When Labatt Breweries launched its "Cheers. To friends" campaign for Blue, the idea was to reflect

FIGURE
3.16

Innovative products make teeth-whitening simpler

Courtesy of Daniel Acker/Bloomberg News/Landov

what guys do with their friends, to their friends, and for their friends. The humorous ads are vignettes of what the boys are up to, such as tying a naked pal to a telephone pole on his birthday, filling an SUV with golf balls, playing a series of pranks, or just hanging out. According to Labatt, "This is a very real part of what guys do together—a true lifestyle approach to selling beer!"[16]

REPOSITIONING

So far, we have discussed only the initial positioning of a product in the marketplace and in the minds of consumers. But the competitive market requires positioning strategies that can be readily changed if necessary. It is unrealistic to assume that the position a brand adopts initially will remain the same throughout its life cycle. Products will be repositioned according to the prevailing environment in the marketplace. **Repositioning** is defined as changing the place that a brand occupies in the consumer's mind in relation to competitive products. There are two primary reasons for repositioning. One, the marketing activity of a direct competitor may change, and two, the preferences of the target market may change.

The process of repositioning is based on a brand's continuous monitoring of such changes. Companies that don't monitor change often lose touch with their customer and suffer in terms of lower sales and declining market share. In the beverage market, consumer trends have shifted away from soft drinks and toward juices, waters, and even milk. To take advantage of this trend, milk producers such as Neilson Dairies have repositioned a variety of ready-to-serve milk products (milk and milkshakes) as a more healthful alternative to soft drinks and has aimed the advertising message directly at the extreme sports crowd, mainly teenaged males. Other ready-to-drink beverages such as Nesquik have followed suit. These repositioning efforts have helped grow the entire milk category.

Neilson Dairy
www.neilsondairy.com

In the Canadian beer market, a product category that is synonymous with lifestyle positioning strategies, Molson Export appealed to macho males. Export was losing market share and year-to-year sales were in decline, so an attempt was made to appeal to a larger cross-section of the beer drinking population. When Export launched the "Had Ex Today?" ad campaign, the ads featured a completely different type of guy—rather than macho, they are somewhat vulnerable and insecure. Television spots emphasized your average guy's age-old dilemma: spending time with your girlfriend versus spending time with your friends. The initial spot showed a guy named Bob fooling around with his girlfriend only to be interrupted by another guy who (thankfully) saves him from having all that sex.[17] The new image repositioned the brand in the minds of male beer drinkers between 19 and 25 years of age. Molson reports that the sales and market share for Export increased as a result of the campaign. Export's image today isn't what it used to be—making it a repositioning success.

If a positioning strategy is working and if the advertising in use continues to perform as expected, a company should avoid the temptation to change things. Sometimes change occurs for the wrong reasons. Should a manager be in a situation where repositioning strategies are being considered, perhaps an old rule of thumb should apply: "If it ain't broke, don't fix it."

SUMMARY

Market segmentation and knowledge of consumer behaviour are important factors in marketing and advertising planning. Both have a direct impact on product positioning, creative strategy, and media strategy.

Adequate knowledge of how needs and motives, personality and self-concept theories, perceptions, attitudes, reference groups, and family influence behaviour is essential input for the development of marketing and marketing communications strategy.

In terms of market segmentation, organizations must identify their target markets as precisely as they can. Good use of information provided by demographic trends (the consumer's age, gender, income, occupation, education, marital status, household formation, and cultural mix), psychographic characteristics (the consumer's activities, interests, and opinions), and geographic variables (the consumer's location by geography or region) allows for a precise definition of the consumer and enhances the quality of marketing and advertising plans. Insights into behaviour responses such as occasion for use, benefits sought in a product, frequency of use, and loyalty also play a role in developing a profile of the consumer segment an organization may choose to target.

Database marketing and management techniques have enabled organizations to form and maintain relationships with individual customers, a concept referred to as customer relationship management. The use of database management systems and data-mining techniques allows an organization to identify customers and prospects most likely to buy or buy in large volume. An organization is now capable of pinpointing a specific household in a neighbourhood and can send personalized, custom-designed marketing offers to that household. Such a practice is possible because technology allows information about households from an endless variety of sources to be combined. As a result, there will be a movement toward direct-response communications and away from mass-media communications in the future.

Positioning a product is an important part of pursuing target markets, and advertising plays a key role in positioning. Positioning involves designing a product or service to meet the needs of a target market, and then creating appropriate appeals to make the product stand out in the minds of the target-market members. Common positioning strategies include head-on comparisons, product differentiation, technical innovation, and brand dominance and lifestyle techniques. As a product matures, factors such as competitive activity and changing consumer preferences dictate a re-evaluation of positioning strategies.

Positioning strategies that are working should be retained for as long as possible. Often, companies adopt new strategies for the wrong reasons—companies tend to tire of things more quickly than do loyal consumers. The old expression, "If it ain't broke, don't fix it," should apply.

KEY TERMS

attitudes 72
behaviour-response segmentation 82
consumer behaviour 67
customer relationship management (CRM) 84
data mining 84
database management system 84

demographic segmentation 75
direct segmentation 84
double targeting 74
geographic segmentation 82
lifestyle advertising 80
market segmentation 74
motives 68

needs 68
perception 70
positioning 85
psychographic segmentation 80
reference group (or peer group) 73
repositioning 91
subcultures 79

REVIEW QUESTIONS

1. Explain the various levels of needs and identify the two basic principles that needs and motivation theory are based on. Provide an advertising example for each level of needs.

2. Briefly explain each of the components of the self-concept. Provide a new example of an ad campaign that uses the looking-glass self or ideal self to its advantage.

3. Briefly explain how knowledge of attitudes and reference groups influences the direction of advertising strategy.

4. What is double targeting? Provide a new example to demonstrate how it is applied.

5. What are the key elements of demographic segmentation, psychographic segmentation, geographic segmentation, and behaviour-response segmentation? Briefly explain.

6. What are the basic trends affecting demographic segmentation in Canada?

7. Explain the concept of positioning in the context of marketing and advertising practice.

8. What is the difference between head-on positioning and brand-leadership positioning? Provide a new example of each.

9. If a brand is using a product-differentiation positioning strategy, what will the advertised message focus on? Provide two examples that show application of this type of positioning.

10. What is repositioning and why does it occur? Briefly explain.

DISCUSSION QUESTIONS

1. Provide some additional examples to show how advertisers use the following aspects of consumer behaviour theory:

   - Social and esteem needs
   - Self-image, looking-glass self, and ideal self
   - Reference groups
   - Role and position in a family unit

2. "The economies of a national creative plan outweigh the need for numerous regional creative plans." Discuss this issue, choosing some products and ad campaigns as examples.

3. "To succeed in the future, products and services must be repositioned to appeal to older target markets." Comment on the implications of this statement.

4. "Companies are well behind in terms of recognizing the changes occurring in Canadian household formation and it is reflected in the types of advertising they are showing." Is this statement true or false? Provide examples to verify your opinion.

5. Will the influence of relationship marketing be that significant on marketing communications in the future? Will companies spend more on direct-response and online advertising and less on traditional mass-media advertising? Justify your opinion.

NOTES

1. James F. Engel, David T. Kollatt, and Roger D. Blackwell, *Consumer Behaviour*, 2nd edition (New York: Holt Rinehart Winston, 1973), p. 5.

2. Hollie Shaw, "Retailers seek elusive key to the shopping man's heart," *Financial Post*, June 5, 2002, p. FP12.

3. A. H. Maslow, *Motivation and Personality* (New York: Harper and Row Publishers, 1954), pp. 370–396.

4. John Douglas, George Field, and Lawrence Tarpay, *Human Behaviour in Marketing* (Columbus, OH: Charles E. Merrill Publishing, 1987), p. 5.

5. Louise Kramer, "Just Dew it: Green soda poised to pass Diet Coke," *Advertising Age*, August 23, 1999, pp. 3, 26.

6. Andrea Zoe Aster, "Back to school," *Marketing*, August 11/18, 2003, pp. 20, 21.

7. Hollie Shaw, "Skip the Chevy—buy yourself a Beemer," *Financial Post*, July 10, 2003, pp. FP1, FP8.

8. Terry Poulton, "The paradox of the working mom," *Strategy Media*, October 20, 2003, p. 19.

9. Barbara Wickens, "How we live," *Maclean's*, November 4, 2002, p. 46.

10. Eve Lazarus, "VanCity makes bold play for gays," *Marketing*, August 19, 2002, p. 3.

11. Jo Marney, "Counting ethnic Canadians in," *Marketing*, June 4, 2001, p. 24.

12. "Demographic Statistics," *The Daily*, Statistics Canada, March 28, 2002, **www.statcan.ca**.

13. Patti Summerfield, "New study reveals demise of brand loyalty," *Strategy*, December 7, 1998, p. 11.

14. David Eggleston, "We've come a long way baby," *Strategy Direct Response*, November 8, 1999, p. D13.

15. "Elastoplast reveals no secrets," *Marketing*, May 26, 2003, p. 3.

16. Michelle Warren, "Labatt smiling over new Blue work," *Marketing*, March 3, 2003, p. 3.

17. Astrid Van Den Broek, "Molson backs Ex over too much sex," *Marketing*, October 2, 2000, p. 3.

Strategic Planning Concepts for Marketing Communications

Learning Objectives

After studying this chapter, you will be able to

- Identify the distinctions and relationships between the various types of planning

- Describe the key variables that comprise a corporate plan

- Outline the organization and content of a marketing plan and marketing communications plan

- Show how integrated marketing communications plans provide solutions to marketing problems

Business planning is an integrated process that involves planning at three levels of an organization: corporate planning, marketing planning, and marketing communications planning. Advertising is one aspect of marketing communications planning. It is important for students to understand the planning process and appreciate the interaction of plans at each level and at different levels. Marketing communications plans are not created independently; they are linked to plans at other levels of the organization. The corporate plan will influence the marketing plan and the marketing plan will influence the marketing communications plan.

There are no design norms against which marketing plans and advertising plans are measured. The design and content of plans vary considerably among organizations, and the structure of them depends on the needs and degree of marketing sophistication of the firm developing the plan. Lengthy, comprehensive plans are not necessarily good plans. A good plan provides direction for a product, service, or company; outlines key activities to be implemented; and provides a means of measuring the success or failure of the plan. In this regard, no limitations are placed on the design, organization, and content of a marketing communications plan.

Business-Planning Process

Strategic business planning involves making decisions about three variables: objectives, strategies, and execution or tactics. Let's first define these planning variables:

1. **Objectives** are statements that outline what is to be accomplished in the corporate, marketing, or advertising plan.
2. **Strategies** are statements that outline how the objectives will be achieved and usually identify the resources necessary to achieve objectives, such as funds, time, people, and type of activity.
3. **Execution (tactics)** refers to tactical action plans that outline specific details of implementation, which collectively contribute to the achievement of objectives. Tactical plans usually provide details of an activity's cost and timing.

FIGURE
4.1
PLANNING MODEL EXHIBIT

Strategic planning: The links
between plans at various
levels of an organization

The corporate plan provides
guidance for the marketing plan
and the marketing plan provides
guidance for the marketing
communications plan. Corporate
plans are strategic in nature while
marketing plans and marketing
communications plans are
strategic and tactical in nature.

A diagram of the business planning process as it applies to marketing and advertising is provided in Figure 4.1.

Strategic Planning

When a company embarks on a **plan** it anticipates the future business environment to determine the course of action it will take. For example, a firm will look at trends in the economy, demography, culture, and technology, and then develop a plan that will provide growth. A typical plan considers the long-term (five years) and the short-term (one year) situation. Each year the plan is evaluated and changes are made where necessary.

Strategic planning is the process of determining objectives (setting goals) and identifying strategies (ways to achieve the goals) and tactics (specific action plans) to help achieve the objectives. A corporate plan originates at the top of the organization and is largely based on input from senior executives. Such plans are usually not elaborate documents, since their purpose is to identify the corporate objectives to be achieved over a specified period. The corporate plan acts as a guideline for planning in various operational areas of the company. Marketing and advertising are two of these operational areas.

In examining Figure 4.1, we find that the business planning throughout the organization begins and ends at the corporate or senior-management level. Senior management formulates the overall strategic direction for the organization and establishes the financial objectives the company should aspire to (sales, profit, return on investment). Then, in accordance with the objectives and directions passed down from senior management, the marketing department develops marketing plans that embrace objectives, strategies, and tactics for individual products, divisions, or target markets.

Marketing plans consider such matters as the marketing mix (product, price, distribution, and marketing communications), target-market characteristics, and control and evaluation mechanisms that determine the effectiveness of the strategies being implemented. Marketing plans are very specific and all activities related to product, price, distribution, and marketing communications are outlined in the plan. With reference to Figure 4.1, our primary concern is marketing communications, which is subdivided into advertising, direct-response communications, online and interactive communications, sales promotion, personal selling, public relations, and event marketing. Advertising can be further subdivided into creative plans and media plans.

As this planning process indicates, each plan is related to another. The saying "A chain is only as strong as its weakest link" is an appropriate description of these relationships. Strategic planning attempts to coordinate all activity so that elements from various areas work harmoniously. In the case of marketing, advertising, and any other form of communications, all activity must present a consistent image of the company or its product in order to create a favourable impression in the minds of consumers. One weak link in the chain can create conflict or confuse the target market. For example, a product's selling price could be set too high in relation to the customer's perception of quality. Such a situation occurred when Chrysler launched the Pacifica, an SUV crossover vehicle. The Pacifica was introduced with significant advertising but was rejected by consumers because the price was too high compared to competitive vehicles. Sales fell well short of expectations and the entire marketing plan had to be re-evaluated. Inconsistent activity spread over numerous company products could seriously disrupt attempts to achieve marketing and corporate objectives.

Chrysler Pacifica
www.chrysler.com/pacifica

The Corporate Plan

A **mission statement** is the foundation of the corporate plan; it is a statement of the organization's purpose. It reflects the operating philosophy of the organization and the direction the organization is to take. Such statements are related to the opportunities the company identifies for itself in the marketplace. Mission statements are market-oriented; they will work for the company only if its products are designed and marketed according to consumers' demands. Stemming from the marketing concept, mission statements recognize customers' needs and consider the competition, the need to build long-term customer relationships, and how to balance corporate goals with societal goals. They may be quite detailed or very brief in content. To understand what a mission statement reads like, consider the following example, one that is quite detailed, but a good reflection of where the company is heading:

Toyota Motor Corporation

Toyota is taking the initiative to achieve solid growth by creating new synergies among people, the environment, and automobiles. Our strategy is to be one step ahead in our pursuit of global motorization and environmental preservation.

Toyota Canada
www.toyota.ca

Toyota, along with the rest of the automobile industry, faces a number of difficult challenges that must be overcome to ensure future growth. We will continue to boldly take on these challenges by creating original solutions across the broad spectrum of our operations to achieve sustainable development.

Through next-generation technology, innovative production engineering, and accelerated globalization of all areas of our operations from development, procurement, and production, to sales and services, we aim to become the leading company in the automobile industry.[1]

Since corporate plans provide direction to all functional areas of the company, they tend to be long-term in nature (encompassing three to five years), broad in scope, and considerate of the overall well-being of the organization. Now let's examine the differences between corporate objectives and strategies.

CORPORATE OBJECTIVES

Corporate objectives are statements of a company's overall goals, and take their direction from the mission statement. They may state what return on investment is desired or what level of sales or market share is desired of a particular market segment. Social responsibility objectives now play a more prominent role in corporate planning. Good objective statements are written in quantifiable terms so that they can be measured for their attainment. Consider the following examples:

- To increase total company sales from $500 000 000 in 20XX to $600 000 000 in 20XX.
- To increase market share from 25 percent in 20XX to 30 percent in 20XX.
- To increase return on investment from 10 percent in 20XX to 13 percent in 20XX.
- To implement a company-wide recycling program by the end of the year.

Objectives like these provide the framework for the development of detailed plans in the operational areas of the organization.

CORPORATE STRATEGIES

After the corporate objectives are confirmed, the organization must identify the **corporate strategies**, which are plans outlining how the objectives will be achieved. The factors considered when strategies are being developed are marketing strength; degree of competition in markets the company operates in; financial resources (e.g., the availability of investment capital or the ability to borrow required funds); research and development capabilities; and management commitment (i.e., the priority a company has placed on a particular goal).

Assuming market growth is the corporate objective, corporations could proceed in an endless range of strategic directions to achieve it. One option is to follow a **penetration strategy**. A company like Coca-Cola, for example, wants to build its leadership position in the world's beverage market. To do so it focuses all of its financial and marketing resources on improving the sales of its soft drink, juice, and water beverages. Coca-Cola will invest heavily in marketing in order to keep its name top-of-mind and to build its distribution network for all of its beverage products.

A second option is an **acquisition strategy** that involves one company buying another company or parts of another company. Recently, Cadbury Schweppes acquired the Adams division of Pfizer Inc. for US$4.2 billion. Adams products include Trident and Dentyne chewing gums, Bubblicious bubble gum, Hall's cough drops, and Clorets breath fresheners. The acquisition makes Cadbury the market leader in the functional confectionery market where growth is double that of the broader confectionery market.[2]

Another common corporate strategy to achieve growth is to invest in research and development to develop **new products**. Alternatively, a company could decide to acquire new products developed by other companies. Both Coca-Cola and Pepsi-Cola have launched a variety of flavoured colas to expand their lines. Pepsi Vanilla, for example, has been very successful. Procter & Gamble invested heavily in research and development to refine and launch the very successful Swiffer mop system. When the company wanted to expand its Crest brand name, it acquired spin-brush technology from another company, and it internally developed Crest White Strips and Crest Night Effects. The addition of these new product lines repositions Crest as a complete oral care product line. See Figure 4.2 for an illustration. Truly new products like these create new revenue

Cadbury
www.cadbury.com

Crest White Strips
www.whitestrips.com

streams for organizations. Such a strategy is proving more effective than simply expanding existing products.

Strategic alliances are now very popular among companies wanting to find ways of reducing costs or improving operating efficiencies. An alliance is a relationship between two or more companies that decide to work co-operatively together to achieve common goals. Toyota and Nissan, arch-rivals in the automotive market, decided to work together on new gasoline-electric hybrid vehicles in order to speed the development of more affordable, environmentally friendly cars. They see working together as a more practical means of recovering the massive development costs of such projects.[3]

Rather than expanding, some companies are consolidating their operations by **divesting** themselves of operations that are not profitable or no longer fit with future plans. Bigger is not always better it seems! Cited above was Cadbury's acquisition of Adams brands from Pfizer Inc. One might question why Pfizer sold off Adams. For Pfizer, the deal represented the first stage of a strategic plan to shed itself of non-pharmaceutical businesses. Pfizer's goal is to stay focused on what it does best—developing and marketing pharmaceutical products. Ironically, Pfizer had acquired Adams brands when it merged with Warner Lambert in 2000.[4]

Pfizer Canada
www.pfizer.ca

FIGURE
4.2
PLANNING MODEL EXHIBIT

Innovative new products create new revenue streams for a company

Marketing Planning

The marketing department operates within the guidelines established by senior management. The objectives, strategies, and action plans developed by marketing are designed to help achieve overall company objectives. Where planning is concerned, the major areas of marketing responsibility include:

1. Identifying and selecting target markets.
2. Establishing marketing objectives, strategies, and tactics.
3. Evaluating and controlling marketing activities.

Marketing planning is the analysis, planning, implementation, evaluation, and control of marketing initiatives to satisfy market needs and achieve organizational objectives. It involves the analysis of relevant background information and historical trend data and the development of marketing objectives, strategies, and executions for all products and services within a company. The integration of various elements of the marketing mix is outlined in the marketing plan of each product. In contrast to corporate plans, **marketing plans** are short-term in nature (one year), specific in scope (since they deal with one product and outline precise actions), and combine both strategy and tactics (they are action-oriented).

While there is no typical format for a marketing plan (e.g., the content and structure does vary from company to company), they are usually subdivided into major sections based on background content and planning content. In terms of background, the company conducts a **situation analysis** (sometimes called environmental analysis) in which data and information about external and internal influences are compiled. It is important to examine happenings that impact on the performance of a brand. External factors that are considered include economic trends, social and demographic trends, and technology trends. As well, information is compiled about the market, the customers, and the competition. In the **marketing plan**, the objectives, strategies, and tactics for the brand or company are clearly delineated. The following is a description of the various elements of a marketing plan. Refer to Figure 4.3 for a summary of the information that is usually included in a marketing plan.

MARKET BACKGROUND—SITUATION ANALYSIS

As a preliminary step to marketing planning, a variety of information is compiled and analyzed. This information includes some or all of the following:

EXTERNAL INFLUENCES

- *Economic trends* Basic economic trends often dictate the nature of marketing activity (e.g., if the economy is healthy and growing, more resources are allocated to marketing activity; if the economy is in a recession, a more conservative approach is often adopted).

- *Social and demographic trends* Basic trends in age, income, immigration, and lifestyle influence decisions on what target markets to pursue. For example, the Canadian population is aging and large cities are becoming more ethnic in nature. These factors necessitate change in marketing strategy.

FIGURE
4.3

Content of a marketing plan:
A sample model

MARKETING BACKGROUND	MARKETING PLAN
External Influences • Economic trends • Social and demographic trends • Technology trends **Market Analysis** • Market size and growth • Regional market importance and trends • Market segment analysis • Seasonal analysis • Consumer date (target user) • Consumer behaviour (loyalty) **Product Analysis** • Sales volume trends • Market share trends • Distribution trends • Marketing communications activities **Competitor Analysis** • Market share trends • Marketing activity assessment **SWOT Analysis*** • Strengths • Weaknesses • Opportunities • Threats	**Positioning Strategy** • Positioning Statement **Target Market Profile** • Demographic • Psychographic • Geographic **Marketing Objectives** • Sales volume • Market share • Profit • Marketing communications • Other **Marketing Strategies** • Product • Price • Distribution • Marketing communications • Marketing research • Budget (total available for brand) **Marketing Execution** (Action plans for each component) • Product • Price • Distribution • Marketing communications • Marketing research • Profit improvement **Budget and Financial Summary** • Budget allocation (by activity, time, area) • Brand profit & loss statement **Marketing Calendar** • Activity schedule by month

Note: Including a SWOT analysis is optional. Many planners believe that you actually conduct a SWOT when the background information is compiled in the first four subsections of the background section of a plan. Other planners believe that such information must be analyzed further to determine priorities. The latter is the intention of a SWOT analysis.

■ *Technology trends* The rapid pace of change (e.g., in computers and telecommunications) influences the development of new products, shortens product life cycles, and influences the communications strategies used to reach customers.

MARKET ANALYSIS

- *Market size and growth* A review is made of trends in the marketplace over a period. Is the market growing, remaining stable, or declining?

- *Regional market importance* Market trends and sales-volume trends are analyzed by region to determine areas of strength or weakness and areas to concentrate on in the future.

- *Market-segment analysis* The sales volume of total market and segments within a market are reviewed. For example, the snack food market and many other food categories are analyzed in terms of regular products and light (diet-related, low-calorie, and low-carbohydrate) products. Consumers' concerns about obesity are causing a change in marketing strategy for most food companies today.

- *Seasonal analysis* An examination is conducted of seasonal or cyclical trends during the course of a year. For example, traditions such as Christmas, Thanksgiving, and Halloween often have an impact on sales volume and affect the timing of marketing activities.

- *Consumer data* Current users of a product are profiled according to factors such as age, gender, lifestyle, and location. The data may consider primary users as well as secondary users and indicate new areas of opportunity.

- *Consumer behaviour* The degree of customer loyalty to the market and individual brands within a market is assessed. Are customers loyal or do they switch brands often? Other factors considered are benefits consumers seek in the product and how frequent their purchases are. Such data indicates the need for strategies that will attract new customers or retain existing customers.

PRODUCT ANALYSIS An assessment of a product's marketing-mix strategy is reviewed at this stage. In the assessment, relationships are drawn between the marketing activity that was implemented over the course of the year and the sales volume and market share that was achieved.

- *Sales volume* Historical sales trends are plotted to forecast future growth.

- *Market share* Market share success is the clearest indicator of how well a brand is performing. Market share results are recorded nationally and regionally, and areas of strength and weakness are identified.

- *New-product activity* The success or failure of new products introduced in recent years is highlighted (e.g., new pack sizes, flavours, product formats, and so on).

- *Distribution* The availability of a product nationally and regionally is reviewed. Distribution is also assessed based on type of customer (e.g., chains and independents).

- *Marketing communications* An assessment of current activities will determine if strategies are to be maintained or if new strategies are needed. A review of expenditures by medium, sales promotions, event marketing, and any other activity is necessary in order to assess the impact of such spending on brand performance.

COMPETITIVE ANALYSIS It is wise to know a competitor's products as well as your own. A review of marketing-mix activities for key competitors provides essential input on how to revise marketing strategies.

- *Market share trends* It is common to evaluate market share trends of all competitors from year to year, nationally and regionally. Such analysis provides insight into what brands are moving forward and what brands are moving backward.

- *Marketing strategy assessment* An attempt is made to link known marketing strategies to competitor brand performance. What is the nature of their advertising, sales promotions, and events and sponsorships? How much money do competitors invest in marketing? Have they launched any new products and how successful are they?

The combination of market analysis, product analysis, and competitor analysis helps provide direction to those managers responsible for developing a new marketing plan and presents senior managers with an overall perspective.

SWOT ANALYSIS

After assembling the market information, the next step is appraising it. While this is not a formal part of the marketing plan itself, a manager should evaluate all information collected and then determine what the priorities are for the next year. This process is referred to as a **SWOT analysis**. The acronym SWOT stands for strengths, weaknesses, opportunities, and threats. A SWOT analysis examines the critical factors that have an impact on the nature and direction of a marketing strategy. Strengths and weaknesses are internal factors (e.g., resources available, research and development capability, and management expertise), while opportunities and threats are external factors (e.g., economic trends, competitive activity, and social and demographic trends.)

"SWOT Analysis: Beyond the Textbook"
www.websitemarketingplan.com/
Arts/SWOT.htm

The end result of a SWOT analysis should be the matching of potential opportunities with resource capabilities. The goal is to capitalize on strengths while improving weaknesses. A SWOT analysis can be conducted at any level of an organization—product, division, or company.

The Marketing Plan

POSITIONING STATEMENT

Positioning refers to the desired image that a company wants to place in the minds of customers about the company as a whole or about individual products—it is the selling concept that helps motivate purchase. The concept of positioning was discussed in Chapter 3. Effective positioning statements are realistic, specific, and uncomplicated, and they clearly distinguish what a brand has to offer.

A **positioning-strategy statement** is a working statement. It is the focal point from which relevant marketing and marketing communications strategies are developed. To demonstrate, consider the dilemma that Toyota faced in Canada. The average age of a Toyota driver is 46 years old. The company urgently needed to attract younger buyers. Their answer was the Toyota Echo, a unique-looking automobile for urban streets. The Echo's positioning statement could read as follows:

> To position Echo as a car of choice for young 18 to 25-year-olds
> (Generation Y), based on the car's fun, funky, and functional styling,
> myriad custom options, and youthful image.

Toyota believes that every generation wants a car to call its own—the Echo will be the car for Generation Y, but it will also be attractive to older Canadians who are "young-at-heart." "The new Echo hatchback combines exciting styling with the confidence of Toyota quality at an extremely competitive price, says Tony Weary, Group Vice President of Toyota Canada. Such a proposition is attractive to a lot of Canadians of all ages."[5]

Toyota recognizes the primary target is net-savvy, so advertisements encourage consumers to visit the "Price Your Toyota" section of the website. Here consumers can configure and price their own unique Echo. An image of the Toyota Echo is included in Figure 4.4.

FIGURE
4.4

The Toyota Echo appeals
directly to Generation Y

TARGET-MARKET PROFILE

At this stage, the manager identifies, or targets, markets that represent the greatest profit potential for the firm. A **target market** is a group of customers with certain similar
needs and characteristics. As discussed in Chapter 3, a target-market description is
devised based on demographic, psychographic, and geographic characteristics.

- *Demographic profile* Characteristics such as age, gender, income, education, and
  ethnic background are considered. Depending on the product and the extent of its
  appeal to the population, some characteristics will be more important than others.

- *Psychographic profile* The lifestyle profile includes three essential characteristics: the
  target's activities, interests, and opinions. Such knowledge provides clues that will
  influence the direction of message strategies (how to appeal to the target) and media
  strategies (how to best reach the target). For example, the much-sought 18- to 25-
  year-old male market is apparently watching much less television than they used to.
  This presents a challenge for marketers wanting to reach them.

- *Geographic profile* Much of Canada's population is urban and certainly there are distinct regional differences that must be considered. Geography will influence decisions

ADVERTISING IN action

Sporty Vehicles Target Youth

Perhaps movies like *The Fast and the Furious* and vehicles like the Honda Civic started it all, but now all carmakers are doing what they can to impress Generation Y (people born between 1977 and 1995), at least those between 18 and 25 years old. These are the sons and daughters of baby boomers now graduating and entering the job market.

Marketers are now focusing on Generation Y because they will become a bigger pool of customers as they age. It is expected that, by 2020, they will represent 32 percent of the population and they will exceed their baby boomer parents' buying power when at their peak. For certain, some brand loyalties must be established now!

Generation Y is the internet generation. They are into PCs instead of TVs, they are tech-savvy and love to download music, and they are skeptical toward the media, which makes them a difficult lot to direct advertising messages at. Advertising and communications strategies that are perceived to be mainstream may not resonate with Generation Y. Automobile marketers will have to look at a different arsenal of communications strategies to reach and motivate this audience.

A marketing research study about new-car buying intentions reveals that Generation Y is much more likely to purchase a compact car or a sports car. In contrast, older generations buy sedans, sports utility vehicles, and minivans. Honda was one of the first companies actively targeting Generation Y. In 2003 they launched the Honda Element, a boxy sports utility vehicle. Ads for the Element showed the great outdoors through the vehicle's rear door or wide-swing side doors. Toyota launched the Scion in 2004 in several different models and firmly believes it will be a car that the youth market will quickly identify with.

Gen-Yers want it all: price, a nice buying experience, and a vehicle they won't be embarrassed to be seen in. Until now, Saturn has been a car for older age groups, but they too have joined the fray. A sporty version of the Saturn Vue, which the company says will do 0 to 96 kilometres per hour in seven seconds, eliminates the need for the apologetic "It's a Saturn." There is even a hybrid version (combination gas and electric power) available for the young, environment-conscious consumer.

And how are marketers reaching Generation Y? Rather than the typical barrage of television commercials, advertisements are being placed in urban magazines and companies are sponsoring events such as rock concerts and extreme sports. Wild postings at construction sites and other downtown locations are also popular. And of course, the internet plays a key role in communicating vivid pictures and in providing the necessary product information—the internet is truly Generation Y's home turf for communications.

Sources: Adapted from Paul Brent, "Saturn gets performance-ified," *Financial Post*, April 19, 2003, p. D010 and Jean Halliday, "To survive, carmakers think young," *Advertising Age*, April 14, 2003, p. S-2.

about regional versus national marketing strategies and will influence how a budget is allocated across the country.

To demonstrate, the following profile might represent a target market for an upscale automobile or someone interested in the services of a financial-planning company:

- *Age:*   25 to 49 years old
- *Gender:*   Male or female
- *Income:* $75 000 plus annually
- *Occupation:* Business managers, owners, and professionals
- *Education:*   College or university

- *Location:* Cities of 100 000 plus population
- *Lifestyle:* Progressive thinkers and risk takers who like to experiment with new products; they are interested in the arts, entertainment, and vacation travel

To demonstrate the importance of understanding your customer and for more insight into how automobile marketers are targeting the youth market, read the Advertising in Action vignette **Sporty Vehicles Target Youth**.

MARKETING OBJECTIVES

Marketing objectives are statements identifying what a product will accomplish during one year. Typically, marketing objectives concentrate on sales volume, market share, and profit (net profit or return on investment), all of which are quantitative (as opposed to qualitative) in nature and measurable at the end of the period. Objectives that are qualitative in nature could include new product introductions, new additions to current product lines, product improvements, and packaging innovations. To illustrate the concept of marketing objectives, consider the following sample statements:

- *Sales volume* To achieve sales of 200 000 units, an increase of 10 percent over the current-year sales.
- *Market share* To achieve a market share of 30 percent in 12 months, an increase of 4 share points over the current position.
- *Profit* To generate an after-budget profit of $600 000 in the next 12 months.
- *Marketing communications* To launch a new advertising campaign in the second quarter that will increase brand awareness from 50 percent to 75 percent among the target audience.

Objectives should be written in a manner that allows for measurement at the end of the period. Were the objectives achieved or not?

MARKETING STRATEGIES

Marketing strategies are essentially the "master plans" for achieving marketing objectives. The importance of having a sound marketing strategy must be emphasized. All elements of the marketing mix and marketing communications mix must act in unison; collaboration is necessary in order to present a consistent and meaningful proposition to new and existing customers. The goal should be to have the right strategy and then work on improving the execution of it as time goes on.

At this stage of the planning process, the role and importance of each component of the **marketing mix** is identified. Priority may be given to certain components depending on the nature of the market, the degree of competition, and knowledge of what motivates customers to buy. For example, brands like Coca-Cola and Pepsi-Cola rely heavily on advertising and distribution strategies to build sales and market share. Wal-Mart dwells on product and price—a combination that offers significant value to consumers across all income groups. Automobile marketers have focused on pricing strategies (incentives and rebate offers) in recent years at the expense of building brand image through advertising.

The amount of money or **budget** will be identified in the strategy section of the plan. Typically, the corporate plan has already identified a total marketing budget for the company. That budget must be allocated across all company products based on the firm's analysis of current priorities or profit potential. Managers responsible for product planning must develop and justify a budget that allows enough funds to implement the strategies identified in their marketing plan, and to achieve the financial objectives identified for the product. The final stage of the budgeting process is the allocation of funds among the activity areas in the plan (advertising, marketing research, consumer promotion, trade promotion, events and sponsorship, interactive communications, etc.).

MARKETING EXECUTION

Often referred to as **marketing tactics**, **marketing execution** focuses on specific program details that stem directly from the strategy section of the plan. In general terms, a tactical plan outlines the activity, how much it will cost, what the timing will be, and who will be responsible for implementation. Detailed tactical plans for all components of the plan (advertising, sales promotion, internet communications, marketing research, etc.) are included here. It should be noted that the ad agency develops a detailed advertising plan in a separate document. If advertising is a key element in overall marketing strategy, then advertising strategy and tactics will be integrated into the marketing plan in summary form in the marketing communications section.

FINANCIAL SUMMARY AND BUDGET ALLOCATION

As a summary of the entire marketing plan, a statistical presentation of key product-performance indicators is commonly included. Variables such as sales, market share, gross profit, marketing budget, and net profit are presented historically. Past performance and trends can be compared to the latest financial estimates in the new marketing plan. A detailed budget is included that indicates all activity areas in which funds will be spent. Major areas such as media, consumer promotion, trade promotion, and marketing research are often subdivided into more specific areas.

MARKETING CONTROL AND EVALUATION

Since clearly defined and measurable objectives have been established by the organization and by the marketing department, it is important that results be evaluated against the plans and against past performance. This evaluation indicates whether current strategies need to be modified or if new strategies should be considered.

Marketing control is the process of measuring and evaluating the results of marketing strategies and plans, and taking corrective action to ensure that marketing objectives are attained. For example, if financial objectives are not being achieved, then new marketing strategies may have to be considered. This is also a good time to re-evaluate the various marketing objectives. Perhaps some objectives were too aggressive, and considering the current dynamics of the market, should be adjusted accordingly. Any modifications to the marketing objective will have an impact on the marketing activities as well. See Figure 4.5 for a diagram of the marketing planning and control process.

Advertising and Marketing Communications Planning

Similar to marketing planning, marketing communications planning involves the development of appropriate objectives, strategies, and tactics. This section will concentrate on advertising planning and planning for the related areas of marketing communications—sales promotion, public relations, event marketing and sponsorships, direct-response communications, and online communications.

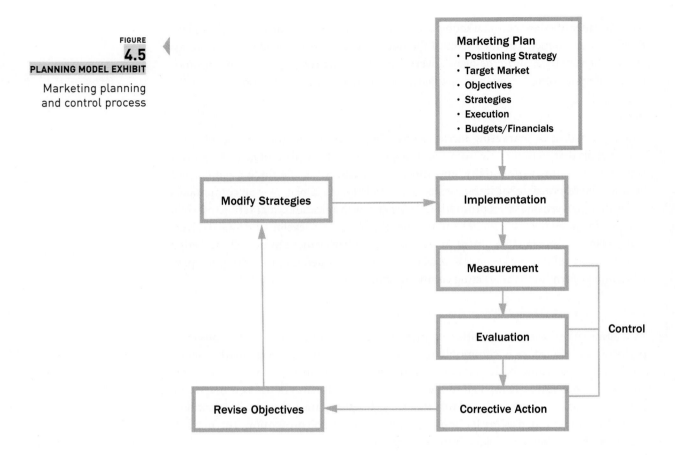

Usually a campaign is designed to resolve a specific problem or pursue an opportunity, so the primary objective of marketing communications must be stated clearly. Marketing communications objectives tend to cover a diverse range of possibilities and could involve

- Creating awareness or building awareness for a product or company

- Differentiating a product from competitive offerings

- Encouraging more frequent use of a product

- Altering perceptions held by consumers about a product

- Offering incentives to get people to buy the product

- Fostering a strong public image of the product or company

The list could go on but the point is that certain types of marketing communications are better than others at achieving certain objectives. Sometimes one form of communications, say advertising, may be enough to achieve the objective while at other times a multi-discipline approach is necessary. Determining which components of the marketing communications mix will be used depends on the nature of the market, competitive activity, and the target market to be reached. As well, the funds available will influence the decision—some activities are much more expensive than others! The key to success is the integration of the various components to produce a unified approach to building the brand (or company).

A **marketing communications plan** is a document usually prepared by the company's marketing communications agency. Or it could be a coordinated effort of several agencies that are doing specialized work (e.g., advertising, public relations, sales promotions) for the brand or company (e.g., an interactive ad agency, a sales-promotion specialist, and an event-marketing specialist). To develop the plan, each agency must be informed about relevant marketing information. In the case of advertising, for example, the client will prepare a document that contains relevant information from the marketing plan. That document is commonly referred to as a **creative brief** (if message is the issue) or a **media brief** (if the issue is media-related). These concepts are discussed in appropriate chapters later in the textbook. Similar documents are prepared for other specialized communications agencies if they are involved in the planning process. The content of a marketing communications plan is included in Figure 4.6.

MARKETING COMMUNICATIONS OBJECTIVES

Marketing communications objectives define the role that advertising and other forms of communications will play in selling the client's product or service and in achieving a stated marketing objective. For example, advertising usually plays a key role in creating brand awareness, sales promotions encourage trial purchases, and public relations helps build and maintain brand image. The various plan components, therefore, work together to help achieve the marketing communications objectives.

A good statement of objectives will make it possible to quantify the success or failure of advertising by establishing the minimum levels of awareness and purchase motivation. It should also provide a description of the target market to be reached by advertising. Consider the following examples:

1. To achieve a minimum awareness level of 75 percent among men and women, 18 to 34 years of age, in urban markets of 500 000 population
2. To motivate at least 25 percent of the defined target market to try the product on the basis of trial incentives to be included in print advertising
3. To improve public awareness of our company's actions in the area of social responsibility marketing
4. To alter consumers' perceptions about brand image so that the views held about the brand are more positive.

As shown above, where possible the objectives should be quantitative in nature (objectives 1 and 2) so that when the campaign is over the results can be evaluated against the plan. Many firms will conduct marketing research to determine the effectiveness of their message and media strategies. For example, if the desired awareness level was not achieved, new strategies will have to be considered for the following year. These objectives also imply that marketing communications will be an integrated effort embracing activities beyond just advertising. In the case of objective 4, it could be assumed that currently held perceptions are negative; some consumer research in the post-campaign stage will reveal if perceptions have been altered favourably.

In the mission statement for Toyota that appeared earlier in the chapter, one of Toyota's goals is to balance economic objectives with social responsibility objectives. See illustrations of the marketing communications Toyota uses to inform the public about how these goals are achieved in Figure 4.7. Toyota's efforts in this area go well beyond its products, and the company is highly recognized through awards for its environmental

FIGURE
4.6
PLANNING MODEL EXHIBIT

Marketing communications
plan: A sample model*

Marketing Communications Objectives

(A selection of possibilities)

- Awareness
- Preference
- Trial Purchase
- Alter Image
- Frequency and Variety of Use
- Promotional Incentives

Marketing Communications Strategies

- Positioning Statement
- Components of Mix
- Budget

Advertising Plan

a) Advertising Objectives

(A selection of possibilities)

- Awareness
- Product Differentiation
- Position or Reposition Product
- Trial Purchase
- Enhance Image

b) Creative Plan

- Objectives (what message)
- Strategies (how to communicate message)
- Execution

c) Media Plan

- Objectives

  Who

  What

  When

  Where

  How

- Strategies

  Target-Market Matching Strategies

  Rationale for Media Selection

  Rationale for Media Rejection

- Execution

  Cost Summaries (budget appropriation)

  Media Schedule (timing, coverage, usage)

Direct-Response Plan

- Objectives
- Strategies
- Tactics
- Budget

Online/Interactive Plan

- Objectives
- Strategies
- Tactics
- Budget

Sales Promotion Plan

- Objectives
- Strategies
- Tactics
- Budget

Public Relations Plan

- Objective
- Strategies
- Tactics
- Budget

Events and Sponsorship Plan

- Objectives
- Strategies
- Tactics
- Budget

Personal Selling Plan

- Objectives
- Strategies
- Tactics
- Budget

*Assumes adequate input from background section of marketing plan.

Note: More detailed discussion of objectives, strategies, and tactics occurs in chapters related to each element of the marketing communications mix.

FIGURE 4.7

Online communications outline Toyota's commitment to social responsibility

initiatives. Complete details are available at the company website, **www.toyota.com**. An illustration of the Toyota Prius, the company's hybrid car (it uses a combination of gasoline and electric power) appears in Figure 4.8. When it comes to fuel efficiency and emissions performance, the Prius sedan is in a class by itself. The Prius offers the best fuel efficiency rating of any mid-size vehicle sold in North America.[6]

FIGURE 4.8

The new Toyota Prius: A fuel-efficient and clean-burning automobile helps Toyota achieve its environmental objectives

MARKETING COMMUNICATIONS STRATEGIES

A **marketing communications strategy** provides a broad outline of how the various elements that comprise marketing communications will be integrated into a plan. As was illustrated by the objectives listed above, the strategy would probably embrace numerous components of the marketing communications mix. For example, advertising would be used to generate awareness; sales promotions would generate trial purchase; public relations and event marketing could help improve brand image; and internet advertising through a website could satisfy both awareness and image objectives.

If the marketing communications plan is a separate document from the marketing plan, then a **positioning-strategy statement** should be included here (positioning was discussed under Marketing Planning earlier in this chapter and in Chapter 3). The positioning strategy statement acts as a guideline for the development of all communications strategies.

This section of the plan should identify the total **budget** that is available for marketing communications activities. It may even allocate the money between the various components of the mix that are included in the plan. For example, what percentage of the total budget will be allocated to advertising, events and sponsorships, public relations, or other activities?

Establishing the budget and allocating amounts to each of the components of marketing communications is a major decision area. There are various methods that can be used to develop a budget. Some methods estimate sales first and then base the advertising budget on sales. Other methods develop the budget first; these methods essentially presuppose that advertising and other forms of communications are an effective means of achieving sales objectives. Regardless of the method used, the advertising budget must be carefully calculated and rationalized by the manager responsible for it so that the advertising plan can be implemented as recommended.

The plan is usually subdivided at this stage with objectives, strategies, and tactics identified for each component of the marketing communications mix that is recommended.

ADVERTISING PLAN

The **advertising plan** begins with a clearly worded list of advertising objectives that outline what advertising will specifically achieve. For example, Pfizer Inc. recently launched the Schick Quattro four-blade razor, a product that goes a step beyond Gillette's three-blade razors. Gillette is the dominant brand leader. Schick's advertising objectives may have been stated as follows:

- To create a 75 percent awareness level for the Schick Quattro razor among 16- to 29-year-old males

- To differentiate Schick from all other razors based on four-blade technology that offers the best possible shave

- To achieve a trial purchase rate of 20 percent among 16- to 29-year-old males

The advertising plan is then divided into two main areas: creative and media. The **creative plan** will document what the nature of the message will be and what strategies and techniques will be used to communicate the message. As indicated by the objectives above, the message will focus on the benefits offered by the four-blade shaving system. The message usually revolves around a key benefit statement (a brand makes a promise of something) and a support claims statement (a statement that gives people a reason to buy the product).

In terms of how the message is communicated, advertisers have a variety of appeal techniques they call upon. Among these appeal techniques are the use of sex, humour, celebrities, product comparisons, and lifestyle associations, to name just a few. As well, the message usually has a central theme so that all messages (print, broadcast, and online) are focused and saying the same thing the same way. See Figure 4.9 for an illustration. Creative planning is discussed in more detail in Chapters 5 and 6.

The **media plan** involves decisions on which media are best suited to reaching the target audience efficiently. Since a lot of money is at stake, making the right decisions is crucial. The goal of the media plan is to provide maximum impact at minimum cost and to reach the target market at the right time. Therefore, numerous strategic decisions must be made. An advertiser must determine which media to use—television, radio, newspaper, magazines, direct mail, the internet, etc.; the best time to reach the target market and how often it must be reached; which markets to advertise in (geographically) and at what weight levels; and timing and length for the media campaign. All information is summarized in a media plan. Media planning is discussed in detail in Chapter 7.

For additional insight into how a marketer matches its message with the interests of its target market, read the Advertising in Action vignette **A Marca Bavaria Sizzles**.

A Marca Bavaria
www.amarcabavaria.com

DIRECT-RESPONSE PLAN

Due to advances in communications technology, companies are now investing more heavily in direct-response techniques to get their message out. Direct response includes direct mail, direct-response television, catalogue marketing, and telemarketing activities. These types of activities can be measured for effectiveness more readily than mass advertising. Consequently, managers who are being held more accountable for producing results are investing in direct-response advertising. Appropriate objectives and strategies are incorporated into the communications plan. Direct-response communications are presented in detail in Chapter 11.

FIGURE
4.9

A humorous, lighthearted strategy communicates the key benefit of Viagra

VIAGRA

Viagra is a bit of a "nudge nudge, wink wink" product. In an effort to lessen the impact of bad jokes on late night TV, Taxi had to turn Pfizer's most famous product into a likable brand that men would feel good about. The agency's first effort, the popular "Good Morning" spot, gave viewers a glimpse of one man's experience with Viagra. This year, Taxi followed this up with a message that took an even broader view, but maintained the same lighthearted tone.

Queen's classic anthem, "We are the Champions," is an iconic song for the target group and speaks volumes about the transformative impact Viagra has on men with erectile difficulties. The men's willingness to celebrate their feelings openly sends a message that using Viagra is nothing to hide.

Images: Pfizer Canada Inc.

A Marca Bavaria Sizzles

So what's on the mind of urban males between the ages of 19 and 29? Seems these folks have a sense of adventure, and of course, women and sex are not far behind. To capture that sense of adventure Molson Canada went all the way to Brazil to cast and shoot a series of commercials for its Brazilian import A Marca Bavaria.

In the first two ads Brazilian women wearing skimpy bathing suits and carnival costumes frolic on the beach and dance floor and—unable to control themselves—throw themselves at Brazilian men. There are all kinds of lingering camera shots and bare midriffs.

Perhaps the most attention-getting spot is one that features Pietra, a Brazilian model. In the spot two guys are relaxing on the beach as a bikini-clad woman emerges from the water, Halle Berry style. One guy reaches into a bucket and pulls out a Bavaria. As he turns the bottle around, the woman turns as well—as if under his command—giving the camera a 360-degree view of her body. The guy tilts the bottle on its side, prompting the woman to get down on all fours, all the while looking at the male seductively, before lying on her stomach. Finally, as he peels the label, she stands up again and undoes the string on her bikini bottoms. Teasing the male, she draws the line there!

Is this style of ad something out of desperation or is it just good marketing by a company that knows its customers? The Canadian beer market is flat, however, and mainstream brands are losing ground to craft brews and imports. New brands like A Marca Bavaria have to get the attention of young, impressionable males.

The beer industry is playing by a new set of rules and is simply reflecting broader social trends and popular culture that is full of sexual images. Television shows such as *Temptation Island*, magazines such as *Maxim* and *Stuff*, and any music video tailored to Generation Y clearly spell out the priorities of this age group. According to Allan Middleton, professor of marketing at York University, "We've gone through a period where you just couldn't use overtly pretty bodies because you were going to get dumped on by everybody. That's pretty well gone now. Now it is considered okay for men to ogle women."

For their part, Molson says it's only giving its target customers what they want. "We believe we depict beautiful women the same way we do attractive men. At the end of the day we have to be relevant to our beer drinkers." Like it or not, that's all that counts!

Sources: Adapted from Michelle Warren, "Molson's Brazilian brew ads sizzle," *Marketing*, May 19, 2003, p. 4 and John Heinzl, "Sex is pretty stale way to sell suds," *The Globe and Mail*, May 9, 2003, p. B10.

ONLINE AND INTERACTIVE PLAN

The internet and other forms of interactive communications are slowly gaining ground among the alternatives that are available to advertisers. Certainly company and product websites now play an integral role in communicating vital information to customers and other publics. In terms of online advertising, companies assess the value of banner ads (ads in various sizes that viewers click on for more information), sponsorship opportunities (advertising on other websites of interest to a brand's or company's target audience), and email opportunities. An example of internet advertising from the Jaguar website is included in Figure 4.10. Interactive communications strategies are presented in greater detail in Chapter 12.

SALES PROMOTION PLAN

If promotion incentives are to be integrated with the advertising activities, a sales promotion section should be included in the marketing communications plan. Objectives of the promotions (e.g., to secure trial purchase, repeat purchase, or multiple purchase)

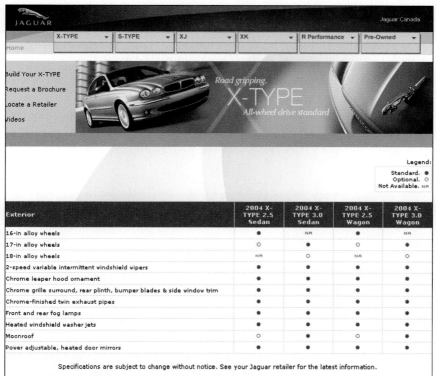

FIGURE
4.10

Advertising on the internet: Websites play a key role in the image-building process

should be documented. A summary calendar outlining the activities, timing, and costs associated with the promotion must be included where applicable. Refer to Chapter 13 for more insight into sales promotion planning.

EVENTS AND SPONSORSHIP PLAN

Events and sponsorship are playing a more prominent role in contemporary marketing. If a company develops an event or participates in one, careful planning is required. A variety of communications elements must be built into the plan to show how the event will be supported. If sponsorship funds are required, the company offers financial support in return for advertising privileges. All of this information is documented in the communications plan. Additional details about event marketing and sponsorships are included in Chapter 14.

PUBLIC RELATIONS PLAN

Public relations can play a key role in launching a new product or generating interest about an existing product. A plan to secure media support for newsworthy information about a product should be developed. The value of such publicity can be worth much more than the value derived from advertising—something the company is paying for. Documentation about public relations activity should be included in the communications plan. Refer to Chapter 14 for more insight into public relations.

PERSONAL SELLING PLAN

Communicating with members of the distribution channel is the job of an organization's sales force. The role of the sales representative is to communicate the benefits of the products offered for sale in terms of how they will specifically resolve a potential customer's problem. As well, the sales representative communicates to the trade any support plans that will help the distributor resell the products (e.g., price discounts and allowances, advertising programs, sponsorships). Coordination of the personal selling effort with other marketing communications activities is crucial.

For some initial insight into what a communications plan looks like and how the various elements of the plan are linked together, refer to the plan that is included in Appendix I.

SUMMARY

The quality of marketing and marketing communications planning in an organization is influenced by the business planning process itself. Business planning is a problem-solving and decision-making effort that forces management to look at the future and to set clear objectives and strategies.

In terms of marketing communications, three different but related plans are important: the corporate plan, the marketing plan, and the marketing communications plan. Each plan involves the development of appropriate objectives, strategies, and tactics, and, when one plan is complete, it provides direction to the next plan. The marketing plan, for example, directs the marketing communications plan.

Corporate planning starts with the development of a mission statement followed by corporate objectives and strategies. Some of the more common corporate strategies include penetrating the market more aggressively, acquiring other companies, implementing new-product development programs, forming strategic alliances with other companies, and selling off unprofitable divisions of a company to consolidate operations.

Strategic marketing planning involves the following steps: conducting a situation analysis, a procedure that reviews and analyzes relevant data and information; conducting a SWOT analysis that highlights the general direction a brand or company should be heading in; establishing appropriate marketing objectives and strategies; identifying target markets; accessing budget support; and establishing measurement and control procedures. The evaluation and control procedure attempts to draw relationships between strategic activity and results. All of this information is included in a marketing plan.

The marketing communications plan identifies the various communications objectives to be accomplished and delineates strategy in several areas. The communications plan is subdivided into specific areas depending on what components of the mix are going to be used. The advertising plan focuses on creative objectives and strategies (what message to communicate and how to communicate it). The media plan states the media objectives by answering who, what, when, where, and how. The media strategies rationalize the use of media alternatives and treat in more detail considerations of timing, market coverage, and scheduling of messages.

Finally, other elements of the integrated marketing communications mix may be included in the plan. If sales promotion, event marketing and sponsorships, public relations, and direct-response and internet communications are important, objectives, strategies, and tactics for each will be included. All plans must work together to achieve the objectives stated in the marketing communications plan.

KEY TERMS

REVIEW QUESTIONS

1. In planning, what is the basic difference between objectives, strategies, and tactics?

2. What is the relationship between a company's mission statement and the company's marketing activity?

3. What is the relationship between a corporate plan, marketing plan, and marketing communications plan?

4. What does the term "situation analysis" refer to and what are the key issues associated with such an analysis?

5. What role does a positioning strategy statement play in the development of marketing strategy?

6. What are the essential components of a target-market profile?

7. Briefly describe the key elements of the marketing strategy section of a marketing plan.

8. How will a precise target-market profile affect the development of creative strategies and media strategies?

9. What is meant by "marketing control"? What are the three basic elements that constitute marketing control?

10. In the planning process, what role does a clearly worded marketing communications objective play?

11. What are the key decision areas of an advertising plan? In considering the key areas, identify the relationships between creative and media strategies.

12. What are the various components of the marketing communications mix?

DISCUSSION QUESTIONS

1. "Good strategy, poor execution" or "Poor strategy, good execution"—which scenario will produce the best results? Support your position with an appropriate rationale.

2. Toyota was used as an example in this chapter to show the relationship between a company's mission and how it has an impact on its marketing communications strategies. Are there other companies that are doing the same? Conduct some online research for a few companies of your choosing and file a brief report on the relationships between mission (the direction a company is heading) and marketing communications.

3. Conduct some secondary research on the internet to determine the type of marketing and marketing communications strategies being implemented by the following companies. What conditions are prompting the use of these strategies?

   a) PepsiCo

   b) Nike

   c) Colgate-Palmolive

   d) United Way

   e) BMO Bank of Montreal

4. Review the Advertising in Action vignette **A Marca Bavaria Sizzles**. Based on your knowledge of target marketing and how important it is to understand your customer, do you feel that this type of message strategy will have an impact on the twenty-something male target audience? Are there better message alternatives that brands like this should consider? Justify your position.

NOTES

1. Toyota Motor Corporation, **www.toyota.com**.
2. David Jones, "Cadbury buys Adams for US$4B cash" *Financial Post*, December 18, 2002, p. FP14.
3. Todd Zaun, "Toyota, Nissan cooperate," *The Globe and Mail*, September 2, 2002, p. B11.
4. David Jones, "Cadbury buys Adams for US$4B cash," *Financial Post*, December 18, 2002, p. FP14.
5. Press release, Toyota Canada Inc., June 10, 2003.
6. Press release, Toyota Canada Inc., August 25, 2003.

THE practice OF ADVERTISING

Target, Position, Advertise! Sometimes It Works. Sometimes It Doesn't.

One of the major problems facing all manufacturers in the automobile business is the aging population. It seems that the average age of a new-car buyer today is somewhere in the 40- to 45-year-old range. Long term, the aging trend is a concern because the cars that suit older people are not the cars that suit younger people.

Compounding the problem is the fact that automobile manufacturers know very little about young people and their needs. Toyota's research tells the carmaker that, by 2010, Generation Y (approximate age 18 to 25 years old right now) will account for about a quarter of the light-vehicle market. By 2020 the figure rises to 40 percent, resulting in 6.5 million units in a 16-million-unit U.S. market, a number that no manufacturer can afford to ignore. What kind of product does this generation require? Answers are needed now if car companies expect to have customers 20 years from now.

Toyota Goes for Generation Y

Toyota is perhaps the first manufacturer to create a brand specifically for Generation Y consumers. The thinking was fairly simple. Each generation needs a car it can call its own. For Generation Y, Toyota created the Scion in two different models. The xB version is a boxy-looking vehicle while the xA version offers a more rounded look. To suit the needs of this target, each model can be customized. Potential owners can select their preferences for transmission, colour, and a range of accessories including illuminated cup holders and sporty mufflers. Toyota's marketing intentions are admirable, but are they workable?

While the Scion has only been available since June of 2003, the car has not attracted the desired target. While it may not be the feeling of all of Generation Y, one 19-year-old female described the

Scion as a "Clown bus." "I laughed when I saw it. That's what everyone thinks we'd like." How wrong they may be.

The average age of the Scion buyer is 35, well above the 18- to 25-year-old target. For now, Toyota says it doesn't matter since the launch of the Scion has helped increase Toyota sales overall. In the longer term there are ramifications Toyota will have to deal with.

Mitsubishi's Plan Worked. Or Did It?

Mitsubishi launched a very successful advertising campaign that showed young people zooming around streets and through tunnels while passengers listened to tunes from the Barenaked Ladies and other Gen-X aimed bands. The advertising strategy worked. It attracted the twenty-something and thirty-something crowd, a target market that the competition could only dream of reaching. The cars, the songs, and the imagery cemented the brand's image with young people, many of whom were enticed into buying Mitsubishis.

Combined with the advertising was a pricing strategy that featured very low financing on purchases. The pricing strategy was a surefire hit among people with little or no credit history. When the cheap credit taps were finally turned off, sales dropped 25 percent and Mitsubishi incurred billions in losses. The strategy cost several senior executives their jobs.

Mitsubishi has since retreated to a more familiar positioning strategy and has dumped the Barenaked Ladies and other bands of similar ilk. According to Ian Beravis, Mitsubishi's senior vice-president marketing, "We're out of the rock video business."

Mitsubishi did retain one element of the former campaign. It continues to offer "spirited cars for spirited people" but this time around they mean "spirited financially viable people." The new advertising approach is to explain that its products are as well made—and better looking—than its biggest Japanese rivals: Toyota and Honda.

Beravis states that people buy Mitsubishis because they stand out from a styling viewpoint. But to really make a move and build market share you have to explain the benefits of the vehicle in comparison to what Toyota and Honda offer. "You don't have to explain why you buy a Toyota or Honda but you do have to explain why you buy a challenger brand like Mitsubishi."

In terms of advertising Mitsubishi is taking an aggressive stance. Direct comparisons with Honda and Toyota are intended to build the brand's credibility. One television spot shows a Mitsubishi Galant effortlessly avoiding debris while the Toyota Camry pulls off the road. Says Beravis, "Cliff-hangers and comparisons with Toyota and Honda will be the standard for Mitsubishi going forward." Mitsubishi may want to exercise some caution, however. Comparisons, especially with brand leaders, can also come back to haunt you.

Volvo, You Say. Will Young People Buy?

Hip-hop music and music videos selling Volvos. It sounds so strange. After all, when you think of a Volvo you may have an image of a rather square-looking vehicle being driven by someone in his or her fifties. Yes, Volvo is a safe vehicle, but will young people actually buy one? Sounds like the ultimate marketing communications challenge!

Volvo Cars of North America is taking a walk on the wild side in marketing its S40 sedan. With a sporty look and feel the S40 is trying to lure twenty-something and thirty-something buyers by tying in with Microsoft's Xbox video games and by showing commercials featuring hip-hop band Dilated Peoples. A co-marketing arrangement with the Virgin Group (music stores) is also part of the S40 repositioning strategy. Present customers of the S40 are in their mid-forties.

The new approach is based on two elements that are culturally relevant to the target: music videos and video games. Why video games? Apparently, the average age of a gamer today is 29 (middle of the target group) and heavy gamers have household incomes of $60 000. They can afford to buy a Volvo.

The new campaign comes at a time when Volvo is on a roll in North America. Unit sales of all makes increased 22 percent in 2003 when compared with 2002. Volvo is hot!

The launch television commercial shows the S40 racing in the environment of Xbox's RalliSport Challenge 2. This is the first time that Microsoft Xbox has partnered with a marketer in a TV commercial. A new song called "By Chance" from Dilated Peoples is featured in the commercial.

The co-marketing deal with Virgin includes S40 banners and signs in all Virgin mega-stores. In addition, Volvo will take the car on tours of stores and provide product specialists to explain details.

You Be the Judge

Analyze each of these brand situations. Is there a good match between the target market, the positioning strategy, and the advertising strategy? Are these companies doing the right thing? To enhance your understanding and response to each situation you may wish to consider the following:

TOYOTA

Visit the Scion website (**scion.com**) to view the Scion. Is this the type of vehicle that will attract Generation Y? If so, what message strategies would you recommend? Alternatively, is the vehicle more suited to an older target?

MITSUBISHI

Mitsubishi has adopted a traditional approach to targeting and positioning but has chosen to make direct comparisons with key competitors in its advertising. Is such a tactic wise?

VOLVO

"Is your image your own worst enemy?" Volvo's image is firmly established: safe, conservative, and suitable for older age groups. Can Volvo successfully position the S40 model to attract a younger target market?

Adapted from Jean Halliday, "Volvo goes after younger buyers," *Advertising Age*, January 26, 2004, p. 8; Jeremy Grant, "Getting a fix on teens' car preferences a hit-and-miss affair," *National Post*, February 10, 2004, p. FP4; Paul Brent, "Mitsubishi kills the video star," *National Post*, 2004.

Creating the Message

In Part Two, the relationships between marketing and advertising were established and a detailed review of the planning process was presented. Clearly, the content of a marketing plan or advertising plan affects the direction of creative planning.

Part Three describes the creative planning process in detail, by differentiating among creative objectives, strategies, and execution considerations.

In Chapter 5, the role of research in the creative evaluation process is examined along with the roles and responsibilities of the client and the agency in the message-development process.

Chapter 6 presents the production considerations for print, broadcast, and interactive media.

PART

3

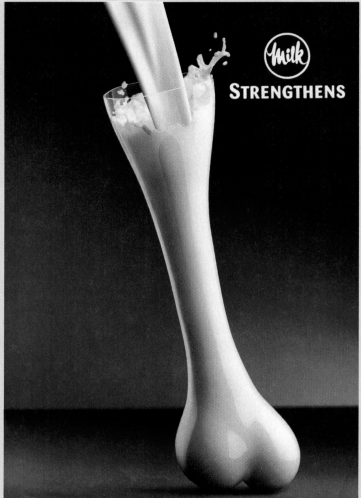

Courtesy: Dairy Farmers of Canada. Photography: Philip Rostron-Instil Productions Inc.

Creative Planning Essentials

Learning Objectives

After studying this chapter, you will be able to

- Identify the basic elements of the communications process
- Distinguish between client responsibility and agency responsibility in the creative development process
- Explain the stages in the creative development process
- Explain the creative briefing process and describe the content normally included in a creative brief
- Clearly distinguish between creative objectives, creative strategies, and creative execution
- Describe the various appeal techniques commonly used in advertising
- Identify the various execution techniques for presenting advertising messages
- Explain the measurement techniques for evaluating creative

Developing the actual message to be advertised is the next step in the advertising planning process. The creative plan is a logical extension of the marketing plan and advertising plan discussed in the previous chapter. Essentially, the marketing plan provides valuable input that must be communicated to the creative team (i.e., art director and copywriter) at the advertising agency.

The actual advertisements that we see, read, and listen to are simply the outcome of the planning process. It is in the planning stages for both creative and media that client–agency interaction is at its peak, and any discussion that takes place results in clear direction for the development of advertising messages.

This chapter focuses on the creative planning process and the relationships between the client and the agency in that process. The initial section examines the creative development process and the roles of clients and agencies in that process. The content of a creative brief is also discussed. The concepts of creative objectives, creative strategies, and creative execution are examined in detail, and numerous advertisements and campaigns are included to illustrate these concepts. Since research plays a role in the creative development process, various evaluation techniques are presented.

The Communications Process

Prior to discussing creative development, it is imperative the reader understand the nature of the communications process (see Figure 5.1). The process begins with a sender (the advertiser) who develops a message to be transmitted by the media (television, radio, magazine, newspaper, internet) to a receiver (the consumer or business user).

FIGURE
5.1

The communications process

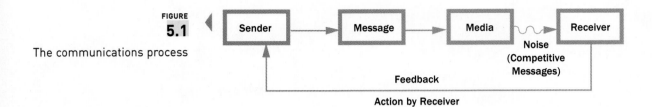

However, competitive products may also be sending similar messages to the same target market. This action is referred to as **noise**. If the message can break through the noise of competitive messages, and if it is relevant to the receiver (i.e., if its benefits satisfy a need), then the product may become a preferred alternative. In this case, positive feedback results in the purchase of the product. However, if the message cannot break through the noise (if it is dull, uses the wrong appeal techniques, or is misunderstood by the target), there is little chance that the product it advertises will be bought. This is a form of negative feedback, and it indicates that creative strategy needs to be re-evaluated.

When deciding what products to buy, a consumer passes through a series of behaviour stages, and advertising can influence each stage. One such model that refers to the various stages is **AIDA**. The acronym stands for *attention, interest, desire,* and *action.* Another model is **ACCA**—*awareness, comprehension, conviction,* and *action.*

It is very difficult to directly link mass advertising to sales (or the desired action as described above); what can be measured is how well the message communicates and whether consumers like or dislike the message and the way it was presented. Effectiveness may refer to how well a message grabs attention, generates awareness, stimulates interest and preference, and leads to the desired action. Therefore, the creative development process starts with clearly defined objectives for these dimensions of consumer behaviour.

An advertisement that succeeds in all of these respects increases the likelihood that consumers will purchase the advertised product. As a consequence, clients and advertising agencies conduct extensive consumer research to evaluate advertising. A potential new ad could be tested with consumers for likeability, persuasiveness, and likelihood of purchase. Scores exceeding the norms for other products in the same category would suggest the advertiser is on to something. A description of each behaviour stage is provided below.

- *Awareness* In the awareness stage, the customer *learns of something for the first time.* Obviously, this learning can occur only if one is exposed to a new advertisement.

- *Comprehension* By the comprehension stage, *interest* has been created. The message is perceived as relevant, and the product, judged from the information presented, is considered useful. The product becomes part of the customer's frame of reference.

- *Conviction* The customer's evaluation of the product's benefits (as presented in the advertising) leads to a decision. The product is viewed as satisfactory, and has gained *preference* in the customer's mind. The customer may be sufficiently motivated to buy the product.

- *Action* In this stage, the desired active *response* occurs. For example, a car advertisement may motivate a customer to visit a dealer's showroom or a website; a coupon may motivate a reader to clip it out for more information or for use in an initial purchase.

The Creative Development Process and Client–Agency Responsibilities

When developing creative, the roles and responsibilities of the client and agency are clearly defined. The client provides the necessary input (information) and evaluates agency recommendations; the agency takes the information and develops appropriate message strategies that will fit with other marketing and marketing communications strategies. The creative development process is subdivided into seven distinct stages. Refer to Figure 5.2 for a visual illustration of the stages.

CLIENT RESPONSIBILITY

The client initially must provide enough market, competitor, and product information so that the agency understands the situation clearly. This information is usually contained in the background section of the marketing plan. The client also plays a role in developing a list of creative objectives. The creative objectives identify the key benefits that are to be communicated to the target market.

Through consultation with the agency's creative team, the client will have some (limited) input in the development of creative-strategy statements. The agency might gain general direction by noting the client's preference for emotional or humorous appeals, but strategy is largely the domain of the agency.

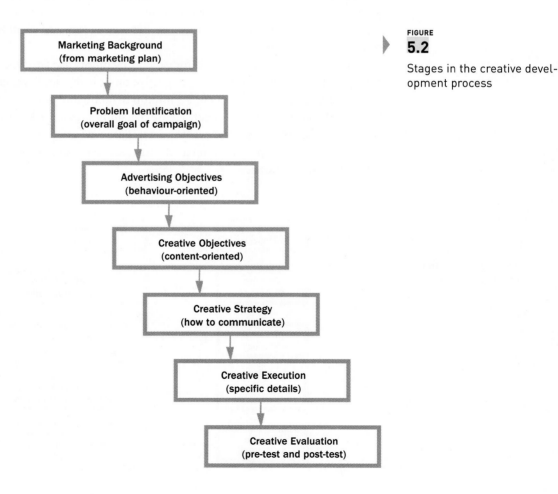

FIGURE

5.2

Stages in the creative development process

The last area of client responsibility is its involvement in the creative evaluation process. Since the client's money is on the line, the client has every right to apply qualitative and quantitative research assessments at any stage of creative execution. Essentially, the client reviews creative recommendations to ensure they match the positioning strategy for the brand.

AGENCY RESPONSIBILITY

The agency first must familiarize itself, through consultation with the client, with the intricacies of the marketplace. Once the creative objectives have been decided, the agency must develop a more precise creative strategy. The creative team, comprising art directors and copywriters, works on numerous ideas and concepts and develops a short list of promising possibilities. Creative execution details are considered so that the product may be presented in a convincing and believable manner. Teamwork is an important component of the creativity process as it provides consistency of thought and style to campaigns that stretch over extended periods. Therefore, it is essential that the copywriter and art director complement each other, appreciate each other's talents, and enjoy working together as a professional team.

When the creative team has completed the creative assignment in the form of rough layouts for print, storyboards and scripts for television, and so on, the ideas are submitted to senior agency personnel for internal approval and then to the client for approval.

Depending on the outcome of the evaluation process, the agency either proceeds with creative execution or goes back to the drawing board to modify or develop new ideas. Very often there are several meetings between agency and client before a campaign concept is finally approved.

There isn't any magic formula for generating innovative advertising concepts. Each advertising agency has a different perspective on how the development process should be handled. Regardless of process, a common denominator is the working relationship between the agency and the client. Figure 5.3 summarizes the key roles of clients and agencies in the creative development process. For some good insight into how agencies meet the challenges posed by their clients, read the Advertising in Action vignette **A Creative Idea Is Born**.

FIGURE 5.3

Client–agency responsibility in the creative development process

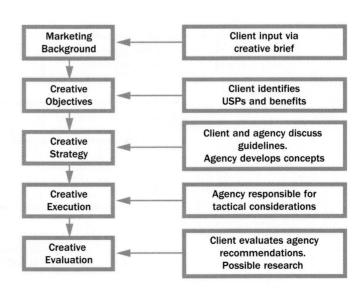

Marketing Background	←	Client input via creative brief
Creative Objectives	←	Client identifies USPs and benefits
Creative Strategy	←	Client and agency discuss guidelines. Agency develops concepts
Creative Execution	←	Agency responsible for tactical considerations
Creative Evaluation	←	Client evaluates agency recommendations. Possible research

A Creative Idea Is Born

Today's advertising industry is more complicated and scientific than ever. Clients and agencies are burdened with layers of bureaucracy and endless reams of research information, both of which are factors that negatively impact the creative process.

In today's environment the role of the creative team is changing. They work more closely with other disciplines in the agency and are more strategically involved with the client. While every agency has its own processes and different ideas about producing good creative, the consumer cares only about what comes out the other end. "Poor creative can result when you get too burdened in your own process, and end up in a narrow alley," suggests Julie Walters, senior vice-president and director of strategic planning at Young & Rubicam.

Ultimately, it is the work of the creatives that is always on the line. If it's off the mark too often, the agency is history! Agencies have to produce ads that will get noticed, be remembered, and, most of all, move product—a challenging task, to say the least. Clients are also different. Nike has its way of advertising and Procter & Gamble has its way of advertising. "If Nike used P&G's techniques, Phil Knight would still be selling shoes from his car." This statement underscores the need for an agency to clearly understand how clients operate and what their expectations are.

How an agency works with a client and approaches an assignment varies—considerably. Rick Davis, the executive vice-president and chief creative officer at MacLaren McCann, compares the past with the present. "Like other departments we used to operate in a silo, hardly talking to anybody from other disciplines at the start of a campaign. Now, clients are demanding more integrated communications and we have responded quickly. We make sure that TV spots, billboards, print ads—everything—acts as if it comes from one place and one thought. Each year we have a three-day planning session where the account group—planners, creatives, and the clients—critique the previous year's ads and brainstorm for the future."

At BBDO, Craig Cooper, vice-president and group creative director, says, "Any great advertising has to have sound, solid strategic thinking behind it. Good creative has to touch and stimulate the consumer in an emotional way." BBDO's definition of creativity is getting more of an impact through advertising than your competitor, with the same level of spending. Cooper says that insight from creative research is helpful, but the creative product is almost always the result of "gut feel—the skills of the writer and art director, combined with their instincts as consumers themselves. All the science in the world does not produce great ads.

"One of BBDO's solutions is to break down the boxes and tap into the knowledge of various disciplines within the agency—the creatives, planners, media, PR, and others—before pencil goes to paper." This core-team approach allows the agency to trace everything back to the client's business problems. A firm understanding of the problems makes selling the advertising to the client that much easier.

Taxi Advertising offers a contrast. Taxi is a small, agile shop where creativity sits firmly in the driver's seat. According to Taxi partner Paul Lavoie, "We don't define creativity as visual or literary expression, but more as a way of thinking." At Taxi a small group of people—planner, writer, art director, and client—take responsibility for creative ideas rather than being caught up in the rigid hierarchy of differentiated roles, responsibilities, and job titles. The partners believe that one small group taking a holistic approach is capable of creating one solution that can affect every dimension of a brand.

For Taxi's approach to prosper, the client must share similar values and principles. It's the core of a sound partnership. "In putting together a creative strategy for a client," Lavoie says, "each of the four-member Taxi squad derives inspiration and direction from the company mantra, 'Doubt the traditional. Create the exceptional.' We blend intuition with hard research. If we don't build our clients' business, we don't deserve to have it."

Source: Adapted from Stuart Foxman, "Canada's Leading Creative Agencies," *Strategy*, June 2000, pp. 1, 2, 6, 11.

Young & Rubicam www.yr.com
BBDO www.bbdo.com
Taxi Advertising www.taxi.ca

The Creative Brief

The starting point for any new advertising project is the creative brief. A **creative brief** is a document developed by the client that contains vital information about the advertising task at hand. The information contained in the brief is presented and discussed with the agency personnel so that copywriters and art directors fully understand the nature of the assignment. The brief is a discussion document; therefore, its content can change based on the discussion that takes place. Sometimes sections are left blank, awaiting discussion between the two parties. For example, creative strategy is the responsibility of the agency, so the client must resist the temptation to offer its preferences in this area. Too much direction by a client sometimes has a negative influence on the creativity of copywriters and art directors.

To understand how client and agency come to agree on an advertising direction, one must first look at the information that both parties analyze and consider when determining what to say in an ad, and how to say it. The brief typically communicates essential background information, a problem statement or overall goal, a list of advertising objectives, a positioning-strategy statement, and a list of creative objectives.

With regard to message delivery, the content and style of an advertisement or campaign is another way a brand (company) can distinguish itself from another. Therefore, the client and agency try to gain competitive advantage by making the right choices about how to present the message.

Once the briefing process is complete, the creative team is in the spotlight. The team, comprising a copywriter, art director, and creative director, is charged with the task of developing the **creative concept** or "big idea" that will be the cornerstone of a campaign. To do so, the team considers information supplied by the client. The only way a creative team can discover ways of solving a client's problems is to fully immerse itself in the product (company) so the members fully understand the present situation.

The next series of sections examine the content of a creative brief in more detail. Refer to Figure 5.4 for a summary of the information that is typically included in a creative brief.

Market Information

MARKET PROFILE   Initially, agency personnel are briefed on happenings in the marketplace. Key issues include the size and rate of growth in the market, identification of major competitors and their market shares, and what their strengths and weaknesses are.

PRODUCT PROFILE The focus then shifts to the brand in question. The agency is briefed on the key benefits the brand offers, benefits that will entice consumers to buy. Typically, the benefits offered are ranked by priority. For example, the key benefit could be economy, safety, variety, durability, or reliability. Once the primary benefit is identified, it should become the focal point of the advertising message.

Glad products (several varieties of garbage bags), for example, offer consumers strength and durability. They are often seen in television commercials taking a beating before they reach their destination at the curb. The "Man from Glad" makes the pitch in a rather convincing manner. A recent print campaign for Glad Kitchen Catchers focused on the tear-resistant qualities of the bag. The illustration in the ad aptly portrays the tear-resistance benefit by showing bags tied together hanging from a window. Refer to the illustration in Figure 5.5 for details.

GLAD
www.glad.com

FIGURE
5.4

Content of a creative brief

MARKET INFORMATION

- Market profile
- Product profile
- Competitor profile
- Target market profile
- Budget

PROBLEM IDENTIFICATION

- Clear identification of the problem advertising will resolve, or
- Overall goal of campaign

ADVERTISING OBJECTIVES

(Appropriate behavioural objectives based on problem or goal)
- Awareness
- Interest
- Preference
- Action
- New image
- New targets

POSITIONING STRATEGY STATEMENT

- Statement of the brand's benefits, personality, or desired image

CREATIVE OBJECTIVES

- List message content objectives
- Key benefit statement
- Support claims statement

CREATIVE STRATEGY

- Buying Motivation
- Tone and Style
- Theme
- Appeal Techniques

CREATIVE EXECUTION

- Tactical Considerations
- Production Considerations

Note: Clients and advertising agencies are unique enterprises. Therefore, the style, structure, and content of this document will vary across the industry. This is a working model to highlight content that could be contained in a brief. The creative strategy section often isn't determined until the client and agency discuss the assignment.

A brand's reputation may also influence the message. While creative direction often changes with time, quite often an important element from previous campaigns is retained in a new campaign. Such an element may have contributed positively to the image of the brand. For example, a good slogan may outlast numerous advertising

FIGURE 5.5

An ad that stresses the key benefits of strength and durability of the product

campaigns because the slogan is closely associated with the brand name and has high recall with consumers. Consider the following examples:

- Maxwell House Coffee: "Good to the last drop"
- Nike: "Just Do It"
- Gillette: "The Best a Man Can Get"
- Volkswagen: "Drivers wanted"

Also, a character or spokesperson may be so closely associated with a product that their presence is expected in advertising. Here are a few examples:

- Kellogg's Frosted Flakes: Tony the Tiger
- Glad Garbage Bags: The Man from Glad
- Pillsbury: The Pillsbury Doughboy
- Michelin Tires: The Michelin Man

Elements such as these have longevity, and therefore must be considered when a new creative direction is contemplated.

COMPETITOR PROFILE A discussion of competitive creative strategies provides a more complete perspective on what is happening in the marketplace. The creative team should know what competitor brands are saying and how they are saying it. The advertiser should analyze the strengths and weaknesses of the competition, and use the analysis as a guideline for creative direction. The direction an advertiser takes may be similar to, or totally different from, that of the competition. Competitive analysis may also have an impact on the tone, style, and appeal techniques used in advertising.

To demonstrate, consider the situation Nissan faced when it launched the Titan, its first full-size truck in Canada. The company knew it had an uphill battle on its hands if it was to compete with the tough truck images held by consumers for brands like the Ford F-150 ("Built Tough"), Chevy Colorado ("Like a Rock"), and Dodge Dakota ("Grab Life by the Horns"). Nissan and its agency decided to present the Titan as a true challenger to these brands right away. Television commercials vividly portrayed the strength and toughness of the vehicle in all kinds of road and off-road situations. A really tough image was projected to potential buyers. At the end of one commercial, a fully loaded Titan hauling a trailer is shown passing a Dodge truck on the highway. The comparison technique does not go unnoticed by viewers.

TARGET-MARKET PROFILE The client must provide a complete profile of the target market, which includes all relevant demographic, psychographic, and geographic information. The better the knowledge of the target market, the easier the task of developing advertising messages. If adequate resources are allocated to the collection of research information—to identifying and understanding the motivations behind consumers' purchases—such information can be used to develop convincing messages. The ability to associate product benefits with buying motives or to present a product in a manner suited to a certain lifestyle is part of developing creative objective and creative strategy statements.

To illustrate the use of target profile information, consider the challenges an advertiser faces when trying to reach the youth and young adult segments. Often categorized as a skeptical group of consumers, the role and influence that advertising has on them is sometimes questioned. In relating to young adults, many advertisers attempt to portray a vision of "young adult cool," hoping that they'll be liked because they're cool too. But the message that young adults get is that the advertising is an attempt to fabricate a culture for them: You're telling me what cool should be. Following such direction leads to failure.

As discussed in Chapter 3, target markets broken down by demographic characteristics and psychographic characteristics are then added to the profile. Descriptive expressions such as Baby Boomers, Generation X, and Generation Y have been coined to describe targets. A firm understanding of the behaviours for these and other targets provides agency creative personnel valuable insights for developing a message strategy.

BUDGET At this stage of the planning process, the client should provide a budget guideline. The amount of money available will determine whether the use of certain media is restricted or eliminated. For example, a budget judged to be small eliminates the use of television. If the budget is large, a multimedia campaign is possible. Either way, the media under consideration influence the creative direction. Refer to Figure 5.6 for a summary of the various factors that influence the development of creative objectives and creative strategies.

FIGURE
5.6

Direct influences on
creative objectives
and creative strategies

Product-Related Influences
- Product characteristics, image, and reputation
- Competitor strengths, weaknesses, and advertising strategy
- Target-market profile
- Budget
- Primary communications objective
- Positioning strategy

Creative Objectives

Creative Strategy

Creative Execution

Problem Identification

Typically, advertising campaigns are designed to resolve a specific problem or pursue an opportunity. In other words, all of the analysis that has occurred so far points the campaign in a certain direction. Perhaps the problem or opportunity is better described as the *overall goal* of the campaign. At this point, what the communications are expected to do is clearly identified. The following are a few generic examples of overall communications goals:

- To create or increase brand awareness
- To position or reposition a product in the customer's mind
- To present a new image (re-image the brand)
- To attract a new target market
- To introduce a line extension

These examples suggest that a campaign must have focus. Attempting to accomplish too many goals at one time only creates confusion in the customer's mind. It is preferable to focus on one primary goal and ensure that it is achieved.

Advertising Objectives

As indicated in the previous section, an advertising campaign typically has a central focus. Therefore, to facilitate the creative thinking process, the overall goal is subdivided into more specific advertising objectives. Advertising objectives may also be referred to as communications objectives. The broader term, communications objectives, is often applied when several different components of the marketing communications mix are being employed.

Advertising objectives focus on behavioural issues such as creating awareness and preference, for these are the things that advertising can accomplish. Objectives are usually expressed in quantitative terms, as they are used to measure the effectiveness of the campaign at a later date.

The stage a product is at in its life cycle and the competitive environment of the marketplace often influence the communications objective. For example, at the introduction and growth stages of the life cycle, the emphasis is on awareness and preference and the message deals with unique selling points. The goal is to differentiate one brand from another. In the mature stage, the message shifts to increasing frequency of use by consumers, to expand the variety of uses current customers have for the product, or to attract new users to the product.

To apply the concept of advertising objectives, consider the following examples that could apply when launching a new product:

- To achieve a brand awareness level of 60 percent among the defined target market within twelve months of launching the product.

- To achieve a trial purchase rate of 25 percent among the defined target market.

Since this is a new product, the objectives deal with awareness and trial. As indicated above, lifecycle and competitive factors influence the objectives. Let's examine a few of these challenges in more detail and see how they influence the direction of the creative.

TO INCREASE AWARENESS AND PREFERENCE Thinking strictly in terms of consumer behaviour, advertising objectives are stated in terms of achieving certain levels of brand awareness and brand preference. Advertising that achieves the desired levels will produce a stronger likelihood of purchase among members of the target audience. Achieving good levels of awareness and preference depends on a host of factors. For example, the impact of the message (how memorable it is) and the media (the impact of the medium itself) combine to influence consumer behaviour.

TO INCREASE FREQUENCY OR VARIETY OF USE When a product is firmly established in the market (mature stage of the product life cycle), the marketing objectives usually reflect an attempt to convert light or casual users into heavy users. Advertising can play a role in this process by showing alternative uses for the product.

Another option for an established product is to encourage current users to use the product more heavily. Since users know the benefits of the product, the costs associated with increasing usage are much less than attempting to attract new users. With reference to the ad for Welch's Grape Juice in Figure 5.7, the brand is positioned as a healthy beverage that should be consumed more frequently. Here, Welch's Grape Juice promises consumers the benefits of grape juice. That promise is reinforced in the body copy, which shows the product being endorsed by the Heart and Stroke Foundation's Health Check Program. Consumers find third-party endorsements like this very convincing.

Heart and Stroke Foundation's Health Check
www.healthcheck.org

TO ATTRACT NEW TARGETS In the case of mature products that are experiencing marginal sales growth or decline, making the product appeal to different user segments represents opportunity. Sprite found itself in this position and has successfully repositioned the brand to appeal to the 16- to 24-year-old age group. Sprite reached this market by partnering with K2 Inc, the leading name in snowboarding equipment. The advertising and promotional campaign was anchored on the insight that snowboarding and the general attitude of "board culture" had broad appeal across the teen market. Snowboarding is a fast growing sport, and 70 percent of newcomers are under the age of 24. To reach this target the creative had to reflect the attitudes and values of the whole snowboarding lifestyle. To mirror the no-hype anti-image of the boarding culture, Sprite's own message became "Image is nothing. Trust your instinct."[1]

TO COMMUNICATE PRODUCT IMPROVEMENTS In the late growth and early mature stage of the product's life cycle, marketing strategies often deal with product changes

FIGURE
5.7

An ad encouraging greater
frequency of use

Another way to get the goodness of grapes.

Drinking a 250ml glass a day of Welch's® Grape Juice is a simple way to get 2 servings of fruit. Welch's® is a proud participant in the Heart & Stroke Foundation's Health Check™ Program.

Courtesy: Cadbury Schweppes Americas Beverages

and improvements to keep the product competitive. This strategy is very popular in the food industry (where advertisements often focus on a product's new and improved taste) and household products industry (where messages focus on improved product performance).

In this situation, advertising messages make the consumer aware of the improvement. This strategy is often used as a defensive measure to entice current users to stay with their current brand rather than switch to a newer brand that may offer trial-purchase incentives. In the advertisement in Figure 5.8, Callaway Golf shows the technological advances it is making with its golf clubs. Such a convincing message will stimulate interest in the products among current customers and with new customers. Golfers tend to be very receptive to messages that promise enhanced performance.

TO ENCOURAGE TRIAL PURCHASE When a product is in the introduction and growth stages of its life cycle, achieving high levels of awareness and trial purchases are key objectives. Sometimes incentives have to be offered to give consumers an extra nudge to buy. If that is the case, the ads will carry a coupon offer, refund offer, or some other incentive. The incentive provides an additional benefit for the customer.

Courtesy: Gallaway Golf Company

FIGURE
5.8

An ad using factual appeals to communicate product improvements

In other situations, the ad alone may be enough to achieve trial purchase. When Unilever launched Axe deodorant, a product aimed directly at 18- to 24- year-old males, they understood that their target preferred to discover brands, rather than being sold to. Therefore, the launch campaign bypassed traditional television ads in favour of banner ads on websites of male magazines such as *Maxim* and *FHM*. The online world is the hub of Generation Y's lifestyle. The banners clicked through to a flashy website that played short video clips. In each clip, an attractive young woman is instantly transformed into a nymphomaniac by a whiff of Axe deodorant. One clip shows a high school cheerleader sprinting onto the football field whereupon she starts to tear off a player's uniform. Such a response by females is referred to as "The Axe Effect."

The campaign was a huge success at getting trial purchases! By year-end Axe had captured 4 percent of the male deodorant market and was threatening the position of brand leaders such as Old Spice and Right Guard.[2] An illustration of Axe advertising appears in Figure 5.9.

Axe Deodorant
www.theaxeeffect.com

FIGURE
5.9

Axe deodorant appeals directly to the instincts of 18- to 24-year-old males

The image of AXE deodorant appears with the permission of Unilever Canada

TO COMMUNICATE PROMOTION INCENTIVES Very often an entire campaign revolves around a special offer from a manufacturer. In the previous section some trial-oriented incentives were mentioned. Other promotional incentives include contests, premium offers, rebate offers, and loyalty programs.

In these situations, advertising may temporarily depart from communicating **unique selling points** in order to focus on the brand name and promotion. For example, the automobile industry frequently switches from image-oriented brand advertising (a long-term strategy) to promote rebates, low financing, and special option packages (sometimes free) as a means of stimulating sales (a short-term strategy). Contests for packaged-goods products also require short-term investment in advertising and in-store merchandising and display activity to spark awareness and interest in the promotion.

Consumers today are looking for better value in the products and services they purchase and, as a result, incentive-oriented advertising is now more prominent than in the past.

TO COMMUNICATE A POSITIVE CORPORATE IMAGE In addition to product-oriented advertising, a company can implement advertising campaigns that benefit the company as a whole. Multi-product firms may run a corporate advertising campaign as part of their "corporate responsibility" positioning.

Shell Oil, for example, is running an ad campaign about sustainable development, being careful not to promise too much. "Solutions for global warming won't come easy the ads say, but you can't find solutions if you don't keep looking. Shell believes that they and other companies are an integral part of society. Says Phillip Watts, chairman of the Royal Dutch/Shell Group of Companies, "When we take a business decision, we try to strike a balance between

Shell Oil
www.shell.com

Courtesy: Shell.

FIGURE

5.10

An ad designed to build and improve corporate reputation with the public

economics, the environment, and social impacts."[3] Making the public aware of their actions improves how people perceive Shell as a corporation. A Shell ad appears in Figure 5.10.

TO ALTER A PERCEPTION OR IMAGE Sometimes a company or a product doesn't seem to be in control of its image, or, as an old saying goes, "perception is reality." Automobiles such as the minivan, for example, possess an image of being the car of choice for mothers with young families. It's the centre of the soccer mom's universe. With primary female consumers switching to sport utility vehicles, makers of the minivan were facing shrinking sales. In a pro-active move Nissan repositioned the Quest minivan as a vehicle for "Yummy Mummies" rather than soccer moms.

Nissan's campaign was based on the notion that mothers have lives beyond their children. They can still go out all night, they can be a lover, a friend, a mother, and be sexy as well. The headline on one of the print ads reads, "Finally, a minivan that goes with anything including heels."[4] Time will tell if Nissan is successful in altering consumers' perceptions of the Quest minivan.

Positioning-Strategy Statement

Positioning refers to the selling concept or message that motivates purchase of a particular brand of product or service. It involves the message or image of the brand (company) to be instilled in the customer's mind. Agency creative people refer to this statement when they are trying to discover the creative concept—that big idea for communicating the message effectively. The positioning statement influences the content of creative-objective statements and creative-strategy statements.

To illustrate the role of a positioning-strategy statement, consider what Gillette Mach 3 is doing with its creative. The positioning statement for Gillette Mach 3 could read:

> To position the Gillette Mach 3 as the most technically advanced disposable razor that delivers the best possible shave consistently.

The essence of their creative concept is captured in Figure 5.11.

FIGURE 5.11

Gillette Mach 3 offers the benefit of the closest shave possible with less irritation

Courtesy of The Gillette Company

Courtesy: The Gillette Company.

FIGURE
5.12

An ad portraying a sound and consistent positioning strategy

Frequently the tagline or slogan portrays or summarizes the positioning strategy. Gillette, for example, has always positioned its shaving and grooming products based on innovation. In the razor product category, Gillette is always making subtle yet important improvements to its products in order to provide users with a "close and comfortable shave." Gillette's well-known slogan "The Best a Man Can Get" that appears in all ads aptly summarizes their positioning strategy. See Figure 5.12 for an illustration.

The creative concept or "big idea" will attract attention to an ad while communicating the key benefit. The slogan plays a key role by ingraining the essence of the positioning strategy in the customer's mind. Competitors send out equally compelling messages. Consider the following examples that show the competitive nature of the luxury automobile market:

- BMW: "The ultimate driving experience."
- Lexus: "The relentless pursuit of perfection."
- Infiniti: "Accelerating the future."
- Jaguar: "The art of performance."

Creative Objectives

Creative objectives are statements that clearly indicate the content of the message to be communicated to a target audience. As indicated above, positioning-strategy statements have a direct influence on what will be said about a product or company. Although the formats for writing creative objectives vary, a common practice is to consolidate what has to be said about a product in a short list of objectives. Here are a few examples that could have applied to the Gillette ad in Figure 5.12:

- To communicate that the Sensor 3 is the best quality disposable razor available
- To communicate that the spring-mounted head automatically adjusts to the contours of the face
- To communicate that the aloe strip offers additional lubrication

The list of objectives is often summarized in the form of a *key-benefit statement* and a *support-claims statement*; in other words, what the most important information to communicate is and on what basis it can be stated. Let's examine each of these elements:

- *Key-benefit statement* This is a statement of the basic selling idea, service, or benefit that the advertiser *promises* the consumer. This benefit or key fact is the primary reason for buying the product over any competitive product. Additional supplementary benefits may be described in another objective statement. With reference to the Colgate toothpaste ad in Figure 5.11 and the positioning-strategy statement described on page 138, the primary benefit of Colgate Total Advanced Fresh is fresh breath. In the Gillette ad in Figure 5.12, Gillette promises the best possible shave from a disposable razor.

- *Support-claims statement* This statement describes the principal characteristics of the product or service, the characteristics that substantiate the promise made in the key-benefit statement. It provides *proof* of promise based on criteria such as technical-performance data or consumer-preference data generated from marketing research. Good support claims give customers a reason why they should buy the product. With reference to Colgate toothpaste again (Figure 5.11), the body copy in the ad invites people to take the fresh breath test, and the use of phrases such as "*clinically proven*" and "*unique system*" helps support the promise made. In the Gillette ad (Figure 5.12) support is offered from tests against competing triple-blade disposable razors and the unique head design that automatically adjusts to the contours of the face. These facts clearly differentiate Gillette Sensor 3 from other brands.

For an additional illustration showing the relationship between positioning strategy, creative objectives, key-benefit statements, and support-claims statements, refer to Figure 5.13.

Creative Strategy

After confirming the message content, the next stage is to develop the creative strategy. In contrast to the first two stages, the agency's creative team plays a dominant role here. In essence, the client pays the agency primarily for the strategy (i.e., the ideas and concepts used in presenting the message). Sound strategies, in accordance with the positioning strategy and the creative objectives, are the foundation of successful advertising campaigns.

FIGURE
5.13

Relationships between positioning strategy and the writing of creative objectives

This example was created for illustration purposes only.

PRODUCT
Levi's Jeans

POSITIONING STRATEGY STATEMENT

To position Levi's as a brand that is proactive in response to changing consumer fashion tastes and preferences. Levi's is to be thought of as a fashionable and hip brand, a brand of choice among lifestyle peers across diverse age groups.

CREATIVE OBJECTIVES

1. To communicate that Levi's offers a fashionable line of blue jeans
2. To communicate that Levi's offers a diverse line of jeans that are suited to the needs of all consumer segments.

KEY BENEFIT(S)

1. Levi's offers in-style jeans
2. Levi's offers an opportunity to satisfy social needs
3. Levi's offers a wide range of styles to suit diverse consumer needs.

SUPPORT CLAIMS

1. Imagery will portray a target consumer being thought of as "trend-conscious" and "cool."
2. The product will be shown as being accepted by peer groups, inferring those who wear Levi's will be accepted.
3. A variety of styles will be shown throughout the campaign to show the diversity of the product line.

The **creative strategy** is a statement of how the message is to be communicated to the target audience. It is a statement of the character, personality, and image that the agency will strive to develop for the client's product or service. Strategy is reflected in the tone, style, theme, and appeal techniques of the advertising. **Tone** and **style**, for example, may be informative, persuasive, entertaining, or warm in nature, to suggest just a few options. The creative team must determine what approach will have the most impact on the target audience. Information gleaned from the target's demographic and psychographic profile influences this kind of decision.

The **central theme** or **"big idea"** is the glue that binds the various creative elements together. It must work in all different media forms if it is to have impact. For a brand like Maytag appliances the central theme is "dependability." The idle repairman who appears in all commercials is the vehicle that communicates Maytag's dependability benefit. Refer to Figure 5.14 for an illustration. For Tim Hortons, the central theme revolves around "True Stories" that are submitted to the company by customers. Tim Hortons has become an icon that portrays a strong nationalist sentiment. A recent instalment of this campaign shows a young male traveller meeting fellow Canadian travellers who notice him by his Tim Hortons travel mug attached to his backpack. Many true stories have been part of this very successful campaign.

These strategic characteristics of ads usually stem from the basic appeal technique that the creative team decides upon. A brand may appeal to a potential buyer on the basis

Tim Hortons
www.timhortons.com

FIGURE
5.14

The central theme of all Maytag advertisements is dependability. The idle repairman communicates the dependability benefit.

Get a whole meal ready, all at once. Without resorting to camera tricks.
How do you get dinner on the table in the real world? The Maytag® Gemini® range. It's the only range with two ovens, so you can cook two different items at two different temperatures and have dinner ready all at once. Plus, you get legendary Maytag performance, in your choice of either gas or electric. The Gemini® range. Another dependable idea, only from Maytag. For information, visit Maytag.com.

of factual information, emotion, humour, or sex, to name only a few of the alternatives available. The following is a discussion of some of the more common creative **appeal** techniques.

POSITIVE APPEALS

When positive appeals are used in advertising, the product promise and benefits (i.e., the primary reason for buying the product) are presented on the basis of a positive, enjoyable experience for the consumer. The mood, tone, and style of the advertising are upbeat, and are intended to leave the consumer with a favourable impression. Canadian Tire effectively uses positive appeals in its campaign that features Ted and Gloria, a cheery but imaginary suburban couple who have taken centre stage in the commercials. They demonstrate an innovative product available only at Canadian Tire and banter on about how the item can make life easier. Canadian Tire has differentiated itself with the Ted and Gloria spots by actually showing what the product does, what makes it different, and how it solves a problem, and the message is presented in a pleasant and positive way.[5]

NEGATIVE APPEALS

For negative appeals, the product promise and benefits presented are based on an experience the potential buyer can *avoid* by purchasing the advertised product or service. Very often the use of fear and anger is associated with negative appeals. To illustrate, CIBC Insurance tackled the issue of rising car theft head-on in a recent campaign. A commercial depicts an architect toiling away in his office, while professionals of another kind are at work on his car. The underlying message is that there is really nothing a car owner can do to stop a thief, so it is essential to have coverage with a good insurance company.

"Tastes awful and it works." By now you are familiar with that famous phrase coined by Buckley's Cough Mixture. Since Buckley's started attacking itself with the awful taste message, the brand has experienced new popularity and a "positive" increase in sales. Their success is based solely on their negative style of advertising.

Buckley's Cough Mixture
www.buckleys.com

FACTUAL APPEALS

In this appeal technique, the promise and benefits are presented in a straightforward, no-nonsense manner. The benefits are stated in a factual way and any visuals that are employed usually state the obvious. Products that appeal to the rational buying motives of consumers such as proprietary medicines—cough and cold remedies, nasal sprays, and liniments (which relieve the tension of aching muscles)—tend to employ a direct, here's-what-the-product-does approach.

Products in other categories can also use this strategy successfully. For example, a headline of a print ad for the Olympus digital camera states that it "Resists water, dust, snow, and imitation." Body copy goes on to explain the versatility of the camera in a very straightforward, simple manner. With only a few words and a compelling, attention-grabbing visual, Olympus effectively communicates its message. The Olympus ad appears in Figure 5.15.

COMPARATIVE APPEALS

When comparative appeals are used, the benefits of the advertised product are presented through comparison of those attributes that the product shares with competitive brands—attributes that are important to the target market, usually the primary reason why consumers buy the product. Comparative appeals can be indirect, in the form of a comparison with other unidentified leading brands, or direct, with the other brand mentioned by name.

In recent years, the use of comparative appeals has come to the foreground through campaigns dubbed as the "Cola Wars" or the "Burger Wars." In the soft drink market Pepsi-Cola will challenge Coca-Cola in taste comparisons, and in the burger market Burger King will claim that their flame-broiled hamburgers taste better than those cooked by other means by their competitors. Comparative campaigns present an element of risk for the initiator, usually the number-two brand in a market. To participate in a potential battle with a competitor requires long-term financial commitment by the initiator, since there is always the danger of retaliation by the market leader. This commitment factor demands that advertisers of a product analyze the competitive situation carefully before deciding to proceed with a comparative campaign.

HUMOROUS APPEALS

When an advertiser uses humorous appeals, the promise and benefits of the product are presented in a lighthearted manner. Advertisers often use humour but do so with reservation. Many advertisers feel a campaign will suffer from premature wearout after a few

FIGURE
5.15

A straightforward message communicates the key benefits of the Olympus camera

Resists water, dust, snow, imitation.
Take it to the beach. Take it to the ski slope. Take it anywhere. Four megapixels, 3x optical zoom lens and five easy scene programs in a compact, all-weather body. No other digital camera gives you all this. Stylus Digital. **Designed to do more.**

exposures: when the humour is familiar, it is no longer funny. Also, the use of humour allows for a great deal of creative latitude, and some advertisers argue that the humour gets more attention than the product. If brand-name recall is low after research testing, the problem is often attributed to the excess use of humour in advertising.

In spite of certain drawbacks, a humorous strategy can work. Successful campaigns tend to use a pool of commercials in order to keep the message fresh. Bud Light has done this effectively for years with its Bud Light Institute campaign. The fictitious institute (**www.budlightinstitute.ca**) is dedicated to providing ingenious solutions to everyday chores and responsibilities so that guys 25 to 35 years old can get out with their buddies more often. In the commercials, the rather naïve but understanding wife or girlfriend always falls for the excuses their males present.

Corby Distilleries' attempt to reposition Canadian Club rye to a twenty-something target market employed humour effectively in a commercial titled "Ouch." It featured a group of sports fans in a bar, drinking whisky and watching a soccer game on television. The commentator's voice indicates that the scene is England. The spot cuts to a similar scene in Jamaica, then India, then Sweden, and each time the language changes accordingly. As one of the players is kicked in his most sensitive spot, the viewer sees subsequent shots of each bar scene in rapid succession. All of the spectators wince simultaneously and make an emphatic "ouch" sound. The lighthearted, humorous approach actually had broad appeal across all age groups. The tagline for the campaign is "151 countries. One rye. Canadian Club."[6]

EMOTIONAL APPEALS

Advertisers who use emotional appeals successfully do so by arousing the feelings of the audience or by showing the psychological satisfaction that can be gained by using the product. It seems ironic that a sports utility vehicle would use emotional appeals, but there is a movement afoot to present these gas-guzzling vehicles as more environmentally friendly. A commercial for the Jeep Liberty Renegade shows the SUV driver using a spear to cut a hole in the ice in order to reunite a helpless seal pup with its mother. Not knowing what the driver is going to do with the spear initially, the viewer's emotional reactions vary from fear and helplessness to joy when the pup and mother are reunited. The intent of the ad is to show that SUVs can be friendly to the environment when used responsibly.[7]

The Tim Hortons "True Stories" campaign described earlier in the chapter provides another good example of the emotional appeal technique. The spots show an emotional connection between their customers and the company. Through visual imagery and words, all of the ads say that you don't know what you're missing until you're away from it—an important lesson in life! Things just aren't the same without Tim Hortons coffee.

Campaigns that promote awareness of social causes also use emotional appeals. To illustrate, consider some of the images in television commercials for campaigns that discourage drinking and driving or that encourage people to stop smoking. Seeing a distraught man sitting on a curb in the dead of night after a fatal accident, wishing he had made a wiser decision earlier on, or hearing a young boy talk about all the good times he had with his father who has died of cancer, does tug at the heartstrings of the viewing audience. Emotional advertising has impact!

SEXUAL APPEALS

The use of sexual appeals is popular and appropriate in certain product categories. Categories such as cosmetics, colognes, perfumes, lingerie, and alcoholic beverages use sexual appeals as an effective motivator. Refer to Figure 5.16 for an illustration.

How about oral sex and beer? That combination recently raised eyebrows. A now-famous ad for Carlsberg beer features a woman discussing her new boyfriend with a couple of friends. Using a subtle downward hand gesture, her friend alludes to his prowess at giving oral pleasure. "I don't even have to ask," the woman murmurs unbelievingly. When the man joins the group a moment later, he is greeted by approving glances all around. As one veteran creative said, "It's a whole new twist on the tired old beer phrase, 'It goes down great.'"[8]

When developing a launch campaign for an aphrodisiac called Klimax, Laboratories Mauves requested the ads show different situations that demonstrate the effectiveness of the product. Their creative guideline to the agency was to be "edgy" but not "distasteful." The drink will make people lose their inhibitions. In one print ad there is a shot of an attractive female with rug burn on her knees. In another ad, probably aimed at gay men, there is a shot of gym showers (open concept) with five bars of soap on the floor.[9] While visual imagery is always in the eye of the beholder, there is an element of humour in these ads as well.

Advertising of this nature is risky, but it does reflect general trends in society. People are now more accustomed to seeing provocative imagery and language in television shows, movies, and music videos. These trends open up new doors for advertisers.

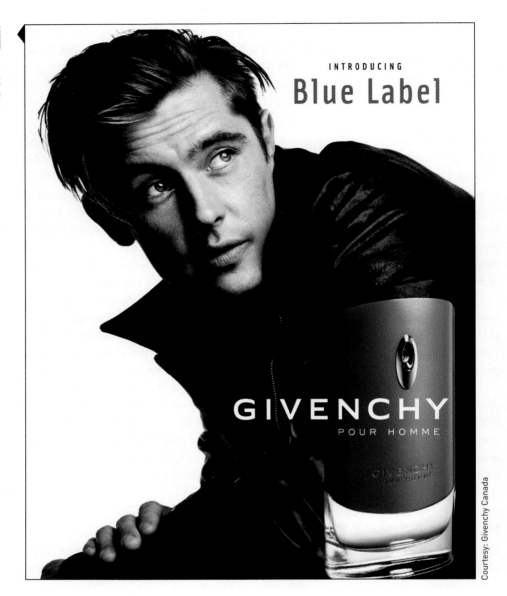

INTRODUCING
Blue Label

GIVENCHY
POUR HOMME

Courtesy: Givenchy Canada

LIFESTYLE APPEALS

Advertisers who use lifestyle-appeal techniques are attempting to associate their brand with the lifestyle (*lifestyle* refers to activities, interests, and opinions) of a certain target audience.

The key to the success of this type of campaign is in the association. If an individual feels part of the lifestyle, then he or she is likely to view the product favourably. That favourable opinion may lead to a purchase, even if only on a trial basis. Lifestyle appeals are becoming increasingly popular, owing to the greater availability of psychographic information on Canadian consumers.

A company like Labatt Breweries certainly sees the value in such information and uses it to develop advertising campaigns. The lifestyle appeal technique is aptly demonstrated in the "Cheers. To Friends," campaign for Labatt Blue. In a format similar to a reality TV show (the commercials were shot on video rather than film), the campaign depicts realistically what guys do when they hang out with their friends. The

ADVERTISING IN action

A Strong, Relevant Idea Works Wonders

Absolut Vodka is the third largest international premium spirit in the world. The brand is available in 125 markets and is the number two brand of premium vodka worldwide. Of course, Absolut didn't always hold such a lofty position. Much of its success is due to very creative advertising—in fact, a relatively simple idea that has been working for over 25 years.

In today's marketing environment, managers are constantly under pressure to improve sales and market share. Consequently, they often experiment with new ideas without ever giving any one idea a long enough chance to accomplish something. It's almost a trial-and-error mindset. In contrast, consistent application of strong, relevant campaign ideas proves time and again to be the surest way to build lasting brands. No advertiser has demonstrated this more than Vin & Spirit, Sweden's state-owned alcoholic beverage company and producer of Absolut Vodka.

In 1979, Vin & Spirit launched a new vodka product for export. It was made using a distillation method called rectification, a Swedish invention. The brand's positioning would underscore the product's traditional Swedish origins. That strategy quickly changed when TBWA Advertising, New York, landed the account for the U.S. market. The agency soon came up with a campaign idea that made the bottle the hero and quickly turned Absolut into a fashion icon.

Art director Geoff Hayes, while doodling in front of the television one day, sketched the outline of a magazine ad that was to be titled Absolut Perfection. The black-and-white ad—still in use today—shows a photograph of the bottle against a black background. The bottle is bathed in a circle of light, while a halo hovers just above it.

That ad was the beginning of a campaign that has used more than 700 (and counting) executions of the clear, largely nondescript glass container. "We haven't changed the concept yet, and that's what is unique about the campaign," says Mats Persson, vice-president of Vin & Spirit. Classic ads in the long-running campaign include Absolut Attraction (1983), in which a martini glass bends toward the vodka bottle, and Andy Warhol's 1985 painting, which was commissioned by V&S and drew immediate worldwide press.

Richard Lewis, account director at TBWA, describes the campaign as "a tree with many branches." The branches are associated with different themes, including the visual arts, fashion, and scenes from famous cities.

The campaign works, so there is absolutely (pardon the pun) no incentive to change things. Absolut is the leading imported brand of vodka in the United States and it ranks third on the spirits list worldwide behind Bacardi Rum and Smirnoff Vodka. Canada is the third largest market for Absolut after the United States and Sweden.

Source: Adapted from Patrick Allossery, "A message in a bottle," *Financial Post*, December 3, 2001, p. FP6.

---

ads actually feature real groups of friends rather than actors. The spots include a montage of scenes with guys doing everything from tipping over an outhouse, with an unsuspecting chum inside, to filling one guy's car with golf balls, and leaving another guy tied to a chair in an elevator wearing only his underwear and two hockey sticks. After the words "You can feel the love" appears the tagline "Cheers. To Friends." The core message is intended to reflect the attitude of Blue's target market.

Lifestyle advertising is problematic because little attempt is made to differentiate one brand from another. Usually, the advertisements focus on the lifestyles of the target market instead of the product benefits. Therefore, if such a technique is overused in a product category, a brand can expect to benefit only marginally from its use.

For additional insight into the importance of having a sound creative strategy, read the Advertising in Action vignette **A Strong, Relevant Idea Works Wonders**.

147

Creative Execution

The **creative execution** stage of the creative development process is concerned with two main areas: tactical considerations regarding how to present the message (and generate impact on the audience) and production considerations regarding the media to be used.

TACTICAL CONSIDERATIONS

At this stage, the agency's creative team evaluates specific ideas on presenting the client's product or service. These ideas, often referred to as "tactics," are simply more precisely defined strategies. Tactics undertake to answer questions such as the following:

- What is the best or most convincing way to present a product so that the consumer will be motivated to take the desired action of purchasing the product?
- Does the advertisement use a demonstration, a product (brand) comparison, a testimonial, or a celebrity spokesperson?

PRODUCTION CONSIDERATIONS

As indicated earlier, the media budget has probably already restricted the use of certain media. Budget considerations may also affect the production of advertising messages. Considering the media to be used, the client must communicate to the agency any production restrictions. For example, if television is being used, what is the desired commercial length (15 or 30 seconds)? How many commercials will be needed (one commercial, or a pool of commercials on the same theme)? If print ad is being used, what are the size specifications (one page or less)? Are there any restrictions on the use of colour (black-and-white, spot-colour, or four-colour process)? How often should the brand name be registered?

Once the strategy has been developed, the creative team must decide how to best present the product so that the message will have maximum impact on the target market. Tactical decisions are made. The following are some of the more commonly used presentation tactics.

TESTIMONIALS   In a **testimonial** ad, a typical user of the product presents the message. Since real people are used, as opposed to professional models and celebrities, the message is usually perceived as believable even though the presenter works from a carefully prepared script. As indicated in the strategy section, Tim Hortons uses testimonials effectively in a campaign called "True Stories." In each television commercial, someone has a story to tell about how Tim Hortons plays an important and enjoyable role in his or her life. Wal-Mart develops television and print ads that feature store employees delivering the message. Such a strategy is quite different from the image and lifestyle campaigns of competitors such as Sears and The Bay. Perhaps this strategy is part of Wal-Mart's desire to have a folksy and local image despite the fact it is the world's largest retailer. It also saves the company money!

ENDORSEMENTS Essentially there are two types of **endorsements**: associations or other organizations, and celebrities. Brands like Crest and Colgate have, for years, used the endorsement of the Canadian Dental Association (a professional association) in their advertising. The ad for Welch's Grape Juice that appears in Figure 5.7 includes an endorsement from the Heart and Stroke Foundation—an appropriate organization to endorse the health benefits of the product. When a celebrity is used, the advertiser attempts to capitalize on the popularity of a "star." Stars from television, movies, music, and sports form the nucleus of celebrity endorsers. Tiger Woods, for example, appears frequently in television and magazine advertising for Buick automobiles. Jazz musician Diana Krall has proven to be a worthy spokesperson for Chrysler automobiles, even though she only plays a small role in television commercials.

A potential danger of celebrity endorsements is overexposure if the celebrity is associated with too many brands. Overexposure cheapens the image. Wayne Gretzky, for example, represents many brands even though he has retired from hockey. Among them are Ford, McDonald's, Post Cereal, CIBC, Campbell Soup, Imperial Oil, and Tylenol. The more ads he appears in, the less special the occasion is. A greater threat is the erosion of his credibility, a consequence of promoting products about which he has no expertise. And, of course, if the "star" stumbles à la Kobe Bryant, the brands the star endorses may also stumble. There are risks if a brand is too associated with a star!

In this age of more sophisticated consumers, the advertiser must be very careful if it selects this method of presenting its product. It must be careful about whom it selects to present the product. Among the techniques deemed unbelievable by consumers, endorsements by celebrities rank the highest (72 percent of respondents in a survey). Ads that feature the company president ranked second highest, at 68 percent.[10]

PRODUCT DEMONSTRATION   The use of a **demonstration** is quite common in advertising focused on the product performance. Several execution options are available to the advertiser. For example, a "before-and-after" scenario is a common strategy for diet-related products, where the message implies usage by the presenter. Such a technique is suitable for both print and television media, although with television the technique is much more effective. A second strategy is to simply show the product at work—a technique commonly used for advertising household products such as oven cleaners, tub and tile cleaners, and floor wax. Typically, such advertisements show how easy the product is to use. In a print ad, Dawn detergent stacks dishes extremely high to substantiate its products claims. See the illustration in Figure 9.17.

EXAGGERATED DEMONSTRATIONS—TORTURE TESTS   In a **torture test**, the product is exposed to exaggerated punishment or the situation the product finds itself in is exaggerated in order to substantiate a product claim that is known to be of interest to consumers. For example, truck brands, such as the Ford F-150 and Dodge Dakota, show the vehicle pulling things it could not pull—a ship for example. People see the exaggeration and draw a conclusion about how strong and tough the vehicle is.

The BMW Mini is a small automobile with a "cute" reputation, not exactly the image BMW wanted for its small but high performing vehicle. A series of TV commercials was developed to highlight safety, speed, and spaciousness. To demonstrate how much space there is, one commercial shows a male and a female suddenly popping up in the front seat while putting their clothes back on. If that wasn't enough to make the point, a second female pops up from the back seat while putting her clothes back on. Message delivered!

BMW Mini
www.mini.com

PRODUCT AS HERO   If the **product-as-hero** technique is employed, the advertiser presents a problem situation (e.g., using negative appeal strategy), which is quickly resolved when the product comes to the rescue. The advertisers of Glad Garbage Bags have used this technique effectively for many years. In many commercials, other garbage

FIGURE 5.17

A demonstration of how effective and efficient Dawn detergent is.

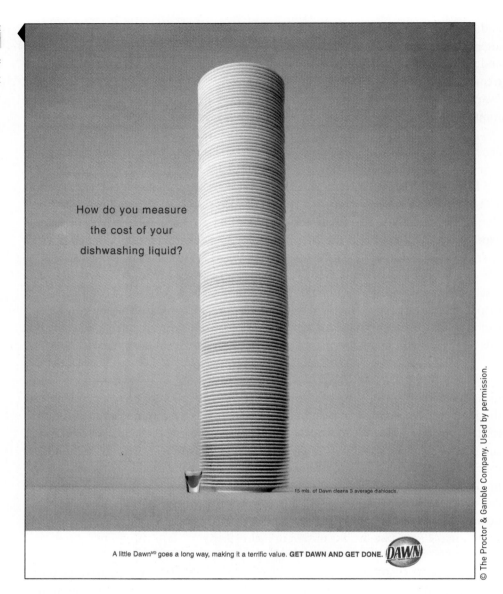

How do you measure the cost of your dishwashing liquid?

15 mls. of Dawn cleans 3 average dishloads.

A little Dawn^MD goes a long way, making it a terrific value. **GET DAWN AND GET DONE.** *DAWN*

bags are shown ripping open, leaving a mess. The obvious message is that the use of Glad Bags prevents such situations. In this example, the execution effectively dramatizes the durability of the Glad product.

In Figure 5.18, a print advertisement for Cascade 2 in 1 ActionPacs, some typical dishwashing problems are presented—baked-on grease, sticky pans, and so on. Not a job for standard dishwashing products. No problem, though, for Cascade 2 in 1, a new product that combines the best benefits of Cascade and Dawn in one product. It not only gets the dishes cleaner, but does the job faster as well.

PRODUCT COMPARISONS   For product comparisons to be used successfully, the attribute singled out for comparison must be of value or highly interesting to the target market. So as not to mislead the consumer in the message, the competitor must be identified fairly and properly, and the advertiser must be able to substantiate its claims with independent, objective research. Duracell once used the phrase "The CopperTop tops them all," a superiority claim, but was forced to change to "Nothing tops the CopperTop," a parity claim, because it could not prove the superiority claim when

FIGURE
5.18

An ad using the product-as-hero technique

challenged by Energizer in court.[11] Legal and ethical considerations aside, if used properly comparative advertising can present a convincing argument to consumers.

There are many critics of comparative advertising techniques. The most obvious drawback is the fact that one product's advertising budget is providing free exposure for another product. Comparative ads can also leave a consumer confused as to which brand is actually better. Certainly, the execution must deliver the message clearly and emphatically to the consumer in order to avoid any confusion.

PRE-PRODUCTION CREATIVE EXECUTION

With creative strategy and tactical details confirmed, attention shifts to production requirements of the campaign. Production requirements are often determined by media usage. For example, storyboards must be prepared for television, scripts for both radio and television, and layouts and designs for print advertisements.

Very often the content of the ad, if not the budget, restricts or makes necessary the use of certain media. For example, demonstrations are effective on television, while factual details are best left to magazines and newspapers. If sales promotion activity is to be part of the creative execution, a media mix may be required, with broadcast media used to build awareness and print media used to communicate details. Consideration must also be given to how traditional forms of advertising will be linked with web-based communications. A consistent look and theme should be common to all forms of media.

In addition, the pre-production stage should review any mandatory items that must appear in an advertisement or commercial—for example, should brand and company logos appear in a certain place; how many times should the package be shown (in the case of a television commercial)—or directions as to whether the execution is to be consistent across all forms of media. Specific details about design, layout, and production are presented in Chapter 6.

Refer to Figure 5.19 for a summary of the key elements and considerations for the various aspects of communications planning.

For an applied illustration of advertising objectives, creative objectives, and creative strategies, refer to the advertising plan that is included in Appendix II.

Creative Evaluation and Research

CLIENT EVALUATION

Creative can be tested at numerous stages of the development process. The first step is usually a qualitative assessment by the client to determine if the message conforms to the strategic direction that was provided the agency. This evaluation is conducted by means of a "managerial approach." In this evaluation, a client must resist the impulse to assess the creative on personal, subjective bases. However, if a "to proceed or not to proceed" decision must be made, the client reserves the right to conduct consumer research prior to making the decision.

Clients using the **managerial approach** for evaluating creative may apply some or all of the following criteria:

1. ***In terms of content, does the advertisement communicate the creative objectives and reflect the positioning strategy of the brand (company)?*** The client reviews the creative for the primary message and support claims outlined in the creative brief.
2. ***In terms of how the ad is presented (strategy and execution), does it mislead or misrepresent the intent of the message? Is it presented in good taste?*** The client must be concerned about the actual message and any implied message since they are responsible for the truthfulness of the message. Legal counsel often has the final say regarding message content. Consumers also lodge complaints about ads they find offensive or that encourage risky behaviour. Consumer complaints forced the Ford Motor Company to pull an ad for the Ford Focus. There were complaints about a scene in which a female shopper pushes a male clerk into the hatchback of her car. For some reason the ad was perceived to condone violence, which clearly wasn't the intention.
3. ***Is the ad memorable?*** Breaking through the clutter of competitive advertising is always a challenge, and a lot of advertising that is approved doesn't quite cut it. Is there something that stands out in the ad that customers will remember? What will they take away from the ad? For example, the idle repairman (see Figure 5.14) has been used for years to portray how dependable Maytag appliances are. Characters

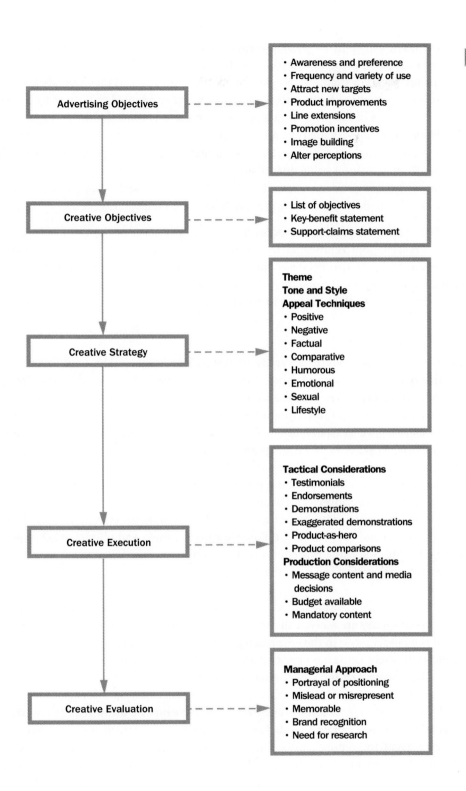

FIGURE
5.19

A summary of the key elements and considerations of creative planning

Planning Model Exhibit

like this play an integral role in providing continuity of message from one medium to another. Over an extended period of time the character becomes synonymous with the brand. So memorable are the characters that the public misses them if they are not included. The loveable A&W Root Bear is one of those characters.

4. ***Is the brand recognition effective?*** There must be sufficient brand registration in the ad. Some companies go as far as to stipulate how many times the package

should be shown in a television commercial. Nonetheless, the creativity of the commercial or print ad should not outweigh the product; it should complement the product. For example, people often recall funny ads and they can talk knowledgeably about the humorous situations that were presented until they are asked for the name of the product that appeared in the ad. So much for the laughs!

5. ***Should the advertisement be researched?***   When it comes to assessing the impact and effectiveness of the advertisement, subjective judgments by the client have the disadvantage of not being quantifiable. Prior to spending money on production, the client may decide to conduct consumer research to seek quantifiable data that will help the decision-making process. Better safe than sorry!

The evaluation process can occur at virtually any stage of the creative execution process. A television commercial, for example, could be evaluated by consumers at the storyboard, rough-cut, or finished commercial stage. While it is not practical to test commercials at all stages, if the quality or effectiveness of the commercial is ever in question, the client should conduct research to avoid costly and embarrassing errors in judgment.

RESEARCH TECHNIQUES

Creative evaluation involves a variety of research techniques. The objective of most **creative research** is to measure the impact of a message on a target audience. Creative research is conducted based on the stage of creative development. It is either a pre-test or a post-test situation. **Pre-testing** is the process by which an advertisement, commercial, or campaign is evaluated before final production or media placement, so that the strengths and weaknesses of a strategy and execution may be determined. Post-testing is the process of evaluating and measuring the effectiveness of an advertisement, commercial, or campaign during or after it has run. **Post-testing** provides information that can be used in future advertising planning.

Among the more common techniques used to measure the effectiveness of creative are recognition and recall testing, opinion-measure testing, and physiological response testing. Post-testing using procedures such as inquiry tests and controlled experiments also measures the effectiveness of the message.

RECOGNITION AND RECALL TESTING   In **recognition tests**, respondents are tested for *awareness*. They are asked if they can recall an advertisement for a specific brand or any of the points made in the advertisement. For example, consumers who have read a publication where an ad has appeared are asked if they remember the editorial content of an advertisement or the advertisement itself. Are they aware of the brand name that was advertised?

In **recall** tests, respondents are tested for *comprehension*, a measure of the impact of advertising. The test can be an **aided recall** situation (some information is provided to the respondent to stimulate his or her thinking) or an **unaided recall** situation (no information is provided). In either situation, respondents are asked to recall specific elements of an advertisement or commercial, such as its primary selling points, the characters used in it as presenters, and its slogan. Test scores are usually higher for tests where some aid is provided.

Two of the more common methods for collecting recognition and recall information are Starch readership tests and day-after recall tests. A **Starch readership test** is a post-test recognition procedure applied to both newspaper and magazine advertisements. The objectives of a Starch readership test are to measure how many readers have seen the ad and what percentage of those who saw it read it.

In terms of procedure, a consumer is shown a magazine and, once he or she has read it, an interviewer goes through the magazine ad by ad with the respondent. For each advertisement in the magazine (the entire magazine is "Starched"), respondents are divided into three categories:

- *Noted*   The percentage of readers who remember seeing the ad in this issue.

- *Associated*   The percentage of readers who saw any part of the ad that clearly indicated the brand or advertiser.

- *Read Most*   The percentage of readers who read half or more of the written material.

The Starch readership test offers several benefits: the client can measure the extent to which an ad is seen and read; by reviewing the results of other ads that were tested, the extent of clutter breakthrough can be determined; and by reviewing scores obtained by other products in previous tests, various layout and design options can be evaluated for effectiveness.

In the broadcast media, particularly television, the use of **day-after recall testing (DAR)** is quite common. As the name implies, research is conducted the day after an audience has been exposed to a commercial message for the first time. By means of a telephone-survey technique, a sampling of the client's target market is recruited and asked a series of questions so that their exposure to, and recall of, particular commercials may be determined. Once it has been determined that a respondent saw the commercial, they are asked what the ad actually communicated. Specific information is sought about the primary selling message, what the respondent likes and dislikes about the ad, about areas of disbelief or confusion, and purchase motivation.

The actual quantified measures obtained in a DAR test are described as total-related-recall levels. **Total related recall** measures two dimensions of the test commercial: intrusiveness and impact. **Related recall** refers to the percentage of the test-commercial audience who claim to remember the test execution and who are also able to substantiate their claim by providing some description of the commercial.[11] The higher the percentage is, the more intrusive the message with respect to the audience. For measuring the impact a commercial has made on an audience, the total-related-recall score is broken down into categories: unaided (by brand-name mention) versus aided; specific versus non-specific; communication-objective or selling-message playback; and central-situation playback.

OPINION-MEASURE TESTING **Opinion-measure testing** exposes an audience to test-commercial messages in the context of special television programs. In terms of procedure, a group of people are seated around television monitors, or they view commercials in a theatre environment where they view ads and respond to a series of questions.

The test commercial is usually presented twice during the program, in cluster situations. Also included in the cluster is a set of control commercials, against which the test commercial or commercials (sometimes more than one commercial is being tested) can be compared. The position of the test commercial is different in each cluster. The test measures three key attributes: the audience's awareness of the commercial based on brand-name recall; the extent to which the main idea of the ad is communicated; and the effect the commercial could have on purchase motivation (e.g., the likelihood of the respondent buying the brand). This final measure is based on a comparison of pre-exposure brand purchase information and post-exposure brand preference data.

This procedure is often referred to as a *forced-exposure test*, a name that suggests its potential weakness: the artificial environment in which it occurs. However, the results for commercials are compared to results from previous tests, and since the procedure remains constant, the data should provide reasonable direction to advertisers.

PHYSIOLOGICAL TESTING Advertisers also have access to a variety of physiological testing methods that measure involuntary responses to a specific element of an advertisement. In an **eye movement-camera test**, consumers read an advertisement while a hidden camera tracks their eye movements. Such a test gauges the point of immediate contact, how a reader scans the various components of an ad, and the amount of time spent reading it. The **pupillometer test** measures a person's pupil dilation to determine the level of interest in the ad. In a **voice-pitch-analysis test**, a person's voice response is taped. It measures changes in voice pitch caused by emotional responses.

Testing procedures and the need for them are controversial issues in the industry, particularly among advertising agencies, whose work is being tested. Many creative directors argue that too much testing defeats the creative process (it stifles creativity) and that what people say in research and do in the real world can be completely different. Nevertheless, clients like to know how customers will react to their messages, preferably before they spend money on them.

INQUIRY TESTS (SPLIT-RUN TESTS) Perhaps the most meaningful tests are those that measure an ad's actual influence on a target audience: did the target actually purchase the product or take advantage of a special offer because of the ad?

With an **inquiry** or **split-run test**, an advertiser can measure the effectiveness of two or more advertisements at once. For example, an advertiser can run two different ads with the same coupon offer (the coupon being pre-coded differently for each of the two ads). The number of coupons redeemed for each ad may be indicative of the relative strength of the overall ad. Small-scale tests of this nature are excellent for determining which advertisement should be more widely distributed. This procedure can be adapted for use by direct-response advertisers who use return coupons of a "send for more information" nature.

CONTROLLED EXPERIMENTS To measure the potential impact of advertising activity on sales, an advertiser could set up a **controlled experiment** situation in which the advertising activity used in a test market differs from that used in a control market. To implement this type of test, the advertiser would select two markets that were closely matched in terms of demographics, shopping habits, and media-consumption habits. In the control market, a given set of planned marketing activities would prevail. In the test market, the advertising variable would be altered: different media might be used, or the expenditure level or weight of advertising might vary. Sales would be monitored closely in both markets so that test results would be obtained and conclusions about advertising effectiveness reached.

SUMMARY

The communications process begins with a sender (the advertiser) developing a message that is sent by the media to the receiver (the consumer or business user). From this fundamental understanding of communications, advertisers deliver messages to customers with the objective of prompting some kind of action (e.g., buying the product). Before such an action occurs, the consumer passes through several stages of behaviour: awareness, comprehension, conviction, and then action.

The creative development process begins with a creative brief, which is a discussion document prepared by the client. The brief includes the appropriate background information that creative personnel require prior to undertaking a new creative challenge. The content of a creative brief includes market background information, product information, competitor product and advertising information, target-market profile, budget, clear identification of the problem that advertising will resolve, the advertising objectives, positioning-strategy statement, and a list of creative objectives.

Creative objectives are statements that clearly indicate the information to be communicated to a target audience. They include a key-benefit statement and a support-claims statement. The key-benefit statement identifies the primary benefit and makes a promise to consumers about what the product will do. The support-claims statement provides details that substantiate the promise made. The client is usually responsible for developing the creative objectives.

Creative strategy is the responsibility of the agency and is concerned with tone, style, theme, and appeal techniques. Some common appeal techniques include positive and negative approaches, the use of factual information, comparisons with competitor products, humour, emotion, and sex and lifestyle appeals.

At the creative execution stage, the primary concern is to make an impact on the target market. Considerations in this area include the use of testimonials, endorsements, product-as-hero tactics, demonstrations, or torture tests. The final stage, creative evaluation, occurs when the client management appraises and approves (or disapproves) of the agency's creative recommendations. It may also involve conducting consumer research to evaluate the potential impact the advertisement or campaign will have on the target market.

Should research be necessary, a variety of pre-test and post-test techniques are available. If recognition and recall of the message is of concern, a Starch readership test, a day-after recall test, and an opinion-measure test can be implemented. These tests generate data regarding brand identification and message comprehension. In post-test situations, inquiry (split-run) tests and controlled experiments are undertaken.

KEY TERMS

REVIEW QUESTIONS

1. Briefly describe the four behavioural stages that a consumer passes through prior to making the decision to buy a product.

2. Briefly describe the key responsibilities of clients and agencies in the creative development process.

3. What is a creative brief, and how is it used by an advertising agency?

4. What are the stages in the creative development process? Briefly describe each stage.

5. In the context of creative development, what is the role of the positioning-strategy statement?

6. What are the components of creative objective statements? Briefly describe each component.

7. What is the difference between creative strategy and creative execution?

8. Identify and briefly describe the factors that influence the direction of creative objectives and creative strategies.

9. Briefly describe the various appeal techniques commonly used in advertising.

10. Explain the differences among the following types of creative execution: demonstration, exaggerated demonstration, and product-as-hero. Provide a new example of each.

11. What is meant by the "managerial approach" to evaluating creative output? Briefly describe the criteria that comprise such an evaluation.

12. What is the difference between pre-testing and post-testing of creative?

13. What is the difference between recognition testing and recall testing?

14. What does a Starch readership test measure?

DISCUSSION QUESTIONS

1. "Humorous advertising campaigns are effective in the short term, but do little to achieve long-term objectives for a product or service." Agree or disagree, citing some specific examples to substantiate your position.

2. "Comparative advertising: Is it wise to acknowledge a competitor while you pay for the ad?" What is your opinion on this style of advertising?

3. Conduct some secondary research (online or otherwise) and compare and contrast the creative strategies being used by the following brands. Are the strategies similar or different?

   a) Coca-Cola and Pepsi-Cola
   b) Guess jeans and Levi's jeans
   c) Canadian Tire and Home Depot

4. The "managerial approach" for evaluating creative was discussed in the chapter. Do you think this activity by the client impedes the creative process in the advertising agency? Discuss.

5. Review the Advertising in Action vignette **A Strong, Relevant Idea Works Wonders**. Research some of the images that have been used in this campaign. Why do you think this campaign has been so successful at building the brand? Can you identify any other long-term campaigns that have also been successful? Why have these campaigns been successful?

NOTES

1. "Sprite Need Gear," *Marketing*, 2002 Promotion Awards.
2. Thomas Mucha, "A message guys love: get sprayed, get girl," *Financial Post*, June 16, 2003, p. FE2.
3. Ellen Roseman, "Most want socially responsible companies," *Toronto Star*, February 1, 2002, p. E2.
4. Paul Brent, "You can be sexy and drive a minivan," *Financial Post*, August 25, 2003, pp. FP1, FP4.
5. Marina Strauss, "Canadian Tire ads demonstrate smarts," *Globe and Mail*, October 10, 2003, p. B10.
6. Lucy Saddleton, "Guys will be guys the world over," *Strategy*, November 19, 2001, p. 7.
7. John Heinzl, "SUV ads drive kinder, gentler course," *The Globe and Mail*, February 28, 2003, p. B9.
8. Wendy Cuthbert, "Racy ads pushing the boundaries," *Strategy*, September 25, 2000, p. 20.
9. Matt Litzinger, "The creative eye," *Marketing*, January 19, 2004, p. 17.
10. Jo Marney, "Credibility and advertising," *Marketing*, June 3, 1996, p. 22.
11. "Marketers move from stores to courts," *Marketing*, January 1/8, 1996, p. 5.

Fresh Citrus Breeze

Scratch and swoon.

Extreme Herbal Mint

Scratch and shiver.

Cinnamon Rush

Scratch and sizzle.

Crest Whitening Expressions. The new toothpaste that whitens your teeth, with an experience that blows your mind. Scratch and sniff all three flavours for a hint of the thrilling sensation to come.

©2004 P&G

Fights cavities.

CHAPTER

6

Design, Layout, and Production

Learning Objectives

After studying this chapter, you will be able to

- Explain the role and functions of copywriters and art directors

- Identify the design principles and creative considerations for developing print, broadcast, and electronic advertising

- Explain the various types of print layout options

- Characterize the functions of the various sections of a television commercial

- Explain the production stages of television and radio commercials

This chapter examines in greater detail the design, layout, and production considerations associated with the execution stage of the creative development process. Focusing on the differences between the various print and broadcast media, it examines the copywriting and art direction function in more detail by presenting the techniques that are used to develop ads for the various media.

A significant amount of a client's advertising budget can be tied up in production expenses. The combination of production expenses and the high cost of media time and space places pressure on the agency to produce creative that sells the client's product or service. Theoretically, the various elements of an advertisement or commercial must work together effectively to present a convincing message. In essence, the message must create a favourable impression in the mind of a consumer as quickly as possible. Further, in the context of integrated marketing communications, the message delivered should be the same in each medium—one sight, one sound, one sell!

For those who earn a living developing advertising messages, the challenge is to stop readers at a certain page, to keep viewers in the room and mentally alert during commercial breaks, or to attract attention to a banner ad so that visitors click on the banner to obtain more information.

Magazine and Newspaper Advertising

In traditional print advertising, the central idea is primarily conveyed through the headline and visual illustration. The elements work together to produce a single message. As a unit, the headline and illustration must attract attention and create sufficient interest so that the reader moves on to the body copy, which, in turn, must sufficiently expand on the promise made in the headline or illustration.

THE COPYWRITING FUNCTION

The major areas of concern for the copywriter are the headline and subheadlines, the body copy, and the signature elements of an advertisement. Each element will be discussed in the context of the influence it is intended to have on the reader.

HEADLINES   The primary purpose of the headline is to command the reader's attention. According to David Ogilvy (co-founder of Ogilvy & Mather Advertising), "Headlines get five times the readership of the body copy. If your headline doesn't sell, you have wasted your money."[1] There is no magic formula for distinguishing a good headline from a bad headline, but some research indicates that short headlines are more effective than long ones. To attract readers' attention, various types of headlines are commonly used.

The **promise of benefit** headline makes an immediate promise to the reader. The promise is substantiated with other body copy and illustrations. A headline for the Oral-B 3D Excel spin toothbrush reads: "The ultimate weapon in the fight against gum disease." The illustration and supporting body copy draw attention to the key features that substantiate this claim. The tagline "Brush Like a Dentist" summarizes the promise by suggesting your teeth will have that "clean teeth" feeling similar to the feeling you have when you leave the dentist. See the ad in Figure 6.1 for details.

A **curiosity** headline makes the reader inquisitive enough to seek more information (to look for an explanation). British Airways used the headline "Upgrade from a power nap to a good night's sleep." A reader might wonder about how an airline can provide a good night's sleep when any seat becomes uncomfortable on a long flight. British Airways has taken positive steps to provide more space on seats and the seats actually convert into beds for more complete comfort. They want their transatlantic customers to be aware of this.

A **question** headline asks a question and encourages readers to search for an answer in the body copy or illustration. This type of headline implies some kind of benefit. Volkswagen uses a clever headline: "Is it possible to go backwards and forwards at the same time?" There is no body copy to explain the headline, only a picture of the uniquely shaped Volkswagen Beetle—a car that looks like it could go both ways. See the illustration in Figure 6.2.

A **news** headline expresses a sense of urgency or announces something new to the reader. Words commonly used in news headlines are "New!" or "Introducing!" or "Finally!" When Gillette launched the new Sensor 3 disposable razor for men it employed a very simple news headline: "New Sensor 3. The Best Disposable Razor You Ever Threw Away." When Acura launched the new Acura TSX, a very sporty-looking sedan, it used the headline: "Give your old car two weeks' notice." The phrase "two weeks' notice" is commonly associated with giving notice when leaving a job. In this case it suggests there is about to be a change, once the reader sees the new car. The bold beauty shot of the car does the rest of the selling.

A **command** headline politely makes a request of the reader to do something. A Campbell's Soup ad has the following headline: "Try something a little different with soup. Don't just stir, stir-fry." The ad goes on to explain the versatility of the soup in a variety of recipes.

A more subtle type of command is to simply reassure the reader that taking action is the right thing to do. When Infiniti launched the FX45, a sporty-looking luxury SUV, the visual showed a forty-something male contemplating the decision to buy while

Oral B
www.oralb.com/home.asp

Volkswagen
www.vw.com

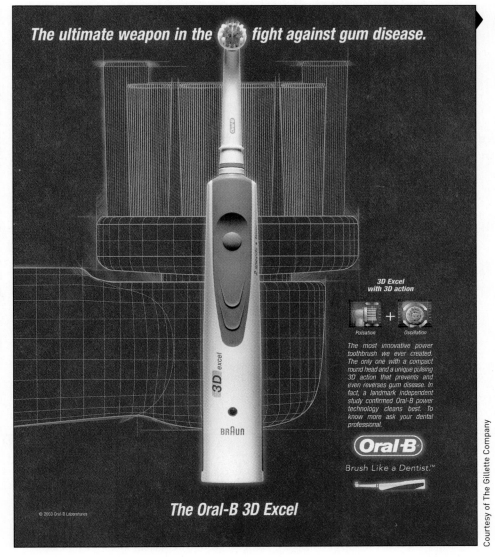

The ultimate weapon in the fight against gum disease.

3D Excel with 3D action

Pulsation + Oscillation

The most innovative power toothbrush we ever created. The only one with a compact round head and a unique pulsing 3D action that prevents and even reverses gum disease. In fact, a landmark independent study confirmed Oral-B power technology cleans best. To know more ask your dental professional.

Oral-B

Brush Like a Dentist.™

The Oral-B 3D Excel

© 2003 Oral-B Laboratories

FIGURE
6.1

An ad with a promise headline

visualizing what it would be like to drive the vehicle. The headline read: "Stop torturing yourself. What you want is what you need."

SUBHEADLINES   A **subheadline (subhead)** is a smaller headline that amplifies the main point of a headline, making it possible to keep the headline short; it acts as a breaker between the headline and the body copy. It more commonly, however, takes the reader directly from the headline to the body copy and/or illustration. Subheadlines are an optional component of a print ad. Many ads run without one. If there is to be a transition it is from the headline to the body copy.

BODY COPY   The **body copy** is the informative or persuasive prose that elaborates on the central theme of the advertisement. The body copy helps create preference by providing information the consumer needs as a basis for making a purchase decision. Body copy is the substantiation—the proof of promise or product claims. It is a device that integrates headline with illustration. The headline announces something new, the sub-

Is it possible to go backwards and forwards at the same time?

Drivers wanted.

Courtesy: Volkswagen Canada Inc.

FIGURE
6.2

An ad with a question headline that provokes curiosity in the reader

head provokes curiosity in the reader, and the body copy and visual of the product provide proof. There are several types of body copy commonly used in print advertising:

1. *"Reason-why" copy* This straightforward copy relates the product's benefits to customers' needs. Typically, reason-why copy methodically resolves a problem the reader may encounter.
2. *Dialogue copy* Dialogue copy delivers a message from a spokesperson's point of view (i.e., in the form of a testimonial or endorsement). Dialogue copy can stand alone, but it is commonly integrated with other types of copy.
3. *Narrative copy* Narrative copy presents a message in the third person. Using this type of copy can be problematic; it must be very good to hold the reader's attention.

How long should body copy be? Advertising practitioners have varying opinions on this subject. Generally, people read more of the copy if they are interested in the product or the idea communicated in the advertisement. Also, people will read more of an ad at a time when they are actually contemplating purchase, particularly if it is a major purchase. The body copy provides the information that helps the consumer decide.

While not discounting the value and importance of body copy, some creative experts believe the complete message should be communicated in the headline and visual. Their point is simple: the first thing people avoid is the body copy—they don't have enough time to read it!

Here are some guidelines that should be considered when working with body copy. Remember, a creative team does not have to follow guidelines to develop persuasive advertising—many believe you have to break the rules to be seen, heard, and read!

1. Short copy is most appropriate for image advertising. The illustration plays a key role in portraying a certain image, and lengthy copy would detract from it.
2. Purchase value has a bearing on copy length. The higher the cost of the product or service, the more likely that the consumer will use advertising as a source of information, and thus more copy is necessary.
3. Copy for new products may be longer than copy for established products. More copy is needed in the informative stage of advertising than in the retentive stage, where short messages are used to remind consumers of product benefits.

SIGNATURE   The final copy element in a print advertisement is the **signature**. Often referred to as a **tagline**, the signature can include a company or product logo and a brand or company slogan. A *logo* or logotype refers to the distinctive copy style that identifies the company or product. Logos are used in advertising to provide a common corporate identity to all products of a multi-product firm (e.g., a corporate logo appears in all ads for individual products). The purpose of the signature is to achieve the following:

1. To summarize the concept or central theme of the advertisement. For example, the logo and slogan can reinforce a key benefit or reinforce a company position that applies to several products. The tagline "Brush Like a Dentist" in Figure 6.1 demonstrates this point.
2. To position the product in the customer's mind. For example, the logo and slogan will appear in all forms of advertising and be selling messages themselves. Recognizing that readers may pass over body copy entirely, the signature must leave an impression with the consumer. In addition, the signature provides continuity from one advertisement to another. The "Drivers wanted" slogan and the Volkswagen insignia (see Figure 6.2) demonstrate this principle. These elements appear in all forms of Volkswagen advertising. Slogans such as "Drivers wanted" become familiar and meaningful to people the more they occur in advertising. Here are some other good examples of signatures and slogans:

   - "Panasonic . . . Ideas for Life"
   - "Canadian Tire . . . Let's get started"
   - "Gillette . . . The Best a Man Can Get"
   - "Visa . . . All You Need"

To demonstrate the concept of transition and the relationships between headlines, illustrations, body copy, and signature, refer to the ads that appear in Figures 6.3 and 6.4. Both ads are for Porsche automobiles. In each ad the bold, striking visual captures the attention of the reader. The eyes then migrate to the headline in the middle of the page that instills curiosity in the mind of the reader. A headline does not have to appear at the top of an ad. The body copy focuses on the key benefit that the headline alludes to. In each ad the body copy is not very long, but in each case it adequately elaborates on the key benefit. Porsche's well-known insignia and distinctive font for the brand name appear in the lower right corner.

Porsche
www3.us.porsche.com/
english/usa/home.htm

FIGURE
6.3

An ad that demonstrates effective transition between illustration, headline, and body copy

Contact us at 1-800-PORSCHE or porsche.com. ©2004 Porsche Cars North America, Inc. Porsche recommends seat belt usage and observance of all traffic laws at all times.

Calling it transportation is like calling sex reproduction.

In trying to describe it, you risk the understatement of the century. The 911 Turbo is driving in its highest form. It is the sum of all our knowledge engineered into a machine that can take the human senses to the redline. Porsche. There is no substitute.

The 911 Turbo

PORSCHE

THE ART DIRECTION FUNCTION

The primary responsibility of the art director is to design the layout of the advertisement. **Layout** refers to the design and orderly formation of the various elements of an advertisement within specified dimensions (size specifications). The layout combines the illustration with the copy and offers an overall impression of what the final advertisement will look like. Advancing computer technology is changing the nature of layout and design procedures. Formerly, the art director would progress through three distinct design stages: the thumbnail sketch, the rough art, and the comprehensive. **Thumbnail sketches** are small, experimental drawings of various ideas and design concepts. Their purpose is to identify a few options that can be used as a basis for more extensive design development.

Rough art refers to the drawing of an ad that is done in actual size (derived from the best of the thumbnail sketches), with the various elements of the ad included so that their size and position are shown—the location of headline, body copy, and illustration. The rough artwork and copy sheet (where precise copy is composed) are usually

The four corners of the world are,
after all, corners.

It takes you where no other sport utility vehicle can. At every corner, your will connects to the road.
An active suspension responds instantly. The stability management system ensures the perfect line.
The Cayenne. Pure Porsche. In a most unexpected form. Learn more at 1-800-PORSCHE or porsche.com.

Introducing Cayenne. The next Porsche.

Courtesy: Porsche

FIGURE
6.4

An ad that demonstrates
effective transition between
illustration, headline, and
body copy

presented by the agency to the client for approval. Again, several options may be presented, with the preferred option progressing to the next stage of design.

In a **comprehensive**, or **comp**, the copy and illustration appear as a highly refined facsimile of what the finished ad will look like. A comp usually includes the actual font styles and sizes and finished photographs or drawings. Given the computer technology available today, the comp is typeset on computer and positioned with the visuals. The ad is then printed in full colour and shown to the client for final approval. Refer to the **Practice of Advertising** section immediately following this chapter for some illustrations of thumbnails, rough art, and comprehensives.

Computer technology has changed the way that ads are prepared. A copywriter's words can be instantly transferred to an art director's layout by computer. The art director chooses a font from a library of typefaces, sets it in position, imports images and logos from a library of images, and commissions artwork as needed. The art director can play with all of the parts until satisfied with a design, and then produce a colour laser printout for client approval. Computer-aided design allows art directors to quickly examine "what if" experiments with raw ideas. For the client, the changes mean shorter production times, lower costs, more involvement in creative, the chance to see a more precise version of the final advertisement at an earlier stage, and the ability to make changes without hassle and expense.

DESIGN PRINCIPLES AFFECTING LAYOUTS

The client and agency strive for distinctiveness in their ads in order to break through the clutter of competition. To achieve that distinctiveness, the art director considers factors such as balance, unity and flow, the use of colour, size alternatives, bleed pages, the use of artwork and photography, and the use of white space.

BALANCE **Balance** refers to the relationship between the left side and the right side of an advertising layout.

    Formal balance occurs when both sides are equal in weight. If different weights are assigned to the various elements of an ad, there is *informal* balance.

UNITY **Unity** refers to the blending of all elements of an ad to create a complete impression. The headline, visual, and body copy must work together to create an impression.

FLOW **Flow** refers to the movement of the reader's eye—from left to right and top to bottom—when he or she is exposed to a print advertisement (see Figure 6.5). When some people scan an advertisement, their eyes move diagonally, from upper left to lower right. Others follow a "Z" pattern, with eyes moving left to right across the top, then diagonally from upper right to lower left, and then across the lower portion of the page to the right corner.

    Such reading patterns suggest the ideal locations for various elements of a print ad. For example, headlines often appear at the top to attract attention and state the key point of the ad. The illustration is used as background to the entire page, or part of the page (say in the middle), with body copy. The signature (summary message) usually appears in the lower right-hand corner of the page, along with any purchase incentives to encourage action. Signatures are strategically located to make an impression on those who skip the body copy. The Oral-B ad that appears in Figure 6.1 and the Porsche ads that appear in Figures 6.3 and 6.4 are good illustrations of balance, unity, and flow.

COLOUR AND CONTRAST Colour, or contrast in colour and style, can be an effective attention-grabber. In a black-and-white medium, reverse printing (white letters on black background) or spot colour may attract more attention. In a colour medium where photography prevails, black-and-white photos, line drawings, or spot colour can distinguish one ad from another. Most magazines publish in full colour, so to be different

FIGURE
6.5

Reader's eye movement

Flow of reader's eye from left to right and top to bottom

Courtesy: Audi of America, Inc.

FIGURE
6.6

An ad that effectively uses spot colour to advantage

and to grab the reader's attention, Audi designed a black-and-white ad that included limited but effective use of one colour (red). The stormy visual imagery (shades of grey and black) offers contrast and places the focus squarely on the automobile. The Audi ad appears in Figure 6.6.

Does colour increase readership? As a rule of thumb, the answer is yes, but factors such as the layout of the ad and how the various elements of an ad fit together also impact readership. In a major study, one-third more respondents remembered seeing the four-colour ads than the black-and-white ads.[2]

SIZE   The decision to use a full page, a double-page spread, or a fractional page (a half page or a quarter page) has an impact on how effectively an advertisement draws readers. Sometimes small ads can achieve the same result as larger ones (which is a boon to the client paying the bill), but generally speaking the full-page ad gets higher readership than a smaller ad. In fact, the degree of improved readership is surprising. Full-page ads receive 71 percent more readership than fractionals, and double-page spreads get 37 percent more readership than single pages.[3] A fractional page ad appears in Figure 6.7.

Audi
www.audi.com

FIGURE 6.7

An ad that occupies only a fraction of a page: one-third of a page in a three-column magazine

BLEED PAGES In the case of a magazine, a **bleed page** is an advertisement in which the dark or coloured background extends to the edge of the page (often explained as an arrangement where the colour appears to run off the page). The Audi ad in Figure 6.6 is an example of an ad that bleeds. Most magazines offer bleed flexibility. A bleed page attracts more attention (21 percent more) and preference (22 percent more) than a non-bleed page.[4] Typically, a majority of ads in magazines are bleeds but some advertisers distinguish their ads by including framed borders or by having white space surround the visual. The Porsche ads in Figures 6.3 and 6.4 adopt the framed approach, using white space to advantage.

ARTWORK VERSUS PHOTOGRAPHY The two basic illustrating devices are photography and drawn (or painted) illustrations. In the case of a four-colour medium such as magazines, logic suggests that colour photography be used, but the end product will, of course, be similar to numerous other ads in the same publication. An artist's drawing—

Courtesy: © The Procter & Gamble Company. Used with permission.

FIGURE
6.8

An ad using drawings as a
primary means of illustration

even a black-and-white drawing—may command a higher level of attention through
contrast. The opposite is true of newspapers. Generally, a good photograph will be most
effective in conveying realism, emotion, or urgency. But there are benefits to using drawings. Drawings allow artists to create the desired impression in their own style. The end
product can exaggerate or accentuate in ways a photograph cannot often match. In
Figure 6.8 a drawing is very effective in communicating the benefits of Charmin—soft-
ness: a true benefit for a sensitive area of the body.

WHITE SPACE   **White space** is the part of an advertisement that is not occupied by other
elements. Margins, for example, are considered white space. The careful use of white
space can be an effective means of providing contrast and of focusing attention on an isolated element. White space is also the means of achieving an uncluttered appearance. The
ad for Volkswagen that appears in Figure 6.2 aptly portrays the use of white space. The
ad is simple and uncluttered. The Mercedes Benz ad in Figure 6.9 also uses white space

FIGURE
6.9

An ad that effectively combines the principles of white space, clarity, and simplicity

effectively. Ads such as these focus on the product. The advertisers believe that clean and simple style of communications is more effective.

CLARITY AND SIMPLICITY Any elements that do not serve a specific function should be eliminated. Too much variety in type style, too many reverses or illustrations, and unnecessary copy should be cut. To achieve the desired impact, the ad should be pleasant to the eye and easy to read.

The Porsche ads that appear in Figure 6.3 and Figure 6.4 aptly demonstrate the principles of white space, clarity, and simplicity. Also note that both ads look the same even though they are for different automobiles. Regardless of which make and model Porsche advertises, all ads look the same. The combination of theme, consistent use of appeal techniques, tone, style, and layout presents a consistent image to current and prospective customers.

All of the above factors are considered in the design of an ad, but there is no magic formula for success. The effect of advertising is in the eye of the beholder. Therefore, when an ad is designed by the creative team, submitted to a focus group for its blessing, and ultimately sent to the client for final approval, everything must be kept in perspective. Relying on old evidence that colour offers more impact than black and white and that full pages produce higher readership than fractional pages is questionable today. The objective is to be noticed and remembered—and that may mean breaking a few rules.

TYPES OF LAYOUTS

The creative team considers the factors discussed in the preceding section when positioning the various elements in an ad for layout. With its decisions depending on the importance of an illustration and the need for explanatory copy, the creative team must blend all elements together to create an overall "look" for an advertisement. Here are some common types of layouts.

POSTER   The **poster** layout relies almost entirely on visual impression. The advertisement is picture-dominant, with a minimum of copy. The Audi ad in Figure 6.6 is an example of a poster layout. The strong visual in the ad combined with a different type of headline that reads "Never Follow" suggests what type of consumer the Audi is trying to attract: bold achievers, people that like to take risks and reflect a certain status in what they own. The ad presents a powerful image—as the old expression goes, "A picture is worth a thousand words."

VERTICAL SPLIT   In a **vertical-split** layout, the copy dominates one side of the ad and the picture dominates the other side (left side versus right side). In a single-page ad, an imaginary line down the middle can divide the page. Vertical splits are popular with a double-page spread (two pages).

HORIZONTAL SPLIT   A **horizontal split** divides the page across the middle. A common format has picture domination at the top and copy domination at the bottom. The Porsche ads that appear in Figures 6.3 and 6.4 are examples of a horizontal split.

MULTIPLE ILLUSTRATIONS   In the **multiple-illustration** layout, a series of illustrations is presented, either in sequence or showing a variety of related features and benefits.

LONG COPY   The **long-copy** advertisement is copy-dominated, with limited or no use for illustrations. The body copy plays a key role in explaining the product's benefits. The ad for Nerds on Site in Figure 6.13 (later in this chapter) is one that effectively combines a strong visual of the product with important body copy.

INSERT LAYOUT   In the **insert layout**, a secondary visual illustration appears as an "insert" on the page. Inserts are commonly used to emphasize the product, package, or special features. The ad for the Mazda Tribute that appears in Figure 6.10 draws the reader's attention to special features by using the multiple-illustration technique.

For more insight into copy and design elements that produce better advertising, see the Advertising in Action vignette **Attention, Interest, Action!**

FIGURE 6.10

An ad that applies the multiple-illustration technique to highlight key features

For an applied illustration of the various copywriting and art direction concepts discussed in this section, refer to the **Practice of Advertising** section that follows this chapter. In this illustration you are exposed to the creative brief, the creative director's thoughts as he was designing the ads, and a variety of ads at various stages of development. This campaign was developed for the Centre for Addiction and Mental Health. Its purpose was to create awareness and understanding of depression, a growing condition in Canada and elsewhere.

Out-of-Home Advertising

Other print media possess different characteristics and present different problems and opportunities for the creative team to explore. Out-of-home advertising is the current term for advertising in formats such as outdoor posters, transit ads, mall posters, shopping carts, and mural ads, to mention a few. These formats usually function as

Attention, Interest, Action!

What does the following mean? "If you want to break through the endless inspiration–procrastination–guilt cycle and achieve personal fitness, simply summon your courage and apply yourself." A copywriter for Nike wouldn't use such a sentence if he or she were really interested in selling shoes. Instead, the writer followed some basic rules for writing copy and came up with that now-famous phrase, "Just Do It." More aptly stated, the difference between a good copywriter and a great copywriter is the ability to convey a message in a short phrase, sometimes breaking a rule of grammar along the way.

What makes good copy and layout? Are there rules that great copywriters and art directors follow? These are interesting questions. Research reveals that when readers leaf through pages of a magazine, the average ad has less than half a second to grab their attention. With such little time to work with, the relationship between copy and illustration has to be readily apparent.

While there is no secret formula for success, here are some tried and true tips to ponder:

- **Successful ads have visual magnetism** An ad should be constructed so that a single component dominates the area—a picture, headline, or text. The more pertinent the picture, the more arresting the headline, the more informative the copy, the better the ad will be.
- **Successful ads select the right target** There should be something in the ad that the reader can readily relate to. The ad should say to the reader, "Hey, this is for you."
- **Successful ads invite the reader into the scene** The art director has to visualize, illuminate, and dramatize the selling proposition.
- **Successful ads promise a reward** Readers must be given a reason to continue reading, for if they do, they will learn something of value. A promise must be specific. The headline "Less maintenance cost" is not as effective as "You can cut maintenance costs by 25 percent."

- **Successful ads back up the promise** A promise is only believable if hard evidence is provided (e.g., comparisons with the competition can be convincing, as are third-party testimonials).
- **Successful ads present the selling proposition logically** The parts of an ad must be organized so that there is an unmistakable entry point and the reader is guided through the material in a sequence consistent with the logical development of the selling proposition.
- **Successful ads talk person-to-person** Copy is more convincing when it talks to the reader as an individual. The writing style should be simple: short words, short sentences, short paragraphs. A more friendly tone results when the copy refers to the advertiser in the first person (as "we") rather than by the company name.
- **Successful ads are easy to read** Magazines and newspapers are loaded with ads in which the copy is too small to read. The typeface selected should be easy to read, should not be printed over an illustration, and should appear black on white.

When clients evaluate creative concepts very often they are afraid to take risks. If they feel uncomfortable about the ad they won't approve it. Yet strong ads almost always contain something that raises an eyebrow or two: an unusual photo, or a headline that smacks readers between the eyes. On the client side, the more people who see the ad, the more likely there will be unwanted design critiques, a source of frustration for agency creative people. If too many people chip away at the sharp edges, you're more likely to end up with a teddy bear— something cute and cuddly but not very effective. So, in terms of evaluation, here are a few fundamentals to consider:

- **Is the single most important benefit properly emphasized?** Don't try to say too much in an ad. Readers pause only briefly as they flip through a publication. Make sure the ad selects the strongest benefit and presents it prominently and persuasively.

continued

- **Is the visual a stopper?** Some managers feel a beauty shot of the product is all that is needed. It is better to dramatize the most important benefit either by showing the product in action or by visualizing the problem and offering the product as a solution.
- **Does the layout have a sense of balance and flow?** Is there a single large visual that catches your eye first? Does the headline work in tandem with the main visual? Is it obvious who sponsored the ad? Are the logo and slogan given their own space as a signature?
- **Is the offer clear?** Think through the offer. What exactly do you want the reader to do? Request a sample? Send for more information? Log on to your website?

In the end, these copy and design fundamentals are certainly food for thought. But advertising is very subjective—so too many guidelines could produce boring advertising. Clients must remember that it is not they who are buying the product. The ad that stops consumers in their tracks and then offers enough motivation to stimulate action is the best design of all. Advertising would be very boring if the formula for success could be bottled and sold to every copywriter and art director. Truly good advertising is in the eye of the beholder!

As an exercise, the reader may wish to analyze some of the ads in this chapter and evaluate them against the criteria described in this vignette.

Sources: Adapted from Bob Lamons, "Guidelines for making better advertising decisions," *Business Marketing*, April 21, 1998, p. 9; "The copy chaser commandments," *Business Marketing*, January 1994, p. 23; Jo Marney, "Gotcha!" *Marketing*, February 22, 1988, p. 14; and "General rules for the perfect print ad," *Marketing*, June 26, 1989, p. B14.

supplemental media and seem to work best when introducing new products, building awareness, and adding reach to a campaign.

OUTDOOR POSTERS

Perception Research Services
www.prsresearch.com

A research study conducted by Perception Research Services (U.S.) indicated that 75 percent of all individuals who see an outdoor board are likely to be drawn to the name of the product advertised, so bold identification of the name is important. In addition, factors such as size and the use of *cut-out extensions* affect the attention-getting ability of the board. Cut-out extensions are outdoor designs that extend beyond the perimeters of the standard space. Cut-outs lead to higher levels of readership and more repeat examination by readers.[5]

Other design factors important for **outdoor advertising** include the simplicity of the design and the use of colour. Since outdoor advertising is often used as a complementary medium (in conjunction with a primary medium such as television), the outdoor message should contain creative concepts from the other media. This method is referred to as the **integrative concept** of creative design.

Here are some basic guidelines for outdoor layout and design:

- Use bold colours and high contrast.
- Use typefaces that are simple, clear, and easy to read.
- Size the copy and place it appropriately in relation to the product.

If simplicity is a key to good advertising, then telegraphic simplicity is the key to good outdoor advertising. If you consider that people drive by a street poster at 100 km/h or rapidly walk by a mall poster, arms loaded with packages, there is not a lot of time to communicate. To illustrate, consider an outdoor ad that was placed by the Cancer Patients Aid Association in India. The only element of the ad was a three-word headline positioned in the middle of the board. It read: "Cancer Cures Smoking." Think about it. That's a very convincing message and it is communicated quickly!

CRAFT AWARDS

ART DIRECTION

TITLE: Cap
PRODUCT: Beer
ADVERTISER: Kokanee Glacier Beer, Toronto
AGENCY: Palmer Jarvis DDB, Vancouver
CREATIVE DIRECTOR: Randy Stein
ART DIRECTOR: Dean Lee
ILLUSTRATOR: Instil Productions
PHOTOGRAPHER: Philip Rostron
PRODUCTION HOUSE PRODUCER: Gina Gallagher
CLIENT SUPERVISOR: Marc Solby
ACCOUNT EXECUTIVES: David Leonard and Adina Neufeld

It's the beer out here.

Courtesy: Columbia Brewery Palmer Jarvis, DDB Vancouver.

FIGURE 6.11

An outdoor ad taking advantage of the monumental

One of the main strengths of outdoor boards is that they invoke our respect for the monumental. Where else are you given the opportunity to shout at the world with letters and images up to seven metres high and 16 metres long? It is a medium that can inspire awe, so copywriters and art directors should take advantage of it. The ad for Kokanee Glacier Beer in Figure 6.11 is a good example of this.

TRANSIT ADVERTISING

Because the transit rider is sometimes moving and sometimes standing still, certain design considerations are particularly relevant to both interior and exterior transit advertising. With **interior transit**, the advertiser can use time to its advantage. The average length of a ride is 28 minutes, so copy and illustrations can be detailed. Alternatively, short and quick messages tend to be read and reread by idle passengers.

Exterior transit advertising reaches pedestrians and travellers in other vehicles. Since travelling displays on buses are often viewed from an angle and a distance, bold type, punchy copy lines, and absolute simplicity are preferable. The impact of a powerful visual must be respected in exterior transit advertising. The ad for Nike in Figure 6.12 is a good illustration of transit advertising.

POINT-OF-PURCHASE ADVERTISING

Point-of-purchase is another form of "reminder" advertising that uses the design concepts of another medium; it may be similar in appearance to ads designed for newspapers or magazines. Point-of-purchase advertising encourages impulse buying and influences last-minute choices between comparable brands. When it comes to retail display materials, which include posters, shelf-talkers (small posters at shelf locations), ad pads (tear-off coupon, contest, and cash rebate offers at shelf level), and floor ads, the design must provide what the point-of-purchase industry refers to as the four *I*'s: impact, identification, information, and imagery.

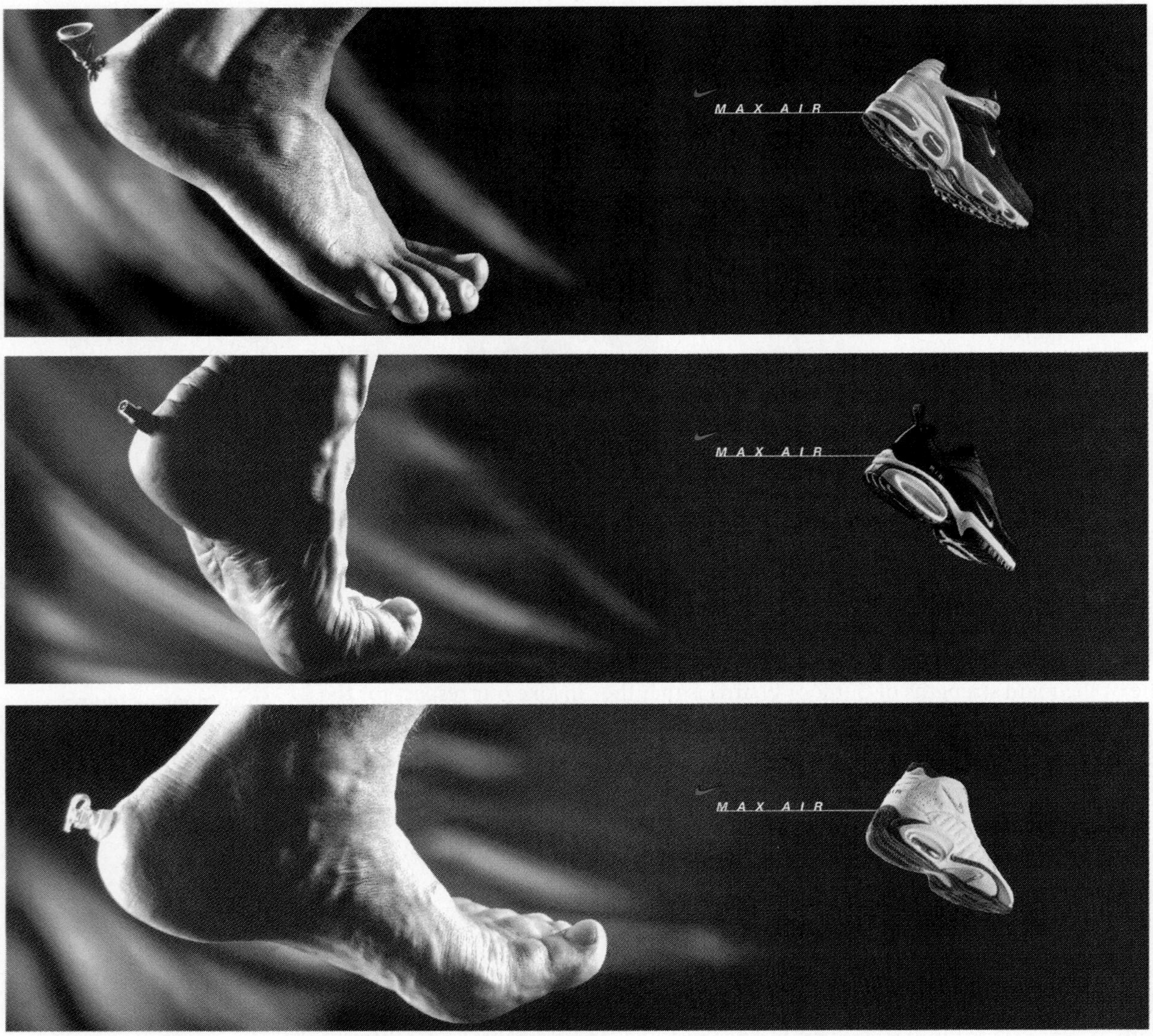

Courtesy: Nike Canada and Cossette Communications-Marketing. Photo by Edward Gajdel.

FIGURE
6.12
A strong visual is important in exterior transit advertising

- ***Impact*** The display must generate immediate impact. It must say "Here I am, buy me."
- ***Identification*** The brand or business name must be boldly displayed. Identification must link the message to the source.
- ***Information*** In a brief format (i.e., in the copy and the illustration), the display must provide the consumer with a reason to buy.
- ***Imagery*** The overall impression must be relevant to the customer. As in a print ad, the various elements of a display must blend together to make a complete message.

Direct-Response Print Advertising

Direct refers to a marketing situation where there is no distributor between the advertiser and the customer. Instead, there is a one-on-one link between the advertiser and customer through a phone call, a letter, or a print, radio, or television ad. With **direct-response print**, the message is communicated through magazines, newspapers, or the mail. A response opportunity is provided for the customer through a toll-free telephone number, reply card, or website address. Direct-response advertising aims to solicit a call for action quickly, either in the form of a purchase or a request for more information. Refer to Figure 6.13 for an illustration.

Since direct mail remains the most widely used form of direct-response advertising, let's focus on some copy and design characteristics of this medium.

1. ***Get the reader's attention***   Since so many people discard direct mail without opening it, there has to be some relevant copy or design element that gets the mail opened. For example, the envelope must function like a headline in a print ad. It should grab the reader's attention. Bright colours, unusual envelopes, and interesting graphics tend to generate more interest.

2. ***Personalize the mailing***   Direct mail is a targeted medium that relies on database marketing for success. With technology advancing rapidly, advertisers have access to accurate mailing lists. Taking the step to personalize each mailing is integral to the one-on-one sales situation referred to earlier. Also, the language in the letter

FIGURE 6.13

A direct-response print ad that effectively combines a strong visual and long copy in a direct-response print offer

Courtesy: Nerds on Site

and other elements of the mailing should be warm and informal and should echo the language of the consumer.

3. ***Include a complete presentation***   Unlike traditional forms of advertising, direct-mail advertising functions as a complete sales message. The copy must grab attention, stimulate interest and desire, provide ample proof of the promise, handle objections, and close the sale. The offer must be compelling and presented in a manner that makes it absolutely irresistible.

4. ***Include multiple pieces in the mailing***   A typical direct-mail piece includes several items (e.g., a letter, pamphlet, involvement device, and an offer of a free gift to encourage immediate action). Direct advertisers believe that many items working together to communicate the same message is more effective than one element alone. And, of course, it should be easy for the recipient to respond. Order cards must be easy to read and fill out. A postage-paid envelope, toll-free number, and website address should be included. A sample direct mailing is shown in Figure 6.14.

FIGURE
6.14

Contents of a typical direct-mail campaign

Courtesy: Canadian Business

Television Advertising

The nature and content of a television commercial are derived from the same base of information as print advertising, but there are obvious differences. Print advertising uses space, whereas television advertising is concerned with the use of time; since the message is delivered within a period of time, the creative team is concerned with the "flow" of the commercial from beginning to end. A television commercial is typically divided into three distinct sections: an opening, middle, and closing.

OPENING

The purpose of the opening section is to grab the viewer's attention and introduce the key benefit before the audience "disappears" physically or mentally. A common means of attracting attention is to present a problem situation that subsequently must be resolved.

MIDDLE

This section's purpose is to communicate the bulk of the message; it must hold the viewer's interest by elaborating, in an interesting manner, on the single most important benefit of the product or service, clearly identifying the name of the product or service.

CLOSING

The closing section of a commercial, which is usually the final few seconds, will definitely resolve the problem. The focus is usually on the product's name and package, if applicable. It may repeat a promise and should suggest some course of action to the viewer (e.g., "Call or write for information," "Visit your dealer for a test drive," or "Visit our website"). A tagline usually appears at the end of a commercial.

Figure 6.15 demonstrates the concept of opening, middle, and closing. In this ad an unattended dog in a house leaps off the table (a place he shouldn't be) when he hears his owners return. These scenes demonstrate that Pine-Sol cleans the dirt you see and the dirt you don't see. Examine the script and the pictures to capture the flow of the ad.

Pine-Sol
www.pinesol.com

DESIGNING TELEVISION COMMERCIALS

In designing a television commercial, the creative team first develops the **central concept** or **theme** and then creates a story around it. For example, the central theme of the Labatt Blue campaign called "Cheers. To Friends" revolves around the pranks that good friends play on each other. For arch-rival Molson Canadian and its campaign called "I AM Canadian," the theme revolves around patriotism and all things Canadian.

Labatt Blue
www.labattblue.ca

In the development stage, the creative team is concerned with the sequence of events in the ad, and the team creates a storyboard for this purpose. A **storyboard** is a set of graphic renderings (an artist's rough version of a finished commercial) in a television-frame format, with appropriate copy showing what the commercial will look like. An alternative to the storyboard is a complete **script**, which details in words the audio and visual elements of the commercial. It is common to have the description of the visual on one side, and the audio on the other. Clients approve advertising campaigns on the basis of the script and storyboard, so the combination of the two items must plant a good visual impression in their minds. Once approved, the script and storyboard act as the guideline for producing the commercial.

"DOG TIRED"

Video: *Open on a shot of a dog lying on a kitchen table. Camera stays on dog, still just lying on table.*

Super: *Pine-Sol cleans the dirt you know about.*

Video: *The dog then hears his owner returning home and jumps off the kitchen table.*

SFX: *Car pulling in, keys opening door.*

Video: *The dog settles into his same comfortable position, except now under the kitchen table.*

Super: *And the dirt you don't.*

Video: *Cut to a mid-shot of Pine-Sol Original bottle.*

Super: *The thorough clean.*

FIGURE
6.15

A television spot with a well-defined opening, middle, and closing

CREATIVE CONSIDERATIONS FOR TELEVISION

The creative team must consider several factors when trying to design a television commercial that will stand out from the clutter of competition. Given the context in which commercials appear (six or more in a cluster during a station break), the need for a commercial to break through a viewer's perceptual barriers is paramount.

UNITY   **Unity** refers to the visual and aural flow of a broadcast commercial, from the customer's perspective. Viewers do not distinguish between the opening, middle, and closing sections of an advertisement as they watch. Instead, they perceive the ad as a continuum of action focused on a central idea. The commercial, therefore, must flow logically: it presents the problem or situation, and then provides an explanation and solution. In the case of the Pine-Sol commercial (Figure 6.15), the central idea is that Pine-Sol is a reliable product for cleaning visible and hidden dirt—it does a thorough job and that's what the user wants.

INTEGRATION OF AUDIO AND VIDEO   In a commercial, the voice and action should be in unison: if a benefit is depicted, it should be discussed at the same time. The product should be the main element of the commercial; the creative team will consider using sound effects and music, where appropriate, but in so doing they must recognize that their purpose is to enhance the product message, not to overwhelm it. Music can play a special role by grabbing the viewer's attention. If rights are obtained for a popular song, the song must enhance a key benefit. For example, Honda Civic used the song *Who Let the Dogs Out* by Baha Men. The ad featured a dog and owner driving to a destination for a walk. The dog preferred to stay in the car listening to the song on the stereo sound system. Message delivered. Benefit understood!

SPECIAL EFFECTS   Special effects are such devices or techniques as animation, trick photography, or supers. A **super** is copy superimposed onto a picture in a television commercial, as is done with the final tagline in the Pine-Sol commercial (Figure 6.15). Most video production companies use digital video effects (DVE) units that can manipulate graphics on the screen in many different ways—fades, zooms, rotations, and so on. As with sound effects and music, special effects are meant only to enhance the commercial message. No technique should captivate viewers to the point that they focus more on it than the product.

PACE   A television commercial lasts 15, 30, or 60 seconds. Using the time limit as a guideline, the creative team must produce a message that will communicate itself at a suitable **pace**. In recent years, the 15-second commercial has become popular with advertisers, as it saves money in media time. However, scaled-down versions of 30-second commercials do not have the same impact. It is preferable to use the time constraint as a guideline from the beginning and develop an original commercial designed to suit the 15-second period.

The product and product image have an effect on the pace of a commercial. For example, a commercial for a perfume product may suggest romance and use emotional situations in the communications process. In this circumstance, the pace is likely to be slow. In contrast, a commercial for a soft drink like Mountain Dew aimed at a youthful target market may use fast-paced rock music and action sequences to create the appropriate image for the product.

LIVE ACTION VERSUS ANIMATION   **Live action** involves using real-life situations and real people in a commercial. The real people may be amateurs or professional actors. **Animation** is a technique whereby hand-drawn cartoons or stylized figures generated by design software on a computer are given movement and visual dimension. There is an animated television commercial for Charmin that uses this technique. The animation is identical to that which appears in the print ad featured in Figure 6.8. Some commercials combine live action and animation. Do you remember the commercials for Kellogg's Frosted Flakes that showed Tony the Tiger sitting at a table with real people and communicating with them? The Pillsbury Doughboy live-action commercials employ another animation technique.

There are advantages to both live-action and animated ads. A live-action commercial can generate a sense of realism and immediacy. As well, personalities can be used as persuasive presenters, and effective locations can be selected in which to shoot the commercial. The animated commercial is potentially entertaining; the advertiser can use a fantasy situation to advantage, and the commercial will no doubt be unique in its animation techniques. As well, animation is becoming more innovative as technology advances. New computer-assisted television cameras that control camera movement, complex effects from multiple exposures of the same frame, and computer-generated graphics have added to the quality of animated commercials.

In terms of creative execution, choosing the proper format is a key decision. **Format** refers to the best means of executing a strategy, the best means of dramatizing the benefit that has to be expressed. The most common formats are as follows:

1. ***Demonstrations***   In a demonstration, the objective is simply to demonstrate how the product works. There are several options: showing actual usage (e.g., the paper towel cleans up the entire spill), a comparison with a competitor (e.g., a thick ketchup compared to runny varieties), and a before-and-after scenario (e.g., a shirt with a messy spill on it is stain-free when removed from the laundry).

2. ***Narratives***   In a narrative, a story is told during the commercial. Some of the common options in this format include slice of life, vignettes, and little movies. The *slice-of-life* option usually introduces a problem situation that is remedied by using the product (e.g., the product comes to the rescue of the person in the commercial). The *vignette* shows a series of quick stories, one right after the other (e.g., many different people enjoy the use of the product). The *little movie* is one complete story with a short but strong plot, developed characters, and honest dialogue, often emotion-tugging. The "True Stories" campaign for Tim Hortons is a good example. In these ads much time is spent developing the featured character in order to show how his or her lifestyle has a close relationship with Tim Hortons.

3. ***Testimonials and endorsements***   Often referred to as "talking heads," such tactics have proven to be a durable technique in convincing customers about the merits of a product. Testimonials may come from a variety of sources, such as animated characters (e.g., the Pillsbury Doughboy), the common man or woman (e.g., that loveable but vulnerable man in the Goodyear tire commercials), or celebrity endorsers (e.g., Cindy Crawford for Pepsi-Cola, Tiger Woods for Nike and Buick, and Todd Bertuzzi for Gatorade).

TELEVISION PRODUCTION STAGES

The creative team and the account executive are responsible for presenting the storyboard and script to the client for approval. With a significant amount of money on the line at this stage (i.e., actual production costs and the cost of media time), both the agency and client want the message to be right.

Once the client has approved the concept, storyboard, and script, the commercial goes into production. The production process involves four separate stages: securing cost quotations, pre-production, production, and post-production.

COST QUOTATIONS   The task of producing the commercial is the responsibility of a production house (i.e., a specialist in commercial production). Evaluating production cost estimates from various production houses is a critical assignment, as the costs of producing a 30-second, live-action commercial—without celebrity talent—can average $100 000 to $300 000. Some beer commercials have reached into the $500 000 range.[6] The inclusion of celebrity talent, popular music, or a lot of special effects increases the production costs of TV advertising. Smaller advertisers in local markets can produce commercials for much less by using the production services offered by local television stations.

The agency typically solicits estimates from two or three production houses. The busiest production houses in Canada as measured by shooting days are The Partners Film Company and Radke Films. Suppliers such as these bid competitively on the job, with the lowest bid being accepted. To estimate costs, the production house will use the storyboard and script as a guideline and add in other costs normally associated with commercial production. Some of the factors that can cause commercial production costs to be high are as follows: travel to distant locations; using celebrity talent; complexity (which calls for large crews and many cameras); special effects; studio rental charges; the use of animals; the director (good ones are expensive); and additional days for production (time is money).

Production is a one-time cost, except for the talent used in the commercial. Talent can include actors, models, musicians, and so on. Talent is paid union scale for an appearance in a commercial, and an additional payment, known as a **residual**, is made to the performer each time the commercial is broadcast. Therefore, the costs of the talent increase with the frequency and coverage of the media buy. A celebrity may be employed under contractual agreement. Such agreements may call for participation in a certain number of television commercials each year.

PRE-PRODUCTION   At this stage, a meeting is held with representatives of the production house, the agency (i.e., the creative team), and the client. The storyboard and script are reviewed, and final decisions and arrangements are made. Prominent areas of discussion are casting, the use of secondary suppliers (e.g., music specialists, editors, and mixers), and finding appropriate props, costumes, and film locations. Agreement by all parties on all details is essential.

If an announcer is required for the commercial, the identity of the announcer will be determined in the pre-production meeting. Announcers in a commercial do not appear on screen, but are heard as a **voice-over** that communicates a key point.

If music is part of the commercial, the advertiser has several options depending on the price it is willing to pay. For the highest cost, specific music, such as a current rock tune, can be requested (usually such music is under copyright by the original musician or producer). The cost depends on the popularity of the artist and the song, with a range from US$20 000 to US$100 000.[7] Several types of rights packages are available, including sound-alike rights, parody rights, and even original music rights. As an alternative, music writers and arrangers can prepare original music scores. The cost of original music, if produced locally, is much less than the costs of pop or rock music quoted above. Less costly alternatives include the use of pre-recorded music prepared and distributed by recording studios, and the use of public-domain music, which is music whose copyright has expired.

PRODUCTION   The actual shooting (production) of the commercial can be very long and tedious, but—since time is money—every effort is made to complete the task as quickly as possible. However, quality is also paramount. Therefore, when scenes are shot it is common to try several takes to get them right. The director may adjust the lighting, for example, a process that often requires two or three good takes of each scene. However, scenes do not have to be shot in sequence. For example, scenes without sound, which therefore do not require a full crew, can be done last. Finally, considerable time is lost between scenes as cameras are moved, actors briefed, lights reset, and so on. It is important that there be continuity from scene to scene; otherwise, the finished commercial will appear disjointed. As discussed earlier, the concepts of "time" and "flow" are critical to the success of the message.

POST-PRODUCTION   The post-production stage involves putting the commercial together, and requires the coordinated effort of the director, film editor, and sound mixer. The normal procedure is to assemble the visuals and the sound separately, without extra effects such as dissolves, titles, or supers. Post-production activity can be described in a series of steps, which are as follows:

1. *Rough cut* A copy of the original film, referred to as a work print, is used in editing as a way of preventing damage to the original. The film editor reviews all footage and splices together the best takes to form a **rough cut**.

2. *Interlock* The **interlock** is the synchronization of sound and picture by means of a special editor's projector. The synchronized film and sound are projected onto a large screen to provide a feeling of what the finished commercial will be like. At this stage, scenes can be substituted and music added or deleted at the discretion of the creative team or client.

3. *Addition of optical effects* The movement from one scene to another in the rough cut and interlock is usually abrupt. Optical effects, such as dissolves, are added to make the transitions between scenes appear smooth. These dissolve effects involve **fades**, whereby one scene fades away and another gradually appears, and **wipes**, whereby one scene pushes the other away. Other options include the use of split-screen techniques or the addition of **supers** to the film.

4. *Mixed interlock* With the soundtrack and film edited, other audio elements and music can be added in a mixing section. Sound effects dubbed into other elements are called a **mixed interlock**.

5. *Answerprints* In the **answerprint**, film, sound, special effects, and opticals are combined and printed. The answerprint is presented to the client for approval, and duplicates (dupes) are made for distribution to television stations.

Direct-Response Television Advertising

Direct-response television (DRTV) advertising has two distinct formats: the 30-, 60-, and 120-second spot, or the 30-minute infomercial. An **infomercial** presents in more detail the benefits of a product or service and encourages immediate action through the use of toll-free telephone numbers. Some of the more common infomercials are for health-oriented products (e.g., exercise videotapes and workout equipment) and financial-planning products. The shorter direct-response commercials are commonly used to promote small kitchen appliances, audio and videotape offers, compact discs, and magazine subscriptions. The objective of a direct-response commercial is to initiate action by the customer immediately.

Mainstream advertisers are recognizing the benefits of direct-response advertising. The Ford Motor Company was an innovator, but others such as Rogers, Bell, Apple, and Royal Bank have followed. Time has proven that the consumer will no longer be swayed to a brand solely because of the image portrayed in a "linear" 30-second television spot. By allowing the consumer to interact with the brand through toll-free numbers and other interactive means, a closer relationship develops. The customer is one step closer to the purchase decision.

Planning and implementing a direct-response commercial is very different from a 30-second brand awareness/image campaign. Typically, there is much more time to spend on the message. Successful direct-response commercials incorporate a strong offer that gives the viewer a reason to call. Stressing a sense of urgency, offering a discount, or providing free information or a bonus incentive such as a gift are some techniques that help create action. The following are some proven creative techniques used in infomercials:[8]

- Always focus on the product. Extol it, praise it, and sell it.

- Include a strong offer—one that is clear, compelling, and simple. The stronger the offer, the greater the response will be.

- Clearly demonstrate the product in a convincing manner and establish and maintain credibility by using testimonials, research statistics, and judicious use of the brand name.

- Consider a magical transformation, that is, show the need and how it is easily fulfilled. This is similar to the problem-solution technique used in other forms of television advertising.

- Use an appropriate tone and style to communicate the message. The infomercial must consider the brand's image. For example, the tone and style of a Ford F-150 infomercial will be very different from one for EZ Krunch or some other exercise appliance.

Cost must also be considered in the infomercial equation. They can cost between $100 000 and $500 000 to produce when one considers the extent of involvement by producers, writers, directors, musicians, studio rental, travel costs, tapes and dubbing, rough-cut and final editing, talent fees, and contingency fees.

Radio Advertising

As in television execution, radio execution focuses on the effective use of time and on making the commercial flow from beginning to end. The creative team develops the concept or central theme in script form, which indicates the words to be spoken and provides direction regarding the use of sound effects and music.

CREATIVE CONSIDERATIONS FOR RADIO COMMERCIALS

Radio commercials must grab the listener's attention immediately and hold it until the end. This is a challenging task; listeners tend to "tune out" quickly if they are not interested. Radio is often listened to when a person is doing something else (e.g., reading, driving, sunbathing). To command attention, therefore, the ad must be catchy and memorable. Some proven techniques in the creation of radio advertising include the following:

1. Mention the advertiser's name often. Many practitioners suggest that the brand or company should be mentioned three times during a 30-second commercial.
2. Be conversational, but use short words and sentences.
3. Centre the message on one significant idea. Variations of the key message should be made repeatedly.
4. Use sound effects to create a visual image. Radio advertising, to be effective, must activate listeners' imaginations.
5. Make the tone of the radio commercial positive, cheerful, and upbeat.

Figure 6.16 includes a few examples of a radio script. In each script, the creative team has used a combination of humour and sound effects to catch the imagination of the listener. Read each script and visualize the situation—you may even laugh! If you do, you will know it will be an effective radio ad.

FIGURE
6.16

A radio script that includes conversation, sound effects, and a voice-over

These ads are part of a campaign that won the Gold Award in the Radio Campaign classification at the 2003 Marketing Awards.

Source: Courtesy of RETHINK.

Advertiser:	*Playland Amusement Park*
Agency:	*Rethink, Vancouver*

SCRIPT 1

"Father, Son"

SFX:	Amusement park sounds.
Son:	I don't know about that ride, Dad. I'm kinda scared.
Dad:	Son, sometimes we do things in life because they scare us. That's how you grow as a person. It's not easy. But in the end, it's worth it. Now whatta you say?
Son:	(*sucking it up*) All right, Dad. I'll do it.
Dad:	Atta boy.
SFX:	Safety bar being snapped shut on the ride.
Son:	Aren't you getting on with me?
Dad:	(*laughs*) What, are you nuts? Have you seen how fast this thing goes?
SFX:	Ride starting up.
Son:	(*terrified*) Daddy?
Dad:	Don't "Daddy" me, you picked it.
Son:	(*screaming*) Daddy!
Announcer:	Playland. Now open weekends.

SCRIPT 2

"Scream"

SFX:	Rollercoaster going up incline at beginning of ride.
Man:	Whoa, this is going to be great.
Woman:	Yeah! This thing goes really high, doesn't it?
Man:	If you're scared, just hang on to me.
Woman:	Oh-h-h-h.
Man:	Here we go!
SFX:	Rollercoaster rushing down first slope. We immediately hear high-pitched, blood-curdling, girlie screaming that lasts throughout the ride. Every curve and every swoop, the scream gets louder. As we hear the ride slow down and come to an end, the hysterical screaming continues.
Woman:	Honey! Snap out of it! It's embarrassing.
Man:	(*man's screams come to an end*) Oh, sorry.
Announcer:	Playland. Now open daily. Admission includes unlimited access to 25 rides.

TYPES OF RADIO COMMERCIALS

Generally, radio commercials can be divided into four categories: musical commercials, slice-of-life commercials, straight announcements, and personality announcements.

MUSICAL COMMERCIALS For commercials in which music plays a major role, there are several ways of "deploying" music: a commercial may be all music, as in the case of many soft drink ads; music jingles may be interspersed with spoken words; or orchestral arrangements can be used.

SLICE-OF-LIFE COMMERCIALS Much like a television commercial, a "slice of life" situation involves the presentation of a problem and then of product benefits that will resolve the problem. Effective use of listeners' imaginations enhances slice-of-life commercials.

STRAIGHT ANNOUNCEMENTS With these commercials, the message simply states the facts. The message is relatively easy to prepare and deliver. Music may be used in the background.

PERSONALITY ANNOUNCEMENTS This method differs from the first three alternatives in that the advertiser gives up the control of commercial delivery. In a **personality announcement**, the radio host presents the message using his or her radio personality style. The radio station is provided with a **feature sheet** that outlines the key benefits and the product slogan. The host develops the specific wording for the message. Personality announcements have increased in popularity recently. They are different from the other forms and sometimes the message can run longer than the usual time allocation of 30 or 60 seconds. Some advertisers even join in by having a representative engage in conversation with the radio host. Casino Rama does this by featuring fictional reporter Jack Marshall conversing with on-air personalities about upcoming appearances by musical acts. Such a practice allows the casino to get new information about performances out quickly to the public.[9]

RADIO ADVERTISING—THE PRODUCTION PROCESS

In the case of a radio commercial, the finished product is a **mixed tape** that contains all of the spoken words, music, and special effects. For radio commercial production that involves a production house, the basic steps in the process are as follows:

1. Once the client has approved the script and the production costs, the commercial producer selects the studio and the casting director.
2. The casting director finds appropriate actors for slice-of-life commercials and the right voices for announcement-type commercials.
3. If music is required, the decision whether to hire a composer or use stock music is made. Decisions regarding the use of special effects are also finalized.
4. The director supervises rehearsals, and several commercial readings are made so that the agency and client have a selection to choose from.
5. Music and sound are recorded separately and mixed to form a *master tape*. From the master tape, *duplicates* or *dubs* are made. The dubs are sent to radio stations for broadcast.

The Internet

The **internet** is a network of computer networks linked together to act as one. It works just like a global mail system in which independent authorities collaborate in moving and delivering information. Companies that use the internet can set up a site on the World Wide Web to advertise their products and place ads on other sites that are linked to their website. Internet surfers simply have to stop at a website and browse the material.

The most common form of advertising on the internet is the banner ad. A **banner ad** stretches across the screen in a narrow band. Other options include rectangles (a larger box-style format), and skyscrapers (a vertical banner that appears on the sides of webpages). In terms of appearance and design, banner ads are often compared to outdoor posters (see Figure 6.17). The content of the ad is minimal. Its purpose is to stir interest so that the viewer clicks the ad for more information. Once clicked, the viewer sees the ad in its entirety, or

FIGURE
6.17

An illustration of two different sizes of internet ads

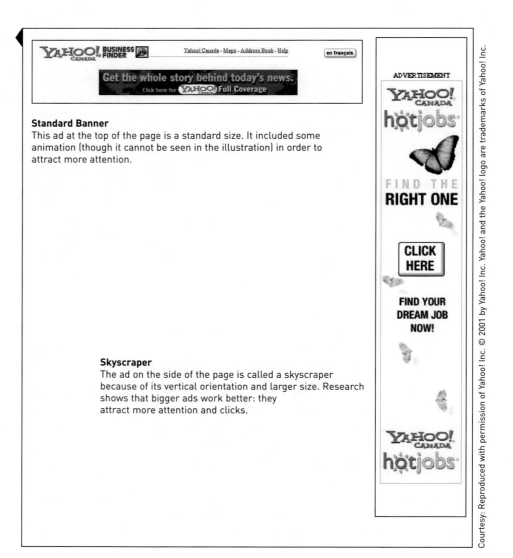

Standard Banner
This ad at the top of the page is a standard size. It included some animation (though it cannot be seen in the illustration) in order to attract more attention.

Skyscraper
The ad on the side of the page is called a skyscraper because of its vertical orientation and larger size. Research shows that bigger ads work better: they attract more attention and clicks.

secures additional information from the advertiser's website. The design characteristics of the banner ad are critical since the goal is to encourage clicking. While design elements on the internet are still in their infancy, certain basic design principles are still useful.

BANNER ADS

Banner ads are either static or animated. If static, the ad appears much like a small print ad or outdoor board. It must communicate just enough information so the viewer clicks on the ad. If the ad is animated, it includes some kind of motion that helps grab the viewer's attention. Higher attention scores produce better click rates. Internet users perceive the internet to be a different medium than traditional mass media. When online, people expect to be entertained and they want to receive information quickly. These behaviours suggest that advertising must also entertain. Here are some tips for improving response rates based on research conducted by DoubleClick and I/Pro:[10]

1. ***Choose words wisely*** Due to the limited amount of space, simplicity should be the rule of thumb. Simple phrases such as "Click here," "Visit now," and "Enter here" tend to improve response rates. A call to action is never out of place.
2. ***Provide an incentive*** Including a free offer boosts response rates 35 percent higher than ads without the word "free." If free is out of the question, offer a chance to win something in a contest, such as a car, trip, or T-shirt. This will drive more people to a site and into a marketing database.
3. ***Add an element of humour*** Ads that make a real point in a very humorous way are effective. Perhaps it is part of the "entertainment" criteria people have for the internet. Regardless, providing some fun along with information is more effective than simply providing information.
4. ***Be specific*** Because of the small space, conciseness and brevity are good guidelines. Be straightforward and don't make viewers guess your message. The goal should be good strong copy, a clear call to action, and an emphasis on impact over design. Why be cute and clever when all you want are results?
5. ***Use colour effectively*** Colour has an impact on all forms of advertising. Using bright colours can help attract a viewer's eye, contributing to higher response rates. Blue, green, and yellow work best, while white, red, and black are the least effective.
6. ***Consider animation*** Animation (movement) can help attract a user's eye. Strategic use of movement grabs attention more effectively than static banners. Animated banners generate more clicks than static banners.
7. ***Size is important*** Research has proven that bigger is better. The bigger the ad, the more intrusive, the more attention, the more "clickthrough." Therefore, the use of rectangles and skyscrapers is preferable, even though they may cost more. The creative decision on size must be weighed against the cost of placing the ad.

WEBSITES

Advertising on the internet is becoming an integral element of a firm's marketing communications strategy. Consumers like to visit websites for information and they do so frequently when collecting information about what products to buy. It is a research tool for comparing products. Consumers want a website to be easy to navigate, offer an enjoyable experience, and provide meaningful information. If the information and experience is not meaningful, it is unlikely they will return. A website has a significant impact on a company's or brand's image and reputation. Here are some tips to improve the design of a website.

1. ***Have a focused concept*** Many sites have floundered because they simply duplicated information that was available in a printed form. Content must be carefully

edited to suit the webpage format. Concise, well-organized, and easily read information offers much more to the viewer.

2. *Have a consistent look* A corporate identity is important. Therefore, keep a consistent look and feel throughout the site by using the logo, graphics, and colours of the company's corporate identity. For example, a viewer would expect to see red at the Coca-Cola website.

3. *Keep scrolling simple* Don't force a viewer to scroll across and down a page. A default screen is not that large, so the actual display may not be visible to a large number of viewers. Introduce the site with single screens of information, allowing content to increase in length as the viewer explores deeper.

4. *Clarity of graphics is essential* Don't use small fonts in graphics. Viewers may be visually impaired, so descriptions should always be available for graphics. A site should be tested with different fonts and font sizes.

5. *Plan for expansion* A site may start at a modest 20 pages, but could grow into hundreds of pages. Begin with an organizational system that allows for easy updates and logical growth.

Web design is a combination of design features and emotional experiences that have the greatest impact on whether a visitor will return to a site. Good content is the most important factor that leads to repeat visits.

More specific information on the strategic implications of interactive media and internet advertising is presented in Chapter 12.

SUMMARY

Numerous tools are employed to penetrate the customer's perceptual barriers. For example, the copywriter is responsible for the headline, body copy, and signature, and the art director is responsible for the illustration; the two join forces to create a complete message—an impression on the customer. In print advertising, the impression is affected by variables such as balance, unity, flow, use of colour and size, white space, clarity and simplicity, and use of artwork or photography in illustrations. Art directors also consider layout alternatives for delivering the message. Among the layouts commonly used are the poster, vertical split, horizontal split, multiple illustration, long copy, and insert layout.

Other print media have unique creative considerations. Out-of-home messages (outdoor posters, transit ads, and point-of-purchase ads) must be simple in design and use bold colours. In these media, strong visual imagery works to the advertiser's advantage. Point-of-purchase advertis-

ing must be brief, but also convincing enough to promote impulse purchasing. Transit ads have a more captive audience (often idle), and, therefore, their messages can be more detailed. In the case of direct-response advertising, the advertiser must grab the customer's attention quickly and use specific techniques that will hold their interest and encourage them to take the desired action.

For television commercials, the element of flow is the critical creative consideration. Variables such as integration of audio and video, the use of music and special effects, and pace of the commercial are also significant in that they, too, have an impact on the viewer. In commercial production there are four stages: obtaining cost estimates, pre-production, production, and post-production.

Radio commercials are also concerned with flow. Effective commercials tend to be positive and upbeat in tone, conversational in nature, and focused on one central idea. Radio ads that involve the listener's imagination have proven to be successful. The production process is very similar to that of television.

Online advertising presents unique challenges for creatives. The most common form of internet advertising is the banner ad. If banner ads are employed they must be clear and concise and include a call to action. Other techniques such as animation, providing incentives, and using appropriate colours have a positive impact on response rates. Website designs must be concise, have a consistent look, offer a simple scrolling procedure, and include fonts of an appropriate size that are easy to read.

KEY TERMS

animated commercials   183
answerprint   186
balance   168
banner ad   190
bleed (bleed page or bleed ad)   170
body copy   163
comprehensive   167
dialogue copy   164
direct-response print   179
direct-response television (DRTV)   186
fade   186
feature sheet   189
flow   168
format   183
horizontal split   173

infomercial   186
insert layout   173
interlock   186
internet   190
layout   166
live-action commercials   183
long copy   173
mixed interlock   186
mixed tape   189
multiple illustration   173
narrative copy   164
outdoor advertising   176
pace   183
personality announcement   189
point-of-purchase (POP) advertising   177

poster   173
residual   185
rough art   166
rough cut   186
script   181
signature (tagline)   165
storyboard   181
subheadline (subhead)   163
super   183
thumbnail sketches   166
unity   168, 172
vertical split   173
voice-over   185
white space   171
wipe   186

REVIEW QUESTIONS

1. Identify the basic elements of a typical print advertisement and describe the primary purpose of each.

2. Briefly describe the various types of headlines.

3. What are the stages in the design of a print layout? Briefly describe each stage.

4. What are the factors affecting the design and layout of print advertising? Briefly discuss the influence of each.

5. Distinguish between the following:

   a) balance versus unity (print advertising)
   b) vertical split versus horizontal split (print advertising)
   c) poster versus long copy (print advertising)
   d) unity versus pace (television advertising)
   e) live action versus animation (television advertising)
   f) rough cut versus interlock versus answerprint (television advertising)

6. What are the design characteristics of an effective outdoor ad?

7. What are the four I's of point-of-purchase advertising? Briefly explain each one.

8. In direct-mail advertising, what copy and design characteristics are critical to success?

9. What are the various sections of a television commercial? Explain the role of each section.

10. In television advertising what does "format" mean? Briefly explain.

11. Identify and briefly explain each stage in the television production process.

12. Identify and briefly explain some of the proven techniques for producing effective infomercials.

13. What are the different types of radio advertising?

14. Identify and briefly explain any two copy and design elements for creating better banner ads.

DISCUSSION QUESTIONS

1. Read the Advertising in Action vignette **Attention, Interest, Action!** in this chapter. Select a few of the advertisements included in the chapter and assess their potential effectiveness in light of the rules of thumb presented in the vignette.

2. Scan a magazine of your choosing and select an ad that you think is effective and one that is ineffective. Evaluate the impact of each ad based on some of the layout and design principles discussed in this chapter.

3. "Tell more, sell more." Discuss this statement in the context of print advertising.

4. Assess the role and effectiveness of the internet for advertising purposes. How important will the internet be in future advertising strategies? What is your opinion?

5. Visit a website of your choice. Analyze the site based on the design elements for websites included in this chapter.

NOTES

1. David Ogilvy, *Ogilvy on Advertising* (Toronto: John Wiley & Sons Ltd., 1983), p. 139.

2. "Design: Colour & Size," from *Marketing Tips*, December 15, 1997, p. 2, a *Marketing* publication.

3. Ibid.

4. *Laboratory of Advertising Performance*, Results reported by Jo Marney, "Sizing up ads: Bigger is better," *Marketing*, n.d.

5. Jo Marney, "Posters turn all heads," *Marketing*, September 8, 1996, p. 30.

6. James Careless, "Where's the price tag?" *Marketing*, January 31, 2000, p. 15.

7. Susan Heinrich, "Tuning up the pitch," *Financial Post*, July 30, 2001, p. PC4.

8. Ian French, "Building a brand in 30 minutes," *Marketing*, December 4, 1995, p. 13.

9. Samson Akaolow, "Radio ads go au naturel," *Strategy*, March 24, 2003, pp. 1, 8.

10. Jim Sterne, *What Makes People Click: Advertising on the Web* (Que Corporation: Indianapolis, IN, 1997), pp. 283–295.

THE practice OF ADVERTISING

An Illustration of Creative Development:

THE DEPRESSION CAMPAIGN FOR THE CENTRE FOR ADDICTION AND MENTAL HEALTH

People in the advertising industry willingly donate their time and expertise in support of worthwhile causes and charitable organizations. When a group of highly talented people join forces to work on a public service project they are committed to, they produce very good advertising.

David Sharpe, vice-president and creative director, and his agency Remtulla Euro RSCG became involved in a public-service project after reading a disturbing article about depression in *The Globe and Mail.* In the article, Michael Wilson (a former finance minister for Canada) was discussing depression and how it affects one's family. His son Cameron committed suicide in 1998 as a result of depression.

Sharpe immediately contacted Wilson (the campaign chair of Mental Health Week in October 2000) to offer his company's services. Soon thereafter, a committee of top marketing, advertising, public relations, and media professionals was working on the project on behalf of the Centre for Addiction and Mental Health. Sharpe was committed to making the public more aware of the illness since he had experienced depression first-hand in his own family.

What you will see develop here is a print and web campaign that made the public more aware and more understanding of depression and what can be done to help those who suffer from it. A creative brief is presented along with the creative director's thoughts as he was developing the strategy for the campaign. That is followed by the creative execution.

Creative Brief: Centre for Addiction and Mental Health Depression Awareness Campaign

BACKGROUND INFORMATION

- 3 million Canadians suffer from clinical depression
- Only one-third of sufferers seek help (there is a fear of being "labelled")
- 80 percent of suicides are by people suffering from depressive illness
- 10 to 20 percent of Canadians will experience one or more episodes in their lives
- 40 percent of cases are diagnosed in people under the age of 20
- Depression accounts for 30 percent of all disability insurance claims in Canada

PROBLEM AND OVERALL GOAL

Recently, four separate centres for alcohol and drug addiction in Toronto (The Clarke Institute for Psychiatry, The Donwood Institute, The Queen Street Mental Health Centre, and The Addiction Research Foundation) centralized operations and began offering help under one roof—the Centre for Addiction and Mental Health. The Centre had a logo but no real identity among the public.

Centre for Addiction and Mental Health   www.camh.net

The public knows little about depression. It is a silent disease with a prevailing stigma surrounding it. Many perceive it to be a simple coping deficiency that "weak" people have and that they will, and can, snap out of it. Or, they are just feeling "blue." Depression is a misunderstood illness.

The **overall goal** of the campaign was twofold:

- To create awareness about depression as a disease and to influence the public's attitudes about how to deal with people suffering from it.
- To make the public aware of the Centre for Addiction and Mental Health and the services it provides.

COMMUNICATIONS OBJECTIVES

- To remove the social stigma that surrounds depression and sell understanding of the disease.
- To encourage those who may have the disease to seek help via a toll-free telephone number and the website.
- To raise awareness of the new Centre for Addiction and Mental Health in the community.

CREATIVE OBJECTIVES

- To communicate that depression is an illness—like asthma or diabetes—and is a result of a chemical imbalance in the brain of sufferers, and that it can in most cases be controlled with modern medication and professional counselling.
- To communicate that people with depression can't help themselves. Those who have it or those who think they may have it need to know they are not to blame, that others suffer just like they do, and that there is compassionate help available to deal with it (a classic case of problem/solution).

CREATIVE STRATEGY

Dramatically portray the real suffering situations (at home, at work, etc.) that people with depression go through every day by using compelling, human, and empathetic headlines and images.

CREATIVE EXECUTION

Rather than talk specifically about the Centre for Addiction and Mental Health, the message will focus on the kinds of real help the Centre provides to the community—in an empathetic way.

Black-and-white ads of various sizes will be placed in the print media; similar images will be depicted on the website. Images will portray empathy and compassion.

Thoughts from the Creative Director on Developing the Ads

VP creative director David Sharpe describes his creative approach this way. "Great advertising is that split-second mental interplay that happens between reading the words in a headline then looking at the accompanying visual. They work in lockstep to create an 'idea' or 'the strategic thought' impressed in an instant on the reader's mind . . . because (hopefully) the idea touched to the core in a memorable human way.

"Since I had experienced the stigma of depression first-hand from family experience, I knew instinctively what my job was—to creatively sell understanding of what these people suffer from each day. I wanted a distinct, empathetic ad that touched the problem and the people with dignity. For example, I could have used a trendy computer font for the copy, but its cold, 'techy' edge would have worked against the dignity I was after. So I used a classic serif font with a simple and modern spin on the look of it.

"I wanted a somewhat stark, dramatic, editorial feel to the ad so I went for a 'real' or sort of 'eavesdropping' look to the people shots. Absent are the trendy computer manipulation effects that would have lessened the credibility of the Centre's 'soul' of serving real people struggling with real problems.

"The elements of the ad were laid out in a grid-like modular format that wouldn't box me in (as grids can sometimes do). This allowed me to fit heads and crop photos but still have a 'family feel.'

"Black-and-white ads were the preferred option (as opposed to colour) because ad space would be easier to secure, especially in smaller communities.

"You will notice that the prominent logo in the ad is not the client's logo but the word 'Depression' in a distinct black box situated in the same place on all ads along with a positive 'non-addy' positioning line that summarizes attitudinally the Centre's mission statement. This is a branding element that provides branding consistency.

"The only copy about the Centre itself is in a small line at the bottom. The intent was to focus on the Centre's heart rather than its head—to show what they actually do for people. And that's the best corporate advertising, when it's not the expected 'look-at-me, aren't we great' corporate fluff out there today that's totally invisible."

The Ads

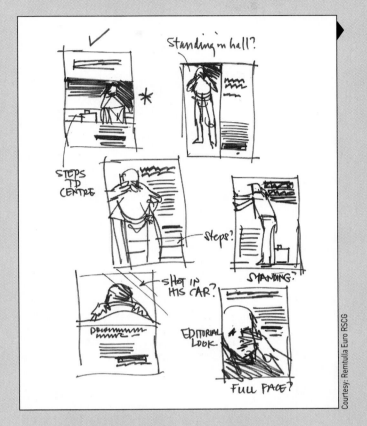

Step 1: Thumbnail Sketches

The creative team experiment with a variety of layouts to find the best location for the various elements of the ad: the headline, body copy, illustration, and signature.

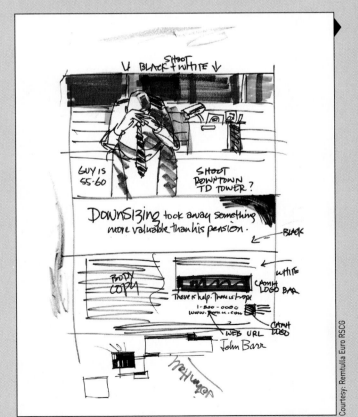

Step 2: Rough Artwork

The idea is roughed in linear form to give the client an impression of what the final ad will look like. When approved by the client, computer art is initiated.

Courtesy: Remtulla Euro RSCG

Step 3: Photography

Photography is shot according to the specifications of the final layout.

Downsizing took away something more valuable than his pension.

It can come on suddenly or creep into everyday life — dramatically changing the way someone feels — causing uncontrollable waves of sadness, anxiety, fatigue, utter hopelessness and even shame.

It used to be called 'feeling blue'.

Today it's called Depression — an illness like Asthma or Diabetes — caused by a chemical imbalance in the part of the brain that controls mood.

Unfortunately only about a third of people with Depression actually seek treatment because of the stigma of having a mental illness. Left undiagnosed and untreated it can cripple families, friends and relationships. In the workplace it's costing over 8 billion dollars a year in lost time and productivity — more than any other health problem. Over the next 20 years, it will become the leading cause of premature death and of workdays lost to disability.

But there *is* help.

Depression is an illness. With modern advances in medication and counselling, it can be treated — just like any illness. Find out what the common signs of Depression are and what help is available by talking to your doctor, calling our 1-800 number or visiting our web site.

(All calls and e-mails will be held completely confidential).   Toronto (416) 595-6111 / www.thereishelp.org

depression
There *is* help. There *is* hope.

Toll free 1-800-463-6273   Centre for Addiction and Mental Health
Centre de toxicomanie et de santé mentale

The Centre for Addiction and Mental Health is an amalgamation of the Addiction Research Foundation, the Clarke Institute of Psychiatry, the Donwood Institute and the Queen Street Mental Health Centre and is affiliated with the University of Toronto. To make a gift to support our work, please call (416) 979 6909. This is the first in a continuing series of vital public education messages about mental health and addiction.

Creative donated by Remtulla EURO RSCG Toronto.   This message is made possible through the generosity of this publication.

Courtesy: Remtulla Euro RSCG

Step 4: Comprehensive Artwork

All elements of the ad are placed in their exact position. Font style and font size for headlines, body copy, and signature are precise and the illustration (photograph) is cropped to fit the specifications of the layout.

This is the final copy for another ad used in this award-winning campaign.

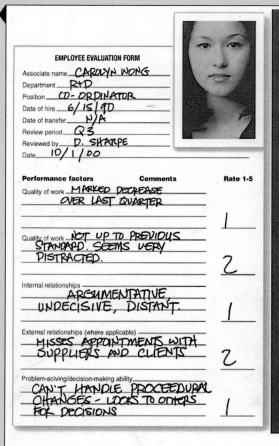

EMPLOYEE EVALUATION FORM

Associate name CAROLYN WONG
Department R+D
Position CO-ORDINATOR
Date of hire 6/15/90
Date of transfer N/A
Review period Q3
Reviewed by D. SHARPE
Date 10/1/00

Performance factors	Comments	Rate 1-5
Quality of work	MARKED DECREASE OVER LAST QUARTER	
Quality of work	NOT UP TO PREVIOUS STANDARD. SEEMS VERY DISTRACTED.	1
Internal relationships	ARGUMENTATIVE, UNDECISIVE, DISTANT.	2
External relationships (where applicable)	MISSES APPOINTMENTS WITH SUPPLIERS AND CLIENTS	1
Problem-solving/decision-making ability	CAN'T HANDLE PROCEEDURAL CHANGES - LOOKS TO OTHERS FOR DECISIONS	2
		1

Her mind isn't on her job. But maybe you're the one who's not paying attention.

It can come on suddenly or creep into everyday life – dramatically changing the way someone feels – causing uncontrollable waves of sadness, anxiety, fatigue, utter hopelessness and even shame.

It used to be called 'feeling blue'.

Today it's called Depression – an illness like Asthma or Diabetes – caused by a chemical imbalance in the part of the brain that controls mood.

Unfortunately only about a third of people with Depression actually seek treatment because of the stigma of having a mental illness. Left undiagnosed and untreated it can cripple families, friends and relationships. In the workplace it's costing over 8 billion dollars a year in lost time and productivity – more than any other health problem. Over the next 20 years, it will become the leading cause of premature death and of workdays lost to disability.

But there *is* help.

Depression is an illness. With modern advances in medication and counselling, it can be treated – just like any illness. Find out what the common signs of Depression are and what help is available by talking to your doctor, calling our 1-800 number or visiting our web site.

(All calls and e-mails will be held completely confidential).

depression
There *is* help. There *is* hope.

Toll free 1-800-463-6273
Toronto (416)595-6111 / www.thereishelp.org

The Centre for Addiction and Mental Health is an amalgamation of the Addiction Research Foundation, the Clarke Institute of Psychiatry, the Donwood Institute and the Queen Street Mental Health Centre and is affiliated with the University of Toronto. To make a gift to support our work, please call (416) 979 6909. This is the first in a continuing series of vital public education messages about mental health and addiction.

Creative donated by Remtulla EURO RSCG Toronto

This message is made possible through the generosity of this publication.

Courtesy: Remtulla Euro RSCG

The Media

All media space was donated. The depression campaign ran in magazines and national and community newspapers. A branded information kit was assembled for distribution via a toll-free telephone number or the website. The web work was coordinated with Infinet Communications, who added their technological expertise to maintain the look and feel of the print ads.

A public relations plan was developed and implemented by National PharmaCom. The public relations initiatives increased consumer access to trustworthy information about depression. Among the initiatives were a website that was "branded" like the print messages, a province-wide speakers' bureau, community education forums in partnership with *Chatelaine* (a large percentage of sufferers are women), and workplace education programs with the Canadian Economic Roundtable on Business and Mental Health.

Campaign Results

The volunteer effort produced excellent results:

- Over $750 000 donated in professional advertising services
- Over $250 000 in donated media space
- Community education forums in Toronto, Ottawa, and London reached more than 400 people including CEOs, senior executives, and health professionals
- More than 600 information kits distributed
- 25 000 web visits from 8 different countries
- 8 corporate enquiries (Steelcase Company of Canada is now working with the Centre to develop a year-long campaign to help employees)
- The campaign recently won a prestigious gold medal at the American Pharmaceutical Marketing Association's Marketing Awards.
- Remtulla Euro RSCG is currently developing the Centre's next campaign, on alcohol awareness. It will contain the same branding elements, empathetic attitude, distinctive typographic treatment, design, and positioning line.

All information and illustrations provided by Remtulla Euro RSCG.

Communicating the Message:

PLANNING MESSAGE PLACEMENT IN TRADITIONAL MEDIA CHOICES

Part Two established the relationships between marketing planning and marketing communications planning; Part Three described the creative planning process. Part Four describes the media planning process.

Media planning involves identifying media objectives, strategies, and execution. Decisions in each area depend largely on budgets. Chapter 7 discusses media objectives and media strategies along with budgetary issues. In Chapter 8, the print media are examined in detail, followed by broadcast media in Chapter 9.

Chapter 10 is devoted to out-of-home media. Planning and buying media time and space varies from one medium to another. Therefore, the unique considerations for the various media are presented in the appropriate chapters.

PART

4

Courtesy: Dick Hemingway

Media Planning Essentials

Learning Objectives

After studying this chapter, you will be able to

- Assess the roles and responsibilities of both client and agency in media planning
- Differentiate among media objectives, media strategies, and media execution
- Utilize terminology used in media planning
- Describe the steps involved in the media selection process
- Identify the factors affecting the size of an advertising budget
- Describe the methods of determining the size of an advertising budget

The process of developing a media plan is very complex. The task of an agency's media planners is to reach the desired target market efficiently. Although this objective may appear to be rather simple, the assignment is complicated by variables such as market information, media reach information, consumers' media habits, and so on. Efficiency in media planning can be loosely defined as "gaining maximum impact or exposure at minimum cost to the client." The agency must develop and execute a plan that meets stated expectations within certain financial parameters.

Essentially, input from the client to the agency becomes the foundation of the media plan. The direction a media plan takes is largely based on the guidelines provided by the client's marketing plan. It is important to realize that the media plan is a subset of a broader marketing communications plan. Therefore, media strategies must be coordinated with other communications and marketing activities.

Media Planning Process

Media carry a brand's selling message to a predetermined target market. The selling success of any advertising campaign, therefore, depends on the effectiveness of the media plan. **Media planning** involves developing a plan of action for communicating messages to the right people (the target market), at the right time, and with the right frequency.

Similar to the creative plan, the media plan must flow from the marketing and marketing communications plan. Both client and ad agency play a role in the media planning process. The client provides the agency's media personnel with background information, along with broadstroke direction for developing the media plan.

Information typically provided to the agency is carefully outlined in a document called a **media brief**. The media brief includes some or all of the following information: a market profile, product media profile, competitor media profile, target-market profile, media objectives, and media budget. Figure 7.1 illustrates a schematic diagram of the media planning process.

FIGURE
7.1
PLANNING MODEL EXHIBIT
Media planning process

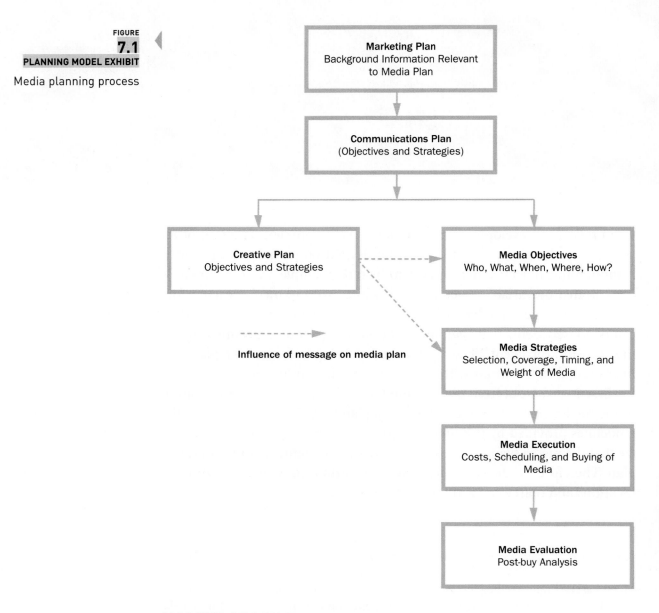

MARKET PROFILE

The market profile reviews the market size and growth trends. It also includes current and historical market-share trends, which give the media planner a perspective on what is happening in the market and the level of competition within it.

PRODUCT MEDIA PROFILE

Prior to developing a new media plan it is wise to review and evaluate past media practices. What media have been used and how effective have they been? A qualitative and quantitative evaluation of the strengths and weaknesses of past media plans provides input for new plans. If little else, such a review should produce strong feelings about what worked and what did not. This information is particularly important if the client is briefing a new ad agency.

COMPETITORS' MEDIA USAGE

A summary analysis of competitors' media usage and spending trends influences the strategic media direction chosen for the product. For example, what media do the competitors dominate? How much do they spend? Where do they spend it? How does competitive information influence the media direction an advertiser should take?

TARGET-MARKET PROFILE

The marketing plan provides the media planner with a precise definition of the target market. All relevant demographic, psychographic, and geographic information available influences media strategy and execution. Knowing the activities and interests of the target market can enable media planners to choose the best times and places in which to advertise. If information about the target's media consumption is known, it too should be communicated to the agency. For example, the medium the target refers to most, how frequently they refer to it, and how long they refer to it is valuable information. The media tendencies of the target market influence the overall direction of the media strategy.

MEDIA OBJECTIVES

A broadstroke definition of what the media plan will accomplish is the client's responsibility. Information regarding who, what, when, where, and how should be provided to the agency. The intent is not to restrict the agency in its thinking; on the contrary, the detailed consideration of these elements will be the responsibility of the agency media planners. Media objectives set priorities and establish guidelines for agency media planners. Media objectives are discussed in detail later in the chapter.

MEDIA BUDGET

Usually, the amount allocated to the media budget has already been established. At an earlier stage (the marketing communications plan), the budget is allocated among activities such as media advertising, sales promotion, and events and sponsorships. The relative size of the budget provides the framework within which media planners must develop strategies and achieve stated goals.

Once the briefing process is completed, the agency media personnel take over. **Media planners** are specialists who put together the detailed media strategies and tactics. They assess all of the input from the client and devise a media strategy and execution plan that will achieve the stated objectives. Media strategy is discussed in detail later in the chapter.

Once the media plan has been approved, **media buyers** purchase the time and space. They interpret the media plan and purchase the best deals available through the various media representatives for the different media vehicles. A media buyer's task is to deliver the maximum amount of impact (against a target audience) at a minimum of cost (client's budget). The sophistication of computers has enhanced the ability of both media planners and buyers to generate more efficient media plans. Once the media plan has been implemented, the agency is responsible for evaluating the plan through a post-buy analysis. A **post-buy analysis** is an analysis of actual audience deliveries calculated after a specific spot or schedule of advertising has run.

The Media Plan

A **media plan** is a document that outlines all relevant details about how a client's budget will be spent: objectives are clearly identified, strategies are carefully rationalized, and execution details are documented with precision.

Media Budget

- Total Budget Available for Media Advertising

Media Objectives

- Who (target market profile)
- What (nature of message)
- When (best time to reach)
- Where (market priorities)
- How (how many, how often, how long)

Note: Media objectives are usually clear, definitive statements

Media Strategy

- Target Market Strategy (Shotgun, Profile Match, Rifle)
- Reach Considerations
- Frequency Considerations
- Continuity Considerations
- Coverage Alternatives
- Timing
- Media Selection Rationale
- Media Rejection Rationale

Note: Media strategies usually expand upon the objective statements by providing details about how objectives will be accomplished.

Media Execution

- Media Cost Summaries
  a. Spending by Media Classification
  b. Spending within Media Classification
  c. Spending by Time of Year
  d. Spending by Region or City
- Blocking Chart
  a. Calendar of Activities
  b. Media Used
  c. Market Coverage
  d. GRPs
  e. Timing

Note: For an applied illustration of these concepts, see the marketing communications plan Schick Quattro in Appendix II.

Since a significant amount of the client's budget is at stake in an advertising campaign, communications between client and agency peak when media plans are presented. Media planners must present and defend their recommendations and be prepared to consider client input. Media plans have been known to undergo numerous revisions prior to final client approval. The structure and content of a media plan is discussed in this section. Refer to Figure 7.2 for a summary of the content.

Media Objectives

Media objectives are clearly worded statements that outline what the media plan should accomplish. Within this framework, media objectives can be subdivided and more precisely defined statements can be developed in response to the questions concerning who, what, where, when, and how. Although answers to some of the above questions are often judged to be strategic elements of the media plan, they are intended to provide broad guidelines for more detailed strategic considerations (refer to Figure 7.3).

The components of media objective statements are as follows:

- **Who?** Who is the target market? A precise definition of the target market, derived from the marketing plan or marketing communications plan, provides the foundation for the media plan. A *target-market profile* defined in terms of demographics, psychographics, and geographics is collected, and media planners use it to match the target with a compatible media profile (those who read, listen to, or watch a certain medium).

- **What?** What is the message to be communicated? A brief summary of the selling message should be included in the objective statement. Note that the creative strategy may already be complete. The message, and the manner in which it is presented, can have an influence on media selection. Conversely, if media decisions are made first, such decisions could influence the direction of creative strategy and execution. Clients do things differently.

- **Where?** Where are the market priorities? This question is critical, as most advertising campaigns are restricted by the size of the budget. Based on directives from the client regarding which regions or cities have priority, and the media planner's ability to work efficiently with little money, decisions must be made whether to reach a few markets more frequently or to reach more markets less frequently. The issue is how far or how many markets will be reached with the budget that is available.

- **When?** When is the best time to reach the target market? Certain product and target-market characteristics have bearing on this question. For example, the fact that a product is sold on a seasonal basis will directly influence media timing. A heavier media schedule in the pre-usage season may be recommended as a way of building awareness prior to the purchase period of the seasonal product. Knowledge of the customer can also influence the timing of advertising messages. For example, is there a best time of the day, or better days of the week, to reach the target? Information about target audience media consumption is useful when making decisions on when to advertise.

- **How?** How many? How often? How long? Several questions must be answered here. These questions are strategic considerations regarding reach, frequency, and continuity. Objective statements on these issues stem from more detailed media strategies. Strategy considerations will be discussed separately in this chapter.

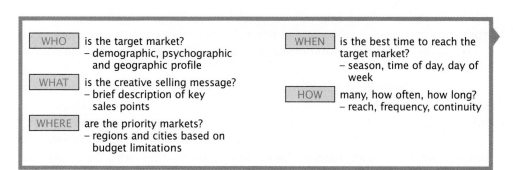

WHO	is the target market? – demographic, psychographic and geographic profile
WHAT	is the creative selling message? – brief description of key sales points
WHERE	are the priority markets? – regions and cities based on budget limitations
WHEN	is the best time to reach the target market? – season, time of day, day of week
HOW	many, how often, how long? – reach, frequency, continuity

FIGURE
7.3

Questions from which media objectives are derived

Media Strategy

Similar to other types of planning, media planning deals with the best way to advertise the product or service within the budget guidelines provided. **Media strategy** focuses on how media objectives will be achieved—it results in a recommendation of what media to use, along with supporting rationale detailing why certain media were selected and others rejected. Consideration is given to a host of factors and decisions must be made on each: which media to use, how often to advertise, for what length of time, what markets to cover. The various factors that influence media strategy are discussed below.

TARGET MARKET

A well-defined customer profile must be provided to media planners. The more precise the target-market definition is, the greater the likelihood that the planners will make a more effective and efficient media recommendation. For products and services whose target markets are more loosely defined (markets that include both sexes, a wider age range, no specific income requirements), the task of selecting the most effective and efficient media is less challenging.

Essentially, the task of the media planner is to match the advertised product's target-market profile with a compatible media profile, such as the readership profile of a magazine or newspaper or the listener profile of a radio station. Theoretically, the more compatible the match, the more efficient the media buy. Depending on the media planner's knowledge about the target market (its characteristics, attitudes, interests, location, and so on), certain matching strategies can be considered.

SHOTGUN STRATEGY The nature of the word "shotgun" suggests that the target market for which the **shotgun strategy** is best suited is more general than other target markets. For example, the target may be described as all adults 18 years and older. The product or service being advertised has widespread appeal. For target markets that are more loosely defined, particularly in terms of demographics, the media selected to advertise the product can be more general in nature.

Members of the audience watching a popular situation comedy during prime time (7:00 p.m. to 11:00 p.m.) will range in age, encompass both sexes, cover the entire range of income groups, and lead all kinds of lifestyles. For advertisers with sizeable media budgets, television is an effective means of reaching a broad target market. The cost of a spot on a popular show like *Survivor* costs about $80 000 tops in Canada, followed by *ER* and *CSI* at about $65 000 apiece. On *Hockey Night in Canada*, the CBC's most popular property, a spot costs about $25 000.[1] While cable channels have fragmented the market and audience reach is now lower on conventional channels and programs, these types of programs still reach a mass audience. For advertisers with more limited media budgets, daily newspapers, transit media, and outdoor media can provide good reach at a lower cost.

Very often advertisers implement a shotgun strategy for launching new products or when advertising for very special occasions. If so, they go for high reach and frequency in order to create awareness. In some cases, a strategy called roadblocking is employed.

Roadblocking involves buying commercial time on all available stations at a fixed time (or approximately the same time) so that viewers can barely avoid seeing the commercial. A roadblock is one of the few ways to reach a mass audience in an increasingly fragmented media landscape and it is ideally suited for an advertiser that has something special to say. When Bell Canada launched its new branding campaign using the theme "Making it simple®" a few years ago, it aired a special two-minute commercial simultaneously on four networks in Ontario. TD Canada Trust also used a roadblock strategy to unveil its first major branding strategy since the merger of the TD Bank and Canada Trust.[2]

PROFILE-MATCHING STRATEGY In the case of a **profile-matching strategy**, the customer target market is carefully defined by demographic, psychographic, and geographic variables. When using this strategy, the advertising message is placed in media whose readers, listeners, or viewers have a similar profile to that of the product's target market. All media do not offer complete compatibility.

Certain media types are characterized as general interest, while others are seen as special interest. Magazines such as *Canadian Living*, *Canadian Business*, and *Canadian Geographic* appeal to a more selective target market, and may be suitable for a profile-matching strategy. *Canadian Living*, for example, appeals to female readers between the ages of 25 and 54 who are college or university educated, have a household income between $50 000 and $75 000, and reside in markets of 100 000 plus population. If that is the brand's target-audience profile, then *Canadian Living* is a wise selection.[3]

Canadian Living
www.canadianliving.com

The same could be said of television programs that appeal specifically to children (e.g., the YTV specialty network offers programs for children and young teens), or sports programs that appeal to a predominantly male audience. Radio is another medium suited to a profile-matching strategy. A radio station's format (e.g., rock, soft rock, news, top 40, and so on) is designed to appeal to a particular demographic group. Advertisers wanting to reach a certain demographic group will select the appropriate stations in a local market.

Examine the profile presented in Figure 7.4. *Canadian Business* reaches over 1 million readers, $2/3$ of them male and $1/3$ of them female, with each issue. These readers possess high household incomes and by occupation they are classified as MOPES—managers, owners, professionals, and entrepreneurs. These readers are four times more likely than average to make business purchase decisions valued at $100 000 plus. The readership profile suggests that advertisers who appeal to a target that is more affluent and upscale should consider *Canadian Business* as an appropriate advertising medium. *Canadian Business* competes for advertisers with *National Post Business* and *ROB Magazine*, a publication of *The Globe and Mail*.

Canadian Business
www.canadianbusiness.com

RIFLE STRATEGY A **rifle strategy** is a matching strategy used in situations where the target market can be precisely defined by some common characteristic, such as employment in a certain industry, having a certain occupation, or having a particular leisure-time interest or hobby. It is the common characteristic that makes this audience a target. In many situations, a specific medium can reach this target market.

An interest in recreational downhill skiing or snowboarding, for example, could be the common characteristic of a group. The demographic profile of such a group could be diverse, but the fact that all members of the group ski or snowboard is important to equipment manufacturers. A specific medium can be used to reach each target group. *Ski Canada* or *Le Ski* would be an appropriate medium to select for a rifle strategy to reach skiers and *Snowboard Canada* could be used to reach snowboarders. Should the interest or activity in common be fashion, a publication such as *Elle Canada* or *Elle Quebec* would be a good choice. *Elle* is a magazine that covers trends in fashion, beauty, and lifestyle. Its editorial content is much more focused than a magazine like *Chatelaine* or *Canadian Living*. Enthusiasts look to these kinds of publications for information about products that are advertised there.

FIGURE
7.4

Readership profile
of *Canadian Business*
magazine

Canadian Business readers are passionate—about their businesses, their careers, and their lives. They're driven, motivated people who are highly receptive to products and services that help them reach their goals quickly.

Each issue reaches:

- Over 1 million readers
- Canadians who are four times more likely than average to make business purchase decisions valued at $100 000+
- A subscriber base that includes 4200 executive members of Canadian Manufacturers & Exporters, a group responsible for $500 billion in annual sales, 80 percent of Canada's manufacturing production, and 90 percent of its merchandising exports.

Total readers: 1 021 000
Male readers: 696 000
Female readers: 325 000

	Audience	Index
DEMOGRAPHICS		
Household income $75 000+	338 000	150
Household income $100 000+	197 000	190
Senior managers/owners	57 000	239
Professionals	84 000	185
Managers/owners/professionals	315 000	184
BUSINESS PURCHASING INVOLVEMENT		
Make business purchase decisions	283 000	196
Value of purchase decisions: $50 000	87 000	255
: $100 000	59 000	288
FINANCIAL		
Value of savings/securities $100 000+	95 000	169
Own RRSPs	533 000	146
Own mutual funds	479 000	156
Own stocks or bonds	244 000	175
Automotive		
Purchased new vehicle last 12 months	243 000	128
Spent more than $30 000 on recent purchase	154 000	181
TECHNOLOGY		
Use computer/telephone banking	403 000	136
Use computer at home and work	773 000	132
Have cellular/PCS phone	493 000	128
TRAVEL		
Stayed in luxury hotel in last 12 months	104 000	161
One or more business trips in last 12 months	288 000	214
Travelled outside Canada last 12 months	269 000	138

Source: Reprinted by permission of *Canadian Business*.

A summary of the various target-market-matching strategies appears in Figure 7.5.

NATURE OF ADVERTISING MESSAGE

Creative strategy and media strategy should be developed simultaneously for a coordinated effect in the marketplace. However, the nature of the message, determined by the advertiser's needs, often influences the media selection process. If factual details such as technical data and performance ratings must be communicated, print media is a practical option along with a website on the internet. If an emotional connection between product and target is the objective, then broadcast advertising through television and radio are preferred choices. If a promotion, such as a contest, is part of the advertising campaign, a combination of media could be recommended as the means of achieving a variety of objectives (e.g., television to create awareness and print and point-of-purchase material to communicate details on how to enter). If the objective is brand-name awareness among a general cross-section of a population then outdoor advertising and transit media are good alternatives.

REACH/FREQUENCY/CONTINUITY/FLEXIBILITY

These strategic factors are grouped together because of their interaction in the media planning process.

<figure>

FIGURE
7.5

Key aspects of target-market-matching strategies

```
┌─────────────────────────────────────────────┐
│              Shotgun Strategy                │
└─────────────────────────────────────────────┘
```

Target market covers a wide cross-section of the population; therefore, media options that have a diverse reach are appropriate (e.g., conventional television networks, daily newspapers, outdoor advertising, and transit advertising).

```
        ┌─────────────────────────────────────┐
        │       Profile-Matching Strategy     │
        └─────────────────────────────────────┘
```

Target market is described by certain demographic, psychographic, geographic variables. Media options with audience profiles that are a close match are selected (e.g., magazines, radio, business newspapers and journals, and special interest television networks).

```
            ┌───────────────────────────┐
            │      Rifle Strategy       │
            └───────────────────────────┘
```

Target market precisely defined by a special characteristic such as a hobby, sport, or occupation. Media options that specifically reach the target are selected (e.g., special-interest consumer and business magazines, special-interest cable channels, direct mail, online and interactive communications).

</figure>

REACH **Reach** is the total, unduplicated audience (individuals or households) potentially exposed one or more times to an advertiser's schedule of messages during a given period (perhaps a week). It is expressed as a percentage of the target population in a geographically defined area (e.g., a television station might reach 30 percent of a metropolitan market). To explain the principle of reach, assume that a message on a particular station was seen by 40 000 households, in a geographic area of 100 000 households. Reach is calculated by the formula

$$\text{Reach} = \frac{\text{Number of households tuned in}}{\text{Number of households in area}}$$

To complete the example,

$$\text{Reach} = \frac{40\ 000\ (\text{tuned in})}{100\ 000\ (\text{in area})}$$

$$= 40\%$$

The dynamics of reach apply to all media forms. The only variation is the time frame for which reach is expressed. It may be weekly on television and radio and monthly in magazines and out-of-home media (outdoor and transit).

FREQUENCY **Frequency** is the average number of times an advertising message has been exposed to a target audience (an individual or a household) over a period of time, usually a week. Reach and frequency variables are considered together in media planning. The media planner must delicately balance reach and frequency objectives within budget guidelines.

In any given market, households receive different numbers of exposures due to their different viewing habits. As a result, media planners think of frequency in terms of **average frequency**. The terms *frequency* and *average frequency* mean the same thing. Frequency is calculated by dividing the total possible audience by the audience that has been exposed to the message at least once (reach).

Therefore, average frequency is based on the formula

$$\text{Average frequency} = \frac{\text{Total exposures of all households}}{\text{Reach (households)}}$$

To illustrate this formula, let us assume that the total exposure of all households is 180 000, and the total number of households reached in one week is 50 000. The average frequency is as follows:

$$\frac{180\ 000}{50\ 000} = 3.6$$

A common dilemma faced by the media planner is whether to recommend more reach at the expense of frequency, or more frequency with less overall reach. The stage of the product life cycle a brand is in plus the size of the media budget often dictates which variable gets more attention. For example, a new product that has a high awareness objective may place greater emphasis on reach (and frequency if there is enough budget). A mature product that is trying to defend its position may opt for more frequency directed at a defined target audience.

IMPRESSIONS **Impressions**, or **total exposures**, refers to the total number of commercial occasions or advertisements scheduled, multiplied by the total target audience (households or people) potentially exposed to each occasion. A media plan's impressions are usually referred to as *gross impressions*. You calculate it by multiplying the actual number of people who receive a message (reach) by the number of times they receive it (frequency). To illustrate the concept of impressions, let's assume that a message on a television station reached 100 000 people, and that the message was broadcast three times a week for eight weeks. The calculation for the number of impressions would be

$$\text{Impressions} = \text{Reach} \times \text{Frequency}$$
$$= 100\ 000 \times 3$$
$$= 300\ 000$$

Therefore, over the eight-week schedule, the gross impressions or exposures would be 2 400 000 (300 000 × 8).

GROSS RATING POINTS The weight (amount) of advertising in a market is determined by a rating system. Media weight is expressed in terms of gross rating points. **Gross rating points (GRPs)** are an aggregate of total ratings in a schedule, usually in a weekly period, against a predetermined target audience. It is a description of audience delivery without regard to duplication or repeat exposure to the media vehicles, thus the word *gross*. Reach multiplied by frequency results in GRPs.

To explain the principle of GRPs, let us assume that an advertiser buys media time in Toronto at weight level of 200 GRPs. When calculating GRPs, a percentage figure for reach is used. The desired GRP level is achieved by manipulating both variables: reach and frequency. Therefore, if reach is 20 percent, the frequency would have to be 10 to achieve the 200 GRPs (10 × 20). If reach is 25 percent, the frequency would be 8 to achieve 200 GRPs (25 × 8).

To further illustrate this concept (GRPs = Reach × Frequency), let us assume that a message reaches 50 percent of the target households three times in one week. The GRP level would be 150 (50 × 3). If the message reaches 40 percent of the target households with an average frequency of 4.6 per week, the GRP level would be 184 (40 × 4.6).

The reach of a television program is also referred to as a rating. If, for example, *CSI* reaches 30 percent of households with televisions in its weekly time slot, the show has a 30 rating. Therefore, another way calculating GRPs is to multiply a show's rating by the frequency of messages on that show. Here is an illustration:

Audience	Rating	Number of Spots	GRPs
18–49 years	30	2	60
18–49 years	25	3	75
18–49 years	20	2	40
Total		**7**	**175**

In this example, the advertiser scheduled seven spots over the period of a week on shows with various ratings. This resulted in a weight level of 175 GRPs for the week. Typically, an advertiser will vary the weight levels over the duration of the schedule and by geographic market. Markets that are given priority, for whatever marketing reason, will receive higher GRPs than less important markets.

Decisions about reach and frequency are difficult. Traditional wisdom suggests frequency is the more important variable—you have to drive the message home before consumers will take action! But what is the reaction of consumers if they are exposed to the same message too many times? Will it hurt or help the brand? Some media traditionalists believe three ads get awareness, six ads get interest, and nine ads lead to possible action. At 12 ads the consumer is tuning out the message. Further, it is more efficient to add a new medium rather than adding weight to an existing medium if the goal is to maximize effective reach. Watching a brand splurge on repetitive television commercials is almost like watching an impending train wreck.[4]

Traditional buying models are based on the goal of eliciting the three *A*'s: *awareness*, *attitude*, and *action*. But there is a threshold at which an advertiser starts to turn the consumer off.[5] Therefore, many advertisers are buying into a relatively new concept called "recency." **Recency** is a model that suggests advertising works best by reminding consumers of a product when they are ready to buy.[6] With recency the key issue is the *timing* of the advertising; with traditional models the key issue is the *weight* of the advertising. For more insight into the concept of recency, refer to the Advertising in Action vignette **Shattering the Paradigm: How Does Advertising Work?**

CONTINUITY **Continuity** is the length of time required to ensure that a particular medium affects a target market. A single theme or selling proposition is delivered over that time period. For example, will the schedule be four weeks long, six weeks long, or eight weeks long? Media planners must juggle the reach, frequency, and continuity factors to obtain maximum benefit for the dollars invested in media. Quite often the continuity is the first of these variables to "give way" when budget (that is, lack of budget) becomes a key factor.

Only an exceptional advertiser would purchase media time on an annual basis (52-week schedule). More moderate advertisers tend to stretch dollars over a one-year period by purchasing media time in "flights." **Flighting** refers to the purchase of media time in periodic waves separated by periods of inactivity, a tactic that stretches media dollars over an extended period of time. A **hiatus** is an inactive period between flights. To understand the application of continuity and flighting, refer to Figure 7.6.

FLEXIBILITY **Flexibility** is the ability to modify media spending plans throughout the period that advertising is scheduled. Flexibility is not a variable that influences the media selection process. It is, however, important from the client's viewpoint, since rapidly changing conditions in the marketplace or within the company may require that media tactics be changed on short notice.

The flexibility of the chosen media—that is, whether the media will allow cancellation by a client who is in a profit-squeeze situation—must be known prior to media purchase. The various media stipulate lead times required for notification of cancellation. For

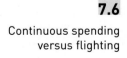

FIGURE 7.6

Continuous spending versus flighting

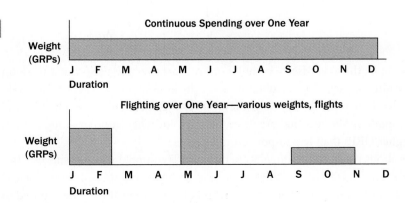

Shattering the Paradigm: How Does Advertising Work?

The traditional thinking is that advertising does not begin working until perhaps the third exposure. This approach is based on learning theory, from experiments showing that the ability to remember a random sequence of numbers is dependent on the number of exposures the subject has had to the sequence. One model that describes the sequence of how advertising works is called "AIDA," namely *awareness*, *interest*, *desire*, *action*. Another is called the "funnel" model, with the sequence being *awareness*, *knowledge*, *attitudes*, and then *behaviour*.

But there is a growing body of evidence suggesting that advertising can first influence behaviour and attitude changes follow, not the other way around. The traditional view of how advertising works is that media planning assumes there is no value to the initial two exposures. The emphasis is to ensure a certain minimum of frequency, namely three or more, within a given time frame.

Research conducted by John Philip Jones of Syracuse University (U.S.) and Colin McDonald of McDonald Research (U.K.) indicates the initial exposure is more powerful at influencing behaviour than subsequent ones. If so, the implications to strategic media planning are profound, with the emphasis shifting to reach, while minimizing excessive frequency.

This new approach has come to be known as "recency," with media consultant Erwin Ephron (U.S.) being one of its most articulate proponents. Advertising is less about learning than reinforcement, which calls for different tactics. Ephron suggests that advertising bursts with long hiatuses are not as effective as continuous weights covering more weeks. Another key aspect of implementation, he suggests, is to disperse messages widely.

Lowell Lunden of LLunden & Associates Limited (Canada), Strategic Media Explorers, defines recency as "the discipline of delivering media messages in a way that maximizes the likelihood of reaching the most people with the message at a time close to when a purchase decision will be made." Recency might be described as "Just-In-Time Communications™." Success is based on the finding that if recency is properly executed with creative that works, a single impression can influence behaviour if it is delivered at the right time.

Lunden has done in-field Test vs. Control experiments in Canada, demonstrating the success of different ways to implement recency. He consults primarily with advertisers and their ad agencies to foster an understanding of recency media planning and its implications.

While the goal of advertising should be to build a brand's power in the long term, Lunden believes it is irresponsible for advertisers to accept a continued lack of measured success in the short term and to simply continue spending behind the same creative. Powerful creative tends to be memorable, linked to the brand, relevant, fresh/current/unpredictable, and likeable. The problem is that too often advertising does not work. "Half of my advertising is wasted," it is said, "I just don't know which half." But there is more truth to this than people realize.

Misinterpretations of how recency can be effectively implemented are common. The biggest risk is spreading advertising too thinly, running more duration but below some threshold level. Another risk that advertisers must minimize is wearout of creative. Executing recency can help minimize commercial wearout, which is a bigger problem than people realize. The challenge is to cost-effectively produce different executions of creative, including multimedia, to help maintain high attention levels.

When implemented and measured properly, recency can help in building more powerful advertising. But the success of any advertising effort is dependent on having creative that works, and on media executed with individual brand objectives and the competitive environment in mind. Currently, Canadian advertisers lag behind U.S. and U.K. advertisers in implementing recency.

Source: This vignette was prepared by Lowell Lunden, President & Chief Learning Officer, LLunden & Associates Limited, Strategic Media Explorers, **www.recency.ca** or **www.jitcommunications.com**.

example, local television stations allow cancellations on four weeks' written notice. However, the booking must run a minimum of four consecutive weeks. A media plan is, after all, exactly that: a "plan." During the year, reality sets in; that is, profit objectives of a short-term nature begin to look better than advertising objectives of a long-term nature.

Conversely, an advertiser may decide to purchase additional media. Competitive activity might dictate heavier-than-planned spending in a certain market. Often media time is sold well in advance of either air date or publication date, but the advertiser should be aware of the options that are available on short notice. Assuming that the creative material is readily available, newspapers and radio offer short-notice purchase flexibility.

For a summary of issues relating to reach, frequency, and continuity, refer to Figure 7.7.

MARKET COVERAGE

Market coverage or **coverage** refers to the identity and number of markets in which advertising occurs over the course of the media plan's execution. Several coverage options are available to the advertiser. Market selection is often based on factors such as the level of distribution in a market (i.e., the availability of the product or service) and the importance of an area in terms of the sales volume generated there. An additional factor affecting market choice comes into play when an advertiser decides either to correct a problem or to pursue an opportunity through advertising. In either situation, the result is a disproportionate increase in media spending in the area of concern. Assuming there is an overall ceiling on spending, such a move involves a decrease of advertising in another region. Several market coverage plans are available to an advertiser.

NATIONAL COVERAGE National coverage requires media coverage wherever the product is available. Assuming that a product is widely distributed, the advertiser can select

FIGURE 7.7

Some key issues related to reach, frequency, and continuity

Reach	The total audience exposed one or more times to an advertising schedule of messages in a given period
Frequency	The average number of times a message has been exposed to a target audience over a period of time, usually a week
Continuity	The length of time required to ensure a particular medium affects a target market

Are these strategic variables equally important or does one take precedence over the others? A media plan that emphasizes all three variables will be very costly and is beyond the scope of the average brand. Therefore, media planners must determine which element is to be given priority.

The most difficult decision for a media planner is frequency. How many times

does the planner schedule the message to elicit action without overexposing the audience to the message? Too much exposure can turn off the audience the advertiser is reaching, a self-defeating principle.

Decisions about these variables are dictated by the size of the budget and the nature of the problem that advertising has to resolve.

media that have national scope. Network television and national magazines are obvious choices. If urgency is a criterion in the decision-making process (as it usually is when launching a new product or reacting to a competitive activity), newspapers in major metropolitan areas, which provide national coverage, are excellent vehicles to use.

REGIONAL COVERAGE   If an advertiser chooses to advertise regionally and allocate media dollars accordingly, some equitable system of allocation must be developed so that all regions benefit from advertising. All regions do not require the same level of advertising weight; competitive advertising and promotion factors vary among regions, and this variance affects regional allocations and causes either upward or downward adjustments.

Assuming that Canada is divided geographically into five regions and that the regional volume importance (the contribution to total volume) as shown below is accurate, an advertiser would allocate $1 million in media dollars according to the chart below.

This example considers only the level of brand development in each region. Additional considerations could be factored into the regional equations so that a more accurate allocation could be calculated. For example, one could compare the total volume of the product category in each region to regional brand development to identify areas where potential increases and decreases in spending could be productive. For example, if a brand was underperforming in a region that was growing in importance, more advertising weight could be allocated to that region. When funds are being allocated and media are being purchased on a regional basis, media such as regional television networks, selective spot television, radio, regional editions of magazines, and newspapers are attractive alternatives.

Geographic Regions	Regional Volume Importance (%)	Media Budget ($)
Atlantic	8	80 000
Quebec	28	280 000
Ontario	40	400 000
Prairies	12	120 000
British Columbia	12	120 000
Canada	100	1 000 000

KEY MARKET PLAN   A **key market plan** is a media plan according to which time and space are purchased in urban markets that have been identified as priorities. Providing coverage only in key markets is often considered an option when budget constraints do not allow for much flexibility. In this situation, the advertiser uses a predetermined system to prioritize markets. Key markets could be identified nationally or regionally— according to population, for example.

To illustrate, let us assume that a product had reasonably good national distribution, but only enough funds to advertise in a selective list of markets. The media objective would therefore be to achieve adequate levels of reach and frequency in all cities of over 500 000 inhabitants. The media planner would consider the reach, frequency, and continuity factors for each market, and allocate the budget equitably to the cities in question. What cities would this plan cover? The following illustration indicates that media spending would be distributed among nine cities, which comprise 50.5 percent of the Canadian population.

While this system appears equitable, at least in the example, some cities and areas may never receive advertising support. Such decisions often create conflict between marketing/advertising managers and regional sales managers, who argue that they are short-changed in the media allocation process. The illustration, for example, does not include any city in the Atlantic region. The advertiser would have to drop the population requirement to just below 400 000 to accommodate Halifax. Even then, the markets of London, Kitchener-Waterloo, and St. Catharines-Niagara are ahead of Halifax.

Markets	Population (000)	Canadian Total (%)
Toronto	5 040	15.9
Montreal	3 603	11.4
Vancouver	2 156	6.8
Ottawa-Hull	1 127	3.5
Calgary	1 105	3.2
Edmonton	977	3.1
Quebec City	707	2.2
Winnipeg	694	2.2
Hamilton	692	2.2
Total	16 011	50.5

Source: Canadian Media Directors' Council *Media Digest*, 2003–2004, p. 5.

Key market-coverage plans can accommodate media that have a more urban orientation or are more local in nature. Potential media alternatives include spot television, radio, daily and community newspapers, city magazines, outdoor media, and transit media.

SELECTIVE COVERAGE PLAN   In contrast to other market coverage plans, a selective plan does not consider level of distribution, population by area, geographic product development, and the like. Instead, it attempts to reach a desired target market regardless of geographic location. Advertisers use a **selective coverage plan** with a *rifle* media strategy when a target market can be narrowly defined by a common characteristic.

A selective coverage plan works because of the nature of the advertised product, the common characteristic of the target market, and the availability of a specialized medium. For example, *Photo Life* magazine would be an advertising vehicle appropriate for reaching a photography enthusiast, and *Golf Canada* would effectively reach people interested in golf. Direct-response advertising techniques such as direct mail or direct-response television offer the industrial or business advertiser a good opportunity to approach prospects on a selective basis. In the case of direct mail, the use of specialized mailing lists can effectively match sellers with buyers, regardless of their geographic location. Now, advertisers can use the internet to reach prospects individually. Email marketing programs are becoming quite popular.

BEST TIME TO REACH TARGET

Media strategy must consider the best time to reach the intended target market. The best time could refer to the best time of year, the best season, the best time of day, or the best

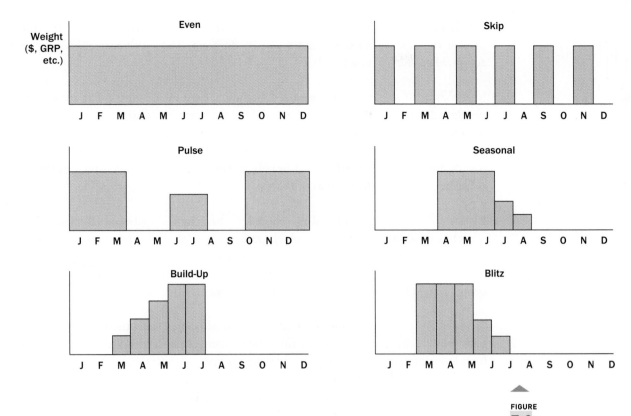

FIGURE
7.8

Media scheduling options

day of the week. If a new product is to be launched into the market, should the advertiser intensify reach and frequency initially, or gradually build intensity over a longer period? These questions are addressed when decisions about scheduling media are being made. In most cases, the advertiser works within a budget restriction, so the money available must be stretched over the entire planning period. Several scheduling options are available to advertisers. Refer to Figure 7.8 for a diagrammatic representation of each.

EVEN SCHEDULE   According to the **even schedule**, media time and space are purchased in a uniform manner over a designated period. This schedule is usually a practical option for the largest of advertisers, which need to advertise on a steady basis, perhaps due to competitive factors. However, advertisers should be cautious about such a spending approach. Consistent levels of advertising for extended periods can be wasteful. The goal is to spend at a level necessary to achieve the desired action. An even spending pattern is not very common, but it does serve as a basis for comparison with the other alternatives.

SKIP SCHEDULE   With a **skip schedule**, media time and space are purchased on an "alternate" basis—every other week or month. In terms of media usage, skip can refer to alternating media—magazines one month, television another month. A skip schedule is one method of stretching media dollars over an extended period while maintaining the effect of advertising in the marketplace.

PULSE SCHEDULE   **Pulsing** refers to the grouping of advertisements (spending of media dollars) in flights over a predetermined length of time. **Flights**, as mentioned earlier, are the periodic waves of time in which the product or service is advertised. In this case, a flight would be followed by a hiatus in a continuous cycle throughout the year. The grouping of advertisements in flights contributes to the synergistic effect desired. In any particular flight, the weight of the advertising (reach and frequency) and the duration of the advertising (continuity) can be different. The result resembles a pulsing action when shown on a schedule.

SEASONAL SCHEDULE   A **seasonal schedule** is used for products that are sold and purchased at traditional times of the year. Media advertising is usually heavy in the pre-season, and then tapers off in the purchase season. Products may advertise lightly at other times of the year, but will increase weight considerably in the pre-selling season. RRSPs, for example, are advertised heavily in January and February—the deadline for contributions is usually the end of February.

BUILD-UP SCHEDULE   A **build-up schedule** is characterized by low initial media weight, often due to selective use of media, which gradually builds to an intensive campaign in subsequent time periods, with an increase in media weight and the use of additional media. The build-up strategy is often associated with new product launches (e.g., new movies being released by Hollywood studios). Such a strategy is often called a *teaser campaign*.

BLITZ SCHEDULE   The **blitz schedule** is often associated with the introduction of a new product, an event for which multimedia campaigns are implemented. To create high levels of awareness during the introductory period, advertising saturates the market and then gradually tapers off. Another feature of this schedule is that certain media will be used less frequently, or eliminated, as time goes on.

COMPETITIVE MEDIA STRATEGIES   Prior to committing to a plan, media planners should analyze competitors' media usage and expenditure patterns. What the competition does can help planners recommend a media direction for their own product. Should the media recommendation follow a similar pattern or should a unique strategic direction be recommended?

Assume that a product has a large media budget and dominates other products because it is extensively advertised on television. Does a competitor attempt to compete at the same level in television (assuming adequate funds are available) or should its media planners choose another medium or media combination so that, by dominating the different media, the product can reach a similar target market? If funds are not adequate to allow direct competition, a different media strategy must be considered. In this situation, the use of more selective media, which reach a defined target market, may be the most efficient and competitive approach to media planning.

MEDIA ALTERNATIVES   As indicated earlier, the advertiser can choose among television, radio, newspaper, magazines, out-of-home, direct response, and the internet. Each medium has its own advantages and disadvantages, so selection is largely based on the nature of the product, the description of the target market and the media they refer to most often, and the budget available. Typically, an advertiser will not rely solely on one medium but will select a combination of media to achieve the stated objectives of the campaign. They may identify a primary medium and support it with secondary media. As explained earlier, television may be ideal for creating awareness and for emotionally connecting with consumers while print may be ideal for communicating details and appealing to consumers on a rational basis. Combinations of media, therefore, may be the best bet!

Currently, television and newspapers attract the lion's share of advertising investment in Canada. However, advertisers are slowly moving away from conventional media forms aimed at the mass market and toward media forms that offer greater targeting potential. One of the controversies in the industry right now is the effect the internet is having on television viewing. While conflicting reports have been published, it appears that as people spend more time online they are spending less time watching television and reading newspapers. Such behaviour has to be considered when a media strategy is being developed.

Detailed discussion of the advantages and disadvantages of each medium is included in Chapters 8 through 12.

BUDGET Essentially, all media strategy decisions are affected by the budget. For example, a small budget can restrict the use of media, extent of coverage, and reach and frequency levels; a sizeable budget can provide considerable flexibility with respect to the same factors. A large budget allows flexibility in the media selection process, since a multimedia campaign can be considered. Media planners who face restrictions or smaller media budgets must be more selective in the evaluation process. The size of the budget (small or large) means that media planners face different challenges when trying to allocate funds efficiently.

To maximize the potential of scarce media dollars, media planners often recommend a primary medium that provides an effective and efficient means of reaching a target market. Such a plan is referred to as a **concentrated media strategy**, since most media dollars are allocated to a primary medium. The advantage of a concentrated strategy is potential media cost savings, since the purchase of one medium in larger quantities creates higher discounts. Then, after considering additional factors such as reach, frequency, and market coverage, media planners will recommend secondary media. Secondary media are often used selectively, and serve to complement the primary medium. The result is a **media mix** that maximizes the use of scarce media dollars.

Alternatively, a media planner could recommend that media dollars be distributed more equitably among several media types. Such a strategy allows the advertiser to reach the same target market in different environments—if members of the target market are not watching television in their leisure time, they may be reading or surfing the internet. The strategy of distributing media dollars more equitably across several media is often referred to as an **assortment media strategy**. Figure 7.9 summarizes the effect of budget size on media strategy.

For an introduction to a rather unique media strategy read the Advertising in Action vignette **GM's 24-Hour Blitz.** This vignette presents the key details and rationale behind a General Motor's new product launch campaign.

Media Execution

The final stage in the media planning process is media execution. **Media execution** is basically the process of fine tuning the strategy and translating it into specific action plans. These action plans, or tactics, can be divided into the following areas: evaluating cost comparisons so that a particular medium may be chosen over another; scheduling specific media in a planning format (calendar or blocking chart); developing budget summaries that outline media spending details; and buying the media time when the client approves the plan.

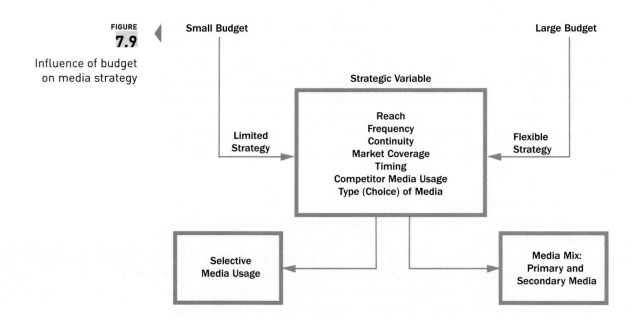

FIGURE 7.9

Influence of budget on media strategy

MEDIA SELECTION PROCESS

Media selection can be viewed as a "funnelling" process, since the focus of the process is moving from the general types of media to a specific medium (see Figure 7.10). The process is based on a three-stage decision system that involves selecting the general type of media to use (media strategy), selecting the class of media within the type, and selecting the particular medium.

The *first* decision is selecting the *type of media* that will best allow the advertisers to meet the objectives for the product and to execute the advertising strategies devised for the product. In the selection process, the various media types are evaluated and compared on the basis of how effectively and efficiently they reach the target market.

The *second* decision involves comparing the *class options within the type of media* recommended. Such a decision often depends on the overall target-market matching strategy being employed: shotgun, profile matching, or rifle. For example, if magazines are recommended, what class of magazine should be used? Will it be general interest, specific interest, or a magazine tailored to the needs of men or women? If television is recommended, will it be a conventional network such as the CBC or CTV, a specialty

FIGURE 7.10

Media selection process

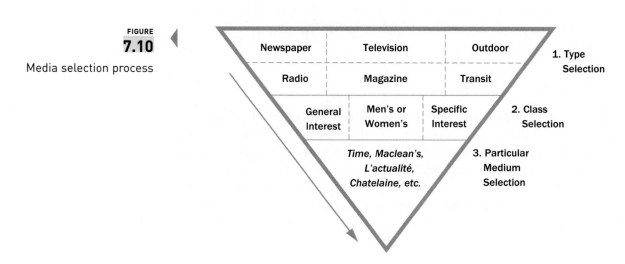

GM's 24-Hour Blitz

November 12, 2003 is a day now referred to as C-Day. *C* stands for Chevrolet. In 2004, General Motors launched six new Chevrolet models in Quebec, and did it with a bang—a one-day media blitz! A more usual media strategy is to stretch a schedule over a longer period, giving consumers time for the message to sink in. Chevrolet actually spent 20 percent of its annual Quebec budget for Chevrolets in one day.

The campaign was orchestrated by Cossette Communication Group of Montreal and comprised

- 7 television spots scheduled throughout the day on all major networks and stations;
- 336 radio spots in Montreal and Quebec City;
- 700 superboards, billboards, subway, and university mobile boards;
- 1.5 million four-page newspaper inserts;
- Saturation coverage on the Canoe website; and
- An on-air contest giving away five new Chevrolets on a high-profile radio network

Typical of a blitz strategy, the campaign started with high impact and then tapered off. Some of the less costly elements ran for an extended period. The goal of the campaign was to move market share. In the long term (two years) the objective was to increase share from 21 percent to 25 percent, an aggressive target given the competitive nature of the market. As well, the ads were designed to dispel Chevrolet's image as being the car "my uncle" drives.

The ads are targeted at the cool and hip thirty-something crowd. All of the models are small and sporty with a European style—everything that Quebecers look for in their cars. Quebecers buy smaller cars at a much greater rate than do people in any other province.

A blitz strategy of this magnitude has some benefits and drawbacks. On the positive side, the blanket coverage has a reinforcing effect, with print and internet ads complementing the more rapid-fire television and billboard ads. Awareness of the new models is almost a given. On the negative side, consumers are exposed to a lot of information in a short period. Can they absorb it? It could be information overload.

One critic of the campaign stated, "This comes across as more brawn than creativity. It's like a gigantic loudspeaker, but it's not clear if the consumer is responding to the tune being played." Only time will tell.

A bonus of such a unique campaign was the publicity it generated. The media did their part as every Quebec daily ran a story about the one-day campaign. There was also TV, radio, and magazine coverage. Cossette estimates the PR value alone to be worth $150 000. Not bad for a one-day effort!

You be the judge. Is this strategy a wise investment for General Motors? Should they have gone with something more conventional?

Sources: Adapted from Bertrand Marotte, "GM puts pedal to the metal in Quebec," *The Globe and Mail*, November 14, 2003, p. B8 and Danny Kucharsky, "One Day Wonder," *Marketing*, February 2, 2004, pp. 10–12.

General Motors Canada www.gmcanada.com

cable channel that has a specific theme (such as the Outdoor Life Network or MuchMusic), or a selective spot at a local market television station?

The *third* decision of the media planner is recommending which *particular medium* within a class provides the most cost-efficient means of delivering the advertiser's message. For example, if the female or male head of the household is the intended target market, and magazines have been recommended, which publications are most cost-efficient? The recommendation would have to consider magazines that appeal to both genders such as *Canadian Geographic, Cottage Life*, and *Harrowsmith Country Life*, among others. Depending on funds available, one publication or all three might be recommended. If television is recommended for a key market plan, which network, or which station or stations (to be purchased locally) should be part of a key media buy? The decision is largely based on how cost-efficient the medium is at reaching the intended target.

Cost **efficiency** is based on a mathematical model called CPM (cost per thousand). **CPM** is defined as the cost incurred in delivering a message to 1000 individuals. In the case of magazines, the data required for the calculation are the cost of a comparable advertisement in each publication and the circulation figures. The CPM calculation allows for easy comparison of magazines that have different rate structures and circulations. The formula for calculating CPM is as follows:

$$CPM = \frac{\text{Unit Cost of Message}}{\text{Circulation (in thousands)}}$$

The CPM comparison of the three magazines is as follows:

Magazine (National Edition)	Cost ($) (1P, 4 colour)	English Circulation (in thousands)	CPM
Canadian Geographic	14 590	233.2	62.56
Cottage Life	8 930	71.3	125.24
Harrowsmith Country Life	8 100	129.1	66.44

Source: Canadian Media Directors' Council *Media Digest*, 2003–2004, p. 45.

These magazines compete for advertising revenue in the general interest category. The figures reveal that *Canadian Geographic* and *Harrowsmith Country Life* reach their respective audiences at a lower cost per thousand than does *Cottage Life*. Both *Canadian Geographic* and *Harrowsmith Country Life* may be given priority in a media buy due their efficiency (the lower cost per thousand) at reaching the target audience. Note, however, that the same calculation can be made based on actual readership (instead of circulation) of the magazine. This may result in different CPMs and different decisions. Readership is discussed in more detail in Chapter 9.

The sample decisions outlined above are based solely on cost efficiency. Other, more qualitative factors are often considered in the decision-making process. Factors such as editorial content, quality of reproduction, and demographic selectivity can lead the media planner to prefer one magazine over another, even if the preferred magazine's CPM is greater than the other magazine's.

Another factor that could enter into the selection process is the method by which the magazine is distributed. Some magazines are given away or are a combination of paid circulation and unpaid circulation. If magazines are to be compared, the common factors should be the cost of the ad and paid circulation. The inclusion of unpaid circulation could make a magazine look better than one that relies solely on paid circulation. There are those who believe that readership is higher in a magazine a consumer pays for.

Similar calculations can be made for other media. In television for example, the cost of the commercial divided by the size of the viewing audience (in thousands) produces a CPM figure. This calculation helps determine which show to advertise on. Generally, high demand shows such as *Friends, ER,* and *CSI* have high CPMs and low demand shows have low CPMs. To demonstrate, the average CPM on the CBS Network (U.S.) in prime time in 2003 was $22.63. That considers the popularity of all shows and the cost of all advertising spots. A popular television show on the same network cost $300 000 plus, resulting in a CPM of $37.63. Supply and demand determines the cost of television advertising.[7]

To broaden the perspective on tactical considerations, let us review some of the decisions that will affect what other media forms are chosen for use. The following is a brief outline of some critical factors involved in evaluating broadcast, print, or other media.

Some tactical considerations for broadcast media are:

- What levels of reach and frequency are required? Which is more important—reach or frequency?

- In which days or months will commercials appear? (Seasonality often affects costs.)

- Will commercials be placed in prime time or fringe time, or a combination of both? Prime time is much more expensive.

Some tactical considerations for print media are:

- How many advertisements will appear, and on which day (newspapers), weeks, or months (magazines)?

- Will preferred positions, such as covers in a magazine or specific pages in a newspaper, be purchased?

- Must special creative options be considered, such a *gatelegs* (multiple-page foldouts), *flexform* advertising (advertising that doesn't conform to a normal geometric shape), or use of spot or full colour?

- What are the reach and frequency objectives?

Some tactical considerations for other media are as follows:

- For outdoor advertising, what markets will be purchased, and what locations are preferred within a market?

- For outdoor advertising, what kind of billboard will be used (poster or spectacular)? There are considerable cost variations.

- For transit advertising, what markets will be purchased? Will interior or exterior transit be purchased, or a combination?

In deciding on the best media strategy and execution there are a lot of variables that must be considered. Companies and brands face unique situations, so the strategies they employ will certainly be different. Certain media-consumption trends also affect the decisions on what media to employ and how much money should be invested into them. Some companies have taken media strategy and execution a step further by investing in convergence media strategies with one large media outlet. The outlet controls a variety of media in broadcast and print. For insight into this relatively new practice, read the Advertising in Action vignette **Media Strategy: Does a Convergence Strategy Work?**

MEDIA SCHEDULING AND BUDGETING

With the media selection process complete, planners proceed to the final stage in developing the media plan: formulating a media schedule and related budget summaries. This portion of the planning document outlines for the advertisers how, where, and when the media expenditures will occur. The media schedule is normally presented in a calendar format, often referred to as a blocking chart. A **blocking chart** outlines in one or two pages all of the details of the media execution (e.g., media usage, market coverage, weight levels, GRPs, reach, frequency, and the timing of the campaign).

Media Strategy: Does a Convergence Strategy Work?

The term *convergence* suggests that things come together. In a media strategy sense, if things come together, the net result will be greater impact on the target audience. At least that's the theory.

In recent years there has been much convergence in the Canadian media. What were once separate companies are now huge media conglomerates. Bellglobemedia, for example, owns *The Globe and Mail*, CTV, TSN, The Comedy Network, ROB TV, and the Discovery Channel. Beyond these media outlets, the BCE empire includes Bell Canada, Bell Mobility, Bell ExpressVu, and internet sites such as Sympatico-Lycos and various *Globe and Mail* sites.

With so many media holdings, Bell is trying to figure ways of making all of their media interests attractive to advertisers. The premise is simple. If an advertiser buys a package deal (all media outlets bundled together) the advertising rates will be lower. In total, however, the advertiser could spend a lot more on the package, so such a strategy is not for everyone. Before pursuing such a strategy, the advertiser must be confident that all of the media outlets reach the target audience.

Cadillac was one of the first advertisers to buy into a convergence media strategy. Their plan consisted of three half-hour TV shows airing on CTV, TSN, Discovery, and Report on Business Television; 17 vignette interstitials airing in rotation on the same channels and **innovatingtomorrow.com** website; three supplements in *The Globe and Mail*; and articles in *ROB* magazine. As you can see, this campaign is more than a media buy—it embraces program content in broadcast and editorial content in print.

Such a strategy made sense to the managers responsible for marketing Cadillac. The brand was struggling and its core buyers were getting older. Cadillac had to generate some excitement with the next generation of status-conscious consumers. The media strategy was designed to cut the clutter of traditional advertising by developing relevant program content that would appeal to the new target—males aged 35 to 44 making upper-level incomes. They are entrepreneurs, executives, and business people on the rise.

The campaign was designed around three pillars: leadership in technology, leadership in design, and leadership in business. By building television shows, webpages, and newspaper features around these pillars, the content would be relevant to the target audience and echo the Cadillac brand equities—without the risk of turning off audiences with blatant pitches written into the content itself.

"Leadership in technology" is demonstrated by such tech-toys as a voice-activated navigation system available in all Cadillac models. "Leadership in design" stems from the dramatic planes and curves of the new models, particularly the CTS sports model. "Leadership in business" is based on the brand's status symbol roots.

The Cadillac campaign is one that combines advertising in the media with program content that is of interest to the target. It goes well beyond branded content, a strategy that simply places the product in a program. The content of the show is based on the values that Cadillac represents. Cadillac will sponsor the shows and the audience will see their ads, but the shows are not about GM or Cadillac.

It is not known how much Cadillac invested in this media strategy, but it is in the millions, and the results of the effort are not determined at this time. However, in defending such a unique strategy, GM advertising manager Cathy Cooper says, "Bellglobemedia has a lot of media properties which are very appropriate for our target. The program content is of interest to our audience and is very much in line with what our advertising message is."

Sources: Adapted from Chris Powell, "GM drive huge convergence deal," *Marketing*, February 4, 2002, p. 4 and Duncan Hood, "When the rubber hits the road," *Strategy*, June 3, 2002, pp. 28–29.

Cadillac www.gmcanada.com/english/vehicles/cadillac/cadillac.html

Accompanying the blocking chart are budget allocation documents. Typically, the media budget classifies spending allocations according to product (for multi-product advertisers), medium, region, and time of year (months and quarters).

Detailed expenditure plans are important to the client for budget control purposes. As indicated in the strategy section of this chapter, flexibility in media planning is important, due to the possibility of rapidly changing conditions throughout a planning cycle. Budget control documents are referred to often, particularly when cancellations are being considered.

For an applied illustration of the content of a media plan (media objectives, strategies, and execution), refer to the Advertising Plan that appears in Appendix II.

MEDIA BUYING

The media buyer purchases the time and space according to the media plan, requiring the buyer to interpret the work of the media planners and to make decisions regarding actual buys. Buyers are also charged with the responsibility of making replacement buys if the original choice is unavailable.

Time is often a critical factor in the buying process. For example, in broadcast television, the CBC and CTV networks are booked in late June to cover a 52-week period, starting in September, with bookings being non-cancellable. Spot television can be purchased any time during the year, assuming local-market availability. There is cancellation flexibility with selective spot buying.

The media buyer acts as a "negotiator" with media representatives. He or she must maximize the efficiency of the media budget by seeking favourable positions and negotiating the best rates possible in light of the guidelines in the media plan. In essence, the buyer fulfills the schedule by implementing the plan.

The media-buying process is a complicated process involving numerous companies. The industry now uses an electronic data interchange (EDI) system in all four stages of a media buy: the purchase order, order acknowledgment and request for changes, invoice, and payment. EDI helps reduce costs and speeds up the payment process.

THE ROLE OF COMPUTERS IN MEDIA PLANNING

The process of media planning and buying has always been a complicated task, so it is not surprising that computers now play a prominent role. User-friendly software developed by organizations such as BBM Bureau of Measurement, Nielsen Media Research, and Telmar-Harris Media Systems lets media planners and buyers alike make reasoned, detailed decisions. BBM currently uses two media planning programs: microBBM and micro-TV. Both software programs let buyers analyze who's watching what and where they're watching it, using data downloaded from BBM's website.

Nielsen Media Research also has two TV-ad planning tools: Media Master and Media Advisor. Both tools define the overall task and the general solution and then lead planners to specific applications needed to answer their questions. For example, Media Advisor lets a planner create custom demographics, such as women between the ages of 35 and 49 who are professionals and who have a household income of $70 000. The software identifies television programs that reach these women.[8]

Telmar-Harris provides advertisers and agencies with a host of computer media planning and analysis services for most major media. Their software allows a media

Nielsen Media Research
www.nielsenmedia.com

Telmar-Harris
www.ca.telmar.com

planner to analyze and use data in databanks provided by companies such as the BBM Bureau of Measurement (television and radio), NADbank Inc. (newspapers), and the Print Measurement Bureau (magazines). Telmar-Harris offers a complete range of software for all media, and it can be used in a microcomputer or online environment. The software does all of the quantitative assessments for reach, frequency, GRPs, and CPMs, many of the concepts discussed in this chapter. In the context of media planning, software allows planners to maximize reach at the least cost.

The Media Budget

Determining the amount of money to spend on marketing communications generally, and advertising specifically, is a problematic process the manager must face each year. How much does each component of the marketing communications mix deserve?

The investment payback from some expenditures can be calculated relatively precisely, but the payback from advertising remains rather vague—that direct link to sales or profit just isn't there. Organizations must realize that investment in advertising requires a long-term commitment if a plan is to have a chance at success. To think otherwise is foolish, but chopping advertising budgets in midstream is a common phenomenon when advertisers try to protect short-term profit margins. Such decisions are questionable as they conflict with the long-term expectations of the brand, and they can accentuate the rough financial situation by reducing revenues further. Regardless of the size of a business, managers should resist the temptation to cut budgets without just cause.

FACTORS AFFECTING BUDGET SIZE

To develop an advertising budget, the manager analyzes a host of factors that will influence the size of the budget. When these factors are examined collectively, they provide insight into the amount of money required for advertising. A discussion of each factor follows.

SIZE OF CUSTOMER BASE   In terms of the size of the customer base, a clear distinction can be made between consumer markets and industrial markets. Organizations directing consumer products at mass target markets tend to rely more heavily on advertising, while organizations directing products at industrial markets, which represent a more selective and geographically centred audience, rely more on personal selling. If viewed from a budgeting perspective, a competitive advertising budget is essential for the long-term success of any product in a consumer-oriented market. For industrial products, the money available for promotion will be wisely spent if less is allocated to conventional advertising than to personal selling and sales-promotion budgets. Direct-response and internet communications are useful for reaching both consumer and industrial targets.

DEGREE OF COMPETITION   The amount of money spent on advertising by competitors may be the single most important influence on the size of a product's advertising budget. If nothing else, it is a useful indicator of how much money the company will have to spend to remain competitive. Information on competitors' advertising spending is available to consumer-goods advertisers through marketing research firms such as Nielsen Marketing Research. While past expenditures are well known, the advertising manager must also predict with reasonable accuracy what the main competitors will spend next year, for these projected expenditures can help him or her develop and justify a budget.

A decision must be made regarding how competitive the brand will be with respect to advertising expenditures. In many markets, the competition is so intense and the media spending so high that an advertiser might be forced to spend more than it would like. In the battle for soft-drink supremacy between Coca-Cola and Pepsi, is it realistic for either brand to reduce its investment in advertising? Both brands compete in a segment of the beverage industry that is experiencing flat growth year to year, so to protect market-share advertising spending has to remain competitive. In the process, profits may have to be sacrificed.

STAGE IN THE PRODUCT LIFE CYCLE Advertising is more important in the introductory and growth stages of the product life cycle than in the mature and decline stages.

In the **introduction stage**, the advertiser is mainly concerned with creating a high level of awareness for the new product. In relation to sales, the investment in advertising will be extremely high. Since the objective is brand development, it is quite common to have an advertising expenditure that exceeds the projected return in sales. Initial losses are offset by profits made in the longer term.

In the **growth stage** competition is present, so the competitors' advertising budgets enter the picture. A manager is concerned about two objectives: continuing to build awareness, and creating brand preference in the customer's mind. Accomplishing both objectives costs money. Securing growth and improving market share in a competitive environment is a challenge and requires a budget that will attract users of competitive brands. Consequently, a brand may wind up spending much more on advertising in this stage than it would like to.

When the brand enters the **mature stage**, most advertisers shift the strategic focus from brand development to profit maximization. Rather than spending money on advertising, there is a conscious effort to preserve money wherever possible. Being in a maintenance position, the budget should just be enough to sustain market share position while increasing bottom-line profitability. If life-cycle extension strategies such as product modifications, new packaging, and new varieties occur, there may be a temporary need to invest in advertising to make consumers aware of new things.

In the **decline stage**, profit motives take priority. Advertising budgets are generally cut significantly or withdrawn entirely. Profits that are generated from brands in this stage are allocated to brands that are in their developmental stages.

PRODUCT CHARACTERISTICS The nature of the product (the degree of its uniqueness) and its perceived value to potential customers can have an influence on the amount of money that is spent on advertising the product.

Assuming a **high-interest unique selling point** exists, an advertiser must invest heavily in advertising to establish in consumers' minds the perceived value of the unique selling point. For example, when Nabob Coffee introduced the vacuum-sealed package format as a new way of preserving its product's freshness (it sealed out the staling effect of oxygen), the company increased its advertising budget and used a "break the rules" style of advertising (the new package was shown pounding on, and then breaking open, the traditional package of brand leader Maxwell House) to communicate its unique advantage. The combination of the new package (offering a better, fresher product) and a significant investment in advertising made Nabob the number-one roast coffee brand in Canada.[9] Once the brand is established, or when adequate levels of brand loyalty have been achieved, the investment in advertising can be reduced.

For product categories in which brands have only **marginal unique selling points** (i.e., its unique selling points are easily duplicated), the amount spent on advertising is determined by the overall objectives for the brand and the degree of competition. For example, if a brand like Wisk laundry detergent wants to be competitive with leaders such as Tide and Sunlight, brands that traditionally spend heavily on advertising, then Wisk will have to spend at similar levels. Conversely, Wisk may choose a different strategic approach and focus on other areas of marketing or marketing communications where the competition is less intense. For example, Wisk may focus on price incentives such as coupons and cash refunds or simply market the product at a lower price.

MANAGEMENT PHILOSOPHY ABOUT ADVERTISING   The size of a company and the attitude and perceptions of senior executives about the value of advertising often determine the financial resources available for marketing communications. For example, expense-oriented managers who consider only the short term may be reluctant to spend scarce dollars on advertising; investment-minded managers, however, are more willing to take budget risks to encourage long-term brand development. They will see a plan through to the finish before passing judgment on the investment. For a summary of the factors influencing the budget and budgeting methods, refer to Figure 7.11.

FIGURE 7.11

Factors influencing size of budget and budget methods

Factors Influencing Budget Size	
Customer Base	Consumer goods require larger budgets than industrial goods due to size and location of customers
Degree of Competition	Assuming growth is the objective, a brand must be at or above competitor advertising spending levels
Stage in Product Life Cycle	Introduction and growth require significant budgets (awareness and trial); spending is reduced in maturity (retention) and non-existent in decline
Product Characteristics	High interest USPs require high investment to promote benefits; marginal USPs should look at less costly alternatives
Management	The perception of the value of advertising is questioned (short-term expense orientation versus long-term investment orientation

Budgeting Methods	
Percentage of Sales	A predetermined percentage of forecast sales is allocated to advertising
Fixed Sum/Unit	A predetermined dollar amount per unit sold is allocated to advertising
Industry Average	The average amount spent on advertising by competitors (historical or forecast) spending is allocated to advertising
Advertising Share/ Market Share	Invest at a level to retain share (ad share equals market share); invest at a level to build market share (ad share is greater than market share)
Task (Objective)	Define the task; determine the activities to achieve the task; associate a cost with the activities

BUDGETING METHODS

Annual sales and profit projections are normally established at the corporate level of an organization. These projections often become guidelines for developing potential advertising budgets. An advertising budget can be developed in a variety of ways, each with its own pros and cons. Since no one method is ideal for all situations, it may be wise to compare a variety of methods so that the budget is realistic, given the competitive situation in the marketplace. Discussion of the various methods follows.

PERCENTAGE OF SALES   If a company uses the **percentage-of-sales** method, it usually forecasts the sales-dollar volume for the forthcoming year and allocates a predetermined percentage amount of those sales to advertising. Management determines the percentage to be used. Percentages often used are past industry averages or simply the percentage the company has used in the past. This method of developing a budget has an obvious shortcoming. The philosophy underlying the method is that advertising results *from* sales, whereas the wiser manager prefers to believe that advertising results *in* sales.

This method is popular largely due to its simplicity, and because it relates advertising expenditures directly to sales. If used, the budget implications are very predictable. If sales decrease, so does the budget, and vice versa. The percentage-of-sales method may be appropriate for companies and products that face very similar market conditions year after year. However, if conditions are volatile, the advertising expenditure should change with the market.

Note: Depending on the competitive situation, on the stage the product has reached in the life cycle, and on other factors, the actual percentage allocated to advertising may vary as time passes. For example, a company may allocate to a new brand a very high percentage of the sales, perhaps 200 percent (two dollars in advertising for one dollar in sales), in order to establish the brand's position (thus sacrificing short-term profit). Conversely, a mature brand with a high level of annual sales will be allocated a reduced percentage (perhaps 5 to 10 percent) since maximizing profit is the motivation at this stage.

FIXED SUM PER UNIT SOLD   The **fixed-sum-per-unit-sold** method of budgeting is very similar to percentage of sales in that the volume of product sold has a direct influence on the size of the brand's advertising budget. According to this method, the company allocates a predetermined amount to advertising for each unit sold. For example, the Chrysler minivan spends more on advertising per unit than many of its competitors. Chrysler sees value in advertising and its goal is to defend its leadership position in a hotly contested market segment. In 2003, Chrysler spent $79 million on media advertising with unit sales of 215 000, an average investment in advertising of $368 per unit. Honda Odyssey, the second-ranked minivan, spent only $293 per unit.[10] There is a significant gap in spending between the market leader and market challenger.

This method is suitable for products with a high unit price (appliances, automobiles). Similar to the percentage-of-sales method, the major weakness of this method is that the budget fluctuates with changes in sales volume.

INDUSTRY AVERAGE (COMPETITOR SPENDING)   Advertisers using the **industry average** approach base their advertising budgets on what competitors are spending. Depending on the performance objectives established for a product, the advertiser could

Chrysler Minivan
www.chrysler.com/town_country

choose to lag behind, to be equal to, or to exceed the spending of the competition. Using competitors' past expenditures as a starting point, advertisers attempt to forecast competitive advertising expenditures for the next year, and then to position their own budgets accordingly.

An advertiser may also review historical industry averages as a starting point. For example, if a cosmetics company knows that the cosmetic industry historically spends 15 to 20 percent of revenues on advertising, then this range would provide a "safe" starting-point figure for a particular brand's budget. Industry averages provide a good preliminary guideline. However, the influence of other variables may force the advertiser to modify this "starting-point budget." An alternative approach simply examines the average spending patterns of your closest competitors. For example,

Brand A	$400 000
Brand B	200 000
Brand C	300 000
Industry Average	**$300 000**

Using this method, we see that Brand B falls behind its competitors. Assuming advertising is equally important to all brands, the company that produces Brand B would not anticipate much in the way of improved brand performance if the budget remains at $200 000.

TASK (OBJECTIVE) METHOD The budgeting methods discussed so far fail to acknowledge that advertising is a potential means of achieving marketing objectives. Which comes first, the chicken or the egg? In contrast to other methods, the task or objective method shows how advertising can affect sales. The task method involves a few basic steps: defining the task, determining the type and quantity of advertising needed, and determining the cost of the advertising recommendation.

- *Defining the task* The task of advertising is often expressed in communications terms; usually, it is described as the task of achieving a specified level of brand awareness (e.g., "to increase brand awareness for Brand X from 60 to 75 percent in the next year").

- *Determining the type and quantity of advertising* The difficult part of the task method is determining the most efficient and effective ways of achieving the desired objectives. The myriad media options available suggest that knowledge and experience in media planning are essential for determining reasonable and reliable budget estimates. A detailed understanding of the strategic variables discussed earlier in the chapter—reach, frequency, continuity, impressions, and GRPs—is essential.

- *Determining the cost of the advertising recommendation* This last step in the process is more mechanical. Presuming there is agreement as to objectives and the type and quantity of advertising required (i.e., the first two stages), the costs are calculated arithmetically according to media. Production costs are estimated, and the sum of all media and production variables becomes the advertising budget.

Since many variables are considered in the task method, it is often viewed as the most scientific of the various methods. It is also argued that if the input variables (media-planning variables such as reach, frequency, and continuity) are incorrect, serious miscalculations for a budget will follow. Further, this method does not consider the profit objective of the brand or company. Once a budget figure is arrived at, the company must decide if it can afford to spend that much on advertising. If it can't, the objectives of the plan must be re-evaluated and the plan altered accordingly.

SHARE OF ADVERTISING/SHARE OF MARKET   Share of advertising, or **advertising share**, refers to the amount invested in advertising by one brand expressed as a percentage of the total category investment in advertising (e.g., Tide's investment in advertising may be 20 percent of the total invested by all laundry detergents).

This method is based on the premise that advertising plays a key role in motivating consumers. A brand that spends at a level where advertising share equals market share can reasonably expect to retain its market-share position. Brands that want to grow in a market and increase market share will have to increase spending so that advertising share is greater than market share. Consider the example in the table below and the consequences it presents:

Brand	Market Share (%)	Projected Advertising Budget ($)	Advertising Share (%)	Consequences
A	40	5 000 000	50	Share increase
B	30	2 500 000	25	Decrease
C	20	1 500 000	15	Decrease
D	10	1 000 000	10	Maintenance
	100	10 000 000	100	

If the projected budgets came close to equalling actual spending that year, advertising expenditures for Brand A would have been at a level greater than Brand A's market share, while those for Brands B and C would have been below market share. As a consequence, we would expect Brand A to achieve share increases while B and C would suffer market-share declines.

The use of this method requires an advertiser to review competitors' media spending. It produces a good starting point (guideline) for developing a budget. However, it does not consider profit objectives. A preoccupation with what competitors are spending may force a company to spend more than it can afford.

This chapter has presented the various components of a media plan and demonstrated how the budget influences the nature and direction of a plan. For an applied illustration of how the budget and the media objectives influence media strategy and the selection of specific media, refer to the Practice of Advertising section following Chapter 10. Also refer to the Advertising plan that appears in Appendix II.

SUMMARY

In the media-planning process the client is responsible for providing the agency with adequate background information, which is usually contained in the marketing plan. Using this information, the agency develops a detailed media plan and assumes responsibility for selecting, scheduling, and buying media time and space.

The media plan flows logically from the overall marketing strategy and marketing communications strategy. The media plan is divided into three basic sections: media objectives, media strategies, and media execution. Media objectives are statements that outline *who* (i.e., what the target market is), *what* (i.e., what the selling message is), *where* (i.e., where the markets to advertise in are located), *when* (i.e., when is the best time to reach the target market), and *how* (i.e., how often and for how long one should need to reach the target market). These objectives act as the framework for more detailed strategies and tactics.

Media strategy deals with the selection of appropriate media to accomplish media objectives. Strategies are affected by variables such as the characteristics of the target market; the nature of the message; reach, frequency, and continuity; flexibility of the plan; the degree of market coverage desired; the best time to reach the target; competitive influences; the pros and cons of the various media alternatives; and the budget.

Media execution is the section of the media plan that outlines the specific tactics for achieving the media objectives. In these detailed action plans are the specific media usage recommendations and summaries of how media funds will be allocated. Once the client approves the media plan, the agency media buyers negotiate the best possible prices with media representatives.

Whether the budget devised is appropriate for a media plan depends largely on the marketing sophistication of the organization. A variety of factors influences the potential size of an advertising budget, including the size of the customer base, the degree of competition the product will face, the stage the product has reached in the product life cycle, the product's characteristics, and management's commitment to advertising.

Advertisers can select from a variety of methods when determining the size of an advertising budget. Commonly used methods include percentage of sales, fixed sum per unit of sales, industry average, and the task or objective method. Since each method offers benefits and drawbacks, it is recommended that a company use several methods and compare the results of each before committing to a final budget.

KEY TERMS

REVIEW QUESTIONS

1. Identify and briefly explain the basic roles and responsibilities of the client and agency in the media planning process.

2. What are the basic differences between media objectives, strategies, and tactics?

3. Identify and briefly describe the components of media objective statements.

4. Describe the differences between

   a) profile-matching strategy
   b) shotgun strategy
   c) rifle strategy

5. Briefly explain the impact that reach, frequency, and continuity have on strategic media planning.

6. What are gross rating points (GRPs), and how are they calculated?

7. What is the difference between a key-market media plan and a selective market plan?

8. What is a pulse media schedule? What strategic variables combine to create the pulsing effect?

9. Briefly explain the difference between a build-up media schedule and a blitz media schedule.

10. What is the difference between a concentrated media strategy and an assortment media strategy?

11. What are the stages in the media selection process?

12. What is CPM? How is it calculated? What purpose does it serve?

13. Identify and briefly describe the factors that influence the size of an advertising budget.

14. Contrast the strengths and weaknesses of the percentage-of-sales budgeting method with those of the task (objective) budgeting method.

15. How does the product life cycle influence the amount of money a company or brand invests in advertising?

DISCUSSION QUESTIONS

1. "Media planning is an activity that should be in the hands of specialists." Discuss, in the context of clients doing their own media planning, the use of a full-service agency and a media-buying service (a specialist).

2. "The client is at the mercy of the agency's media recommendations." Is this a problem? Discuss.

3. "The budget should be based on the media plan, not the media plan based on the budget." Discuss from the perspectives of both the client and the agency.

4. Read the Advertising in Action vignette **Shattering the Paradigm: How Does Advertising Work?** Conduct some secondary research on the issue of recency. Is it suitable for all products or should it be used selectively? What is your opinion of this media strategy? What are the advantages and disadvantages of such a strategy?

5. Review the Advertising in Action vignette **Media Strategy: Does a Convergence Strategy Work?** What is your opinion of the media strategy employed by Cadillac? Identify other possible benefits and drawbacks of such a strategy. Are there other products that should take advantage of such an opportunity?

NOTES

1. Rick Westhead, "Networks wooing ad dollars," *Toronto Star*, June 10, 2003, pp. D1, D13.

2. John Heinzl, "Viewers get caught in ad roadblocks," *The Globe and Mail*, October 19, 2002, p. M1.

3. Canadian Living, **www.canadianliving.com**.

4. Tom Hespos, "Reach and the Law of Diminishing Returns," *Media Post*, January 6, 2004, **www.mediapost.com**.

5. Andrea Zoe Aster, "How much is way too much," *Marketing*, August 16, 1999. p. 4.

6. Chris Daniels, "Media buying gets scientific," *Marketing*, July 31, 2000, pp. 11, 12.

7. Bradley Johnson, "Low CPM can spell bargain for buyers," *Advertising Age*, May 19, 2003, p. 10.

8. James Careless, "TV buys make easy easier," *Marketing*, January 31, 2000, p. 22.

9. John Bell, "Be a brand surgeon," *Marketing*, January 22, 2001, pp. 11, 12.

10. Jean Halliday, "Chrysler innovates to keep lead in heated minivan war," *Advertising Age*, December 15, 2004, p. 4.

Print Media: Newspapers and Magazines

Learning Objectives

After studying this chapter, you will be able to

- Identify the classifications of newspapers and magazines available to the Canadian advertiser

- Explain the advantages and disadvantages of newspapers and magazines as advertising media

- Assess the considerations and procedures involved in buying newspaper and magazine space

- Understand the basic terminology used in newspaper and magazine advertising

- Assess the influence of technology on the print media

Newspapers in Canada

Toronto Star
www.torstar.com

In Canada, there are currently 105 *daily newspapers* with a total average daily circulation of 4.7 million copies. The largest daily is the *Toronto Star*, which has an average Monday to Friday circulation of 454 992. Of the 105 dailies in Canada, 93 are published in English and 12 in French. Only 32 dailies publish a Sunday edition.[1]

The term "circulation" in print media refers to the number of issues sold. **Circulation** is defined as the average number of copies per issue of a publication that are sold by subscription, distributed free to predetermined recipients, carried within other publications, or made available through retail distributors.

Newspapers rank second to television in Canada, controlling 17 percent of net advertising revenues.[2] That revenue is generated from four advertising sources: retail advertising, classified advertising, general (national advertising), and inserts (e.g., retail flyer advertising).

Community newspapers are generally smaller-circulation newspapers published once a week (sometimes more often in larger markets) and directed at a local target audience. There are just over 1200 English and French community newspapers in Canada. Penetration of community newspapers is quite high, as 58 percent of English Canadians (18 years+) and 71 percent of French Canadians (18 years+) read a community newspaper each week.[3]

From an advertising viewpoint, the demographic profile of community newspaper readers closely matches that of the entire population. Among adults they have a fairly even reach among all age, education, income, and gender brackets. There is a modest skew in the direction of older readers.[4] Therefore, community newspapers are truly an advertising medium for the local market, appealing more to independent advertisers. A weekly newspaper stays in the home longer than a daily, owing to its weekly distribution cycle.

NEWSPAPER FORMATS

Canadian newspapers are published in two formats: tabloids and broadsheets. **Tabloids** are flat, with only a vertical centrefold, and resemble an unbound magazine. They are usually produced in one section. In terms of size, the tabloid page is 8 to 10 $^3/_4$ inches wide by 11 to 15 inches in depth. The highest-circulation tabloids in Canada are *Le Journal de Montréal* (259 600), the *Toronto Sun* (202 100), and the *Vancouver Province* (159 600). In total, 19 tabloids are published in Canada.

Broadsheets are much larger newspapers. A broadsheet page is $11^1/_2$ to 13 inches wide by 21 to $22^1/_2$ inches deep. The majority (86) of Canadian daily newspapers are

FIGURE
8.1

Canada's top 10 daily
newspapers

Market	Newspaper	Circulation (000s)
Toronto	*The Toronto Star*	455.0
Toronto	*The Globe and Mail*	318.0
Montreal	*Le Journal de Montreal*	259.6
Toronto	*National Post*	251.8
Toronto	*The Toronto Sun*	202.1
Montreal	*La Presse*	185.6
Vancouver	*The Vancouver Sun*	180.9
Vancouver	*Vancouver Province*	159.6
Montreal	*The Gazette*	141.5
Ottawa	*Ottawa Citizen*	134.0

Source: Canadian Media Directors' Council *Media Digest*, 2003–2004, p. 38.

published in broadsheet format, the largest being the *Toronto Star*, with an average daily circulation of 454 992, *The Globe and Mail* (318 100), the *National Post* (251 800), and the *Vancouver Sun* (180 900). Canada's largest daily newspapers and their circulations are listed in Figure 8.1.

Newspaper Readership Highlights

Readership data about newspapers is compiled by an industry-sponsored measurement organization called NADbank Inc. This organization provides advertisers, advertising agencies, and daily newspapers with accurate and credible information on newspaper readership, retail data, and consumer behaviour. NADbank conducts an annual survey among 31 000 adults representing 86 percent of Canada's urban population. The nature of information produced by NADbank includes weekday and weekend readership, demographic profiles of readers, product ownership and purchase intentions, and media habits (e.g., other media referred to).

NADbank Inc.
www.nadbank.com

Among the adult population in Canada, newspapers reach 58 percent of males and 48 percent of females on a daily basis.[5] Readership tends to increase marginally on weekends, a time when people have more time to read. By region (Atlantic Canada, Quebec, Ontario, Prairies, and British Columbia), and by age in each region, readership does not vary that much. There is, however, a tendency for readership to increase as a person's level of income and education increases. For a summary of newspaper readership by key demographic variables refer to Figure 8.2.

Types of Newspaper Advertising

The revenues generated by advertising significantly offset the production and overhead costs of publishing a newspaper. Advertising accounts for roughly 60 percent of newspaper space. The advertising layouts are put into position first; the editorial content is then arranged around the advertising. A larger newspaper results from an increase in

FIGURE
8.2

Readership of daily
newspapers by
demographic characteristic

This type of information is compiled from surveys conducted by NADbank Inc. each year. NADbank data cover 67 newspapers in 45 urban markets and represent 93 percent of the total daily newspaper circulation in Canada.

Demographic Characteristic	% Canadian Adults (18+)
GENDER	
All Adults	53.5
Women	48.8
Men	58.4
INCOME	
$75 000+	37
$50 000–$74 999	28
$30 000–$49 999	18
$20 000–$29 999	10
Less than $20 000	8
EDUCATION	
College or University Grad	32
Some Post-Secondary	31
High School Grad	23
Some High School	12
COMMUNITY SIZE	
1 million +	52.6
150 000–1 million	56.8
Less than 150 000	54.1

Source: Adapted from Canadian Media Directors' Council *Media Digest*, 2003-2004, pp. 34, 36.

advertising revenues. For example, the Wednesday edition of many daily newspapers is often much thicker than the other days' editions, in part because of the addition of preprinted inserts by supermarket and department store chains. The same could be said of Friday or Saturday editions when television guides and other inserts are included.

There are two broad forms of advertising: *display* and *classified*. **Display advertising** is defined as any advertisement appearing in any part of the publication, excluding the section of classified ads. Display advertising can be subdivided into two types: *general* or *national advertising* and *retail advertising*. Preprinted inserts are another form of advertising that produces revenues for a newspaper. Let's examine the various types of advertising in greater detail.

GENERAL ADVERTISING (NATIONAL ADVERTISING)

General advertising, or **national advertising**, is sold to advertisers and advertising agencies by a national sales department or a media representative firm. Advertisements of this kind normally feature products or services marketed on a national or regional basis, through a network of local retailers. Included in this category are advertisements for brand-name food and beverages, automobiles, airlines, banks and other financial institutions, computers, and telecommunications products and services. Ads placed by national advertisers very often include a **hooker** (also called a **tag**), which identifies local retailers where the product can be purchased; a hooker is usually placed at the bottom of the advertisement. General advertising is usually placed by advertising agencies on behalf of the advertiser (the client).

RETAIL ADVERTISING

As the name suggests, **retail advertising** is used by such businesses as department stores, supermarkets, drug stores, restaurants, and shopping malls. Retail ads usually stress sale items and specials, or they re-advertise national brands that are carried by the retailer at special prices. Another important function of retail ads is the communication of store location and hours of operation. Most daily newspapers have a sales department that is responsible for selling retail ad space. As indicated earlier, retail advertising generates most of the newspaper's revenues.

CLASSIFIED ADVERTISING

Classified advertising appears in a much-read section of the newspaper, and in many of the larger dailies it has a full section to itself. It produces a considerable amount of revenue for a newspaper. Classified ads provide readers with opportunities to buy, sell, lease, rent, or obtain a variety of products and services such as jobs, houses, apartments, cars, recreational vehicles, and furniture.

PREPRINTED INSERTS

Preprinted inserts, often referred to as **free-standing inserts**, are inserted into the fold of the newspaper and look like a separate, smaller section. On any given day, it is not uncommon for a newspaper to include several different inserts. Large users of inserts include supermarkets, department-store chains, and automotive and hardware chains, to name a few. Daily newspapers and weekly newspapers receive additional revenues from the distribution of preprinted inserts.

Newspapers as an Advertising Medium

An advertiser must assess the use of newspapers in the context of the problem that advertising has to resolve and the objectives of a campaign. This section presents the case for selecting or rejecting newspapers for advertising purposes.

ADVANTAGES OF NEWSPAPERS

GEOGRAPHIC SELECTIVITY Newspapers serve a well-defined geographic area (town, city, trading zone, and so on), so they are attractive to local merchants. For the national advertiser, newspapers offer placement on a market-by-market basis. The advertiser can select specific newspaper markets or all the markets in a region. Therefore, newspaper advertising is useful for national advertisers following a key-market media strategy.

Although predominantly local in nature, Canada's two largest dailies illustrate how newspapers can expand coverage into regional markets. The *Toronto Star* has excellent penetration in trading zones surrounding Metropolitan Toronto, and *The Globe and Mail* publishes an Ontario edition and a national edition. Approximately 40 percent of *The Globe and Mail's* circulation is outside of Metropolitan Toronto.[6]

Globe and Mail
www.theglobeandmail.com

COVERAGE AND REACH As indicated in the readership highlight section, newspapers effectively reach a broad cross-section of the adult population. Current readership statistics show that newspapers effectively reach 58 percent of adults 18 years of age and over. The medium also offers high reach among all household income, occupation, and education groups. For all of these demographic variables, readership increases proportionately to income, education, and occupational status. For advertisers with loosely defined target-market profiles, newspapers represent significant reach opportunity.

FLEXIBILITY Newspapers provide several forms of flexibility. It is a medium where ads can be placed with short lead times, say two to three days. Therefore, it is a useful medium for reacting to unforeseen competitive activity. In terms of creative execution, an advertiser can take advantage of flexform advertising. **Flexform** refers to an advertisement that does not conform to normal shapes. Editorial may intertwine with the ad in a variety of ways. Oddly shaped advertisements stand out from the clutter surrounding them.

READER INVOLVEMENT Newspapers are a highly personal medium, and readership is habit-forming. Since subscribers pay for the newspaper, and since the content is news and current information, newspapers are a closely read medium. Although readership patterns (how a newspaper is read) vary among individuals, readers do tend to go through the entire paper. Such reading tendencies suggest a high possibility of exposure for products and services advertised in newspapers. The most popular sections of a newspaper are the local news, national news, and entertainment.

CREATIVE AND MERCHANDISING CONSIDERATIONS Since newspapers are a closely read medium, and since there are many size options, advertisers are able to present messages that include long copy or factual information (as is not the case with broadcast media). Also, newspapers offer merchandise tie-in opportunities, such as co-operative advertising with local distributors or ads containing coupons or other promotional incentives geared toward trial purchase or building loyalty. Newspapers are often referred to as the "sales action" medium. To illustrate, newspapers can help support product launches with coupon promotions or other direct-response (e.g., toll-free numbers and website) activity. See the ad in Figure 8.3 for an illustration.

EDITORIAL SUPPORT Newspaper content can offer positive benefits to advertisers. For example, a luxury automobile that is targeted at business executives can be placed in an appropriate section of the newspaper—the business section. Similarly, an ad for a sports and recreation product would be seen by readers of the sports section. It should be noted, however, that requests for specific positions in the newspaper add to the costs of advertising. For specific page or location requests, an advertiser must pay a position charge. Position charges are discussed in the media-buying section of this chapter.

SUITABILITY FOR SMALL ADVERTISERS To retail advertisers, particularly local-market independents, newspapers offer high reach and flexibility at relatively low cost compared to other media. Also, retailers lacking advertising expertise can draw upon the creative servic-

FIGURE
8.3

A newspaper ad that
includes a sales incentive
to generate action

es of the newspaper, usually at no extra cost. Retailers and automobile manufacturers and dealers are among the largest investors in newspaper advertising across Canada. For insight into why Lexus chose newspapers as the primary medium to launch the new ES 300 model, read the Advertising in Action vignette **The Relentless Pursuit of Perfection**.

Lexus
www.lexus.ca

DISADVANTAGES OF NEWSPAPERS

SHORT LIFESPAN "There is nothing as stale as yesterday's news." This phrase sums up any newspaper's biggest drawback—a short life. Since a daily newspaper is around for only one day or less, the likelihood for an advertisement to receive exposure is drastically reduced if the newspaper is not read on the day of distribution. To reach the audience an ad may have to be placed several times during the week.

LACK OF TARGET-MARKET ORIENTATION Excluding newspapers like *The Globe and Mail* and *National Post*, which have a more selective target-market reach (a reach determined by demographics), newspapers in general reach a very broad cross-section of the

The Relentless Pursuit of Perfection

Luxury automobiles and daily newspapers: good combination or not? Initially, one might think that upscale magazines are a better media choice, but for some reason Lexus opted for newspapers as the primary medium when the new Lexus ES 300 was launched in 2002.

Ad agency DCC Communications' challenge was to create a unique campaign idea that was different from all other competitors—something impactful and compelling, something that would stick in the minds of readers, listeners, and viewers.

Lexus was looking for an integrated media strategy. As a package the media that would be chosen would have to effectively convey the Lexus message: "The Relentless Pursuit of Perfection." The media strategy and execution would have to hit the audience in a relevant and meaningful manner.

Marketing research would play a role. From research it was learned that Lexus buyers viewed the ES 300 as a personal oasis of tranquility and freedom. These findings were a delight to Lexus since they were in keeping with the "Relentless Pursuit of Perfection" theme and would become the cornerstone of the creative strategy.

While Lexus is a relatively young brand, it has a well-defined brand image. The media chosen would have to respect that image, yet offer impact and visibility. The agency recommended newspapers as a key component of the overall media strategy for the launch. Newspapers were well suited for showcasing the comfort and serenity of driving the vehicle. It was also ideal for accentuating many of the intangible qualities associated with the car.

Since the target market represents less than one half of one percent of Canada's population, targeting efforts were essential. This target has a list of relevant newspapers they read, and within those newspapers there are specific sections that are "must reads." *The Globe and Mail* and *National Post* were ideal choices.

The agency recommended newspapers for several reasons. First, newspapers can communicate a compelling proposition in an environment that doesn't overshadow the message. Second, an impressive and dramatic message such as a bold and vivid photograph of a luxury automobile in a newspaper will stay in the reader's head. Third, a newspaper provides a one-on-one environment, an environment where a story can be communicated in a meaningful way, and at a time when the reader is relaxed.

The launch campaign for Lexus was a success, and to this day Lexus continues to allocate a significant portion of its media budget to newspapers. In fact, the 2003 launch of the RX 330, a luxury sport utility vehicle, used the same newspapers and inserts in those newspapers as the primary medium. It's a good match for the very select target market Lexus is pursuing.

Source: Adapted from Keith McDevitt, "Driving the message home," *Marketing*, February 4, 2002, p. 12.

population. For advertisers using a shotgun strategy (mass reach), newspapers serve a purpose. But advertisers wishing to reach a target market that is upscale in terms of income, occupation, or education must recognize that newspaper advertising will reach many who are not in the target market, resulting in a wasteful spending of an advertising budget. Therefore, advertisers with well-defined targets may find other media more appropriate and efficient.

CLUTTER Clutter is the extent to which a publication's pages are fragmented into small blocks of advertising and/or editorial. Generally, 60 percent of a newspaper's space is devoted to advertising. Therefore, making an ad stand out and make an impression on the reader is a challenging creative task. The inclusion of advertising inserts on certain days compounds the clutter problem, as does the hasty manner in which people read newspapers. Including colour will increase an ad's attention-grabbing ability, but colour is an added cost.

POOR REPRODUCTION QUALITY   Advertisers may compare newspapers to magazines on any number of bases. With respect to quality of print reproduction, newspapers compare very poorly. Detracting from the quality of the print production in newspapers are the quality and speed of the printing presses and the poor quality of newsprint used. As newspapers continue to shift to offset presses (magazine presses) the quality of reproduction, particularly for colour ads, will improve.

HIGH COST   The high cost of newspaper advertising is a problem faced by national advertisers. As an advertiser adds markets to its list in order to reach regional or national market coverage objectives, the cost of newspaper advertising suddenly becomes quite high. For example, the cost of running a $1/_2$ page black-and-white ad in five key markets (1MM+ population) involves 16 daily newspapers. The cost of the space would be $157 500. The addition of one colour to the ad increases the cost another $39 600. If the ad runs in full colour the cost increase is $58 200.[7] This example demonstrates that advertisers must consider alternative media if they wish to increase regional or national coverage for a product, or if the product's target market is precisely defined.

Buying Newspaper Space

Newspaper space is sold on the basis of agate lines or modular agate lines. An **agate line** is a non-standardized unit of space measurement, equal to one column wide and $1/_{14}$-inch deep. For **broadsheets**, standard pages are $11^1/_2$ inches wide with column widths of $1^1/_{16}$ inches. The number of columns ranges from 7 to 10, so full-page lineage ranges from 1800 to 3150 agate lines. In **tabloids**, the number of columns ranges from 5 to 10 and full-page lineage ranges from 875 to 1050 agate lines. A majority of broadsheets and tabloids use agate lines to determine the size of an advertisement.

A **modular agate line** is a standardized unit of measurement equal to one column wide and $1/_{14}$-inch deep. Standard column widths are $2^1/_{16}$ inches in broadsheets. A modular agate line is wider than an agate line.

Readers should note that the lines and columns referred to here are not physical lines and columns. They are invisible lines and columns that the newspaper industry refers to for the purposes of measuring the size of an ad.

The basic procedure for buying newspaper space is to determine the size of the ad either in agate lines or modular agate lines. In either case, the cost is calculated by multiplying the width of the ad (number of columns) by the depth of the ad (inches of depth). *One column inch* of depth equals *14 agate lines*. Other factors that influence costs include the number of insertions, creative considerations such as the use of colour, and position charges, if applicable. The following section includes some examples of how to calculate the costs of newspaper advertising.

At one time, the newspaper industry attempted to standardize newspaper ad sizes to a modular format by dividing a newspaper page into newspaper units. But, facing higher costs, newspapers started to downsize and reformat. Such action reduced the production benefits gained by standardization to modular format. This causes confusion when agencies are dealing with all kinds of newspapers.

To simplify matters, some newspapers offer standard-size ads that are easier to understand in terms of size. With reference to *The Globe and Mail* (see Figure 8.4), some

FIGURE 8.4

Some standard size options in newspapers

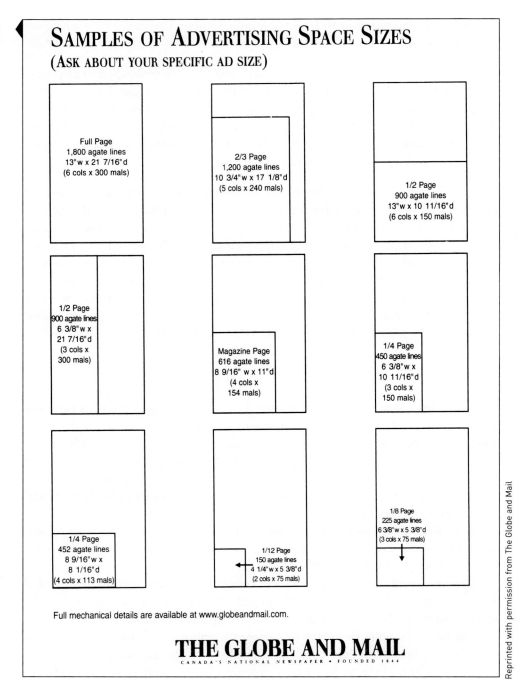

of the standard-size options include full-page (1800 agate lines), half-page (900 agate lines), magazine page (616 agate lines), and quarter-page (453 agate lines).

DETERMINE SPACE SIZE

For the sake of example, let's assume that space is being purchased in agate lines. The size of the ad is 4 columns wide by 12 column inches deep. Considering that each column inch of depth equals 14 agate lines, the size of the ad would be calculated by the following formula:

$$\text{Number of columns wide} \times \text{inches of depth} \times 14$$
$$4 \times 12 \times 14 = 672 \text{ agate lines}$$

If the size of the advertisement were 6 columns wide by 8 inches deep, the size of the ad in agate lines would be:

$$6 \times 8 \times 14 = 672 \text{ lines}$$

These two examples illustrate that different configurations of ads (combinations of width and depth) may produce the same size of ad in terms of space occupied and rates charged for the space.

The calculations above would be the same for modular agate lines. The only difference is that the modular agate line is slightly wider than the agate line. Before calculating the costs of an ad the planner must be aware of what system the newspaper is using: agate lines or modular agate lines.

Newspaper space can be sold on the basis of **modular units**, though only a few daily newspapers use this system. If this system is used, the size of the ad is expressed in terms of units of width and units of depth (e.g., 2 units wide by 5 units deep). In effect, the page is sectioned off into equal-sized units with each unit being 30 modular agate lines deep. Therefore, to calculate the actual size of an ad that is 2 units wide by 5 units deep, the calculation would be as follows:

$$\text{Number of columns wide} \times \text{units deep} \times 30$$
$$= \text{Modular agate lines } 2 \times 5 \times 30 = 300 \text{ MAL}$$

RATE SCHEDULES

Line rate is defined as the advertising rate charged by newspapers for one agate line or one modular agate line. With regard to rate schedules, several factors must be noted. First, rates charged by line go down as the volume of the lineage increases over a specified period. Second, costs for the addition of colour or preferred positions are quoted separately. Third, the line rates may vary from one section of the paper to another. For example, the transient rate (the highest rate paid by an advertiser) for advertisers in *The Globe and Mail's* News and Report on Business sections is higher than in *The Globe Review*, Technology, Travel, and Special Interest sections. See Figure 8.5, The *Globe and Mail* rate card, for more details about line rates.

In the chart in Figure 8.5, the rates quoted start with a **transient rate**, which is defined as a one-time rate or base rate that applies to casual advertisers. Discounts are offered to advertisers purchasing volume lineage over a more extended period of time, usually one year.

To illustrate how costs are calculated in newspapers, let's develop a hypothetical plan and consider the use of agate lines and modular agate lines. For the sake of accuracy, however, it should be noted that *The Globe and Mail* does quote rates in terms of space occupied measured by modular agate lines.

Newspaper	*The Globe and Mail*—National Edition, News Section
Size of Ad	4 columns wide × 10 column inches deep
Rate	Transient Rate—General Advertising
Frequency	Once

The first calculation would determine, as follows, the total number of agate lines:

$$4 \text{ columns wide} \times 10 \text{ column inches deep} \times 14 = 560 \text{ lines}$$

The next step would be to multiply the number of agate lines by the line rate by the frequency to determine the cost of the insertion. In this case, the transient rate would apply because there are not enough lines to earn a discount.

$$560 \times \$31.89 = \$17\ 858.40$$

FIGURE
8.5

The Globe and Mail rate card

THE GLOBE AND MAIL
CANADA'S NATIONAL NEWSPAPER • FOUNDED 1844

Advertising Rates effective January 1, 2004

General Rates

Canada's largest and leading national newspaper is, without a doubt, the No. 1 choice for reaching affluent and educated Canadians from coast to coast*.

Industry studies repeatedly confirm that The Globe and Mail dominates the national newspaper market in Canada – and by a widening margin.

The Globe and Mail is a unique medium with the most educated, influential, affluent and loyal readers in Canada – an audience you can't find anywhere else.

No matter what you need to advertise, The Globe and Mail delivers more of your best prospects in numbers too significant to ignore.

When quality prospects with money to spend and intent to purchase matter to your media buy, buy The Globe and Mail.

NEWS, REPORT ON BUSINESS, FOCUS
Report on Business appears Monday through Saturday – National Edition only.
Focus appears every Saturday.

Monday to Friday

MALS**	National	Ont/Que	Metro
Transient	$31.89	$27.53	$25.35
900	30.93	26.72	24.59
1,800	30.15	25.91	23.87
3,600	29.35	25.19	23.16
5,400	28.38	24.36	22.43
7,200	27.90	23.99	22.09
10,000	26.95	23.17	21.35
13,000	26.47	22.77	20.96
16,000	26.00	22.38	20.60
20,000	25.65	22.10	20.36
25,000	25.20	21.69	19.98
32,000	24.72	21.27	19.59
43,000	24.39	20.98	19.35
58,000	23.76	20.43	18.83
75,000	23.12	19.87	18.30
100,000	22.32	19.16	17.65
135,000	21.53	18.49	17.03
175,000	20.57	17.66	16.28

Saturday

MALS**	National	Ont/Que	Metro
Transient	$33.47	$28.91	$26.62
900	32.48	28.05	25.83
1,800	31.66	27.22	25.06
3,600	30.82	26.46	24.33
5,400	29.80	25.58	23.54
7,200	29.31	25.19	23.19
10,000	28.30	24.34	22.42
13,000	27.79	23.92	22.01
16,000	27.29	23.49	21.63
20,000	26.94	23.21	21.38
25,000	26.47	22.77	20.98
32,000	25.97	22.33	20.58
43,000	25.61	22.03	20.32
58,000	24.95	21.46	19.76
75,000	24.27	20.86	19.22
100,000	23.45	20.13	18.53
135,000	22.60	19.41	17.88
175,000	21.59	18.54	17.09

GLOBE REVIEW, TRAVEL
Globe Review appears Monday through Saturday.
Travel appears Wednesday and Saturday.

Monday to Friday

MALS**	National	Ont/Que	Metro
Transient	$19.89	$17.24	$15.82
900	19.16	16.60	15.21
1,800	18.60	16.11	14.74
3,600	17.94	15.63	14.13
5,400	17.47	15.11	13.71
7,200	17.26	14.91	13.60
10,000	16.72	14.44	13.18
13,000	16.40	14.19	12.94
16,000	16.16	13.97	12.76
20,000	15.95	13.80	12.58
25,000	15.70	13.56	12.37
32,000	15.41	13.29	12.14
43,000	15.21	13.14	11.98
58,000	14.89	12.84	11.71
75,000	14.56	12.56	11.46
100,000	14.13	12.21	11.12
135,000	13.70	11.84	10.77
175,000	13.10	11.30	10.29

Saturday

MALS**	National	Ont/Que	Metro
Transient	$20.88	$18.09	$16.61
900	20.13	17.44	15.97
1,800	19.52	16.91	15.48
3,600	18.85	16.41	14.85
5,400	18.34	15.87	14.41
7,200	18.11	15.66	14.28
10,000	17.56	15.16	13.83
13,000	17.22	14.90	13.58
16,000	16.98	14.66	13.40
20,000	16.75	14.48	13.21
25,000	16.50	14.24	12.99
32,000	16.19	13.97	12.75
43,000	15.97	13.80	12.58
58,000	15.63	13.49	12.30
75,000	15.30	13.20	12.03
100,000	14.85	12.82	11.68
135,000	14.40	12.43	11.31
175,000	13.76	11.87	10.82

Advertising rates shown are per line per day.

* SOURCE: NADbank 2002, 37 National Markets.

** Volume rates based on modular agate lines.
All rates are gross. Prices in Canadian dollars.

YOU ALSO NEED TO KNOW:
Any advertising published by The Globe and Mail in the newspaper or any of its other publications may, at our discretion, be published, displayed, retained and archived by us and anyone authorized (including any form of licence) by us, as many times as we and those authorized by us wish, in or on any product, media and archive (including print, electronic and otherwise).

All advertising must meet Globe and Mail terms and conditions – ask for a printed copy from your Globe and Mail advertising representative.

Toronto:
tel (416) 585-5111
toll-free 1-800-387-9012
fax (416) 585-5698

Montreal:
tel (514) 982-3050
toll-free 1-800-363-7526
(from NFLD, NS, PEI, NB, PQ)
fax (514) 845-8766

Western Canada:
tel (604) 685-0308
toll-free 1-800-663-1311
(from BC, AB, SK, NT)
fax (604) 685-7549

United States and international advertising representatives:
Publicitas, New York, NY
tel (212) 599-5057
fax (212) 599-8298

on-line media kit at **globeandmail.com/advertise**

As indicated in the rate schedule in Figure 8.5, the cost of each advertisement will be less if the *volume of lines purchased* meets or exceeds the line requirements on the volume scales. To illustrate the effect of such a situation on costs, let's assume the same information as in the preceding example, with one change. This time, the ad will run 10

FIGURE
8.5

continued

General Rates

SPORTS AND STYLE

Style appears Saturday.
Sports appears daily.

Monday to Friday

MALS**	National	Ont/Que	Metro
Transient	$15.14	$13.15	$12.04
900	14.60	12.65	11.59
1,800	13.99	12.27	11.09
3,600	13.49	11.89	10.59
5,400	13.13	11.50	10.28
7,200	13.10	11.35	10.20
10,000	12.76	11.00	9.94
13,000	12.51	10.82	9.77
16,000	12.32	10.64	9.67
20,000	12.18	10.51	9.57
25,000	11.95	10.33	9.40
32,000	11.75	10.14	9.26
43,000	11.59	10.00	9.14
58,000	11.34	9.79	8.93
75,000	11.09	9.58	8.70
100,000	10.74	9.29	8.47
135,000	10.44	9.01	8.19
175,000	10.03	8.66	7.82

Saturday

MALS**	National	Ont/Que	Metro
Transient	$15.90	$13.81	$12.64
900	15.33	13.28	12.17
1,800	14.69	12.88	11.63
3,600	14.16	12.48	11.13
5,400	13.79	12.08	10.80
7,200	13.76	11.92	10.70
10,000	13.40	11.56	10.44
13,000	13.13	11.35	10.25
16,000	12.94	11.16	10.16
20,000	12.79	11.04	10.04
25,000	12.55	10.85	9.88
32,000	12.34	10.66	9.72
43,000	12.17	10.50	9.59
58,000	11.91	10.27	9.38
75,000	11.63	10.05	9.15
100,000	11.29	9.75	8.90
135,000	10.96	9.46	8.60
175,000	10.52	9.08	8.22

COLOUR CHARGES

National	Ont/Que	Metro
$8,204	$7,460	$6,863

NOTICES

Appointment Notices	$55.00
Financial Notices/Tombstones	40.13

GLOBE CAREERS

Includes 3 insertions – Wednesday, Friday and Saturday or Monday	$40.50

REGIONAL EDITIONS

Eastern Edition

Monday to Friday	$7.25 transient
Saturday	7.61 transient

Includes Ottawa, Quebec and Atlantic Canada.

Western Edition

Monday to Friday	$8.94 transient
Saturday	9.39 transient

Includes British Columbia, Alberta, Manitoba and Saskatchewan.

Eastern and Western editions published daily in front news.

Colour subject to availability.

RESERVATIONS AND CLOSINGS

Issue Day	Space Booking	Pub-set Material
Mon.	Thurs. 4.30pm	Wed. 4.30pm
Tues.	Fri. 4.30pm	Thurs. 4.30pm
Wed.	Mon. 4.30pm	Fri. 4.30pm
Thurs.	Tues. 4.30pm	Mon. 4.30pm
Fri.	Wed. 4.30pm	Tues. 4.30pm
Sat.	Thurs. 4.30pm	Wed. 4.30pm
Mon. Careers	Thurs. 2:00pm	Wed. 2:00pm
Wed. Careers	Mon. 2:00pm	Fri. 2:00pm
Fri. Careers	Wed. 2:00pm	Tues. 2:00pm
Sat. Careers	Thurs. 2:00pm	Wed. 2:00pm
Wed. Travel	Fri. 4:30pm	Fri. 4:30pm
Sat. Travel	Tues. 4:30pm	Tues. 4:30pm
Sat. Style	Tues. 2:30pm	Mon. 4:30pm
Saturday Review	Thurs. 10:00am	Wed. 4:30pm

All deadlines are based on Eastern Standard Time.

Complete deadlines listed on our Web site: globeandmail.com/advertise

Colour advertising
4 business days in advance for space booking and material.

Double truck
4 business days in advance for space booking and material.

COPY CHANGES

News, Report on Business, Sports, Globe Review (excluding Weekend Review)
2:00pm day prior to publication date.

Wednesday Travel:
Monday 4:30pm.

Style: Thursday 12:00pm.

Saturday Travel/Review:
Thursday 4:30pm.

Saturday Books:
Thursday 12:00pm.

ADDITIONAL INFORMATION

- Deadlines and specifications available separately.
- There is a $68.00 production charge for ads under 50 MAL that are not camera-ready.
- Minimum display space in News, Style, and Report on Business is 30 MAL; unless specified, it is 15 MAL in other sections.
- Advertising columns 251 MAL or more in depth are charged full column depth.
- Double Trucks: Gutter is charged as full column.
- Regional copy changes: $500 per plant.
- Position charge: +25 per cent.
- Front News Banner: +50 per cent.
- Page 3, News: +40 per cent.
- Pages 2 & 3, ROB: +40 per cent.
- Charge for Globe and Mail box number: $68.00.
- Charge for affidavits: $68.00.

- Cancellation charge: 50 per cent for ads cancelled after deadline. No cancellations for colour advertising two days prior to publication. No cancellations accepted the day prior to publication.
- The Publisher shall not be liable for errors in advertisements beyond the actual space paid. No liability for non-insertions of any advertisement.
- Not responsible for return of advertising material.

NEWSPAPER SPECIFICATIONS

Complete mechanical and digital specifications available separately.

Number of columns: 6.

Column width: 50mm
11.9 picas
1.96" (approx. 1 15/16")

Column depth: 300 modular agate lines for full page ads (1,800 lines per 6 column page).

THE GLOBE AND MAIL

CANADA'S NATIONAL NEWSPAPER • FOUNDED 1844 • GLOBEANDMAIL.COM

times (twice a week, Monday and Wednesday, for five weeks). In this case, the total lines purchased would be as follows:

4 columns wide $\times$ 10 column inches deep $\times$ 14 $\times$ 10 insertions = 5600 lines

Based on the rate schedule (Figure 8.5), the rate per line in the national edition would be $24.41. Therefore, the total costs of the campaign would be calculated as follows:

Total lines purchased × line rate = Total cost

5600 × $28.38 = $158 928

Where the cost of the advertisement in the original example was $17 858.40, the cost of each advertisement in this campaign would be $15 892.80 ($158 928 divided by 10 insertions). For additional illustrations of how to calculate costs, refer to Figure 8.6. The next example will consider modular agate lines.

Newspaper	Globe and Mail Metro Edition
Number of columns	6 columns wide
Units of depth	4 units deep
Edition Metro	—
Frequency	4 times

The calculation for the number of modular agate lines is as follows:

6 columns wide × 4 units deep × 30 × 4 insertions = 2880 MAL

The cost calculation for this number of lines would be:

Total lines purchased × the line rate

2880 × $23.87 = $68 745.60

SPACE CONTRACTS AND THE SHORT RATE

To facilitate the use of the volume-discount scale, large advertisers usually enter into a **space contract** with newspapers. This space contract is an agreement with conditions:

- The advertiser estimates the amount of lineage required for one year, but does not guarantee the purchase.
- The advertiser is billed during the year by the newspaper at the estimated rate.
- The advertiser agrees to a rate adjustment at the end of the year (positive or negative) based on the actual lines purchased.

To illustrate the use of a space contract, let's assume the estimated lineage for the national edition of *The Globe and Mail* (refer to Figure 8.5) was 10 000 modular agate lines for a one-year period. The corresponding line rate would be $26.95. At the end of the year, the actual MAL purchase totalled 9000. What is the effect on costs for the advertiser?

Since the advertiser estimated that 10 000 modular agate lines would be purchased, the rate billed by the newspaper was $26.95 per line. However, since the advertiser purchased only 9000 lines, which was less than estimated, the line rate actually charged at the end of the year would be based on the $27.90 line rate. The difference between the two line rates is referred to as the **short rate**. In this example, the calculation would be as follows:

Costs based on estimated line rate (rate for 10 000 lines):

9000 lines × $26.95 = $242 550

Costs based on actual line rate:

9000 lines × $27.90 = $251 100
Balance due newspaper = $8550

The advertiser would therefore owe the newspaper $8550, according to the terms of the space contract. Conversely, if the advertiser purchased more than the estimated number of lines and graduated to the next level up on the volume scale, the newspaper would give the advertisers a rebate. For the benefit of advertisers contemplating more extensive use of newspaper advertising, space contracts can be backdated so that previous advertising volume can be grouped together to earn volume rates. Transient rates apply to unsigned space contracts and backdating policies vary from one newspaper to another, but a 90-day period is quite common.

POSITION CHARGES

Since a disadvantage of newspaper advertising is clutter, advertisers and agencies normally request positions in the newspaper that are deemed to be favourable. The request may be for a particular section, or it could be for the first few pages of the newspaper. In the case of a broadsheet, advertisers commonly request a position "above the fold." To keep advertisers satisfied, a newspaper will do its best to accommodate requests, but there are no guarantees that requests will be honoured.

As mentioned above, the privilege of having a preferred position in a newspaper comes at a higher cost—that cost is referred to as a **position charge**. The position charge is normally quoted as a percentage increase over the insertion cost. Referring to *The Globe and Mail*'s rate card (see the "additional information" section in Figure 8.5), we see that a specific position request adds 25 percent to the cost of the insertion. The advertiser usually justifies the additional expense of a position request by referring to the improved recognition and recall that will result from the better position. Also note that an ad appearing on page 3 of the News section increases cost by 40 percent, and a banner ad on the front page increases the cost by 50 percent.

Newspaper publishers reserve the right to place advertisements at their discretion, unless a preferred position charge is paid. The placing of advertisements anywhere within the regular printed pages of a newspaper is referred to as **ROP (run of press, run of paper)**.

COLOUR CHARGES

Although newspapers are often referred to as the black-and-white medium, colour is available to advertisers willing to pay for it. Additional costs are incurred as the number of colours increases. Colour charges are normally quoted on the basis of spot colour or full colour. With reference to *The Globe and Mail*'s rate schedule in Figure 8.5, the addition of full colour adds $8204 to the cost of an ad. There are minimum size requirements for ads that include colour. Refer to Figure 8.6 for cost examples that include colour and position charges.

Does the use of colour justify the additional expense? In making this decision, the advertiser must weigh the potential impact of colour on the reader against the cost of colour. Much research has been done on the impact of colour in newspaper advertising. The research finds that full colour draws readers to ads (noted scores are higher) and keeps them more involved in the message. Colour also boosts in-depth reading by 60 percent compared to black-and-white ads. Colour has more of an impact on readers than does the size of the ad.[8]

MULTIPLE-PAGE CHARGES

Multiple-page charges apply to advertisers that use multiple pages in a single issue of a newspaper. For example, supermarkets, department stores, and shopping malls often use double-page spreads, referred to as a **double truck**, or multiple pages to advertise

FIGURE
8.6

Illustrations of calculating
newspaper advertising costs

Refer to the rate card in
Figure 8.5 to see where line
costs were obtained.

The following illustrations consider two aspects of newspaper buying: the addition of colour and requesting specific locations

ILLUSTRATION 1—ADDITION OF COLOUR

Newspaper:	The Globe and Mail, National Edition, News Section
Size of Ad:	6 columns wide by 12 column inches deep
Colour:	All ads full colour
Frequency:	8 insertions
Timing:	1 insertion each Wednesday for 8 consecutive weeks

The cost calculation would be as follows:

Total Number of Lines
$(6 \times 12 \times 14) \times 8 = 8064$ lines

Cost of the Ad (in black & white)
$8064 \times \$27.90 = \$224\ 985.60$

Additional Colour Cost
$\$8204 \times 8 = \$65\ 632.00$

Total Cost
$\$224\ 985.60 + \$65\ 632.00 = \$290\ 617.60$

ILLUSTRATION 2—POSITION REQUEST

Newspaper:	The Globe and Mail, Metro Edition, News Section
Size of Ad:	6 columns wide by 8 column inches deep
Colour:	Black and white
Frequency:	10
Location Request:	page A5 (news section)

The cost calculation would be as follows:

Total Number of Lines
$(6 \times 8 \times 14) \times 10 = 6720$ lines

Cost of Ad
$6720 \times \$22.43 = \$150.729.60$

Position Charge (add 25%)
$\$150\ 929.60 \times 1.25 = \$188\ 412.00$

weekly specials. In this situation, reduced line rates apply based on the number of pages purchased. Double-truck and multiple-page rates may or may not be quoted on a newspaper's rate card but are available by contacting the newspaper.

PREPRINTED INSERTS

Preprinted **inserts**, such as advertising **supplements** for supermarkets and department stores, are inserted into and distributed by most newspapers. Costs are usually quoted on a CPM (cost per thousand) basis, with rates increasing with the size of the insert. For example, a 24-page catalogue insert would cost more than a four-page folded insert. Insert rates are quoted separately on newspaper rate cards.

SPLIT RUNS

A **split run** occurs when an advertiser uses the full circulation of the publication but has different material appearing in two or more regions. Split runs can be used for testing the effectiveness of various advertisements that are under consideration. For example, an advertiser may want to test some variations in layout and design. To do so, the various ads are placed in the same newspaper but they are distributed to different areas. The action generated in each region is compared to determine which ad was more effective. If the ads contained coupons of the same value, redemption rates would determine which ad was most effective in stimulating action.

INSERTION ORDERS

Details of a newspaper ad are communicated via an insertion order. The **insertion order** specifies pertinent details including the size of the ad, the dates of its insertion, use of colour, position requests, and the line rate to be charged. Closing dates and cancellation dates may also be included.

To verify that an advertisement actually ran, the agency or the advertiser receives a "tear sheet" from the newspaper. As the name implies, a **tear sheet** is an ad that the newspaper personnel extract from the newspaper to illustrate to the advertiser how it actually appeared. Should there be any problems with the ad, such as poor production quality, the advertiser or agency might request a **make good**, a rerun of an ad at the publisher's expense.

COMPARING NEWSPAPERS FOR EFFICIENCY

In larger metropolitan markets, where several newspapers compete for advertising revenue, advertisers must decide which papers to place advertising with. If using a shotgun strategy, the advertiser may use all newspapers. Conversely, if budgets are limited and target markets are more precisely defined, the advertiser may be more selective in the decision-making process.

Since the circulations and the costs of advertising (line rates) vary among newspapers, the advertiser must have a way of comparing the alternatives. To make this comparison, the advertiser may use a standard figure called the CPM. **CPM** is the actual cost of reaching 1000 readers in a market. The formula for calculating CPM is as follows:

$$CPM = \frac{\text{Unit Cost of Message}}{\text{Circulation (in thousands)}}$$

To illustrate the concept of CPM, advertisers wanting to reach adults in the Toronto market would choose among three daily newspapers. See Figure 8.7 for specific details of how the newspapers are compared.

As shown by Figure 8.7, the newspaper CPM is strictly a quantitative figure and the results vary considerably. If the advertiser's decision regarding what newspaper to use were based solely on this principle, the decision would be an easy one—the *Toronto Star* and *Toronto Sun* have lower CPM. Not shown in a CPM calculation is the demographic profile of the readers of the various newspapers. The *Toronto Star* and *Toronto Sun* offer mass appeal to a broad cross-section of the Toronto population at very reasonable costs compared with those of *The Globe and Mail*. However, if the target market is more upscale in terms of income, occupation, and educational background *The Globe and Mail* might be selected, despite the higher CPM. See Figure 8.8 for a profile of the *Globe and Mail* reader compared to the population at large.

FIGURE
8.7

Comparison of newspapers
based on CPM: Cost of
reaching 1000 people

Printed with permission
of CARD, Rogers Media
Publishing, Toronto, Canada

Specifications	Toronto Star	Globe and Mail	Toronto Sun	National Post
Ad Size	900 lines	900 lines	900 lines	900 lines
Cost per Line	$17.89	$29.46	$7.53	$15.28
Ad Cost (rate × lines)	$16 101	$26 514	$6 777	$13 752
Circulation	440 901	414 946	208 907	247 690
CPM	$36.52	$84.20	$32.44	$55.52

Analysis: The CPM for the Toronto Star and Toronto Sun are close. Both papers would have a similar readership profile. The Globe and Mail reaches an audience characterized by higher education, higher income, and professional occupations. The cost of reaching a more upscale reader is much more. The CPM for the National Post is lower than The Globe and Mail even though the readership profile is similar. The National Post is a newer paper trying to establish a circulation base. Its advertising rates are lower during this time to attract advertisers.

Source: Adapted from *Canadian Advertising Rates and Data*, November 2003.

In summary, CPM is a quantitative figure that fluctuates with changes in the line rate or circulation: the higher the circulation, the lower the CPM. Advertisers can use it as a base guideline for comparing the varying cost efficiencies of specific newspapers that reach a mass target market.

Magazines in Canada

Currently, 1600 magazines are published and distributed in Canada, 550 of which are classified as consumer magazines. Magazines are classified in many ways—by content and audience reached, by circulation, by frequency of publication, and by size and format.

CONTENT AND AUDIENCE REACHED

In terms of content and audience reached, publications fall into two major categories: consumer magazines and business magazines. Both categories include general-interest and special-interest publications. In both consumer and business magazines, the content is such that it has high interest among a precisely defined target market.

CONSUMER MAGAZINES

Canadian Advertising Rates and Data indexes 50 sub-classifications of consumer magazines, with the classification based on the publication's content and audience. There is a strong base of general-interest magazines, as well as a host of specialized classifications such as art and antiques, children, entertainment, hobbies, sports and recreation, and women's. Popular, high-circulation magazines in their respective categories include *Reader's Digest* (General Interest classification), *Maclean's* (News classification), *Chatelaine* (Women's classification), *Flare* (Fashion classification), and *Style at Home* (Homes classification).

BUSINESS MAGAZINES

Business magazines can be broadly subdivided into subject areas such as trade, industry, professional, and institutional. Sub-classifications of these general areas would include broadcasting, engineering construction, food and food processing, hardware trade, hotels and restaurants, photography, and telecommunications. Business publications tend to be very specialized, their content appealing to a particular industry,

FIGURE

8.8

Demographic profile of *Globe and Mail* readers

THE GLOBE AND MAIL
ON-LINE MEDIA KIT AT ADRATES.GLOBEANDMAIL.COM

NATIONAL EDITION
Weekday and Saturday Readership Facts

Updated March 31, 2003

% COMPOSITION

GENDER	GLOBE AND MAIL WEEKDAY (M-F)	GLOBE AND MAIL SATURDAY	ADULT POPULATION
Male	58.1%	53.1%	48.7%
Female	41.9	46.9	51.3

AGE DISTRIBUTION	GLOBE AND MAIL WEEKDAY (M-F)	GLOBE AND MAIL SATURDAY	ADULT POPULATION
18-24	7.8%	7.3%	12.1%
25-34	20.2	18.4	19.6
35-49	32.3	30.5	32.2
50-64	25.6	26.6	20.8
65+	13.8	17.3	15.3
Age 25-54	64.2	60.5	61.3
Average Age	46.1 yrs	47.7 yrs	45.0 yrs

MARITAL STATUS*	GLOBE AND MAIL WEEKDAY (M-F)	GLOBE AND MAIL SATURDAY	ADULT POPULATION
Married/ Living Together	66.6%	65.0%	60.9%
Single/ Widowed/ Separated/ Divorced	33.4	35.0	39.1

LEVEL OF EDUCATION	GLOBE AND MAIL WEEKDAY (M-F)	GLOBE AND MAIL SATURDAY	ADULT POPULATION
Some Post-Secondary	22.6%	23.3%	32.1%
University Graduate +	60.4	61.5	29.1
Post-Grad. Degree	25.3	25.8	8.8

EMPLOYMENT STATUS	GLOBE AND MAIL WEEKDAY (M-F)	GLOBE AND MAIL SATURDAY	ADULT POPULATION
Self-Employed	15.4%	16.5%	11.5%
Other Employed	55.5	50.2	51.4

% COMPOSITION

OCCUPATION	GLOBE AND MAIL WEEKDAY (M-F)	GLOBE AND MAIL SATURDAY	ADULT POPULATION
Management (Senior/other)	24.7%	21.5%	14.1%
Professionals	9.5	8.6	4.3
Net MPs (Senior/ Other mgmt; Professionals)	34.2	30.0	18.4
Other White Collar	20.2	20.3	17.7

PERSONAL INCOME	GLOBE AND MAIL WEEKDAY (M-F)	GLOBE AND MAIL SATURDAY	ADULT POPULATION
$50,000+	46.0%	44.3%	24.4%
$60,000+	31.9	30.4	13.4
$75,000+	20.3	19.1	6.8
$100,000+	11.1	10.5	3.1
Avg. Personal Income	$55,194	$53,808	$38,148

HOUSEHOLD INCOME	GLOBE AND MAIL WEEKDAY (M-F)	GLOBE AND MAIL SATURDAY	ADULT POPULATION
$50,000+	78.7%	76.5%	59.8%
$60,000+	66.5	64.7	46.1
$75,000+	54.7	52.6	32.8
$100,000+	36.7	34.9	17.7
Avg. Household Income	$87,693	$85,507	$65,185

HOUSEHOLD COMPOSITION*	GLOBE AND MAIL WEEKDAY (M-F)	GLOBE AND MAIL SATURDAY	ADULT POPULATION
Adults only	65.7%	69.0%	64.6%
Adults with children	34.3	31.0	35.4

DWELLING*	GLOBE AND MAIL WEEKDAY (M-F)	GLOBE AND MAIL SATURDAY	ADULT POPULATION
Own	76.0%	76.9%	69.6%
Rent	24.0	23.1	30.4

SOURCE: NADbank 2002 Total Readership Study

BASE: 37 National Edition Readership Markets (Toronto EMA included)

* Repercentaged – excluding Don't Know/Not Stated

Average Issue Weekday Readership: 950,100

Average Issue Saturday Readership: 1,019,100

Six-day Cumulative Net Reach: 2,475,400

CONTACT INFORMATION:

Toronto
tel 416.585.5600
toll-free 1.800.387.9012
fax 416.585.5682

Montreal
tel 514.982.3050
toll-free 1.800.363.7526
(from NFLD, NS, PEI, NB, PQ)
fax 514.845.8766

Western Canada
tel 604.685.0308
toll-free 1.800.663.1311
(from BC, AB, SK, NT)
fax 604.685.7549

United States and international advertising representatives
Publicitas, New York, NY
tel 212.599.5057
fax 212.599.8298

Reprinted with permission from The Globe and Mail.

trade, or professional group. With a very well-defined target audience, such specialized publications allow an efficient use of media dollars by advertisers.

Business magazines can also be classified as horizontal or vertical. A **horizontal publication** appeals to people who occupy the same level of responsibility in a business—the senior management level, for example. Horizontal publications tend to be more general in content, dealing with subjects such as business issues and trends, management information systems, effective business management principles, and so on. Examples of horizontal business publications are *Canadian Business, National Post Business, ROB Magazine*, and *Profit*. Also classified as horizontal are those publications aimed at people who have functions in their companies similar to those discussed in the magazine. A magazine such as *Modern Purchasing* would be directed at the purchasing managers and agents in any number of different industries.

Vertical publications appeal to all levels of people in the same industry. All specialized classifications and corresponding magazines fall into this category. *Canadian Grocer*, for example, appeals to those people employed in the food processing and food distribution business in Canada, while *Foodservice & Hospitality* magazine appeals to those employed in the restaurant, hotel, or food service industry.

CIRCULATION BASE (DISTRIBUTION)

Canadian magazines are distributed on the basis of **paid circulation**, which refers to subscriptions and newsstand sales. Magazines such as *Maclean's, Time, Chatelaine, Flare*, and *Canadian Business* are paid-circulation magazines and rely on subscriptions, newsstand sales, and advertising space to generate revenues.

Some magazines are distributed on the basis of **controlled circulation**. In this case the magazine is distributed free to a predetermined target market (e.g., a target defined by demographic segment, geographic area, or job function). A controlled-circulation magazine generates revenue from advertising space only. Typically, receivers of the magazine are in a unique position to influence sales, so they are attractive to advertisers wanting to reach them.

Homemaker's/Madame au Foyer is an example of a widely distributed women's magazine that combines paid circulation with controlled circulation (about 15 percent of their circulation receives the magazine for free). Other magazines, many of which have a city-lifestyle orientation, are examples of controlled-circulation magazines. Included in this group are publications such as *Ottawa City Magazine, OttawaLife*, and *Vancouver Magazine*. These are distributed to selected households, apartments, condominiums, and hotels in a defined geographic area.

FREQUENCY OF PUBLICATION AND REGIONAL EDITIONS

The frequency of publication varies considerably from one magazine to another. The more common frequencies are monthly and weekly; more limited frequencies are biweekly, bimonthly, or quarterly. Numerous magazines offer regional editions. Popular consumer magazines such as *Canadian Living/Coup de Pouce, Chatelaine* (English and French), and *Maclean's* offer advertisers regional flexibility in reaching geographic targets. The following is a sampling of magazines, their respective publication frequencies, and regional flexibilities:

Magazine Publications	Frequency of Editions	Regional
Canadian Business	24 bimonthly	1
Reader's Digest	12 monthly	16
Maclean's	52 weekly	14
Chatelaine (Eng. & Fr.)	12 monthly	7
Flare	12 monthly	6

SIZE AND FORMAT

Canadian magazines are published in three distinct sizes: digest, standard, and larger size. Owing to the rising costs of production, mailing, and distribution, there is currently a trend toward smaller publications.

A **digest-size magazine**'s approximate dimensions are $5^1/_2$ inches $\times$ $7^1/_4$ inches (140 cm $\times$ 184 cm), with a two-column printing format. *Reader's Digest /Sélection du Reader's Digest* is a good example of this type of format. The dimensions of a **standard-size magazine** are 8 $\times$ 11 inches (203 cm $\times$ 279 cm), with a three-column format. Among the popular magazines that appear in this size and format are *Maclean's, Chatelaine, Canadian Business,* and *Equinox.*

Some magazines are produced in a **large-size format**. The dimensions of larger magazines vary from one publication to another. *Marketing* is a large-size business publication, with dimensions of $11^1/_4$ inches $\times$ $16^1/_4$ inches (286 cm $\times$ 413 cm). It is published in a five-column format. The *National Post Business* magazine uses a wider-than-normal two-column format.

National Post
www.nationalpost.com

MAGAZINE CIRCULATION AND READERSHIP HIGHLIGHTS Magazines are sold to advertisers on the basis of circulation and readership. It is a very competitive market where advertisers often have choices to make between various magazines. Circulation and readership figures are verified by independent data collection organizations: Audit Bureau of Circulations, Canadian Circulations Audit Board, and the Print Measurement Bureau.

The Audit Bureau of Circulations (ABC) issues standardized statements, referred to as publisher's statements, verifying circulation statistics for paid circulation magazines and most daily newspapers in Canada. A **publisher's statement** includes the average paid circulation for the past six months, paid circulation for each issue in the last six months, new and renewal subscriptions, and a geographic analysis of **total paid circulation**.

The Canadian Circulations Audit Board (CCAB) provides similar information but its focus is primarily on business, trade, and professional publications. It also provides data for selected consumer magazines and community and daily newspapers. The data provided by ABC and CCAB offers two benefits to advertisers. First, they can analyze circulation trends to determine which magazines are more popular. Second, they can determine how effective a publication is at reaching their target market.

The Print Measurement Bureau (PMB) tracks the readership of all magazines from year to year. Readership information is collected in an annual research study. The readership data that is collected is cross-referenced with other data of interest to advertisers. That data includes product and brand usage data, retail shopping habits, and lifestyles. When analyzing what magazines to select for advertising, comparisons are made between circulation and readership among a selection of prospective magazines. Wise managers will look at both statistics when making decisions. It is possible that a magazine with a lower circulation has more readers per copy than a magazine with higher circulation, resulting in a higher readership level. **Readers per copy** refers to the average number of people who read a single issue of a publication. For a summary of circulation and readership data for a selection of magazines refer to Figure 8.9. In each of the classifications in Figure 8.9, the magazines listed compete with each other for advertisers. How efficient they are at reaching the target is an important influence on what magazines an advertiser chooses.

Print Measurement Bureau
www.pmb.ca

FIGURE
8.9

Circulation and readership of
selected magazines

In their respective classifications each of these magazines competes for advertisers. Advertisers use circulation and readership data to determine which magazines to select and with what frequency. Readers per copy data is compiled from an annual research study conducted by the Print Measurement Bureau.

Classification / Magazine	Average Circulation	Readers per Copy	Total Readership
BUSINESS			
Canadian Business	82 807	11.3	935 719
ROB Magazine	337 288	2.4	809 491
National Post Business	226 129	6.1	1 384 000
WOMEN'S			
Canadian Living	543 826	8.4	4 568 138
Chatelaine	707 779	6.0	4 246 674
Homemaker's	501 402	3.9	1 955 468

Analysis: Although the circulation of Canadian Business *is much lower than the other two business magazines, its readers per copy are much higher.* Canadian Business *actually has a higher reach than* ROB Magazine. *All three magazines in the business classification are good advertising buys.* Canadian Living's *circulation is only 75 percent of* Chatelaine's *circulation but it has many more readers per copy. Despite the lower circulation,* Canadian Living *reaches slightly more readers than* Chatelaine. *Both magazines are a good advertising buy. Similar comparisons can be made in other classifications of magazines.*

Source: Adapted from data contained in Canadian Media Director's Council *Media Digest,* 2003–2004, pp. 56, 46.

Magazines as an Advertising Medium

Magazines offer advertisers a unique set of advantages and disadvantages. This section presents some of the strategic considerations for using or rejecting magazines for advertising purposes.

ADVANTAGES OF MAGAZINES

TARGET-MARKET SELECTIVITY Magazines are often referred to as being a "class" medium rather than a "mass" medium. Both consumer magazines and business magazines have target audiences that are well defined by some combination of demographic and psychographic variables. Therefore, advertisers with well-defined target markets can select specific magazines by using a profile-matching strategy (i.e., by selecting magazines whose audience closely matches the product's target market). The profile-matching strategy becomes a little more complicated when a group of comparable magazines competes for the same target audience. Nevertheless, demographic selectivity is the primary advantage of magazines.

GEOGRAPHIC FLEXIBILITY Numerous high-circulation consumer magazines offer regional editions. An advertiser wishing to advertise in a certain area, such as the Prairies or the Atlantic provinces, may make use of the flexibility offered by regional editions—provided, of course, that the regional readership is similar to the advertiser's target market. Regional editions also provide advertisers with the opportunity to increase spending on an as-needed basis geographically, while holding the line on spending in other areas of the country.

Currently, 31 publications offer some form of geographic flexibility. The largest such publications are *Maclean's* (14 editions), *Canadian Living* (12 editions), and *Reader's Digest* (16 editions). Regional editions for *Maclean's* include Eastern Canada, the Atlantic Provinces, Quebec and Ontario, Ontario, Ontario and Western Canada, and Western Canada. They also publish city editions for Toronto and Montreal.

The growth of city magazines, such as *Toronto Life* and *Vancouver Magazine*, gives advertisers demographic selectivity and geographic flexibility. Although city magazines are most suited to local advertisers because of their regional nature, they also appeal to national advertisers because of their demographic selectivity.

LIFESPAN Because of the relative infrequency (in comparison to newspapers) of magazine publication (weekly, biweekly, monthly), the advertiser gets the benefit of longevity. Magazines remain in the home and are read intermittently over a period of time; hence, readers may be exposed to an advertisement several times during the lifespan of the magazine (which means that the product gets repeat exposure at no extra cost). Some magazines, such as *Canadian Geographic*, may be retained in the home permanently as part of a collection.

ENVIRONMENT Magazines are purchased and read because the editorial content interests the reader; therefore, advertisers' messages may benefit in terms of prestige and believability from being associated with the magazine and the quality it represents. The receptiveness of the audience may also result in the magazine being read at a more leisurely pace; this reading creates the potential for more detailed communications in advertising.

QUALITY OF REPRODUCTION Magazines are printed on high-quality paper, by means of a four-colour process that creates a high-quality and attractive presentation of both editorial and advertising content. Recent innovations, such as bright metallic inks that create a striking visual effect, have added to the quality of reproduction.

CREATIVE CONSIDERATIONS In terms of creative strategy and execution, magazines offer some flexibility. For example, most magazines offer gatefolds (multiple-page foldouts), double-page spreads, and bleeds. They can also accommodate special features such as scent strips, **pop-up coupons** (coupons with a perforated edge appearing on top of an advertisement for a product), and even product samples. Although the use of such options may increase the cost of advertising, the resulting distinction and potential impact on the reader may justify the additional expense. See Figure 8.10 for an illustration.

PASS-ALONG READERSHIP Magazine space is sold to advertisers at costs that are based not only on the magazine's circulation but on the number of readers it reaches. As well as being exposed to its primary readers, a magazine may be exposed to other readers. The actual readership of the magazine will be much greater than the circulation. A **primary reader** is a person who qualifies as a reader because he or she lives (works) in the household (office) where the publication is initially received. Additional readers, called **pass-along readers**, are those that do not live (work) in the household (office) where the publication is originally received. The concept of pass-along readers was discussed earlier in the chapter. The combination of primary readers and pass-along readers equals **total readership**.

Maclean's
www.macleans.ca

Canadian Geographic
www.canadiangeographic.ca

FIGURE
8.10

An illustration of a magazine insert (tip-in) that includes a sample of the product

When CP Hotels changed its name to Fairmont Hotels & Resorts, a change necessitated by a merger, magazines were used as the primary medium to communicate the new branding strategy to the public. For insight into this media campaign, read the Advertising in Action vignette **Fairmont Grows with New Name**.

DISADVANTAGES OF MAGAZINES

LEAD TIME   Magazine use requires the advertiser to carefully plan production well in advance of the issue date. Since the layout and design of the magazine are finalized at an early point (in comparison to newspapers), advertisers must deliver finished production materials to the publisher well before the publishing date. Lead times may vary from one publication to another, but for a monthly magazine, six to eight weeks is the average lead time required for materials. For a weekly magazine, an average of four weeks is required. Long lead times do not allow advertisers the flexibility of changing advertising content should market conditions so warrant, nor can they increase advertising weight on short notice.

CLUTTER   **Clutter** in magazine advertising refers to the clustering of ads near the front and back of the magazine. Advertisers can partially overcome the problem by ordering

Fairmont Grows with New Name

For as long as anyone can remember, CP Hotels was the name behind such icons as the Château Frontenac, Banff Springs, Château Laurier, and Royal York. Why would a Canadian hotel chain drop the CP name in favour of Fairmont, a popular brand in the United States?

In 2000, CP acquired Fairmont and instantly became the owner of 36 properties in Canada, the United States, Mexico, and the Caribbean. Fairmont was now the dominant player in the North American luxury hotel segment. To grow even further, it made perfect sense to adopt the Fairmont name on all hotels. The CP name would mean very little to people in the United States.

The advertising objective was to establish the Fairmont name as the top-of-mind luxury hotel and resort chain on the continent. The challenge was to establish share of voice in the marketplace and, in the longer term, build brand equity.

Research studies revealed that primary target members were vociferous readers. In fact, they read as many as 15 magazines a week. The target was defined as affluent baby boomers 40 to 55 years of age. They live in larger cities, control 55 percent of U.S. wealth, and account for 58 percent of all luxury sales in North America. Household income is in excess of $US150 000.

A creative strategy was born based on a five-point positioning strategy that would be a reference point for all future marketing activities. The strategy states that Fairmont hotels promise the best address, grand architecture, style that is both timeless and classic, and an unforgettable stay.

To create awareness and to start building brand equity in the Fairmont name, the company launched a blitz campaign in magazines all across the continent, including *Maclean's*, *Elm Street*, *Toronto Life*, *Vancouver Magazine*, *ROB Magazine*, *Canadian Business*, *Forbes*, *Vanity Fair*, *The New Yorker*, *Vogue*, and almost every travel magazine in North America. Considering the target profile, magazines were the obvious choice as primary medium. Fairmont rounded out the media plan with direct-mail and email advertising initiatives and alliances with other travel-related companies.

Source: Adapted from Peter Vamos, "Fairmont Hotels puts on an ad blitz," *Strategy*, January 29, 2001, p. 6.

Fairmont Hotels www.fairmont.com

preferred positions (covers), assuming such positions are available. Although covers are available only at higher cost, the resulting impact may justify the additional expense. Other position requests, such as being on the right side (as opposed to the left side), are available at no additional cost, but the publisher will not guarantee the position.

COST Magazine production costs, particularly for four-colour advertisements, are significantly higher than newspaper production costs. Because of these high production costs and because of the cost of space, magazines may not be an efficient buy for the local or regional advertiser, particularly if the regional target is small. Although many magazines offer regional editions, the absolute cost of advertising does not decline proportionately with the decline in circulation. In fact, the cost of reaching the regional reader is actually higher. National advertisers, with their larger budgets, can consider regional editions and the higher costs associated with them when market conditions warrant such activity.

FREQUENCY Although mass-circulation magazines offer high reach to the advertiser, and specialized magazines offer selective reach, magazines do not offer the advertiser much opportunity to *frequently* reach the audience, because the distribution frequency of magazines is low. Building frequency using one publication is extremely difficult for advertisers. They can overcome this problem by adding magazines that reach similar target markets, but such a solution is expensive. Placing two or more ads for the same product in the same issue of a magazine will build frequency, but it is not a common tactic.

Magazines are often a medium of choice among consumer-goods advertisers that want to reach fairly specific targets with a message. Generally speaking, magazines are useful when a profile-matching media strategy or a rifle media strategy is in place.

ADVERTISING FEATURES OFFERED BY MAGAZINES

Magazines have some special features that make the medium attractive to potential advertisers. The use of these features adds to the cost of advertising, however, so advertisers must carefully weigh the additional cost of these features against the potential impact their use will have on readers. These features include bleeds, gatefolds, preferred positions, inserts and reply cards, and split-run availability.

BLEEDS The term **bleed** refers to a situation where the coloured background of an ad extends to the edge of the page. An ad can bleed on some or all sides of the page, depending on creative strategy and execution. Most magazines offer bleeds, and either build bleed charges into published four-colour rates or quote the additional costs separately. An example of a bleed ad is shown in Figure 8.11.

GATEFOLDS A **gatefold** is an advertisement that folds out of a magazine, spanning two, three, or four pages. Gatefolds are usually used on special occasions. For example, a car manufacturer may use gatefolds when launching a new line. The most common position for a gatefold is the magazine's inside front cover. Magazines are now experimenting with gatefolds as part of the front cover (e.g., a one-page foldout from the side of the cover or a window-style foldout from the middle of the cover). Since gatefolds are not used very frequently and require significant lead times, most magazine rate cards state that rates are available on request. See the illustration of a front-page gatefold in Figure 8.12.

PREFERRED POSITIONS Obtaining a **preferred position** in a magazine involves requesting a specific position within the magazine. Since the potential for an advertisement to be seen is very great if it is positioned on the inside front or back covers, such positions command a higher price than others. While the cost of cover positions varies from one magazine to another, an increase of 15 to 20 percent above a normal page is common. Position charges are demonstrated in the magazine media-buying section of this chapter.

INSERTS AND REPLY CARDS Practically any size of business reply card, small multiple-page insert, or booklet can be bound into a magazine. Business reply cards are common in business publications, as are pop-up coupons and small recipe booklets in consumer publications. **Tipping** (gluing) items such as recipe booklets or small product catalogues is now very popular. The brochure or catalogue is easily removed once the magazine is purchased. The illustration in Figure 8.10 is an example of a **tip-in**. Advertisers usually must contact the publisher for rates and availability information.

SPLIT-RUN AVAILABILITY In a similar way to newspapers, a selected group of consumer magazines offers split-run availability. In this case, different ads may appear in different regional editions. Assuming that all conditions are constant and that each of the two or more ads contains a coupon, split-run availability can help advertisers determine which ad is more effective; they can compare actual customer responses to the coupon.

Courtesy of Generals Mills

FIGURE
8.11

An example of a bleed ad

Buying Magazine Space

The procedure for buying magazine space begins with deciding on the size of the ad, which involves choosing from among the variety of page options sold by the magazines under consideration. The rates quoted are based on the size of page requested. Other factors that could influence the cost of advertising in magazines include the frequency of insertions and appropriate discounts, the use of colour, guaranteed-position charges, and the use of regional editions.

SIZE OF AN ADVERTISEMENT AND RATE SCHEDULES

Magazines offer a variety of page options or page combinations. For example, *Canadian Geographic* sells space in the following formats: double-page spread, double half-page spread, one page, two-thirds page, half-page digest, half-page horizontal, and one-third page. See Figure 8.13 for illustrations of various magazine ad sizes.

The size selected for the advertisement determines the rate to be charged. Magazine rates are typically quoted for all page combinations sold on the basis of full

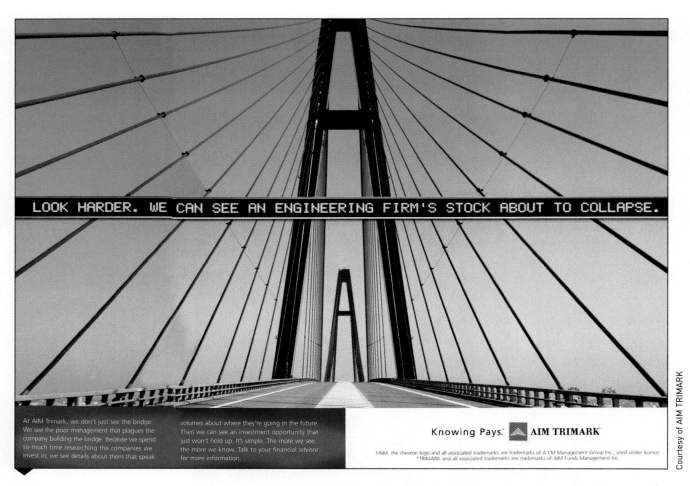

LOOK HARDER. WE CAN SEE AN ENGINEERING FIRM'S STOCK ABOUT TO COLLAPSE.

At AIM Trimark, we don't just see the bridge. We see the poor management that plagues the company building the bridge. Because we spend so much time researching the companies we invest in, we see details about them that speak volumes about where they're going in the future. Then we can see an investment opportunity that just won't hold up. It's simple. The more we see, the more we know. Talk to your financial advisor for more information.

Knowing Pays. ▲ AIM TRIMARK

†AIM, the chevron logo and all associated trademarks are trademarks of A I M Management Group Inc., used under licence
*TRIMARK and all associated trademarks are trademarks of AIM Funds Management Inc.

FIGURE
8.12

An ad that folds out from the front cover of a magazine: A real attention-grabber

colour. Rates may also be quoted for black-and-white ads and black-and-white ads with one colour added.

To illustrate how costs are calculated, let's consider a simple example. Assume an advertiser would like to purchase a one-page, four-colour ad in *Canadian Geographic* for January/February and March/April (see Figure 8.14). *Canadian Geographic* is a bimonthly publication. Since the frequency of the advertising does not reach the first discount level (three insertions), the advertiser would pay the one-time rate. The cost calculation would be as follows:

One-page rate × number of insertions = Total cost

$14 990 × 2 = $29 980

DISCOUNTS

Advertisers that purchase space in specific magazines with greater frequency will qualify for a variety of discounts. The nature of these discounts may vary from one publication to another. Some of the more common discounts offered by magazines include frequency, continuity, and corporate discounts.

In magazines, a **frequency discount** refers to a discounted page rate, with the discount based on the number of times an advertisement is run. The more often the ad is run, the lower the unit cost for each ad. In the *Canadian Geographic* rate card, the unit rate is reduced when the ad is run 3 times, 6 times, 9 times, and 12 times.

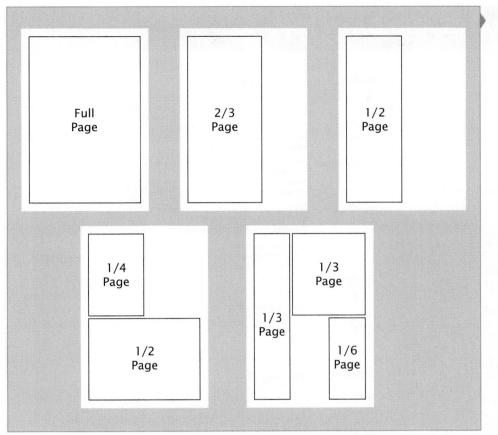

FIGURE
8.13

Various sizes of magazine ads

A **continuity discount** is an additional discount offered to advertisers that agree to purchase space in consecutive issues of a magazine (such as buying space in 12 issues of a monthly magazine). When continuity discounts are combined with frequency discounts, lower unit costs per page of advertising result.

Large advertisers that use the same magazine to advertise a variety of products (note that such an advertiser would have to be a multi-product firm whose products have similar target markets) may qualify for corporate discounts. A **corporate discount** involves consideration of the total number of pages purchased by the company (all product lines combined), resulting in a lower page rate for each product. Therefore, products that do not advertise frequently in a particular magazine may obtain a very favourable page rate if other company product lines advertise frequently in that magazine. As an alternative to using pages as the means of calculating volume discounts, magazines may use dollar volume purchased as the guideline, and offer a percentage discount on total advertising dollar volume.

COLOUR AND POSITION CHARGES

Additional costs for the inclusion of colour, or for a **guaranteed position**, are quoted separately on the rate card. For a guaranteed position, such as the back cover or the inside front and inside back covers, the additional costs are usually in the plus 15 percent to 20 percent range when compared to the cost of a regular page. Rates for guaranteed positions are usually quoted as a percentage or a dollar amount increase over the normal four-colour page rate. As for any regular page, the unit rate for a cover decreases as the frequency increases.

FIGURE

8.14

Canadian Geographic rate card

RATES AND DATA 2005

Publishing Schedule 2005

Issue	Features and Supplements	Closing Date (Insertion orders & materials)	On Newsstand
Jan/Feb 2005	100th Anniversary of Alberta and Saskatchewan	November 24, 2004	December 27, 2004
Mar/Apr 2005	Travelling from Labrador-Churchill Falls, 20 yr. Anniversary	January 26, 2005	February 28, 2005
	Travel & Adventure — Spring/Summer	January 19, 2005*	
May/June 2005	10th Anniversary Annual Report on the Environment	March 30, 2005	May 2, 2005
	Canadian Environment Awards	N/A	
July/August 2005	Parks & Conservation; Golf Islands National Park	May 25, 2005	June 27, 2005
	C² — Summer 2005	May 18, 2005*	
Sept/Oct 2005	Liveable Cities	July 27, 2005	August 29, 2005
Nov/Dec 2005	TBA	September 28, 2005	October 31, 2005
	Travel & Adventure — Winter	September 21, 2005*	
Jan/Feb 2006	TBA	November 23, 2005	December 26, 2005

*Closing date for supplements only.

Get on the plan!

Canadian Geographic is a leader in Canadian publishing. Its editorial tradition began 75 years ago thanks to The Royal Canadian Geographical Society. Today, the flagship magazine is published six times a year and it is the cornerstone of a recognized, respected and dynamic Canadian brand.

Canadian Geographic **delivers:**

- one of Canada's largest and most devoted readerships through paid circulation

- a stable consumer market — our subscribers, on average, make a five-year commitment to our magazine

- the second-largest dual audience in the country

Share the success!

2005 Advertising Rates

National	1x	3x	6x	9x	12x
IFC spread	30,700	29,770	28,880	28,010	27,165
OBC	17,890	17,350	16,835	16,325	15,840
IBC	17,155	16,630	16,130	15,645	15,170
Double-page spread	26,690	25,890	25,110	24,360	23,630
Full page	14,990	14,575	14,135	13,705	13,295
Double half-page spread	17,560	17,030	16,515	16,020	15,545
2/3 page	11,920	11,560	11,210	10,875	10,550
1/2-page digest	10,890	10,565	10,245	9,935	9,635
1/2-page horizontal	10,650	9,265	8,985	8,715	8,440
1/3 page	7,150	6,940	6,725	6,510	6,320

East/West Split Runs	1x	3x	6x	9x	12x
DPS	20,020	19,425	18,840	18,275	17,730
Full Page	11,270	10,930	10,600	10,285	9,980

Supplements (Travel & Adventure, C²)					
DPS	15,300				
Full Page	8,500				
1/2 Page	6,000				

All rates listed in gross Canadian dollars.

Your **country** — your **magazine**.

FIGURE
8.14
continued

RATES AND DATA 2005

Mechanical specifications

Non-Bleed Ads

Ads that are not intended to bleed must be sized to fit within the non-bleed sizes listed above.

Bleed Ads

- Ads that are intended to bleed must be sized to be trimmed to the bleed sizes listed above.

- All live matter (text, images not to be trimmed) must be kept within the non-bleed measurements. Any matter that extends past the non-bleed safe area may be trimmed due to folding and bindery variations.

- Any image or background colour intended to bleed must extend a minimum of 1/8" past the trim dimensions on all four sides of the ad. Right or left hand positioning is not guaranteed.

- Be aware of common crossover limitations in "double-page-spread" configurations (adjoining pages can shift up to 1/8" in the binding process on certain copies).

Author's Alterations and Late Fee

Changes to supplied material will be made only when accompanied by written instructions from the client. Changes will be made only if received before the ad submission date, and clients may be charged an AA fee of $80/hr depending on the production stage. *Canadian Geographic* endeavours to comply with all advertisers' changes, but assumes no responsibility for errors or omissions resulting from requested changes. Requested changes are assumed to be final. A courtesy proof will be sent to the client upon request. Any material supplied after the published submission date will be subject to a charge of $80.

Production Requirements

Canadian Geographic does not accept film. Electronic files must be supplied. Any charges incurred to convert film to electronic format will be charged to the client.

- Upon confirmation of an ad booking, each ad will be assigned a reference number. This number must be included in the file name and marked clearly on the supplied proof.

- Electronic files must be supplied as Mac QuarkXpress 5.0 (or earlier) with all support files and fonts included, or PDF (Press Optimized). Extra charges may be applied to convert PC files.

- Acceptable removable media include 100 mb Zip, 1 or 2 Gb Jaz, or CD.

- Compressed files must be saved as self-extracting archives (.sea).

Generic Book Specifications

Trim Size	8" x 10 ⅞"
Bleed	Minimum 1/8" bleed
Colour	CMYK throughout
Printing	Web Offset, coated stock, Staccato.
Binding	Perfect bound

Standard Unit Sizes

	Non-Bleed AD	Bleed Ad Trim Size*
Full Page	7" x 10"	8" x 10 ⅞"
Double-page spread	15" x 10"	16" x 10 ⅞"
Double half-page spread	15" x 4 ⅞"	16" x 5 ¼"
1/2-page horizontal	7" x 4 ⅞"	8" x 5 ¼"
1/2-page digest	4 ½" x 7 ⅜"	5 ¹⁄₁₆" x 7 ⅞"
2/3 page (two column)	4 ½" x 10"	5" x 10 ⅞"
1/3-page vertical	2 ³⁄₁₆" x 9 ⅞"	2 ¹¹⁄₁₆" x 10 ⅞"
1/3-page square	4 ½" x 4 ⅞"	5 ¹⁄₁₆" x 5 ¼"

* Any image or background colour intended to bleed must extend a minimum of 1/8" past the trim on all four sides

- Type should be converted to outline when possible (Adobe Illustrator, Macromedia Freehand, Corel Draw).

- Press-ready proof must be supplied to guarantee accurate colour reproduction.

- *Canadian Geographic* will not assume responsibility for type reflow or accurate colour reproduction if all necessary fonts, support files, and press-ready proofs are not included.

General Information

Acceptability: The content and design of all advertisements are subject to the publishers' approval.

Commissions: 15% of charges for space, position and colour allowed to recognized agencies.

Cash Discount: 1% on net if paid within 15 days of date of invoice.

Terms: Net 30 days; 2% interest charged per month on overdue accounts; 24% per annum.

GST: Rates do not include Goods and Services Tax. Where applicable, a 7% GST will be added to the price of all advertising and services in *Canadian Geographic.*

Shipping:

1. All insertion orders and contracts are to be sent to:

Canadian Geographic Enterprises
Advertising Sales Office
495 King St. West, Suite 301
Toronto, ON M5V 1K4
Telephone: (416) 360-4151
Fax: (416) 360-1526
E-mail: adsales@canadiangeographic.ca

2. All creative should be shipped to:

Canadian Geographic Enterprises
Production Manager
39 McArthur Avenue
Ottawa, ON K1L 8L7
Telephone: (613) 745-4629
Fax: (613) 744-0947
E-mail: elston@canadiangeographic.ca

For FTP information contact your
Advertising Coordinator:
Telephone: (416) 360-4151
E-mail: adsales@canadiangeographic.ca

Your **country** —
your **magazine**.

MAGAZINE BUYING ILLUSTRATIONS

To illustrate the cost calculations of buying magazine space, let's develop a few examples based on the *Canadian Geographic* rate card (Figure 8.14) and on the following information:

Example 1:

Size of ad: One-page, four-colour ad
Number of insertions: One-page ad to run in 4 issues

The calculation for this buying plan will be as follows:

Costs for one-page, four-colour:

Base rate   = the 3–5 times rate
$14 575 $\times$ 4 = $58 300

Example 2:

Size of ad: Double-page spread, four-colour ad
Number of insertions: 6 issues

The calculation for this buying plan will be as follows:

Costs for DPS, four-colour:

Base rate   = the 6–8 times rate
$25 110 $\times$ 6 = $150 660

SPACE CONTRACTS AND THE MAGAZINE SHORT RATE   To facilitate the use of discount scales offered by magazines, larger advertisers usually enter into a space contract with magazines they use frequently. The space contract provides an estimate of the advertising space required for a one-year period. At the end of the year, adjustments are made (whether positive or negative) when actual usage of space is known. Should advertisers not meet their estimates, a short rate would be due the publisher. To illustrate, let's assume the advertiser estimated that 12 four-colour pages would be purchased in *Canadian Geographic*, but by the end of the contract period only eight pages had been purchased. The advertiser would be billed as follows:

Ran eight times but paid the 12-times rate:
8 $\times$ $13 295 = $106 360

Earned only the 8 times rate of $14 135:
8 $\times$ $14 135 = $113 080
Short rate due publisher = $6720

In this example, the advertiser owes the magazine $6720, according to the terms of the space contract. Conversely, if the advertiser purchased more than the estimated amount, to the point where another frequency discount plateau was reached, the magazine would rebate the difference to the advertiser.

MAGAZINE INSERTION ORDERS   Depending on the extent of an advertising campaign with any particular magazine, the advertiser may decide to enter into a space contract with the magazine or place an insertion order on an as-needed basis. To obtain the best possible rate, large advertisers will opt for the space contract. The space contract is not an order for a specific amount of space; rather, it protects the advertiser's right to buy space at a certain rate. Publishers retain the right to announce increases in rates at predetermined levels.

When the advertiser is ready to run an ad, an insertion order is sent to the magazine. The insertion order specifies the date of issue, the size of the ad, any applicable position requests, and the contracted rate. The advertiser must be aware of the closing date for placing ads. The **closing date** usually refers to the deadline for the insertion order and material due at the publication. In some cases, however, the insertion order date is a few weeks in advance of the material date. The **insertion order date** is the last date for ordering space and the **material date** is the last date for having production material at the publication.

COMPARING MAGAZINES FOR EFFICIENCY

Assuming that a decision has been made to use magazines with the understanding that magazines usually have a well-defined target audience based on demographic variables, advertisers must choose particular magazines in which to advertise. Since costs and circulation figures vary, the advertiser must have a way of comparing alternatives. As with newspapers, **CPM** is an effective quantitative means of comparing competing magazines.

In most magazine classifications, there is usually a group of publications competing for the same market. For example, *Chatelaine*, *Homemaker's*, and *Canadian Living* compete against each other in the women's classification. Although the editorial content varies from one magazine to another they do reach a similar target, so advertisers must look at the efficiencies of each.

Figure 8.15 contains the comparative calculations for three of the magazines in the women's classification. In terms of a purely quantitative measure, *Homemaker's* offers the best efficiency in reaching the target market. The CPM of *Homemaker's* is considerably lower than that of *Canadian Living* and *Chatelaine*. However, *Chatelaine* and *Canadian Living* rely solely on subscriptions and newsstand sales for readers, while a portion of *Homemaker's* readers get the magazine free. This could affect readership. Large advertisers are likely to select a combination of these three magazines. By doing so they are expanding their reach. The question is, how much weight does each magazine receive?

FIGURE
8.15

Comparative statistics used when making magazine buying decisions

	Chatelaine	Canadian Living	Homemaker's
1 page, 4-colour	$41 750	31 865	21 260
Circulation	704 779	543 826	501 402
CPM	$59.23	$58.59	$42.40

CPM is calculated by dividing the cost of the ad by the circulation in thousands. For *Chatelaine* the calculation would be $41 750 divided by 704.8. That results in a CPM of $59.23. On a purely quantitative basis *Homemaker's* appears to be the most efficient magazine for reaching the target audience these magazines reach. *Homemaker's* has the lowest CPM.

Source: Adapted from Canadian Media Directors' Council *Media Digest*, 2003–2004, p. 45.

Technology and the Print Media

The information age and the electronic revolution together have changed the very nature of newspaper and magazine publishing. While the printed format remains the dominant form, major daily newspapers and national magazines have launched websites and some have launched their own television shows on specialty networks.

The major newspapers and magazines referred to in this chapter (*The Globe and Mail*, *National Post*, *Toronto Star*, *Chatelaine*, *Canadian Geographic*, and *Canadian Living*) have websites, as do many others. For an advertiser of the magazine, the addition of a website means they can reach the same audience profile but in a different way. The typi-

FIGURE

8.16

Home page for
Canadian Geographic

cal website includes the key news and feature articles from the publication. Ads in the form of banners (small rectangular or square ads) and sponsorship opportunities are available on these websites. Rates for banner ads are quoted separately from magazine rates. More details about banner advertising and all other forms of internet advertising are included in Chapter 12. For an illustration of a magazine's website, see Figure 8.16.

Newspapers and magazines are also expanding into television. Some examples include ROBtv, a *Globe and Mail* venture; *Canadian Home Workshop*; *Money Sense*; *Cottage Life*; and *Canadian Gardening* (all four have magazines with the same name). All of these publications are creating synergies among different forms of media. They represent integrated marketing communications opportunities for advertisers wanting to reach the same target market but in different ways.

It is the popularity of specialty TV that has inspired more publishers to spin off their own series, a trend that has sparked advertisers to become more aggressive in reaching a well-defined target audience. *Canadian Home Workshop* already had a website, so the television show was a natural extension. The show is a means of extending the trademark and offers advertisers new opportunities. The magazine attracts big-name advertisers such as Canadian Tire, Wal-Mart, and Home Depot. The magazine believes these advertisers will want to extend their reach to their television audience, comprising men 25 to 45 years old. This trend of extending brands into other media is in its infancy—there is lots of room for growth for other newspapers and magazines. In fact, the specialty networks are looking for content from other sources; such content lowers their production costs.

SUMMARY

With respect to print media, the primary alternatives for an advertiser are newspapers and magazines.

Newspaper advertising is divided between daily and weekly publications. Dailies and community newspapers attract both national and local advertisers, though they are more suited to local-market advertisers. A newspaper is published in one of two formats: the broadsheet, which is the larger, folded newspaper; and the tabloid, which is the smaller, flat newspaper. All newspapers receive revenues from four different types of advertising: national or general advertising, retail advertising, classified advertising, and preprinted inserts (flyers distributed via a newspaper).

As an advertising medium, newspapers offer the advertiser geographic selectivity, local-market coverage, and flexibility. Major disadvantages include the short lifespan, the lack of target-market orientation (demographic distinctions), and clutter. The rates charged an advertiser decrease as the volume of lines purchased increases, and rates are increased by position requests and requests for the use of colour.

Magazines are classified according to factors such as size and format, frequency of publication, circulation base, content, and audience reached. As an advertising medium, magazines offer target-market selectivity, quality in reproduction and editorial environment, and a longer lifespan than other media. On the negative side, significant lead times are required for materials, the use of colour raises costs, and clutter remains a problem.

Additional features of magazines that make them an attractive advertising medium include the use of bleeds, gatefolds, inserts, and reply cards. Magazine advertising rates depend on the size of the ad, the frequency of insertion, and the use of colour. A variety of discounts are available to advertisers that choose magazine advertising, with frequency and continuity being the most important factors reducing the cost of advertising.

Newspapers and magazines are now expanding their content on websites and television shows. The goal of such offerings is to provide synergies among publishing, the internet, and television and to present new advertising opportunities for their magazine advertisers.

KEY TERMS

273

REVIEW QUESTIONS

1. What is the difference between a tabloid and a broadsheet?

2. What are the differences among general advertising, retail advertising, and classified advertising?

3. What are the advantages and disadvantages of using newspapers as an advertising medium?

4. In a city where more than one daily newspaper dominates the market, how would you determine which newspaper to advertise in, assuming you could select only one? What factors would enter into your decision?

5. Provide an explanation for the following newspaper terms:
   a) hooker
   b) MAL
   c) transient rate
   d) short rate
   e) split run
   f) ROP colour
   g) tear sheet
   h) make good
   i) flexform
   j) position charge

6. Calculate the total cost of the following newspaper campaigns based on the information provided:

   ### Campaign 1
Newspaper:	*The Globe and Mail*
Edition:	National edition, Report on Business section
Size of Ad:	4 columns wide by 10 column inches deep
Colour:	Black and white
Frequency:	10 ads (2 ads each week—Tuesday and Thursday)

   ### Campaign 2
Newspaper:	*The Globe and Mail*
Edition:	Metro edition, Sports section
Size of Ad:	6 columns wide by 12 column inches deep
Colour:	Black and white only
Frequency:	8 ads (2 ads each week—Wednesday and Friday)

7. What are the advantages and disadvantages of using magazines as an advertising medium?

8. What is the difference between the following pairs of magazine terms:
   a) Paid-circulation magazine versus controlled-circulation magazine
   b) Vertical publication versus horizontal publication
   c) Primary reader versus pass-along reader

9. Provide a brief explanation of the following magazine terms:
   a) digest ad
   b) bleed ad
   c) gatefold
   d) tipping (tip-in)
   e) reply cards
   f) insertion order date
   g) material date
   h) space contract
   i) split run
   j) preferred position

10. Calculate the cost of the following magazine campaigns using the information provided:

    ### Campaign 1
Magazine:	*Canadian Geographic*
Size:	½ spread
Frequency:	4 ads
Colour:	Full colour
Edition:	National

    ### Campaign 2
Magazine:	*Canadian Geographic*
Size:	⅓ page
Frequency:	8 ads
Colour:	Black and white
Edition:	National

11. Identify and briefly describe the various discounts frequently offered by magazines.

12. How does the magazine short rate work?

13. Explain the CPM concept as it applies to the purchase of advertising space in magazines.

DISCUSSION QUESTIONS

1. Newspapers like the *Toronto Star*, the *Vancouver Sun*, and *The Globe and Mail* charge higher rates to advertisers requesting specific sections and specific pages for their ads. In some cases the additional charge is as much as 40 to 50 percent more. Do the benefits gained outweigh the costs involved? What is your opinion?

2. "Paying a premium price for a cover position (inside front, inside back, or outside back) in a magazine is always a wise investment." Discuss this statement.

3. "The location of an advertisement in a newspaper is the key factor in determining the success of the ad." Discuss this statement in the context of other variables you judge to be important.

4. Read the Advertising in Action vignette **The Relentless Pursuit of Perfection**. Are there other media choices that you could recommend for the Lexus ES 300 or any other Lexus model? Remember, you are trying to attract and motivate a very selective target market. Justify your media recommendation.

NOTES

1. Canadian Media Directors' Council *Media Digest*, 2003–2004, p. 34.
2. Ibid, p. 10.
3. Ibid, p. 40.
4. Jim McElgunn, "Community press demographics," *Marketing*, June 26, 1995, p. 14.
5. Canadian Media Directors' Council *Media Digest*, 2003–2004, p. 38.
6. Based on data from *Canadian Advertising Rates and Data*, Rogers Media, September 2000, p. 23.
7. Canadian Media Directors' Council *Media Digest*, 2003–2004, p. 36.
8. *Outstanding Newspaper Advertising—Thirteen Creative Principles*, Canadian Newspaper Association, n.d., p. 12.

Courtesy: Dick Hemingway

CHAPTER

9

Broadcast Media: Television and Radio

The latest statistics available reveal that 99 percent of Canadian households are reached by both television and radio. Further, 65 percent of Canadians live in multi-set households and 85 percent of Canadians live in households equipped with cable or satellite. On an average day, 76 percent of Canadians view television at least once.[1] Such spectacular penetration and reach suggests that the potential impact of broadcast media on their audience is enormous. From an advertising point of view, the placement of messages in broadcast media offers the same high reach/high impact potential.

A variety of new technologies are changing the landscape of conventional broadcasting. These technologies are having an impact on viewership—it is lower now. Technologies such as digital television, the internet, and personal video recorders are changing the nature of television viewing. A television market that was once controlled by a few conventional broadcasters is now a fragmented market with many participants. The competition for eyeballs is intense!

This chapter examines the use of television and radio as advertising media and examines the advantages and disadvantages of each; it reviews the variety of rates and discount structures available to advertisers; and, finally, it examines the new technologies that are affecting the traditional broadcasting industry.

The Canadian Television Market

The television market is divided between conventional **national networks** and stations, specialty cable channels, and pay-TV. The conventional networks include CBC Television, CTV, Radio-Canada, and TVA. Both the CBC and CTV serve English Canada, reaching 99 percent of English-language households, while Radio-Canada and TVA serve French Canada, reaching 99 percent of French-language households.

CBC
www.cbc.ca
CTV
www.ctv.ca

Global TV
www.canada.com/globaltv

Both the CBC and CTV operate **regional networks**: the CBC, for example, has Atlantic, Central, Western, Pacific, and North networks. CTV operates regional networks in Ontario, Atlantic Canada, and Saskatchewan. Global TV is a prominent network in Ontario, reaching 97 percent of households.

A multitude of **specialty networks** is available to viewers. Some of the more popular specialty networks are TSN, Space, Rogers Sportsnet, Showcase, Discovery, MuchMusic, CBC Newsworld, and The Weather Network. Recently added to the television mix are a group of digital specialty networks available for additional fees through cable suppliers. This group includes The Biography Channel, ESPN Classic Canada, Leafs TV, MenTV, NHL Network, Pride Vision, and many more. Pay-per-view options are also available to cable subscribers.

Trends Affecting Television and Television Advertising

The landscape of the Canadian television industry is changing. Several factors are converging on the industry that signal potential loss of advertising revenues in the future. These factors include a decline in viewing trends, particularly among males 18 to 34 years old, the growth and penetration of specialty networks, and new technologies such as the internet and personal video recorders.

VIEWING TRENDS Conventional television networks such as the CBC and CTV are concerned about the time viewers spend watching television. Generally speaking, viewers are spending less time each week with television. One of the primary reasons for the drop-off is the internet. Time spent online takes away from time spent watching television. Networks typically obsess over the 18- to 34-year-old segment of the population, and in 2003 there was a noticeable drop-off (6 to 8 percent) among males in this age group. Apparently males have strayed toward personal video recorders, DVDs, and video games. They are device oriented, more apt to spend time online, and still watch television.[2]

Similar patterns are also being detected in younger age groups. Teens, for example, are the tuned-in generation, but they are tuned in to the internet, cell phones, and personal digital organizers. In 2003, McDonald's in the United States announced the company would shift more of its media dollars into digital media as younger consumers spend more time online and less time in front of the tube.[3] Other prominent advertisers are sure to follow.

PENETRATION OF SPECIALTY NETWORKS

In Canada there are 43 specialty networks and 44 digital networks. These networks, combined with traditional broadcasters such as the CBC, CTV, and Global, provide so much choice for viewers that audiences have become fragmented. Fewer viewers for popular prime time shows mean lower advertising rates and less revenue for all networks. From purely an advertising perspective, television is viewed as the optimal mass medium—it delivers a large audience quickly. Once this advantage disappears, advertisers will invest their advertising dollars elsewhere.

In more positive terms, the specialty channels do offer some targeting capability, though the audience that the advertiser reaches is usually smaller than on conventional networks. Advertising rates are adjusted accordingly. Specialty networks such as YTV and MuchMusic, for example, tap into Canada's tween market. According to YTV's Tween Report, there are 2.5 million tweens spending $1.7 billion a year of their own money while influencing about $20 billion in family purchases. Such economic power is referred to as "kidfluence."[4] Advertisers wanting to reach this market have an avenue to do so. Other networks such as ROBtv (business orientation), TSN (sports orientation), and HGTV (house and garden maintenance) are examples of networks attractive to advertisers that want to reach specific demographic and psychographic targets.

THE INTERNET

Internet access has seen steady growth, with 75 percent of all Canadians now online. The 18- to 24-year-old age group is by far the most highly connected segment, using multiple connection devices (computers, cell phones, and personal digital assistants) to hook up to the internet. They have grown up with the internet as part of their lifestyle.[5]

A recent survey reveals that television is the biggest casualty of internet usage, with 27 percent of respondents saying their television watching has fallen as a consequence of being online.[6] As the price of technology drops and more Canadians go online, the competition for an audience will be more intense. The shift from television to the internet by Canadians in all age categories has caught the attention of advertisers, and many have already reallocated their budgets accordingly. Advertising funds haven't necessarily been channelled into the internet, but rather all other media are being re-evaluated.

To combat this trend, a phenomenon referred to as **media convergence** has taken hold. Through ownership of different media, a company such as BCE can deliver the same content (and advertising messages) in the various media it controls. BCE's portfolio includes the CTV Network (conventional network), CTV Sportsnet, CTV Newsnet, The Comedy Network, and the Outdoor Life Network (all specialty networks), *The Globe and Mail*, Bell ExpressVu (satellite provider), and the internet sites Sympatico-Lycos and **globeandmail.com**. Media buyers are evaluating converged media strategies. The premise is simple: if the advertiser doesn't generate sufficient reach in one medium (e.g., television), additional reach is possible by advertising on other media outlets controlled by the media company. Packaged deals embracing numerous different media outlets produce economies of scale when buying the media time.

PVRs (PERSONAL VIDEO RECORDERS)

PVRs will revolutionize television programming and television advertising. A PVR allows consumers to digitally record and store their favourite shows for viewing later. Going a step further than a VCR, the PVR allows for time-shift programming and skips the commercials—a frightening thought for the networks and advertisers. Two companies, TiVo and Replay, offer machines that can store between 8 and 28 hours of programming. Bell ExpressVu (a satellite provider in Canada) is planning a similar device and will offer it as an option to its existing base of customers.

PVRs are still in their infancy, but as their penetration grows advertisers will have to look at alternatives such as sponsorships and branded content opportunities if they want to deliver a message via television.

Television Viewing Highlights

BBM Canada
www.bbm.ca

Media-viewing data is collected by two prominent and competing organizations in Canada: BBM Bureau of Measurement and Nielsen Media Research. The BBM is divided into two divisions: BBM TV and BBM Radio. BBM TV collects viewing data through a combination of electronic observation and diaries.

The electronic observation, or people-meter service as it is referred to, collects minute-by-minute viewing behaviour from more than 5000 individuals across Canada. This information is a valuable resource for advertisers and agencies in terms of assessing the value of their advertising expenditure, and for networks in terms of identifying what programs are popular or unpopular. An illustration of basic BBM data appears in Figure 9.1.

The diary is issued three times a year to a panel of viewers in the top 40 markets across Canada. The data is compiled on the basis of time period, program, and trend. The data is used to determine the rating of a program. **Ratings** are audience estimates expressed as a percentage of a population in a defined geographic area. For example, if a show has a rating of 20, it reaches 20 percent of that market's population.

Nielsen Media Research also employs people-meter technology to collect viewing data. The Nielsen Television Ratings are an ongoing count of television audience size and composition. From a nationwide sampling of 3350 households, the company produces the National Nielsen Television Index (NTI), representing the national Canadian TV viewing universe. The report provides viewing information 24 hours a day for the entire year. Data are organized on the basis of age, education, income, and occupation of its members. Nielsen also conducts local market measurements in Toronto/Ontario, Vancouver/Victoria, Montreal Francophone, and Calgary/Alberta.

FIGURE
9.1

The most popular shows on Canadian television by audience size

Top Programs - Total Canada
January 26-February 1, 2004

bbm CANADA

Rank	Program	Broadcast Outlet	Weekday	Start time	End time	Total 2+ AMA(000)
1	Survivor: All Stars	Global	......S	22:52	23:58	3611
2	Super Bowl	Global	......S	17:56	22:51	3560
3	American Idol 3	CTV	.T.....	20:00	21:00	3151
4	American Idol 3	CTV	..W....	20:00	21:00	3110
5	Fear Factor	Global	M......	20:00	21:00	1894
6	Friends	Global	...T...	20:00	20:32	1767
7	CTV Evening News	CTV	MTWTF..	18:00	19:00	1637
8	The Apprentice	Global	...T...	20:59	22:00	1596
9	C.S.I.	CTV	...T...	21:00	21:59	1557
10	NHL Hockey	CBC	.....S.	19:00	22:00	1516
11	My Big Fat Obnoxious Fiance	Global	M......	21:00	22:00	1493
12	Law & Order: SVU	CTV	.T.....	22:00	23:00	1356
13	ER	CTV	...T...	21:59	23:00	1348
14	Will & Grace	Global	...T...	20:32	20:59	1341
15	Average Joe II: Hawaii	Global	M......	22:00	23:00	1333
16	Law & Order	CTV	..W....	21:59	23:00	1301
17	C.S.I.:Miami	CTV	M......	22:00	23:00	1235
18	Without a Trace	Global	...T...	22:00	23:00	1186
19	Jeopardy/Access Hollywood	CTV	MTWTF..	19:30	20:00	1147
20	Global 5:30pm News	Global	MTWTF..	17:30	18:30	1086

BBM Canada Meter Service

Understanding this report ...
This chart shows the Top 20 TV programs for national networks for the week indicated. Programs are ranked based on their AMA(000). AMA(000) is the average minute audience in thousands. The chart also indicates the broadcast outlet on which the program aired and the program's start and end time (shown in Eastern Standard Time).

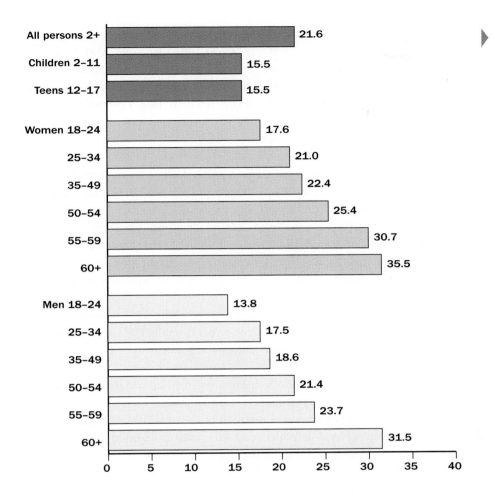

FIGURE
9.2

Weekly hours of television viewing in Canada by age group

Source: BBM Bureau of Measurement.

Generally speaking, Canadians spend more time with television than they do with any other medium. All people aged two years and older watch 21.6 hours of television each week, and the number of hours escalates with age. People over the age of 60 spend more than 30 hours a week watching television. Refer to Figure 9.2 for some specific data about television viewing by age and gender.

The data collected by BBM Bureau of Measurement and Nielsen Media Research reveal other key trends. By **daypart**, a block of time in a programming schedule (e.g., a half-hour or one-hour period), prime time (7:00 to 11:00 p.m. Monday to Sunday) attracts the most viewers. While accounting for only 20 percent of viewing hours, prime time generates 45 percent of total viewing time.

On a seasonal basis there is a drop-off in viewing in the summer, a reflection of consumers changing their patterns when the weather is warmer. After all, why watch reruns on television! Generally speaking, viewing drops by about 25 percent in the summer. Advertising rates charged for summer shows reflect the viewer drop-off.

Television as an Advertising Medium

As an advertising medium, television offers numerous benefits—but there are also some drawbacks. The advertiser must assess the merits of using television in the context of the problem that advertising is trying to resolve.

ADVANTAGES OF TELEVISION

IMPACT AND EFFECTIVENESS OF MESSAGES Compared to all other media, television stands out as a multi-sense medium. Advertisers can use the combination of sight, sound, and motion that television offers to create maximum impact on the viewing audience. It is a medium that is ideally suited for delivering an emotional message. Television viewing requires only passive involvement; viewers can do something else as they receive messages from the television.

HIGH REACH Television's reach is astounding, particularly in prime time. As Figure 9.1 indicates, a commercial shown on any of the top 20 shows in Canada has the potential to reach more than one million viewers. Further, television reaches a broad range of demographics and in many cases mirrors the Canadian population on specific demographics, making it an extremely attractive medium for advertisers targeting fairly general audiences. Nielsen audience data confirms that shows that are ranked in the top 10 during prime time (comedy, reality, and drama shows) are equally attractive to adult males and females.[7]

Consumer-packaged-goods advertisers, financial institutions, telecommunications companies, and producers of high-priced consumer durables such as automobiles and computers all value the high reach available from television.

FREQUENCY POTENTIAL Television is an expensive medium in absolute-dollar terms, but advertisers with large budgets can use television effectively to build frequency. For example, an advertiser may purchase more than one spot within a certain program or during a certain time of day. Alternatively, an advertiser could build frequency by purchasing the same time slot in a program over a continuous period—perhaps 13, 26, or 52 weeks. In either case, owing to viewers' loyalty to a certain program or to the appeal a certain time period has for a particular target market, the target audience will be exposed to the same commercial message over an extended period. Strategically, the advertiser wants just enough frequency to prompt action—too much repetition could have a negative impact on the viewer.

SOME DEMOGRAPHIC SELECTIVITY Television is primarily a mass-reach medium, but it has some potential for demographic selectivity. Because of the various age and sex classifications that television reaches, television advertising can reach certain demographic groups effectively at certain times. Further, certain types of programs may attract upscale, white-collar professional groups while other programs may attract a predominantly blue-collar crowd. Programs such as *Hockey Night in Canada* and *Blue Jays Baseball* are sold to advertisers on the strength of their potential to reach males of all ages. Specialty networks such as YTV, TSN, and MuchMusic effectively reach selective audiences. MuchMusic is available in 6.8 million homes and is very popular with the 13–34 age group. YTV, a youth-oriented channel, is popular with kids of all ages. For advertising purposes YTV effectively reaches a group referred to as tweens (10- to 14-year-olds).[8]

COVERAGE FLEXIBILITY Network advertisers receive good national coverage on both of the national networks (CBC and CTV). However, advertisers that—despite smaller budgets—still want to use television can purchase commercial time from individual

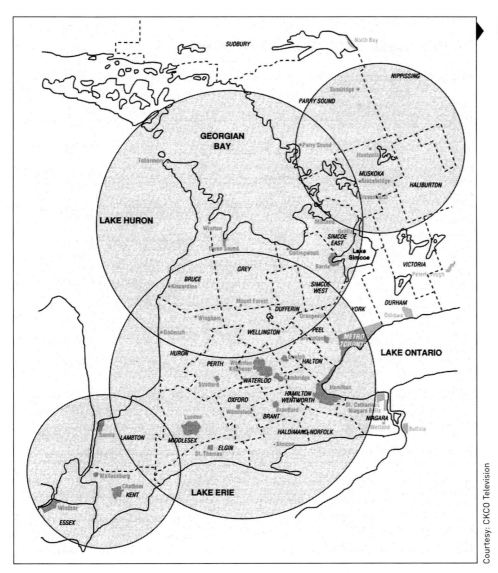

Courtesy: CKCO Television

FIGURE 9.3

Sample coverage map of a local television station

stations. Thus, advertisers can be selective regarding markets they advertise in. Consideration of variables such as competition and opportunity markets helps advertisers determine which markets to purchase. For network advertisers, additional advertising on selected stations can be used to increase the weight of advertising in a particular market when needed, perhaps to counter competitive spending. As Figure 9.3 illustrates, an advertiser placing commercials on Kitchener's CKCO-TV would effectively cover southwestern and south central Ontario.

DEMONSTRATION CAPABILITY Television offers creative flexibility. It is the appropriate medium for verifying a product's claims because it can show the product being used, which provides proof. Convincing demonstrations provide potential customers with a reason to buy the product. In addition, television is an effective medium for building consumers' awareness of and ability to identify the packages of products, particularly the packages of new products.

DISADVANTAGES OF TELEVISION

HIGH COST Television offers high reach potential and relatively low CPMs, but in real spending terms it is very expensive. The cost of a prime-time 30-second commercial on CBC can be as high as $52 000; on the CTV network it can be as high as $80 000, though the average costs are not near that high.[9] In addition to the cost of media time, television advertising involves high production costs; these costs for a finished commercial range between $150 000 and $250 000. To counter the high costs of television advertising, many advertisers are choosing 15-second commercials. However, those 15 seconds are sold at a premium rate of 65 to 70 percent of the cost of a 30-second commercial. The Global Television Network is experimenting with five-second commercials—dubbed dot spots—that are available in sets of six during prime-time viewing.[10]

The use of shorter commercials adds to the clutter problem on television but, all things being equal, if the creative impact of those commercials is as effective as a 30-second commercial the advertiser will save money.

CLUTTER Television **clutter** refers to the clustering of too many commercials during a program break or taking too many breaks during a program. The level of clutter has a direct bearing on both viewing patterns and message recall. Viewers are likely to reach for the remote control when a program pauses for a commercial in a cluttered environment or they are apt to leave the room temporarily. Such behaviour negates much of the reach potential of television.

Since this clustering occurs at planned intervals, and since a certain percentage of the audience may leave the viewing area during the break, many feel that particular placement within a **cluster** is important. Generally, the first and last positions in the cluster are preferable.

LACK OF TARGET-MARKET SELECTIVITY As indicated by the list of advantages, television offers high reach to mass audiences, with some potential for reaching target markets that are defined in terms of age and sex. However, for advertisers with target markets precisely defined in terms of a combination of demographic, psychographic, and geographic variables the use of television advertising is wasteful, since the message reaches many people outside the target definition. If there is wasted reach there is a reduction in cost efficiency. Consequently, advertisers should consider other media that reach their target markets more efficiently.

AUDIENCE FRAGMENTATION TV viewing itself is static. While the number of channels has increased dramatically over the past decade, the total number of viewers hasn't grown. The viewing audience is fragmented in such a manner that the size of the potential audience reached is reduced while the costs of reaching those who do watch is increased. The efficiency of television is becoming an issue. Audience **fragmentation** is the result of several factors: the intrusion of U.S. based stations (that accounts for 12 percent of Canada's viewing audience in prime time), the penetration of specialty networks and satellite television suppliers, and the introduction of new digital stations. For some homes television is a 600-channel universe!

COMMERCIAL AVOIDANCE Viewers watch the shows, but do they watch the commercials? If viewers do leave the room during commercial breaks the size of the audience is reduced. Avoiding commercials is an issue. In fact, a recent study conducted by Decima Research pegged television commercial avoidance at 57 percent.[11]

Remote control devices make it easy for viewers to switch channels during commercial breaks; they literally surf the dial until they think the break is over, a phenomenon referred to as **zapping**. Many viewers record shows and play them later. In such cases the viewer fast-forwards through the commercial breaks; a practice referred to as **zipping**. The latest technology, the PVR (personal video recorder), allows the viewer to record shows without tape and it automatically eliminates the commercials. Advertisers are searching for alternative television advertising strategies to counter these behaviours.

LACK OF PLANNING FLEXIBILITY To plan and buy television advertising space requires significant lead time. For example, network buys are negotiated in June for a complete broadcasting year that commences with the new fall program schedule in mid-September. Network contracts are usually non-cancellable, and spot advertising can be cancelled only on the basis of a minimum run and a specified notice period (e.g., advertising must run for four weeks, and four weeks' notice must be given prior to cancellation). Facing this contract, advertisers must be prepared to make an investment in television advertising.

CREATIVE LIMITATIONS Television is a multi-sense medium offering significant impact capabilities, but a television commercial is very short—the normal length is 30 seconds. Considering the behaviours of viewers discussed earlier in this section, advertisers are even using 15-second commercials in an attempt to break through the clutter. From a creative perspective it is questionable whether a 15-second commercial can achieve the same communications results as a 30-second spot. In both cases time is essential, and, as a result, only simple messages can be effectively communicated. Simply editing a 30-second spot down to a 15-second spot may not work! Research evidence from the United States confirms that shorter spots are less effective than 30-second spots among advertisers in packaged-goods product categories.[12]

Products and services whose selling points need to be communicated via long copy are better suited to print media. Television advertisements must focus on one major benefit of a product if communications are to be effective. Alternatively, a television commercial should direct viewers to a website where more detailed information is available.

For additional insight into the behaviours of television viewers and the effectiveness of television advertising, refer to the Advertising in Action vignette **What Really Happens During Commercial Breaks?**

Television is frequently the medium of choice when an advertiser wants to reach a large audience quickly, say in the case of a new product launch. For an applied illustration of recommending television as part of a media plan, refer to the advertising plan in Appendix II.

Television Advertising Alternatives

When buying television time, advertisers choose between network advertising (either national or regional), selective-spot advertising, sponsorship opportunities, and local market spot advertising. In addition, advertisers are now looking at branded content opportunities. Branded content involves integrating the product right into the television show.

What Really Happens During Commercial Breaks?

What do you do during a commercial break—do you grab a snack, visit the washroom, or grab the remote control and start surfing? Some research studies have concluded that viewers avoid as much as 60 percent of all commercials. Now, advertisers have the PVR to contend with, an electronic recording device that is capable of recording shows while skipping over the commercials. Zero messages delivered!

Another concern that advertisers have about television advertising is clutter—there are simply too many commercials! U.S.-based shows that are broadcast in Canada are shorter than they used to be and that is the source of the problem. A recent study by the Association of Canadian Advertisers found that 80 percent of the TV hours it monitored contained an average of 15 minutes of commercial time. The legal limit is 12 minutes.

Viewer behaviour is another problem. Research conducted in the U.S. by the Roper Organization revealed some interesting insights about viewer behaviour. It found that men switch channels more frequently than women (31 percent versus 22 percent), and younger people more frequently than older (33 percent versus 29 percent). Demographically, multi-person households with higher incomes, a college-educated member, children under 18, and a VCR (the ideal household that advertisers want to reach) showed a greater frequency of channel zapping. It seems that the presence of a remote-control device

has led to "viewing-on-the-fly." Considering these behaviours, does any commercial stand a chance of being noticed?

Perhaps the answer is better programming—programming that will hold the viewer's interest so that they won't want to miss anything. Many critics of television are emphatic when they say the quality of TV programming has gone down. And many popular shows that do surface are fads that attract large audiences initially and then die off. Shows like *Who Wants to Be a Millionaire?* and the *Survivor* series fall into this category. Other observers say the shows are so mindless that a viewer can watch three or four shows at the same time simply by surfing the dial. Why bother watching the commercials?

A research study from the United Kingdom concluded that people who have specifically chosen to watch a program are more likely to remain present for the commercial breaks within it. Their reasons to leave the screen—or the room—are few. This helps explain the popularity of shows like *Friends*, *CSI*, and *ER*—millions of people want to watch these shows each week.

The U.K. study also concluded that better-quality programs grabbed higher attention levels with the audience. For advertisers, the message is clear: place ads on the right (quality) shows. The networks will have to demonstrate the quality of their programs to justify advertising rates, or advertisers will continue to migrate to alternative media.

Sources: Adapted from Sheila Byfield, "What people really do during commercials," *Strategy*, March 26, 2001, p. 19; Patrick Allossery, "Global's dot spots increase TV clutter," *The Financial Post*, March 31, 2000, p. C3; and John Heinzl, "Pest control ads give viewers the creeps," *The Globe and Mail*, April 7, 2000, p. M1.

NETWORK ADVERTISING

Network advertising is suitable for advertisers whose products and services are widely distributed and who have relatively large media budgets. All stations composing the network carry a set of programs at a certain time—usually prime time, with some daytime. The network sells the commercial time. The advertiser must supply one commercial to a central source, and the message is fed across the entire network all at once. Network advertising offers an advertiser substantial reach at relatively low cost. *American Idol*, for example, reaches more than 3 million Canadian viewers each week on the CTV network at a cost of $75 000 per spot, a CPM of $25.00. A national spot on *Hockey Night in Canada* costs $25 000 and reaches 1 500 000 viewers for a CPM of $16.67.[13]

NATIONAL-SPOT OR SELECTIVE-SPOT ADVERTISING

At a regional level or local station level, stations fill in the balance of programming time with non-network programs and sell commercial time directly to clients wanting to advertise in that market. Alternatively, the local station that carries network programs may have the opportunity to sell some advertising time directly to advertisers during the network program. For example, in network shows such as *Marketplace*, *The Fifth Estate*, or *Hockey Night in Canada*, a certain portion of the commercial time available is allocated to local stations for **selective-spot sales**. In either case, advertisers would purchase time from the individual station, be it CBLT Toronto, CBOT Ottawa, or CBUT Vancouver. Each station from which time is purchased would require a copy of the commercial.

Selective-spot advertising offers several advantages to advertisers. First, it provides a network advertiser the opportunity for incremental coverage in key markets where more frequency is desired. Second, advertisers with smaller budgets or advertisers following a key-market media strategy can choose only markets that are important to their situation (e.g., markets where they have good distribution).

SPONSORSHIP OPPORTUNITIES

In response to changing client needs, the major networks actively market sponsorship opportunities that will integrate television advertising with other marketing and promotion efforts. Television **sponsorship** allows advertisers to take "ownership" of television properties that are targeted at their consumer audience. If the fit is right, the advertiser can leverage the sponsorship by extending the package to include consumer and trade promotions, and alternate media exposure.

The most prominent and ongoing sponsorship in Canada is *Hockey Night in Canada*, a Saturday-night institution. Both major beer companies in Canada, Molson and Labatt, have taken turns holding the primary sponsorship position on *HNIC*. At the end of the contract period the rights for *HNIC* are up for renewal and various sponsors bid for the lead sponsorship position. The cost of the sponsorship depends on supply and demand.

L'Oréal Canada was the lead sponsor on the extremely popular *Canadian Idol* show in 2003. L'Oréal's sponsor package included traditional 30-second spots, opening and closing **billboards**, a major presence in the backstage area of the *Canadian Idol* website, and sponsorship announcements during on-air promotions for the show. The real coup of L'Oréal's agreement was the inclusion of its products in several in-show segments. *Canadian Idol* reached an average audience of 2.06 million each week, peaking at 3.6 million for the final show. The asking price for the sponsorship package was $2.3 million, but it is not known what L'Oréal actually paid.[14] Negotiations between buyers and sellers play a key role in establishing the final price.

L'Oréal Canada
www.loreal.ca

From a targeting perspective, *Canadian Idol* was a perfect match for L'Oréal. The show over-delivered on the 18- to 34-year-old female demographic. To reach this age group it was by far the best property of the summer.

BRANDED CONTENT

Branded content refers to the visible placement of branded merchandise in television shows and films. In any given show, numerous products are given exposure; such exposure has more credibility with the audience than regular advertising. To maximize the potential of a branded content strategy the product should be more than just a prop; it should be integrated into the show in some manner.

Programs that teach, demonstrate, or advise, such as the do-it-yourself home and decorating shows, are proving to be good opportunities for products to be integrated in a natural and positive way. Home Depot, for example, has already formed partnerships with shows such as *Designer Guys*, *Home to Go*, and *Trading Spaces*.

The popular show *Sex and the City* actually developed an entire episode around the development of a fake advertisement for Absolut vodka. The episode shows Samantha Jones (Kim Cattrall) striking a deal for her latest lover to appear in a fake Absolut ad called "Absolut Hunk." In the ad a budding young model poses in the buff, save for a strategically placed Absolut bottle. The ad eventually winds up on a billboard in Times Square. The ad set off a craze for a new drink called Absolut Hunk, which the girls drink on the show. This branded content concept was Absolut's first venture ever into television advertising and they were pleased with the results. Much positive publicity was generated.[15]

LOCAL ADVERTISING

Local advertising is similar to selective-spot sales. The local television station sells the time to local market advertisers (retailers, restaurants, entertainment facilities, and so on). In contrast to network and selective-spot advertising, local advertising is non-commissionable. Since local-market advertisers do not usually work with an advertising agency, the individual television stations provide assistance in the development and production of commercials for local clients.

Television Advertising Rates and Buying Procedures

INFLUENCES ON TELEVISION ADVERTISING RATES

The convergence of numerous factors influences advertising rates on networks and individual stations. Generally speaking, popular programs with large audiences command higher advertising rates. What follows is a discussion of the major factors that influence advertising rates.

SUPPLY AND DEMAND For the CBC, CTV, and Global TV, advertising costs are based on fundamental economic principles, mainly the availability of supply and the demand exerted on that supply by competing advertisers. Under such conditions, prospective advertisers outline their advertising needs in terms of desired reach levels, frequencies, seasonal implications, the ratio of prime time to fringe time, and the budget available. The network assembles a package and then the price of the advertising is negotiated between the agency's media buyer and the network sales representative. This system places added pressure on media buyers, since the rate that their clients pay depends largely on their ability to negotiate.

NATURE OF THE ADVERTISING PURCHASE The negotiation process described above occurs well in advance of a media schedule, usually in late spring for the following broadcast year. Major networks such as the CBC, CTV, and Global operate in a similar manner. They book time in mid to late June to cover a 52-week period starting in September. Each spring, upon announcement of its fall schedule, the network establishes a *declaration date* (referred to as D-Day), at which time most advertisers place their orders for the coming broadcast year. Every effort is made to accommodate each order as placed. If overbooking should occur as a result of the volume of orders, preference is allocated according to the following priorities: (1) incumbency position, (2) length of contract, (3) volume of contract, and (4) start date. Large-budget advertisers that have advertised on network programs in the past (incumbents) are given priority in this system. Approximately 70 percent of available commercial time on the networks is sold on or near the declaration date. This procedure of selling so much space at one time is referred to as the **upfront buying**. Part of the buying process involves gambling on what new shows will be popular.

TYPES OF PROGRAMS   Network and selective-spot advertising is sold on the basis of a regular program schedule that is established for the entire year. However, certain programs within a schedule may be designated as special buys and are sold separately to potential advertisers. Examples of such programs include drama specials, miniseries, and sports programs such as the annual *Academy Awards* (*Oscars*) broadcast, *Hockey Night in Canada*, and the *World Figure Skating Championships*.

In the case of sports programs, hockey and baseball broadcasts appeal largely to a particular viewing audience (that is, males aged 18 to 49) and, as a result, are attractive to a particular type of advertiser. Since the network is seeking sponsors willing to make a long-term commitment over the entire season, separate rates and discount schedules apply to those that make such a commitment.

DAYPARTS (TIME OF DAY)   Television can be divided into three broad time categories: *prime time*, *fringe time*, and *daytime*. Since the type of audience and size of audience vary according to daypart, so then must the rates for commercials within the dayparts. **Prime time** is usually designated as the viewing hours between 7 and 11 p.m. Most network shows are scheduled during prime time, and the shows with the largest audiences are usually scheduled between 8 and 10 p.m. (*Fear Factor*, *CSI*, and *Law & Order*, etc.). Advertising rates in prime time vary from show to show based on popularity and reach potential. As discussed in Chapter 7, each show has a rating and the rating places advertising rates within a certain dollar range. As mentioned above, estimating the ratings for new shows is difficult. For advertising purposes it is safer to buy time on established shows where audience estimates are based on past experience.

Fringe time is usually defined as the time preceding or following prime time. For example, early fringe would be 4 to 6 p.m., and late fringe 11 p.m. to 1 a.m. In early fringe time, viewing is somewhat lower among the adult population but is high among kids returning home from school. As a result, early fringe rates are lower than prime time rates. Program content in this time period usually consists of comedy reruns, music videos, and talk shows. Late fringe includes talk shows and movies. Viewing is lower in the late fringe period so advertising rates are adjusted accordingly.

Daytime television runs from early morning (sign-on) to 4 p.m. The reach potential of television is relatively low in the morning, except for the potential to reach young children. Television rates are lowest during the day. However, audiences increase during the day and the rates are increased accordingly. The types of programs scheduled during the daytime range from news and information in the early morning, to kids' shows in the morning, to soap operas and talk shows in the afternoon.

For a complete illustration of a weekly program schedule and the costs of advertising by daypart, refer to Figure 9.4.

LENGTH OF COMMERCIAL   Most advertising rate schedules are based on the purchase of 30-second units. Commercials that are longer in length—60, 90, and 120 seconds—are usually sold at two, three, and four times the 30-second rate.

Recently, 15-second commercials have become popular, as have **"split 30s"** (two 15-second commercials for the same product, one appearing at the start and one at the end of a commercial cluster). A split commercial may also involve different products of the same advertiser. Such a commercial strategy is sometimes referred to as "piggybacking." Fifteen-second commercials pose scheduling problems for networks and stations, and

FIGURE
9.4

Sample program
schedule—CKCO
Television

WINTER 2004 PROGRAM SCHEDULE

	MONDAY	TUESDAY	WEDNESDAY	THURSDAY	FRIDAY	SATURDAY	SUNDAY	
06:00			LOCAL NEWS (REPEAT)			OWL TV	ACORN: THE NATURE NUT	06:00
06:30						KINGDOM ADVENTURE	KIDS @ DISCOVERY	06:30
07:00						KATIE AND ORBIE		07:00
07:30			CANADA AM/NEWS ROTATION			D'MYNA LEAGUES	GOOD MORNING CANADA	07:30
08:00								08:00
08:30						GOOD MORNING CANADA		08:30
09:00			REGIS & KELLY (S ABC)				PAID PROGRAMMING	09:00
09:30								09:30
10:00			BALANCE (CDN)			DAILY PLANET		10:00
10:30			DAILY PLANET (CDN)					10:30
11:00			THE VIEW (S ABC)			ANIMAL PLANET		11:00
11:30								11:30
12:00			NEWS AT NOON			CTV TRAVEL	QUESTION PERIOD	12:00
12:30								12:30
01:00			BALANCE (CTV)			PAID PROGRAMMING	W-FIVE	01:00
01:30			THE BOLD & THE BEAUTIFUL (S CBS)					01:30
02:00			VICKI GABEREAU (CDN)			BALANCE		02:00
02:30						BALANCE	SUNDAY AFTERNOON MOVIE	02:30
03:00			GENERAL HOSPITAL (S ABC)			THE ASSOCIATES		03:00
03:30								03:30
04:00			OPRAH (S CBS)			MYSTERIOUS WAYS		04:00
04:30							SUNDAY AFTERNOON MOVIE	04:30
05:00			DR. PHIL (CBS)			MYSTERIOUS WAYS		05:00
05:30								05:30
06:00			NEWS AT SIX			LOCAL NEWS	LOCAL NEWS	06:00
06:30								06:30
07:00			E TALK (CDN)			W-FIVE (CDN)	ALIAS (PRE ABC)	07:00
07:30			JEOPARDY (S ABC)					07:30
08:00	SIMPLE RULES (PRE ABC)	AMERICAN IDOL (S FOX)	CORNER GAS	COMEDY NOW (CDN)	JOAN OF ARCADIA (S CBS)	SUE THOMAS F.B. EYE	COLD CASE (S CBS)	08:00
08:30	DEGRASSI: NG (CDN)		AMERICAN IDOL (S FOX)	COMEDY NOW (CDN)				08:30
09:00	THE O.C. (PRE FOX)	ACCORDING TO JIM (S ABC)	THE WEST WING (S NBC)	C.S.I. (S CBS)	CHARMED (WB)	LAW & ORDER	LAW & ORDER: CI (S NBC)	09:00
09:30		SCRUBS (S NBC)						09:30
10:00	CSI: MIAMI (S CBS)	LAW & ORDER: SVU (S NBC)	LAW & ORDER (S NBC)	ER (S NBC)	THIRD WATCH (S NBC)	LAW & ORDER: SVU	ELEVENTH HOUR	10:00
10:30								10:30
11:00			NATIONAL NEWS					11:00
11:30			NEWS AT 11:30 PM					11:30
12:00		THE DAILY SHOW WITH JON STEWART			LAW & ORDER ROTATION	SEX FILES	EBERT & ROEPER AND THE MOVIES	12:00
12:30		ETALK DAILY				ELLEN STRIP	DREW CAREY (REPEAT)	12:30
01:00				CTV LATE NIGHT MOVIE	CTV LATE NIGHT MOVIE	CTV LATE NIGHT MOVIE	DREW CAREY (REPEAT)	01:00
01:30		PAID PROGRAMMING					PAID PROGRAMMING	01:30
02:00								02:00

REG & SEL SALES	NET, REG & SEL SALES	*NET ONLY ITALICS*	KIDS PROGRAMMING	SELECTIVE SALES	PAID PROGRAMMING-NO SALES	
REGIONAL SALES	*NET ONLY ITALICS*					

Revised: February 5, 2004

their policies for acceptance vary. On average, the rates for 15-second commercials range from 65 to 70 percent of the 30-second rate. Split 30s may be accepted at the 30-second rate or range as high as 120 percent of the 30-second rate, depending on the network.

BUYING TELEVISION TIME

In recent years, dramatic changes have occurred in television advertising. Factors such as audience fragmentation, conflicting viewing data from competing electronic data providers, the introduction of optimizers, and demographic and lifestyle influences have created a need for new approaches to buying and selling television time.

As discussed earlier, media buying in television is a very complicated process that requires a high level of expertise on both sides of the negotiating table (i.e., among the media buyers who represent clients and among sales representatives who represent the networks and individual stations). In a textbook of this nature it is not possible to illustrate the negotiation process, as there is so much variation among the networks. Instead, a brief overview of some of the key points for the major networks is presented below. Also, a few illustrations of specific media buys are included in this section. The concept of media optimizers will be discussed in more detail in the technology section of this chapter.

NATIONAL AND REGIONAL NETWORK RATES The supply and demand system is based on a standard **grid card** with varying price levels. The highest level on the CBC is in the $50 000 range and at CTV as high as $80 000 for a high-demand, 30-second spot in prime time. Average rates in prime time are much lower. In this type of system, rates are adjusted periodically and are affected by factors such as inventory of time available, projected audiences, continuity, and seasonality. When the agency and the network negotiate the rates, client-oriented factors come into play such as competition for time, budget available, the ratio of prime time to fringe time required, and the program mix desired. Canadian media directors have estimated the average rates of buying 30-second spots on all Canadian networks based on these factors. For a summary of these rates, refer to Figure 9.5.

Both the CBC and CTV networks offer advertisers regional packages. The CBC offers advertisers four regional alternatives: Atlantic (New Brunswick, P.E.I., Nova Scotia, and Newfoundland), Central (Ontario and Montreal English), Western

Network	# of Stations	Basic Range	Basic Average
NATIONAL			
CBC Full	34	100–52 000	6 500
CBC MetroNet	17	100–25 000	N/A
CTV	22	2 500–80 000	12 000
Radio Canada	13	200–25 000	N/A
REGIONAL			
ATV	3	450–3 300	700
CBC Regional			
Atlantic	6	100–2 800	N/A
Central	12	100–21 000	N/A
Western	12	100–7 500	N/A
Pacific	6	100–4 200	N/A
SPECIALTY			
CBC Newsworld	1	250–1 000	650
Comedy	1	40–1 600	350
MuchMusic	1	1 050–3 000	2 025
TSN	1	500–20 000	N/A
YTV	1	150–4 500	1 250

Source: Adapted from Canadian Media Directors' Council *Media Digest*, 2003–2004, p. 29.

FIGURE

9.5

Estimated costs of network commercials (30 seconds) in prime time, 2003

(Manitoba, Saskatchewan, and Alberta), and Pacific (British Columbia). In addition the CBC offers a package of 11 key markets referred to as the MetroNet network.

In the case of **spot sales**, advertisers purchase time from any of the 17 CBC-owned stations that constitute the CBC network or the 18 stations that form the CTV network. Agencies can negotiate rates with member stations individually. Commercial material must be supplied to each station purchased.

LOCAL-MARKET TELEVISION RATES Spot announcement rates established by local stations also depend on the daypart (time classification) in which the commercial is scheduled to appear, projected audience size, and the time of year. As is shown by Figure 9.6, the highest rate charged for advertising was $4900 for a spot on *CSI* (Thursday 9–10 p.m.). Other popular shows in prime time include *ER* ($4320) and *Law & Order* ($2840). Reduced rates are offered in fringe and daytime periods.

Similar to the networks, the local-market station offers a continuity discount to advertisers booking a 52-week contract. In addition, some television stations may offer a seven-day reach plan. The **reach plan** is an interesting concept for television; it is more commonly used in radio as a way of selling off non-peak time. Commercials are rotated vertically throughout the day and horizontally during the week. Since the demographics of the audience change throughout the day, the number of people reached in a particular target group will vary with the schedule. However, with respect to the entire viewing audience, reach will be maximized and the plan is purchased at a discounted rate, a trade-off that must be considered against daypart scheduling.

GROSS RATING POINTS The concept of gross rating points (GRPs) was introduced in Chapter 7. When purchasing commercial time in specific television markets, media buyers request a certain level of GRPs, basing their request on the reach and frequency objectives of the advertiser. The GRP concept offers a way of measuring the advertising weight levels in a market in terms of reach and frequency variables; it is based on the formula

$$\text{GRPs} = \text{Reach} \times \text{Frequency}$$

Assume, for example, that a commercial message reaches 20 percent of target households in a market, and the commercial is scheduled five times in a week. The GRPs (weight) would be 100 [Reach (20) × Frequency (5) = 100]. In another week, the reach may be 25 percent and the frequency four; in that case, the GRP level would remain at 100. Consequently, from week to week in a television advertising flight, the actual number of commercials varies depending on the estimated reach of the programs the ads appear on.

Since reach figures and GRPs are discussed in the media negotiation process, it is impossible to illustrate the concept in a buying plan in this book. However, to illustrate the basic use of a television rate card, and to illustrate the fact that rates fluctuate according to daypart, a few examples will be developed.

If we use the CKCO-TV Kitchener rate card (Figure 9.6) in conjunction with the buying-plan examples below, we come up with the media cost calculations listed here.

TELEVISION BUYING ILLUSTRATIONS

Plan 1 Information	
Jeopardy:	2 spots per week
CSI Miami:	1 spot per week
Law & Order:	1 spot per week
(all spots run 52 weeks per year)	

Cost Calculations

On the basis of the above information, the advertiser qualifies for a continuity discount, which will be considered in the following cost calculations (the costs are taken from Figure 9.6).

FIGURE

9.6

CKCO-TV rate card

CKCO KITCHENER
2003-2004 RATE CARD

REVISED EFFECTIVE: June 02/03
30 SECOND - PUBLISHED RATE (GROSS)
FOR INTERNAL USE ONLY
RATES ARE PROTECTED FOR 5 WORKING DAYS

PRIME

DAY	TIME	PROGRAM		GROUP #	FALL SEP 15/03-DEC 14/03	WINTER DEC 15/03-FEB 22/04	SPRING FEB 23/04-JUN 6/04	SUMMER JUN 7/04-SEP 12/04	52 WEEK SEP 15/03 - SEP 12/04
M-F	557-7P	EARLY NEWS	0	015	$1,170	$990	$1,170	$990	$1,040
SA-SU	558-7P	WEEKEND NEWS	0	162	$670	$570	$670	$570	$590
M-F	7-730P	WHEEL OF FORTUNE	SIM	160	$930	$800	$930	$800	$830
M-F	730-8P	JEOPARDY	SIM	001	$690	$590	- $690	$590	$610
MO	8-830P	8 SIMPLE RULES	PRE	193	$1,740	$1,480	$1,740	$1,480	$1,540
MO	830-9P	WHOOPI	PRE	152	$1,030	$880	$1,030	$880	$920
MO	9-10P	THIRD WATCH	PRE	091	$1,630	$1,390	$1,630	$1,390	$1,450
MO	10-11P	CSI MIAMI	SIM	192	$2,720	$2,310	$2,720	$2,310	$2,410
TU	8-9P	AMERICAN JUNIORS	SIM	114	$1,010	$860	$1,010	$860	$900
TU	9-930P	ACCORDING TO JIM	SIM	102	$990	$840	$990	$840	$880
TU	930-10P	LESS THAN PERFECT	SIM	175	$440	$380	$440	$380	$390
TU	10-11P	LAW & ORDER SVU	SIM	092	$1,720	$1,470	$1,720	$1,470	$1,530
WE	8-830P	MY WIFE AND KIDS	SIM	285	$750	$640	$750	$640	$670
WE	830-9P	DEGRASSI: THE NEXT GENERATION	0	286	$190	$160	$190	$160	$170
WE	9-10P	THE WEST WING	SIM	042	$2,420	$2,050	$2,420	$2,050	$2,140
WE	10-11P	LAW & ORDER	SIM	076	$2,840	$2,410	$2,840	$2,410	$2,520
TH	8-828P	JUST FOR LAUGHS - GAGS	0	292	$170	$140	$170	$140	$150
TH	828-9P	SCRUBS	SIM	265	$970	$830	$970	$830	$860
TH	9-10P	C.S.I.	SIM	068	$4,900	$4,160	$4,900	$4,160	$4,340
TH	10-11P	ER	SIM	049	$4,230	$3,600	$4,230	$3,600	$3,750
FR	8-9P	JOAN OF ARCADIA	SIM	123	$600	$510	$600	$510	$530
FR	9-10P	CHARMED	0	062	$440	$380	$440	$380	$390
FR	10-11P	BOOMTOWN	SIM	067	$1,210	$1,030	$1,210	$1,030	$1,070
SA	7-8P	W-FIVE	0	039	$190	$160	$190	$160	$170
SA	8-9P	SUE THOMAS F.B.EYE	0	172	$380	$320	$380	$320	$340
SA	9-10P	COMEDY HOUR	0	142	$170	$140	$170	$140	$150
SA	10-11P	THE OSBOURNES	0	030	$400	$340	$400	$340	$350
SU	7-8P	ALIAS	PRE	081	$1,050	$900	$1,050	$900	$930
SU	8-9P	COLD CASE	SIM	128	$1,410	$1,200	$1,410	$1,200	$1,250
SU	9-10P	LAW & ORDER CI	SIM	103	$2,330	$1,970	$2,330	$1,970	$2,060
SU	10-11P	NIP/TUCK	0	137	$1,010	$860	$1,010	$860	$900
SU	10-11P	COLD SQUAD	0	0	$170	$140	$170	$140	$150
TU	8-9P	AMERICAN IDOL	SIM	0	$2,620	$2,230	$2,620	$2,230	$2,220
WE	830-9P	AMERICAN IDOL	SIM	0	$2,300	$1,950	$2,300	$1,950	$1,950

Jeopardy	$610 × 2 × 52 = $63 440
CSI Miami	$2410 × 52 = $125 320
Law & Order SVU	$1530 × 52 = $79 560
Gross Cost	= $268 320

Assuming an advertising agency purchased the advertising time for the advertiser, a further calculation would be as follows:

Client is billed by agency	$268 320
Agency retains 15-percent commission	$ 40 248
Media CKCO-TV receives	$228 072

Plan 2 Information

The rates in this example are also based on the CKCO-TV rate card (Figure 9.6).

Wheel of Fortune	1 spot (8 weeks; February 23 to March 16)
According to Jim	2 spots (8 weeks; February 23 to March 16)
CSI	1 spot (10 weeks; February 23 to March 30)

Cost Calculations

In this example, the continuity discount does not apply. The calculations would be as follows:

Wheel of Fortune	$930 × 8 = $7 440
According to Jim	$990 × 2 × 8 = $15 840
CSI	$4900 × 1 × 10 = $49 000
Total Cost	**= $72 280**

Assuming the time was purchased by an advertising agency, a further calculation would be as follows:

Client is billed by agency	$72 280
Agency retains 15-percent commission	$10 842
Media CKCO-TV receives	$61 438

The buying and selling of television time evolves with changing market conditions. Many networks in the United States (Canada will soon follow) are rethinking the upfront buying process. The networks are contemplating launching new shows throughout the entire year rather than at one time, usually September and October. Such a change will definitely have an impact on media planning and media buying. In the existing system advertising agencies have a vested interest in getting all bookings committed up front in order to reduce the cost of buying, and maintaining the buy in terms of person-hours required. For the networks such long-term commitments from advertisers ensures a steady cash flow and costs are also reduced.

The American networks now find that shows launched in late spring and even the summer are garnering larger audiences than shows in the traditional heavier viewing months. It proves that good programming will attract an audience regardless of season. For the record, the most watched show on a regular basis in Canada in 2003 was *Canadian Idol.* The audience averaged slightly over 2 million viewers for each show during July and August. As well, advertisers who properly execute **recency** (a media strategy that emphasizes the timing of advertising instead of weight of advertising) have a negotiating advantage in this new media-buying environment. These advertisers require fewer top-rated shows and as a result need not commit so much of their television budget up front.

DISCOUNTS OFFERED BY TELEVISION

A variety of discounts are available to television advertisers, depending on the extent of their advertising commitment. In general terms, discounts are based on the amount of advertising time purchased, on seasonal factors, and on other factors important to the network or station.

FREQUENCY, VOLUME, AND CONTINUITY DISCOUNTS

A **frequency discount** is usually earned through the purchase of a minimum number of spots over a specified period of time. Offered on a percentage basis, the discount increases with the number of spots purchased in the stated period of time. For example, the purchase of 5 to 10 spots per week may earn a 5-percent discount, 11 to 15 spots per week a 10-percent discount, and so on.

A **volume discount** is linked to the dollar volume purchased by the advertiser over a 52-week period. The greater the volume purchased, the greater the discount. A network such as the CBC or CTV would typically offer a volume discount range from 2 percent to 10 percent.

A **continuity discount** is earned when advertisers purchase a minimum number of designated spots over an extended period (usually 52 weeks, but the period may be shorter). The value of the continuity discount may increase with the number of spots purchased. For example, purchasing a minimum number of prime-time spots, perhaps two per week over 52 weeks, may earn the advertiser a 4-percent discount. If the number increases to three spots, the discount may move to 6 percent, and so on.

SEASONAL DISCOUNTS

The time of year has an effect on potential reach and the size of the television viewing audience. Television viewing drops off in the summer season. Consequently, **seasonal discounts** are available to advertisers wishing to purchase commercial time in non-peak seasons. The peak television season is mid-September to mid-February (the new television season each year). Viewing is lighter in the spring (mid-February to mid-June) and lightest in the summer (mid-June to mid-September). Reruns are shown in non-peak seasons.

Networks and stations usually offer summer discounts in the 20- to 25-percent range during this period because of the decline in television viewing. Viewing drops off by a similar percentage for all age groups except teens.

PACKAGE PLANS

Networks and stations offer **package plans** to sell off fringe or daytime spots at a discount, sometimes in combination with the purchase of prime time. The nature of such plans varies considerably. For example, an advertiser that purchases two prime-time spots per week in a popular American series may be required to purchase equivalent time in a prime-time Canadian series and/or equivalent time in daytime periods. Essentially, advertisers that demand the premium time spots must be prepared to make sacrifices through the purchase of less desirable time as well.

ROS (RUN OF SCHEDULE)

Run of schedule refers to a discount offered by a station to an advertiser that allows the station to schedule a commercial at its discretion during any time in the programming day.

PRE-EMPTION RATES **Pre-emption** is a situation in which a special program, such as a miniseries, an entertainment special, or a hockey playoff, replaces a regularly scheduled program. Advertisers are usually determined well in advance, and they pay premium prices for the right to sponsor such shows. Advertisers of the originally scheduled show are credited with equivalent commercial time at a later date.

MEDIA OPTIMIZERS: A PLANNING TOOL

Buying advertising time on television more efficiently is always the objective, and new software technology is playing a much bigger role in achieving that objective. TV optimizers are the highest expression of technology in media. An **optimizer** is a software program that searches the immense Nielsen TV ratings database for daypart or program combinations that increase target reach (or reduce the cost of buying it).

Procter & Gamble is one company that is advancing the use of optimizers. P&G's objective was to buy time more cheaply by negotiating around high-cost dayparts. With optimizers, agency media planners can investigate complex viewing targets and consider variables such as co-viewing and circumstance of viewing. They can study the viewer and duplication patterns of programs, dayparts, and networks, and determine how many targeted rating points in a venue is enough for a brand.[16] To get on board, the investment for an agency is substantial. So far, it is the domain of the larger agencies, which have demanding clients.

The Canadian Radio Market

As of 2004, 274 AM and 667 FM radio stations were operating in Canada. Collectively, these stations reach 93 percent of all people aged 12 and over. FM reaches 80 percent of the same group of people. The average listener spends more than 21 hours a week with the radio when all locations for listening are included (home, work, automobile. etc.).[17] Radio broadcasting in Canada is divided between the Canadian Broadcasting Corporation, which is funded by the government (or, more precisely, by the taxpayers of Canada), and independently owned and operated stations that survive on advertising revenues. All AM and FM stations are self-regulating, with no restrictions on the number of commercial minutes or on the placement of these minutes.

Trends Influencing the Radio Industry

The radio industry is changing but at a much slower rate than television. On the horizon are digital audio broadcasting and internet radio. As these technologies develop there will be a negative impact on tuning in for traditional AM and FM stations. Both technologies signal the future of radio broadcasting.

DIGITAL RADIO

Digital radio is coming to Canada, and with it a variety of new opportunities for advertising and reaching niche audiences that will revolutionize the medium. Thus far, the penetration of digital radio is low as the cost of a digital receiver is very high (like any new technology). Digital audio broadcasting (DAB) offers several advantages: sound of compact disc quality, perfect sound reception within a station's coverage area, and the ability to compress 15 signals into the transmitter space now used by one. It is anticipated that radio will follow the growth of television by introducing specialty radio stations that will focus on specific topics (e.g., specialized sports, news, business news).

Of all the radio stations in Canada, only 57 broadcast in a digital format. These broadcasts offer the same programs heard on existing AM and FM stations. Listeners of these broadcasts are few because you need a digital receiver to tune in. General Motors of Canada will become the first automaker to offer DAB radio in several of its models (2003).[18] It seems that the future of radio will be in digital broadcasting. The high costs of entry are the stumbling block for many stations.

INTERNET RADIO

There are about 5000 radio stations online around the world. Online radio offers listeners sound quality that is better than CD quality. Currently, the online radio stations are commercial-free, but on-air advertising revenue is certainly the objective for the immediate future. Traditional radio stations and the advertising industry have mixed feelings about the new medium. Broadcasters concede that an online presence is essential, but none are willing to abandon the traditional radio in favour of a new technology with an unproven revenue stream.[19] As the old saying goes, however, "he who hesitates is lost." Those stations that jump in early will benefit the most. While firm information about internet listening is not yet available, some industry experts estimate 30 percent of consumers with a web connection now listen to online stations.

If stations aren't broadcasting online they are establishing a web presence of some kind. Stations moving in this direction firmly believe they are giving current listeners every opportunity to access the station. The primary goal is to increase the loyalty and hours tuned in of their established listeners while attracting new audience. A problem with going online is cost. Local radio stations have discovered that a web presence is expensive, and cost is a deterrent.

Radio Listening Highlights

The BBM Bureau of Measurement compiles listening data in a survey (diary) format three times a year in over 115 radio markets in Canada. The diary also collects data about product usage and consumer lifestyles. Market reports are published for nine key urban markets and six regions (Atlantic, Quebec, Ontario, Manitoba Saskatchewan, Alberta, and British Columbia) three times a year. Tuning data covers 22 demographics for over 30 dayparts. Other standard data include market share, audience profiles, and listening locations tuning.

AM VERSUS FM

Radio signals are transmitted two ways: **AM (amplitude modulation)** and **FM (frequency modulation)**. AM refers to the height at which radio waves are transmitted. AM stations transmit waves by varying amplitude. Frequency refers to how fast waves travel in thousands of cycles per second (kilohertz). FM transmits waves by varying frequency. FM frequencies are above the static and noise level of AM. This results in clearer reception and better sound on FM stations. FM radio is more effective than AM in reaching all age categories. In recent years, FM stations have taken market share from AM stations. Currently, FM accounts for 80 percent of all tuning. Refer to Figure 9.7 for AM and FM audience-share data by age classification.

TUNING HOURS: HOW MUCH, WHEN, AND WHERE

The average listener spends almost 22 hours a week with radio and all age categories except teens spend about an equal amount of time listening. Refer to Figure 9.8 for details. By time of day radio is the inverse of television. Radio is much more popular in

FIGURE 9.7

AM and FM share of tuning by age classification

Canada	Reach		Share	
	AM %	FM%	AM%	FM%
12+	38.5	80.4	26.3	73.7
Women 18+	39.1	80.2	27.3	72.7
Men 18+	43.0	80.2	27.1	72.9
Teens 12–17	14.7	82.6	6.0	94.0

Source: BBM, Fall '02, Canadian Media Directors' Council *Media Digest*, 2003–2004, p. 32.

FIGURE 9.8

Weekly hours of radio listening in Canada

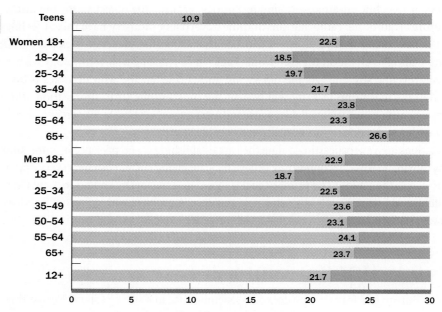

* The average listener spends 22 hours a week with the radio.

FIGURE 9.9

Radio listening by time of day

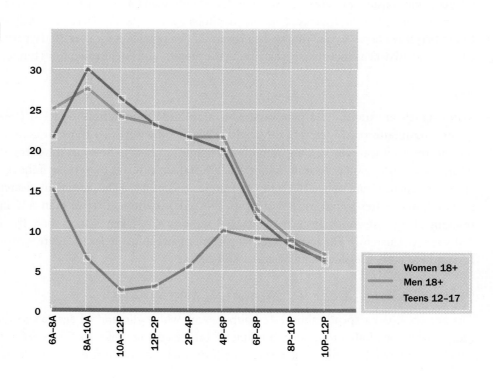

the morning and as the day progresses listening tapers off. The use of radio during the day is high since people tune in when they wake up, while they travel to work, and when they are at work. Refer to Figure 9.9 for details.

One of radio's advantages is its mobility. Listeners can be reached on various occasions. Among all listeners 12 years and older listening from the home accounts for 50 percent of listening time. Listening in automobiles ranks second and accounts for 25 percent of listening time and listening from work accounts for 23 percent of listening time.[20]

Radio Station Formats

One of the major advantages of radio is its ability to reach selective target audiences. The audience reached depends on the format of the station. **Format** refers to the type and nature of the programming offered by an individual station. Basically, the content is designed to appeal to a particular target group, usually defined by age and interests.

The most popular radio-station formats in Canada are adult contemporary, news/talk, and CHR (contemporary hit radio). **Adult contemporary (AC)** stations play popular and easy-listening music, current and past, and generally appeal to an audience in the 25- to 49-year-old range. In recent years the AC format has lost some ground and today the battle for supremacy is a virtual dead heat between AC (25.8 percent market share) and news/talk (25.5 percent market share).[21]

News/talk stations focus on frequent news reporting and listener call-ins to discuss newsworthy current issues. Some stations focus specifically on news niches (e.g., sports). News/talk is a fast-growing segment that is helping to revitalize AM radio (e.g., CFRB and 680 News in Toronto). In the **sports talk** niche, Toronto has The Fan 590. CHUM radio has a list of stations across the country devoted to full-time sports talk and related programming. Sports talk reaches a male audience in the 25- to 54-year-old range.

Contemporary hit radio (CHR) stations play the latest hits, mainly rock, and appeal to teens and 18- to 34-year-old adults. Top-40 stations are popular in urban markets but they have been losing ground to other formats in recent years.

Album-oriented rock (AOR) stations play a continuous collection of rock albums. They are quite popular with teens and adults. Basically, AOR acts as an alternative to the CHR stations, and appears more frequently on FM than on AM.

Country stations play a variety of country music ranging from classic hits to current chart-toppers. The music played is in the contemporary or traditional Nashville or bluegrass genre. Audiences tend to be blue-collar and cover a much wider cross-section of age ranges. The popularity of country music has drifted off in recent years.

Classical music stations are popular in Toronto (CFMX-FM) and Montreal (CJPX-FM) and across the country on CBC Radio Two. Other stations integrate some classical music into a station's program schedule to reflect **audience flow**, or as a programming alternative in markets served by only one radio station. Classical music generally appeals to more mature age groups with more extensive educational backgrounds and with occupations that require more extensive education.

In recent years, the **gold** format has waned in popularity. Gold, strictly an AM-station format, is targeted at the coveted baby boomers who prefer music from the 1960s, 1970s, and 1980s. There is little hope of any share improvement until the CRTC allows the format to move to FM. Gold is the only format legislated off the FM band. Refer to Figure 9.10 for a summary of station format trends in Canada.

The variety of radio formats in urban markets reflects each individual station's desire to be successful. Finding the right niche (a niche that is underserved in a market)

CHUM Radio
www.chumlimited.com/radio

FIGURE
9.10

Radio format and listening
share trends

Format	Market Share 2000	Market Share 2002
Adult Contemporary	26.7	25.8
News/Talk	21.7	25.5
Contemporary Hits	18.6	14.5
Classical	7.1	6.3
Album-Oriented Rock	7.4	6.1
Country	5.8	5.3
Classic Rock	3.3	4.6
Adult Standards	1.1	2.9
Modern Rock	2.0	2.8
Gold	3.0	1.6
Sports	0.9	1.6
Full Service	2.4	1.0

Source: Adapted from Patrick Bohn, "Adult Contemporary Rules," *Marketing*, July 22, 2002, p. 10.

makes a station attractive to a particular group of advertisers. The main considerations are the age demographics of the local market and the number of competitive stations appealing to similar target audiences. Based on the degree of competition for a listening audience (e.g., competition to reach a particular demographic group), stations often change their format to reach a target that is underserved.

Radio as an Advertising Medium

Radio offers advertisers several advantages and disadvantages. Selecting radio as an advertising medium depends on the problem that advertising is trying to resolve.

ADVANTAGES OF RADIO

TARGET-MARKET SELECTIVITY Because they tend to adopt a specific music format (adult contemporary, contemporary hit radio, country, gold, and so on), radio stations appeal to more precisely defined demographic groups than television stations do. Consequently, advertisers can use a profile-matching strategy and select stations with audience profiles that closely match their target market. Even in smaller markets, where music formats change within a single station and the audience flow varies by daypart, the advertiser can schedule radio commercials at the appropriate time of day so that dollars will not be wasted reaching people outside the target. For example, advertisers for soft drinks, snack foods, and fashion aimed at a youthful target would concentrate their advertisements in the evening time block, when the youthful target market is most likely to be listening.

REACH POTENTIAL Since radios are almost everywhere—with multiple receivers in the home, carried around by teens with portable stereos, in the car, and at the beach—radio has the potential to reach large audiences, particularly if advertisers place ads on several stations in an urban market.

The morning is the most popular listening time. Since the reach is highest in this time period, it is the most expensive time of day to advertise. The mobility of radio has a positive influence on reach potential. As indicated earlier in the chapter, tuning into the radio when travelling in an automobile accounts for 25 percent of all listening time. Another factor affecting reach potential is portability. Radio is a popular medium outdoors in the summer, when people are away from competitive media. Many stations charge higher rates in the summer because of this higher reach potential.

FREQUENCY Radio is usually referred to as a **frequency medium**, a name that suggests radio's probable foremost advantage. If target-market selectivity is used, an audience can be reached on several occasions throughout the day or week (vertical and horizontal rotation plans) at a relatively low cost. For local advertisers wanting to advertise sales, radio is a preferable medium; numerous announcements can be scheduled before and during the sale to stimulate immediate response from consumers. For national advertisers, the radio can boost frequency in key markets as needed. Because radio offers frequency at a reasonable cost, advertisers can use it to supplement the reach of other media in a campaign.

COST The low cost of radio advertising attracts local clients for whom advertising otherwise would not be affordable. Radio advertising is cost-favourable in two areas. First, production costs are much less than they are for television, and changes to copy can be made on short notice. Second, in terms of time, the basic cost for each spot is relatively low (making radio an efficient means of reaching selective audiences), and numerous discounts are available for larger-volume advertisers. The combination of reasonable cost and frequency potential makes radio a good medium to supplement other media in a total campaign.

FLEXIBILITY Radio offers flexibility in three areas: creative, time scheduling, and market scheduling. In terms of creative, copy changes can be made on short notice to meet the needs of changing competitive situations as well as the needs of local markets. With respect to scheduling, the lead time required is short (two weeks or less); however, demand for popular stations in urban markets is quite high. Nonetheless, schedules can be "heavied up" (i.e., advertising can be increased) on short notice if the competitive situation so dictates.

Radio is an ideal medium for advertisers who are following a key-market strategy. Since stations are local in nature and reach a specific demographic, an advertiser can select popular stations in each urban market it has designated as a priority. Consequently, the advertiser is not paying for any wasted reach. Several leading national advertisers allocate significant budgets to radio advertising. Among them are Goodyear, Labatt, Molson, and the Dairy Farmers of Canada.

For more insight into the benefits of radio advertising, read the Advertising in Action vignette **Radio Helps Build Brands**.

DISADVANTAGES OF RADIO

AUDIENCE FRAGMENTATION While reach potential is high, the audience is fragmented due to station format and to the demographic groups that competing stations appeal to. An advertiser wishing to reach the teen audience in urban markets may have to purchase several stations to achieve adequate reach levels. Listener loyalty to a certain station contributes to the fragmentation problem. The net effect of fragmentation is that radio is recognized as a low-reach/high-frequency medium.

Radio Helps Build Brands

Media planners often view radio as a supplementary medium; it plays a supporting role so it can't be recommended for building brand awareness. Recent marketing research conducted by the Radio Marketing Bureau, however, along with some real case studies, strongly suggests that radio can definitely help create awareness and build a brand.

The objectives of the Radio Marketing Bureau's research were to challenge the perception of radio as simply a tactical medium and to show national advertisers that radio is effective in establishing a brand and for reaching specific target groups. "If your campaign can increase perception of your brand as more valuable and increase top-of-mind awareness, then there's a better chance the consumer will actually purchase."

The case studies were based on pre- and post-test data for brands in the packaged goods, automobile, and alcohol beverage categories. The research revealed that radio did improve brand perceptions and it did encourage greater levels of consumption.

In one test for a mature packaged-goods brand, multiple-use radio messaging aired in tandem with national television brand advertising. The pre-wave survey found purchase intent similar in both the radio and TV markets, but post-wave the consumers in the radio market were 19 percent more likely to consider purchasing the brand than those in the TV-only market. In the automotive category a similar test produced a 12 percent increase in purchase intention.

Bill Ratcliffe, president of Millward Brown Goldfarb, the company that conducted the research, observed that, in markets where radio was used, the level of awareness didn't necessarily increase, but for more important measures such as purchase intention it did. He cautions, "When approaching a multimedia effects model, you have to make sure you are looking at a variety of brand health measures and not just awareness because you could be totally misled."

Goodyear is a firm believer in the power of radio. In fact, the company is contemplating investing more in radio advertising and less in television advertising in the future. It currently uses both—it's simply a matter of reallocation to potentially save a lot of money.

Goodyear's consistent use of the vulnerable Goodyear guy (actor Tom Sharp) on both radio and television over the past decade means radio listeners actually visualize the character. When consumers are asked questions about advertising they often attribute awareness to television when there are no spots running at the time. Such data confirms the power of radio! Goodyear believes that radio is ideal for the automotive product category. Consumers listen to the radio when they drive. If their car has a problem, there is no better time to reach the customer.

Source: Adapted from Patti Summerfield, "A cheaper way to build brands," *Strategy Media*, July 26, 2003, p. 4.

Radio Marketing Bureau www.rmb.ca
Goodyear www.goodyear.com

MESSAGE RETENTION Several factors restrict the retention ability of radio messages. First, radio messages are short; there is limited opportunity for the communication of details in 30 seconds. Sixty-second commercials offer more creative flexibility, but they are less popular because of costs. Second, radio is a background medium; therefore, attention levels of listeners are potentially lower. Third, clutter is a problem, particularly on AM stations. Finally, radio is only a sound medium; as a result, there is no chance for the customer's mind to register the way a package looks (an important consideration for a new product), and there can be no product demonstration. Some of these weaknesses may be overcome with the introduction of digital radio and online radio (refer to the technology section of this chapter for details).

MEDIA-PLANNING CONSIDERATIONS   For local-market advertisers, the advantages of radio outweigh the disadvantages. For national advertisers purchasing a large number of radio markets, other media factors must be considered. Generally speaking, radio time is in high demand, particularly among leading stations in urban markets. This demand makes it difficult for media buyers to purchase the specific times desired by their clients. Also, since there are more than 900 commercial stations from coast to coast, it is a difficult medium to coordinate in a media buy.

The industry has consolidated in recent years and various radio networks have become much larger. The CHUM Radio Network, Corus Radio Network, and Telemedia Radio Network, for example, offer packaged media buys in all of their stations coast-to-coast. This helps alleviate some of the problems associated with planning and buying media time.

Radio Advertising Rates and Buying Procedures

The rates paid by radio advertisers are affected by several factors: the season or time of year in which commercials are placed; the daypart or time of day for which the commercials are scheduled; the utilization of reach plans; and the availability of discounts offered by individual stations. The type of advertiser (national or local) also has an impact on the basic rate charged to advertisers.

INFLUENCES ON RADIO ADVERTISING RATES

SEASONAL RATE STRUCTURES   The rates charged by radio stations are often influenced by seasonal fluctuations in listening. Generally, radio rates fluctuate with the seasons, as follows:

Time Period	Rate
May–August (summer) and December	Higher
September–October	Mid-range
March–April	Mid-range
January–February	Lower

DAYPARTS   Since the size and nature of the audience varies according to the daypart, different rates are charged for each. Generally, the dayparts are classified as follows:

Classification	Time
Breakfast	6 to 10 a.m.
Midday	10 a.m. to 4 p.m.
Drive	4 to 7 p.m.
Evening	7 p.m. to midnight
Nighttime	Midnight to 6 a.m.

Dayparts vary from one station to another, with some stations having more or fewer classifications than those listed above. In addition, weekend classifications are often different from weekday ones, as the listening patterns of the audience change on weekends.

REACH PLANS Radio advertisers can either purchase specific time slots and schedule a particular **rotation plan** during the length of the media buy, or they can purchase a reach plan. For the first option, a rotation plan, the advertiser specifies the time slots and pays the corresponding rate associated with it. Two types of rotation plans are available:

- **Vertical rotation:** the placement of commercials based on the time of day (within various dayparts)
- **Horizontal rotation:** the placement of commercials based on the day of the week (same daypart on different days)

Earlier in the chapter, potential reach was identified as an advantage of radio. However, since listening levels and the type of audience vary with the daypart, radio stations have developed reach plans in order to maximize reach. In a **reach plan** (or a **total audience plan**, as it is often called), commercials are rotated through the various dayparts in accordance with a predetermined frequency, in order to reach different people with the same message. Reach plans vary from station to station. In many cases, the reach plan covers the entire week, while in other cases a separate reach plan is implemented on weekends.

With reference to Figure 9.11, reach-plan spots are equally divided among breakfast, daytime, drive time, and evening/Sunday dayparts. For the advertiser, the benefit of the reach plan is twofold. First, the reach potential is extended, and second, the rates charged for the reach plan collectively are lower (because of the discounts) than those that would result from the individual purchase of similar time slots. Reach plans do require a minimum spot purchase on a weekly basis.

TYPE OF ADVERTISER Radio advertising rates vary with the nature of the advertiser. National advertisers are charged the general (national) rate that is generally higher than rates charged to local advertisers (retail establishments, restaurants, and so on). Rates for national advertisers are commissionable to recognized advertising agencies at the rate of 15 percent. Retail rates, being lower, are non-commissionable, but owing to their importance in the local radio station's revenue mix stations offer production assistance either at no cost or at reasonable cost to encourage retailers to advertise. On average, local advertisers contribute 75 percent of a radio station's revenue.

DISCOUNTS OFFERED BY RADIO

Advertisers that purchase frequently from specific stations qualify for a variety of discounts. While the criteria for earning discounts vary, the discounts are similar in nature.

A **frequency discount** is a discounted rate earned through the purchase of a minimum number of spots over a specified period of time, usually a week. Having earned such a discount, advertisers are referred to a lower-rate grid schedule, or they could be quoted a percentage discount, such as 5 percent for 15 to 20 spots per week, 8 percent for 21 to 30 per week, 10 percent for over 31 spots, and so forth.

With a **volume discount**, the advertiser is charged a lower rate for buying a large number of spots; the discount might be 5 percent for 260 spots, for example, or 10 percent for 520 spots.

With a **continuity discount**, the advertiser is charged a lower rate for making a contract buy that covers a specified period of time. At intervals of 26, 39, and 52 weeks, advertisers are charged according to a discounted grid schedule, or the percentage discount offered increases with the length of the contract.

As discussed earlier in the chapter, radio can increase advertising reach—in other words, can gain access to a different audience—by rotating commercials through the various dayparts. To increase reach, stations offer **reach plans** or **total audience plans** that require advertisers to purchase a minimum weekly number of spots in return for a packaged discount rate, such as 16 spots per week divided equally among four dayparts.

It is quite common for independent radio stations to be controlled by one owner (e.g., two AM stations in different markets, or an AM/FM combination in the same market). Advertisers receive a discounted rate called a **combination rate** if they air commercials on more than one station. A station may offer additional discounts to advertisers if allowed to vertically and horizontally rotate commercials through a schedule at its own discretion. This is referred to as a **run of schedule** rate.

BUYING RADIO TIME

No doubt, a strategic plan will guide the buying of radio commercial time. In order to get the best possible rate from a station or network of stations, all details of the plan must be known by the radio station. Factors such as volume and frequency (the total number of spots in the buy), the timing of the schedule in terms of time of day or season in which the plan is scheduled, and continuity (the length of the plan) collectively have an impact on the spot rate that is charged the advertiser. It places an advertiser on a particular grid with the station. Refer to Figure 9.11 for a listing of grid rates and how an advertiser arrives at a certain grid. For advertisers that purchase large amounts of time, the discounts just described usually apply.

To illustrate some basic cost calculations used in buying radio time, let's develop some examples based on the rate card shown in Figure 9.11.

EXAMPLE ONE—BUYING INFORMATION

30-second spots	15 drive spots per week
10 breakfast spots per week	12-week schedule

Based on the length of the schedule (12 weeks), the advertiser does not qualify for a continuity discount. Therefore, the first calculation is to determine the total number of spots in the buy, to see if the advertiser qualifies for a volume discount.

Total number of spots	= spots per week × number of weeks
Breakfast	= 10 per week × 12 weeks = 120
Drive	= 15 per week × 12 weeks = 180
Total spots	**= 300**

Based on the total number of spots (300), the rate charged will be from grid 3. In this case, the 30-second rate is $88 for breakfast and $79 for drive time. The cost calculations are as follows:

Total Costs	= number of spots × earned rate
Breakfast	= 120 spots × $88 = 10 560
Drive	= 180 spots × $79 = 14 220
Total cost	**= $24 780**

FIGURE
9.11

CHET Radio
rate card

This rate card has been created to demonstrate to the reader the key factors that influence a radio media buy: spot rates, reach plan rates, volume discounts, and continuity discounts. Discounts are not usually published in *Canadian Advertising Rates and Data*.

CHETRadio

640 AM

| All Talk!
24/7 |

NEWS ON THE HOUR EVERY HOUR

30-sec spot rates

Daypart / Grid	1	2	3	4	5
Breakfast 6:00 to 10:00 am	109.00	98.00	88.00	79.00	72.00
Daytime 10:00 am to 3:00 pm	92.00	82.00	73.00	64.00	58.00
Drive 3:00 to 7:00 pm	98.00	88.00	79.00	70.00	63.00
Evening and Sunday	76.00	68.00	65.00	57.00	49.00

Reach Plan – 30-sec. spots

Breakfast 25% Daytime 25% Drive 25% Evening and Sunday 25%	88.00	79.00	71.00	62.00	54.00

Discount Schedule

Contract Buy (Continuity)		Volume (Spots)	
14 to 26 weeks	Grid 3	250	Grid 3
27 to 39 weeks	Grid 4	450	Grid 4
40 to 52 weeks	Grid 5	700	Grid 5

EXAMPLE TWO   The advertiser would like to evaluate a reach plan (involving 16 commercials per week) against a specific buying plan. Details of each plan are as follows:

Plan A—Reach Plan (30-second spots) Information
Involves 16 spots per week
Rotated between breakfast, drive, day, and evening/Sunday
Runs for 16 weeks, June through September

Plan B—Specific Plan (30-second spots) Information
8 breakfast spots per week
8 drive spots per week
16-week schedule

Cost Calculations for Plan A   In this case, the advertiser qualifies for a continuity discount because of the 16-week schedule. Based on the rate card, the earned rate would be under grid 34 in the reach plan. The earned rate is $71 per spot. Therefore, the cost of the reach plan is

Total cost	= total number of spots × earned rate
	= (16 weeks × 16 spots/wk) × $71
	= $18 176

Cost Calculations for Plan B   The total number of spots in the buy are

Breakfast	= 8 spots per week × 16 weeks = 128 spots
Drive	= 8 spots per week × 16 weeks = 128 spots
Total spots	= 256

Based on this calculation the advertiser does not qualify for a volume discount, but since the contract runs for 16 weeks, a continuity discount does apply. The advertiser is charged the rate from grid 3. Therefore, the total costs for Plan B are as follows:

Breakfast	= 128 spots × $88 = $11 264
Drive	= 128 spots × $79 = $10 112
Total cost	**= $21 376**

In conducting a comparative evaluation of Plan A and Plan B, the advertiser must weigh the more selective reach potential of Plan B against the savings of Plan A. Perhaps the advertiser wants to reach business commuters in drive time to and from work. With Plan A, the advertiser can reach a somewhat different audience by means of a daypart rotation of spots. The net result is a cost difference of $3200 in favour of Plan A. Should the advertiser decide to go with the cost savings of Plan A, or with the more selective reach of Plan B at greater cost? Would you like to make the decision?

SUMMARY

The Canadian television market comprises public networks, private networks, cable television networks, pay-TV networks, and direct-to-home broadcasting (satellite television). How people view television varies according to the time of day and the season. Television viewing tends to be lowest in the morning, somewhat higher in the afternoon, and highest in the evening. In terms of seasonal changes, viewership is much lower in the summer.

A trend in the industry is the gradual movement away from conventional mass-market television toward specialty channels that appeal to niche targets (e.g., YTV, HGTV, and TSN). Of even greater concern is the impact the internet and personal video recorders will have on television-program and advertising-message viewing. There will be less exposure to advertising.

As an advertising medium, television's primary advantages include high reach, message impact and effectiveness, frequency (for large advertisers), some demographic selectivity, demonstration capability, and coverage flexibility. Disadvantages include high cost, audience fragmentation, clutter, and commercial avoidance.

Depending on the degree of coverage they desire, advertisers can purchase television time from the national networks, for national or selective spots, or from local stations. To compensate for clutter and commercial avoidance, advertisers are taking advantage of sponsorship and branded-content opportunities. These strategies offer product exposure during the programs. The rates an advertiser pays are affected by supply and demand, type of program purchased, and the daypart. The cost of television time is highest in prime time (7–11 p.m.). Discounts are generally offered on the basis of frequency, volume, continuity, and season.

In terms of planning and buying television commercial time, computer software is playing a key role. Referred to as optimizers, the software allows planners to search Nielsen databases for the best program combinations to increase target reach.

In contrast to television viewership trends, radio listenership peaks in the morning (6–10 a.m.) and tapers off as the day progresses. Radio signals are transmitted in three ways: AM, FM, and digital. FM is presently the most popular form of transmission, but digital audio broadcasting is expected to grow in the next decade. Internet radio is also growing and will continue to steal market share from conventional stations.

As an advertising medium, radio offers target-market selectivity, reach and frequency potential (based on its relatively low cost), and coverage flexibility. Radio's ability to reach selective targets is based on the format of the station. Currently, adult contemporary, contemporary hit radio, and news/talk are the most popular station formats. Disadvantages include audience fragmentation, problems associated with message retention, and clutter.

Radio rates are affected by several factors: season, daypart, reach plans, and the type of advertiser (local advertisers pay lower rates). Advertisers are offered discounts based on frequency, volume, continuity, and the use of package plans (reach plans).

KEY TERMS

REVIEW QUESTIONS

1. What is the purpose of the various time classifications in television and radio?

2. What are the primary advantages and disadvantages of television advertising for the national advertiser? For the local advertiser?

3. Explain the difference between network advertising and national or selective-spot advertising.

4. Identify and briefly explain any three factors that influence the cost of television advertising.

5. Identify and briefly explain the television discounts that are based on the amount of time purchased by advertisers.

6. Explain the following television terms:
   a) branded content
   b) fragmentation
   c) sponsorship
   d) daypart
   e) zipping
   f) zapping
   g) clutter
   h) upfront buying
   i) prime time versus fringe time
   j) package plans
   k) ROP
   l) pre-emption rates
   m) GRPs

7. Calculate the cost of the following television campaign on CKCO-TV. Assume an agency commission of 15 percent. What amount does CKCO-TV actually receive? Use the rate card in Figure 9.6 to do your calculations.

   Information: CKCO-TV
   Alias; 1 spot per week for 13 weeks
   The West Wing; 1 spot per week for 13 weeks
   Early News; 3 spots per week for 52 weeks

8. What does "station format" refer to in radio broadcasting?

9. What are the major advantages and disadvantages of radio advertising for the national advertiser? For the local advertiser?

10. Identify and briefly explain any three factors that influence the cost of radio advertising.

11. What is a reach plan, and what benefits does it provide the advertiser?

12. Calculate the cost of the following radio campaign. Use the rate card in Figure 9.11 to do your calculations.

    CHET Radio
    30-second spots as follows:
    Breakfast; 4 spots per week; Mon–Fri; 28 weeks
    Drive; 4 spots per week; Mon–Fri; 28 weeks
    Daytime; 8 spots per week; Mon–Fri; 28 weeks

    Now calculate the cost of a 16-spot reach plan for 28 weeks. How much money is saved compared to the original calculation? Is the reach plan a better deal?

13. If you made the decision to use radio in a city such as Toronto, Ottawa, or Vancouver, on what basis would you select specific stations? Discuss your reasons.

14. Briefly explain the following radio terms:
    a) audience flow
    b) combination rate
    c) vertical rotation
    d) horizontal rotation
    e) reach plan
    f) frequency discount
    g) volume discount
    h) continuity discount

DISCUSSION QUESTIONS

1. "Expanded penetration of specialty networks, pay TV, and direct-to-home television will have an impact on traditional television viewing patterns and will influence the media selection process of advertisers." Discuss this trend from the viewpoint of the advertiser.

2. What impact will the internet have on the future of television viewing and television advertising? Discuss.

3. The television industry is moving in the direction of channel specialization (i.e., niche channels to reach selective targets). Will this trend continue? If so, is this trend a benefit or drawback for companies using television to deliver advertising messages? Justify your position.

4. Identify some additional strategies advertisers should be taking to counter the problem of commercial avoidance (either viewers leaving the viewing area or viewers using PVRs to avoid messages). Should funds be reallocated to other media? Present a position on this issue.

5. Is branded content a viable means of advertising? Will too much branded content harm the credibility of television programs and the advertiser's reputation? Evaluate the issues surrounding this form of advertising and present a point of view.

6. Target-market selectivity is the key benefit of radio advertising. On what basis can the radio industry exploit this advantage? Discuss appropriate strategies the industry might use to attract advertisers.

7. Read the Advertising in Action vignette **Radio Helps Build Brands**. Is the potential of radio advertising underestimated? Should more advertising dollars be allocated to radio? Conduct some secondary research on the issue and present a point of view.

8. Is internet radio a threat to conventional radio broadcasters? If so, what strategies should conventional broadcasters be implementing now or in the near future? Discuss.

NOTES

1. Canadian Media Directors' Council *Media Digest*, 2003–2004, p. 13.

2. Seana Mulcahy, "Unnerved by young men," *Media Post*, **www.mediapost. com**, January 5, 2004.

3. Jim Kirk, "Viewer shifts unnerve industry," *Chicago Tribune*, January 2, 2004, **www.chicagotribune.com/business/chi-040102018**.

4. Lianne George, "This ain't OshKosh B'Gosh," *National Post*, April 19, 2003, pp. SP1, SP7.

5. Canadian Media Directors' Council *Media Digest*, 2003–2004, p. 55.

6. Patrick Brethour, "Women narrow Internet gender gap," *The Globe and Mail*, March 27, 2001, pp. B1, B2.

7. Bruce Classen, "Big But Stupid vs. Small But Smart," *Marketing*, October 28, 1996, p. 15.

8. Canadian Media Directors' Council *Media Digest*, 2003–2004, p. 19.

9. Ibid. p. 29.

10. Patrick Allossery, "Global's dot spots increase TV clutter," *Financial Post*, March 31, 2000, p. C3.

11. Patti Summerfield, "Commercial avoidance rampant," *Strategy*, March 12, 2001, pp. 1, 2.

12. Chuck Ross, "Study: Shorter spots less effective," *Advertising Age*, October 4, 1999, pp. 3, 65.

13. CPM calculations are based on data in Canadian Media Directors' Council *Media Digest*, 2003–2004 and BBM audience data.

14. Chris Powell, "Idol worship," *Marketing*, November 10, 2003, p. 11.

15. Sara Minogue, "Absolut free storyline," *Strategy*, November 8, 2003, p. 19.

16. Erwin Ephron, "Where's robobuyer?" *Advertising Age*, May 1, 2000, p. 45.

17. Canadian Media Directors' Council *Media Digest*, 2003–2004, p. 32.

18. Mark Evans, "Digital hits world of radio," *Financial Post*, January 16, 2002, p. FP7.

19. Keith Damsell, "FM Canada.com plays the Net," *The Globe and Mail*, August 16, 2000. p. B7.

20. Canadian Media Directors' Council *Media Digest*, 2003–2004, p. 33.

21. Patrick Bohn, "Adult contemporary rules," *Marketing*, July 22, 2002, p. 10.

Courtesy: Dick Hemingway

Out-of-Home Media

Out-of-home media include outdoor advertising, transit advertising, and various forms of in-store and point-of-purchase advertising. This chapter presents the basic types of out-of-home advertising alternatives, the advantages and disadvantages of each alternative, and the procedures for buying media space for each.

Out-of-home advertising and the variety of alternatives included in its domain represent a highly visible and effective alternative for advertisers. Think about it. If you drive a car, travel by transit, or stroll through shopping malls, you are constantly exposed to out-of-home advertising messages. Out-of-home advertising messages reach a massive cross-section of a city's population 24 hours a day, seven days a week. In 2001, the combination of outdoor and transit advertising generated net revenues of $310 million, which accounted for 3 percent of net advertising revenues in Canada.

This media segment is growing at a faster rate than other forms of media. The current popularity of outdoor advertising is perhaps due to the specialization and fragmentation that has occurred in other media, especially television and magazines. Another factor affecting growth stems from a shift in the thinking behind media planning. Many planners now pay more attention to when and why consumers come in contact with media and advertising messages. These planners believe that the proximity and timing of an advertising exposure and the consumer's mindset at the time of that exposure are emerging as critical factors in the communications planning process. The concept of recency is one component of this new way of thinking. For additional details about recency, refer to the Advertising in Action vignette that appeared in Chapter 7 titled **Shattering the Paradigm: How Does Advertising Work?** Many forms of out-of-home advertising actually reach the consumer when they are in a position to make a buying decision! Finally, with the population becoming increasingly mobile, particularly in urban markets, outdoor advertising provides a quick and convenient way to get a message to consumers.

Outdoor Media Research

The Canadian Outdoor Measurement Bureau (COMB) is responsible for compiling reliable data and information about outdoor advertising. COMB audits the circulations of outdoor posters, superboards, mall posters, backlit posters, and transit shelters. Circulation data for all media except mall posters are based on municipal and provincial traffic counts and are converted into circulation based on an established traffic-variation factor. COMB uses an average occupancy factor of 1.75 per vehicle. Mall counts are based on head counts conducted by an independent organization in each market location. COMB maintains a national database of all media products and publishes the data in *Market Data Reporter*, a quarterly publication.

Sellers of outdoor media also rely on research data that they integrate with sophisticated software programs to help plan campaigns. For example, Mediacom, a Toronto-based company, uses a system called SMART—Strategic Mapping and Response Tool. This database is based on Statistics Canada data, traffic flow and traffic volume information that is continually being added to the system. Referred to as geodemographic mapping, it has helped advertisers such as Western Union and Bell Canada implement campaigns that target specific ethnic neighbourhoods with advertising in the appropriate language.[3] Outdoor has never been considered a targeted medium, but the combination of information and technology is changing things.

In Canada, the primary out-of-home alternatives include outdoor media and transit media. In addition there are various other options such as street-level advertising, and a host of other miscellaneous opportunities.

Mediacom
www.mediacom.com

Outdoor Advertising

POSTERS The **poster** is the most commonly used form of outdoor advertising (see Figure 10.1 for an illustration). Posters are either horizontal or vertical and are commonly

Courtesy: Dick Hemingway

FIGURE
10.1

An illustration of an outdoor poster

referred to as **billboards**. The poster is composed of 10 or 12 sheets of special paper designed to withstand the wear and tear of outdoor conditions. To maximize reach potential, posters are strategically located on major routes within, or leading to, the business and shopping districts of a community. To maximize the frequency of the message, and to extend the daily viewing by consumers, posters are often illuminated. Advertisers can purchase poster space either in single panels or as a "showing." A **showing** refers to the buying of multiple panels to achieve a desired level of reach and frequency in a market.

BACKLIT POSTERS A **backlit (backlight) poster** (often called a backlight) is a luminous sign containing advertising graphics printed on translucent polyvinyl material. Colour reproduction and impact are among the advantages offered by a backlit poster. At night, the lighted display takes on a three-dimensional effect. Backlit posters are strategically located at major intersections and high-volume traffic routes. The primary advantage of backlit posters is the image enhancement they offer; there is strong visual impact in the day and night. The cost of producing backlit posters is quite high, but the opportunities for exposure are estimated to be twice that of a standard poster.

Scrolling backlights are a recent innovation for high-traffic areas. The messages are timed to change with the flow of traffic so that everyone gets a chance to see the message from three different advertisers.

SUPERBOARD (BIGBOARD) AND SPECTACULARS A **superboard** or **spectacular** is an oversized display unit positioned at high-volume traffic locations. Typically, it extends from a rectangular format to include space extensions (i.e., the product itself may extend beyond the frame of the board), flashing neon lights, and electronic messages that can change quickly to meet an advertiser's specifications.

Some recent innovations include the "superflex" board, a hand-printed or screen-printed flexible vinyl sheet that is stretched over the standard superboard frame, and a computer-designed 3-D billboard that produces a product replica as large as 16 metres high. An example of a 3-D board appears in Figure 10.2. The new "trivision" board is a three-sided board that rotates. Each rotation has louvres that change the ads so that as

FIGURE 10.2

Example of superboard advertising

Courtesy: Dick Hemingway

many as 40 or 50 advertisers can be at one location. Boards of this nature are ideal for prime locations where no new billboard space is available.

Since spectaculars are usually one-of-a-kind structures fabricated at high expense, they require a long-term commitment from the advertiser. Spectaculars are beyond the budgets of most advertisers.

MALL POSTERS   Unlike all other forms of outdoor advertising, **mall posters** do not rely on vehicular traffic. Typically located inside shopping malls, these backlit posters are seen at eye level by passing pedestrians as they walk through the mall's aisles. These posters reach consumers at a crucial time, a time when they are making buying decisions, so they are a good outlet for retailers and branded products available right in the mall. The very presence of a message on a mall poster may encourage impulse buying. As a medium, mall posters are a good secondary vehicle in a multimedia campaign. They are ideal for reinforcing a brand's primary selling message.

The quality and impact of mall posters is advancing. Some malls hang oversized wall murals from various structures so that the advertising message is clearly visible to passersby. Refer to Figure 10.3 for an illustration of an indoor mall wall mural.

TRANSIT SHELTERS   A **transit-shelter** unit consists of two street-level backlit posters that are incorporated into the design of glass-and-steel transit shelters. Each shelter has two faces that are backlit from dusk until dawn. Transit-shelter units are located on busy public-transit routes and offer advertisers high levels of potential exposure to motorists, pedestrians, and transit riders. Transit-shelter advertising offers the advertiser strong visual impact, as the colour reproduction is of superior quality. These units are sold to advertisers on the basis of site-selection flexibility. That is, advertisers can select sites that reach certain age, income, or ethnic groups or they can concentrate on a geographic trading zone, depending on the target they would like to reach. Refer to Figure 10.4 for an illustration of transit-shelter advertising.

ELECTRONIC SIGNAGE   **Electronic** outdoor posters are relatively new. These units display advertising messages electronically, with ads from numerous advertisers displayed

Courtesy: Dick Hemingway

FIGURE
10.3

Examples of wall-mural advertising in an indoor mall

10.4

Examples of transit-
shelter advertising

Courtesy: Dick Hemingway

Courtesy: Dick Hemingway

on a rotation basis around the clock. Ads are typically 10 to 15 seconds in length. These signs offer tremendous flexibility, as an advertiser can change the message quickly if necessary. They are generally located in high-traffic areas in large urban centres across Canada. Prime location means heavy weekly frequency can be achieved.

STREET-LEVEL ADVERTISING **Street-level units** are rear-illuminated and are positioned adjacent to high-traffic streets in the downtown cores of major markets. Many of these signs are now popping up along sidewalks and in hard-to-target urban areas where there is a good deal of pedestrian foot traffic in the daytime. The signs are visible to vehicle traffic as well. The ads appear much like they do on a transit shelter except the street level unit is a stand-alone structure that contains only the advertising message.

FIGURE
10.5

An illustration of
wall-mural advertising

WALL BANNERS AND MURALS **Banners** are large PVC vinyl banners framed and
mounted on the outside of a building. They can be moved and reused. **Mural** advertisements are hand-painted outdoor extravaganzas on the sides of buildings. They are very
large, often the entire height of the building. They can be three-dimensional, which adds
to their attention-getting capability (see Figure 10.5).

Outdoor as an Advertising Medium

Many advertisers overlook or ignore the benefits of outdoor advertising, yet it is a medium
that is excellent at reinforcing a message communicated in another medium, like television
or magazines. This section presents the benefits and drawbacks of outdoor advertising.

ADVANTAGES OF OUTDOOR ADVERTISING

TARGET REACH AND FREQUENCY Outdoor advertising provides advertisers with the
opportunity to reach a very large cross-section of a market's population in a short period.
Depending on the weight level purchased (GRPs) and on the strategic location of outdoor
boards on busy thoroughfares, outdoor advertising has the potential for multiple exposures. According to Viacom data (Viacom is one of Canada's largest sellers of outdoor
space), up to 90 percent of a city's traffic is concentrated on 10 percent of the streets (streets
where outdoor boards are located), and significant exposure levels are achieved during the
first two weeks of a campaign.[4] From that point on, reach potential is marginal.

TARGETING FLEXIBILITY Advertisers that want to advertise only in certain areas have
the flexibility to do so with outdoor advertising. Outdoor units can be purchased on a
regional basis (perhaps for an entire province or for an area within a province) or on a
market-by-market basis. Within major metropolitan markets, advertisers can use outdoor posters to target neighbourhoods based on a combination of demographic and
geographic characteristics. Other advertisers may choose transit shelters that are close to
high schools if the goal is to reach teenagers. Advertisers that want to increase weight

Viacom
www.viacom.com

levels in selected markets can use outdoor advertising to supplement a national campaign in another medium.

SIZE AND QUALITY OF MESSAGE Backlit posters, mall posters, and transit-shelter advertising units all offer advertisers high reproduction quality. Although the messages communicated by outdoor advertising must be short, a strong visual impression can attract the attention of passersby. As the old saying goes, "A picture is worth a thousand words." If the goal is to create a monumental impression on consumers, outdoor boards have such capability (see the illustration in Figure 10.6).

COMPATIBILITY WITH OTHER MEDIA Outdoor advertising can reinforce the message of other media in two ways. First, it can extend the total reach and frequency of a campaign beyond what a single medium can do. Therefore, it is a good complementary medium—a good means of reinforcing important sales messages. Second, outdoor advertising can increase the total number of impressions made on a target market that may consume another medium lightly. For example, a light viewer of television, who is hard to reach regardless of the weight level purchased, may be easier to reach via outdoor advertising.

CREATING PRODUCT AWARENESS Traditionally regarded as a complementary medium, outdoor advertising can also be effective in generating product awareness when used as a primary medium, particularly if a shotgun media strategy is used (e.g., if an advertiser wanted to reach all adults aged 18 to 49 in specified markets). To illustrate,

FIGURE
10.6

An outdoor poster that makes a strong visual impression

Courtesy: Dick Hemingway

outdoor boards are commonly employed in "teaser" campaigns. For automobile manufacturers wanting to plant a fast impression in the minds of new car buyers, outdoor posters are an ideal medium. When Harvey's Restaurants launched the Big Harv, a mouth-watering, six-ounce burger, vivid and tempting creative appeared on outdoor boards. The boards were ideal bait for their primary target market—young adult males.

COST When the absolute cost of outdoor advertising is evaluated in terms of reach potential—the opportunities for exposing consumers to outdoor messages—the medium begins to seem a fairly efficient media buy. Using Toronto as an example, and assuming an advertiser purchased standard outdoor posters sold by Viacom for a four-week period at a 75 GRP level, we would calculate the CPM (cost of reaching a thousand people) as follows:[5]

$$CPM = \frac{Cost}{Population\ (000)}$$

$$= \frac{278\ 419}{4551.1}$$

$$= \$61.18$$

This represents the cost of reaching a thousand people once. Therefore, when the daily travel patterns of people are considered (and thus the potential for multiple exposure), the cost efficiencies of outdoor advertising improve.

DISADVANTAGES OF OUTDOOR ADVERTISING

CREATIVE LIMITATIONS   The nature of the outdoor advertising medium (that is, people pass by outdoor ads either in a vehicle or on foot) is such that it must rely on instant visual impact to get attention. The message itself must be short and simple to read, and it must quickly draw attention to the brand name. Creative limitations are a bit of a myth to Brian Harrod, a former creative director at several prominent Canadian ad agencies. According to Harrod, "If you can't present an advertising idea on an outdoor board, it isn't simple and focused enough to be an effective advertising idea."[6] Examine the ad in Figure 10.7—I'm certain you will agree it is a creative piece of outdoor advertising.

LACK OF TARGET-MARKET SELECTIVITY The broad reach potential of outdoor advertising (it reaches all adults and children) makes it impossible for an advertiser to focus on a target market. Therefore, due to wasted circulation, the cost-per-thousand figures which show efficiency may be deceptively low (since the medium reaches many people who would never purchase the product).

COSTS Costs of outdoor advertising are high in two areas. First, the costs of producing finished materials for vehicles such as backlit posters, mall posters, and transit shelters are high (printing on a plastic vinyl material is expensive). Second, the absolute cost of buying media space is high. A four-week showing of horizontal outdoor posters in Canada's top three markets (Toronto/Oshawa/Hamilton, Montreal, and Vancouver) at a 25-GRP level would cost between $185 000 (for 105 panels) and $229 000 (for 155 panels) depending on the minimum and maximum number of panels desired. At 50 GRPs, the range is $349 000 (for 211 panels) to $376 000 (for 308 panels).[7]

LACK OF PRESTIGE Outdoor advertising does not always enhance the image of the product, whereas advertising in a quality magazine can rely on the surrounding editorial content to aid in image development. Also, the association of the product with a

FIGURE
10.7

A classic example of
creativity in outdoor
advertising

medium that clutters the landscape may have a negative impact. Many critics of outdoor advertising refer to it as "pollution on a stick."

UNOBTRUSIVE MEDIUM Despite the reach and frequency potential of the medium, people who pass by may not notice outdoor ads. Unless the message catches the attention of passersby, the outdoor board will blend into the background and not break through the consumer's perceptual barriers. In urban downtown locations, the clustering of outdoor advertising may prevent any single message from being noticed.

For more insight into the effectiveness of outdoor advertising, see the Advertising in Action vignette **The Big Picture Is Booming**.

Buying Outdoor Media Space

Regardless of the outdoor advertising format under consideration (posters, superboards, mall posters, and so on), there are similarities in the media-buying process. Outdoor space is sold in four-week periods and is available on a market-by-market basis. Advertisers can purchase a single market, a group of markets (composing a regional buy), or a national buy if strategy demands it and budget permits it.

Media space is purchased on the basis of the advertising weight level desired by the advertiser, expressed in terms of GRPs (gross rating points). As indicated in the Media Strategy section of Chapter 7, GRP is a weighting factor that combines reach and frequency variables. In the case of outdoor advertising, GRP is defined as the total circulation of a specific outdoor advertisement expressed as a percentage of the market's population. With reference to Figure 10.8, on a weekly basis a weight level of 100 GRPs delivers exposure opportunities equal to the population of a market. A weight level of 50 GRPs offers one-half the exposure opportunities, and so on for the various weight levels.

The Big Picture Is Booming

Outdoor advertising is catching the attention of more and more advertisers. In 1991, outdoor advertising accounted for only 1.5 percent of advertising revenues. Today it represents 3 percent and accounts for $310 million in annual spending. Viacom, the largest supplier of outdoor advertising space, estimates that 25 percent of its business now comes from packaged-goods companies, and that business has fuelled the growth in outdoor.

Why has there been so much growth in outdoor advertising? There are several reasons. First, the medium offers much better quality—high-resolution video displays make earlier moving billboards look crude by comparison. Second, new digital printing technologies are flourishing and flashy projects like the Dundas Square project in Toronto incorporate the latest gadgetry. Dundas Square is the Times Square of Toronto—it features two multimedia towers at the corner of Yonge and Dundas streets. The towers include LED video screens, neon signs, backlit signs, and banners.

Advertisers offer another key reason for growth in outdoor advertising. One of their major concerns is the fragmentation of TV and magazines—these media have become increasingly specialized. At one time television was the prime medium because it was so captive, but that image has waned with the proliferation of channels and because people watching TV have a remote-control panel in their hands. Channel surfing means a lot of commercials go unnoticed. Unlike TV, outdoor lets you reach "anyone and everyone," says Aileen Grant of the Dairy Farmers of Ontario. From her perspective, outdoor is "one of the last mass media vehicles available and that is important for a product like milk."

Perhaps there is an economic argument that favours outdoor advertising. An advertiser can reach Canada's top 10 markets with outdoor posters for two months at a cost of $550 000. That's 60 days of continuous exposures. By comparison, a single 30-second commercial during a popular prime-time television show like *ER* that covers the entire network costs approximately $50 000. It takes only 11 TV spots to spend $550 000. Of course, the needs and objectives of the advertiser must be addressed when selecting various media.

Labatt Breweries of Canada recently revamped its marketing budget to incorporate more outdoor. According to Audrey Yates, national media manager, "Labatt once looked upon outdoor as an extra; it is now integrated into the communications strategy." Like other organizations, Labatt has to do more with less. Yates notes that "Labatt now tries to develop campaigns in print, broadcast, and outdoor that work in concert, utilizing the strengths of the different media. The company has found that print and broadcast are effective for telling stories, while outdoor is most suited to reinforcing a basic message about the product."

A limitation of outdoor advertising cited by many observers is its inability to tell a story. People driving by have only a few seconds to look. Geoffrey Roche, a prominent creative director and former CEO of Roche Macauley & Partners Advertising, disagrees: "The beauty of outdoor is that you have to be simple. Unlike television there are no props. It's very pure; there's nowhere to hide." Roche says the litmus test of a good advertising campaign is whether it works as a billboard. If the idea can be boiled down to a simple graphic and caption, then he knows he's on to something. That sounds like good advice for any copywriter or art director. Like the old adage says, "A picture is worth a thousand words." In the case of outdoor advertising, that picture can be a pretty big one.

Sources: Adapted from John Heinzl, "Billboards enjoy boom times," *The Globe and Mail*, June 16, 1999, p. M1 and Fawzia Sheikh, "A New Home Out of Home," *Marketing*, April 21, 1997, pp. 8, 9.

Dundas Square www.ydsquare.ca/home.htm

OUTDOOR ADVERTISING—RATES AND DISCOUNTS

All outdoor advertising rates are quoted on a four-week basis. Both posters and transit shelters are sold on the basis of a four-week minimum purchase. The other options (backlits, mall posters, and superboards) have a 12-week minimum purchase requirement. To illustrate outdoor cost calculations, let's consider a few media-buying examples. Rates and data from Figures 10.8 and 10.9 are used to calculate costs.

OUTDOOR BUYING PLAN: EXAMPLE 1

Medium:	Transit Shelters (Viacom)
Markets:	Toronto/Hamilton (CMA), Montreal District, Calgary (CMA), and Halifax (CMA)
Weight:	50 GRPs weekly
Contract Length:	16 weeks

According to Figure 10.8, the costs for a four-week period for each market would be as follows:

Toronto/Hamilton	$127 200
Montreal	69 636
Calgary	24 258
Halifax	9 009
Total	**232 649**

Since the length of the contract is 16 weeks, the cost of the markets above would be multiplied by a factor of four (16 weeks divided by four-week rates). The gross cost would be calculated as follows:

$$\$232\ 649 \times 4 = \$930\ 596$$

While not shown in this particular illustration and rate card, outdoor media usually offer advertisers volume discounts (e.g., a reduced rate based on dollar volume purchased) and continuity discounts (e.g., a reduced rate for extended buys such as 12 weeks, 16 weeks, etc.).

OUTDOOR BUYING PLAN: EXAMPLE 2

Medium:	Outdoor Posters (Viacom)
Markets:	Toronto (CMA), London (CMA), Calgary (CMA), Winnipeg (CMA)
Weight:	Toronto and London at 50 GRPs; Calgary and Winnipeg at 25 GRPs
Contract Length:	16 weeks

Using the data from Figure 10.9, we would calculate the appropriate costs for each market over a four-week period as follows:

Toronto	$185 613 × 4 =	$742 452
London	17 880 × 4 =	71 520
Calgary	20 608 × 4 =	82 432
Winnipeg	9 869 × 4 =	39 476
Total Cost		**= $935 880**

FIGURE
10.8

Outdoor rate card for
transit shelters

OUTDOOR

PMB
Associate

The Poster Network

Data confirmed for Mar./04 CARD

TRANSIT SHELTERS:

Market	Population	25 DAILY GRPs approx panels	4-week net rate	50 DAILY GRPs approx panels	4-week net rate	75 DAILY GRPs approx panels	4-week net rate	100 DAILY GRPs approx panels	4-week net rate
ATLANTIC									
St. John's(CMA) Nfld.	162,200	6	$3,180	11	$5,214	17	$8,058	23	$10,534
Mount Pearl (C) Nfld.	23,700	1	500	2	1,000	3	1,500	4	2,000
Halifax(CMA) N.S...	347,000	9-10	4,730	18-20	9,009	28-30	13,513	36-40	18,018
Sydney(C) & District	44,200	1	800	2	1,525	3	2,288	4	3,050
Annapolis Valley ESA	94,900	3	1,080	6	2,160	9	3,060	11	3,685
Saint John(C)	63,800	2-3	1,167	4-5	2,223	6-7	3,334	8-9	4,445
Total Atlantic	735,800		11,457		21,131		31,753		41,732
QUEBEC									
Quebec City District	494,000	13-15	10,254	26-28	19,531	39-43	29,297	51-57	39,063
Chicoutimi/ Jonquiere	105,900	4-5	2,048	8-9	3,901	11-13	5,852	15-17	7,803
Trois Rivieres District	95,400	4-5	1,624	8-9	3,093	11-13	4,639	14-16	6,185
Sherbrooke(CMA) ..	148,600	3-4	1,962	6-7	3,736	9-10	5,604	11-13	7,473
Montreal District	3,067,100	48-54	36,559	96-106	69,636	147-157	104,454	192-212	139,273
Hull C & District	196,100	7	2,415	14	4,610	19	6,915	25	9,580
Shawinigan (CA) & District	53,100	3	1,855	5	2,925	5	2,925*	5	2,925*
Total Quebec	4,160,200		56,717		107,432		159,686		212,302
ONTARIO									
Toronto(CMA)/ Hamilton(CMA)	5,290,000	82-90	66,780	165-175	127,200	247-287	190,800	332-352	254,400
Toronto(CMA)	4,654,300	72-78	68,116	146-156	129,746	216-236	194,618	291-311	259,491
Hamilton(CMA)	635,700	15-17	9,987	29-33	19,024	45-49	28,536	59-65	38,048
Stratford(CA)	28,200	3-4	2,193	3-4	2,193*	3-4	2,193*	3-4	2,193*
London(CMA)	412,700	7-8	5,264	14-16	10,026	22-24	15,039	28-32	20,053
Windsor(CMA) & District	326,900	8-9	4,386	17-19	8,355	26-28	12,533	34-38	16,710
Sarnia(CA)	81,200	3-4	2,295	6-7	4,371	8-9	6,557	10-12	8,743
Owen Sound(CA)...	29,400	2-3	819	2-3	819*	2-3	819*	2-3	819*
Barrie(CA)	162,200	5-6	1,685	11-13	3,210	16-18	4,815	16-18	4,815*
Sault Ste. Marie(CA)	77,600	2	876	4	1,752	5	2,190	7	3,066
Timmins(C)	39,700	2	1,060	4	1,956	6	2,544	7	2,877
Sudbury(CMA)	155,600	3	2,025	6	3,870	9	5,535	12	7,020
Total Ontario	6,603,500		83,143		163,752		243,025		320,058
PRAIRIES/B.C.									
Winnipeg(CMA)	624,400	8-9	6,544	16-18	12,465	24-26	18,698	31-35	24,930
Regina(CMA)	178,100	3-4	2,148	7-8	4,091	10-12	6,137	14-16	8,183
Calgary(CMA)	950,500	19-21	12,735	37-41	24,258	55-61	36,386	75-81	48,515
Grande Prairie C	152,500	1	260	1	260	1	260	1	260
Edmonton (CMA) ...	893,600	18-20	12,716	35-39	24,220	52-58	36,330	70-76	48,440
Vancouver CMA	1,998,800	27-31	26,925	54-60	51,300	82-90	76,950	111-119	102,600
Total Prairies/B.C.	4,797,900		61,068		116,334		174,501		232,668
Canada	16,297,400		222,385		408,648		608,965		807,398

*GRP level not available. †Secondary rep. agreement in place.
For single panel buys contact rep.
2024–2350

The length of the contract is 16 weeks. Therefore, the cost for each market is multiplied by a factor of four (16 weeks divided by a four-week rate). Should volume and continuity discounts apply, they would be deducted from the gross amount shown in this illustration.

FIGURE
10.9

Rate card for outdoor posters

VIACOM OUTDOOR

PMB Associate

Audited by COMB

The Poster Network

Data confirmed for May/04 CARD

Markets	Pop'n	25 DAILY GRPs app. pan.	25 4-week net rate	50 DAILY GRPs app. pan.	50 4-week net rate	75 DAILY GRPs app. pan.	75 4-week net rate	100 DAILY GRPs app. pan.	100 4-week net rate
ONTARIO									
Kingston (CA)/ Belleville (CA)/ Brockville (CA) & Dist.	308,800	7-8	8,254	14-16	15,723	22-24	23,584	28-32	31,445
Kingston (CA)	139,500	3-4	5,278	6-7	10,054	9-11	15,081	12-14	20,108
Ottawa(ESA)	798,800	21-23	31,554	41-45	60,104	61-67	90,155	81-89	120,207
Peterborough (CA)	96,500	5-6	3,582	10-12	6,805	10-12	6,805*	10-12	6,805*
Peterborough (CA)/ Lindsay (CA) & Dist.	130,700	7-8	4,390	15-17	8,341	15-17	8,341*	15-17	8,341*
Toronto (CMA)/ Hamilton (CMA)/Osh- awa (CMA)	5,587,700	72-78	93,958	145-155	178,968	215-235	268,451	290-310	357,935
Toronto (CMA)	4,654,300	58-64	97,447	116-126	185,613	177-187	278,419	232-252	371,225
Oshawa (CMA)	297,700	8-9	7,568	16-18	14,415	25-27	21,623	25-27	21,623*
Hamilton (CMA)	635,700	14-16	14,546	28-30	27,708	41-45	41,561	54-60	55,415
Kitchener (CMA)	404,600	7-8	10,127	15-17	19,290	15-17	19,290*	15-17	19,290*
Kitchener(CMA)/ Brantford (CA)	486,300	10-12	12,280	21-23	23,391	21-23	23,391*	21-23	23,391*
St. Catharines/ Niagara (CMA)	354,500	10-12	9,772	20-22	18,614	30-34	27,921	30-34	27,921*
Brantford (CA)	81,700	3-4	3,859	3-4	3,859*	3-4	3,859*	3-4	3,859*
Woodstock (CA)	31,700	1	879	2	1,340	2	1,340*	2	1,340*
London (CMA)	412,700	7-8	9,387	15-17	17,880	22-24	26,820	22-24	26,820*
Windsor (ESA)	452,100	9-10	8,965	19-21	17,076	28-30	25,614	37-41	34,153
Sarnia	81,200	2-3	2,259	4-5	4,303	4-5	4,303*	4-5	4,303*
Owen Sound (CA)/Colling- wood (CA) & Dist.	202,500	12-14	11,000	24-26	20,953	35-39	31,429	47-53	41,905
Barrie (CA)/Oril- lia (CA)/ Central Ont.	319,900	10-11	16,552	18-20	31,528	27-29	47,291	36-40	63,055
Barrie (CA)	162,200	5-6	9,737	10-12	18,546	15-17	27,819	20-22	37,093
Sault-Ste-Marie (CA)	77,600	2	1,620	4	3,240	6	4,860	8	6,480
Sudbury (CMA)/ North Bay (CA)/North Shore & Dist.	235,000	8	7,400	15	13,125	23	19,665	30	25,350
Thunder Bay (CMA)	113,200	3-4	2,303	5-6	4,386	8-9	6,579	10-11	8,773
Timmins (CA)/ Kapuskasing/ Kirkland Lake & Dist.	107,800	5	3,590	10	6,920	16	10,464	21	13,209
Timmins (C)	39,700	2	1,570	3	2,232	5	3,405	6	3,870
Total Ontario:	9,700,500		224,163		425,892		620,208		794,628
PRAIRIES/B.C.									
Winnipeg (CMA)	624,400	7-8	9,869	13-15	18,799	19-21	28,198	26-28	37,598
Brandon (CA) & Dist.	38,300	2-3	2,028	2-3	2,028*	2-3	2,028*	2-3	2,028*
Regina (CMA)	178,100	3-4	3,500	6-7	6,668	9-10	10,001	11-13	13,335
Yorkton (CA)	16,000	2-3	1,648	3-4	2,318	3-4	2,318*	3-4	2,318*
North Battleford (CA)	15,900	2-3	1,245	3-4	1,556	4-5	2,334	5-6	3,112
Rural Saskatche- wan	437,000	1	820	—	—	—	—	—	—
Moose Jaw (CA)	30,400	2-3	1,189	3-4	2,265	4-5	3,398	5-6	4,530
Saskatoon (CMA)	212,900	4-5	4,001	7-8	7,620	10-11	11,430	12-14	15,240
Calgary (CMA)	950,500	16-18	20,608	31-35	39,254	31-35	39,254*	31-35	39,254*
Edmonton (CMA)	893,600	14-16	18,332	28-30	34,918	41-45	52,376	54-60	69,835
Vancouver (CMA)	1,998,800	33-37	71,225	33-37	71,225*	33-37	71,225*	33-37	71,225*
Total Prairies/ B.C.:	5,395,900		133,645		186,651		222,562		258,475
Total Canada:	21,172,300		519,626		907,927		1,259,318		1,574,577

*GRP level not available.

For single panel buys contact rep.

2020–2290

Transit Advertising

Transit riders represent a captive audience that often has a need for visual stimulation. Bored with travelling on buses and subway cars, riders frequently read advertising mes-

Courtesy: Dick Hemingway

FIGURE
10.10
Interior transit card
advertising

sages. In fact, they may read the same message over and over again. Further, if they are habitual transit users, there is potential for the message to be seen repeatedly. The major forms of transit advertising include interior transit cards, exterior transit cards, station posters, superbuses (painted buses), subway online, and station domination.

INTERIOR CARDS

Interior cards or **car cards** are print advertisements contained in racks above the windows of public transit vehicles (i.e., in buses, streetcars, subway cars, and light rapid transit cars). Transit cards are available in a variety of sizes depending on the needs of the advertiser. Interior cards located above windows have a horizontal orientation. Given that the audience is captive and that the average travel time in a transit vehicle is estimated to be 30 minutes in major markets, the advertiser has the flexibility to include longer copy, which is not an option with other out-of-home media.[8] An interior transit illustration is included in Figure 10.10.

Another interior option is the door card. **Door cards** are positioned on both sides of the doors on subways, LRTs, and GO trains. They tend to have a vertical orientation. Passengers are exposed to these ads while in transit or when exiting the vehicle—assuming it is not a rushed exit.

EXTERIOR BUS POSTERS

Two options are available in the **exterior bus poster** format. The first is a *king poster* (larger format) located on the side of surface transit vehicles only. It is 139 inches × 30 inches (353 cm × 76 cm) in size. The second option is called a *seventy poster* (smaller format) that is either located on the side or tail of surface transit vehicles. The unique characteristic of exterior bus posters is their mobility. They move through every area of a city and are seen by motorists, transit riders, and pedestrians. An illustration of an exterior bus poster is shown in Figure 10.11. A relatively new option is the tail poster. *Tail posters* appear in the back window of surface vehicles.

SUPERBUSES AND BUS MURALS

The **superbus** allows an advertiser to "own" a whole bus. The advertising is printed onto a vinyl product that is applied to all sides of the bus except the front. The advertiser has access to all interior advertising space as well (see Figure 10.12).

FIGURE
10.11

An exterior transit ad

Unlike other transit advertising, the painted buses are generally contracted for a minimum one-year period, although six-month rates are available. Rates for painted bus advertising vary considerably. In a market the size of Toronto, the 52-week rate for one bus is $98 985; in Hamilton, the rate is $28 400. **Bus murals** are also available in selected markets. Murals appear on the driver's side and/or the tails of buses. These are applied using vinyl products and are sold for commitments of 12 weeks or more. In Toronto, the cost of a mural for 52 weeks is $75 830 (about 75 percent of the cost of a superbus for a comparable period of time).[9]

STATION POSTERS AND BACKLITS

Station posters are advertisements located on platforms and at the entrances and exits of the subway and light rail transit systems in Canada. They are available in a variety of sizes, and the most common of these is called the station poster. The station poster is the same size as a transit shelter or mall poster. Standard size specifications encourage cross-usage

FIGURE
10.12

An illustration of superbus advertising: A painted streetcar

of various out-of-home media. Station posters fall into two broad categories: platform posters and subway backlits (see Figure 10.13). **Platform posters** are located on the subway wall opposite the rider waiting on the platform. In the Toronto subway system, posters are also attached to steel pillars in the area between rail lines. Passengers waiting on both platforms are exposed to these messages.

The second option is the subway backlit. The **backlit poster** is a vinyl poster with rear illumination. Backlits are usually located along station walls and above and below escalator stairwells throughout the Toronto and Montreal subway systems and the GO Transit system in southern Ontario. Light rail transit systems in Vancouver, Edmonton, and Calgary also offer a variety of backlit and poster options.

A recent innovation in subway backlits is "triples." **Triples** are three transit shelter ads placed side by side, giving advertisers greater impact capability. The same ad may appear on all three boards, or each panel may be used for a different part of a message.

SUBWAY ONLINE

These are digital news centres located in the top 10 subway stations in Toronto. With video capabilities, these centres serve up the latest news, sports, weather, and time. Advertising is sold in 20-second units and is limited to 10 advertisers. The limited number of advertisers increases the likelihood of exposures among passengers waiting at a station.

STATION DOMINATION

The Toronto and Montreal transit systems are testing various new concepts and exploring new opportunities to maximize the effectiveness of an advertiser's message. One of these concepts is station domination, an opportunity that gives a single advertiser control of every advertising space in a subway station. According to Richard Bridgman, vice-president for TDI Media, the company that sells the ad space, "Advertisers today are on the lookout for new ways to stand out amid the out-of-home clutter, and are quite open to the kinds of opportunities we have to offer."[10]

Toronto Transit Commission
www.city.toronto.on.ca/ttc

FIGURE

10.13

Subway poster advertising

Courtesy: Dick Hemingway

FIGURE 10.14

Some innovative advertising concepts in subway stations

Some of the concepts being tested in subway stations include **stair risers** (ads that appear on the sides of steps), **ceiling decals** in vehicles, and **floor advertising**. An example of station-domination advertising appears in Figure 10.14.

Transit as an Advertising Medium

ADVANTAGES OF TRANSIT

CONTINUOUS EXPOSURE AND CREATIVITY
Commuters tend to be creatures of routine, so they are exposed to messages daily. With the average transit ride in major markets over 30 minutes, passengers can relieve their boredom by reading the ads. This provides some creative opportunity, as longer copy can be used and riders can be more involved. In this regard, transit advertisements are a good vehicle for reinforcing the messages of in-home media.

REACH AND FREQUENCY Like outdoor advertising, transit advertising reaches a mass audience quickly. Transit riders cut across all demographics, with the heaviest concentration in the adult category. Consumers generally encounter the message more than once because of daily riding patterns, and the combination of high reach and frequency translates into an extremely high number of impressions on the target market. Factors such as the rising costs of running a car and the increasing numbers of commuters travelling to and from a city each day for work have had a positive effect on the reach potential of transit.

FLEXIBILITY Certain transit media are flexible because the message can be changed easily. For example, a portion of a poster can display a permanent message and another portion can display a short-term message that can be changed periodically. Should creative direction change, new execution can replace the old execution quickly. In terms of geography, transit markets can be purchased on an individual basis, so it is a good complementary medium to add reach and frequency in a total advertising campaign.

MARKET COVERAGE In any given market, transit advertising covers all sectors of an urban/suburban community—industrial, commercial, and residential areas—where other forms of out-of-home media may not be available.

COST On a market-by-market basis the dollar outlay for transit media space is relatively low, and considering the number of consumers reached the cost per thousand is low. Essentially, transit is a cost-efficient medium that reaches a mass audience. As a result, it is attractive to smaller-budget advertisers and to larger-budget advertisers needing a complementary medium to reach urban customers.

DISADVANTAGES OF TRANSIT

LACK OF TARGET-MARKET SELECTIVITY In large urban markets, transit use reflects the general, non-specific demographic and socio-economic characteristics of those markets. Therefore, for an advertiser attempting to reach a precisely defined target, the use of transit results in wasted circulation. Consequently, the cost-per-thousand efficiencies, which are based on high reach of a mass audience, may be artificially low.

MEDIA ENVIRONMENT Transit advertising is not granted the status of an important advertising medium. In the case of interior transit, the environment is often cluttered and crowded (particularly during peak-usage periods such as rush hour), a circumstance that makes the messages both less visible and less attractive. This environment may detract from the prestige of the product.

CREATIVE LIMITATIONS While transit advertising offers good colour reproduction, the actual amount of space it provides advertisers to work with is quite small. In the case of exterior bus posters and platform posters, there is a bit more creative flexibility. However, as indicated in the previous section, some new and innovative concepts such as station domination are being tested. This option and the opportunities it presents offer greater creative potential.

Both outdoor advertising and transit advertising are often the choice of media planners when the target market description is fairly broad in scope (e.g., age, income, occupation, and lifestyle) or if specific geographic markets (e.g., cities) are important. As mentioned earlier in the chapter, planners now perceive outdoor and transit as a timely medium. That also factors into media recommendations. Both outdoor advertising and transit advertising can be purchased on a local market-by-market basis.

Buying Transit Advertising

Pattison Group
www.jimpattison.com

Transit advertising rates are affected by variables such as the number of markets being covered, the length of the showing (which affects discounts), the weight level desired in any given market, and the size of the space required. Transit space is generally sold on the basis of four-week minimums and is available on a market-by-market basis. Advertisers can purchase space in a group of cities in a region to qualify for greater discounts; major Canadian-market cities might constitute a group, or cities within a geographic region. Viacom and the Pattison Group are among the largest sellers of transit advertising space in Canada. Collectively, they represent the majority of urban transit properties across Canada.

The first thing to consider when purchasing transit space is the weight level desired in each market. As in outdoor advertising, transit weight is expressed in terms of GRPs (gross rating points), with GRP referring to the total circulation of a showing expressed as a percentage of a market's population. For an illustration of the GRP concept and its effect on costs, refer to Figure 10.15.

As indicated earlier, all rates are based on the purchase of a four-week period, starting with a base rate for each market purchased. Usually, a **continuity discount** is available to advertisers that meet predetermined time commitments (e.g., 12, 24, and 52-week periods), with the percentage of the discount increasing with the time commitment.

MEDIA-BUYING ILLUSTRATIONS

Let's consider a few media-buying examples, using the rates and data in Figure 10.15 as a basis for calculating the costs. Please note that all rates are quoted for a *four-week period.*

TRANSIT BUYING PLAN: EXAMPLE 1

Medium:	Exterior King Bus Posters
Markets:	Toronto, Winnipeg, and Hamilton
Weight:	75 GRPs in Toronto; 50 GRPs in Winnipeg and Hamilton
Contract Length:	20 weeks

According to Figure 10.15, the costs for specified markets for four weeks at the specified GRP levels would be

Toronto	$ 114 450
Winnipeg	$ 12 135
Hamilton	$ 12 730
Total Cost (4 weeks)	**$139 315**

Therefore, the total cost for the 20-week contract would be

$$\$139\ 315 \times 5 = \$696\ 575$$

In this example, the length of the contract is 20 weeks, so the rate for four weeks is multiplied by a factor of 5 (20 weeks divided by the 4-week rates).

FIGURE
10.15

Exterior and interior transit rate card

VIACOM
O U T D O O R

Data confirmed for Mar./04 CARD

Rates are **net**.
KING BUS POSTERS: 139" x 30"

FLEET:
ATLANTIC:
St. John's 58
ONTARIO:

Hamilton	192	Sarnia	30
Oakville...	55	Timmins	21
Toronto (TTC only)...............................	2175	TTC (TTC only-Superkings)................	274

PRAIRIES:

Winnipeg	536	Saskatoon...	106
Regina	88		

Market:	25 GRPs Panels	Rate	50 GRPs Panels	Rate	75 GRPs Panels	Rates	100 GRPs Panels	Rate
Newfoundland								
St. John's	7	1,565	15	3,225	22	4,635	30	6,180
TOTAL ATLANTIC	7	1,565	15	3,225	22	4,635	30	6,180
Hamilton......................	18	6,565	36	12,730	54	18,705	72	24,425
Oakville......................	6	2,180	11	3,885	17	5,875	22	7,510
Sarnia	3	750	6	1,500	9	2,250	13	3,250
Timmins	3	850	6	1,400	6	1,400*	6	1,400*
Toronto (TTC only)	95	43,550	190	80,670	286	114,450	381	143,285
Toronto (TTC only- Superkings)	95	51,235	192	99,400	192	99,400*	192	99,400*
TOTAL ONTARIO	125	$53,895	249	$100,165	372	$142,80	494	$179,870
Manitoba								
Winnipeg	23	6,125	47	12,135	70	17,705	94	23,270
Saskatchewan								
Regina	7	1,666	15	3,440	22	4,860	29	6,160
Saskatoon	8	1,900	17	3,990	25	5,525	34	7,225
TOTAL PRARIES...........	38	$9,691	79	$19,475	117	$28,090	157	$36,655
TOTAL NATIONAL..........	170	$65,151	343	$122,583	511	$175,405	681	$222,705

STANDARD INTERIOR TRANSIT POSTERS: 35" x 11"

FLEET (Standard Interiors/Super Interiors):
ATLANTIC:
St. John's 58
ONTARIO:

Chatham...	7	Sarnia	30
Hamilton	192	Timmins...	21
Oakville..	55	Toronto (TTC only).............................	2460

PRAIRIES:

Winnipeg	536	Saskatoon...	106
Regina	88		

Market:	1/4 Showing Panels	Rate	1/2 Showing Panels	Rate	3/4 Showing Panels	Rate	Full Showing Panels	Rate
Newfoundland								
St. John's....................	15	270	29	495	44	720	58	925
TOTAL ATLANTIC	15	$270	29	$495	44	$720	58	$925
Chatham	2	28	4	55	6	80	7	95
Hamilton......................	48	800	96	1,580	144	2,235	192	3,000
Oakville......................	14	230	28	450	41	665	55	890
Sarnia	7	84	15	180	23	276	30	360
Timmins	6	81	11	149	16	216	21	284
Toronto (TTC only)	780	17,475	1,560	33,898	2,340	48,250	3,120	62,565
TOTAL ONTARIO	857	$18,803	1,714	$35,539	2,570	$51,722	3,425	$67,194
Manitoba								
Winnipeg.....................	134	2,230	268	4,465	402	6,695	536	8,925
Saskatchewan								
Regina	22	225	44	450	66	595	88	750
Saskatoon..................	26	265	53	540	79	710	106	900
TOTAL PRARIES...........	182	$2,720	365	$5,455	547	$8,000	730	$10,575
TOTAL NATIONAL..........	1,054	$21,683	2,108	$41,489	3,161	$60,442	4,213	$78,694

2004 rates published courtesy of Viacom Outdoor

TRANSIT BUYING PLAN: EXAMPLE 2

Medium:	Standard Interior Cards
Markets:	Toronto, Winnipeg, Regina, and St. John's
Weight:	(three-quarter showing, or 75 GRPs); Winnipeg, Regina, and St. John's (half showing, or 50 GRPs)
Contract Length:	Toronto 16 weeks; other markets 24 weeks

According to Figure 10.15, the costs for the specified markets are

Toronto	$ 48 250
Winnipeg	$ 4 465
Regina	$ 450
St. John's	$ 495
Total	**$53 660**

Therefore, the total costs for the contract would be

Toronto (16 weeks):	$48 250 × 4 = $ 193 000
Other markets (24 weeks):	$ 5 410 × 6 = $ 32 460
Total cost:	**$227 530**

The multipliers (4 and 6) are used in the above example because the length of the contract is different in Toronto (16 weeks) compared to the other markets (24 weeks). Any continuity discount that is available would be deducted from the total cost above.

Other Forms of Out-of-Home Advertising

Advertising is everywhere! There always seems to be a unique means of reaching consumers when they least expect it. Some of the more unique and innovative vehicles for sending messages include elevator advertising, arena and stadium advertising, taxicab advertising, and theatre-screen advertising. The stream of new advertising vehicles continues to grow. Here are some of them.

AIRPORT DISPLAY ADVERTISING

Essentially, this is outdoor advertising located at major airports. Included in the range of options are baggage cart advertising, outdoor posters and spectaculars on roads leading to and from the airport, and backlits inside the terminals. Backlits are offered in a variety of shapes and sizes and a scrolling option is available (i.e., the poster scrolls to reveal a new advertising message). Clear Channel Communications is a major supplier of airport advertising in North America.

WASHROOM ADVERTISING

Mini-posters (30 × 40 cm) are available in washrooms at universities, colleges, fitness facilities, hospitals, and health-care facilities. According to research conducted by Cossette Communication, 68 percent of people aged 15 to 24 in Toronto, Vancouver, and Halifax are aware of washroom ads in restaurants and bars. Zoom Media and New Ad Media are major suppliers of advertising space in this medium.

Zoom Media
www.zoom-media.com
New Ad Media
www.newad.com

ELEVATOR ADVERTISING

This sort of advertising uses glass display cases on side panels adjacent to the control panels in high-rise elevators. The Elevator Network has taken elevator advertising a step further. Slim-line televisions installed in elevators in major office towers deliver up-to-date news and information along with ads. Clorets gum, a Warner-Lambert product, selected this medium because of the profile match. According to category manager John Vares, "The audience profile is slightly older and upscale in office towers and the environment is one where self-consciousness about bad breath could occur."[11]

The Elevator Network
www.hirise.ca

BUILDING WRAPS

Building wraps or **glass murals** are a new medium that creates curiosity in the minds of passersby. They might say: "How'd that get there?" The Abcon Media Group introduced this medium by placing giant vinyl murals on Toronto office buildings. Labatt Breweries tested the glass mural concept and found its novelty brought about positive publicity, an absolute bonus for an advertiser. A Bud Light mural 68 feet high and 57 feet wide was pasted to the side of a glass-faced office building at Yonge and St. Clair (a major intersection). According to Gino Cantalini, director of marketing at Labatt, there were two objectives: "make a large, local impact and bring the Bud Light Institute to life." An ad with a headline "Coming Soon" announced that it was the Bud Light Institute coming soon (the Institute is not real!). Onlookers had a rather baffled look after reading the message. Objectives accomplished![12]

FOOD COURT VIDEO SCREENS

The Digital Advertising Network (DAN) offers full-motion video screens in mall food courts across the country. The screens show 15-minute video loops that combine supplied programming from TV shows like Headline Sports and CHUM Fashion Television with 15-, 30-, and 60-second ads from various advertisers (see Figure 10.16). Companies that have quickly jumped on this medium include Coty, Nike Canada, Sears, and McCain Foods—all products that can be readily purchased in shopping malls. Says Skip Beloff, executive VP sales at DAN: "You're speaking to the consumer at a point where they can make a buying decision."[13]

SPORTS AND ARENA ADVERTISING

Sports advertising appears in the form of signs affixed to arena boards, backboard signs placed on backstops and outfield fences, plastic signboards on golf courses, and poster advertising on ski-lift towers. Where sporting events occur, an ad is not far behind.

Within arenas and stadiums there are numerous advertising opportunities. For example, in the SkyDome in Toronto, advertisers can take advantage of backlit signs on concourses, fixed signs in the bowl or seating area, product displays in concourses, on-deck circle signs, commercial time on the world's largest video screen (the JumboTron), and temporary signs during special events. One of the more recent innovations is the rotating sign (usually three different messages) that is seen behind home plate in many major league ballparks and on the sidelines of NBA basketball games.

In hockey arenas such as the Air Canada Centre (Toronto) and GM Place (Vancouver) there is on-ice advertising, where an ad is painted right into the ice in the neutral zone (between the blue lines). Signs can also be located behind the players' benches and penalty box. Advertising at a sports venue starts right at the front door, with

companies paying megabucks to have a facility adorned with their names. The Bell Centre in Montreal and the Corel Centre in Ottawa are two more examples of such arenas.

TAXICAB ADVERTISING

Taxicab advertisements are roof-mounted backlit panels or poster advertising on the backs of cab trunks. Taxi-wraps are now available in Toronto—similar to bus wraps, this makes the taxi look like the product logo or package.

CINEMA ADVERTISING

Cinema advertising embraces TV-style commercials on screen, slides on screen, and print ads and displays in theatre lobbies. On-screen commercials are usually 60-second or 90-second spots that are shown just before the start of the feature presentation to a captive audience. Cineplex Odeon Network offers over 1000 screens in 93 markets across Canada. The cost of a 30-second commercial is $268 500 for a four-week period. Projected monthly, average impressions range from 2.9 million to 4.8 million nationally.[14]

WILD POSTINGS

Wild postings are ads that are slapped on the hoarding at construction sites. Once the domain of concert promoters and sports promoters, they are now a strategic element of many mainstream advertisers' media plans. Mercedes-Benz (an upscale brand) used wild postings to launch their entry-level C-coupe hatchback. According to Joanne Caza, director of marketing at Mercedes, "People noticed them. They thought they were fun."[15]

Wild postings are cheaper than traditional billboards and they can be targeted to specific neighbourhoods. They give a brand a hip, urban feel that appeals to the hard-to-reach youth market. Unfortunately, they can be torn down easily and to date there is no means of measuring their effectiveness. In most cases the owners of the construction

Mobile Media

It's everywhere! It's everywhere! Just when you thought you had seen everything, a new media concept pops up out of nowhere. When it comes to outdoor advertising, the sky is literally the limit.

Is it possible to mount an advertising message on the hubcaps of taxis? Wheels rotate, so you would think it is impossible. E-Caps is a new mobile media product that places ads over the wheels of taxis. The hubcap-like discs don't rotate, which attracts attention because the car appears to glide along the road.

Buses and subways have carried ads for years, so why not taxis, trucking fleets, and tourist rickshaws? Mexx Canada cruised the streets of Montreal with an 18-foot illuminated shop window. The window included 10 mannequins wearing fashions from the fall/winter Mexx City collection for young men and women. The roving window was seen as a very urban way of presenting fashion to a very urban clientele. It grabbed the attention of onlookers! According to Julie Brisson, marketing director for Mexx Canada, "Marketing is like fashion—you've got to innovate. If you don't it's boring."

Mobile advertising is becoming popular due to the fragmentation factor affecting television and print media. Marketers are looking for new ways of reaching mass audiences, and outdoor ads in general are one of the few ways of reaching a mass audience. In the old days cars used to go down the main streets using a loudspeaker to announce an event that was about to happen. Today we have a company called Motomedia that operates a fleet of trucks in Toronto, Ottawa, Calgary, and Vancouver that are equipped with illuminated advertising signs. They travel through neighbourhoods of interest to the advertiser.

Put your mind to work. Can you come up with another brilliant advertising medium? Remember, these concepts were nothing more than ideas only a few years ago. Follow through. You might just hit the jackpot!

Sources: Adapted from John Heinzl, "Anything that moves," *The Globe and Mail*, May 11, 2001, p. M1 and Larry Harding, "Taking It to the Streets," *Marketing*, November 19, 2001, p. 18.

Mexx www.mexx.com

site are paid by the advertisers for the privilege of putting up the signs. More permanent versions of wild postings are starting to appear at construction sites. Much like an oversized outdoor poster, the advertising message is painted on the boards that surround the construction site (see Figure 10.17).

Students are advised to check the out-of-home section of *Canadian Adverting Rates and Data* for more information about the diverse range of out-of-home media alternatives. It seems that out-of-home advertising is everywhere. Quite frankly, it is! Entrepreneurs keep pushing the boundaries. For more insight into the latest innovations in out-of-home advertising, see the Advertising in Action vignette **Mobile Media**.

Point-of-Purchase Advertising

Point-of-purchase (POP) advertising can be defined as advertising or display materials set up at a retail location to build traffic, advertise a product, and encourage impulse buying. Unlike other forms of advertising, point-of-purchase is positioned where the product or service is immediately available to consumers. Thus, it closes the gap between consumer advertising and actual sales. Gerald H. Long, president and chief executive officer of R. J. Reynolds Tobacco Company, pointed out the effectiveness of point-of-purchase when he stated: "Each form of advertising has its role, but, in very candid terms, POP is the only form that is at hand when consumers reach for their money."[16]

FIGURE
10.17

An illustration of wild posting advertising; permanent painted ads at construction sites

Courtesy: Dick Hemingway

Point-of-Purchase
Advertising International
www.popai.org

The main reason for using point-of-purchase advertising is to remind consumers of a product just before they make a purchase decision. This medium can provide a finishing touch to a well-integrated advertising and promotion program. Studies conducted by the Point-of-Purchase Advertising Institute (POPAI) in the United States reveal that, when the imagery of a television commercial is graphically repeated in an in-store display, sales increase significantly. Further, it is estimated that as many as 70 percent of brand purchase decisions are made right in the store.[17] Point-of-purchase advertising also plays a very important role in a self-service retail environment.

Some of the more common types of point-of-purchase advertising include exterior signs, modular display racks, display shippers, display cards, audiovisual displays, and vending machines.

EXTERIOR SIGNS

The primary function of a store sign is to identify the business. The style and lettering of the sign (i.e., the store logo) becomes familiar to customers in the market area and helps to draw them to the business. The logo style of the business sign is integrated with other forms of store advertising. The McDonald's "golden arches" exemplify the familiar sign that can be seen from a great distance by passing motorists or pedestrian traffic. For most retailers, store signs and logos play a prominent role in message strategy and execution.

MODULAR DISPLAY RACKS

A **modular display rack** is a permanent display unit provided by a manufacturer to display a certain line of merchandise. These types of units are usually made of wire and metal (e.g., candy and gum counter displays, potato-chip racks in variety stores) or plastic materials. The primary advantage of a display rack is that, for as long as the display rack remains, the merchandise is located outside its normal environment, by itself, away from the competition. Signage can be appended to the display unit to help draw attention to it. Depending on the size of the unit, a poster, shelf poster, or tear-off ad pad can be integrated into modular displays to communicate special sales or promotions.

DISPLAY SHIPPERS

A **display shipper** is a cardboard shipping carton that converts into a temporary in-store display when opened and assembled. Designed to encourage impulse purchases, display shippers are often used to merchandise seasonal products. Display shippers for Halloween candies and for the summer barbecue season (exhibiting barbecue-related products such as spices and sauces) are quite common. They are very common in grocery and drugstore outlets, and are usually sold through the head office of the retail organization. The displays are used at the discretion of store management, and can be assembled by store personnel or the manufacturer's field sales representative. A display shipper appears in Figure 10.18.

DISPLAY CARDS

Display cards include paper or paperboard posters, shelf talkers (small-size posters that hang from the store shelves where the product is located), and tear-off ad pads that often include coupons or other purchase incentives. Designed to encourage impulse purchases, these forms of advertising can be used with display shippers or on displays that are set up at the ends of aisles or other store locations. Their primary role is to draw the customer's attention to something special and prompt a decision to buy. Manufacturers commonly use tear-off ad pads to promote contests, refunds, and other sales promotion activity.

FIGURE
10.18

An illustration of a display shipper; shipping carton unfolds to form a temporary display

Courtesy: Dick Hemingway

AUDIOVISUAL DISPLAYS

Large department stores and national chain stores now use **audiovisual** displays frequently. These displays can be short-term in nature; they can promote the sale of a special line of merchandise while it is on sale. For example, television monitors and videocassette units are sometimes integrated into aisle displays to draw attention to special offers.

Some retailers have integrated TV monitors into effective long-term programs. Home Hardware has implemented an in-store advertising program that combines a product demonstration and commercial in a 30-second message. Referred to as a *demomercial*, it shows a simple yet effective demonstration of how a featured product works. Typically, the spot shows a flaw in an existing product and then introduces a solution in the form of a nifty Home Hardware item. Viewers can find the item only in a Home Hardware store.[18] The home improvement market is very competitive, so programs like this provide a bit of a competitive edge. Canadian Tire also shows demomercials in its stores.

VENDING MACHINES

Vending machines are a traditional component of soft-drink merchandising programs. Now available are vending machines with vivid and colourful faces that quickly grab the attention of passersby. Their design has advanced considerably to the point where the face panels (plastic front panels illuminated by interior lights) resemble a backlit poster. Soft drink and snack food brands sell significant volumes through vending machines, so it is not uncommon to see backlit-style machines for Coca-Cola, Pepsi-Cola, and Nestlé candy bars (Smarties, Kit Kat, Coffee Crisp, etc.).

Automated banking machines, another form of vending, have proven to be an overwhelming success for financial institutions and are capable of offering many more services in the future. Scotiabank has already printed out Burger King and Swiss Chalet coupons on bank machine receipts and experimented with some third-party ads for Coca-Cola and the two restaurants.[19] Potentially, this medium represents new revenue (advertising revenue) for the banking industry and private ATM operators.

OTHER POINT-OF-PURCHASE ADVERTISING

Supermarket chains and convenience store chains have been particularly innovative regarding new forms of in-store advertising and merchandising concepts. Often developed by independent media advertising companies, the merits of these concepts are sold to potential advertisers.

Among the options are grocery cart advertising, shelf ads, and floor ads. **Grocery cart advertising** uses full-colour posters that are attached to the ends of shopping carts. Shoppers facing an approaching shopping cart are exposed to the message, while the shopper pushing the cart also sees a message from inside the cart. **Shelf ads** include shelf pads, recipe cards, and promotional materials that are appended to store shelves and temporary displays. A relatively new innovation is floor ads. **Floor ads** are portable floor mats (often called **ad-tiles**) that will not scuff or peel and that carry advertising messages. Floor ads cut through the clutter of other forms of in-store advertising. These three options provide advertisers with last-minute exposure right at the point of purchase.

For additional insight into the role and importance of point-of-purchase advertising, read the Advertising in Action vignette **The 70 Percent Factor**.

The 70 Percent Factor

In modern-day supermarket and drugstore retailing there is a battle going on between national brands and private-label brands. Many large chains such as Loblaws, Sobeys, Safeway, and Shoppers Drug Mart are placing greater emphasis on their own brands. Consequently, many national brands are being squeezed out—they're not in a display bin and they're not on the shelf.

Despite this tug of war, retailers never forget the widely cited fact that at least 70 percent of all buying decisions are made at the point of purchase, and that displays, promotions, and contests that promote national brands play a big role in making the cash register ring. The branded products appreciate the 70 percent factor and as a result allocate considerable marketing funds toward in-store messaging. In many cases, budgets previously allocated to traditional advertising are increasingly migrating to retailer-specific national promotions often supported by television commercials.

Smart grocery retailers today have given up trying to compete with Wal-Mart and Costco on price. Instead, they are emphasizing the shopping environment and the shopping experience. Part of that experience involves effectively promoting what they sell—giving shoppers additional reasons to buy certain products. From the manufacturer's perspective, it has become more important than ever for their products to shout at consumers from the store shelves: "Buy me! Buy me!"

Beyond special displays that usually include posters and ad pads announcing something special, technology has entered the scene to upgrade the image of in-store advertising. Both Mountain Dew and Dr. Pepper tested a new concept called Visi-strobe. It is a motion-activated device attached to the bottom of a selection of bottles in a refrigerator. A sensor is activated when customers walk by. Suddenly the Mountain Dew container lights up and the product looks like a lighter shade of green or red. Something unexpected catches the consumer's eye. The curious will buy!

Another good reason to focus on in-store advertising and promotion is the high degree of impulse buying that occurs. A recent research study revealed that 30 percent of grocery shoppers make spur-of-the-moment purchase decisions every time they shop. Therefore, the brand that offers a little motivation in the store stands to benefit the most. Simply put, marketers cannot underestimate the potential impact of point-of-purchase advertising. It's a medium that gets the wallets out!

Sources: Adapted from Kate Fitzgerald, "In-store media ring cash register," *Advertising Age*, February 9, 2004, p. 43.

Point-of-Purchase as an Advertising Medium

There are numerous pros and cons to point-of-purchase (POP) advertising. Advertisers who use this medium do so because it is the last opportunity to reach a target audience before an actual purchase decision is made. In this section the merits of point-of-purchase advertising are explored.

ADVANTAGES OF POINT-OF-PURCHASE ADVERTISING

IMPULSE PURCHASING In the case of frequently purchased product categories such as candies, snack foods, toiletries, and beverages, point-of-purchase advertising stimulates impulse purchasing. Furthermore, research studies indicate that more than two-thirds of all purchase decisions are made right in the store. Such unplanned behaviour creates ample opportunity for point-of-purchase advertising to influence last-minute decisions. It is often referred to as the "last chance" medium.

MESSAGE REINFORCEMENT While the display itself stimulates action, the incidence of consumer action increases when the display visuals are used to supplement the advertising done in other media (e.g., in-home media). Point-of-purchase reinforces prior messages, finalizing sales to consumers who have been preconditioned by other forms of advertising.

MESSAGE RECEPTIVENESS POP addresses the message to consumers when they are shopping (i.e., it appeals to the right audience in the right place, at the right time). Since consumers generally shop in stores whose merchandise they can afford, the selling message is visible to the desired target audience.

LAST CHANCE (DECIDING FACTOR) IN SALE For product categories where impulse buying is not a factor (such as expensive durable goods), point-of-purchase material can be used to inform and educate consumers. Automobile dealers rely heavily on the colour brochures in their showrooms to communicate essential details about their various product lines. These types of advertisements go home with the customer, are consulted in detail, and play a major role in bringing the customer back to the showroom. As indicated earlier in the chapter, home improvement chains have started using in-store television commercials to promote their own unique product lines. Such information presented at just the right time could produce a sale.

MERCHANDISE TIE-INS Point-of-purchase advertising promotes the trial of new products, new packaging, and new sizes and flavours. It draws attention to warranties, rebate programs, contests, and other forms of promotional activity. It is also an effective vehicle for developing cross-promotions with related products sold in the same store (soup and crackers, potato chips and dips, bandages and antiseptics, and so on).

DISADVANTAGES OF POINT-OF-PURCHASE ADVERTISING

PLACEMENT The most eye-catching display will be ineffective if it is not located in the appropriate position in the store. The problem facing the retailer is the limited area in which to place the abundant display material available from manufacturers. If good placements are not found, the displays will not achieve sales objectives.

CLUTTER Consider the number of displays you are exposed to while walking through a drug, grocery, or hardware store. Assuming a retailer grants a manufacturer permission to erect a display or poster material, the manufacturer's display will face considerable competition from other products in commanding consumers' attention. Due to clutter, some displays will be relegated to poor locations (and then they may as well not be there at all).

WASTE Some displays and other point-of-purchase materials never get erected in the store. Manufacturers generally require permission from the retail store's head office to erect display units in corporate-owned retail stores such as Loblaws, Safeway, A&P, and Shoppers Drug Mart. Even if permission is granted, if and how the display units will be utilized is often left to the discretion of store managers. Securing co-operation from retail managers is the responsibility of the field sales force. This task can be difficult at times.

SUMMARY

Out-of-home media are composed of a variety of outdoor poster options, transit advertising, and point-of-purchase advertising. The various forms of outdoor advertising are posters, backlit posters, superboards and spectaculars, mall posters, electronic signs, street-level advertising, transit shelters, wall banners, and murals. Outdoor advertising offers high target reach and frequency and geographic flexibility. It is an effective medium because it can reinforce the message that appears in other media. Among the weaknesses of outdoor advertising are the lack of target-market selectivity and the creative limitations related to the speed at which people pass by.

There are various forms of transit advertising, including interior and exterior cards, interior door cards, superbuses and bus murals, a variety of station posters, and station domination. Among the new media vehicles are stair risers, ceiling decals, and floor ads. Transit advertising offers continuous exposure (a result of transit users' consistent travel patterns) and high reach and frequency against a general target market. The major weaknesses of the medium are the lack of target-market selectivity and the creative limitations owing to space restrictions.

Some new and unique forms of advertising media include airport display advertising, washroom advertising, elevator advertising, building wraps, food-court video screens, sports and arena advertising, taxicab advertising, and cinema advertising.

Point-of-purchase advertising is effective in stimulating impulse purchases and reinforcing a message delivered by another medium. A drawback of point-of-purchase is the lack of use by retailers because of the abundance of display material they receive from suppliers. As well, too many displays in a store reduce the impact of any individual display. POP advertising is often referred to as "last chance" advertising. It reaches consumers at a critical moment, that point in time when brand decisions are made and wallets are about to be opened.

KEY TERMS

REVIEW QUESTIONS

1. Briefly explain the difference between an outdoor poster, a backlit poster, and a spectacular.

2. Identify and explain two advantages and two disadvantages of outdoor advertising.

3. Using the rate card in Figure 10.9, calculate the net cost of the following outdoor campaign:

   Medium: Viacom outdoor posters
   Markets: Halifax, Montreal ESA, Toronto, Vancouver District
   Weight: Toronto and Montreal 50 GRPs; Halifax and Vancouver 25 GRPs
   Time: 16 weeks in all markets

4. What is the difference between an exterior king poster and an exterior seventy poster?

5. Explain briefly the nature of the following transit advertising vehicles: interior cards, station posters, triples, and station domination.

6. What are the major types of transit advertising?

7. What types of products or services are suitable for transit advertising?

8. Identify and briefly explain two advantages and two disadvantages of transit as an advertising medium.

9. Using the rate card in Figure 10.15 calculate the cost of the following campaign:

Medium: King bus posters
Markets: Toronto, Halifax, and Winnipeg
Weight: Toronto 50 GRPs; Halifax and Winnipeg 75 GRPs
Time: 12 weeks

10. Identify and briefly describe the major types of point-of-purchase advertising.

11. Explain the following terms in the context of the term in parentheses:

a) superboard (outdoor)
b) mural ads (outdoor)
c) 75 GRPs (outdoor)
d) backlit poster (outdoor)
e) superbus and bus murals (transit)
f) continuity discount (transit)
g) building wraps (outdoor)
h) display shipper (point-of-purchase)
i) floor ads (point-of-purchase)

12. Identify and briefly explain two advantages and two disadvantages of point-of-purchase advertising.

DISCUSSION QUESTIONS

1. "Out-of-home media are primarily recognized as a means of complementing other media forms." Is this statement true or false? Discuss this statement, assuming the role of marketing manager—first for a television station, and then for an outdoor advertising company.

2. Read the Advertising in Action vignette **The Big Picture Is Booming**. The vignette states that Labatt has shifted funds into outdoor advertising as part of their integrated communications strategy. Do you see other consumer-goods brands following suit? Is this an effective media strategy for Labatt and others to follow? Explain your position.

3. There is statistical evidence showing point-of-purchase advertising to be effective in prompting purchase response, at least in the short term. Should advertisers be spending more or less on this form of advertising in the future? Should investment in this form of advertising come at the expense of traditional brand advertising in the mass media? Discuss these issues, using examples of your choice.

4. Naming rights to arenas and advertising inside arenas such as the Air Canada Centre and GM Place are suddenly popular. What potential benefits do you see for advertisers that pursue this media strategy? Do you think arena advertising is effective? Explain your position.

5. Read the Advertising in Action vignette **Mobile Media**. Based on the examples cited in the vignette, do you think that delivering messages by moving the medium around the city is effective at reaching a target market, or will the message simply get lost in the urban landscape? Assess this medium and explain your position.

NOTES

1. Canadian Media Directors' Council *Media Digest*, 2003–2004, p. 10.
2. Joe Mandese, "New outdoor media options challenge conventional media planning wisdom," *Media Post*, August 14, 2003, **www.mediapost.com.**
3. Patti Summerfield, "The last mass medium goes niche," *Strategy*, September 24, 2001, p. 25.
4. Canadian Media Directors' Council *Media Digest*, 1993–1994, p. 6.
5. *Canadian Advertising Rates and Data*, November 2003, p. 473.
6. Brian Harrod, "The true test of a great idea," *Marketing*, April 12, 1999, p. 42.
7. Canadian Media Director's Media Council *Media Digest*, 2003–2004, p. 50.
8. "Out-of-home evolution," *Marketing*, January 30, 1995, p. 15.
9. *Canadian Advertising Rates and Data*, November 2003, p. 489.
10. Laura Pratt, "TDI shaking up the transit business," *Strategy*, September 25, 2000, p. 28.
11. Mary Klonizalis, "The view on the way to the top," *Marketing*, April 12, 1999, p. 36.
12. Chris Powell, "Here, there and everywhere," *Marketing*, November 19, 2001, pp. 11, 13.
13. Ibid., p. 13.
14. Based on data from *Canadian Advertising Rates and Data*, November 2003, p. 509.
15. John Heinzl, "Mainstream advertisers go wild for wild postings," *The Globe and Mail*, n.d.
16. "In-store merchandising," in "The Power of P.O.P.," insert in *Marketing*, n.d., p. 1.
17. Ibid.
18. Chris Powell, "Show & Tell," *Marketing*, February 24, 2003, p. 13.
19. Rob Ferguson, "Advertising teller machines," *Toronto Star*, January 6, 2002, p. C1.

THE practice OF ADVERTISING

Media Strategy and Execution:
AN INNOVATIVE LOCAL MARKET CAMPAIGN YIELDS POSITIVE RESULTS FOR CAMPBELL'S SOUP

The solutions to one advertiser's problems are not the same as those of another. How an advertising agency recommends the use of media depends on a host of factors: the characteristics of the target market and their media consumption; the importance of reach and frequency to the advertiser; the nature of the message; and the budget available.

If significant funds are available, then an agency can embark upon a multimedia campaign, if necessary. In contrast, if funds are scarce, then more unique and innovative ways to employ media must be explored. Here is a story of one brand that met with great success by implementing a unique, local-market campaign, where the primary strategic consideration was the timing. For now let's just refer to it as "Targeting by Timing."

This campaign was judged the Best Plan Overall in the annual Best Media Plan competition sponsored by *Strategy* magazine. It was submitted in the under $500 000 budget category but was the outright winner of the competition regardless of budget size. The media plan was created by OMD Toronto with creative prepared by affiliate agency BBDO.

Background

In the dead of winter there's nothing better for you than a hot bowl of soup. At least that's what mother always used to say! Is this the makings of a media plan for Campbell's soup? You bet!

Soup has a distinct advantage over many other product categories during the cold Canadian winter, so when some new ideas were being considered by OMD Canada, Campbell's media agency, they posed the question: Why not connect cold weather to hot soup with a precedent-setting multimedia campaign that would run only on days when the temperature dropped below -5°C?

The thinking behind the idea was fairly simple. Soup has a warming effect. It's comfort food. Simple idea, but from a media logistics point of view it would be difficult to implement. Would it be possible to schedule messages only on days when temperatures in Toronto were below -5°C? Securing co-operation from media vendors would prove to be challenging, but things did fall into place.

Media Objectives

In Canada, the condensed soup market is flat and Campbell's is the dominant brand leader. Being a mature brand in a mature market calls for marketing activities that encourage current customers to buy more product. Soup has to be portrayed as a suitable alternative on hot meal occasions (cold winter days). A media strategy was devised to achieve the following media objectives:

- To position Campbell's soup as a hot meal opportunity on cold winter days (the brand would be directly linked to cold days)
- To increase frequency of use during the peak season for consumption (January and February)
- To bolster the association between the soup and the cold weather and ultimately encourage consumers to get a can out of the cupboard
- To focus the campaign only on the Toronto market largely due to budget restrictions

343

Creative Strategy

The actual ads in the campaign showed a thermometer with the temperature dropping right into a Campbell's soup can. In addition to the well-known slogan "M'm! M'm! Good!" was the tagline: "Warm up with Campbell's." The colours red and white (Campbell's soup colours) played a prominent role in the message (see Figure 1 for an illustration).

The Media Plan

The media plan embraced four key components: The Weather Network which aired a series of 10-second spots, the weather pages of the *National Post* and *Toronto Star*, radio spots during traffic reports, and internet scroll messages on the Weather Network's home page and messages emailed to individuals signed up to the Weather Network's database.

Falling temperatures triggered all campaign activity. Whenever the temperature dropped below -5°C, guerrilla tactics were deployed. The result was a pulsing kind of strategy that provided for great message continuity. The soup achieved excellent exposure on days when it was needed most.

Media vehicles that offered maximum flexibility were chosen within a weather-related environment, further enhancing the creative message. Multiple media messages would reach consumers on "weather-triggered" days. All media space was secured with only 24-hour advance bookings. The Weather Network advised other media partners when these days were expected to ensure a mutual call to action for placing Campbell's ads.

TELEVISION

The Weather Network, being a very credible information source, provided a desirable environment for the ad described in the Creative Strategy section. Campbell's dominated the network on cold-weather days. Since consumers' visits to the Weather Network are not that long, the 10-second spots were scheduled with heavy frequency to maximize the number of daily occasions.

NEWSPAPER

Banner ads (ads that extend across the bottom of a page) were placed in the weather pages of the *National Post* and *Toronto Star*. Ad location was a critical component of the campaign, so securing banner positions was a critical negotiation detail up front.

RADIO

Radio spots were scheduled in the afternoon drive period (3 p.m. to 6 p.m.) to serve as a pre-dinner reminder to encourage consumers to consider soup. The ads included blowing wind and an announcer stating: "Can't stand the cold! Get into the kitchen! Warm up tonight with a hot bowl of Campbell's

Courtesy of Daniel Acker/Bloomberg News/Landor

FIGURE

1

soup. . . ." The ad was announcer-read (by a DJ) and included sponsorship mentions. The ads were run on weather-triggered days when the DJ could give the impression of being cold.

INTERNET

A banner ad appeared on Canadian city weather pages during the 4 p.m. to 7 p.m. time period. The ads were scheduled for heavy frequency during the pre-dinner period when log-ins to check weather and live-traffic cameras are most popular. Campbell-sponsored emails were sent to the Weather Network database.

OUT-OF-HOME

Digital video messages appeared in food courts and other outdoor video signs on weather-triggered days. The Digital Advertising Network (the media supplier here) incorporates weather content into its regular messages, so it was an ideal environment for the

Campbell message. The 10-second television spots were adapted for this medium.

The Results

Philip Donne, president of Campbell's Soup Company, was so impressed with the novelty of the campaign that he gave it quick approval. "What better way to tap into the feeling that hot soup is great on a cold day . . . than to get involved with the weather, and to break through the clutter in a way that no one else has done."

Campbell's sales rose by 6 percent in the February/March period, clear indication that the campaign had impact. Website traffic (at the Campbell's site) increased by 11 percent. Print ads encouraged consumers to visit the Campbell's site for preparation ideas.

Based on this initial success, Campbell's is planning to extend the campaign to other cities next year.

Adapted from "Planners turn meteorologists for Campbell," *Strategy Media*, April 19, 2004, p. 5 and Terry Poulton, "Minus five degrees? It's Campbell's time," *Strategy Media*, March 10, 2003, p. 12.

Communicating
the Message
INTEGRATED MEDIA CHOICES

Organizations are adopting the concept of integrated marketing communications, looking beyond traditional media choices to different and effective ways of communicating with customers. The result is a communications plan that combines traditional and non-traditional media, producing a synergistic effect. Part Five focuses on non-traditional media choices.

Chapter 11 examines the growing field of direct-response communications, while Chapter 12 discusses the emerging role of the internet. These media are attracting attention as marketers adapt to a changing marketplace. The remaining two chapters discuss non-media alternatives: Chapter 13 examines sales promotion and Chapter 14 discusses public relations and event marketing.

PART

5

Direct-Response Media

Learning Objectives

After studying this chapter, you will be able to

- Describe the various types of direct-response advertising

- Explain the advantages and disadvantages of various forms of direct-response advertising

- Assess the factors considered in, and procedures used for, buying direct mail

- Assess the strategies for delivering effective messages via direct-response techniques

Direct-response advertising is a form of media advertising that communicates messages directly to marketing prospects. Direct mail is the most common means of delivering these messages, but other forms of direct communication such as direct-response television, direct-response print, and telemarketing now play a more significant role. These forms of communication are discussed in this chapter. The internet and other forms of interactive communication are discussed in Chapter 12.

Direct-Response Advertising

Direct-response advertising is one segment of the direct-marketing industry and it now plays a major role in influencing consumer purchase patterns. Gone are the days of brand managers relying on television commercials. In today's competitive environment a manager must deliver bottom-line results, and direct-response advertising does just that. Marketers are attracted to direct response because of its targeting capabilities, its sophisticated measurement devices, and its ability to account for all dollars spent.

While no firm figures are available for direct-response television, direct mail presently accounts for $1.5 billion in net advertising revenues in Canada, or about 15 percent of all advertising revenues.[1] As an advertising medium, direct mail ranks third, just behind newspapers (17 percent of net advertising revenue) and television (26 percent of net advertising revenue). Further, direct-response advertising generates $51 billion in annual sales in Canada, and generates employment for more than 480 000 Canadians.[2]

The trend toward direct response has been building. Banks were the first of the major marketers to enter the direct-response arena, but have been recently joined by packaged-goods companies, automobile manufacturers, and retailers such as Shoppers Drug Mart and HBC. These companies are allocating greater portions of their marketing and marketing communications budgets to direct-response techniques.

The shift to direct response follows on the heels of companies adopting software technology that encourages database-management techniques and the implementation of customer-relationship management programs. Firms can now design and develop programs that reach customers individually and efficiently. Such capability offers significant competitive advantage. And the ability to reach customers directly with a message is a lot cheaper than delivering messages through the traditional mass media.

Direct-response advertising is advertising through any medium designed to generate a response by any means (such as mail, television, a print ad, and telephone) that is measurable. If traditional mass media are used, the message will include a toll-free telephone number, mailing address, or website address where more information can be secured.

The major forms of direct-response advertising are direct mail, direct-response television (DRTV), and telemarketing.

- *Direct mail* is a form of advertising communicated to prospects via the postal service.
- *Direct-response print* is a response-oriented message delivered to prospects by magazine or newspaper advertisements.
- *Direct-response television (DRTV)* is a form of advertising communicated to prospects via television commercials (e.g., 30-minute infomercials or messages seen on cable channels, or 60-second commercials on conventional television stations that encourage people to buy something immediately by telephone).
- *Telemarketing* involves the use of telecommunications to promote the products and services of a business.

Direct mail is currently the primary medium for delivering direct-response advertising messages; however, due to advancing electronic technology, it is expected that direct-response television will play a much stronger role in the communications mix in the future.

Direct Mail

Direct mail is by far the most common form of direct-response advertising. The use of mail is widespread due to its ability to personalize the message (the name can be included in the mailing), the need to send lengthy messages (e.g., copy-oriented sales messages along with reply cards and contracts that are returned by prospects), and its ability to provide a high degree of geographic coverage economically (e.g., the mailing can be distributed to designated postal codes anywhere in Canada). There are numerous options available to companies wishing to use direct mail. Sometimes these options are combined to form a convincing package of information.

SALES LETTERS

The most common form of direct mail, the **letter**, is typeset, printed, and delivered to household occupants or to specific individuals at personal or business addresses. Letters are usually the primary communication in a mailing package, which typically includes a brochure, reply card, and postage-paid return envelope. Refer to Figure 11.1 for an illustration.

FIGURE
11.1

A personalized
direct-response
sales letter

22 -65 -6705   T5 (F)
Keith J. Tuckwell
170 Greenlees Dr.
Kingston ON   K7K 6P5

Dear Keith,

As I was going through our records I noticed it's been four years since we last saw you. During that time, I certainly hope you've been keeping up with your eye exams.

Nothing is more important for protecting your vision. If you'd like, give me a call and I can arrange an appointment for you.

I'm writing you now because there's never been a better time to get new glasses. Some wonderful new styles have come in recently. Rimless glasses from Europe and Ray-Ban® for indoor and outdoors – there's dozens of exciting new styles and accessories for you to see.

Best of all, for a limited time, you can **save $90 on eyeglasses or sunglasses — any frame and lens combination, in any prescription.**

Add in our 30-Day No-Risk Guarantee, 30-Day Price Match and One-Year Breakage Protection and you'll see that LensCrafters is hard to beat.

It's been much too long since we've seen you! Please, make an appointment for an eye exam today, and afterward, come let us help you find a pair of new glasses you'll absolutely love.

Sincerely,

Susan Napier

Susan Napier, General Manager
613-384-0743

P.S. Please don't gamble with your precious sight. Schedule an eye exam soon.

In Quebec, completed eyewear and guarantees provided by the Independent Doctors of Optometry Next to LensCrafters℠.

Your VIP# is 19062498. As part of our regular business practices, LensCrafters collects the name and address of its customers. LensCrafters uses such information solely to notify you of new products and services, to provide you special offers and discounts and, if applicable, to send you eye exam reminders. Because you are a customer of LensCrafters we assume that we have your permission to send our informational mailings to you. If you would prefer not to receive further mailings, you may have your name removed from our mailing list by simply calling 1-800-406-5034. Thanks for being a customer at LensCrafters.

LEAFLETS AND FLYERS

Leaflets and **flyers** are usually standard letter-sized pages (8½ by 11 inches) that offer relevant information and accompany a letter. Leaflets expand on the information contained in the letter and generate a response (i.e., the recipient takes action).

FOLDERS

Folders are sales messages printed on heavier paper, and often include photographs or illustrations. They are usually folded, and are frequently designed in such a way that they can be mailed without an envelope. See Figure 11.2. **Postage-paid reply cards** are an important component of a folder if the objective is to stimulate immediate action.

FIGURE
11.2

An illustration of a folder
mailed to past customers

STATEMENT STUFFERS

Statement stuffers, or **bounce backs** as they are often called, are advertisements distributed via monthly charge-account statements (such as those one receives from Sears, The Bay, or Visa). Capitalizing on the ease of purchasing by credit, such mailings make it very convenient to take action. In this case one order leads to another, and the prospect is reached at very low cost. Usually, the credit card number is the only information the seller requires. .

VIDEOCASSETTES AND CD-ROMS

Organizations now send serious prospects information by more sophisticated means. Videos are popular for demonstrating how a product works, how nice a resort destination looks, how well an automobile performs, and so on. In business-to-business markets, the **CD-ROM** is useful for presentation purposes (when combined with personal selling practices) and for letting customers review things on their own time. Similar to the videocassette, the CD-ROM aptly portrays how a product works. As well, technical information about a product that is hard to communicate in hard copy is easily accessed on a CD-ROM. These are but a few applications for these media. They can be part of a direct-mail campaign or a follow-up to a direct-mail campaign (e.g., for those who requested more information from the original mailing).

Direct-Mail Strategy

Essentially, an organization has the option of delivering a mail piece by itself or delivering an offer as part of a package that includes offers from other companies. This is the difference between solo direct mail and co-operative direct mail.

Solo direct mail, or **selective direct mail**, refers to specialized or individually prepared direct-mail offers sent directly to prospects. With this strategy, the marketing organization absorbs all of the costs. Solo direct-mail pieces are commonly employed in business-to-business communications, supplementing the messages frequently communicated via traditional business publications. The growth of database marketing by consumer goods organizations has led to greater usage of solo direct mail by these organizations. Due to the degree of personalization, response rates to this type of mailing tend to be much higher than for a co-operative mailing. Refer to Figure 11.3 for an illustration of a solo direct-mail piece.

From the Office of the Publisher

CARD
THE MEDIA INFORMATION NETWORK

One Mount Pleasant Rd, 7th Floor, Toronto ON M4Y 2Y5

Professor Kip Tuckwell
Pres
Tuckwell Marketing Ltd. xxT5(F)
170 Greenlees Drive
Kingston, ON K7K 6P5

"CARD never leaves my desk. It is where I go for valuable up-to-date information."
Rob Young, Senior Vice President of Planning & Research, Harrison, Young, Pesonen & Newell Inc.

"CARD is an integral part of my day. I couldn't do my job without it."
Ruth Klosterman, Director of Strategic Resources, Zenith Optimedia

Dear Marketing Manager,

It's clear where top Canadian advertising executives get their information...

...CARD, Canadian Advertising Rates & Data! Every monthly edition of **CARD** has over **8,000 changes** -- vital, time-sensitive information you need to invest your advertising dollars wisely. Successful media executives **know** they can't afford to be even a month behind - and **CARD** is the only publication that delivers the latest information. You'll find complete listings for over 4,500 media outlets... 529 advertising agencies... 150 Canadian and international media reps and their account lists... information on discounts... promotions... value-added packages... bonus circulation... contacts... and more!

Plus you get valuable extras with your CARD subscription, including FREE access to CARDonline®!

Like **CARDonline,** the only source in Canada that delivers the latest information. **CARDonline** includes **The Media Assessment Program,** a very powerful tool that allows you to search, select and compare media alternatives. This new functionality will improve and expand your research capabilities...giving you and your business the best available options to meet your needs.

Included in your subscription, you will also receive 2 issues of **Ethnic Media & Markets.** Look at ethnic publications and listen to ethnic broadcasters. Discover emerging opportunities in new markets you must consider.

You get this whole strategic package - for the price of CARD alone!

I guarantee your satisfaction or you may cancel at any time and receive a prompt refund on unserved issues. Get this unique and powerful information package that the top media executives are using **NOW!**

Sincerely,

Bruce Richards
Publisher

P.S. ARM YOURSELF WITH WHAT YOU NEED TO WIN - GET **CARD** TODAY! Just use the postage paid envelope or, for faster service, phone or fax your completed order form now.

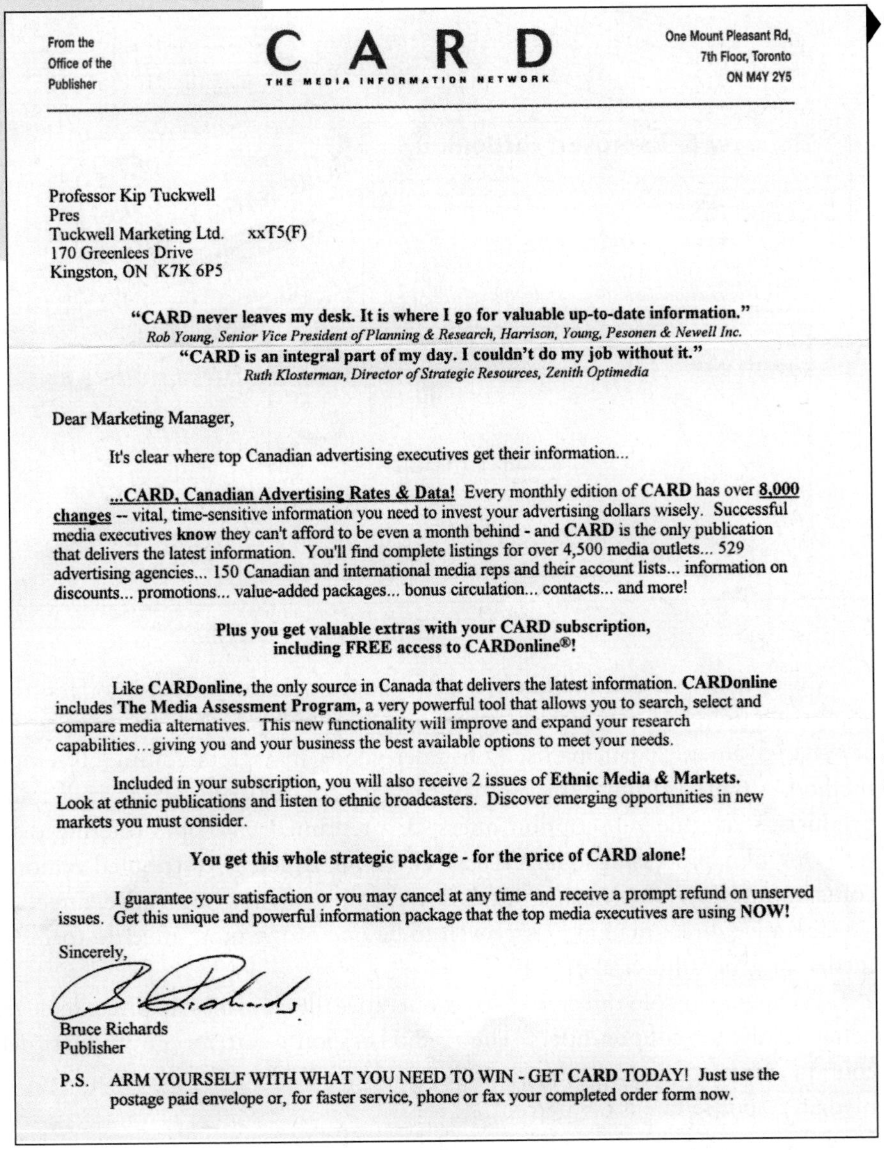

FIGURE **11.3**

Sample content of a solo direct-mail offer

Published with permission of CARD—Rogers Media Inc.

FIGURE
11.3

continued

Co-operative direct mail refers to envelopes containing special offers from non-competing products. Since many companies may be involved in the mailing, the costs are shared among participants. Consumer-goods marketers commonly employ this method. A typical mailing contains coupons for a variety of grocery, drug, and related products, magazine subscription offers, or preprinted envelopes offering discounted rates for film processing. The Val-Pak envelope, which is distributed nationally but contains ads for local businesses, is an example of a co-operative direct mailing. Co-operative direct mailing has proven to be one of the most effective forms of print media for generating trial purchase.

In comparing solo direct mail to co-operative direct mail, solo direct mail generates better results for coupon offers. The median response rate for all products delivering coupons via co-operative direct mail is 1.2 percent, whereas with solo direct mail the median response rate is 6.5 percent.[3]

Direct Mail as an Advertising Medium

Direct-mail marketing has been around for a long time, but it was an activity that traditional advertisers such as packaged-goods companies, banks and financial institutions, and automobile manufacturers avoided for a long time. These industries were turned off by the negative images associated with direct-marketing techniques. Now, these very industries and the leading companies within them are among the largest users of direct mail. Clearly, the advantages of direct mail are an attraction to companies that want to deliver messages to customers one-on-one.

ADVANTAGES OF DIRECT MAIL

AUDIENCE SELECTIVITY Using direct mail, advertisers can pinpoint and reach targets that are precisely defined in terms of demographics, assuming that the organization acquires lists identifying the primary prospects. A good list results in minimal circulation waste. Additional discussion of lists appears in the media-buying section of this chapter. As well, a company's own customer list is a good starting point for any direct-mail campaign.

HIGH REACH Solo direct mailings reach everyone the advertiser would like to reach—unlike other media, which reach only a portion of the target. For example, a life insurance or credit card organization that wants to reach all university graduates may be able to obtain access to such a list of students. For co-operative direct mailings (i.e., mass distribution to selected Canadian households), the national reach potential is very high. In this case, there is much circulation waste but the response rates are usually adequate to cover the costs of mass mailings.

GEOGRAPHIC FLEXIBILITY A proper mailing list offers an advertiser not only demographic selectivity but also the opportunity to deliver direct-mail messages to specific geographic locations. This advantage appeals to retailers and other local businesses that want to confine mailings to certain areas. National advertisers can also use direct mail to isolate geographic areas they would like to concentrate on; say, for example, an area where sales are lower than average.

CREATIVE FLEXIBILITY Like advertising in business publications, direct mail offers the flexibility to include long copy in advertisements (the longer the better, according to some practitioners). Since various pieces are often included in a single mailing, there is also flexibility in terms of style, length, and format. Generally speaking, a combination of formats in a single medium is effective. In this area, only imagination, budget, and applicable postal regulations limit the advertiser. Finally, because direct mail provides the opportunity to include items that will reach desired targets (e.g., free sample packets), it is a good medium for distributing coupons, free samples, and trial offers. Figure 11.4 is a personalized mailing from Energizer Canada that includes product information, free samples, and a coupon offer for a variety of Energizer battery products.

ADVERTISER CONTROL In using solo direct mail, the advertiser retains control over such variables as the circulation and the quality of the message. The message is printed by one source, which results in a consistent quality of reproduction. This consistency contrasts the situation that advertisers encounter when they run an advertisement in a variety of different newspapers, when the quality of reproduction varies from one newspaper to another.

Published with permission of CARD—Rogers Media Inc.

FIGURE 11.4

A personalized mailing that includes product information, free samples, and a trial coupon offer

EXCLUSIVITY   Another advantage of direct mail is that mailings delivered to the household do not compete with other media at the time they are received, although they do compete for attention with other mail. This exclusivity contrasts the circumstances of ads in newspapers and magazines, which compete with other ads and with editorial content as well as with the clutter of television advertising, where much channel surfing occurs.

MEASURABILITY   The success of a direct-mail campaign is measured in one way—the sales generated by the mailing. As a general rule, business-oriented direct mail receives 15 percent of the responses within the first week of the mailing. Early responses, used in conjunction with historical conversion patterns, can be used to project sales for a longer period of time. In this regard, the success of a direct-mail campaign can be determined in a short space of time. Similar calculations cannot be made when using traditional forms of mass advertising. For co-operative direct mailings, coupon redemption rates are higher than for coupons distributed by newspapers or magazines.

DISADVANTAGES OF DIRECT MAIL

HIGH COST PER EXPOSURE   When the absolute costs of production, renting or purchasing lists, fulfillment (i.e., stuffing and sealing envelopes), and mailing are tallied, the total can be higher than it is for other print alternatives. Remember, though, that the selectivity of the medium reduces waste circulation.

ABSENCE OF EDITORIAL SUPPORT In comparison to magazines, which have the support of editorial content (which provides the real reason for consumers to read), direct mail stands alone. It must grab attention without assistance; therefore, it is imperative that the message be designed in a format that combines verbal and illustrative elements attractively.

IMAGE AND LIFESPAN Direct mail is not a prestigious medium. Many consumers perceive direct mailings to be "junk mail," and they are promptly discarded when they reach the household. Many consumers do not perceive the special offers to be all that special. Direct mailings to businesses may suffer the same fate (i.e., they may be discarded), particularly if several mailings from different suppliers are received at the same time. However, the physical form of direct mail enables consumers to retain it for future reference.

POTENTIAL DELIVERY DELAYS Other print media have specific issue dates, so the time of message exposure is precisely controlled. Since direct mail relies on the postal service, and since it is delivered third class, there are no delivery guarantees. It is possible that a mailing will arrive at a destination after the offer has expired or the advertised event has occurred.

For more insight into the benefits derived from direct-mail communications, see the Advertising in Action vignette **Direct Mail and the Web: A Winning Combination for Harley Davidson.**

Buying Direct Mail

Three basic steps are involved in buying direct mail: obtaining a proper prospect list, conceiving and producing the mailing piece, and distributing the final version.

OBTAINING DIRECT-MAIL LISTS

The **direct-mail list** is the backbone of the entire campaign. Both the accuracy and definition of the list can have a significant bearing on the success or failure of a campaign. Companies recognize that it costs about six times as much to acquire a new customer as it does to keep an existing one.[4] As a result, companies are compiling databases to keep track of existing customers and are forming relationships with them through the mail and electronic means. Lists are secured from internal sources and external sources.

INTERNAL SOURCES There is no better prospect than a current customer. Therefore, a company's internal database must be monitored and updated routinely. For example, Canadian Tire accumulates considerable data on customers through its own credit card. As well, HBC (The Bay, Zellers, and Home Outfitters) accumulates considerable data about its customers through its HBC Rewards program. Data-mining techniques allow these companies to determine who their heavy customers are, what they buy, how much they buy, and how often they buy. For companies placing value on repeat business, this information can be used to develop new offers that will be of interest to current customers. Getting current customers to buy more is a much easier challenge than trying to attract new customers. In direct mail terms, an internal customer list is referred to as a **house list**.

As an alternative, companies can take steps to form lists of potential customers. Such customers are referred to as **prospects**. As Figure 11.5 illustrates, Jaguar Canada collects valuable information about customers that it can use in the future. Specifically,

Jaguar Canada
www.jaguar.ca

Direct Mail and the Web: A Winning Combination for Harley Davidson

How do you get a new target market to take a test drive on a Buell motorcycle? Some innovative thinking by promotions agency Square Peg and its online partner IC Group met the challenge and then some. Key to the campaign was a direct-mail effort that made potential customers aware of an online and in-store sweepstakes contest called "Nothing Beats a Buell."

The overall goal of the campaign was to increase retail traffic, encourage demonstration rides, and ultimately increase sales of Buell motorcycles. A secondary objective was to capture essential customer information so that Harley could communicate with prospects on an ongoing basis. The campaign would target experienced riders, new riders, and females.

A sweepstakes strategy was designed to drive traffic to the website and to stores. Customers who registered at the Buell website could win a cash prize while customers who visited a store to take a test drive would be eligible to win the grand prize—a free Buell motorcycle!

The direct-mail campaign used subscriber lists from extreme sports and motorcycle magazines. A mailing to 60 000 potential customers encouraged recipients to visit the website. As well, there were online banner ads on the *Canadian Motorcycle Guide* site, print advertising in industry publications, and point-of-purchase material in stores. Creative strategy and execution used the tagline "Nothing Beats a Buell Between Your Legs." The tagline may be somewhat controversial, but the product category is motorcycles.

Harley Davidson was very satisfied with the results of the campaign. There were 26 000 entries for the contest, 7000 of which came online. There was a 14 percent increase in web hits and an 18 percent increase in web traffic during the promotion period. Over 1200 visitors took a demonstration ride and sales increased significantly. In fact, Buell's market share in the sport bike category increased from 1.3 percent to 2.9 percent. Such good results reinforce the potential impact of direct-mail advertising messages.

Source: Adapted from Kristen Vinakmens, "How to put a Buell between their legs," *Strategy Direct + Interactive*, November 3, 2003, p. 13.

Buell Motorcycles **www.buell.com/en_ca**

Jaguar will be able to mail directly to customers information about new car models they are interested in. This information-oriented postcard appeared in a national magazine with a full-page ad for a Jaguar automobile.

EXTERNAL SOURCES People who have a history of responding to mail offers tend to be attractive prospects for new offers. Buying by mail is part of their behaviour. Therefore, the challenge is to find prospects that have a demographic profile—and perhaps a psychographic profile—that mirrors the profile of current customers. A **list broker** can assist in finding these prospects. The buyer provides the broker with the profile of the target customer, and the broker supplies a list of possible prospects on a cost-per-name basis. Generally, a high-quality list is developed through a **merge/purge** process on a computer, whereby numerous lists are purchased, combined, and stripped of duplicate names.

TargetSource, a database-management company, is an example of a list broker that classifies names by behaviours and interests. Some of their classifications include proven mail-order buyers, hobbies, sports enthusiasts, outdoor enthusiasts, investments, and nutrition and diet. They also provide lists based on demographic characteristics such as income, employment, marital status, presence of children, and type of dwelling. The base rate for names is $110/M ($110 per thousand). As the quality of the list requested

FIGURE
11.5

A reply card that collects valuable information about potential customers

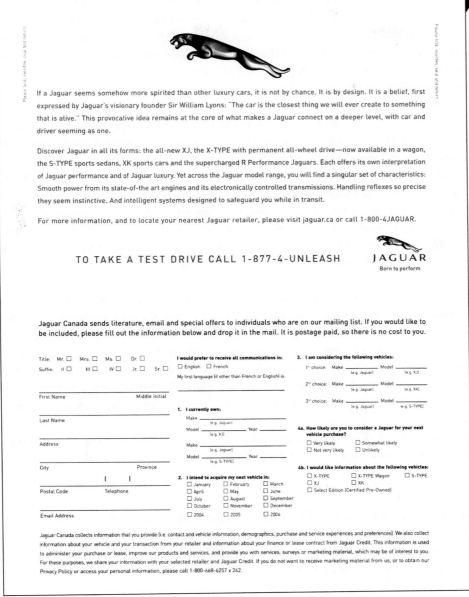

becomes more sophisticated or specialized, the rate per thousand increases. For example, for each demographic characteristic requested add an extra $10/M.[5]

Canada Post also supplies information that is vital to the accurate targeting of messages. For example, a postal code can isolate a small geographic area—say, a city block—and can then be combined with census data to provide relevant statistics regarding the ages and incomes of homeowners in the area, and whether children are present in the households.

A few types of lists are available: response lists, circulation lists, and compiled lists.

Canada Post
www.canadapost.ca

RESPONSE LISTS   A **response list** is a list of proven mail-order buyers. Such lists include book-of-the-month-club buyers, tape and CD music buyers, or people who order from co-operative direct-mailing firms. Because these lists include proven mail-order buyers, they tend to cost more. For example, TargetSource, the list broker referred to earlier, charges an additional $15/M for proven mail-order buyers in Canada.

CIRCULATION LISTS **Circulation lists** are magazine subscription lists that target potential customers by an interest or activity. A publishing company, for example, sells its list of subscribers to any other business that is interested in a similar target. Rogers Media offers a consumer database (English) comprising unduplicated active subscribers to *Maclean's*, *Chatelaine*, and *Flare*. A total of about one million names are available at a base cost of $125/M.[6]

PC Magazine
www.pcmag.com

PC Magazine, a leading publication for trends and information about computer hardware and software, makes its list available to marketing organizations. An organization could advertise in the magazine in a rather cluttered environment, or rent names and deliver a specific message by mail in an uncluttered environment to a cross-section of *PC Magazine* subscribers. As a target market, the magazine reaches an audience described as follows: average age 45, average household income $82 000, college graduates 66 percent, home PC users 97 percent, specify brands of computer products for purchase 97 percent, and access the internet regularly 95 percent. The base cost of the *PC Magazine* list is $170/M. Advertisers of the magazine are entitled to a reduced rate of $155/M. The magazine reaches 963 470 subscribers monthly, and a Canadian-only list is available.[7]

COMPILED LISTS **Compiled lists** are prepared from government, census, telephone, warranty, and other publication information. These are the least expensive of the lists and are not always personalized. For example, a business firm may be identified on the list, but not the appropriate contact person within the firm. Names of business prospects are compiled from print sources such as the Standard Industrial Classification (SIC), Frasers Canadian Trade Directory, or Scott's Industrial Index. Provincial and national associations such as the Canadian Medical Association commonly provide mailing lists of their physicians—or, in the case of other associations, lawyers, teachers, and accountants. A list broker, for example, could compile a list of a cross-section of professionals from various occupations if that is what a client required.

Frasers Canadian Trade Directory
www.frasers.com

PRODUCTION

When designing a direct-mail package, the advertiser usually engages the services of a specialist organization. In Canada, numerous full-service direct-marketing and direct-response agencies meet the needs of clients. Among them are the Carlson Marketing Group, Grey Direct, and OgilvyOne Worldwide. As the Ogilvy name suggests, this company positions itself as a leader in one-to-one communications consulting. Many of the larger traditional agencies, recognizing the growth and opportunity in direct-response communications, have formed direct-response subsidiaries. Grey Direct, mentioned above, for example, is a subsidiary of Grey Advertising Worldwide.

Grey Direct
www.greydirect.com

Once the mailing package is designed, it is ready for printing. Various factors such as size, shape, number of pieces, use of colour, and other variables influence the cost. Costs are usually quoted on a per-thousand basis, with larger runs incurring lower unit costs. Once printed, the mailing pieces are turned over to a letter shop that specializes in stuffing and sealing envelopes, affixing labels, and sorting, binding, and stacking the mailers. Once this task is complete, the mailing units are sent to the post office or a private carrier for distribution.

DISTRIBUTION

The most common means of delivery is Canada Post. A number of options are available through the postal system: first-class mail, third-class mail, and business reply mail.

FIRST-CLASS MAIL Although it is more costly, some direct mail is delivered first class. The advantages of first class are quicker delivery (if time is important), the return of undeliverable mail, and mail forwarding if the addressee has moved.

THIRD-CLASS MAIL Most direct-mail pieces—whether single pieces, bulk items, catalogues, or co-operative mailings—are delivered third class. The advantage over first class is the cost savings.

BUSINESS REPLY MAIL For the benefit of the recipient, an individual can respond at the expense of the advertiser. A pre-printed reply card or envelope is included in the direct-mail package. Postage-paid return envelopes are an incentive aimed at improving the rate of response. Refer to Figure 11.6 for an illustration.

Courtesy: New Brunswick Department of Tourism & Parks

FIGURE

11.6

A postage-paid reply card makes it easier for consumers to respond

Media Buying: Co-operative Direct Mail—An Example

The procedures for estimating the costs of solo direct mail and co-operative direct mail are similar. Taken into consideration are factors such as the distribution costs, printing costs, mailing costs, and costs associated with fulfillment. As indicated previously, an advertiser can either undertake all of these costs or share the costs with others in a co-operative mailing program. For this example, we will assume a co-operative direct-mail program will be undertaken in the Open & Save Co-operative Mailings package. The distribution costs for Open & Save Co-operative Mailings are included in Figure 11.7.

FIGURE
11.7

Rate card for Open & Save
Co-operative direct-mail
packages

Transcontinental Publications G.T. Inc. Open & Save Co-operative Mailings

Data confirmed for Sept./00 CARD

Transcontinental Publications G.T. Inc., 25 Sheppard Ave. W., Ste. 100, North York, ON M2N 6S7.
Phone: 416-218-3620. Fax: 416-218-3631. Email: petrellaj@transcontinental.ca

CLOSING DATES: 2000:

A Panel (Qty. 2,553,900):

Program:	Closing:	In-Home:
Jan.	Dec. 5	Jan. 3-14
March	Jan. 21	Mar. 1-10
May	Apr. 5	May 2-12
Sept.	Aug. 7	Sept. 4-15
Oct.	Sept. 17	Oct. 18-28

B Panel (Qty. 883,200):

Program:	Closing:	In-Home:
Jan.	Dec. 5	Jan. 3-14
March	Jan. 21	Mar. 1-10
May	Apr. 5	May 2-12
Sept.	Aug. 7	Sept. 4-15
Oct.	Sept. 17	Oct. 18-28

C Panel (Qty. 2,871,650):

Program:	Closing:	In-Home:
Jan.	Nov. 16	Jan. 3-14
March	Jan. 21	Mar. 1-10
Sept.	July 14	Aug. 28-Sept. 8
Oct.	Sept. 17	Oct. 18-28

Quebec Urban Panel (Qty. 1,154,350):

Program:	Closing:	In-Home:
Jan.	Dec. 5	Jan. 10-21
Sept.	Aug. 14	Sept. 11-20

Quebec Rural Panel (Qty. 1,082,000):

Program:	Closing:	In-Home:
Jan.	Dec. 5	Jan. 3-14
Sept.	Aug. 7	Aug. 28-Sept. 8

COMMISSION & CASH DISCOUNT: Net 20 days.

GENERAL ADVERTISING: Rates effective March 12,1998. 50% due on closing, balance Due upon completion of mailing.

Under 250,000	$16/M	Over 4,000,000	$12/M
250,000-4,000,000	13/M	C Panel-Rural/Quebec	12/M
Market split charges, each			$600
Postal stn. selections, extra			4.00/M
Cover flash, extra			$1.50/M

Samples, Booklets etc. avail. on request.
All dist'n rates are F.O.B. Toronto.

MECHANICAL REQUIREMENTS

Max. folded size: 5-1/2 x 8-1/2.
Req'd 5 weeks prior to in-home date. Prod. costs extra.
All mat'l must be suppl. in cartons. Based on suppl. inserts not exceeding 3.5 grams in weight. If overweight 65¢/gram/thousand premium will be charged. End fold units will carry 10% surcharge of earned space rate. Rates avail. on request for both samples & booklet inserts. Submissions must be accompanied by a sample to exact size & weight.

PERSONNEL

G.M.: John Petrella.
Client Services: Dawn McKeating.
Prod. Mgr.: Pat Watson.

BRANCH OFFICES/REPRESENTATIVES

Montreal H3A 2A6: 2001 Université, Ste. 840.
Phone: 514-499-0317.

CIRCULATION

☞Circulation statement outdated since 02-97

2104–2835

Courtesy: *Canadian Advertising Rates and Data*

INFORMATION: OPEN & SAVE CO-OPERATIVE MAILINGS

The offer:	1 page folded ad (3¾ × 8½ inches) that includes a $1.50 coupon
Redemption rate:	3 percent
Distribution:	2 million households

COST CALCULATIONS

Distribution costs (cost to insert an offer into an envelope) 2 000 000 × $13/M	= $26 000
Printing costs (estimated cost) 2 000 000 × $6/M	= $12 000
Redemption costs (estimated at 3 percent of total coupons distributed) 2 000 000 ×.03 × $1.50	= $90 000
Total cost	**= $128 000**

Depending on how the coupon offer is returned, there could be additional costs for the advertiser. For example, there is a handling fee provided to the retailer for conducting the coupon transaction. As well, coupons are usually sent from the retailer to a clearing house for processing. The clearing house pays the retailer and provides periodic reports to the advertiser about how many coupons are being redeemed. The advertiser pays a fee for this service.

Direct-Response Television

The forms of direct-response television include 60-second (or longer) commercials that typically appear on cable channels, and infomercials. In each case, the use of toll-free telephone numbers and credit cards makes the purchase more convenient for the viewer. An **infomercial** is a commercial that runs for longer than 12 continuous minutes. Typically, the message is presented in a program-like format lasting 30 minutes. An offer or the benefits of a product or service is presented in great detail. The range of products employing this technique is endless, from exercise equipment to financial investment opportunities. The 12-minute figure is important since the CRTC imposes a ceiling of 12 minutes per hour on advertising time for regular commercials. Infomercials are exempt from this ceiling.[8]

The nature of direct-response television advertising has changed over time. Once regarded as schlock, direct-response advertising was associated with "o-matic" types of products. Today, DRTV is redefining itself. While there are still two-minute direct-response commercials, there are also 60-second, 30-second, and even 10-second spots. Infomercials no longer exclusively revolve around get-rich-quick concepts; in fact, highly informative, well-produced commercials have been created for many blue-chip companies.

The spectrum of direct-response advertisers now includes pharmaceutical companies, banks and financial institutions, automobile manufacturers, technology companies, and not-for-profit organizations. In Canada some of our mightiest mainstream marketing organizations, such as Ford, Bell, and TD Bank, have embraced direct-response television. This diversity is self-perpetuating, so it is likely that advertisers and their agencies will continue to test innovative approaches, thereby broadening the discipline.

Direct-response television commercials are classified into two categories:

- *Traditional* An infomercial that stresses the "buy now, limited time offer" approach; it tries to sell as much as possible at the lowest cost per order.
- *Corporate/Brand* An infomercial that establishes leads, drives retail traffic, launches new products, creates awareness, and protects and enhances the brand image.

One good reason why short and long direct-response commercials are popular is that they elicit measurable audience response. This is traditionally done through 1-800 telephone numbers or website addresses. The activity (response) that occurs via telephone or the website immediately following the commercial allows an advertiser to measure the success of the offer immediately.

To keep the cost of commercial placement as low as possible, the shorter commercials (30 seconds and 60 seconds) usually use run-of-schedule (ROS) time blocks rather than program-specific purchases. The ROS strategy provides the advertiser flexibility by time of day. As well, the spots will cost less, allowing more spots to be scheduled. Frequency of message is another factor that affects the success of a direct-response television campaign. Refer to Figure 11.8 for a summary of some advantages and disadvantages of direct-response television advertising.

For more insight into infomercials and their potential impact on viewers, refer to the Advertising in Action vignette **Ford Goes a Step Further**.

Direct-Response Print Media

It is common for advertisers to communicate direct-response offers through newspapers and magazines. Both options are good for fielding leads for future marketing programs and for getting prospects to take action immediately. Since newspapers are a local-market medium, an organization that has adopted a key-market media strategy can target prospects geographically. Local-market retailers that want to employ direct-response strategies may do so through their local daily or weekly newspaper.

Magazines are a good alternative for advertisers targeting specific audiences based on demographic or geographic characteristics. For example, a company such as Intrawest that markets year-round travel destinations (their destinations include Whistler Blackcomb, Mont Tremblant, and Blue Mountain) will place direct-response

Intrawest
www.intrawest.com

FIGURE
11.8

Advantages and disadvantages of direct-response television advertising

ADVANTAGES

- *Message Content*—numerous benefits can be communicated in detail
- *Demonstration*—added time allows for lengthier and more dramatic demonstrations
- *Cost*—production and media costs of short commercials are less than traditional TV
- *Flexibility*—message can be altered if necessary

DISADVANTAGES

- *Time*—even a 60-second commercial faces time constraints
- *Lifespan*—commercials are fleeting; frequency is necessary
- *Image*—consumers often skeptical about message; are claims believable

Ford Goes a Step Further

In a relatively short period, DRTV has gone from being the poor cousin of the advertising world to becoming one of the fastest-growing segments of the direct-marketing industry. The rapid rise is the result of an incredible number of brand advertisers who have embraced the medium. These advertisers have discovered that a careful and disciplined approach to DRTV can produce impressive results.

In a first for the automotive industry, Ford of Canada used infomercials to sell F-150 series trucks. According to Dean Tesser, Ford's director of marketing, "We're challenging the status quo of what truck advertising should be. Our national campaign for the F-series truck incorporates mass media, including TV, print, outdoor, radio, online marketing, and consumer events, in addition to its first ever infomercial. We wanted to go one step further than any of our competition."

The infomercial does make Ford stand out, since it places emphasis on response mechanisms while competitors rely heavily on mass television ads. A research study in the United States conducted by Cap Gemini Ernst & Young reveals that television commercials are less influential than direct mail. In Canada, a research report by Maritz Research observed that television commercials ranked seventh among various media influences that affect consumers' car buying decisions. Given this data, automobile marketers may want to re-evaluate their media mix.

TV is primarily used to establish brand image while media such as newspapers are used to present immediate offers that encourage purchase activity. Direct-response communications can be very beneficial in maintaining communication with existing customers, and automakers are becoming aware of that fact. The Ford F-series campaign was the largest and most integrated ever undertaken by the company and it began by targeting 100 000 existing customers with a direct-mail information piece and poster announcing the launch of the F-150.

The entire campaign embraced TV, radio, newspaper, magazine, ebusiness, online, cross promotion and consumer events, and an infomercial. Uniquely Canadian creative positioned the new F-150 as the quietest, most luxurious yet "Ford tough" truck, a strategy that was in keeping with Ford's overall ad message of "Built for life in Canada."

The infomercial was created to communicate all of the truck's benefits. The 30-minute spot was loosely based on the reality TV show *Fear Factor*. The infomercial showed four participants competing in driving exercises that would be daunting if not impossible in their current trucks but effortless in the F-150. "The message was imbedded in the infomercial and that is why people tuned in," says Tesser. "It was like watching a television program." Results indicate that Ford exceeded its objectives five-fold. The most interesting result was that 50 percent of consumers who responded to the infomercial have never owned a Ford product. The creative was reaching a new consumer. So, satisfied with the results, Ford is following up with a new infomercial for the all-new 2004 Freestar minivan.

Source: Adapted from Bernadette Johnson, "Automakers rev up DM," *Strategy Direct + Interactive*, November 17, 2003, pp. 11, 12.

Ford Canada www.ford.ca

ads in travel magazines or in general-interest magazines that reach higher income households. Their ads always include a 1-800 telephone number and a website address so that prospects can obtain more information or book a vacation. Provincial governments follow a similar strategy. The print media is ideal for showing colourful pictures of local tourist attractions. Inquiring minds will get in touch for more specific information. See the ad for Prince Edward Island in Figure 11.9 for an illustration.

Another print-media alternative is the insert. An **insert** is a single- or multiple-page document inserted loosely or stitched directly into a publication. Sometimes an insert is strip-glued (a gum-like glue) directly onto a page. In these cases an advertiser usually places an ad and then attaches the insert on top of the ad. This type of insert

FIGURE 11.9

An illustration of direct-response print advertising

is referred to as a **tip-in**. See Figure 11.10 for an illustration of an insert. This Prince Edward Island insert was stitched into the magazine so that it appeared on top of the print ad that is included in Figure 11.9. Note that the government of Prince Edward Island is collecting valuable database information that can be used in future marketing efforts.

Telemarketing

Telemarketing is a booming business in North America. Much telemarketing activity is conducted at call centres. A **call centre** is a central operation from which a company operates its inbound and outbound telemarketing programs. According to a study conducted by the provincial government of British Columbia, the call-centre industry is worth $60 billion in North America and is a $15-billion industry in Canada—a quarter of the total.[9]

Canadian-based call centres are the focal point of North American operations for many companies. In fact, telemarketing is working so well that it now constitutes a leading chunk of marketers' budgets, almost double what is spent on television advertising.

FIGURE
11.10

An illustration of a direct-response insert that was distributed with a magazine ad

According to the Canadian Marketing Association (CMA), $3 billion was spent on telemarketing in 2001 compared to $1.5 billion for television advertising. The CMA states further that the $3 billion investment produced $17 billion in sales in Canada in 2001.[10]

There are two types of telemarketing: inbound and outbound. **Inbound telemarketing** refers to the reception of calls by the order desk, customer inquiry, and direct-response calls often generated through the use of toll-free 1-800 or 1-888 numbers. **Outbound telemarketing**, on the other hand, refers to calls that a company makes to customers to develop new accounts, generate sales leads, and even close a sale.

Many consumers voice displeasure with outbound telemarketing practices, citing aggressive and sometimes abusive behaviour by callers. They also object to the timing of such calls that frequently occur between 5:30 and 7:30 p.m. Such an attitude exists even though legitimate organizations are trying to contact consumers in a highly professional manner. From the marketer's perspective, the timing of the call is critical and those hours that consumers object to are the hours when a majority of consumers are at home. Marketing organizations do recognize the consumer's right to privacy and are taking steps to ensure that all government-legislated guidelines and policies are followed. As well, the CMA has self-regulating policies that organizations follow in all forms of direct-marketing practice.

Given that telemarketing is not a well-liked practice by consumers, perhaps the future success of telemarketing lies in inbound telemarketing. Organizations will have to integrate 1-800 telephone numbers into their other forms of advertising, thus encouraging consumers to make an inbound call. Alternatively, as many companies are now doing, the creation and implementation of customer-relationship management programs allow for communications with customers in a variety of formats. By communicating by telephone, mail, and the web, there is less reliance on the telephone.

The use of call centres is expected to grow because of the cost efficiencies of telemarketing. The cost of contacting a customer is so much lower than other forms of communications that marketers are willing to tolerate the negative reactions of consumers. Much like a game where the law of averages kicks in, the marketer knows that for every so many calls made, someone will respond in a favourable way. As well, if a particular offer is not being well received by consumers, the marketer can change the offer on the spot in order to make it more appealing. Such flexibility is not possible in any form of mass communications.

FIGURE
11.11

Some telemarketing
applications

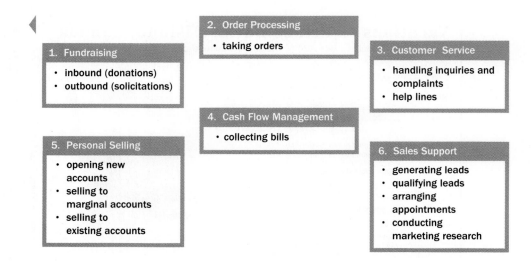

FIGURE
11.11

Some telemarketing
applications

The development of database software and phone system technology makes it cost-effective for companies to link their database to the phone. Delta Hotels, for example, has a very busy call centre in New Brunswick that services its North American operations. It receives an average of 2000 calls a day. In addition to taking reservations, the call centre provides services such as servicing its Privilege Card members, handling consumer complaints, and supporting the sales efforts of its business accounts.[11] For Delta Hotels, telemarketing plays a key role in managing customer relationships. For a list of telemarketing applications, see Figure 11.11.

As indicated above, the primary advantage of telemarketing is its ability to complete a sale for less cost than is needed to complete a sale using such techniques as face-to-face sales calls or mass advertising. However, to be effective, proper training and preparation of telemarketing representatives need to be as comprehensive as they are for personal selling. Planning the message is as important as the medium itself. For additional details, see the strategic planning discussion that follows.

The primary drawback to telemarketing is the fact that consumers react negatively to it. A survey conducted by Ernst & Young concluded that 75 percent of Canadians consider marketing calls unwelcome and intrusive; they are ranked as one of the least desirable sales techniques. Further, 51 percent of people think there are too many calls, and they react to them by hanging up.[12] Despite this behaviour, organizations see the advantages, such as call reach and frequency and cost efficiency, outweighing the disadvantages.

STRATEGIC CONSIDERATIONS FOR TELEMARKETING

For telemarketing to be effective, the nature and quality of the message must be considered in the context of the medium that will deliver the message. How important is a carefully prepared yet flexible script for a telemarketing campaign? Organizations that want to move into the telemarketing arena must take steps to ensure that they do it right. In this regard, some tried and true principles of telemarketing communications should be considered.

Telemarketers face a common problem largely due to poor telemarketing. Consumers view telemarketing as an intrusion or invasion of their privacy, hence their reluctance to accept and listen to callers. Technology, combined with an oversimplified approach at an inappropriate time, leaves people with these kinds of feelings. Successful telemarketing is a process that requires knowledge, skill, and care. Here are some of the elements of successful scripting.

- *Focus on the relationship* Selecting people with whom you have a relationship will produce higher campaign results. Telemarketing is good for securing repeat business from present customers.

- *Adjust the script approach to your audience* A well-tested verbatim script works well for marketing a simple or low-cost product. A guided or outline script is more suited to a business-product environment, where numerous unplanned objections occur.

- *Empathize with the receivers* Approach each prospect as an individual with unique needs.

- *Establish rapport and gain attention quickly* Clear identification of the caller, the company, the relationship, and the reason for the call should occur in the first sentence. Every phrase should reflect honesty and sincerity to place the recipient at ease.

- *Keep it short and simple* There is power in simplicity. Use short words and sentences. Write the script in the same way as you speak.

- *Be prepared* Practice and role-play are important before making a call. Receive feedback to fine-tune the presentation.

- *Make it easy to say yes* Structure the offer to reduce risk. Offer a free trial, discount, or return option. Show the savings and easy payment terms. Test various offers to make sure that the one selected produces the best results.

SUMMARY

Direct-response advertising is one of the largest advertising media in Canada. The major forms of direct-response advertising are direct mail, direct-response television, and telemarketing.

Direct mail is the most prominent form of direct-response advertising. A direct mailing usually includes a sales letter, leaflet or flyer, folder, and statement stuffer. Advertisers choose between solo direct mail and co-operative direct mail. Solo distribution is much more expensive than co-operative distribution.

The primary advantages of direct mail for advertisers are its audience selectivity (which makes it an excellent medium for the business advertiser), high reach potential, and geographic flexibility. Disadvantages include the absence of editorial support and poor image. The success of any direct-mail campaign largely depends on the quality of the list the advertiser uses. Lists are available from list suppliers and other secondary sources such as directories and trade indexes. Lists that are provided by brokers are rented on a cost-per-thousand basis. Canada Post is also a large supplier of information for direct-mail advertising and is the largest distributor of direct mail.

Advancing technology has spurred growth in direct-response television and telemarketing. There are two forms of direct-response television: 30-second and 60-second (or longer) commercials on cable channels, and infomercials. An infomercial is usually a 30-minute commercial that looks much like a television show. Infomercials are becoming more popular with traditional advertisers and are used to establish leads, build image, and launch new products. They are effective in communicating information that involves a lot of details or in situations where the advertiser wants to expose an audience to a lengthy list of product benefits.

Advertisers that are targeting customers based on demographic, psychographic, and geographic characteristics often place ads in newspapers and magazines. The ads include a call to action and customers can easily respond through the 1-800 telephone number or website address included in the ad. Direct-response inserts are another print-media alternative. Inserts are placed loosely in the newspaper or magazine or stitched directly into the magazine, much like a normal page. It is also common for an advertiser to place an ad and an insert in a publication at the same time.

The ad creates awareness and interest while the insert stimulates action.

There are two types of telemarketing. Inbound telemarketing refers to the reception of calls by an order desk, usually through a toll-free number. Outbound telemarketing refers to calls made by a company to customers to generate leads and even close a sale. Companies are attracted to telemarketing because of the relatively low cost. Quite simply, telemarketing is far less expensive than face-to-face communications or mass advertising. A drawback is the negative perceptions people have about this communication technique. Consumers tend to dislike the persistence of telemarketers and the timing of their calls, usually in and around the dinner hour.

The primary advantages of all forms of direct-response advertising are targeting capability and accountability. From a marketing planning perspective the impact of any direct-response offer can be measured while the communications is in progress or shortly thereafter. No form of traditional mass media has such capability. The advancement of computer and communications technology will continue to encourage much greater use of direct-response communications. Direct-response advertising will play a more prominent role in the communications mix in the future.

KEY TERMS

bounce backs   352
call centre   366
CD-ROM   352
circulation lists   360
compiled lists   360
co-operative direct mail   354
direct mail   350
direct-response advertising   350

direct-response print   350
direct-response television (DRTV)   350
inbound telemarketing   367
infomercial   363
insert   365
list broker   358
merge/purge   358

outbound telemarketing   367
postage-paid reply cards   351
response list   359
solo direct mail   353
statement stuffers   352
telemarketing   350

REVIEW QUESTIONS

1. What are the major forms of direct-response advertising?

2. Identify and briefly explain the components of a direct-mail package.

3. What is the difference between a solo direct-mail campaign and a co-operative direct-mail campaign?

4. What are the advantages and disadvantages of direct-mail advertising for a business-product advertiser (e.g., a manufacturer of business equipment)?

5. How important is the mailing list in a direct-mail campaign? Briefly explain.

6. Explain the differences between a response list, a circulation list, and a compiled list.

7. What is a list broker and what functions does a list broker perform?

8. Explain the following terms as they relate to direct-response advertising:
   a) bounce backs
   b) house list
   c) insert
   d) merge/purge
   e) infomercial
   f) inbound telemarketing versus outbound telemarketing
   g) call centre

9. What are some of the advantages and disadvantages of telemarketing for selling products and services?

DISCUSSION QUESTIONS

1. "The dollars an advertiser invests in direct-mail advertising are wasted owing to the low image of the medium." Discuss.

2. "Persistent invasion of consumer privacy will be the undoing of the direct-response advertising industry." Is this statement true or false and does it depend on the type of direct response an advertiser uses? Discuss.

3. "Direct-response television will play a more prominent role in future television advertising campaigns for traditional advertisers such as banks, automobile manufacturers, and insurance companies." Is this statement true or false? Discuss.

4. Conduct some secondary research on the DRTV business. Has the image of DRTV really changed? What companies are using this technique, and how successful have they been with it?

NOTES

1. Canadian Media Directors' Council *Media Digest* 2003–2004, p. 10.
2. John Gustavson, Keynote Address, 2003 CMA National Convention and Trade Show, April 29, 2003.
3. NCH Promotional Services Ltd., 2003.
4. Franzi Weinstein, "Short, sweet and smarter creative," *Marketing*, April 29, 1996. p. 17.
5. ICOM Information & Communications Inc., **www.i-com.com**, 2004.
6. Direct Mail Services, List Rental Data Card, Rogers Communications, 1998.
7. Costs obtained from Ziff Davis, PC magazine, **www.dmipublic/ directmedia. com/datacard/dmicards**.
8. Canadian Media Directors' Council *Media Digest*, 2002, **www.cmdc. ca/ media**.
9. Eve Lazarus, "The new call centre Mecca," *Marketing Direct*, February 12, 1001, p. 24.
10. Lesley Young, "Hanging up on telemarketing," *Marketing Direct*, August 25/September 1, 2003, p. 11.
11. "Comprehensive efforts for Delta," *Strategy*, February 19, 1996, p. 18.
12. Mary Gooderham, "Level of antipathy a wake-up call for telemarketers," *The Globe and Mail*, May 7, 1997, p. C11.

DARE TO **BREAKAWAY** AND LEAD THE CHARGE. SHOW THE WORLD HOW YOU **DANGLE** AND DANCE. IT TAKES THE RIGHT **GEAR** TO **SCORE** AND REAP THE REWARDS. AND WHEN IT ALL COMES TOGETHER, YOU WRITE YOUR OWN TICKET.

LIGHT IT UP

Login   Register

Courtesy: Nike Canada and Henderson BAS

CHAPTER

12

Internet Communications

The internet allows organizations to reach prospects in their own environment with a message that is active and interactive in nature compared to passive, traditional forms of advertising. With traditional advertising, organizations target customers, but with the internet, customers target information that is of interest to them. Control has shifted from the advertiser to the customer. The internet is a different medium; and it is a medium that all consumers are spending more time with each year. Therefore, advertisers and advertising agencies must critically evaluate how online communications will be integrated with other message and media strategies.

Interactive Advertising

In the 1950s, media planners faced the problem of determining how television would fit into the advertising world. Television was a brand-new medium that would upset the status quo for radio, newspaper, and magazines. Existing media survived the onslaught, but their share of the advertising pie would change forever. Now, advancing technology has thrust upon us another medium that is revolutionizing how companies look at advertising, and certainly how they allocate money among the various media.

Companies are exploring new forms of advertising made available by the internet and, in many cases, are adding an online component to their traditional media advertising. These new media are providing progressive companies with a means of reaching what was once thought to be an unattainable goal: a personal, one-to-one relationship with customers involving continuous interaction in the pre-transaction, transaction, and post-transaction phases of a purchase. The internet seems to offer unlimited communications potential.

Currently, advertisers and advertising agencies are struggling in terms of how to integrate internet communications with the traditional media mix. Many advertisers remain skeptical of the benefits that online communications deliver, but case study after case study reveals that the internet, combined with another medium like television, produces substantial increases in brand awareness scores, brand sponsorship associations, and message recall.

"The internet is substantially different. It's a bit of direct response, it's a bit of broadcast, it's a bit of print, and it's a bit of technology."[1] Some things do appear certain, however. First, like television in the 1950s, it will eventually play a major role in communicating information about goods and services, and such communications will result in more electronic purchasing by customers. Second, like television, the internet will not replace existing media. Instead, it will complement the communications programs that are implemented in the mass media.

The Internet

The **internet** is a network of computer networks linked together to act as one. It works just like a global mail system in which independent authorities collaborate in moving and delivering information. The **World Wide Web** is the collection of **websites** on the internet. Organizations using the internet set up a site on the World Wide Web. They might use the site to distribute information, or they can place ads on other sites that are linked to their own website. Internet users actively go to websites that interest them and browse the material for as long as they like. Unlike any other type of medium, the consumer controls whether he or she wants to see the information. Despite the consumer's control, advertisers view the internet as a cost-effective way of delivering a message.

Most websites on the internet are commercial in nature. For example, a company website delivers important information about the company and/or its products to visitors. It also provides a means of collecting information about visitors (e.g., through contests and surveys). If managed properly, the internet is one component of a database-management system. The information collected at a website can be used to identify prospects and better market products in the future. To demonstrate how important online communications are, recent research conducted by Starcom IP Syndicated Research showed that 74 percent of Canadians researched product information online, and 30 percent of those actually purchased online.[2]

While the web is primarily used for delivering information, the statistics cited above clearly indicate the need for organizations to be thinking long term and building in transaction capabilities. Once consumers and organizations adapt to the web's capabilities (e.g., accept its ability to allow consumers and vendors to communicate information and then handle orders directly online), organizations will be able to take advantage of ecommerce opportunities.

INTERNET USER PROFILE

Interactive Advertising
Bureau of Canada
www.iabcanada.com

All kinds of studies by numerous marketing research companies have been conducted to determine the profile of internet users. Needless to say, the profiles vary and they are constantly being updated. Keeping accurate track of internet usage is like keeping track of a moving target. According to a new Canadian study, *Keeping Up with the Consumer*, conducted by the Interactive Advertising Bureau of Canada, the internet ranks as the number three medium behind television and radio in terms of time spent with a medium. That information alone should make marketing organizations think about reallocating their advertising dollars. Teens, for example, are spending upwards of 15 hours a week online.[3]

A Statistics Canada survey shows that the internet is an ideal medium for reaching a target market described as male and female between the ages of 15 and 44, college or university educated, with household income of $40 000 plus, and having a slightly urban skew. The internet reaches a very desirable target market and has the capacity to reach people individually rather than collectively. It seems essential that advertisers learn how to use this medium correctly. For a more complete profile of internet users, see Figure 12.1.

FIGURE
12.1

A profile of Canadian internet users (percentage of households)

Demographic	1997	2001
All Canada*	29.0	60.2
Home Access	16.0	48.7
EDUCATION		
Less than High School	8.9	29.9
High School/College	30.6	64.6
University Degree	59.2	85.8
AGE		
Under 35	37.3	76.2
35–54	28.5	74.1
55–64	20.7	52.5
65 plus	9.3	19.3
INCOME		
$23 000 or less	12.2	31.6
$23 000–$40 000	18.0	51.8
$40 000–$70 000	32.2	70.1
$70 000 plus	53.5	87.3

* Internet access from home, work, school, public library, or some other location

Sources: Adapted from the Statistics Canada publication "Connectedness Series," Catalogue 56F004, September 2003, and from Statistics Canada CANSIM database **http://cansim2.statcan.ca**, Tables 358-0002, 358-0003, 358-0004, and 358-0005.   Adapted from the Statistics Canada publication "Canadian Social Trends," Catalogue 11-0008, Winter 2001, pp. 6 and 10.

INTERNET CULTURE AND BEHAVIOUR

The internet as the centre of the commercial universe is a long way off largely due to the attitudes and behaviours of internet users. Trends indicate that internet usage is increasing each year, but consumers are not necessarily using it to purchase goods and services. Presently, Canada is among the three countries with the highest proportion of internet users, along with the United States and South Korea.[4]

The primary activities of internet users vary by gender and age. Teenagers and young adults (20 to 24 years old) spend as much as 15 hours a week online and use the internet primarily for email, searching for information, accessing online chat services, and playing games.[5] Older age groups (45+ years) spend only about six to eight hours a week online, much less time than younger people. This group uses the internet primarily to search for product information, access online news sites, and search for health and medical information.[6] For a comparison of internet usage by various age groups, refer to Figure 12.2.

Since a primary purpose of internet usage is for online information gathering, it starts to become clear that online advertisements—assuming they are well designed, well targeted, and properly placed—will be useful tools for consumers as they engage in product research over the internet. The internet's primary purpose should be the transfer of important company and product information in a cost-effective manner. It should be viewed as a complementary medium that supports communications strategies that are implemented by traditional media. As the commercial aspects of the internet continue to expand, users will become more accustomed to online advertising, just as they have in any other medium.

FIGURE
12.2

Internet usage varies
by age category

Activity	15–17	18–19	20–24	55+
Email	72	70	70	87
Search for Information on Goods and Services	60	65	70	57
Access Chat Lines	71	63	48	—
Play Games	65	59	50	20
Access Online News Sites	36	49	52	54
Electronic Banking	4	9	18	19
Purchase Goods or Services	11	13	24	12

The survey was designed to reveal how younger age groups and older age groups use the internet.

Sources: Adapted from Michelle Roterman, "Wired young Canadians," *Canadian Social Trends*, Winter 2001, p. 6 and Cynthia Silver, "Older Surfers" *Canadian Social Trends*," Winter 2001, p. 10. Statistics Canada General Survey, 2000.

At the present time, people on the internet seem to act and respond differently than typical consumers. They tend to be information-oriented, intelligent, and have a strong sense of community. The internet represents a medium that allows them to get up-to-date information instantaneously. Details are attractive, while commercialism is not. Because of this attitude, organizations must reconsider the nature of their communications strategy. Information must be viewed somewhat as a "loss leader." It should be provided on the assumption that it will create goodwill, brand interest, and, in the future, some form of purchase.

If the primary goal is to deliver useful information, the typical internet user wants to be entertained in the process. To satisfy this need an organization should view some entertainment as useful, but it should not overshadow the information that is there to help build a business. As well, the company must learn how to present information effectively online. The rules of traditional print and broadcast advertising do not apply.

Marketing Communications Online

The internet provides access to customers all over the world and delivers information in ways that traditional print and broadcast media cannot. Traditional media are passive by nature. In contrast, communications on the internet go both ways—it is an interactive medium. The potential offered by the internet in terms of communication leaves little doubt that it will become an important medium among advertisers looking to reach large numbers of people in a cost-effective manner.

ONLINE ADVERTISING

In Canada, the investment in online advertising continues to climb. The Internet Advertising Bureau estimates that Canadian online advertising revenues for 2004 will be $200 million, representing more than a 30 percent increase from $150 million in 2003 and a more than 100 percent increase over the $97 million in 2001.[7] Despite these significant growth increases, revenues generated from online advertising remain a very small portion of all Canadian advertising revenues.

Several factors hold back organizations from doing more online advertising. First, marketers and agencies must develop more expertise with the medium in order to create effective online strategies. Second, online publishers need to stop cluttering their sites with annoying pop-ups that serve only to frustrate users, and finally, the industry must establish universal formats, rates, and measurements so that the medium can be compared with other media.

Just what is internet advertising? The internet introduces a new characteristic previously unknown to mass media, that of "interactivity." Increasingly, online advertising will employ richer interactive media, multi-faceted interactive marketing strategies, and sophisticated data collection, feedback, and targeting. For now, **online advertising** is defined as the placement of electronic communication on a website, in email, or over personal communications devices connected to the internet. While the ultimate goal of most forms of advertising is to motivate the purchase of a brand, online advertising is useful for:

- Creating brand awareness
- Stimulating interest and preference
- Providing a means to make a purchase
- Providing a means to contact an advertiser
- Acquiring data about real/potential consumers

Based on these objectives, the essential role of the internet is to communicate vital information about a company and its products. When a company quotes a website address in other forms of communications, it finds that interested buyers start to visit its site for new information. Such action could trigger an online or offline purchase. Therefore, organizations shouldn't neglect traditional forms of advertising. Very often, the best way to advertise a web-based company is through traditional media.

Advertising in the traditional media should always provide a website address and encourage customers to contact the site for additional information. While this practice is becoming commonplace, research shows that 60 percent of website visitors are there because the site was mentioned in a print ad (53 percent because of a television ad).[8]

With reference to Figure 12.3, the home page and a subsequent page for Holiday Inn, it can be seen how the hotel chain uses the internet to communicate with current and prospective customers in more complete detail than is possible in other media. From the home page, a traveller need only click on an icon of interest, for example "special offers" or "specific destinations," for more information. A customer wishing to reserve a room can do so online. If such a transaction occurs, then the loop from creating awareness and interest to making a sale is complete—all done online!

The travel industry is one that has embraced online communications and ecommerce opportunities. All hotel chains, rental car companies, and airlines now have websites that allow people to book directly. There are also many dedicated travel sites through which customers can book online. Travel is one of the top five online purchases, and it is growing fast!

As indicated earlier, however, online transactions are not yet the norm. In fact, even though dollar sales online are growing each year, the number of companies exiting ecommerce exceeds those that are entering. For every two that started selling online in 2000, five stopped.[9] There has been a lot of roadkill on the information highway! Clearly, organizations have a lot to learn about online communications and ecommerce.

THE ONLINE ADVERTISING INDUSTRY

The online advertising industry consists of sellers, buyers, advertising agencies and web design companies, and infrastructure companies. On the selling side there are website

FIGURE

12.3

Selected webpages
from Holiday Inn

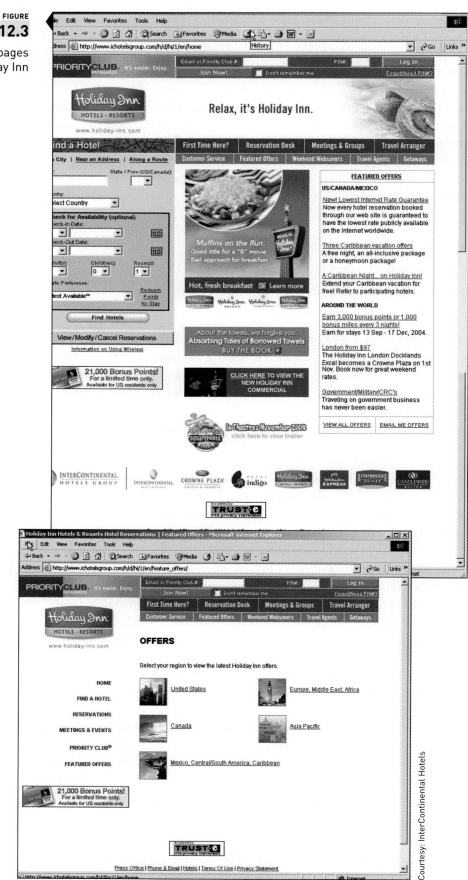

publishers that provide the content, and advertising networks that sell the media to advertisers and agencies. An **ad network** is a specialist company that represents a host of websites and serves as a sales force for participating publishers. Among the largest networks in Canada are Yahoo! Canada, Canoe, and 24/7 Canada. These sites are often the starting point of a person's online browsing session. They offer various advertising opportunities that include banner ads in a variety of shapes and sizes, rich media, sponsorships, and permission-based email.

Other popular sites for placing ads are the information and entertainment sites such as **Canada.com**, **google.ca**, and **sympatico.ca**. Television and radio websites such as **chumtv.com** and **tsn.ca** are also popular. Third party sites such as these represent targeted opportunities since they reach certain gender and age segments with frequency. The same advertising options mentioned above are available at these sites.

On the buying side there are advertisers, traditional advertising agencies, and interactive agencies. Data from the United States indicate that companies in financial services, web media, retail, telecommunications, and travel industries are among the largest advertisers using online media. The sum of all advertising efforts by companies in these industries represents approximately 75 percent of advertising impressions made online.[10]

Traditional advertising agencies have taken a cautious approach to the internet's potential, though several have ventured into the field. Consequently, boutique shops have popped up and they have pioneered online advertising. Rebellium.com, for example, a start-up in 1998, offers a deep understanding of technology that complements their marketing and creative expertise. Such a combination offers clients complete solutions for their communications needs. Among Rebellium's clients are Telus Mobility, Canon Canada, The Loyalty Group (Air Miles), and the Government of Ontario.

Infrastructure companies service the industry and provide the software tools to help publishers and advertisers deliver results through internet advertising. Key areas include traffic management, targeting and personalization, and advertising management. Today, web publishers can measure everything that occurs on a website and everything that occurs within a web ad. There are also ratings companies similar to those used in the television industry. Nielsen/NetRatings and comScore Media Metrix are leading providers of traffic measurement. Web measurement is discussed in detail later in the chapter.

Targeting and personalization are the primary advantages of online advertising. As such, targeting and personalization software companies are vital to the industry. Finally, there are companies that specialize in logistics and ad placement. Their software automatically places, rotates, reports, and bills all the required components of a web-based ad campaign.

Online Advertising Models

The internet presents a variety of opportunities to advertisers. Currently, banner advertising comprises the majority of advertising, accounting for about 58 percent of all ad revenue.[11] Unfortunately, results achieved from banner ads have been short of expectations and as a result advertisers are looking more seriously at sponsorships and email advertising. Prior to examining the basic models, some basic terminology should be understood. The terms defined below relate to how internet ads are measured for effectiveness.

- **Impressions** Also called *ad views,* these are the number of times a banner image is downloaded onto a user's computer. Impressions are the standard way of determining exposure for an ad on the web.

- *Clicks (clickthroughs)* Refers to the number of times that users click on any banner ad. Such a measurement allows an advertiser to judge the response to an ad. When viewers click the ad they are transferred to the advertiser's website or to a special page where they are encouraged to respond in some way to the ad.

- *Clickthrough rate* The percentage of ad views that result in an ad click. The percentage indicates the success of an advertiser in attracting visitors to click on their ad. For example, if during one million impressions there are 20 000 clicks on the banner, the clickthrough rate is 2 percent. The formula is clicks divided by ad impressions.

- *Visitor* A unique user of a website.

- *Visit* A sequence of page requests made by a visitor at a website. A visit is also referred to as a *session* or *browsing period* .

A site's activity is described in terms of visits and visitors, the former always being larger than the latter because of repeat visitors. A site that can report, for example, that it had eight million page views, 100 000 visitors, and 800 000 visits last month would be doing very well. It means that the average visitor returns to the site eight times each month, and views 10 pages on each visit. That's incredible **"stickiness"** (most sites don't do that well!).

BANNER ADVERTISING

A **banner ad** usually refers to third-party advertising on a website. In terms of design, banner ads stretch across a page in a narrow band; their appearance is much like that of an outdoor poster or a banner ad that stretches across the bottom of a newspaper page. This style of banner is static in nature and the content is minimal. Smaller versions of the banner (e.g., half the width, smaller rectangles and squares) are referred to as **buttons**. To improve clickthrough rates, the industry has introduced larger sizes and integrated new technologies to make the ads more interactive—that is, more tempting to click on!

Newer formats include skyscrapers, rectangles, animated banners, and interactive banners. A **skyscraper** is a tall, skinny oblong that appears at the side of a webpage. The **rectangle** is a larger box. It is not as wide as a banner but offers more depth. The thinking behind these sizes is quite simple: the bigger the better. Larger ads provide an opportunity to deliver a more complete message, even if the user doesn't click on them. Research does indicate that larger size ads do achieve higher scores for brand awareness and message association. Refer to Figure 12.4 for additional details.

FIGURE
12.4

Ad size improves scores for various advertising measures

Size of Ad	Brand Awareness	Message Association	Purchase Intent
Banner	1.8	2.4	0.2
Skyscraper	2.7	3.9	1.4
Large Rectangles	3.1	8.5	3.3

Larger rectangles seem to offer the greatest benefit. The data represent the point above the statistical baseline that helped increase the brand measure in absolute terms and are based on an aggregate of all online campaigns tested.

Source: Reprinted with permission from the January 13, 2003 issue of *Advertising Age*. Copyright Crain Communications Inc. 2003.

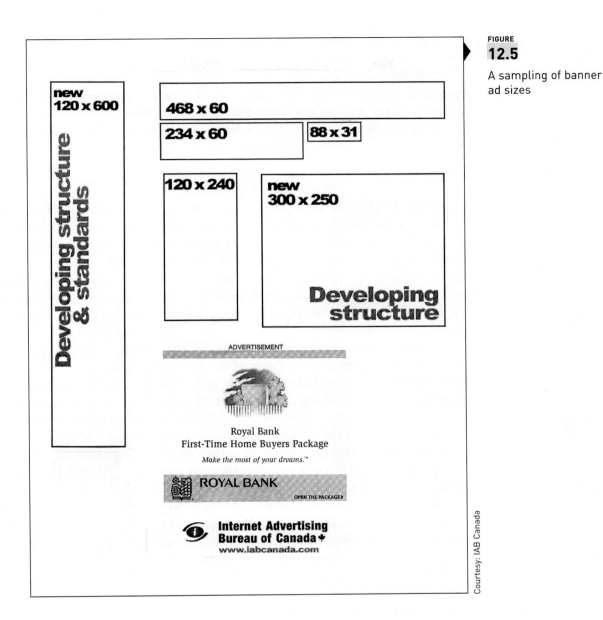

Courtesy: IAB Canada

FIGURE
12.5

A sampling of banner
ad sizes

See Figure 12.5 for some sample sizes of ads and an actual ad for Royal Bank in one of the newer sizes. Larger ads have several advantages over traditional banners. In addition to being harder to avoid for consumers, they allow advertisers to include a longer message. Even if users don't click, a full message is delivered.

The **animated banners** is the type that spins or has some form of action. It is a series of frames shown repeatedly on the screen. Animated banners are now quite popular, and their clickthrough rates are much higher than banners without animation.

INTERSTITIALS

An **interstitial** is an ad that pops onto the screen and interrupts users; this type of ad is often referred to as a "pop-up" or a "pop-under." Interstitials come in different sizes and have varying levels of interactivity, from static to animated productions. A pop-up or pop-under appears on a computer screen without warning and, therefore, does grab the user's attention.

A potential disadvantage of the interstitial is its intrusiveness. Since it is not asked for, the user could object to receiving it and view the brand negatively. So pervasive are these ads that consumers now rank pop-ups as more annoying than both spam and telemarketing. Such a high annoyance factor has led many websites to withdraw this form of online advertising for fear of losing their audiences. Consumers generally agree that advertising is necessary to support the web but suggest some guidelines are necessary to encourage proper usage of ads by advertisers.[12]

RICH MEDIA

The boom in high-speed internet service has fuelled the growth of rich media advertising. **Rich media** generally allows for greater use of interaction with animation, audio and video, and advanced tracking and measurement capabilities. Viewing such banners usually requires special software such as Flash, Shockwave, or Javascript. Ads that embrace these technologies are sometimes referred to as a **superstitial** and are the internet's version of a television commercial. This form of advertising now includes full-page "screen stealer" ads a person can't avoid, banner ads that expand when someone slides a mouse across them, and tiny icons that zip from nowhere across a screen.[13]

Streaming media involve the continuous delivery of small, compressed packets of data that are interpreted by a software player and displayed as audio or full-motion video. The similarity to television advertising makes it attractive to traditional advertisers. Rich media lends itself well to branding efforts and is ideally suited for products that require a "show and tell" element, such as cell phones. Such ads grab the viewer's attention more quickly and can deliver the message on a more emotional level.

A recent study in the United States found rich media ads are twice as effective in lifting message association and that the clickthrough rate of rich media ads is six times higher than standard banner ads.[14]

Message association was an issue for Adidas when it planned a recent online campaign. Adidas ran a streaming media video of its popular "Impossible is Nothing" television commercial featuring Muhammad Ali and daughter Laila, who is also a boxer. Over a two-week period the video prompted five million streams and created heightened brand awareness among 12- to 24-year-old consumers, a target Adidas wanted to reach. The campaign was an attempt to reach a teen audience that is dedicated to sports. Post-analysis of the online effort revealed a 75 percent lift in associating the message with the brand and a 24 percent lift in people remembering they saw the ad online. At the Yahoo! home page there was a 125 percent spike in usage of the search term "Adidas," with the highest interest among males 13 to 17 years old. Adidas was quite satisfied with the results.[15]

Adidas
www.adidas.com/ca/

SPONSORSHIPS

Sponsorships are the second most popular advertising tool (14 percent of advertising revenue in 1999) and are projected to grow in popularity. With a **sponsorship**, an advertiser commits to an extended relationship with another website. For example, a skin-care product might sponsor a weather site. Chapstick, a product associated with both hot and cold weather, does just that. Sponsorships are popular advertising opportunities at sports websites. On **TSN.ca**, for example, the various fantasy sports leagues (hockey and football pools) are sponsored by Ford trucks. Ford's slogan "Built Ford Tough" plays a prominent role on the various pages devoted to these leagues. At **ESPN.com**, Sears and Craftsman sponsor a feature called the Power Rankings, a good association for a brand name that is prominent in the power tool business. These sponsors are targeting the content based on the assumption that an audience comes to that website because they

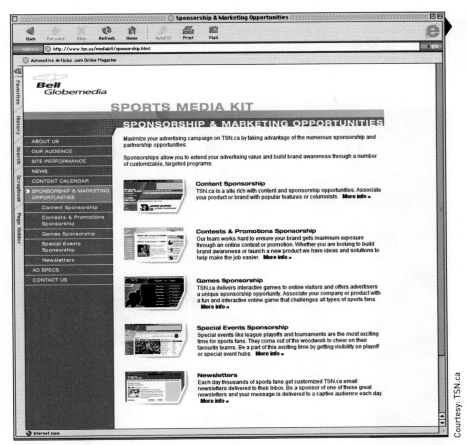

FIGURE

12.6

Sponsorship opportunities available at TSN.ca

are interested in sports. For an illustration of the sponsorship opportunities available at TSN refer to Figure 12.6.

Southwest Airlines has a multi-year agreement to be the official sponsor of the National Hockey League (NHL). This deal includes website advertising and two television spots per game on national and regional cable broadcasts. Sponsorships make up the majority of Southwest Airlines' online initiatives, and effectively support what the company is doing offline. Similar deals have been struck with the NFL, NBA, and several local teams including the San José Sharks, Phoenix Suns, and L.A. Lakers. According to Anne Murray, Southwest's director of marketing, "The outcome is a direct connection with a core population of business travelers who are largely male and who are both sports fans and travelers."[16]

Sponsorships allow an advertiser to have a successful ad campaign without necessarily having to drive traffic to its website. Consumers trust the brands that they visit repeatedly for information on the web. Therefore, a second brand (a sponsor) may be perceived more positively through the sponsorship association.

EMAIL ADVERTISING

One of the most promising applications in online advertising doesn't use flashy graphics or oversized banners. **Permission-based email**, in which a user chooses to receive messages from a particular advertiser, is growing quickly. Other commonly used terms for permission-based email include *direct email* and *email marketing*. This form of advertising is relatively inexpensive, response rates are easy to measure, and it is targeted at people who want information about certain goods and services (see Figure 12.7).

12.7

A sample of permission-
based email

An offshoot of email advertising is **sponsored email**. Many internet sites that mail information to subscribers now include a short message from a sponsor, along with a link to its website.

Email advertising is very similar to direct-mail advertising in terms of how it operates. The difference, though, is that email advertising is generating higher response rates. Unlike banner advertising in its various forms, sending sales messages by email seems quite acceptable to internet users since they agree to accept the messages (i.e., users can subscribe and unsubscribe to email advertising as they wish).

Similar to direct mail, the success of an email ad campaign depends on the quality of the list. There are two kinds of lists: a rented email list and an in-house list. The **rented list** is usually obtained from a list broker. Typically, these lists include "opt-in" names and addresses. **Opt-in** means the people on the list have agreed to receive direct email.

Email advertisements sent to lists that are not opt-in are called *spam*. **Spam** refers to the inappropriate use of a mailing list. It is unsolicited "junk" email. Spam is rapidly becoming a major problem on the internet. With so much spam being sent, consumers are frustrated. They fear participating in the collective life of the internet or withdraw or learn to conceal their email addresses as **someone@nospam.com**. More importantly, spam email destroys trust in the internet, which is what the success of a company's online marketing strategy hinges on.[17]

In the age of database marketing, the compilation of an in-house list is essential. Since all forms of advertising should invite people to visit a website, the site should include a section where people can sign up for email newsletters or email updates that

ADVERTISING IN action

Email Magic

It seems that email marketing has quite a different image among consumers compared to direct-mail marketing. Simply put, the consumers' willingness to accept sales messages via email makes it a very attractive marketing opportunity for business organizations. That's exactly what TD Waterhouse discovered with its "Score with TD Waterhouse" promotion, a joint venture with the Toronto Raptors basketball franchise.

The objective of the promotion was to leverage TD's relationship with the Raptors (TD Waterhouse was a new Raptors sponsor in 2001), and to do so in an interactive environment—apparently communicating online is the preferred environment of current customers.

Why email? TD Waterhouse is one of many companies that are flocking to email. According to a survey conducted by 24/7 Media, email is an important part of the marketing mix, with 55 percent of respondents claiming that it is "very important" in helping achieve overall marketing objectives. Further, email is one of the fastest-growing segments online. Most marketers think the internet is all about building a website, but they should be thinking email—people spend 80 percent of their online time sending and receiving emails. Sharp marketers take advantage of this behaviour!

The TD Waterhouse campaign was based on a contest promotion. Participants were given the option of receiving emails containing biweekly contest updates, notification of special offers from TD Waterhouse, and *The Raptor Insider*, a team newsletter. The promotion drew 10 000 entrants in the first two weeks: 78 percent requested contest updates, 55 percent agreed to receive TD offers, and 27 percent signed up for the newsletter. This was the start of a significant customer database.

According to D'Arcy McDonald, alliance marketing manager at TD Waterhouse, "Our objective was to bring someone who through the normal course of their day wouldn't interact with us and give them a very positive experience. If we're confident in delivering on that, that person will be more prone to consider us when it comes time to make an investment."

Cool prizes and incentives helped make the promotion a success: the grand prize was a trip for two to Orlando, Florida, for a Raptors/Magic game, three nights' hotel accommodation, $1000 spending money, and a $2500 deposit in a TD Waterhouse direct trading account.

While TD's promotion was designed to attract new customers, email marketing helps achieve other marketing objectives. In fact, its most popular use may be customer retention and customer service. And the advantages are many: it is considerably cheaper than traditional direct mail (25 cents compared to $2 for direct mail), it is more efficient, and it allows marketers unprecedented interaction with customers.

In comparison to banner ads, where click rates on average are less than 1 percent, and direct mail, where response rates average 1 to 3 percent, the industry average response for permission-based email—as opposed to spam—is estimated at 11 percent. As well, feedback can be received within 48 hours. With email, advertisers can tell if it was opened, how long it was read, and if it was forwarded to someone else. It offers unprecedented measurability. Clearly, marketers not into email advertising will have to reconsider their position, and soon!

Source: Adapted from Chris Powell, "The Magic in E-mail Marketing," *Digital Marketing*, April 23, 2001, pp. 10, 11.

TD Waterhouse www.tdwaterhouse.com
Toronto Raptors www.nba.com/raptors

could announce the introduction of new products. Online promotions such as contests provide another opportunity to secure email addresses. Sending email to customers and prospects that specifically request the mail will almost always work better than using a rented list. In accordance with internet etiquette, in-house lists should not be rented to another organization—"permission rented is permission lost." The concern for privacy is always an issue in internet marketing. For more insight into email advertising, see the Advertising in Action vignette **Email Magic**.

COMPANY WEBSITES

Traditional forms of advertising can tell a story but not necessarily the complete story. The size of a page or the amount of time available are often restricting factors. Therefore, traditional media combined with effective website content gives an advertiser ample opportunity to tell the whole story. It is now very common for advertisers to include their website address in all forms of marketing communications. An American study indicates that 60 percent of website visitors are there because the site was mentioned in a print ad and 53 percent because of a television ad.[18]

To demonstrate how traditional media and websites can be combined, consider the nature of automobile advertising. Typically, automobile makers show unique and vivid visual images of their latest makes and models in television ads and glossy print ads. These ads project image but do little in terms of telling potential buyers about design and technical specifications. That task is best suited to the website.

Toyota Canada, for example, recently overhauled its website in order to accommodate the needs of its visitors. Toyota's goal was to tap into the consumer's online information-gathering process. According to David Brinson, national manager for PR and marketing, "Consumers now arrive at showrooms with an almost predestined vision of what they want. We have to provide them the best knowledge and information to help them make decisions." Toyota's design and communications strategy was structured to flow logically with the consumer's thought process when shopping. After the "Welcome to Toyota" introduction, consumers move to model offerings, then to information areas such as safety and how to choose a colour, then to a car configuration page, and finally to a price quote and financing information.[19] Refer to the illustration in Figure 12.8 for details.

Marketing research conducted by the Internet Advertising Bureau shows that media combinations that include television, print, and websites generate higher awareness and preference scores than just television and print. Colgate-Palmolive now reveals that online communications are the most cost-effective means of reaching 18- to 49-year-olds for Colgate Total toothpaste. The brand altered its media mix by increasing the online component from 7 percent to 11 percent of the budget. Television advertising was reduced from 78 percent to 74 percent of the budget. Colgate believes it generated higher preference scores in a more economical manner with this mix.[20]

Volkswagen is an example of another company that places high value on web-based communications. For insight into their latest online communications, read the Advertising in Action vignette **Research Leads to New Volkswagen Site**.

Volkswagen Canada
www.vw.ca

TEXT MESSAGING

Text messaging (also called **short message service** or SMS) is the transmission of text-only messages on wireless devices such as cell phones. Cell phones today are used for more than just phone calls. People are playing games, taking pictures, and sending them to people all over the world. Teens and young adults have been attracted to text messaging because of its portability and low cost. To them, email is too slow—kids want instant messaging, whether using their cell phones or online chat services such as ICQ. Text messaging is already enabled on most cell phones in Canada purchased within the past few years.

Labatt Blue is on the leading edge of text-message technology and was the first to launch a nationwide campaign in Canada. The campaign was a pilot project for the wireless communications industry and, if successful, could clear the way for full commercialization of text-message campaigns. The Labatt Blue text message campaign asked users to text message the word "play" to the special six-digit number "24-blue" (242583) to sign up and play "Labatt Blue's Cup Crazy Trivia Challenge." Players receive

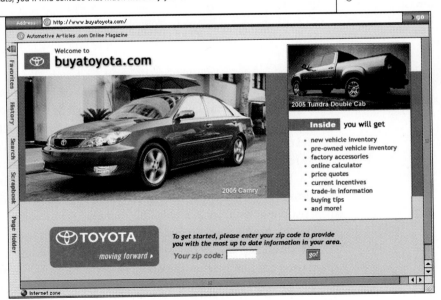

FIGURE
12.8
Toyota places high priority on web-based communica- tions: Print ads create an image and web-based com- munications provide details

TOYOTA
the feeling never ends

Shy

Toyota Corolla. Everyone feels different.

You're the type that likes to keep to yourself. Crowds aren't exactly your style. So it's nice to have a 130 horsepower ULEV VVT-i engine to help take you away from it all. And with ample interior space, 6-speaker CD stereo, wood-grain trim and available leather seats, you'll find solitude that much more enjoyable.

2004 Corolla LE

Address http://www.buyatoyota.com/   go

Automotive Articles .com Online Magazine

Welcome to
buyatoyota.com

2005 Tundra Double Cab

Inside you will get

- new vehicle inventory
- pre-owned vehicle inventory
- factory accessories
- online calculator
- price quotes
- current incentives
- trade-in information
- buying tips
- and more!

2005 Camry

TOYOTA
moving forward ▸

To get started, please enter your zip code to provide you with the most up to date information in your area.

Your zip code: go!

Internet zone

Research Leads to New Volkswagen Site

In 2002, Volkswagen discovered that 82 percent of new vehicle purchasers in North America visited the manufacturer's website before buying and that consumers often visited the manufacturer's site a year ahead of the purchase. That information had a direct impact on the nature and content of Volkswagen's web-based communications.

Volkswagen already had a good North American site, **VW.com**, but was able to identify some basic cultural differences between English Canadian and American consumers. As a result, a new site, **VW.ca**, was introduced.

According to Tesa Aragones, ebusiness leader for Volkswagen America, "Canadian Internet customers' usage was growing more quickly than that of United States customers and there are cultural things we can take advantage of to help those customers connect to the VW brand in a relevant way." For example, lifestyle promotions involving skiing, music, and film sponsorships that are uniquely Canadian justify the new English-language site. A French-language site that serves Quebec consumers already exists.

The company's tracking of customer behaviour showed that Canadian leads submitted through **VW.com** were up 30 percent in 2003 (at the French site leads were up a staggering 60 percent). The closing ratio (people who submit leads and then proceed to an actual purchase) was 30 percent, much higher than any other medium where tracking is possible. Apparently, 15 percent of Volkswagen's total sales volume in North America can be matched back to people who submit leads online.

The new **VW.ca** site was designed from the ground up to function effectively as a research tool and information source. Volkswagen even lists competitor models so consumers can make comparisons immediately. "It's an extremely shrewd move on Volkswagen's part to establish trust and credibility with consumers," says Geoff Linton, marketing professor at Conestoga College. Having lots of competitive information makes comparisons easy and it saves the consumer valuable time in the information-gathering process.

Once the consumer has built their vehicle at the website they are encouraged to visit a dealer for a price quote. The experiential nature of the site is bound to impress potential buyers and, from that experience alone, consumers will form a favourable impression of Volkswagen. From a design perspective, some observers say it is the automotive equivalent of Apple computers: sleek, stylish, and hip. Now let's see what impact it has on sales!

Source: Adapted from Samson Okalow, "Volkswagen launches English Canadian site," *Strategy*, May 3, 2004, p. 12.

---

three NHL Stanley Cup trivia questions each week for six weeks and can message back the answers from a multiple-choice list. The goal of the campaign was to connect Blue drinkers with their brand, as well as introduce the brand's website, **labattblue.ca**.[21]

Text messaging has been enthusiastically adopted by teens and young adults who are largely responsible for its explosive growth. The possibilities for using text messaging seem endless. For example, advertisers could use it to offer instant, personalized messages to target customers provided they have information about what the customer wants along with their cell phone number. A retailer, for example, that develops an opt-in phone list could send out electronic coupons and notices about special sales or other promotions.

In advancing this communications model the industry must be mindful of the spam problem that plagues the online advertising world. Adverse reactions from wireless subscribers can be anticipated if text-message marketing becomes a new avenue of aggravation for consumers.

Audience Measurement

As with other media, accurate measurement is very important if the internet is to attract advertisers. The web is more accurate at capturing measurement information than any other medium, largely due to the technology that is built into it. Without being overly technical, web measurement comes from information that is captured by the computer housing a website—the server. In other words, an internet service provider (ISP), such as Yahoo, Sympatico, or Microsoft, captures information about users through an internet protocol address. Every computer has an internet protocol (IP) address in numeric code that uniquely identifies a particular computer on the internet. The codes are dynamically assigned by the ISP each time a computer logs on.

The information that is captured can be accumulated and then used to compile data about usage: page views, number of unique visitors, number of visits, and how long each visit lasted. Many companies have their own servers and can determine the effectiveness of their communications efforts by analyzing the data in their web server's log files. Several third-party research organizations audit the information and publish data that can be used by advertisers to better plan campaigns.

The collection of accurate information is enhanced by the placement of *cookies* in a user's personal computer. A **cookie** is an electronic identification tag sent from a web server to a browser to track a person's browsing patterns. The irony of cookies is that users agree to accept them while giving up private information about how they use the internet. The average person does not understand what cookies are or how they are used. People often object to cookies—they believe they are an invasion of privacy. To ease the mind somewhat, it must be pointed out that a cookie cannot link information directly to an individual because the cookie is nothing more than a numeric text file. All tracking is done numerically. Cookies usually reside in a computer's hard drive, and the owner can delete them if they wish.

The acceptance of cookies allows a website to be personalized to the user's experience. For example, if a user configures a "My Yahoo!" page, it is a cookie that allows the server to remember the user's preferences. Most users want the benefits of personalization, and once they understand the cookie's function they have no objection.

AUDITING WEBSITE TRAFFIC

In addition to web usage data provided by individual websites, independent third parties provide information about web usage. Being independent, these parties legitimize the internet as an advertising medium by providing reasonably accurate estimates of traffic at a website. Similar organizations exist for other media and advertisers are accustomed to the data they provide. To determine which sites to advertise on, a potential advertiser will want to know how many people visit a prospective site and how often they visit. For advertisers already using a particular site, an audit will determine how much traffic there is to a particular ad (e.g., how many impressions there were and what the clickthrough rate was).

A variety of organizations are involved in web measurement in Canada. Nielsen/NetRatings is a partnership between Nielsen Media Research, ACNielsen, and NetRatings Inc. Nielsen Media Research is a pioneer in audience measurement in the broadcast media and NetRatings offers proprietary measurement software. Another measurement company, comScore Media Metrix, provides monthly reporting on the digital media. Both companies provide data about online media usage, visitor demographics, and online buying power. Such information is useful for planning, buying, and selling internet-based advertising.

Nielsen Net Ratings
www.nielsen-netratings.com

comScore
www.comscore.com

The Internet as an Advertising Medium

The internet offers numerous advantages and disadvantages. Thus far, the internet has offered high expectations but, being a new medium, the lack of experience among advertisers and their agencies has been a problem. As time progresses and everyone gains more experience the true benefits of the internet will be realized.

ADVANTAGES OF THE INTERNET

TARGETING CAPABILITY   Since the internet is based on technology, advertisers have a new range of targeting capabilities. As discussed in the previous section, a person's browsing behaviour and personal preferences can be recorded by inserting cookies on a hard drive. Once one's preferences are known, an advertiser can target the individual with ads that are of potential interest. Significant database information is available to companies that want to pursue direct-marketing and advertising opportunities online. In effect, internet advertising is a convergence of traditional advertising with direct marketing (see Figure 12.9).

TRACKING AND ACCOUNTABILITY   Advertisers can track how internet users interact with their brands while learning what they are interested in. Advertisers can get timely, detailed reports on the success of their campaign. Some email marketing campaign tools allow a company to watch for results in real time. Banner ads can be tracked the next day—with detailed numbers of impressions and clickthroughs. Many websites that sell advertising provide these detailed reports to clients online. Using software such as DoubleClick's DART, a client can log in at any time and view the reports up to the previous day. Such measures gauge the effectiveness of the advertising investment. These measurements are difficult—if not impossible—to generate for traditional media.

A company can also track how often a user visits and how that visitor moves through its own website. The type of information that a user wants can be recorded and used for marketing purposes at a later date (e.g., permission-based email opportunities).

TIMING   The internet doesn't sleep—messages can be delivered 24 hours a day, 7 days a week, 365 days a year. As well, the content of a campaign can be changed at a moment's notice if need be. Technology allows for constant monitoring of a campaign for success or failure, so changes, updates, or cancellations can be made much more quickly than in any other medium.

INTERACTIVITY AND ACTION   Internet users like to be entertained along the way. That being the case, companies have an opportunity to interact with prospects and customers and develop more meaningful relationships with them. Users tend to return often to sites they enjoy. Therefore, appropriate interaction and providing information that makes a visit worthwhile can produce sufficient motivation for a prospect or cus-

FIGURE 12.9

Online advertising is the convergence of traditional advertising and direct marketing

Traditional advertising through the mass media delivers messages to create awareness and interest in a product. Direct marketing sends out an offer and allows a customer to buy goods directly from the source. Online advertising does both if websites accommodate ecommerce opportunities.

tomer to make an online purchase. No other medium can move a consumer from awareness to action as easily as the internet can. Specific software is available that allows organizations to pursue customer-relationship management objectives.

DISADVANTAGES OF THE INTERNET

SELECTIVE REACH

As indicated earlier in the chapter, the internet remains the domain of a middle- to upper-class market in terms of availability and frequency of use. While more than half of Canadians have access to the internet, the majority do not yet perceive the internet as a medium for advertising and commerce, though perceptions are gradually changing. The internet is primarily used for email and collecting information. For the internet to be an effective advertising medium it must be more readily available to the masses, and perceptions regarding its commercialism must change. Both will occur with the passing of time.

CONSUMER FRUSTRATION

Consumers are starting to feel frustrated, even harassed, by the constant barrage of unsolicited emails and the presence of pop-up ads that arrive unexpectedly. Advertisers who persist in using these practices will ultimately suffer the wrath of frustrated consumers. It is not inconceivable that consumers will spend less time online or use the internet only for selective purposes in the future. This perception is in sharp contrast to the industry's notion that email marketing will become one of the most commercial internet applications.

PRIVACY CONCERNS

Consumers are very concerned about how information about them is collected and used by marketing and advertising organizations. While the internet has the capability of taking a consumer from awareness to action (purchase), the transfer of credit card information is the most widely cited reason for resisting online purchases. It is a situation where consumers' perceptions override reality. The consumer whose credit card is stolen or misused is not responsible for paying for unauthorized charges. The Canadian Bankers Association says it is no more dangerous to use a credit card online than it is to use it anywhere else.

Consumers perceive a loss of privacy, since access to many sites involves complex registration procedures. With registration, customers give up information about themselves that can be used for marketing purposes at a later date.

Internet Advertising Rates and Buying Media Space

Several different advertising models are available. Traditional advertisers are accustomed to gross rating points and verified cost per thousand (CPM) comparisons before making critical media decisions. Attempts to use CPM figures on the internet have created some controversy, but they remain the most popular model. Other pricing models include *pay for performance* and *flat fees*.

CPM MODEL

CPM is the price charged for displaying an ad one thousand times. Advertisers and agencies tend to be comfortable with this model since it is the same as that used by traditional advertising media. The calculation for CPM is cost divided by impressions (number of impressions divided by 1000). For online advertising, an organization pays a rate for every 1000 impressions made. Therefore, if the total number of impressions was 500 000 and the CPM was $40.00, the total cost of the advertising campaign would be $20 000 (500 000 impressions / 1000) × $40.00.

CPM rates vary based on the level of targeting desired by the advertiser, and they range anywhere from $10.00 to $100.00. The options include *run of site, run of category,* and *keyword targeting.* With reference to the rate card for **Canada.com** shown in Figure 12.10, if the run of site or run of network is selected the rates charged are those quoted for the various sizes and styles of advertising for ads that will appear anywhere on the website. For example, a banner ad costs $13/M and a skyscraper ad costs $20/M. If targeting requests are applied, a 10 percent premium is charged for each targeted request. Volume discounts are also available based on the total dollar value of advertising purchased. To demonstrate, consider the following buying example:

EXAMPLE 1

Type of Ad:	Banner
Impressions Desired:	2 000 000
CPM:	$13.00
Cost Calculation:	(2 000 000/1 000) × $13 = $26 000

In this example the advertiser earns a 5 percent discount, so the net cost would be $24 700 ($26 000 × .95).

EXAMPLE 2

Type of Ad:	Skyscraper
Impressions Desired:	1 500 000
CPM:	$20.00
One target request:	+10%
Cost Calculation:	(1 500 000/1 000) × $20 × 1.10 = $33 000

In this example the advertiser earns a 10 percent volume discount, so the net cost would be $29 700 ($33 000 × .90).

CPM rate cards vary from one site to another, but rest assured the busier sites in terms of traffic charge a higher CPM for all of the options that are available. Popular sites such as Canoe, Sympatico.ca, Yahoo!, and various sports and media sites (TSN, The Score, *The Globe and Mail*, etc.) attract significant traffic and price their CPMs accordingly.

While these rates are the rates quoted, the reality of the situation is quite similar to offline advertising. CPM rates are negotiable and depend on factors such as length of the campaign, season, and relationship between client and vendor. Effective negotiation skills in the media-buying process could result in lower CPM rates.

PAY-FOR-PERFORMANCE MODEL

Advertisers must remember that the purpose of the banner is to stir initial interest so that the viewer clicks the ad for more information. Once clicked, the viewer sees the ad in its entirety, usually via a link to the advertiser's home page. Since clicking is the desired action, many advertisers feel they should pay on the basis of cost-per-click instead of CPM. The benefit of such a system is clear: the advertiser knows from the start what the internet campaign will cost per click.

This system tends to devalue advertising and punish the website financially if the ad does not attract an audience. In the offline advertising world, the media are not responsible for an action being taken. That is left to the message! Web publishers should not be treated differently than offline publishers.

FIGURE

12.10

Online advertising rate card
for Canada.com

BANNERS: $13 CPM

- 468 × 60 pixels/GIF format and rich media
- Placement: Headers on all pages of Canada.com

BUTTONS: $10 CPM

- 120 × 90/GIF format
- Placement: near right hand top of most Second Level pages

SKYSCRAPERS: $20 CPM

- 120 × 240, 120 × 600, or 160 × 600 pixels
- GIF format and Rich Media
- Placement: fourth column

POP-UP AND POP-UNDER WINDOWS: $35 CPM

- File size limits: GIF format—15K/Rich Media formats—15K initial download/25K in total
- Placement: Available on most Canada.com pages

INTERSTITIALS AND SUPERSTITIALS: $60 CPM

- All pricing based on run of network rotation

TARGETED REQUESTS

- A 10% premium is charged for each applied target specification

VOLUME DISCOUNTS

$15 000–$25 000 5%

$25 000–$50 000 10%

$50 000–$75 000 12%

$75 000–$100 000 15%

$100 000+ 20%

Source: Adapted from CanWest Media Sales, a division of CanWest Interactive Inc., **Canada.com/aboutus/advertising/rate_ card.html** (June 2003).

If the success of an ad is based on the clickthrough rate, then many current campaigns are not doing very well. In fact, latest industry surveys peg the average click rate at about 0.5 percent. The quality of the creative (e.g., its cleverness, its animation), along with a certain degree of targeting, can improve the clickthrough rate. As stated earlier in the chapter, clickthrough rates for rich media advertising are much higher than for static banner ads.

From a publisher's perspective the clickthrough system has several drawbacks. First, the publisher has to rely on the quality of the advertiser's message (the banner) for advertising revenue. If it does not stimulate clicks it will not generate revenues for the website. The job of the media is to offer access to an audience, not to share in the responsibility for the quality of the advertising itself. Second, such a model discounts completely what a banner can do to build brand image. There has to be an advertising cost associated with this benefit. To date, advertising rates based on clickthroughs are the exception rather than the rule.

FLAT-FEE MODEL

Some websites charge a flat fee for advertising—typically, a set amount for the length of time the ad appears on the site. Sponsorships, for example, are usually sold on a flat-rate basis rather than on the number of impressions. The *Maclean's* website, for example, charges $1000 net per week (net means the agency commission has been deducted) for one banner at the top of the home page with two rotations. Rates on other pages of the site are lower.[22] Fee structures vary from one site to another. Lower traffic sites are more likely to use the flat-fee system.

Strategic Considerations for Internet Advertising

In assessing the potential of advertising on the internet, a company must understand that it is a medium capable of dramatically expanding the type and nature of information about the company and its products. The challenge of internet communications is to draw potential consumers into a website, hold their attention, develop a relationship with them, and subtly move them to a transaction. Given the nature of the internet user discussed in this chapter and the nature of the medium itself, it is imperative that visitors to a site feel that they have gained from the experience. Since the medium is so new, a company cannot refer to a list of tried-and-true principles for successful internet advertising. However, on this learn-as-you-go journey, and based on limited experience thus far, communications companies have identified some basic principles of interactive communications:[23]

1. *The consumer perspective is paramount* Sites developed from a company perspective (e.g., let us tell them what we want them to know), rather than a consumer perspective, inevitably fail.
2. *The consumer is in control* The internet is all about browsing and finding new experiences. The challenge is to let the visitor come away with something of benefit (information or the product itself).
3. *Entice consumers with experience* Attempts must be made to draw the viewer into the content. Consumers must want to have the experience and must want to go out looking for it.
4. *Integrate experience, content, and corporate messages* Unlike television, there is opportunity to attach meaningful corporate information to the advertising message. By doing so, a better and stronger company image is created.
5. *It's an active medium* To keep consumers returning, it is important to constantly change, update, and evolve the internet site.
6. *Listen and respond to consumers* Visitors provide a company with information. A company can track what items they are most interested in, and even how to reach them in the future. Gathering and analyzing this information is crucial to improving the site.
7. *Encourage two-way communication* The integration of email and fast response times is key to building a successful relationship with consumers.
8. *Design for transaction* While commerce on the internet is in its infancy, a company should be transaction-ready. Like all forms of marketing, the ultimate goal is to make a sale.

SUMMARY

Companies are turning away from traditional advertising media such as television and newspapers and toward direct-response and interactive communications. The internet appears to be a strong media alternative for the future.

The key elements of the internet are email and World Wide Web sites. Both are efficient ways to communicate information. Currently, the internet is widely used for information purposes, but advertisers are finding that the online advertising when combined with other media produces substantial increases in brand awareness and brand sponsorship associations. Internet users tend to be younger, highly educated, and earn above-average incomes. These demographics make them an attractive target for advertisers.

Advertisers must tread carefully so as not to offend users. Unlike traditional media, the challenge for advertisers is to create interesting interactive communications without alienating users. Information is somewhat of a loss leader, but the provision of good information will create goodwill, brand interest, and in the longer term lead to an online or offline purchase.

The online advertising industry is composed of sellers, buyers, and infrastructure companies. On the buying side are advertisers and advertising agencies. The selling side embraces a host of large independent websites along with advertising networks that represent a host of smaller websites. Web measurement is an important and controversial aspect of the internet. In this area, independent third-party companies such as Nielsen/NetRatings and comScore Media Metrix provide audited data that assists advertisers and agencies in planning advertising campaigns. Data compiled by these and other research organizations legitimize the internet as an advertising medium.

In terms of advertising, organizations purchase banner ads on various websites. They may also take advantage of sponsorship opportunities or advertising on third-party sites. The intent of a banner ad is to stimulate just enough interest so that the viewer clicks the ad for more information. When clicked, the viewer is transferred to the advertiser's website for more details. Banner ads are available in a variety of standard sizes. Larger size banner ads have proven to be more effective than smaller ones. Many advertisers have moved to rich media, the internet's version of television advertising. With rich media the ads are streamed to a person's computer and are displayed as audio or full-motion video.

Sponsorships are another advertising option. With a sponsorship the advertiser commits to an extended stay at a particular website and perhaps sponsors a unique feature of the site. Sponsorships are quite popular on sports and business websites. Permission-based email also represents significant opportunities for advertisers. Using opt-in mailing lists and lists generated from in-house databases, email represents a cost-effective way to reach prospects and current customers. Advertisers must be wary of consumers' frustration with spam, the receiving of unwanted junk email.

As an advertising medium, the internet offers targeting capability at a very reasonable cost and tracking capabilities that measure effectiveness of campaigns in a variety of ways (clicks, leads, and purchases). As well, the interactive nature of the medium provides an environment that fosters the building of solid relationships with customers. The fact that the internet is open 24/7 means that an advertiser's message is always at hand. Some drawbacks of the internet include selective reach (higher-educated and higher-income groups are the main users), consumers' frustration with unwanted email and pop-up ads that appear on screens, and the perception among users that advertisers are invading their privacy.

Online advertising rates are typically quoted on a cost-per-thousand impressions basis. Other options include cost per clickthrough and flat fees. Currently, the CPM pricing model is the model used most frequently by websites and online advertising networks.

KEY TERMS

REVIEW QUESTIONS

1. What characteristics make the internet user different from users of traditional media?

2. In terms of communications, what is the primary role of the internet? What strategies should a potential advertiser apply when communicating with an internet user?

3. Explain the following terms as they relate to advertising on the internet:
   a) click
   b) clickthrough rate
   c) ad network
   d) impression
   e) visit

4. What is banner advertising and how does it work?

5. Identify and briefly explain the various types of banner ads.

6. What is an interstitial and what are the basic benefits of this form of online communications?

7. Briefly explain how an online advertising sponsorship works.

8. Briefly explain the following internet communications terms:
   a) permission-based email
   b) opt-in
   c) spam

9. What is a cookie and how does it work?

10. Identify and briefly explain two advantages and two disadvantages of internet-based advertising.

11. What is the CPM pricing model and how does it work? What factors influence the price charged in the CPM model?

12. If the CPM is $30.00 and the banner ad campaign achieves 1.5 million impressions, what is the total cost of the campaign?

13. If the total cost for a banner campaign was $30 000 and the impressions generated total 1.2 million, what is the CPM for the campaign?

14. How is a pay-for-performance advertising model different from the CPM model? What are the drawbacks for the web publisher if the pay-for-performance model is used?

DISCUSSION QUESTIONS

1. What is your opinion about advertising on a website? Will it play an expanding role in the communications mix in the future? If so, what media will suffer? Defend your position.

2. "Persistent invasions of consumer privacy will be the undoing of internet-based advertising." Is this statement true or false? Conduct some secondary research online to update the status of this issue. Report on your findings.

3. Visit the Yahoo! website or another portal website of your choosing and type a few keywords in the search box. Use general search terms such as *finance, hockey, music, movies,* and so on. Do the ads on the search results page seem targeted in any way and are they linked to the keyword? Report on your findings.

4. The receipt of spam and the presence of pop-up ads on computer screens were presented as key issues that consumers object to. Conduct some online secondary research to update the position of consumers and advertisers on these issues. Will spam and pop-ups continue to be a problem in the future? Report on your findings.

NOTES

1. Bernadette Johnson, "Advertisers revisiting the Web: Study," *Strategy*, February 12, 2001, pp. 1, 14.

2. Samson Okalow, "Marketers retool sites to explore Web research boom," *Strategy*, May 3, 2004, p. 11.

3. Samantha Yaffe, "Are marketers undervaluing the Internet?" *Strategy Media*, March 8, 2004, p. 1.

4. Ibid., p. 6.

5. Michelle Rotermann, "Wired young Canadians," *Canadian Social Trends*, Winter 2001, pp. 4–7.

6. Cynthia Silver, "Older surfers," *Canadian Social Trends*, Winter 2001, pp. 9–12.

7. Samantha Yaffe, "Are marketers undervaluing the Internet?" *Strategy Media*, March 8, 2004, p. 1.

8. "Information still killer app on the net," *Advertising Age*, October 6, 1997, p. 48.

9. "Big corps dominate online sales," *Digital Marketing*, April 2001, p. 2.

10. Nielsen/Net Ratings, **www.nielsen-netratings.com/news**.

11. Canadian Media Directors' Council *Media Digest*, 2002–2003, p. 53.

12. Pete Blackshaw, "Pull the plug on pop-ups," *Advertising Age*, November 3, 2003, p. 24.

13. Shelley Emling, "Rich media ads on Internet fuel recovery," *Financial Post*, June 16, 2003, p. FP24.

14. Risa Goldberg, "It's not just about buttons and banners anymore," *Dynamic Logic: Beyond the Click*, February 19, 2004, **www. dynamiclogic. com/beyond_0602.php**.

15. Kris Oser, "Adidas mines possibilities with Web effort," *Advertising Age*, May 3, 2004, p. 79.

16. Sara Wilson, "Southwest flies far with sponsorships," *Imedia Connection*, November 10, 2003, **www.imediaconnection.com/content/features.111**.

17. John Gustavson, "Can the spam," *Marketing Direct*, April 7, 2003, p. 13.

18. Kate Maddox, "Information still killer app on the net," *Advertising Age*, October 6, 1997, p. 48.

19. Samson Okalow, "Marketers retool sites to exploit Web research boom," *Strategy*, May 3, 2004, p. 11.

20. Tobi Elkin, "Net advantages," *Advertising Age*, February 10, 2003, p. 29.

21. Kristin Goff, "The latest annoyance: Spam on your cell phone," *Edmonton Journal, Calgary Herald,* and *Ottawa Citizen*, May 1, 2003, **www.n5r. com/articles/article_68.asp**.

22. *Maclean's* Online Media Kit, **www.macleansmediakit.com/home.html**, November 2003.

23. John Long, "Online and onside," *Marketing*, May 15, 1995, p. 16.

CHAPTER

13

Sales Promotion

This chapter examines the various sales promotion activities that are often integrated into a marketing communications program or marketing program. In the context of marketing communications planning, the manager must evaluate the contribution that sales promotion activity will make to the achievement of overall objectives. Assuming sales promotions are a worthwhile strategy, decisions are made regarding the types of promotions to implement. For example, some promotions are good at achieving trial purchase while other promotions are good at achieving multiple purchases or for building brand loyalty.

Initial discussion reviews the nature and intent of promotion activity in general. The various types of consumer promotion and trade promotion activities are presented, followed by a discussion of how sales promotions are integrated with other marketing communications strategies.

Sales Promotion

Sales promotion can be defined as activity that provides special incentives to bring about immediate response from consumers, distributors, and an organization's sales force; in other words, it encourages the decision to buy. Sales promotion plans are developed with three groups in mind. The *consumer*, or final user, must be motivated to take advantage of the promotion offer. The *distributor* must actively support the promotion to achieve its goals—greater volume of sales, higher profit margins, inventory movement, and so on. Finally, the *sales force* must be motivated to sell the promotion to the trade at the wholesale and retail levels, in order to make the promotion work successfully for the firm.

Sales promotion activity can be subdivided into two broad categories: consumer promotions and trade promotions. **Consumer promotions** refer to those activities that are designed to stimulate consumer purchase, in effect to help pull the product through the distribution channel. Common types of consumer promotion activities include coupons, free sample offers, contests, cash-back offers, and a variety of frequent-buyer (loyalty) programs. **Trade promotions** refer to those activities designed to encourage distributors to purchase additional volume and provide additional support to stimulate consumer purchase. In effect, trade promotions help push the product through the distribution channel. Common types of trade promotion activities include price discounts and allowances, co-operative advertising funds, and point-of-purchase display materials.

SALES PROMOTION PLANNING Promotion planning relies on input from the overall marketing plan—specifically, the marketing objectives and strategies. The sales promotion plan can be developed by the advertising agency, but more often a specialist agency does it. Regardless of who develops the plan, there is a direct relationship between advertising and sales promotion. Traditional thinking meant that the advertising agency created a national advertising campaign to position the product or service in the marketplace while the promotion plan complemented the advertising: it helped create demand for the product, encouraged trial purchase, and/or built loyalty through repeat purchase incentives. Today, however, the buzz is about integrated marketing. Therefore, sales promotions are not viewed as separate entities. They are planned at the same time to ensure that synergies are achieved across all forms of communications.

PROMOTION OBJECTIVES

Like other elements of the marketing mix, promotion activity must complement the total marketing effort. Thus, each element of the mix is assigned a goal based on what it is capable of contributing to the overall plans. As with other plans, promotion objectives should be realistically achievable, quantitative in nature (for measurement purposes), directed at a carefully defined target, and capable of being evaluated and modified when necessary.

It should be noted that the objectives for consumer promotions and trade promotions are quite different, but they complement each other when implemented. Objectives of consumer promotions focus on achieving *trial purchase* and *repeat or multiple purchases* and *building brand loyalty*. Trade promotions focus on *selling more volume* of merchandise and encouraging *merchandising support* among channel members that buy and resell products. These objectives are examined in detail in appropriate sections of this chapter.

PROMOTION STRATEGY

Promotion strategy focuses on the selection of the best promotion activity to meet the objectives. There are two basic types of promotion strategy: *pull* and *push*.

In a **pull strategy**, the organization creates demand by directing promotional efforts at consumers or final users of a product. Pull strategies tend to rely on a mixture of media advertising and consumer promotion activities. These activities cause consumers to search for the product in stores; by asking for the product, they can put pressure on the retailer to carry it. The promotion activities considered include coupons, samples, contests, and premiums.

In a **push strategy**, the organization creates demand for a product by directing promotional efforts at intermediaries, who in turn promote the product among consumers. Push strategies tend to rely on a mixture of personal selling and trade promotion techniques to create demand. These trade promotions include a variety of financial incentives referred to as listing allowances, performances, and co-operative advertising allowances. For a visual impression of the concept of pull and push promotion strategies refer to Figure 13.1.

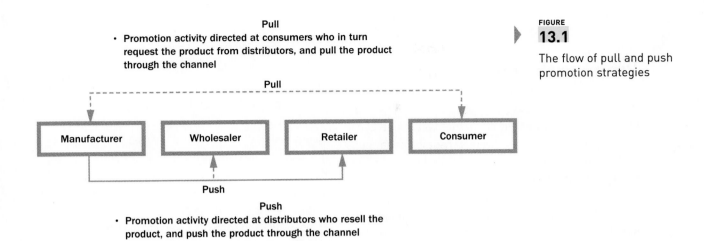

FIGURE
13.1

The flow of pull and push promotion strategies

Most firms feel that attention must be given to both final users and channel members; thus, it is very common for firms to combine push and pull promotion strategies. Companies such as Kraft Canada, Colgate-Palmolive, Apple, and IBM all advertise their products heavily to end users while their sales force sells the products among business customers or channel members using a combination of trade promotion and personal selling. For a promotion to succeed it must be advertised to create awareness; the promotional message must be integrated with long-term message strategies that focus on building a brand's image. Having a great promotional concept is just the start of a promotion plan. For more insight into the need for effective integration with other forms of marketing communications see the Advertising in Action vignette **Promote the Promotion!**

Kraft
www.kraftcanada.com

Consumer Promotion Planning

Consumer promotion is any activity that promotes extra brand sales by offering the consumer an incentive over and above the product's inherent benefits. It is designed to pull the product through the channel by encouraging consumers to take immediate purchase action. The most common objective of consumer promotion activity is to have the consumer make a *trial purchase*. In the case of a new product, the marketer is concerned that the initial trial and consumer acceptance of the product occur quickly. Even when a product is firmly established on the market, marketers will still attempt to secure trial purchase by non-users (see Figure 13.2).

A second objective of consumer promotion activity is to *protect loyalty* by offering incentives that encourage repeat purchase. For example, a coupon distributed via the product itself is a good vehicle for maintaining customer loyalty—a reward for patronage. Current customers are also very likely to use media-delivered coupons for products they normally purchase, in order to save money. Since the purchasers are already "sold" on the product's benefits alone, they view the coupon as an added bonus.

A third objective of consumer promotion activity is to encourage *multiple purchases*. Promotions fulfilling this objective are designed to "load up the customer" or "take customers out of the market" for a time. A well-conceived contest that encourages multiple entries, a cash refund whose value increases with the number of purchases made, or a coupon that stipulates a certain number of purchases are examples of promotions that will achieve the multiple purchase objective. Refer to Figure 13.3 for an illustration.

Promote the Promotion!

Without integration big ideas go absolutely nowhere. Marketers must invest in ideas that will shape consumer perception and motivate consumer behaviour. In the context of sales promotions the big idea must be something the sales force can sell, the trade will display, and the consumer will respond to.

Kraft Canada's recent back-to-school promotion met the criteria. Their value-rich offer was simple: "Every Pack Wins Crayola." The promotion brought Kraft and Binney & Smith (the maker of Crayola) together in a powerhouse promotion that also leveraged Kraft's relationship with YTV. The heart of the promotion was a school bus display made out of preformed cardboard that was filled with Kraft products featuring images of Crayola products. The uniqueness and impact of the display helped secure valuable floor space in stores.

The "Every Pack Wins Crayola" offer was easy for consumers to understand as all details were carefully explained by point-of-purchase material and on the packages of 29 different Kraft and Christie products. The sheer size, uniqueness, and complexity of the in-store displays were a real attention-grabber.

Kraft and Crayola made excellent partners. Kraft food products that were ideally suited for younger age groups were the primary products in the promotion (e.g., Kraft Peanut Butter, Oreo cookies, and Ritz crackers, to name just a few). Crayola benefited from an image boost in grocery stores, and the affiliation with Kraft provided an opportunity to showcase some of their new products.

The trade was impressed by the quality of the point-of-purchase materials, including the giant school bus. They responded favourably by allowing huge displays of Kraft products. YTV offered custom television spots, online support, and promotion announcements in numerous programs.

While all participants benefited from the promotion, consumers were the ultimate winners. The cost of their purchases was offset with free Crayola products.

Source: Adapted from Matthew Diamond, "Leveraging the Big Idea, *Marketing*, October 6/13, 2003, p. 34.

Crayola www.crayola.com/canada/index.cfm

FIGURE
13.2

A consumer promotion that encourages trial purchase

Courtesy: Nestle Canada

FIGURE
13.3

A coupon offer (financial incentive) that encourages consumers to make multiple purchases

Types of Consumer Promotion Activity

The major types of consumer promotion activities implemented in Canada include coupons, free sample distribution, contests such as sweepstakes or instant wins, cash rebates, premiums, frequent-buyer or loyalty programs, and delayed payment incentives. A survey conducted by NCH Promotional Services among packaged-goods companies (i.e., food, household goods, personal care products, and pet food manufacturers) revealed that 77 percent of the manufacturers viewed coupons as their most important form of consumer promotion activity. Following in order of importance were sampling, contests, cash refunds, and premiums.

COUPONS

Coupons are price-saving incentives offered to consumers to stimulate quicker purchase of a designated product. The array of products and services that use coupons is endless. Coupons are used to discount the price of movie and theatre tickets, to lower the price of restaurant meals, and to encourage purchase of a brand of breakfast cereal. Marketing organizations use coupons more frequently than any other type of consumer promotion. In 2003, the latest year that statistics are available, companies in the packaged-goods industry alone distributed a total of 2.6 billion coupons in Canada. A total of 97 million coupons for consumer-packaged-goods items were redeemed by consumers for a total savings on goods purchased of $105 million. The average value of a redeemed coupon is $1.08.[1] The most recent trends in coupon distribution and redemption among packaged-goods manufacturers are outlined in Figure 13.4.

OBJECTIVES OF COUPON PROGRAMS   The traditional objectives associated with coupon promotions are to get non–brand users to make a trial purchase of a brand, to maintain current users, to speed up acceptance of a new product, and to encourage current customers to repurchase the brand (build loyalty). Coupons also help to attract users of competitive brands, encourage multiple purchases, and increase seasonal sales.

How effective are coupons in achieving these objectives? In a report on coupon usage issued by Nielsen Promotional Services in 2003, it was found that 86 percent of households used coupons within the past year, 65 percent stated that they had used at least one coupon during the last month, and 36 percent of all households used at least one coupon in the last week.[2] Coupons are a resource that households refer to when planning shopping trips. These statistics tend to uphold the view that coupons are an excellent promotion if the marketer's objective is trial or repeat purchase. The Nielsen

Characteristic	2001	2003
Quantity Distributed	2.67 billion	2.60 billion
Quantity Redeemed	122 million	97 million
Average Face Value Coupons Distributed	$1.25	$1.23
Average Face Value Coupons Redeemed	$1.05	$1.08
Consumer Savings	$128 million	$105 million

Source: Resolve Corporation, formerly NCH Promotional Services Ltd., 2004.

study also provided some interesting regional information. Apparently, Quebec grocery shoppers use coupons more frequently. Coupons are also redeemed by all levels of society regardless of factors such as age, income, and ethnic background.

The stage the product has reached in its life cycle also has an impact on the objectives of a coupon promotion. When a product is in the introduction and growth stages, trial purchase is the marketer's main objective, so media-delivered coupons are popular. As the product moves into maturity and marketers become concerned with repeat purchase by current customers, they attempt to defend their consumer franchise by means of product-delivered coupons. If an objective is still to attract competitive-brand users (which is important, even at the mature stage), media-delivered coupons remain necessary. Coupons delivered in stores will encourage trial purchase and repeat purchase (brand loyalty). See Figure 13.5 for further insight into consumers and coupon usage.

METHODS OF COUPON DISTRIBUTION Coupons can be delivered to consumers in four different ways: by the product, by the media, in-store at the point of purchase, and electronically.

FIGURE
13.5

The power of a coupon

Never underestimate the impact of a coupon offer. It is a tried-and-true promotion device that definitely achieves certain marketing objectives. Further, Canadian households use them frequently, as evidenced by the number of coupons distributed and redeemed annually. Here are a few important facts about coupons:

1. The most common objective of a coupon offer is to increase product and brand usage. Getting trial purchase, encouraging brand switching, and inducing immediate purchase are less important.
2. In a fiercely competitive marketplace, coupons give consumers a reason to buy a national brand instead of a private-label brand.
3. Nine out of ten households use coupons: 70% of Canadian households have used coupons in the past month.
4. Coupons are used more frequently in households that have 3+ members and a household income of $30 000+. The use of coupons increases with age.
5. On average, 50% of consumers in the past three months were influenced by a coupon to buy a brand that they would not have bought without a coupon.

Source: Wayne Mouland, NCH Promotional Services, "85% of Consumers Used Coupons Last Year," press release, March 2001.

Product-delivered coupons appear in or on the package. One kind of product-delivered coupon, the *in-pack self-coupon*, is redeemable on the next purchase of the same product. The package is usually "flagged" somehow to draw attention to the coupon included inside the package. An *on-pack self-coupon* usually appears on the back or side panel of the package and is valid for a future purchase of the same product. An **instantly redeemable coupon** is valued when the product carrying the coupon is bought and the coupon is removed from the package. Another variation is the **cross-ruff** (or cross-coupon), an in-pack or on-pack coupon valid for the purchase of a different product. Tetley used such a tactic when it packed product information and a trial coupon for a new line of specialty teas in regular packages of tea. Refer to Figure 13.6 for an illustration. Such coupons also encourage the consumer to buy complementary products. For example, a tea or coffee brand may carry coupons for a brand of cookies, and vice versa.

Media-delivered coupons are coupons distributed through a newspaper, magazine, co-operative direct-mail package, or by an online source. The Shop & Save envelope or the Val-Pak envelope received by households are examples of a co-operative direct-mail package; they are delivered numerous times each year and contain coupons for a range of non-competing products.

Savvy shoppers now look to online sources for valuable money-saving coupons. A consumer can select specific goods and services, survey the discounts offered, and then print the coupons off. **Save.ca** offers Canadian packaged-goods marketers the opportunity to provide coupons online. According to Wayne Mouland, vice-president of NCH Promotional Services and a leading expert on coupon trends in Canada, "Online coupons are the fastest growing method of coupon distribution but they only account for 1 percent of all coupons distributed and redeemed."[3] See Figure 13.7 for an illustration.

FIGURE
13.6

A cross-coupon offer. Harvest Crunch offers a coupon for Chewy Granola and Tide offers a coupon for Bounce

Sample of an online-generated coupon

Among media-delivered coupons, the **freestanding insert (FSI)** is the most popular method of placing coupons directly in the homes of consumers. A freestanding insert (FSI) is a preprinted advertisement in single or multiple-page form that is inserted loose into newspapers. Distribution statistics reveal that 65 percent of all direct-to-consumer coupons are distributed by FSIs.[4] Free-standing inserts are marketed by distribution organizations that use such names as "The Coupon Clipper" and "Shop and Save."

The category of **in-store-delivered coupons** includes coupons distributed by in-store display centres and dispensing machines usually located near the store entrance, on the shelves via shelf pads (the consumer tears off a coupon that can be redeemed instantly), or by handout as the customer enters the store.

In recent years, **electronic coupons** distributed by supermarket loyalty cards have increased in popularity with leading chain stores. Such coupons eliminate the need for consumers to clip coupons and, because the discounts are registered by the swipe of a card, the consumer doesn't even think about the discounts they are getting. Such coupons negate the purposes of a coupon, which are to generate excitement and competition among brands, encourage new consumers, or re-interest those who have gone to another brand.[5]

A benefit of electronic coupon cards is that retailers and manufacturers know who the customer is (the customer signed up for the card), so an incredible database is developed that can be used in future relationship-marketing programs.

COUPON REDEMPTION BY MEDIA The **redemption rate** is the number of coupons returned to the manufacturer expressed as a percentage of total distributed coupons. With reference to the figures that appear in Figure 13.8, there is clearly a consumer preference for in-store coupons. The statistical information in Figure 13.8 shows that in-

Media	Range	Average
FSI	0.1–1.8%	0.6%
In-Store	1.2–32.7%	9.8%
In/On Pack	0.3–51.4%	6.1%
Direct Mail Addressed	1.9–22.6%	6.5%
Direct Mail Unaddressed	0.1–3.3%	1.2%
Magazine	0.1–7.0%	0.8%
Charity	0.5–28.5%	16.9%
Other	0.3–30.6%	2.7%
Internet	0.3–14.9%	3.9%

Source: Resolve Corporation, formerly NCH Promotional Services Ltd., 2003.

FIGURE
13.8

Average redemption rates by method of delivery

store coupons (those that are instantly redeemable) have the highest average redemption rates (an average of 9.8 percent) among coupon offers.

The impact of delivering coupons by direct mail should not be underestimated. As the statistics in Figure 13.8 indicate, the average redemption rate for addressed direct mail is 6.5 percent and unaddressed direct mail 1.2 percent, compared to magazines at 1.0 percent. Since both media distribute coupons to generate trial purchases, it can be observed that direct mail does a better job than magazines. Redemption rates for newspaper and magazine coupons are relatively low compared with redemption rates for coupons distributed by other methods.

The method of delivery is only one factor that influences the rate of redemption for a coupon promotion. Other factors that play a major role are the face value of the coupon and the consumer's perception of the value of the discount offered by the coupon in relation to the price of the product.

COUPON COST AND REVENUE CALCULATIONS The costs of a coupon promotion should be monitored closely by the marketing organization. A variety of factors have an impact on the total costs of a coupon promotion: the method of distribution, which affects delivery costs and redemption costs; the printing costs; the handling costs for the retailer and clearing house (the latter being the agent responsible for redeeming coupons, paying retailers, and reporting redemption and cost information to the marketing organization); and the coupon's face value.

The marketer should weigh the costs of a coupon promotion against the potential revenues to ensure that a positive financial payout will result from the activity. The difference between revenues and costs would be the return on investment. The costs associated with a coupon offer include the monetary value of the coupon, distribution, printing, redemption, and handling fees. Retailers and a central clearing house such as Nielsen Promotional Services receive handling fees. Revenues can be estimated based on the value of the product sold by the manufacturer multiplied by the number of purchases generated by the coupon offer. Figure 13.9 illustrates in detail how to evaluate the financial payout of a coupon offer.

The revenue calculation also considers the misredemption of coupons. A coupon is misredeemed if it was not used to purchase the product, but was sent to the clearing house anyway—this is a common occurrence in the industry. The illustration in Figure 13.9 considers a misredemption rate of 20 percent (80 percent are redeemed on an actual purchase).

FIGURE
13.9

Evaluating the financial
impact of a coupon offer

Coupon Promotion Plan	
Face Value of Coupon	$1.00
Handling Charge for Retailer	$0.15
Handling Charge for Clearing House	$0.05
Distribution Cost (direct mail)	$16.00/M
Distribution	3 million households
Printing Cost (digest size ad with coupon)	$8.00/M
Redemption Rate	2.5%
Retail Price of Product (Manufacturer receives 65% of retail price when distributors' mark-ups are deducted)	$4.49

The cost and revenue calculations are as follows:

Costs	Cost Calculation	Total	Grand Total
Distribution	3 000 000 × $16/M	$48 000	
Printing	3 000 000 × $8/M	$24 000	
Coupon Redemption	3 000 000 × .025 × $1.20	$90 000	
Total Cost		**$162 000**	**$162 000**

Revenues	Revenue Calculation	Total	Grand Total
Per Unit of Revenue	$4.49 × .65	$2.92	
Total Revenue	3 000 000 × .025 × 0.80 × $2.92	**$175 200**	**$175 200**
Return on Investment			**$13 200**

Note: A misredemption rate of 20% is included above, hence the 0.80 factor in the revenue calculation.

FREE SAMPLES

A **free sample** is a free product distributed to potential users either in a small trial size or in its regular size. Sampling is considered to be the most effective method of generating trial purchase, as it eliminates a consumer's initial financial risk. Therefore, it is commonly practised when a company is introducing a new product or a line extension of an existing product (e.g., a new flavour if it is a food product). Unlike any other type of promotion, sampling is the only alternative that can convert a trial user to a regular user solely on the basis of product satisfaction.

The most frequently used method of sample distribution is in-store. There are several variations on in-store sampling: product demonstrations and sampling in stores, saleable sample sizes (small replica pack sizes of the actual product), and cross sampling. **Cross sampling** refers to an arrangement whereby one product carries a sample of another product (e.g., a regular-sized box of Cheerios cereal carries a small sample package of Lucky Charms cereal). The popularity of one brand is used to secure the trial usage of a less popular brand.

Other alternatives for delivering free samples include co-operative direct mail (provided the sample is small and light enough to be accommodated by the mailing envelope), home delivery by private organizations, event sampling, and, finally, by sample packs that are distributed to specific target markets. Several companies specialize in the distribution of samples in Canada.

Sampling programs tend to be an expensive proposition for the marketing organization because of the product, packaging, and distribution costs. In spite of these costs, sample promotions rank second in popularity among marketers, so clearly the potential long-term benefits outweigh the short-term costs. Further, sampling combined with a coupon is the best way to gain trial and convert trial to immediate purchase. On the downside, a sample is the fastest and surest way to kill an inferior product.[6] See Figure 13.10 for an example of a product sample offer.

Companies are discovering new ways of delivering samples while at the same time generating positive publicity for the brand involved in the promotion. Some refer to it as **on-site sampling**; others call it **experiential marketing**. Regardless of what it is called, it involves potential customers interacting directly with the product. Lady Speed Stick used experiential marketing to help dramatize a unique selling point—the brand doesn't leave white residue on clothing. Rollerblading females would weave their way through downtown streets wearing T-shirts that read "Tired of white residue." Arrows pointed to the corners of their shirt where perspiration marks form. Curious pedestrians were shown

Courtesy: Unilever Canada

FIGURE
13.10

Free sample offers distributed directly to households

Colgate-Palmolive Canada
www.colgate.ca

Nike
www.nike.com/canada

how lady Speed Stick does not leave residue and were given a sample of the product. According to Carolyn Thompson, product manager at Colgate-Palmolive Canada, "The sampling program was innovative, interactive, and the action—rollerblading and gliding—induces perspiration and ties nicely to the sub-brand name."[7]

Nike has also been successful with experiential marketing. In a venture called the Nike Trial Van, a van loaded with shoes makes pit stops at running events in Toronto and Vancouver where interested consumers can try on a pair of shoes (as many as 15 different styles are available). Runners can take them for a test run for as long as they like. Nike expects tens of thousands of consumers to be exposed to the promotion. This type of promotion is an attempt by Nike to rebuild market share from the grassroots level. The Trial Van reaches the hard-core customer who is unimpressed with flashy advertising.[8]

CONTESTS

Contests are designed and implemented to create temporary excitement about a product. The structure of a contest usually entails incentives for consumers to purchase; entrance often requires, for example, submission of a label or product symbol (or facsimile) and an entry form. Consumers are encouraged to enter as often as possible, resulting in multiple purchases by many consumers.

As a marketing vehicle, contests tend to attract the current users of a product but are less effective in inducing trial purchases than are coupons and samples. Consequently, contests are most appropriate in the mature stage of the product life cycle, when the aim is to retain present market share. *Sweepstakes* and *instant wins* are two major types of contests.

A **sweepstakes** contest is a chance promotion involving a giveaway of products and services of value to randomly selected participants who have submitted qualified entries. Prizes such as cash, cars, homes, and vacations are given away. Consumers enter contests by filling in an entry form, usually available at point-of-purchase or through print advertising, and submitting it along with a proof of purchase to a central location where a draw is held to determine winners. The odds of winning depend on the number of entries received. Usually, an independent organization selects the winners on behalf of the sponsor company.

A **game (or instant win)** contest is a promotion vehicle that includes a number of predetermined, pre-seeded winning tickets, in the overall fixed universe of tickets. Packages containing winning certificates are redeemed for prizes. Variations of this type of contest include collect-and-wins, match-and-wins, and small instant-wins combined with a grand prize contest. Restaurants such as McDonald's and Tim Hortons use this promotion vehicle frequently. McDonald's runs a game fashioned after the board game Monopoly, and Tim Hortons offers "RRRoll Up the Rim to Win" every spring.

Contests are governed by laws and regulations, and any company that runs one must publish the following information: how, where, and when to enter; who is eligible to enter the contest; the prize structure, value, and number of prizes; the odds of winning and the selection procedure; and conditions that must be met before a prize can be accepted (e.g., a skill-testing question must be answered).

A contest requires a significant investment in media advertising. In effect, the focal point of a brand's advertising switches from the product to the contest in an attempt to build excitement for the brand. To create awareness for the contest, a multimedia mix is frequently used (e.g., broadcast media to generate excitement and print media to communicate details). Point-of-purchase advertising is essential. It is common for entry forms to be available at point-of-purchase or at a website.

Because of consumer involvement, contests are usually well received and supported by the retail trade; indeed, they are often launched with trade promotion programs to encourage feature pricing and maximize display activity at retail. As can be seen by the illustration in Figure 13.11, Canada Dry is celebrating 100 years of Canadian refreshment with a contest offer. Canada Dry supported the promotion with print advertising, point-of-purchase advertising, and online communications.

Gillette is a company that uses contests frequently. They see contests as an ideal promotion offer that is useful for a cross-section of brands. Since the same customer is buying many Gillette brands (razors, shaving cream, deodorants) it makes sense to include numerous brands in the contest. All participating brands share the costs of the contest. An illustration of a fairly recent Gillette contest appears in Figure 13.12. The contest is targeted at both male and female customers and the prizes have a family orientation.

The success of a contest depends on the consumer's perception of the value and number of prizes to be awarded and of the odds of winning. Contest prizes should also match the image of the product (e.g., a quality product must offer quality prizes). In terms of

Canada Dry
www.canadadry.com

FIGURE
13.11

A print ad announcing Canada Dry's "Refreshing Escape" contest

FIGURE

13.12

Point-of-purchase advertising creates awareness for a Gillette multi-product contest

attracting participation, automobiles generate the highest number of entries, but vacations and trips are the prizes most offered by sponsoring companies. When designing a contest, the marketer must consider the above factors and must either develop a high-value grand prize that will attract attention and create excitement (as in the case of the Gillette contest cited above) or have prizes of less value awarded frequently to compensate for the disappointment factor associated with most contests ("I'll enter, but who ever wins?").

Tim Hortons runs one of the most popular and successful promotions in Canada—an instant-win promotion. For insight into its promotion activities, read the Advertising in Action vignette **RRRoll Up the Rim**.

CASH REFUNDS (REBATES)

A **cash refund**, or **rebate** as it is often called, is a predetermined amount of money returned directly to the consumer by the manufacturer after the purchase has been made. It is a reward for buying a product within the promotion period. For packaged-goods companies, cash refunds are a useful promotion technique in the mature stage of the product life cycle; they effectively reinforce loyalty by tempting consumers to make multiple purchases.

The most common type of refund is the single-purchase refund, in which a consumer receives a portion of his or her money back for the purchase of a specified product. However, refunds are designed to achieve different objectives; hence, they can be offered in different formats. Refunds encourage consumers to make multiple purchases and stock their pantries. For example, the value of a refund may escalate with the number of items purchased; hence, the consumer is encouraged to make multiple purchases. An offer could be structured as follows: buy one and get $1.00 back; buy two and get $2.00 back; and buy three and get $5.00 back.

In refund offers where multiple purchases are necessary, slippage generally occurs. **Slippage** happens when a consumer starts collecting proofs of purchase for a refund

RRRoll Up the Rim

How do you know when you have a successful promotion? Perhaps it's when the *Royal Canadian Air Farce* comedy troupe spoofs the idea on television. It's proof that you've worked your way into the cultural fabric of Canada. And that's what happened with the Tim Hortons "Roll Up the Rim" promotion. Like the call of the loon, "RRRoll up the rim to win" has hit the airwaves for 17 consecutive springs.

The promotion began in 1987 as a way to boost coffee sales during the summer, but it has evolved into a national obsession that draws customers to the doughnut shops year after year, win or lose. Customers are powerless to resist the temptation of winning something as small as a doughnut or muffin or as large as a colour television, bicycle, or automobile.

According to Ron Buist, director of marketing services at TDL Group (the corporate name for Tim Hortons), one of the keys to success is the KISS principle: "Keep it simple, and whenever possible, silly too. We want it to be fun, and most of all we want it to be easy to play." This promotion proves that a simple idea coupled with a memorable advertising slogan can generate a huge payoff for a company. The company won't discuss sales figures, but one Ontario franchisee says business climbs by 10 to 15 percent during the promotion.

It was a radio spot developed in 1993 featuring an actor with a thick Scottish accent rolling the letter R in the slogan that really got the ball rolling (pardon the pun). The ad drew a few complaints about how it was stereotyping Scots, but it also launched the slogan into the psyches of consumers. The Scottish accent has been dropped, but the rolling R remains in all forms of advertising.

The "Rrroll Up the Rim" promotion demonstrates the application of some important planning variables. To have a chance at being successful, a promotion contest should be easy to play, deliver a consistent theme, and include a catchy and memorable phrase. The advantage of having this kind of long-running promotion is self-evident. It becomes less of a promotion than a brand unto itself. "Roll Up the Rim" has become recognized as its own entity, much as a product would.

"Roll Up the Rim" is a well-known promotion, but each year it receives significant media advertising support to ensure success. A combination of television and radio advertising creates awareness and interest and drives traffic to the stores. Point-of-purchase material provides more details in the stores.

Sources: Adapted from Laura Pratt, "Roll Up the Rim major player for Tim Hortons," *Strategy*, May 22, 2000, p. 22; Liza Finlay, "Perpetual promos," *Marketing*, May 31, 1999, pp. 11–12; and John Heinzl, "Tim Hortons rrrolls up a winner," *The Globe and Mail*, March 24, 1999, p. B29.

offer, but neglects to follow through and submit a request for the refund. In effect, the manufacturer does not pay for the purchases induced by the promotion. Slippage is a significant factor. In a survey of grocery shoppers, it was found that one-half of all refund participants sometimes neglect to submit a request for a refund even after they have bought the product with the intention of using the refund offer.[9]

Strategically, refund offers for packaged goods items should be advertised at point-of-purchase (a retail store), since it is the optimum time when consumers make brand purchase decisions. Ad pads are the medium most frequently used for advertising refund offers on consumer goods. Print media, particularly newspaper, is the medium most often used for promoting manufacturers' rebates on durable goods.

Rebates accomplish such objectives as the liquidation of inventory prior to the introduction of new models and the generation of sales during traditionally weak periods or at times when interest rates on loans are high. Offers of $1000 or $2000 back are quite common in the automobile industry when the economy takes a bit of a downward spin and new cars aren't selling.

PREMIUM OFFERS

A **premium** is an item offered free or at a bargain price to encourage consumers to buy a specific product. The goal of a premium offer is to provide added value to new and repeat purchasers. McDonald's and other fast-food restaurants consistently use premiums because they are effective with its primary target (families) and they reinforce the company's goal of offering value to consumers. Recently, fast-food restaurants have focused their premium efforts on characters from popular movies. McDonald's, for example, has a 10-year promotion agreement with Disney to distribute toy characters. It is part of its never-ending battle to be the preferred choice among young customers.

Premiums are usually offered to consumers in three ways: either as a mail-in (e.g., send in proofs of purchase and the item will be returned by mail), as an in-pack or on-pack promotion (e.g., an item is placed inside a package or attached to a package), or by a coupon offer distributed by in-store shelf talkers. Distributing premiums with a product is popular as it provides instant gratification. Refer to Figure 13.13 for an illustration.

FIGURE
13.13

A package-delivered premium offer influences decisions at point of purchase

Courtesy: Dick Hemingway

In recent years beer and alcohol companies have embraced premiums. Bob Chant, director of public relations with Labatt, says "Giveaways are increasingly important. They are an ongoing element of our marketing mix." Lately, Labatt and Molson have been in a battle over which company offers the best value-added proposition to customers. To entice purchases the beer companies have offered free miniature Stanley Cups, T-shirts with appropriate brand logos, baseball caps with brand logos, extra bottles of beer, golf balls, and on and on it goes. A recent Molson Canadian in-case promotion offered Ontario drinkers a one-in-five chance of winning Roots watches, wallets, and vests, an example of how creative, and extravagant, giveaways have become.[10]

The use of premiums achieves several objectives: they increase the quantity of brand purchases made by consumers; they help to retain current users; and they provide a merchandising tool to encourage display activity in stores. A good premium offer enhances differentiation between similar competing products.

LOYALTY (FREQUENT-BUYER) PROGRAMS

Canadian retailers and various service industries such as airlines, credit cards, and hotels have made frequent-buyer or loyalty programs popular. A **loyalty program (frequent-buyer program)** offers consumers a small bonus, such as points or "play money," when they make a purchase. The bonus accumulates with each new purchase. The goal of such an offer is to encourage consumer loyalty, and that's what a program like Shoppers Drug Mart's Optimum rewards program does. In this program, shoppers accumulate points that are redeemable on future purchases. The card is an integral component of Shoppers' new customer-relationship-management program. Shoppers can electronically cross-reference transaction data and tailor offers and services to specific customers in-store or by email. The company already has more than one million email addresses in its database.[11]

Starbucks recently unveiled a dual-use credit card in conjunction with Visa that allows customers to earn a percentage of each transaction toward the purchase of food, beverages, and merchandise at its stores. Customers using the card receive 1 percent back in "Duetto Dollars" that can be redeemed in stores. Starbucks believes the incentive will entice customers to visit stores more often. Unlike some rewards programs that take an eternity to accumulate points, the Starbucks proposition is almost instantaneous.[12]

Canadian Tire's program is, perhaps, the best-known and longest-running (over 47 years) frequent-buyer program in Canada. It rewards regular shoppers who pay for merchandise with cash or a Canadian Tire credit card with Canadian Tire "money" worth up to 5 percent of the value of the purchase. Canadian Tire now allows customers to collect virtual money on the company's house credit card, its website, and its affiliate MasterCard. Canadian Tire money captures the essence of a rewards program because customers really can purchase something for free.

DELAYED PAYMENT INCENTIVES

In a **delayed payment incentive** promotion, a consumer is granted a grace period during which he or she pays no interest or principal for the item purchased. Once the purchase is made from the retailer, a finance company assumes the agreement and charges interest if full payment is not made by the agreed-upon date.

Leon's Furniture pioneered the delayed payment concept in Canada with promotions called the "Don't Pay a Cent Event" and the "No Money Miracle." From Leon's' perspective, this kind of incentive is but one part of an overall package that includes

Starbucks
www.starbucks.com

Canadian Tire Money
www2.canadiantire.ca/
CTenglish/ctmoney.html

A combination offer; coupon and contest offer encourage trial and repeat purchases

good value, good prices, and wide selection. Other retailers such as The Brick and Future Shop offer similar incentives periodically during the year. Even automobile manufacturers will entice consumers with delayed payments during seasonal slow periods. The combination of low financing rates, cash rebates, and no payments for three months are compelling reasons to buy a car . . . now!

COMBINATION OFFERS

To maximize the effectiveness of a promotion, marketers often combine the consumer promotion techniques discussed in this chapter. For example, it is quite common to combine a trial coupon offer with a premium or contest promotion. The coupon will get the initial purchase and the premium or contest will encourage repeat or multiple purchases. See Figure 13.14 for an illustration of a combination offer.

Goals	Coupons	Sampling	Refunds	Contests	Premiums
To generate trial on existing products	*	*			
To gain trial on new products	*	*			
To speed acceptance and first purchase of a new product by consumers	* *	* *	*		
To encourage multiple purchase of a new product and pantry loading	*		* *		*
To encourage repurchase among current users	*		*	*	*
To provide an extra tool to the sales force	*	*	*	*	*
To increase seasonal sales	*				
To help gain extra listings	*	*			
To help gain off-shelf product displays	*	*		* *	
To increase advertising effectiveness	*		*	* *	*
To add excitement and focus to in-store displays				*	
To focus brand advertising at specific target groups				*	*

Source: Wayne Mouland. NCH Promotional Services Ltd.

FIGURE
13.15

Consumer promotions best suited for achieving specific objectives

For a comparison of sampling and other promotion techniques that are best suited for achieving specific goals, see Figure 13.15.

Trade Promotion Planning

Trade promotion is promotional activity directed at distributors to push a product through the channel of distribution; it is designed to increase the volume purchased and encourage merchandising support for a manufacturer's product. For any new product, the objective of trade promotion activity is to *secure a listing* with distributors (wholesale and retail). A **listing** is defined as an agreement made by a wholesaler to distribute a manufacturer's product to the retailers it supplies. If, for example, the head office of Sobeys or A&P agrees to purchase a specific product, then it is available to all Sobeys and A&P retail stores. To secure a listing, manufacturers will offer distributors a combination of trade allowances and co-operative advertising allowances, which will cover the costs of the listing, of obtaining distribution, and possibly of selling the product at a special introductory price.

A second objective of trade promotions is to *build volume*, either on a seasonal basis or on a preplanned cyclical basis throughout the year. For example, it is quite common for a company to offer trade allowances and other merchandising programs quarterly for key products. The availability of trade allowances encourages retailers to purchase heavily during the promotion period to support the manufacturer's promotion, and to "load up" at the end of the promotion to improve profit margins on products that will be regularly priced at retail after the promotion period. Very often large retailers will carry inventories that will tide them over from one promotion period to another—a situation that manufacturers should be concerned about, because incremental volume sold on deal, particularly at the end of a promotion period, will reduce the sale of merchandise at regular prices. Short-term volume gains may not be to the manufacturer's advantage over a long period.

In the case of seasonal products, allowance programs are essential means of encouraging wholesalers and retailers to stock up before the season and to promote the product in the season. For example, sunscreen will be promoted in the spring, canning and preserving supplies in the late summer, baking supplies in the late fall before the holidays, and school supplies in the late summer.

A third objective is to *secure merchandising support* from distributors. For many products sold through drug, grocery, hardware, or department stores, manufacturers will offer complete promotion programs to encourage display activity, feature pricing, and retail advertising support. Programs of this nature are often agreed to in a signed contract or promotion agreement, and the distributor is reimbursed only when the performance requirements of the agreement are met.

Types of Trade Promotion Activity

The most commonly used types of trade promotion activity are trade and performance allowances, co-operative advertising, retail in-ad coupons, dealer premiums, collateral material, dealer-display material, and trade shows.

TRADE ALLOWANCE

A **trade allowance** is a temporary price reduction designed to encourage larger purchases by distributors (wholesalers and retailers). Such price reductions may be offered in the form of a percentage reduction from list price, a predetermined dollar amount off list price, or as a free-goods offer (e.g., buy 10 cases, get one free). These allowances can be deducted from the invoice immediately, and in such cases are called *off-invoice allowances*. Or they can be offered on the basis of a *bill-back*, in which case the manufacturer keeps a record of the amount of merchandise shipped to distributors and, when the deal period is over, issues a cheque to reimburse the retailers for the allowances they have earned.

PERFORMANCE ALLOWANCE

A **performance allowance** is an additional discount (over and above a trade allowance) offered by manufacturers to encourage retailers to perform a specific merchandising function (e.g., display the product at retail, provide an advertising mention in a retail flyer, or offer a lower price at retail for a short period). Before paying the allowance, the manufacturer requires proof of performance from the retailer.

CO-OPERATIVE ADVERTISING ALLOWANCE

Co-operative advertising allowances are funds allocated to pay for a portion of a retailer's advertising. The weekly specials advertised by major supermarket chains, for example, are partially sponsored by the manufacturers whose products are part of the ads in any given week. In some cases, a manufacturer may agree to pay half of the retailer's cost of advertising (media and creative) if the retailer agrees to feature the manufacturer's product for a specified period. Frequently, the manufacturer provides advertising material that can be integrated into the retailer's own advertising.

To maximize the effectiveness of allowances offered to the trade, manufacturers combine the various allowances to develop a fully integrated promotion plan. The effective combination of all allowances can build short-term volume, possibly secure automatic distribution of a product to retail stores, encourage retail display activity, and obtain an ad in a weekly flyer at a reduced retail price for a specified period. Complete package plans combining the various allowances are attractive to retailers—the financial rewards are much greater, and the package facilitates the efficient use of advertising dollars to support the retailer's own advertising and merchandising activities.

To generate even more impact with trade customers and consumers, integrating trade promotions with consumer promotions and media advertising support is an effective combination. Such a multi-faceted approach gives retailers tangible reasons to get behind the promotion, a win-win situation for the manufacturer and the retailer.

RETAIL IN-AD COUPONS

A **retail in-ad coupon** is a coupon printed in a retailer's weekly advertising, either in run-of-press newspaper advertising or in supplements inserted into a newspaper. These coupons are redeemable on national brands and are paid for by the manufacturers, not by the retailer. Such programs are the result of an agreement struck between the manufacturer's sales representative and the retailer's buyers. Usually, the funds to cover the cost of these coupons come out of the trade promotion budget, hence their inclusion as a trade promotion activity even though they are designed to encourage consumer response. This type of coupon program is appropriate for achieving the following promotion objectives: reducing trade inventories, building distribution levels, gaining trade support at store level, and ensuring that some of a brand's trade spending is passed on to the consumer in the form of a lower retail price.

DEALER PREMIUMS

A **dealer premium** is an additional incentive offered to a distributor by a manufacturer to encourage special purchase or to secure additional merchandising support from a retailer. Premiums are usually offered in the form of merchandise (e.g., a set of golf clubs, or other forms of sports- and leisure-oriented equipment and clothing); the value of the premium increases with the amount of product purchased by the retailer. Their use is often controversial. Some distributors forbid their buyers to accept premiums because they feel only the individual buyer, rather than the organization, benefits. Such a situation, often referred to as "payola," may lead a buyer to make unnecessary purchases and ignore the objectives of the distributor. The other side of the argument is that the purchase of a manufacturer's products at a large savings (through allowances and premiums) offers direct, tangible benefit to the buying organization.

The extent of payola can be considerable (e.g., banknotes, liquor, airline tickets, vacations). These practices are perceived by many to be unethical, and perhaps they should not occur. Nonetheless, some dealings do occur under the table, so students should be aware of it.

COLLATERAL MATERIAL

To facilitate the selling process, the sales force must provide considerable data in the form of **collateral materials** to customers (e.g., dealers, wholesalers, retailers, industrial companies). These materials include price lists, catalogues, sales brochures, pamphlets, specification sheets, product manuals, and audiovisual sales aids prepared by the manufacturer. Electronic brochures available through company websites are now very popular for communicating lengthy and complex information.

DEALER-DISPLAY MATERIAL (POINT-OF-PURCHASE)

Dealer-display material, or **point-of-purchase material**, consists of self-contained, custom-designed merchandising units, either permanent or temporary, that display a manufacturer's product. It includes posters, shelf talkers (small posters that hang from store shelves), channel strips (narrow strips containing a brief message attached to the channel face of a shelf), advertising pads or tear pads (tear-off sheets that explain the details of the promotion), and display shippers (shipping cases that convert to display bins or stands when opened). The use of such displays and materials is at the discretion of the retailers, whose space they occupy. The role of the manufacturer's sales representative is to convince the retailer of the merits of using the display. Retailers usually have an abundance of manufacturer's display material to choose from, so they can be selective.

TRADE SHOWS

Manufacturers often introduce new products or advertising campaigns to their dealer network and the public at large at trade shows. **Trade shows** are typically organized by an industry association each year to demonstrate the latest products of member manufacturers. There are, for example, toy shows, automobile shows, computer shows, and appliance shows. The unique benefit of a trade show is that it allows buyers and other decision-makers to come to a central location to secure the most recent product information from suppliers. For retailers and manufacturers, it is an important opportunity to develop a prospect list that the sales force can follow up on. Thus, participants compete for visitors' attention at the show and usually invest considerable sums to build unique and enticing display exhibits.

Home Depot sees great value in trade shows. According to Pat Wilkinson, director of marketing for Home Depot, "Trade shows are a key piece of a larger integrated marketing program. It is an interactive way of talking to customers outside the store." Enhancing the home in the age of cocooning is a trend that Home Depot is tapping into. Home Depot is also a large sponsor and advertiser on various decorating and home renovation shows on the HGTV network. Such shows are now quite popular and they reach Home Depot's customers.[13]

Home Depot
www.homedepot.ca

Trends in Sales Promotion Planning

In marketing communications planning, the first strategic decision is to determine the relative importance of the various mix elements. The degree of importance has a direct impact on the amount of money that is allocated to any element. The same decision procedure is used when allocating funds between consumer promotion and trade promotion. For some time there has been a trend toward more spending in trade promotions at the expense of advertising and consumer promotions. Several factors have played a role in creating this trend:

- *Media fragmentation* Consumers today have so many broadcast and print advertising options to choose from that the impact of any one option is not as significant as it used to be. For example, television networks have lost significant numbers of viewers to cable channels and the internet. If traditional forms of advertising are not as effective as they once were, advertisers have no alternative but to evaluate other forms of communication.

- *Demand for accountability* Organizations today prefer to invest in activities where return on investment can be measured. Managers realize that all forms of communication do help in one way or another, but if a certain activity can demonstrate measurable results then it will be the preferred option. Trade promotions do increase sales during the promotion period so the results of this investment are tangible.

- *Buying-power concentration* There has been considerable consolidation in many retail markets (e.g., department stores, supermarkets, and home and hardware chain stores). As a result, fewer outlets have much more power over the manufacturers that supply them with goods. For example, many manufacturers face considerable pressures to keep prices down from powerful retailers like Wal-Mart. In the supermarket sector, one large chain, Loblaws and its various other banners, controls 40 percent of all food sales in Canada. Demand from such huge retailers forces manufacturers to spend more on trade promotions than they care to. The result is an imbalance between push strategies and pull strategies, a concept discussed earlier in the chapter.

Continued high-level spending on short-term activities such as trade promotion by manufacturers may inhibit the achievement of long-term marketing objectives for any given product. It must be noted, however, that the large numbers of mature products that require only limited levels of advertising receive high levels of trade promotion support. Brand objectives are different in the mature stage of the product life cycle. This skews the overall spending average in favour of trade spending. In contrast, small numbers of new products that are in the introduction or early growth stage of the life cycle spend heavily on advertising and consumer promotion—their goal is to generate awareness and trial purchase.

Given these trends, it is essential that marketers maximize the effectiveness of their in-store promotions, and to do so requires that consumer and trade promotion plans be carefully integrated. For more insight into this issue, see the Advertising in Action vignette **Value-Added Promotions Increase Sales.**

Value-Added Promotions Increase Sales

If the trend toward trade promotions continues, it can be forecast with reasonable accuracy that tactical in-store programs and trade marketing will unseat branding and advertising as the prime focus for many national brands. A frightening thought for many marketers!

The importance of in-store marketing is being driven by three main trends: corporations are being run by financial-oriented executives that are demanding accountability for every dollar spent; media fragmentation; and consolidation of retail distribution channels. In-store marketing budgets in Canada are growing dramatically because the trade is so concentrated here. Powerful retailers such as Wal-Mart, Canadian Tire, and Loblaws have incredible power over their suppliers. More importantly, however, they have the power to sell a lot of product, so manufacturers must exploit that potential.

Research indicates that retail shoppers do respond to in-store promotions. In fact, 72 percent of respondents in one research survey said they purchased a product due to a promotional offer. As well, 70 percent said they would try a new brand if the promotional offer is perceived as a good one.

Powerful retailers will support national brands, but will only do so if the manufacturer considers their goals as well as its own. From the retailer's perspective, the promotional activity must drive traffic to the stores and build incremental sales and profits.

With so much at stake in the soft drink and snack food product categories, PepsiCo has figured out the vital role and importance of in-store merchandising. The company sees in-store merchandising activities as a vital means of communicating with consumers at a critical time—decision time! PepsiCo has several primary brands that can be merchandised together—Pepsi-Cola products and Frito-Lay products being the most obvious combination. PepsiCo has been particularly successful at selling its ideas to retail partners when it pairs up Pepsi with complementary lines from their product portfolio. This is a strategy the company refers to as "power of one." PepsiCo believes that retailers are more likely to buy into a promotion when there are more players involved, because there is a potential to increase their sales.

A recent Super Bowl promotion involving Pepsi-Cola, Frito-Lay, and Gatorade incorporated miniature football stadium displays built out of Pepsi cases. The displays were a one-stop shopping destination for Super Bowl party planners! On the importance of such activities, Richard Burjaw, director of marketing for Pepsi-Cola, states, "When you get the customer to the point of sale, it always helps to close the sale with some reminders and some attention-grabbing in-store theatre."

Source: Adapted from Lisa D'Innocenzo, "Selling to the store," *Strategy*, February 9, 2004, pp. 1, 6.

Sales Promotion Integration with Marketing Communications

Sales promotion activity is not usually the focal point of a brand's marketing strategy. In most cases, it is used to supplement regular brand advertising. Regardless of the promotional direction the company or brand takes, it must ensure that the strategies employed are integrated with other marketing communications strategies so that synergies are created and objectives are achieved. Strategic decisions must be made on frequency of promotions, the relationship between the product and the promotion, the creative strategy, and the media strategy.

FREQUENCY OF PROMOTION ACTIVITY

How frequently an activity should be used depends on the type of activity. Once a year is usually adequate to generate excitement for a brand (a contest might be used in peak season to counter competitive activity, or once during a traditionally low season to stimulate incremental volume). In general, coupon activity can be implemented much more frequently than cash refunds, premium offers, and contests, and is less disruptive to the regular sales message. There is a risk that too much promotion can cheapen the image of a brand.

PROMOTION/PRODUCT RELATIONSHIPS

In the case of contests, sweepstakes, and premiums, the promotion offer must fit the product image and be attractive to the target market. In a contest situation, the prize must be of interest to the target market. For example, an all-expenses-paid vacation in Disneyland may be appropriate for a soup or cereal manufacturer, but inappropriate for the producer of an expensive gourmet coffee. If the target market is not interested, the promotion will fail.

CREATIVE STRATEGY

The marketer must consider that a promotion might be disruptive to the continuity of the regular sales message. It is possible that consumers not interested in the promotion will look elsewhere for product satisfaction. To avoid this potential problem, separate but integrated message strategies must be considered for promotion activity. Since a promotion is an added incentive, it temporarily becomes the unique selling point. It is logical, then, to integrate the offer into the regular sales message. The combination of a strong ongoing sales message with the added bonus of a promotion offer should help achieve both short-term and long-term objectives for the advertised product.

When assessing the relative effectiveness of a promotional advertisement (particularly a print advertisement), marketers typically analyze the response generated by the specific advertisement or campaign. In a coupon promotion, how many coupons were redeemed? For a contest, how many entries were received? For a premium offer, how many premiums were shipped? Such evaluations provide direction for the design of subsequent promotion-oriented advertisements.

The ideal promotion offer draws attention to the ad and conveys a message about the product. Also, a strong association between the promotional offer and the advertised product tends to increase advertising recall and persuasiveness.

Marketers should analyze their promotion planning efforts, giving consideration to the following questions:

- Does the promotion support the product image?
- Does the promotion distract the reader's attention from copy points that describe product qualities?
- Should the promotion offer be the most prominent feature of the ad, or should it be secondary to the product sales message?

MEDIA STRATEGY

Commitment to a sales promotion plan requires commitment to media advertising support. For any consumer promotion to have a chance, the target market must be made aware of the activity and the specific details of the promotion offer. Usually, a media mix is required to achieve the communications objectives of a promotion plan and the budget is spent in a concentrated period to generate high levels of awareness for the promotion.

BROADCAST MEDIA To create awareness and encourage consumers to respond quickly is largely the responsibility of television and radio. High-impact advertising in a short period (a blitz campaign) is quite common. In the case of a contest or sweepstakes promotion, television and radio can create excitement and convey a sense of urgency (to get consumers to take advantage of the offer—*now*!). As well, television and radio can direct consumers to websites where more detailed information about the promotion is available.

PRINT MEDIA Various combinations of print media are used to create awareness, and, more importantly, to communicate essential details of the promotion offer. Consumers are conditioned to look for details at point of purchase, so this medium is a must for contests and other offers. For complex promotions such as contests, a well-balanced media mix is required. For a premium offer, free sample, or coupon, the marketer can be more selective.

In addition to advertising the promotion to the consumer, the marketer must take appropriate action to notify the trade. As discussed earlier in this chapter, consumer promotion and trade promotion activity (the combination of pull and push) is often integrated into a complete plan to maximize impact on, and response from, both customer groups—consumers and distributors. Therefore, the marketing organization must provide the sales force with appropriate sales aids (promotion literature and display material) so that more effective presentations can be made to distributors. In terms of media, marketers can use selective direct mailings to all distributors, or place advertising in appropriate trade journals to reach wholesale and retail buyers. Such advertising should provide promotion details and encourage retailers to build inventories and participate in display activities to derive maximum benefit from the promotion.

For an applied illustration that integrates consumer and trade promotion strategies with other communications strategies, see the plan that appears in Appendix II.

SUMMARY

The advertising manager must consider the impact that sales promotion activity will have on the achievement of marketing objectives, so a sales promotion plan is often developed concurrently with the advertising plan. Sales promotion activities are designed to encourage immediate purchase response by consumers and distributors. In comparison to media advertising, where the objective is to build an image, sales promotion encourages action immediately. There are two categories of sales promotion activity: consumer promotions and trade promotions.

Consumer promotions are designed to pull the product through the channel of distribution. Specific objectives are to achieve trial purchase by new users and to achieve repeat and multiple purchases by current users. The types of activities commonly used to achieve these objectives include coupons, cash refunds, samples, contests, premium offers, loyalty (frequent-buyer) promotions, and delayed-payment incentives.

Each type of promotion is better suited for certain objectives. Coupons, for example, are good at encouraging trial and repeat purchases depending on the method of distribution. Samples are effective for trial purchase and are appropriate for use when launching a new product. Refunds, premiums, and contests are better suited for maintaining loyalty and are more commonly used by brands in the mature stage of the product life cycle.

Trade promotions are designed to help push the product through the channel of distribution. Specific marketing objectives are to secure listings and distribution, build volume on a preplanned cyclical basis, and achieve merchandising support from distributors. Trade promotion activities that help achieve these objectives include trade allowances, performance allowances, co-operative advertising, retail in-ad coupons, dealer premiums, point-of-purchase display materials, collateral materials, and trade shows.

Sales promotion is generally regarded as supplemental activity that supports regular product advertising. Its goals tend to be short-term, but the increasing usage of frequent-buyer promotions has shifted sales promotion planning to a long-term orientation. Sales promotion activity should not disrupt regular product advertising. In planning promotions, the manager must guard against running them too frequently so as not to harm the image of the product. Promotions that are implemented should complement the existing image of the product. From a media-strategy perspective, a combination of broadcast and print advertising is recommended as the means of creating awareness and communicating the details of the promotion offer.

KEY TERMS

cash refund   412
consumer promotion   399
contests   410
coupons   403
cross sampling   408
dealer premium   419
delayed payment incentive   415
electronic coupons   406
freestanding insert (FSI)   406

frequent-buyer program   415
game (or instant win)   406
media-delivered coupons   405
performance allowance   418
premium   414
product-delivered coupons   405
pull strategy   400
push strategy   400

redemption rate   406
retail in-ad coupon   419
sales promotion   399
slippage   412
sweepstakes   410
trade allowance   418
trade promotion   400
trade shows   420

REVIEW QUESTIONS

1. What are the objectives of the consumer promotion and trade promotion activities?

2. Explain the difference between a pull promotion strategy and a push promotion strategy.

3. What types of coupon distribution are appropriate for the early stages of the product life cycle? For the later stages? What is the relationship between the method of coupon distribution and a promotion's objectives?

4. What are the major reasons that marketing firms use coupons?

5. What benefits come from a manufacturer's implementation of a free sample promotion offer?

6. What is experiential marketing and what benefits does it provide the marketing organization?

7. What elements contribute to the success of a contest offer?

8. Briefly describe the following consumer promotion terms:
   a) Cross-ruff
   b) Redemption rate
   c) Instantly redeemable coupon
   d) Instant-win promotions
   e) Rebate
   f) Delayed payment incentive
   g) Slippage

9. What is the objective of a consumer premium offer and when is the best time (e.g., product life cycle) to use a premium offer?

10. Briefly explain the nature of a loyalty (frequent-buyer) program.

11. What is the difference between a trade allowance and a performance allowance?

12. What role does co-operative advertising play in the development of a manufacturer's product?

13. Briefly describe the following trade promotion terms:
   a) Retail in-ad coupon
   b) Dealer premium
   c) Collateral material

DISCUSSION QUESTIONS

1. "Spending less advertising money directly with consumers, and more advertising money with the trade, will ultimately harm a brand's consumer franchise." Discuss this statement from the manufacturer's viewpoint.

2. The trends of marketing budget allocations and the merits of various consumer and trade promotion techniques have been presented in this chapter. If you were responsible for developing a promotion plan for a brand in the introduction stage of the product life cycle, what balance would you recommend between consumer promotion, media advertising, and trade promotion? Justify your position by using examples of your choice.

3. Conduct some secondary research on the Canadian coffee market (or another popular market of your choice) to determine what brands are the leaders in the market. Assume you are the brand manager for Maxwell House roasted coffee (or a popular brand in the other market you choose). What promotion strategies would you recommend to build brand loyalty considering your market share and stage in the product life cycle? Be specific and justify your recommendations.

4. Conduct some secondary research on the role and importance of trade shows. Will trade shows play a more prominent role in the marketing mix and marketing communications mix in the future?

NOTES

1. Wayne Mouland, "Coupon Distribution Grows in Changing Market," press release, NCH Promotional Services Ltd., March 2004.

2. Wayne Mouland, "Those who use them, use them a lot," *Marketing*, February 10, 2003, p. 29.

3. Ibid.

4. Ibid.

5. Lara Mills, "Are coupons dying," *Marketing*, November 21, 1995, pp. 10, 11.

6. A Special Presentation on Coupon Promotion Fundamentals," *NCH Promotional Services Ltd.*, 1998.

7. Geoff Dennis, "Sampling growth spurs creativity," *Strategy*, May 20, 2002, pp. 1, 10.

8. Samson Okalow, "Nike Trial Van goes hardcore," *Strategy*, June 2, 2003, p. 5.

9. "A Marketer's Guide to Promotion," *NCH Promotional Services Ltd.*, 1996, p. 4.

10. Jason MacDonald, "More giveaways in beer markets," *Marketing*, June 25, 2001, p. 2.

11. "Shoppers launches creative loyalty program," *Marketing*, December 18/25, 2000, p. 21.

12. Josh Fineman, "Starbucks unveils dual-use credit card," *Financial Post*, October 14, 2003, p. FP10.

13. Marina Strauss, "Home Depot takes show on the road," *The Globe and Mail*, October 3, 2003, p. B10.

CHAPTER

14

Public Relations and
Event Marketing
and Sponsorships

Learning Objectives

After studying this chapter, you will be able to

- Identify the role of public relations and event marketing and sponsorships in achieving organizational objectives.

- Describe the various types of public relations activities

- Identify the steps involved in the public relations planning process

- Assess the usefulness of a variety of public relations tools

- Evaluate public relations and event marketing and sponsorships as a communications medium

- Identify the unique considerations involved in the planning and evaluation of event marketing programs

For many organizations, for quite a long time, public relations was an afterthought—something a company got involved with when it faced bad times. It was perceived as a reaction-oriented tactical vehicle for correcting problems that cropped up. Surprisingly, it wasn't until the 1990s, the era when integrated marketing communications took hold, that organizations recognized the true value of public relations. Public relations is now perceived more as a strategic tool that can be integrated with other forms of communications. It is another link in the chain that helps an organization achieve its objectives.

Event marketing and sponsorships have gradually increased in importance over the past few decades. At one time the decision to participate in an event was at the whim of a senior company executive—and the events selected were sexy and interesting to them. Now, event marketing is a very sophisticated activity and, because of its target marketing capability, companies are integrating events and sponsorships with other marketing communications programs.

This chapter examines the increasingly important role that public relations and event marketing and sponsorships can play in an organization. In-depth discussion about developing policies and procedures, strategies, and plans for public relations and event marketing are presented in this chapter.

Defining Public Relations

Public relations consists of a variety of activities and communications that organizations undertake to monitor, evaluate, and influence the attitudes, opinions, and behaviours of groups or individuals who constitute their publics. The word "public" is a crucial aspect of the definition. An organization's publics are varied and include shareholders, employees, suppliers, the government, distributors (wholesalers and retailers), and consumers. The word "relations" is important, for it signifies the organization is involved in a relationship with these publics and that relationship should be a positive one. For the relationship to be positive, the nature of communications between the organization and the various publics should be open, honest, and forthcoming.

Prior to examining public relations in detail, students should clearly understand the basic differences between advertising and public relations. While each form of communication approaches a situation from a different perspective, they do work together to build a strong and positive image for a company or brand.

Public relations is distinguished from advertising in two ways:

1. While advertising is primarily concerned with product image, public relations concerns itself more frequently with corporate image. For example, it spreads good news about an organization or helps remedy a problem situation that suddenly arises. In the latter situation, an organization is often at the mercy of the media, for the media determine what information is communicated to the public.
2. Advertising is controlled and paid for by a sponsor, whereas public relations is a form of communications controlled by the media and not paid for directly by the company that the media story concerns. The media determine the amount and content of the message, constrained only by the known facts of the situation presented. Organizations, however, can and often do include paid advertising as part of their public relations activity.

At the product level, **publicity** is used to help market goods and services. Publicity is one aspect of public relations; it is the communication of newsworthy information about a product, service, company, or idea, usually in the form of a press release. Publicity is designed to familiarize the public with the features or advantages of a product, service, or idea. Typically, publicity attends the launching of a new product, the opening of a new store, a technological breakthrough, or the achievement of some milestone. Since publicity is usually not paid for by the sponsor, the sponsor accepts whatever media coverage it receives. A good report about a company can make a company credible with the public. It can be more convincing than advertising, as there is an implied endorsement by the media.

The Publics

Public relations has to be sensitive to two different publics: internal and external. **Internal publics** involve those whom the organization communicates with regularly. These parties are close to the day-to-day operations of the organization and include employees, distributors, suppliers, shareholders, and regular customers. Employees, for example, must be educated about an organization's policies and procedures, and they should know about the direction a company is heading in order to help the company prosper. Internal communications in the form of email, bulletin boards, newsletters, posters, and displays are means of keeping employees tuned in.

External publics are not close to the organization and are usually communicated with infrequently. They include the media, governments (all levels), prospective shareholders, the financial community, and community groups. Communicating externally involves the use of an intermediary—the press. Both the broadcast and print media have considerable influence on public opinions so the smart organization calls upon their services to promote their cause. The press can positively or negatively influence an organization's reputation. Given such power, it is in the best interests of an organization to develop positive media relations.

The Role of Public Relations

The role of public relations is varied but generally falls into six key areas: corporate public relations, reputation management, publicity generation, developing sound relationships with the media, developing positive relationships with the community, and fundraising by not-for-profit organizations.

CORPORATE PUBLIC RELATIONS

As suggested earlier, public relations can play a vital role in building and protecting the image of a company. A smart company today takes a proactive stance and communicates loud and clear the good things it is doing. For example, a company may communicate with its publics in the form of **corporate advertising**. Corporate advertising may communicate to the public what the company is doing in terms of social responsibility, or show how it helps resolve customers' problems.

A company may also be active in the area of **issue management.** Communications in this realm informs the public about where a company stands on an issue that is important to its various publics. For example, a company's stance on environmental issues may be of utmost importance. Is the company taking a proactive stance on protecting the environment? If it is, then a loud and clear message should be sent to the public.

These kinds of messages can be delivered to the public by paid advertising or through public relations. If a company chooses to advertise it will do so through corporate advertising. Corporate advertising is a form of paid communication that undertakes the task of creating a positive attitude and goodwill toward a company. Corporate advertising does not sell a product but, since the objective is to enhance the image of a company, there could be some long-term and indirect effect on sales. The direct influence of corporate advertising is difficult to measure. Figure 14.1 shows an example of corporate advertising.

Another alternative is advocacy advertising. **Advocacy advertising** is any kind of public communication, paid for by an identified sponsor, that presents information or a point of view on a publicly recognized, controversial issue. The objective is to influence public opinion. The Ontario Attorney General's campaign to stop drinking and driving was initiated to reduce the number of accidents caused by people driving while under the influence of alcohol.

REPUTATION MANAGEMENT

Public relations is also a vital form of communication for a company during a crisis. It simply makes good business sense to invest in a program to protect a reputation that takes years to build and only seconds to lose. How a company manages its public relations during a crisis often influences the final outcome in the public's mind. For instance, a drug manufacturer may face an angry public when a drug it markets is linked to certain unexpected health problems. When the press gets hold of such a story and informs the public, a company has to be instantly ready to go into crisis-management mode.

The textbook case of doing it right is Johnson & Johnson Inc.'s handling of the Tylenol crisis in the 1980s. Disaster struck when seven people in Chicago died after taking Tylenol pills that were laced with cyanide. The company immediately withdrew the product from all store shelves within days, at a cost of $110 million, and had chief executive James Burke go on TV to explain the company's actions. Burke also made himself available to news programs such as *60 Minutes.* The company went on to pioneer tamper-proof packaging that was ultimately adopted by the entire industry, and reintroduced the

Courtesy: Epcor

FIGURE
14.1

An illustration of corporate advertising

product. Within four years Tylenol regained its lost market share and was once again the leading brand.[1] This story verifies that a proactive approach to solving a problem plays positively with the public.

Throughout such a process, the most critical element is leadership. Crises breed fear and confusion, and stakeholders want assurances that someone is in control. A strong leader, willing to be visible on all issues, is essential. When the existing leadership is compromised or tainted by scandal, the best approach is to bring in new leadership with a strong reputation and a commitment to transparency.[2] For some additional tips on how an organization should handle a crisis situation, refer to Figure 14.2.

An organization's leader must be trained to handle the barrage of reporters when they are placed in the media spotlight—glaring lights and reporter scrums can be intim-

"The Tylenol Crisis, 1982"
http://iml.jou.ufl.edu/projects/
Fall02/Susi/tylenol.htm

> **How well an organization manages a crisis situation has a direct impact on how the public perceives the outcome. Here are some vital tips to ensure effective communications with the public:**
>
> ### ONE INDIVIDUAL MUST ASSUME A LEADERSHIP ROLE
>
> People want strong leadership and a sense that decision makers are in charge and have a plan.
>
> ### PEOPLE NEED MORE THAN INFORMATION
>
> They need moral support, a human touch, and a single face with which to identify their hopes for recovery. The 9/11 recovery plan in New York, for example, was led by mayor Rudolf Giuliani.
>
> ### PEOPLE NEED A CONSISTENT MESSAGE
>
> A strong leader will provide consistency and amplify the essence of the message when necessary. A consistent approach to messaging offers reassurance.
>
> ### TIMING IS EVERYTHING
>
> Once the issue has been contained, advise the public that you are open for business again. The message must offer reassurance and provide proof of appropriate actions that have been taken.
>
> Source: Adapted from David Weiner, "The SARS Crisis: Lessons Learned," a public relations advertising feature, *Marketing*, 2003.

idating. They must be prepared to act quickly and show that they have control of the situation. Company presidents and high-level executives must also meet the demands of a more sophisticated and more demanding consumer audience or suffer the consequences of their wrath.

PRODUCT PUBLICITY

A primary objective of public relations is to generate news about a product or service a company is marketing. **Publicity** is news about a person, product, or service that appears in the print or broadcast media. Essentially, publicity must be newsworthy. With regard to publicity, what seems like news to a company may not be news to the media. Opportunities to communicate newsworthy information include the launch of a new product, revealing new information based on research evidence (e.g., a discovery), securing a significant contract that will generate new jobs, and achieving significant sales and profit results.

Newsworthy information is usually communicated by a press release or press conference. These are the major tools of the trade and are discussed in detail in the next section. Information is carefully prepared and distributed to the media in such a way that editors are tempted to run all or parts of the story. The preparation of such information is the responsibility of a public relations firm. Similar to advertising, public relations is a highly specialized field that requires experience and expertise to implement a plan properly. Public relations practitioners have established contacts with media editors over the years, and they rely on their relationships with editors to get their clients' information into the news.

To demonstrate how publicity works, consider the launch of Axe deodorant in Canada in 2002. Axe is a leading brand globally. Media advertising showed Axe-wearing young men fending off females who couldn't resist the Axe scent. Unilever, the company marketing Axe, issued press releases to draw the media's attention to consumer immersion activities that would be taking place. These activities included mobile marketing and sampling programs everywhere young men are found—the cinema, retail, college campuses, music events, and a cross-country Axe Angels tour where guys could mingle with the Angels and check out all of the Axe scents.

Lifestyle events that bring young men and women together with activities they love—music, parties, and fun—were also part of the publicity plan. Axe launch parties were held at prominent nightclubs in Toronto and Montreal.[3] The Axe launch was also supported with an interactive website, **www.TheAxeEffect.com**. At the site young men could actually purchase a booklet titled *Coping with All the Ladies: The Axe Wearer's Handbook*. See Figure 14.3 for an illustration.

Product placement is the insertion of brand logos or branded merchandise into movies and television shows and is another tactic for generating publicity. Industry experts agree that BMW sparked the trend toward placements when its new Z3 Roadster appeared in the James Bond film *GoldenEye*.

Product placement or branded content, as it is often called, has morphed into a media strategy more so than a public relations strategy. This topic was discussed in Chapter 7. Nonetheless, product placement does generate all kinds of publicity for

FIGURE
14.3

The Axe website attracts a young male audience

Courtesy: Unilever Canada

brand names when the press starts talking and writing about it. As Uma Thurman slices and dices her way through the film *Kill Bill*, the yellow-and-black Asics sneakers she wears proved to be a runaway hit. "It's probably one of the most perfect product placements we've ever had," said Dina DeFazio, spokeswoman for Asics' U.S. headquarters. Shoes literally sold out in weeks following the launch of the film. Asics didn't even pay to have its sneakers included in the film. They were simply suggested to Miramax, the film's producers, by a prominent, trend-setting retailer in New York.[4]

Product placement is now so blatant that the brand is integrated right into the script of the movie. *Castaway*, starring Tom Hanks, was nothing more than an extended commercial for FedEx. In addition to featuring countless FedEx packages and logos, the film even managed to accommodate a brief history of the courier's corporate rise. Product placement is a double-edged sword—too much can seem blatant and end up turning off consumers, while too little makes the effort a waste of time. According to Jeff Swearingen, vice-president of marketing at Frito-Lay Canada, "It's less about the number of placements and it's more about the quality. One good placement makes all the economics work."[5] Frito-Lay's potato chips played a prominent role in the movie *Slapshot 2*, a quintessential Canadian hockey story.

MEDIA RELATIONS

Generating publicity is the responsibility of a media relations expert. **Media relations** specialists are employed by public relations companies, and their primary responsibility is to develop unique and effective relationships with the media that cover the particular industry in which they specialize (e.g., financial information, computer hardware and software, automobiles, retailing). Their role is to get industry analysts on board, to the point where they will communicate favourable information about a company or brand.

The relationship between a media specialist and a reporter is one that develops over time. It is predicated on characteristics such as respect, honesty, accuracy, and professionalism. Reputation for fair play is crucial; once a reputation is lost, a PR practitioner cannot function effectively. In this regard, a specialist has to treat all media outlets fairly. Showing favouritism to one media outlet over another on a breaking story of high media value could backfire on the specialist and his or her client in the long run. The media do not forget!

COMMUNITY RELATIONS AND PUBLIC AFFAIRS

In an era of social responsibility, companies are placing high value on programs that foster a good public image in the communities in which they operate. Many companies encourage their employees to give back to the community; some even provide a few hours of work time each week to get involved. Community relations officers of large organizations arrange community events and often provide funds or other resources to sponsor community events and teams. It's all part of being a good corporate citizen. Tim Hortons, for example, uses the phrase "We never forget where we came from" in its advertising. In a public relations sense, the company gives meaning to this phrase through numerous community sponsorships that include funding the Timbits Minor Sports program (hockey and soccer), supplying jerseys to league teams, providing free ice skating for families in hundreds of communities during the holidays, and sending thousands of underprivileged kids to camp every year through the Tim Horton Children's Foundation.[6] The annual Camp Day (an in-store fundraising promotion) raises more than $4.8 million annually to support camp activities.[7]

Public affairs involves programs and strategies to deal with governments. As indicated earlier, governments (federal, provincial, and local) establish laws and regulations that dictate how companies conduct business. It is quite common for a company to hire another company that specializes in lobbying. **Lobbying** involves activities and practices that are designed to influence government policy decisions. Naturally, a company or an industry wants government policy to conform to what's best for business. Needless to say, governments have to balance economic well-being with social and environmental well-being, and therein lies the conflict among business, governments, and special-interest groups (e.g., groups that attack companies on the basis of their handling of environmental issues).

FUNDRAISING

Public relations can play a key role in the marketing mix in the not-for-profit market sector. Fundraising, for example, relies heavily on public relations. A national organization like the United Way faces a huge challenge each year. Some people perceive the organization to be a big "money hole" and wonder where all of the donations go. To change this perception, public relations is used to educate the public about how the funds are used in order to predispose people to give, to solicit commitment, and to make people feel good about giving. The goal of fundraising campaigns for the United Way or the Salvation Army is to create a positive image and secure support by sending a message to the public that clearly states what the organization is all about. Refer to Figure 14.4 for an illustration.

Public Relations Planning

Public relations should be as closely linked to a company's bottom line as a financial plan or marketing plan. Strategic communications planning should be based on the business challenges that lie ahead, marketing needs and strategies, and corporate vision. Any plan that is based on these characteristics must now include a comprehensive public relations program.

The nature of a public relations plan is dictated by the situation at hand. Will it be a proactive plan that can be carefully planned in advance and implemented with precision, or is it a reactive plan that is being undertaken only because of some unforeseen circumstance occurring? A public relations plan usually involves five steps: situation analysis, establishing objectives, devising a strategy, executing the plan, and evaluation. Essentially, the process is very similar to developing an advertising plan, though the tools used are very different.

SITUATION ANALYSIS

Before any plan can be devised, a **situation analysis** is conducted to reveal the true nature of the problem to be resolved or the opportunity to be pursued. Clarification is crucial because a good communications strategy has to be focused if it is to be successful. For example, specific plans may be needed to resolve a crisis situation, to launch a new product, or to announce company expansion plans or financial results.

ESTABLISHING OBJECTIVES

Public relations objectives must relate specifically to the achievement of marketing objectives. Typically, marketing objectives relate to achieving specific sales, profits, and market-share goals. Objectives for launching new products are stated in terms generating awareness and trial purchase among the target audience over a period of time. For established products, marketing objectives are stated in terms of increasing use among current users.

FIGURE
14.4

An emotional message
encourages understanding
and helps raise funds

Regardless of the situation or desired outcome, public relations objectives tend to be similar to advertising objectives, for the two disciplines work hand in hand toward a common goal. While not adopted universally, there is a new school of thought about public relations and advertising: PR first, advertising second. PR plants the seed, while advertising harvests the crop. Such thinking is based on the premise that advertising can't start the fire; it can only fan the fire after it's been started. To get something out of nothing, you need the validity that third-party endorsements bring.[8] The Axe deodorant launch example cited earlier in the chapter demonstrates this way of thinking.

With this in mind, public relations objectives are quite similar to advertising objectives. If a new product is being launched, the objectives of both disciplines are focused on creating awareness. For both advertising and public relations, stating objectives in terms of awareness is valid for the key role of both in positively affecting attitudes and causing consumers to act. As marketing campaigns become more integrated and seamless, however, the effectiveness of the various components of the marketing mix and marketing communications mix becomes more difficult to measure.

Realistic expectations of public relations should be stated in terms of what it can influence. Therefore, objectives such as building recognition, creating a positive image, differentiating one brand from another, introducing new products, and building store traffic fall within the realm of a public relations plan.

Publicity objectives can be more sharply focused and be quantitative in nature. Publicity objectives should take into account the media through which the message will be transmitted and the target audience reached by the media. No matter how targeted an audience might be or might not be (in marketing terms), chances are they will be reached by the mass media (e.g., in a news story on television or a story in a general interest magazine or daily newspaper). If so, gross audience objectives (in terms of impressions) can be established.

To demonstrate the concept of gross impressions, consider the case of Smirnoff vodka when it launched a new package and label design in an attempt to attract younger drinkers. A half-page article about the introduction and a picture of the new package design appeared in the *Toronto Star* (the result of a sound public relations plan). The *Star*'s weekday circulation is 440 000 copies. That figure represents the potential minimum number of impressions the Smirnoff article will achieve. Undoubtedly, a similar article appeared in many other newspapers across Canada.

DEVELOPING THE PUBLIC RELATIONS STRATEGY

Similar to a marketing strategy or an advertising strategy, a public relations strategy considers a common set of variables that includes the target market, geographic location, seasonal considerations, and timing. As well, a decision must be made on the most efficient and effective way to reach consumers and cause them to act. A specific task is assigned to public relations (and other communications disciplines) so that the combined efforts are mutually reinforcing and so that all audiences receive the same message.

Strategy deals primarily with "how" the plan will be implemented. In the case of a new product introduction, for example, public relations may be the initial contact point for consumers and the trade customers. The role of public relations is to reach those parties who have the power to influence behaviour, including industry analysts, key media, and consumers classified as innovators and early adopters. The strategic role of public relations should be examined in terms of how well it can do the following:

- Design the timetable so that the message will reach opinion leaders (analysts, trade audiences, and influential media) well in advance of the public.

- Maximize the news value of new product introductions, new advertising campaigns, and event sponsorships.

- Time PR events to reinforce advertising and sales promotion campaigns and/or maintain high visibility between campaigns.

- Reach important secondary markets, defined geographically, psychographically, and ethnically, that might not be targeted by advertising and sales promotion.[9]

Strategically, the PR message has to be different from the advertising message. Public relations is about information and education rather than unique selling points and fancy slogans. Therefore, any claim made in a press release must be substantiated with factual information (e.g., citing consumer research data that confirms a claim or point of view or explaining an issue thoroughly and accurately). For publicity-oriented programs, product news can be dramatized easily. Without drama and fanfare, the press release will wind up in some editor's recycling box.

Consider, for example, the dilemma beer marketers faced when the low-carb craze was exploding. How do you introduce a new low-carb product without implying that your existing products are high-carb or bad-carb?

Labatt carefully designed a public relations strategy that would turn a negative situation into a positive situation. The company launched Labatt Sterling, a beer with just 2.5 grams of carbs, far fewer than the 11 to 17 grams found in regular beers. The media was anxious to know how Sterling would fit into low-carb diets. Labatt's strategy was to sidestep the good-carb/bad-carb issue by pointing out that beer in general has fewer carbohydrates than most people think and fewer carbohydrates than most other beverages. For the consumer who wants to virtually eliminate carbs, you can still drink beer—Sterling beer! That is a much different message than saying, "We think carbs are bad so we've created this new product." That would be detrimental to a vast majority of other Labatt products.

Labatt's PR plan also featured dietitian Lois Ferguson explaining that drinking beer has nothing to do with "beer bellies," but rather it's what is consumed along with beer, such as chips and other snacks, that causes problems. The Sterling PR campaign helped change people's perceptions about beer. The campaign generated over 20 million impressions across Canada. The brand now has 1 percent share of the beer market, an impressive figure for a niche product.[10]

EXECUTING THE PLAN

Executing the plan involves the specific actions and activities that will be used to achieve objectives. In other words, the directives provided in the strategy section of the plan are translated into action plans. The plan will specify what activities will occur, who will do them, when they will be done, and at what cost. The timing and costs of all activities should be integrated into the marketing plan. The importance of executing details cannot be overemphasized. All things being equal, it is how the information is presented that could differentiate one brand from another. The illustration for Labatt Sterling cited above demonstrates the importance of communicating details in an accurate, factual manner. It can make a difference!

To get the message out, public relations has many more options than advertising does. The PR arsenal includes press releases, press conferences, press kits, audiovisual materials, websites, and lobbyists. These tools are discussed in more detail in the next section of the chapter.

EVALUATING EFFECTIVENESS

Like other forms of communication, public relations activities are evaluated through a variety of research methods that can be either qualitative or quantitative in nature. In some way, results achieved should be compared to the objectives that were originally established for the program. If, for example, the objective of a campaign was to alter the public's perception about a company (e.g., the problem dealt with building a better image), a focus group could be used before and after the campaign is implemented. Shifts in attitudes and opinions in the post-campaign group would determine the relative effectiveness of the campaign. Alternatively, a company could conduct a public opinion poll before and after the campaign.

A company likes to know how much exposure was actually received as a result of its public relations activities. This is referred to as **content analysis**. Organizations that keep

Building Share for a 40-Something Brand

When you think of the brand name "Off!" you probably think of mosquitoes. In other words, Off! is not the type of product one enjoys using. Nonetheless, with West Nile virus being a real problem for the past few summers, Off! saw an opportunity to build its business. Public relations would play a key role. Here's the scoop on how the plan evolved and what results were achieved.

PR Objectives

There were four key objectives to be addressed:

1. To build and reinforce SC Johnson's expertise in the insect repellent category

2. To position SC Johnson and its spokespeople as leaders in combating the West Nile virus

3. To generate as many possible brand mentions of Off! products as possible

4. To introduce a new non-DEET line called Off! Botanicals

Regarding the fourth objective, SC Johnson was responding to consumer demand for a chemical-free product alternative.

PR Strategy

The PR strategy placed a focus in two key areas. Messages were designed to educate consumers, mainly females, on the use of a multi-pronged strategy for fighting West Nile. Consumers should remove standing water, wear light-coloured clothing, wear long sleeves, and use an insect repellent like Off! Second, the messages would differentiate Off! from the competition—a difficult challenge when you consider that the only difference between competing products is the concentra-

tion of DEET. To enhance message credibility, Johnson employed expert entomologists as credible sources to go to for West Nile virus protection information.

The strategy for Off! Botanicals was to emphasize the importance of using federally registered insect repellent instead of untested home remedies and health-store concoctions.

PR Execution

The PR campaign was implemented in four phases:

1. Introduce credible spokespeople through targeted, regional media advisories that included credentials and availability.

2. Launch Off! Botanicals in early May through regional news releases. The releases referred to the spokespeople and offered TV visuals, photographs, and prepared quotes.

3. In July, survey results about West Nile virus were released to the public. This aspect of the plan would be released delicately since July was the peak period for West Nile.

4. The final phase involved the release to the media of a series of "camera-ready stories" about choosing insect repellent, choosing a non-DEET repellent, and tips for parents.

Results

The campaign generated approximately 20 million branded impressions and some 80 interviews across a broad cross-section of Canadian media. The budget for the public relations effort was $300 000. In conjunction with other advertising and marketing communications efforts, sales of Off! increased 150 percent in 2003. Not bad for a brand that's 40 years old!

Source: Adapted from Sara Minogue, "Off! Makes a Comeback," *Strategy*, October 20, 2003, p. 19.

Off Botanicals www.mosquitoes.com/botanicals.asp

track of content do exist. They record what is being reported, where, to how many people, over what period of time, in which media, and how the coverage changes over time.[10] This kind of information provides a company with the means to justify its investment in public relations. What was the value of the effort in terms of advertising equivalency?[11]

For additional insight into public relations planning, read the Advertising in Action vignette **Building Share for a 40-Something Brand.**

FIGURE
14.5

Some unique and innovative
public relations tools

Here are some tactical suggestions for getting the media and the public to take notice of a brand or company.

AWARDS

Brand-sponsored awards that support brand positioning and leadership (e.g., Purina dog food sponsors annual awards for dogs that are heroes).

CAUSE-RELATED MARKETING

Corporate or brand support of causes based on the interests of customers (e.g., EPCDR financially supports Alberta's arts communications. See Figure 14.1 for details).

CEOS

The top executive should be the company's most effective media spokesperson (e.g., Bill Gates at Microsoft; Steve Jobs at Apple).

BRANDED MERCHANDISE

Select merchandise that will positively communicate a brand message (e.g., golf shirts, bomber jackets, key chains, etc.).

PLANT TOURS

Make the factory a popular tourist attraction (e.g., virtually every tourist to Smiths Falls, Ontario, visits the Hershey chocolate factory. A free sample is provided at the end of the tour).

ROAD SHOWS

The brand hits the road using a decorated vehicle as a means of attracting attention. Product samples may be given away at each stop (e.g., Shoppers Drug Mart launched their Optimum loyalty card using a Hummer, and Sunlight detergent used a set of vans resembling sunlight boxes for their "Go Ahead. Get Dirty" campaign).

SURVEYS

The results of surveys are a proven way of achieving positive media exposure. Data derived from marketing research should be used for publicity purposes.

TRADE SHOWS

Shows are the ideal launching pad for new products. Be where your customers are (e.g., Comdex shows display the latest gadgetry in computers and telecommunications).

The Tools of the Trade

The tools available to execute public relations programs are diverse. There are those that are used routinely to communicate newsworthy information and those that are used periodically or on special occasions only. This section discusses those vehicles that are used routinely. See Figure 14.5 for information about some unique and periodically used vehicles.

PRESS RELEASE

A **press release** (news release) is a document containing all of the essential elements of the story (who, what, when, where, and why). The release is written in a format that communicates key details early. Editors make quick decisions on what to go with and what to discard. Copies of the release are mailed to a list of preferred editors (e.g., established and reliable contacts based on past relationships), and it can also be distributed by a national newswire service. News releases are distributed at news conferences or sent to the media directly by mail, fax, and email. It is now common for companies to post their press releases on their websites. A sample press release appears in Figure 14.6.

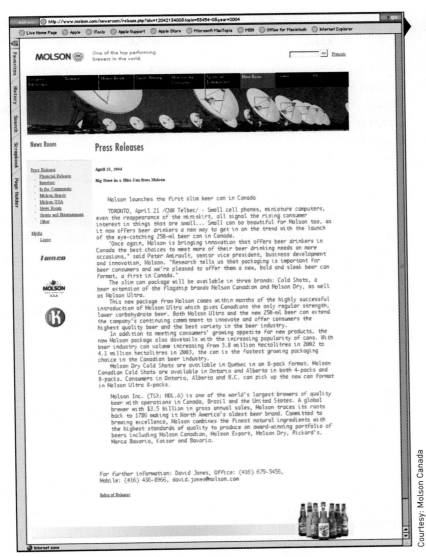

FIGURE

14.6

Molson announces the launch of a new can by press release

PRESS CONFERENCE

A **press conference** is a gathering of news reporters invited to witness the release of important information about a company or product. Because the conference is time-consuming for the media representatives, it is usually reserved for only the most important announcements. A crisis situation, for example, is usually handled by a press conference. A **press kit** is usually distributed at a conference. The press kit includes a schedule of conference events; a list of company participants, including biographical information; a press release; photographs; copies of speeches; videos; and any other relevant information. **Video news releases**—stories prepared by a company for use by television stations—are somewhat controversial. Critics see them as propaganda and object when stations don't mention their origin. Nonetheless, if the shoe fits, the media will wear it—a good video can save the station time and money.

PUBLICATIONS

A publication or **house organ** is a document that outlines news and events about the organization and its employees. It can be distributed internally to employees or externally to suppliers, distributors, shareholders, and alumni. A house organ can be in the form of a newsletter, booklet, brochure, newspaper, or magazine. The objective of the house organ is to generate goodwill and build positive public opinion about the organization. Most colleges and universities have an alumni publication that is well received by former students. They like to know what's going on at the alma mater. The *Annual Report* is a vital publication for publicly held companies. It is a statement of the company's health and wealth and is used to attract new investors and build corporate image. The content of annual reports and other relevant information about a company is now readily available at most company websites.

POSTERS AND DISPLAYS

Posters and displays are a common form of internal employee communications. They communicate vital information regarding safety, security, employee benefits, and special events. Displays and exhibits are a portable and mobile form of communications. An exhibit typically provides a history of an organization, product displays and information, and future plans (e.g., plant expansion, new product innovations). Exhibits are appropriate for shopping malls and colleges and universities. At colleges and universities, an exhibit staffed with company representatives is a useful vehicle for distributing recruitment information to graduates.

Internally, **bulletin boards** are a useful vehicle for keeping employees informed about news and events. For example, social events are commonly announced on boards in central locations (staff lounges, cafeterias, and common areas). **Email** is now a quick and convenient way to communicate important information to employees.

WEBSITES

Corporate and brand websites are now an integral element of marketing communications. Since the purpose of the website is to communicate information about a company, it can be an effective public relations tool. Visitors to a website quickly form an impression about a company based on the experience they encounter at the site. Therefore, the site must download quickly and be easy to navigate. Providing some kind of entertainment or interactive activity also enhances the visit. The website provides an opportunity to inform the public of an organization's latest happenings. Content can vary from financial information to product information to games and contests. It is now quite common to post all press releases about a company on the corporate website. See the illustration in Figure 14.7 for details.

Public Relations as a Communications Medium

Public relations is only one element in the integrated communications mix, but it can play a key role in specific situations. Those responsible for corporate and brand communications should be aware of the basic benefits and drawbacks of public relations communications.

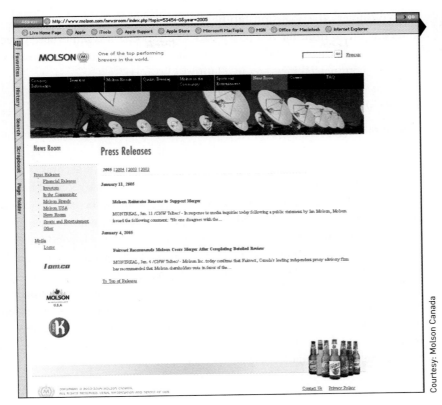

FIGURE 14.7

Companies publish press releases at their websites

ADVANTAGES OF PUBLIC RELATIONS

Public relations is often perceived negatively by the consumer—it is associated with terms such as "spin" and "propaganda." In reality, nothing could be further from the truth. Public relations done properly can be a **credible source of information**. Simply stated, when the message is delivered by an independent third party, such as a journalist or broadcaster, the message is delivered more persuasively than any form of advertising. Further, articles appearing in the media are perceived as being more objective than advertisements. If a company can win favourable press coverage, its message is more likely to be absorbed and believed.[12]

Third-party endorsements by trusted media personalities can **drive up sales**. Here is an illustration to dramatize the point. In 1992, the CBS newsmagazine *60 Minutes* reported that people in France, whose diet is rich in butter and cream and who consume red wine with meals, suffer far fewer heart attacks than Americans do. The report suggested that drinking a moderate amount of red wine could prevent heart attacks by lowering cholesterol. The effect was so astonishing that red wine sales in the United States increased 50 percent after the broadcast. This example points to a peculiarity about public relations: no matter how many millions of dollars are spent on ads, nothing sells a product as well as free publicity, especially something that discusses health claims.[13]

Public relations provides assistance in **building relationships** with consumers and other publics. In today's competitive environment the product alone cannot build consumer confidence. Public relations can help build rapport through an ongoing dialogue with consumers. It is a relationship-building tool that can make a difference—it can separate one brand from the rest of the pack. Such a benefit is important, given the rising costs of communicating via media advertising, the fragmentation of the media, and the clutter of commercial messages in all forms of media.

DISADVANTAGES OF PUBLIC RELATIONS

One of the biggest drawbacks of public relations is the **lack of control** by the company. Through press releases and press conferences, the company does its best to communicate factual information and hopes that it will be presented accurately by the media. Since the media are pressed for time and space, all materials received from companies and selected for use are judiciously edited. If only some of the facts are communicated, the story could be misrepresented or presented in a less than desirable manner. Despite this possibility there are those who believe that any publicity is good publicity!

Catching the eyes and ears of editors is crucial to the success of any public relations program. That is a challenge, considering the enormous amounts of material that flow into media outlets each day. Consequently, the cost of preparing and delivering information may go to **waste**. The senior management of an organization must recognize the waste factor and be prepared to absorb the costs associated with it. Simply stated, what is important to the company and its management group may not be perceived as important by the media. End of story!

Event Marketing and Sponsorships

Event marketing and sponsorships are fast becoming important elements of the marketing communications mix. **Event marketing** is the process, planned by a sponsoring organization, of integrating a variety of communication elements to support an event theme (e.g., Molson's coordination of advertising, public relations, and sales promotion activities for the Molson Indy car races in Toronto and Vancouver).

Event sponsorship is the financial support of an event (e.g., an auto race, a theatrical performance, or a marathon road race) by a sponsor in return for advertising privileges associated with the event. For example, the annual Montreal International Jazz Festival attracts sponsors such as Bell, General Motors, Loto Quebec, Labatt Bleue, and Radio-Canada. Sponsorships are usually offered by the organizer of the event on a tiered basis. For instance, a lead sponsor or sponsors would pay a maximum amount and receive maximum privileges. Other sponsors would pay less and receive fewer privileges.

According to IEG Consulting, a Chicago-based sponsorship measurement firm, the North American sponsorship market is valued at $9.57 billion. Sports sponsorships with revenues of $6.65 billion, or 70 percent of all event sponsorship revenue, attract the lion's share of sponsorship investment.[14] IEG is forecasting a reshuffling of sponsorship investment in the coming years. They project a decline in sports investment and modest increases in spending in other sponsorship areas.[15]

SPORTS SPONSORSHIP

As stated above, sport is the largest segment for event sponsorship investment. On an ongoing basis, the most popular of the sports are auto racing, golf, tennis, and running. Each of these sports attracts an elite group of sponsor companies. In golf, for example, Mercedes and Buick are closely associated with professional golf tournaments, and Cadillac is a featured sponsor for the entire Senior PGA tournament schedule.

In Canada, sports sponsorships are dominated by some of our largest manufacturers, service companies, and retailers. The automobile industry is well represented by companies such as General Motors and Ford, the brewing industry by Molson and Labatt, and the financial industry by RBC Financial Group, BMO Financial Group, Visa, and MasterCard. MasterCard, for example, sponsors at the national level the Canadian Women's Open Golf Championship and at the grassroots level a junior golf development program called Future Links.

How effective is the investment in sports sponsorship? A key indicator of success is the effect the association with a sponsored event has on consumers' awareness of a brand or company. For example, which beer company is closely associated with Blue Jays baseball, which telecommunications company is associated with the Canadian Open Men's Golf Championship, and which brand of beer is the lead sponsor of the WWF (World Wrestling Federation)? If you can't name these companies, then perhaps the companies are not getting a good return for their sponsorship investment. For the record, Labatt Blue sponsors the Blue Jays broadcasts, Bell sponsors the Canadian Open, and Molson Export sponsors the World Wrestling Federation. See the illustration in Figure 14.8.

FIGURE
14.8

Molson Export finds the WWF is a good sponsorship opportunity

Courtesy: Molson Canada

Canadian Olympic Association
www.coa.ca

The grandest of sports sponsorships is the Olympic Games. The Olympics present an attractive yet expensive opportunity for corporate sponsors. Financial support of the Canadian Olympic Association (COA) gives a company the right to run advertising and sales promotion programs in the years and months preceding the Games. Many leading companies renew their commitment to the Olympics each time around because they see great value in participation. For companies operating on a global scale, Olympic participation makes economic sense. Among these companies are Coca-Cola, McDonald's, Kodak, and Visa.

The Olympics is seen as a vehicle to build brand image on a global scale, and building image is the primary benefit that sponsorships offer. A research study conducted by Starcom Worldwide of Toronto revealed that 78 percent of those surveyed said they feel very positive toward companies that are official sponsors of the Olympic Games. Further, 67 percent said that Olympic sponsors are companies "I can trust."[16] In an era of hyper-competitiveness, such positive attitudes toward a company are a means of differentiation.

AMBUSH MARKETING   A recent phenomenon associated with sports-event marketing is the practice of ambush marketing. **Ambush marketing** is a promotional strategy used by non-sponsors to capitalize on the popularity or prestige of an event by giving the false impression that they are the sponsors. Such a strategy works because people are often confused about who the real sponsors are.

Labatt Breweries of Canada walked away from its long-running sponsorship of the Olympic Games due in part to the ambush efforts of arch-rival Molson Inc. While Labatt was sponsoring the Games, Molson was sponsoring Olympics-bound teams or athletes, and that type of association lessened the impact of Labatt's exclusive advertising deal. In the 2002 Olympic Games in Salt Lake City, Labatt was the official games sponsor, but was overshadowed when Molson gave $1 million to the Canadian Hockey Association to sponsor the men's and women's Olympic hockey teams. Molson reaped a marketing windfall when both hockey teams won gold. Both companies ran ads around the winter games, so it was difficult for consumers to judge who was the "official" Olympic sponsor.[17]

VENUE MARKETING AND SPONSORSHIPS   An offshoot of sports sponsorship is **venue marketing**, or **venue sponsorship**. Here, a company or brand is linked to a physical site such as a stadium, arena, or theatre. In Canada, there is GM Place (the Vancouver Canucks play there), the Corel Centre (Ottawa Senators), the Bell Centre (Montreal Canadiens), and the Air Canada Centre (home of the Maple Leafs and Raptors). These companies agree that such sponsorships offer huge opportunities for building or improving their image at a reasonable cost and with minimal risk. Exposure via television broadcasts of games and mentions in the print and broadcast media when the results of games are reported are so frequent that the corporate name is soon closely linked with the building. To an outsider the costs are considerable. For example, General Motors paid $26 million for the 20-year agreement in Vancouver and Air Canada paid $20 million for a 20-year agreement in Toronto.[18] Perhaps Air Canada got a bargain!

ATHLETE SPONSORSHIPS   Rather than sponsoring an event, some companies find that sponsoring a star athlete can pay dividends. Companies will search for an athlete whose image and reputation is a close match to their own. Bell, for example, has been a long-time sponsor of Mike Weir, now a prominent professional golfer who is ranked in the Top 10 worldwide. Bell supported Weir in the lean years but has benefited from Weir's exposure since he has become more successful on the PGA Tour. The benefit of this sponsorship peaked when Weir won the Masters Championship (one of four major championships each year) in 2003.

There are risks associated with "star" sponsorships. Last year's hot commodity can be this year's has-been. While Mike Weir remains a celebrity golfer, he did not make the cut in the 2004 Masters Championship, a clear indication that the fortunes of an athlete can change dramatically in a short period. As a form of protection for the sponsor when dealing with celebrities, ethics clauses must be built into contractual arrangements with stars. The Kobe Bryant scandal (his alleged rape of a young female) in 2003 was a total contradiction to his image and reputation. The fact that he could be involved in such a predicament, and the fact that the court case would get so much public attention and scrutiny, scared off many of his long-time corporate sponsors.

LEVELS OF SPORTS SPONSORSHIPS Sports sponsorship can be subdivided into classifications from global events to local events (see Figure 14.9). While international and national sponsorship programs require significant financial investment, organizations can be involved for much less if they consider **grassroots** participation. Local participation at much lower cost can produce equally attractive results. If the real objective is to reach a target market and sell more goods, consider what Tide detergent and Sunny Delight are doing.

Both Tide and Sunny Delight (Sunny D) are closely aligned with the Canadian Soccer Association. There are more than 700 000 youth soccer players in Canada, and where there are kids playing soccer, there are soccer moms watching. The connection

Canadian Soccer Association
www.canadasoccer.com

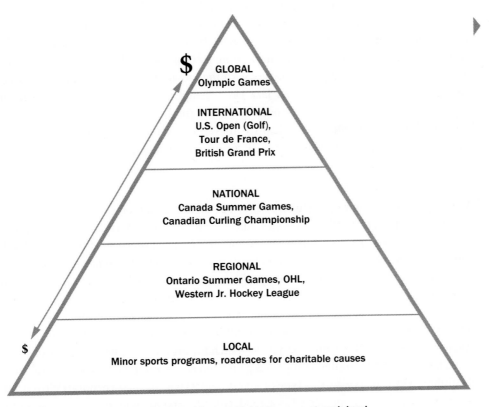

FIGURE 14.9

The levels of sports sponsorship

Costs associated with sponsorship increase at each level.

Costs associated with sponsorship increase at each level.

between muddy soccer uniforms and Tide is obvious, as is the connection between thirsty participants and a healthful fruit-based beverage.

The Tide Mini Soccer program is international in scope but operated locally by member organizations of the Canadian Soccer Association. In a non-competitive environment, the Tide Mini program promotes and teaches basic soccer skills, fair play, fun, good sportsmanship, and teamwork. The program reaches 200 000 children, their parents, and volunteers. Sunny Delight runs a soccer skills program that can be implemented by local coaches. The program tests kids in essential skill areas such as heading, dribbling, passing, and shooting.[19]

ENTERTAINMENT SPONSORSHIP

Corporations invest huge amounts of money to sponsor concerts and secure endorsements from high-profile personalities in the hope that the celebrity–company relationships will pay off in the long run. Companies such as Molson, Coca-Cola, and PepsiCo, which are interested in targeting youth and young adult segments, use entertainment sponsorship as a vehicle for developing pop-music and youth-lifestyle marketing strategies.

In Quebec, for example, Budweiser beer is synonymous with rock music. According to Nicolas Dubé, creative director at Palm Publicité Marketing, "Bud owns rock music in Quebec because we are always knocking on the same door. It is very important to know your target and feed into their mind-set." Unlike the rest of Canada where Bud's target market relates heavily to sports and male bonding activities, Quebecers relate very well to rock. As a result of rock-oriented advertising campaigns, various promotions, and sponsorships, Dubé believes that they could mask the bottle of beer in a poster, and everyone would still know it's a Bud ad.[20] Efforts such as this are designed to attract the young beer drinker who is on the verge of forming lifelong loyalties.

Festivals (film, comedy, and music) offer opportunities to reach a cross-section of adult target audiences. At festivals as popular as the Toronto Film Festival or Festival des Films du Monde in Montreal there are waiting lists for top-level sponsorships. It seems that companies want to align themselves with the movie stars who attend these types of events. The Montreal International Jazz Festival (approaching its 25th anniversary in 2004) reaches a 30-year-plus adult population and the Just for Laughs Comedy Festival reaches all adult age groups. More than 1.7 million spectators attended Just for Laughs in 2003.[21] Such a large reach makes the event a very worthwhile sponsorship investment.

CULTURAL AND ARTS SPONSORSHIP

Arts and cultural event opportunities embrace dance, film, literature, music, painting, sculpture, and theatre. What separates cultural events from sports and entertainment events is audience size. Depending on the sponsor, this can be an advantage or a disadvantage. A company such as Molson prefers the mass-audience reach of a sporting event, whereas Mercedes-Benz or BMW may prefer to reach a more selective and upscale audience through an arts event. Perhaps only 2500 people attend a particular cultural event, but those people most likely fit the demographic and psychographic profile of the target market. Typically, their education level would be above average, as would their income. Such an audience profile would be a good match for promoting a new luxury car.

The primary benefit that companies gain from sponsoring the arts is goodwill from the public. Most firms view this type of investment as part of their corporate citizenship objectives (e.g., they are perceived as a good, contributing member of society). Recently, however, companies are finding ways to capitalize on their sponsorship relationships without wearing out the public welcome. Bell Canada, a long-time sponsor of the Stratford Festival, enhanced its presence at the event through unique signage in the lobby of two theatre venues. Two giant-sized plasma screens looped information about the festival, as well as sponsorship recognition.

Taking a more product-oriented approach, Pfizer Inc. tied its Olay brand name to the production of *Gigi*, becoming the first packaged-goods company to sponsor a play at the Stratford Festival. Stratford offered the ideal demographic: women 35+ who are professionals, highly educated, and have a household income of at least $75 000. Olay conducted on-site sampling of its new Regenerist skin-care products. In both cases, organizers of the festival realized that sponsors wanted closer ties and more meaningful relationships in order to justify continued financial support.[22]

Bell has always invested in the communities it serves and has a varied sponsorship portfolio, which includes major cultural and sporting events that enable it to be present in the community throughout the year. See Figures 14.10 and 14.11 for details.

FIGURE

14.10

A corporate ad that communicates Bell's commitment to the community

FIGURE

14.11

A selection of sponsorships
from Bell Canada

Bell has a varied sponsorship portfolio that includes major cultural and sporting events on a national and local basis. The company has an ongoing presence in the community.

SPORTS

- Bell and the Air Canada Grand Prix (Formula 1 auto racing)
- Bell Challenge Cup (Pee Wee hockey challenge)
- Bell and the Molson Indy (CART auto racing)
- Bell Classic (women's charitable golf fundraiser)
- The Bell Canadian Open (men's professional golf)
- Bell Raptorball (grassroots basketball programs)
- Toronto Maple Leafs (telecommunications sponsor at the Air Canada Centre)
- Ottawa Senators (telecommunications sponsor)
- Toronto Rock Lacrosse (telecommunications sponsor)
- Ottawa Rebels Lacrosse (telecommunications sponsor)
- Canadian Olympic Team

CULTURE

- Bell Encourages Young People to Participate in Expo-Sciences (cross-Canada science exposition)
- Stratford Festival (major sponsor and communications partner)
- Shaw Festival (major sponsor and communications partner)
- Toronto Word on the Street Festival (major sponsor and communications partner)
- Toronto International Film Festival (major sponsor and communications partner)
- Vancouver International Film Festival (major sponsor and communications partner)
- Sprockets—Toronto International Film Festival for Children (major sponsor and communications partner)
- Bell Mobility and the Santa Claus Parade in Toronto
- Just For Laughs Festival, Montreal

Source: Adapted from the Bell Canada website: **bell.ca/en/about/bic/sponsore.ng**.

Strategic Considerations for Event Marketing

Advertisers cannot approach event marketing and sponsorships in a haphazard way. Their primary reason for entering into sponsorships is to create a favourable impression with their customers and target groups. To accomplish this, the fit between the event and the sponsor must be a good one. For instance, Nike sponsors national and international track and field events as well as community-based events such as fun runs. Much of the company's success has been based on event sponsorship and the distribution of merchandise that bears Nike's trademark logo—the swoosh. Generally, event sponsorship is a vehicle for enhancing the reputation of a company and the customer's awareness of a brand. The most effective sponsors adhere to the following principles when considering participation in event marketing.

- *Select events offering exclusivity* The need for companies to be differentiated within events they sponsor calls for exclusivity, meaning that direct competitors are blocked from sponsorship. Also, a concern among sponsors is the clutter of lower-level sponsors in non-competing categories that reduce the overall impact of the primary sponsor.

- *Use sponsorships to complement other promotional activity* The role that advertising and promotion will play in the sponsorship must be determined first. Sponsorship of the proper event will complement a company's other promotional activity. For example, Molson and hockey are a solid connection, forever. Molson advertises extensively during NHL broadcasts while sponsoring the Canadian national women's team and all kinds of adult recreational leagues across the country. Hockey is part of the fabric of Molson.[23]

- *Choose the target carefully* Events reach specific targets. For example, while rock concerts attract youth, symphonies tend to reach audiences that are older, urban, and upscale. As suggested earlier, it is the fit, or matching of targets, that is crucial. Do the demographics of the event audience match as closely as possible the demographics of the target market?

- *Select an event with an image that sells* The sponsor must capitalize on the image of the event and perhaps the prestige or status associated with it. A luxury car such as the Mercedes M-Class sport-utility vehicle may be a suitable sponsor for a significant art or cultural event or a major national golf championship (e.g., The Mercedes Open in Hawaii). The prestigious image and status of such events has an impact on the sale of products that project a comparable image (in this example, the image and status that come with ownership of a Mercedes-Benz automobile).

- *Establish selection criteria* In addition to using the criteria cited above, companies evaluating potential events for sponsorship should consider the long-term benefit such sponsorship offers compared to the costs in the short term. For example, being associated with an event that is ongoing, popular, and successful is wise, as there is less risk for the sponsor. Before committing financial resources to an event, a company should also consider whether it is likely to receive communications exposure through unpaid media sources and whether it will be able to administer the event efficiently. Events that receive substantial media exposure are very attractive. High levels of exposure offset any real or opportunity costs. An organization should establish firm objectives in terms of awareness and association scores, image improvement, and sales so that proper evaluation of the activity can be undertaken.

For more information on how companies have selected opportunities for event marketing, and the benefits they expect to gain from the association, see the Advertising in Action vignette **Labatt Sponsors USA Hockey.**

ADVERTISING IN action

Labatt Sponsors USA Hockey

Has Labatt Blue, a leading national brand of beer in Canada, sold out to hockey in the United States? Given the stature of the brand in Canada, and its association with Canadian hockey, what could possibly prompt a relationship with USA Hockey?

It is hard to believe but Canada's top selling beer is now the proud sponsor of USA Hockey—a program that embraces everything from Canada's arch-rivals, the U.S. national Olympic team (my God!), to adult recreational leagues and grassroots leagues south of the border.

This sponsorship deal makes pure business sense! The beer industry, like so many other industries, and hockey, is an international business. USA Hockey's sponsorship deal is with Labatt USA, a company based in Norwalk, Connecticut. It is owned by Interbrew SA of Belgium, the same company that owns Labatt Breweries of Canada, but it is operated independently from Canada.

Labatt's association with USA Hockey will have national impact, another reason to do it! Labatt Blue is the No. 3 imported beer in the United States. More to the point, being associated with a target audience's entertainment or lifestyle choice allows a marketer to differentiate their offering and connect with their target.

The key component of the deal is the sponsorship of USA Hockey's adult recreational hockey program that will be re-branded Labatt Blue USAdult Hockey. As sponsor of the U.S. men's and women's national teams, Blue will also serve as the official beer of all USA hockey-specific events through marketing and communications initiatives as the national teams advance to the 2006 Winter Games in Torino, Italy.

In rationalizing the decision to support USA Hockey, company spokesperson Geoff Blanck said the deal was more about targeting a specific demographic as opposed to supporting a nation's Olympic dreams. "This is really about hockey. It's not about one country or another." Is there any better way to reach the adult hockey fan and adult hockey player than to be associated with the largest and most renowned hockey organization in the United States?

Source: Adapted from Richard Bloom, "USA Hockey drafts Labatt as official sponsor," *The Globe and Mail*, March 2, 2004, p. B3.

USA Hockey www.usahockey.com

Measuring the Benefits of Sponsorship

One reason many companies are reluctant to enter into sponsorship programs is that results are difficult to measure. Large sums of money are spent at one time for a benefit that may be short-lived. The basic appeal of event marketing is that it provides an opportunity to communicate with consumers in an environment in which they are already emotionally involved. Beyond this, companies conduct marketing research to determine the impact that sponsorship association has. The following indicators, many of which are obtained from research, are used to measure the benefits of sponsorship.

Nokia Brier
www.nokiabrier.com

1. *Awareness* How much awareness of the event within the target group is there, and how well do people recall the brand or product name that sponsored the event? This is an important issue. To illustrate, Nokia is the present sponsor of the men's national curling championships in Canada. But Labatt was the sponsor for so long that the phrase "Labatt Brier" just naturally rolls off the tongue of curling fans. Nokia must find a way of leveraging its association with the Brier in order to make the investment pay off.
2. *Image* What change in image and what increase in the consumer perception of leadership or credibility result from the sponsorship? Market research before and

after event participation may be necessary to identify this benefit. As indicated earlier in the chapter, sponsors who are associated with the Olympic games received excellent scores on image and leadership in post-event marketing research.

3. *New clients* How many new clients were generated as a result of the company's sponsoring an event? It is important to include current and prospective customers in the event. For example, inviting customers to view the event from a **luxury box** and to have them enjoy the trappings associated with the box goes a long way in solidifying business relationships.

4. *Sales* Do increases in sales or market share occur during post-event periods? Participating in an event isn't like dropping a coupon; the actual impact may be longer term. In fact, the real sales benefit may take years to materialize, for it takes time for a sponsor to become closely associated with an event.

5. *Specific target reach* Do the events deliver constituency? Carefully selected events reach specific targets that are difficult to reach by conventional communications. For example, preteens and teens are difficult to reach through conventional media but can be reached effectively through sponsorship of rock concerts and music tours.

6. *Media coverage* What value was derived from editorial coverage? Did the sponsorship result in free publicity for the sponsor? The industry benchmark for sports sponsorship is currently 4:1, meaning $4 in exposure (e.g., free air time) for every $1 spent on sponsorship and its marketing support. Assuming an organization invests in a service to track exposure, it can measure spending equivalencies between free media exposure and comparable advertising.

For sponsorships to be successful, there must be sound business reasons for participating, and the activity must be carefully integrated with corporate marketing and marketing communications plans seamlessly. For every dollar spent on securing the sponsorship rights, an additional investment of $2 to $3 is needed to promote the association with the event. The organization must leverage the use of its website, incorporate the sponsorship into public relations campaigns, and run thematic promotions to get all customer groups (trade and consumers) involved. The various forms of marketing communications must complement each other.

Event Marketing and Sponsorship as a Communications Medium

When assessing whether to be involved with event marketing and sponsorships, an organization weighs the pros and cons of the activity in the context of how well it fits with other marketing and marketing communications strategies. There are numerous advantages and disadvantages of event marketing.

ADVANTAGES OF EVENT MARKETING AND SPONSORSHIP

The primary advantage of event marketing is **target marketing**. Participating in the right event allows an organization to reach its target audience directly and in an environment where the target is receptive to messages (e.g., an auto race where sponsorships are part of the ambience of the event). Sponsorships can also provide **face-to-face access** to current and prospective customers. For example, if a financial services company holds an investment seminar with an open invitation to the public, it will have access to new clients in a non-competitive environment; at such an event the message is delivered to a large group at one time. Finally, participation in the right events and sponsorships enhances a company's **public image**. Whether it's involvement with huge events such as the Olympics, or just supporting local community events, the effect on image is the same. As cited earlier in the chapter, companies that are perceived to be doing good things are liked better and trusted more.

DISADVANTAGES OF EVENT MARKETING AND SPONSORSHIP

The most prominent disadvantage to events and sponsorships is **cost**. Any event on a national or international scale involves significant financial commitment, and to enjoy the benefits of such events the commitment is necessary for an extended period. Opting in and out of big events leaves a confusing image with the public. As indicated earlier in the chapter, successful events must be supported with additional spending on advertising and promotion. One complaint commonly raised by event participants is the **clutter** of advertising and signage at events. If there are too many sponsors the message being delivered by an individual sponsor is diluted; hence, the investment is questionable. As well, the presence of **ambush marketing tactics** by competitors is diluting the product category exclusivity aspect of event participation. Finally, accurately **measuring the effectiveness** of the event or sponsorship in producing sound business results is difficult. It would be nice to know what the return on investment is, but there are so many variables that ultimately contribute to sales and market share performance that the impact of events and sponsorship cannot be isolated.

SUMMARY

Public relations refers to the communications that a firm has with its various publics. Controlled by the media, it is a form of communication for which the organization does not pay, but it is based on information supplied by the organization. Public relations plays a role in developing an organization's image and is an important means of communication in times of crisis.

Two diverse groups are important to an organization, and public relations programs communicate with both of them. *Internal publics* include employees, distributors, suppliers, shareholders, and regular customers. *External publics* include the media, governments, prospective shareholders, the financial community, and community groups.

Public relations plays a key role in delivering corporate-oriented messages and building and protecting the image of a company or brand. As well, it helps generate publicity for the company by distributing news releases to the media. A public relations campaign is planned much like any other communications plan. It starts with a situation analysis and then firm objectives and strategies are devised. Once the plan is implemented, research procedures are undertaken to track the effectiveness of the campaign. Organizations communicate with the various publics through press releases, press conferences, publications, posters and displays, bulletin boards, and videos. Company websites now play a key role in building corporate and brand image.

Event marketing and sponsorship programs are now an important element of a firm's promotion mix, particularly among large Canadian corporations. Sponsorship is popular in three areas, namely sports, entertainment, and cultural events. Unlike other types of promotion, events and sponsorships have an indirect impact on product or company performance. The benefits derived from this activity include goodwill and an increased awareness as opposed to measurable increases in sales or market share.

Organizations must carefully consider certain criteria before jumping into event marketing. They should look for events that offer exclusivity, that complement other marketing communications strategies, that closely match their target market's profile, and that deliver high levels of media exposure. If the right events are selected and the association with the event is leveraged through advertising and promotion, the organization should enjoy high levels of awareness, an improved image, and stronger sales. The latter will likely occur in the long term.

KEY TERMS

advocacy advertising 430
ambush marketing 446
content analysis 438
corporate advertising 430
event marketing 444
event sponsorship 444

house organ 441
lobbying 435
media relations 434
press conferenc 441
press releas 440

product placement 433
public affairs 435
public relations 429
publicity 429
situation analysis 435

REVIEW QUESTIONS

1. What is the difference between public relations and publicity?

2. What is the difference between corporate advertising and advocacy advertising?

3. Identify and briefly explain the role of public relations in the following areas:
   a) Reputation management
   b) Publicity generation
   c) Media relations
   d) Community relations

4. What is lobbying and why is it necessary for organizations to conduct such a practice?

5. What are the key elements of a public relations strategy?

6. What is a press kit and what role does it serve?

7. What is a house organ and what role does it play in an organization?

8. Identify the basic advantages and disadvantages of using public relations campaigns as a means of communication.

9. What is the difference between event marketing and event sponsorship?

10. Briefly explain the following event marketing terms:
    a) Ambush marketing
    b) Venue marketing

11. Identify and briefly explain the essential factors an organization should review when deciding to participate in event marketing.

12. What are the primary benefits an organization gains when it invests in event marketing?

DISCUSSION QUESTIONS

1. "Public relations now plays a more important role in the communications mix of business organizations today." Discuss the merits of this statement, and provide examples to justify your opinion.

2. Assume you are a public relations consultant and Coca-Cola has approached you for advice. They want your recommendation for a celebrity spokesperson to endorse Powerade (a sports beverage), along with a public relations recommendation to announce the signing of the celebrity. Develop a brief plan of action. Be as specific as you can. Provide justification for the celebrity you recommend.

3. Visit the website of the following companies (use other companies if you wish). Evaluate each site as a vehicle for public relations activity. Does the site provide worthwhile information that will create goodwill for the company? Explain.

   a) The Body Shop **the-body-shop.com**
   b) Apple **apple.com**
   c) BMW **bmw.com**

4. If you were the marketing communications manager for any one of the following products, what events would you sponsor? What benefits would you derive from these sponsorships? Be specific.

   a) Budweiser beer
   b) Gillette personal care products
   c) Hallmark cards
   d) Michelin tires
   e) American Express traveller's cheques

5. It seems that measuring the effectiveness or return on investment of event marketing and sponsorships is difficult. If so, is it justifiable for companies to invest significant sums of money in event marketing (e.g., global, international, and national events)? Do the benefits outweigh the costs? What is your opinion?

NOTES

1. Dana Flavelle, "Consumers pay attention if 'sorry' starts at the top," *Toronto Star*, September 10, 2000, pp. B1, B6.

2. Linda Smith, "When the trust begins to rust," *Marketing*, March 1, 2004, p. 12.

3. "Unilever brings world's No. 1 male deodorant brand to North America," press release, **www.newswire.ca/en/releases/archive/August2002/ c4801.html**.

4. Rich Thomaselli, "Asics sneaks are 'Kill Bill' sleeper hit," *Advertising Age*, November 10, 2003, pp. 4, 32.

5. Paul-Mark Rendon, "Casting call," *Marketing*, May 5, 2003, p. 15.

6. Diane Slopek-Weber, The TDL Group, letter to the editor, *Marketing*, May 14, 2001, p. 46.

7. **www.timhortons.com**.

8. Jack Trout and Steve Rivken, *The New Positioning* (New York: McGraw-Hill, 1996), p. 147.

9. Thomas L. Harris, *Value-Added Public Relations* (Chicago: NTP Publications, 1998), pp. 243–244.

10. Chris Daniels, "Carb-charged communications," *Marketing*, March 1, 2004, p. 7.

11. John Burnett, Sandra Moriarty, and E. Stephen Grant, *Introduction to Integrated Marketing Communications* (Toronto: Prentice Hall, 2001), p. 306.

12. Regis McKenna, *Relationship Marketing* (Reading, Mass: Addison Wesley Publishing, 2001), p. 5.

13. Kevin Goldman, "Winemakers look for more publicity," *Wall Street Journal*, September 29, 1994, p. 353.

14. Mark Donnison, "Using equity to make sponsorship soar," *Strategy*, March 12, 2001, p. B9.

15. IEG Inc., "Where the Dollars Go," **www.sponsorship.com/Learn/wheredollarsgo.asp**, November 2003.

16. David Shiffman and Scott Neslund, "Calculating Olympic impact," *Marketing*, October 30, 2000, p. 48.

17. Paul Brent, "Olympics deals not 'exclusive' enough," *Financial Post*, April 5, 2004, p. FP4.

18. Wendy Tanka, "High-tech firms lift their profiles at sports venues," *Rocky Mountain News*, August 15, 1996, p. B16.

19. Canadian Soccer Association website, **www.canadasoccer.com/eng/minisoccer**.

20. Lucy Saddleton, "Cast in rock: Quebec Bud effort targets rockers where they drink," *Strategy*, April 5, 2004, p. 16.

21. Brendan Christie, "Join the party," *Strategy*, April 5, 2004, pp. 15, 16.

22. Sara Minogue, "Enriching the event," *Strategy*, September 8, 2003, p. 15.

23. Richard Bloom, "USA Hockey drafts Labatt as official sponsor, *The Globe and Mail*, March 2, 2004, p. B3.

THE practice OF ADVERTISING

Below the Line Marketing and Marketing Communications

A landscape of increasingly fragmented media, consisting of text messaging, internet, and viral marketing along with traditional staples of television, radio, and print advertising, makes it harder for brands to break through the clutter. Consequently, marketers are looking at promotions, event marketing, and public relations as a means of connecting with their customers.

In the past, marketers perceived promotions and event marketing as activities that would influence sales volume in the short term, and the exact role that public relations could play in building a brand was somewhat of a mystery. That way of thinking is changing—marketers are now devising sophisticated promotions and involving themselves with the softer side of communications to build brands and brand awareness in the consumer's mind over the long term. Businesses are looking for integrated solutions to their marketing problems, and that means opportu-

nities in sales promotion, event marketing and sponsorships, and public relations are rising.

To illustrate how marketers are shifting their priorities, consider the following marketing communications strategies.

Kraft Canada

Packaged goods marketing organization Kraft Canada is constantly running sales promotions for its various product lines, but it has never run one bigger and perhaps more effective than its recent "Every Pack Wins Crayola" promotion. The back-to-school promotion saw Kraft give away more than 500 000 Crayola products when consumers claimed their prizes online through the YTV website.

The Crayola promotion involved 12 different product lines and resulted in huge product displays in Canada's largest supermarket chains (see Figure 1).

FIGURE 1

Courtesy of Tannen Maury/Bloomberg News/Landor

According to Carol Giles, director of customer marketing services at Kraft, "The back-to-school promotion delivered the highest online redemption rate in Kraft history. Combining the strength of two recognized and established brands in the back-to-school market, this unique program aimed to further increase awareness and to reward customers quickly and easily with every purchase."

The promotion was a genuine hit with moms. They saw the incredible value in it. The promotion ran from July to December 2003 and was communicated through television ads, *What's Cooking* magazine, *Not for Adults* magazine, in-store displays, and Kraft's website.

So successful was the promotion that Kraft plans to repeat it in 2004 and also plans to double the number of Crayola prizes.

Molson Breweries of Canada

What's a new product launch without a party? "A party can bring a brand to life," says Justine Rae, manager of events and promotions at Molson Sports and Entertainment. Rae managed the spring 2003 launch of Molson's Brazilian import, A Marca Bavaria. A launch party can play a role in communicating the essence of the brand and where the brand is going to be positioned. It also gives the brand an opportunity to interact with consumers and key influencers. How a brand is reflected at a party is all in the details!

In this day and age it's not good enough to just show people a good time—anyone can do that—it's about creating a brand experience. For A Marca Bavaria, that meant reflecting adventure, sensuality, and fun—qualities that are associated with Brazil and, in Molson's view, beer. Molson opted for a "Passport to Adventure" theme and invitations were in the form of boarding cards.

"Authenticity is a big part of the brand," Rae says. "We actually spoke to people in Brazil to make sure we were targeting and representing things in a positive light." Lush green plants, a feisty Samba band, spicy foods, Brazilian dancers, and plenty of free beer helped "transport" guests from snowy Toronto to tropical Brazil—if only for a few hours.

"If guests are impressed by the event, they'll carry your message to the masses and ignite a buzz among the brand's target audience. It's essential to get the support of key influencers." In Molson's case that

meant bar and restaurant staff and owners, the media, and trendsetters who drive tastes and trends in industries such as fashion and music.

L'Oréal Canada

L'Oréal brand Garnier Fructis sponsored the eighth annual World Ski & Snowboard Festival in Whistler, B.C., in April 2003. The event drew 260 000 resort visits over 10 days.

Garnier Fructis chose this event because Whistler/Blackcomb is the mecca of the board/free-skier movement. These people have the same spirit as Garnier Fructis—free spirit, accessibility, and irreverence. As well, it could be the next new Olympic sport. "It's all about catching the wave at the right time and surfing it for a good number of years."

Involvement with this kind of event does seem out of character for an established company like L'Oréal, but Garnier Fructis desires universal appeal with consumers. It wants to get out with the people, it wants to be more grassroots, and it wants its communications to have a bit of an edge. Garnier wants to be perceived as a street-fighting type of brand.

To maximize exposure at the event the brand set up the Style Zone. "We set up chairs with kids from the mountain who knew the scene and a bit about hair styling. Not professionals, just average kids. The kids learned about the brand's attributes in Garnier Fructis 101. They got consumers styled up—2000 of them in total, mostly kids between 18 and 24 years old, the primary target market for the brand."

Sales results are hard to measure, but L'Oréal is very happy about reaching its target in their environment—an environment that was a mixture of sports, music, and the right venue.

Unilever Canada

Unilever wanted to launch a new Lever 2000 body wash with a splash, but with the Lever 2000 brand not having much marketing support in recent years the company had to find something unique that would resonate with consumers. How about a shower in the streets!

The objective of the Lever 2000 Pure Rain Body Wash was to generate awareness and offer trial sizes as incentives for a sale. The brand was targeted at people 18 to 35 years old.

Experiential marketing in the form of a street-level sampling program was the centrepiece of the

FIGURE

2

The images of Lever appear with the permission of Unilever Canada.

launch. Consumers in high-traffic locations in Toronto, Montreal, and Calgary bumped into merchandisers called the Shower Heads on the streets. In a one-week blitz, the Shower Heads, wearing shower caps and even portable shower stalls, handed out 59-mL-sized samples (see Figure 2).

To create additional buzz, transit shelters in Toronto and Calgary were disguised as large, communal showers, complete with showerheads and water droplets on glass panels. Exterior shelter posters showed a nude male reaching for a towel. Inside, there was a poster of a mirror and wash basin.

Radio played a key role in generating buzz. In Calgary, listeners to Power 107 qualified to win a trip to the rainforests of Belize by taking cordless phones into the shower, on air, and singing songs—a very

high degree of customer involvement to say the least!

About 170 000 samples were distributed in one week, and over a four-week period more than 1.2 million impressions were generated by transit-shelter advertising. The launch was a huge success! According to ACNielsen, the brand took the lead position in the category of Refreshing Body Washes, and it has become the fifth largest body wash in the country.

Unilever successfully tapped in to something good. A recent study from the United States revealed that experiential marketing events are more influential than either television advertising or direct mail in influencing how people make their purchase decisions. By location, consumers show a preference for such events at shopping malls, in stores, and other public events.

Adapted from Fawzia Sheikh, "Casting Off the One-Off," *Marketing*, May 10, 2004, pp. 15–16; Michelle Warren, "Life of the Party," *Marketing*, July 28/August 4, 2003, p. 2; Sara Minogue, "Fructis aims for free skiers," *Strategy*, June 2, 2003, p. 18; and Unilever Canada's Shower Heads Promotion, 2002 Promotion Awards, *Marketing*, 2002.

CASE STUDY 1

INTERCONTINENTAL HOTELS GROUP PLC Holiday Inn Division

The Corporate Group

InterContinental Hotels Group is a leading global hospitality company with more than 3500 hotels and 535 000 guest rooms in 100 countries. Every year more than 120 million people choose to stay at one of the company's lodging brands.

InterContinental operates in all segments of the hotel industry. The market is segmented on the basis of price and quality. The quality criteria include the nature and extent of services and amenities offered by hotels in each segment.

Within the InterContinental Group are the following brands: InterContinental Hotels and Resorts, Crowne Plaza Hotels & Resorts, Holiday Inn, Holiday Inn Select, Holiday Inn SunSpree, Holiday Inn Express, Holiday Inn Garden Court, Holiday Inn Family Suites Resort, Staybridge Suites, and Candlewood Suites. While the list of brands is extensive, InterContinental does not operate all brands in all countries.

The Global Hotel Market

The hotel industry is extremely competitive and is dominated by numerous very large international hotel groups. As of 2004, InterContinental became the international leader in terms of the number of rooms available even though it operates far fewer properties than some of the other large groups. Refer to Figure 1 for a listing of the Top 10 hotel groups based on room availability.

Rank	Group	Country	Hotels	Rooms	% Change (Rooms)
1	InterContinental	GB	3 520	536 318	+4.0
2	Cendant	USA	6 403	518 435	-3.3
3	Marriott	USA	2 656	479 882	+5.7
4	Accor	FRA	3 894	453 403	+2.9
5	Choice	USA	4 810	388 618	+4.0
6	Hilton Corp.	USA	2 161	349 965	+4.0
7	Best Western	USA	4 110	310 245	+0.4
8	Starwood	USA	738	229 247	+1.0
9	Carlson	USA	881	147 624	+4.0
10	Hilton Int.	GB	412	99 364	-1.1

Source: MKG Consulting Database 03/04.

FIGURE 1

Hotel group rankings— Rooms available

In terms of brand (e.g., brands within corporate groups), Best Western is the international leader with Holiday Inn ranking second. Best Western operates smaller hotels, and there are many more of them. Other brand leaders include Comfort Inns & Suites, Marriott Hotels, and Days Inns of America. Refer to Figure 2 for a list of the leading hotel brands internationally.

FIGURE 2

Top 10 hotel brands— International hotel market

Rank	Brand	Group	Hotels	Rooms	% Change (Rooms)
1	Best Western	Best Western	4 110	310 245	+0.4
2	Holiday Inn	InterContinental	1 529	287 769	-1.9
3	Comfort Inns & Suites	Choice	2 366	177 444	+4.5
4	Marriott	Marriott Int.	472	173 974	+5.3
5	Days Inn	Cendant	1 892	157 995	-0.5
6	Sheraton Hotels	Starwood	394	134 648	+0.8
7	Hampton Inn	Hilton Corp.	1 255	127 543	+2.3
8	Super 8 Motels	Cendant	2 086	126 421	-0.3
9	Holiday Inn Express	InterContinental	1 455	120 296	10.2
10	Ramada	Cendant	905	104 636	-9.9

Source: MKG Consulting Database 03/04.

The chart indicates InterContinental is expanding rooms for Holiday Inn Express while reducing the numbers of rooms at Holiday Inn. InterContinental is reacting to the changing needs of travellers. Travellers are requesting value for their money and many are opting to stay at hotels offering good value in the economy segment.

Canadian Operations—InterContinental Hotels

The Canadian market is divided into three segments: luxury, mid-range, and economy. In Canada, in the luxury segment there are several InterContinental Hotels and Crowne Plaza Hotels located in key urban markets. These brands offer consistently high standards, a premium list of amenities and services, a full complement of business services, excellent dining choices, quality fitness facilities, and comprehensive meeting capabilities.

InterContinental's mid-range brand is Holiday Inn. Holiday Inn is a full-service hotel typically situated in convenient locations in and around cities. Holiday Inn offers comfortable guest rooms, restaurants and room service, a restaurant and lounge, swimming pool and fitness centre, meeting rooms, and 24-hour business services.

Holiday Inn Select is also a mid-range hotel but it caters specifically to the business traveller. Throughout Canada and North America they are located near business centres and airports. Select offers business-class rooms, 24-hour business services, and comprehensive meeting services.

Holiday Inn Express is InterContinental's entry in the economy segment of the market. Express appeals directly to value-oriented travellers who do not require an extensive list of services. Express offers comfortable, well-equipped rooms and a free breakfast bar featuring fresh fruit, cereals, and pastries. This segment of the market is growing, so InterContinental plans to expand its presence here.

The Canadian Market

The Canadian hotel industry generates $11.1 billion in revenue (2002). Occupancy rates dropped in 2003 to 59 percent. The industry suffered during the aftermath of the 9/11 disaster. People were simply reluctant to travel. Prior to 2003 occupancy rates were in the 63 percent range. Refer to Figure 3 for a summary of occupancy rates and market revenues generated over the past five years.

Year	Occupancy	Avg. Daily Rate	Revenue ($billion)
1999	66%	$106	10.1
2000	65%	$111	10.6
2001	62%	$114	10.8
2002	62%	$115	11.1
2003	59%	$114	N/A

Source: Hotel Association of Canada, 2004.

FIGURE 3

Occupancy rates and market revenues—Canadian hotel market

As is the case in so many markets, the mid-range segment is being squeezed by growth in the luxury segment and economy segment. Certain factors contribute to this trend: business travellers are cutting back on expenses and/or are holding more meetings online or by other means; the economic situation has reduced the tendency to travel (e.g., people have less disposable income and travel is a discretionary expense); and the expectations of customers in both the business and consumer travel segments are changing. Both segments are looking for better value. Generally speaking, these trends benefit hotels in the economy segment. The luxury segment has not been hit that hard since wealthier customers continue to travel regardless of economic conditions. These customers search for hotels offering premium services. They have the money and are willing to spend it at upscale hotels.

The hotel market is segmented on the basis of price and quality (the extent and diversity of amenities offered). At the top end are hotels like Four Seasons who charge over $250 per night but offer a full complement of personal and business services. At the bottom end are hotels such as Comfort Inn, Quality Inn, and Roadside Inn, all of which are operated by Choice Hotels Canada. Holiday Inn Express competes in this category. Room rates are in the $89.00 to $109.00 range and in most cases offer a free breakfast.

Holiday Inn resides in the middle with competitors such as Radisson, Ramada, and Howard Johnson's. Holiday Inn and others offer a clean room, some business services, a restaurant, and a swimming pool. Rates are in the $119.00 to $159.00 range. As in a lot of other industries today, the mid-market segment is failing. Consumers are either heading up or down—they want luxury on the one hand and discounts on the other hand. Purchase decisions are a matter of priority and trade-offs. Value (perceived value) provided is a primary source of purchase motivation.

In the Canadian market InterContinental and its Holiday Inn brand are not nearly as prominent as they are internationally. Of the Top 10 hoteliers in Canada, InterContinental ranks third in terms of rooms but only ninth in terms of revenue. Revenues for 2002 amounted to $344 million. See Figure 4 for a summary of Canada's largest hotel chains and their revenues.

FIGURE
4

Hotel chains in Canada
ranked by revenue

Rank	Company	Revenue ($millions)
1	Four Seasons Hotels & Resorts	2 845
2	Fairmont Hotels & Resorts	1 922
3	Starwood Hotels & Resorts	742
4	Legacy Hotels	648
5	Best Western	535
6	Westmont Hospitality Group	500
7	Choice Hotels Canada	481
8	Marriott Hotels	366
9	InterContinental	344
10	Royal Host	304

Source: Hotel Association of Canada, 2004.

InterContinental operates just over 100 properties in Canada. Similar to all other hotels, InterContinental must appeal to two distinct target groups: business travellers and recreational travellers (consumers). Business travellers presently account for 65 percent of InterContinental's volume. Recreational travellers account for the remaining 35 percent.

The business travel market has changed in the past few years. Given the trends stated earlier, it can be stated that corporations won't be swayed to travel because they're getting cheaper rates. Canada's hotel room rates remain a bargain when compared to rates in other countries. However, when corporate travellers do hit the road, they're definitely demanding the best possible price. Consequently, lower priced chains like Choice and our own Holiday Inn Express are picking up a lot of corporate business.

Holiday Inn's Product Plans

Throughout Canada and the United States Holiday Inn plans an intensive renovation program commencing in 2003. All new hotels will conform to new standards. The new Holiday Inn prototype will have high-speed access (wireless and land line) in every room, though the company hasn't decided if it will charge for the service. The rejuvenation process will be ongoing and take years to implement. The initial plan is to open 25 new prototypes in the next three years.

The rooms will be designed to accommodate bigger work areas and each will have an ergonomic chair to appeal to the brand's business traveller base, which typically makes up 70 percent of Holiday Inn's reservations.

The company also hopes to appeal to travellers' nostalgia. The hotel sign will be redesigned to remind travellers of the iconic Holiday Inn sign of days past. Company executives believe there is considerable brand equity in that sign.

Each new hotel will have a comfort-food diner with a standardized menu that will include pot roast, meatloaf, and fried chicken. Meals will be offered at affordable prices.

The exteriors of the hotels will have a completely new look and all new hotels will have an indoor swimming pool. The prototype has 145 rooms.

In developing new hotels, Holiday Inn plans to attract franchise developers to build new units while culling older units from the system. Some of the hotels are 40 years old and no amount of renovation can bring them up to the standards demanded by today's business and leisure traveller. As well, with so much urban growth, hotel location is becoming a major factor influencing hotel choice. Many existing Holiday Inns are not in the best of locations any more.

The Marketing Communications Challenge

A new marketing communications plan must be devised to rekindle interest in Holiday Inn. The overall **goal** of the campaign is to attract more travellers to Holiday Inn and Holiday Inn Express. In that regard, particular attention must be given to building a new **brand image** and **creating awareness** for the product and service changes that are being implemented.

Prior to devising the marketing communications plan it is essential that you conduct some secondary research on the Canadian hotel market. From your research you must identify the various market segments and develop a **clear profile of the major competitors** in each segment.

Once you have compiled the necessary background on the market, competition, and customers, the next step is to develop a clearly worded **positioning strategy statement** for Holiday Inn. Your communications plan will then firmly position Holiday Inn in its segment and help win back customers.

The plan should consider **business customers** and **recreational travellers (families)**. As you proceed with the plan you will be able to develop more specific objectives for the various sections. Any and all aspects of marketing communications can be considered for inclusion in the plan. For certain, advertising will play a significant role so you will be developing a creative plan and media plan. Your recommendations may also include other components of the marketing communications mix. It is your plan!

For the purposes of devising this plan, you are only concerned with the Canadian market, that is, you are devising a plan to encourage Canadian travellers to stay at Holiday Inn or Holiday Inn Express. The **budget** is **$2.0 million** for one calendar year commencing **January 1, 2006**.

You may wish to refer to the various **planning models** in Chapter 4 (Figures 4.3 and 4.6), Chapter 5 (Figure 5.4), and Chapter 7 (Figure 7.2). These models will provide the framework for developing your marketing communications plan. Use appropriate sections from these models for presenting your recommendations. Make sure you include adequate background information in order to justify the actions you recommend in the plan section of your document.

Adapted from Ryan Chittum, "Revamp at Holiday Inn," The Globe and Mail, September 23, 2003, p. B14, **www.ihgplc.com**, **www.hospitalitynet.org/news**, *and statistics from the Hotel Association of Canada.*

CASE STUDY 2
MOLSON CANADIAN

Canadian Beer Market

Depending on which company you talk to, Molson or Labatt, both claim to be the market leader in Canada. In a race that is too close to call, each company controls about 42 percent of the market. The remaining 14 percent is controlled by premium import brands and by microbreweries that include companies such as Sleeman's. The premium segment and the microbrewery segment are growing while the mainstream segment is declining slightly.

As of 2002 the Canadian beer market was worth $7.4 billion. Refer to Figure 1 for a regional breakdown of sales. When sales in each region are indexed against the population it is apparent that the Atlantic region and Quebec are overdeveloped beer markets while the Prairies and British Columbia are underdeveloped markets. There is opportunity for growth in the Prairies and B.C.

FIGURE 1

Regional beer sales—Dollars

Province or Territory	Beer Sales (Millions)	% of Beer Sales	% Population	Category Index
Atlantic	602.2	8.1	7.6	106
Quebec	2 069.1	27.9	23.8	117
Ontario	2 772.3	37.4	38.2	98
Prairies	1 064.0	14.1	16.8	84
B.C.	873.1	11.8	13.2	89
Yuk./N.W.T./Nun.	31.9	0.4	0.4	100
Total	**7 412.7**	**100.0**	**100.0**	

Note: The category index is calculated by dividing % sales of a region by % population of a region.

Source: Compiled from Statistics Canada data and Canadian Media Directors' Council *Media Digest*, 2003–2004, p. 5.

Beer Market Segments

The beer market is segmented by type of beer and by origin. The various types of beers include

- *Lagers* Lagers are brewed at cooler temperatures, creating a smoother flavour. They are a pale golden colour with a crisp refreshing taste.
- *Ales* Ales are brewed at cellar temperatures, producing a full-bodied, fruity taste. They are darker in colour ranging from rich gold to reddish amber.
- *Light Beers* Light beers are highly carbonated, and have fewer calories and lower alcohol content. They are light in colour and mild in flavour.
- *Draught* Light or dark, in any style, draught beer is any beer served from a keg or cask. With slightly less carbonation, draught beer is less filling than other beers.
- *Malt* Higher in alcohol content, they offer a rich, full flavour. The colour ranges from deep gold to amber to firelight red.

- *Ice*   A unique brewing process produces a concentrated flavour. The beer is cooled until ice crystals form. It then goes through a unique filtering process that produces a beer with higher alcohol content.

The beer market is also segmented on the basis of origin and the image of the beer. For example, domestic beers have that "mainstream" or "everyday" image whereas imports from foreign countries have a more "sophisticated" image. The segments are described as

- *Domestic Beers*   These are beers produced by the larger national and regional breweries such as Labatt and Molson. Often referred to as mainstream brands, some of the popular brands include Molson Canadian and Canadian Light, Coors Light, Labatt Blue and Blue Light, Budweiser and Bud Light, and Alexander Keith's, among many others.
- *Premium Beers*   These beers are brewed by small, regional microbreweries that emphasize the "craftsmanship" of the brewing process. Some popular breweries in this category include Sleeman's, Brick Brewing, Unibrue, and Creemore Springs. Each company offers a variety of uniquely named brands.
- *Imports*   This category includes brands imported from foreign countries. Both Molson and Labatt have distribution agreements to sell these beers in Canada. Popular brands in this segment include Stella Artois, Guinness, Heineken, Corona, and A Marca Bavaria.

The taste preferences of Canadian beer drinkers are changing. In recent years, Molson and Labatt have found themselves under attack from a burgeoning number of imports. Imports have accounted for about 10 percent of Canadian volume for years but recently have jumped to about 14 percent (2003), marking a fourfold increase in the past decade. There's another significant change as well. Ten years ago this segment was dominated by cheap American beers, but now premium-priced international brands make up three-quarters of this segment. Traditional brand leaders such as Molson Canadian and Labatt Blue are feeling the heat!

According to *The Monitor*, a publication that tracks consumption trends and other trends in the beer industry, trademark brands (the traditional Canadian mainstream brands) now account for only 60 percent of beer sales in Toronto, versus 80 percent a decade ago. While the extent of this trend may not be the same in every city across Canada, it does paint a telling picture of the present situation. Once proud, innovative Canadian brands such as Molson Dry and Labatt Ice have been reduced to discount beers.

For beer marketers the situation is clear. They must react to the fact that beer lovers are looking for distinct tastes. These drinkers want to be seen clutching a premium brand, especially in urban centres. This situation poses a major problem for a brand like Molson Canadian.

Present Situation

Both Molson and Labatt face similar situations. Each company is scrambling in an effort to revitalize key brands that have seen their market share slowly slip away to import brands.

Labatt is better positioned than Molson to deal with this situation. For years Molson Canadian and Labatt Blue have battled with each other to gain the lead position in the market. Just recently, however, Budweiser, "The King of Beers," has quietly slipped into the lead in Canada. With its rugged image and not-so-rugged taste, Budweiser, along with beers like Coors Light and Corona, is profiting from beer drinkers' shift to lighter, sweeter, smoother beers.

Labatt is owned by Interbrew, the world's biggest brewer, and has the rights to distribute Budweiser and Bud Light in Canada. It seems that Labatt is willing to sacrifice market share for its traditional brands like Blue in order to get people to trade over to Budweiser or up to a host of its imported brands that include Beck's and Stella Artois. In contrast, Molson only has one brand—A Marca Bavaria—in the premium beer category. Therefore, if Molson's traditional Canadian brands lose market share the entire company suffers.

It's not all bad news for Molson. The company decided to launch Canadian Light nationally after demonstrating to its U.S. partner Coors that Canadian Light is not hurting sales of Coors Light, the country's top selling light beer, in regions where it is presently sold. Molson holds distribution rights for Coors and Coors Light in Canada.

Canada's Top Brands

While actual market shares by brand are not readily available, the top three brands control between 10 percent and 12 percent of the market. One recent source (a valuation report by JP Morgan) quotes Budweiser's market share at 12.2 percent, Molson Canadian at 10.4 percent, and Labatt Blue at 9.8 percent. Canada's leading beer brands based on dollar sales are listed in Figure 2.

FIGURE 2

Canada's top 10 brands—Dollar sales

Rank	Brand	Type	Brewer
1	Budweiser	Lager	Labatt
2	Canadian	Lager	Molson
3	Blue	Lager	Labatt
4	Coors Light	Light	Molson
5	Blue Light	Light	Labatt
6	Alexander Keith's	Ale	Keith's (Labatt)
7	Export	Ale	Molson
8	Labatt Extra Dry	Lager	Labatt
9	Molson Dry	Lager	Molson
10	Corona Extra	Lager	Cerveceria Modelo

Source: The Beer Store, **www.beerstore.com**.

Consumer Trends

Demographic trends are not on the side of the brewing industry. Older age groups do drink beer but much less of it than before. As well, the 19- to 30-year-old group in the 1980s represented 20 percent of the market, today it represents 18 percent, and by 2007 it will slide to 15 percent. The long-term outlook for the beer industry is somewhat bleak.

Traditional thinking suggests brand choices are made early in life and that drinkers display a sense of loyalty to either Molson brands or Labatt brands. "If you get a young drinker early, they tend to stay with you, that is, they stay within the portfolio of brands offered by one company or the other."

Based on recent trends in beer consumption, present-day beer drinkers are not as loyal as they once were. The influx of imported brands in the premium segment and persistent price battles among brands are causing drinkers to switch brands. In Ontario, for example, the regular price of beer (24-pack) is $35.00 but price discounting has dropped the price of some brands to $24.00. Such discounting has affected consumers' allegiance to brands like Canadian. Ironically, Molson and Labatt created the rapidly growing discount segment by regularly raising prices for brands like Canadian and Blue.

The popularity of "buck a beer" $24.00 cases from Hamilton's Lakeport Brewery and Waterloo's Brick Brewing is proving to be a hit because of the $11.00 price gap. Even Molson (Carling brand) and Labatt (Luck brand) have been reluctantly selling beer at $24.00 a case.

Those drinkers that aren't influenced by price are turning to the imports. With regard to the shift in taste preferences, one bar owner in Toronto sums things up succinctly. "The younger generation likes to try a variety of beers and right now it's like they are not even looking at Canadian brands." Little wonder Molson Canadian is losing ground.

Another factor encouraging switching is the constant barrage of premiums added to cases. T-shirts, golf balls, giant-sized cans of beer, and ball caps have become commonplace in peak beer-drinking seasons. Major brands are differentiating themselves not on the taste of their beer but on the nature of their advertising and sales promotions.

The Battle for Leadership

Both Molson Canadian and Labatt Blue have been battling each other forever. Both brands have held the lead and very often the fate of these brands is determined by the effectiveness of their advertising. Just recently, Budweiser has been added to the race.

Labatt Blue enjoyed considerable success with a campaign called "Out of the Blue." The campaign ran between 1998 and 2003. Blue's launch commercial for the campaign is one of the most memorable on record. The commercial featured a hockey game that spontaneously broke out on the streets of downtown Toronto. It started with a young man carrying a bag and stick. He flicks a crumpled can at someone else's feet. That person pulls out a stick and fires the can into the street. A businessman carrying a briefcase and an umbrella stops to play goalie, with a bicycle rack serving as the net. Men rush out of nearby offices, ties flapping, to join in. Onlookers cheer and do the "wave," until someone yells "Streetcar!" The game ends. There were countless executions of this campaign over the five-year run.

In late 2003 Blue introduced "Cheers. To Friends." Taking a humorous approach, this campaign shows the kind of pranks that guys will do when they are together with friends. The initial spot called "Weekends" depicts guys engaging in frat-style stunts and practical jokes. One victim gets his pants pulled off while sitting in a washroom stall. Another friend is sitting in an outhouse when two friends tip it over. Other spots showed golf balls falling out of cars, men being sprayed by water faucets, and a poor soul taped to a chair half naked going up and down in an elevator. This campaign has not had much impact—Blue's market share continues to slide.

Molson—The Company

Molson is Canada's pre-eminent brewer with over $3.5 billion in annual sales. Founded in 1786, Molson is North America's oldest beer brand and a global brand name with products that include Molson Canadian, Molson Export, Molson Dry, Rickard's, and Brazilian beer brands like Kaiser and Bavaria.

Molson Canadian

Canadian truly exemplifies the pride of Canada's young adults and is a reflection of the pride the company takes in brewing world-class beer. Starting with crystal-clear water, malted barley, and the finest hops, Canadian is slowly fermented to produce a smooth, refreshing beer with a genuine taste. Clean and clear, crisp and cold Canadian is a classic lager. Other brands in the Molson Canadian family include Canadian Light and Canadian Ice.

Molson Canadian Advertising

When Blue's "Out of the Blue" campaign was in mid-stream Molson Canadian launched its "I AM Canadian" campaign. At the time Blue was the market leader and Canadian was the challenger. The launch commercial was the now very famous commercial called "The Rant." In this commercial a character named Joe feverishly yells out what it means to be a Canadian. It represented a strategy based on pure Canadian pride, not American-style flag-waving patriotism but the long-standing Canadian tradition that uses irony and parody to define what it's like to be Canadian against what it is not (i.e., American). The Rant commercial garnered overwhelming publicity and showed that a campaign based purely on Canadian pride could help build a brand—market share moved upwards! The campaign that started in 2000 has had many executions, all revolving around the same theme—Canadian patriotism.

The most recent versions of "I AM Canadian" involve a miserable Molson Canadian beer drinker who becomes a happy camper by making a long trek to the closest beer store—across a lake and through the woods—to get himself a case of his favourite beer. The original spot with this theme featured the Proclaimers hit song "I'm Gonna Be (500 Miles)" throughout. The current spot titled "No Service" features another Proclaimers hit, "I'm on My Way." The spot shows the hero encountering many obstacles along the way, including having to swim across a lake, hike through the woods, and cross a creek before he comes to an open field, where he spots the beer store. The barefooted, shirtless champion believes he has reached his destination only to read a sign that says "No shirt, No shoes, No service." Luckily, two buskers appear and the ingenious trekker swindles one of the men out of his shirt and shoes, buys a case of beer, and returns home happy.

According to Joey Bergstein, vice-president, Molson Canadian, "Many Molson Canadian drinkers equate misery to an empty case of their favourite beer. But the route back to happiness is simple. Make your way, no matter what obstacles you may encounter, to the closest beer store, and your problem is solved."

Molson Canadian's Conundrum

Canadian's market share has slipped. Young beer drinkers are showing a preference for imported beers and craft beers brewed by smaller companies. Canadian's current advertising strategy may be wearing thin. After all, how many years of effective advertising can you get out of one basic idea?

Complicating the situation is the fact that virtually all mainstream brands are interchangeable. They all look and taste the same, regular shelf prices are the same, the bottles are the same, and if one brand is offering a T-shirt, or a feature price, that's enough to make someone switch brands, at least temporarily. This means that advertising is the only option for discriminating one brand from another. History shows that good advertising moves market share. Just how important is one share point in the market? For Molson, a 1 percent share increase (decrease) has a $23 million positive (negative) impact on profit. Therefore, it is absolutely vital that Molson build and protect market share for its most important brand. How to do so is another matter entirely.

If advertising is part of the solution, then something innovative is urgently needed since so many branded campaigns are similar. According to Chris Staples, the creative director and one of the founding partners of Rethink Vancouver, "The best beer advertising is the kind you cannot slap any other logo on. An example of that is Bud Light, which has been consistent in its idea to stand up for Canadian men with the Bud Light Institute campaign." In this campaign men pull every excuse possible out of the book to free up time to do what they do best—have fun! It has helped move the Budweiser franchise into the leadership position in Canada.

The Bud Light Institute is a fictitious organization but it is now synonymous with Bud Light, the brand. The latest television spot in this campaign shows a steaming cup of coffee (the fake cup of coffee 3000) sitting on Johnson's desk at different times of the day. Employees notice the coffee and ask where Johnson is (he must be around somewhere) while the boss compliments Johnson for always being there. All along Johnson is having fun somewhere else. Tagline for the ad is "The Bud Light Institute. Working for you, so you don't have to."

With all that has happened in the beer market in the past few years Molson is contemplating a new direction for Molson Canadian. Perhaps it is time to retire the "I AM Canadian" campaign and move on to something that will really resonate with young beer drinkers. Perhaps not!

The Marketing Communications Challenge

Your advertising agency has been asked to submit new advertising ideas to help rebuild Molson Canadian. Your recommendations will be presented in the form of a creative plan. The overall goal of the campaign is clear: to retrieve leadership status in the Canadian beer market.

You will develop a new creative concept for Molson Canadian that can be executed in any medium. Molson Canadian campaigns typically embrace all the major media alternatives, but using all media is not mandatory. The campaign may also embrace other components of the marketing communications mix.

The budget for the campaign is $3 million. The initial campaign will cover a one-year period commencing May 1, 2006 and ending April 30, 2007. You must also submit a complete media plan that will show how all activities will be scheduled during the one-year period. Production costs will come from a separate budget so you need not be concerned with those costs at this time.

Client Expectations

Prior to developing the plan the client expects you to conduct a secondary research review of the market in order to update essential facts and to further familiarize yourself with the beer market, the competitors, and the brand.

Once the appropriate background information has been collected (no doubt some information you need won't be available, but that is reality), you must assess the information in order to clearly position Molson Canadian in the minds of consumers. In this regard you must devise a clearly worded positioning strategy statement that will represent the brand and provide a guideline for developing the advertising campaign.

From there you must define your primary target market in terms of demographic, psychographic, geographic, and behaviour response characteristics. The campaign will be launched in all areas of Canada *except* Quebec.

For the creative plan, media plan, and any other element of marketing communications that is included in the plan, you must clearly delineate your objectives, strategies, and execution details. Company executives are anxious to hear what your recommendations will be.

It is suggested you use the planning models in the textbook as a guideline for developing your plan. You may wish to refer to the various planning models in Chapter 4 (Figures 4.3 and 4.6), Chapter 5 (Figure 5.4), and Chapter 7 (Figure 7.2). These models provide the framework for developing your advertising plan. Use appropriate sections from these models for presenting your recommendations.

*Adapted from Paul Brent, "Molson to revamp Canadian," Financial Post, May 10, 2004, p. FP4; Bertrand Marotte, "Canadian? This Bud's for you . . . ," The Globe and Mail, April 15, 2004, **www.globeandmail.com;** "Who's No. 1?" Financial Post, April 19, 2004, p. FP4; Paul Brent, "Molson cleans house after sales slump," Financial Post, August 9, 2003, p. FP5; Patti Summerfield, "Big brewers miss out on growing demo," Strategy, May 6, 2002, pp. 1, 16; Lisa D'Innocenzo, "Saving Canadian beer," Strategy, September 8, 2003, pp. 1, 8; "Molson Canadian Drinkers Are on Their Way to Happiness, press release, Canada News Wire, **www.newswire.ca/en/releases/archive/June2002/24, www.molson.com, www.thebeerstore.ca**.*

CASE STUDY 3
DAIRY QUEEN GRILL & CHILL

Dairy Queen is moving in a new direction in an attempt to expand its offerings in the quick-serve restaurant market. The company's newest concept is called Grill & Chill, a concept that presents a new line of menu items along with traditional ice cream favourites.

The Company

Dairy Queen is a leading franchiser of frozen treat stores, with over 6000 outlets in 21 countries. Over 5000 outlets are in the United States. Dairy Queen is an American company with exceptionally strong roots in that market. Canada is its second largest country for outlets with 646. International outlets total 350. In the International group, Thailand is the largest with 147 outlets. Company sales revenue in 2003 was estimated to be US$450 million.

Dairy Queen is popular for its ice cream treats, including Blizzards, sundaes, and cones. Many of the stores serve hamburgers, hot dogs, and fries. A small number of units are company owned; a majority of them are franchised. In addition, Dairy Queen franchises over 400 Orange Julius locations that serve blended fruit drinks and about 30 Karmelkorn stands offering a variety of popcorn treats. The company is owned by Berkshire Hathaway Inc. and is part of Omaha billionaire Warren Buffett's empire.

The Quick-Serve Restaurant Market

The quick-serve restaurant market in Canada is dominated by McDonald's with other chains such as Burger King, Wendy's, and Dairy Queen being distant followers. Refer to Figure 1 for a summary of position and market shares for each company.

Rank	Chain	Share
1	McDonald's	28.4
2	Cara	21.7
3	Tricon Global	14.9
4	Subway	7.2
5	Wendy's	5.9
6	Burger King	5.8
7	A&W	5.3
8	Dairy Queen	4.3
9	St-Hubert	3.3
10	Pizza Pizza	3.2

Note: Cara includes Harvey's and Swiss Chalet; Tricon Global includes KFC, Pizza Hut, and Taco Bell.

FIGURE 1

Quick-serve restaurant market shares

Dairy Queen is different from all of its competitors since its ice cream treats are the primary reason for visiting. Consequently, Dairy Queen also competes with another group of restaurants specializing in ice cream treats and novelties. In this category are companies such as Cool Brands International that franchises and licenses some 5000 frozen yogurt and ice cream outlets under the names I Can't Believe It's Yogurt, Bresler's, Swensen's, and Yogen Fruz.

Another large and resourceful competitor is Allied Domecq Quick Serve Restaurants. In its stable are Dunkin' Donuts, the world's leading chain of doughnut shops, Baskin-Robbins, and Togo's. Baskin-Robbins, well known for always offering 31 flavours of ice cream, operates 5100 outlets worldwide with about half of them located in the United States and Canada.

The Grill & Chill Concept

The Grill & Chill concept is a departure from Dairy Queen's image as an ice cream place. With Grill & Chill the company is out to steal market share from McDonald's and others in that category as well as from more upscale establishments such as Chili's, Applebee's, Kelsey's, and Montana's. In terms of market positioning the Grill & Chill concept fits in between quick-serve establishments and slightly more upscale sit-down establishments. The ultimate goal is a bigger piece of the restaurant pie.

In repositioning Dairy Queen, the Grill & Chill concept prevailed because it's an organic extension of the "Hot Eats, Cool Treats" position. The words also work well together, with "grill" highlighting food and "chill" highlighting the desserts.

The concept was initially tested in two locations in Chattanooga, Tennessee. Both stores were successful and the concept has since been rolled out to about 25 U.S. locations. Presently, the concept is being tested in several small markets in Ontario, British Columbia, and the Maritimes.

The menu offerings are quite different from traditional Dairy Queens. Offerings at Grill & Chill include flame-grilled hamburgers with a choice of toppings, grilled turkey and Philly steak sandwiches, vegetable quesadillas, and breakfast items such as hash browns, eggs, sausage, pancakes, and cinnamon roles baked on site.

Thus far, ice cream has been the bait to get people in, but once there they quickly notice the new decor. The exterior of the stores features a new sign and logo along with two massive fieldstone chimneys. The chimney sends a message of fire, and therefore food. A landscaped patio with high-quality tables and umbrellas makes the building seem warm and inviting. So does the drive-through. Slanted glass, red tiles, and a black and white mural of vintage Dairy Queen speak to the chain's storied history.

Inside, scores of details create a warm and friendly atmosphere. Walking through a large entranceway, customers see a frontlit menu board, instead of a backlit board used in most fast-food restaurants. To the left is the ice cream counter with "Chilled Temptations" written on a blue overhang. A red sign hangs above the hot-food counter, underscoring the Grill & Chill positioning. All interior colours suggest food and restaurant, not ice cream.

The dining room features spacious booths with vinyl seats and moveable tables and chairs encourage guests to sit and linger over snacks and meals. Textured stone tiles cover the floor in high-traffic areas and there is dark wood flooring in the dining area. Unlike fast-food restaurants, Grill & Chill offers limited table service—customers place their order at the counter but are served by an employee. Soft music plays in the background. This adds to the comfort level. Pictures of the Chill & Grill stores are available at the Dairy Queen website, **www.dairyqueen.com**. An online tour of Chill & Grill is also available at the digital edition (June 2002) of *Chain Leader* magazine located at **www.chainleader.com.**

Apparently, the dining rooms are so inviting that drive-through sales in the test restaurants have dropped from the usual 48 percent of sales to 33 percent. Overall, the design has done its job of placing Dairy Queen in customers' minds as a place for food, not just ice cream. Food sales in traditional Dairy Queens account for about 30 percent of sales. In the Grill & Chill test stores food sales have risen to 58 percent of sales. More to the point, total average store sales have almost tripled and in some high-traffic locations have reached $1.5 million.

The casual segment of the restaurant market is growing as people don't seem to mind spending a little more for a higher-quality offering/experience. Prices in Grill & Chill are somewhat higher than prices in traditional Dairy Queens. In contrast, the fast-food segment is experiencing flat growth year to year, a sure sign of a market segment about to enter the early decline stage.

In trying to define what Grill & Chill is, one franchise holder from Ohio said, "Grill & Chill is popping into a niche that's not covered—fast food casual. I have a feeling this will push Dairy Queen in a whole new direction." Customers tend to agree. The Miller family—husband, wife, and four-year-old twins—enjoyed their initial experience. "It's not your typical fast food," said Dale Miller, "but it's still fast."

Dairy Queen has strong roots in smaller markets across North America. The company sees Grill & Chill as suitable for small markets, but the real desire is to establish a stronger presence in major urban markets. According to Charles Chapman, vice-president franchise development, "There's something classic and something new in Grill & Chill. There is a tremendous respect for our heritage, and there's also the thought of what we have to look forward to." In order to be successful with Grill & Chill, Dairy Queen must attract young people and young families, and middle- and upper-middle income households. The test markets will determine how broad Grill & Chill's appeal will be.

The Marketing Communications Challenge

Assume that a new Dairy Queen Grill & Chill will be opening in your market (the city or town where your school is located). Feel free to select another market if you wish. Your challenge is to develop a marketing communications campaign that will introduce the Grill & Chill concept to local market residents. Beyond creating awareness for the name and concept and building a new image for the brand, the plan must also include activities that will entice customers to visit the restaurant for the first time.

The two test stores in Chattanooga generated $750 000 revenue in their first year. The population of Chattanooga is approximately 150 000. The relationship between population and potential sales in Chattanooga may have an impact on how you estimate potential sales in your market.

The Dairy Queen franchise agreement stipulates that franchisees must allocate 6 percent of sales to Dairy Queen's advertising and promotion fund. These funds are used to sponsor national advertising campaigns and to help support local advertising campaigns in markets where Dairy Queens are located. It is also common for local franchisees to enhance their advertising budget in local markets; however, this enhancement comes from their own operating funds and is above and beyond the 6 percent fee. This information along with your projected sales for the first year of operations will help determine how much your advertising budget will be.

The marketing communications plan should include a creative plan that will present and defend how the Chill & Grill concept will be executed. The plan should also include a local market media plan. For both creative and media, appropriate objectives, strategies, and execution details should be included. If other components are added such as sales promotions, public relations, and direct-response activities, they must be supported by appropriate objectives, strategies, and execution details.

You may wish to refer to various planning models in Chapter 4 (Figures 4.3 and 4.6), Chapter 5 (Figure 5.4), and Chapter 7 (Figure 7.2). These models will provide the framework for developing your marketing communications plan. Use appropriate sections from those models for presenting your recommendations. Make sure that you include adequate background information in order to justify the actions you recommend in the plan section of the document.

Adapted from Shawna Richer, "Dairy Queen tests tasty new brands in Maritimes," The Globe and Mail, July 23, 2003, **www.globeandmail.com***; Ron Ruggless, "Dairy Queen heats up, scoops out new niche with grill concept," Nation's Restaurant News, February 18, 2002; "Dairy Queen gets a facelift,"* **www.bison1.com***; Lisa Bertagnoli, "Fit for a queen," Chain Leader, June 2002,* **www.chainleader.com***, and* **www.dairyqueen.com***.*

SCHICK QUATTRO RAZOR

Market Background

MARKET SIZE AND GROWTH

The men's grooming market embraces shaving products, skin care products, hair care products, and fragrances. Combined, these categories represent $US8 billion in sales annually. The Canadian grooming market is estimated to be $C800 million.

ACNielsen data indicate the Canadian razor market to be worth $C270 at retail. With wholesale and retail margins deducted, the value of the razor market at point of manufacture is estimated to be $C190 million.

The grooming market is growing at a rate of +10 percent annually. Such significant growth is attributed to attitude changes among men who pay more attention to grooming, new product introductions, and intense competition between large and resourceful companies in all product categories. Continuous technical innovation is key to sustained growth in this market.

The razor market is growing at an average annual rate of +3 percent. It is much more established than the other product categories in the male grooming market.

MARKET SEGMENTS

The razor market is divided between reusable razors and blades and disposable razors. The reusable segment can be further segmented on the basis of price; regular- or competitively-priced razors and premium-priced razors.

Gillette is a dominant leader in the reusable segment and Bic is the leader in the disposable segment. Both Gillette and Schick are focusing their respective resources on reusable razors with expensive replacement blades. Price does not seem to be an issue in this segment. Male consumers seem willing to pay the price for each product improvement that comes along.

EXTERNAL ENVIRONMENTS INFLUENCING THE RAZOR MARKET

Health and Wellness   There is a growing desire today for men to look and feel healthy.

Demographic Trends   Young men and aging baby boomers are concerned with the looking-glass self as well as their own self-image. The goal of older-aged men is to look and feel young. Young urban males, referred to as "metrosexuals" who dress well and are socially active, are influencing change by making purchases in all grooming categories.

Societal Attitudes   General taboos are breaking down; that is, impeccable grooming tendencies associated with the gay community now transcend all lifestyles.

Media Influences   Images portrayed in "lad magazines" such as *Maxim, Stuff,* and *FHM* promote the ideal body image for young males today. The lads are out to impress the lassies.

MARKET SHARE

Since Energizer purchased the Schick brands from Pfizer in 2002, the battle between Gillette and Schick has intensified. Schick has become much more aggressive from a product development and marketing perspective. Competition on the marketing front is expected to intensify over the next few years. Since 2002 Schick's market share has increased from 10 percent to 14 percent.

Brand Market	Share 2003 (%)
Gillette	76
Schick	14
Bic / Revlon / All Other	10
Total	**100**

Note: Gillette Sensor's market share is 46% and Gillette Mach 3's is 28%.

CONSUMER DATA

Contemporary males of all ages are searching for innovative products that improve appearance. A genuine desire to look and feel better is shaping the male grooming market today.

- Males tend to be brand loyal; once they find the right brand they stick with it.
- Males prefer basic items that offer tangible benefits; they shun products they perceive to pamper.
- Males' interests now extend well beyond shaving; skin care products are becoming more popular with males of all ages.
- Women frequently purchase grooming products for their male spouse or mate.
- Price is not an issue in the purchase decision; quality and performance are important influencers.
- Men spend 51 minutes a day grooming; women spend 55 minutes.

COMPETITOR ANALYSIS

The razor market is dominated by Gillette brands. Schick, other brands, and private label brands are distant followers.

- Gillette's market share is split between two key brands: Gillette Sensor 3 controls 46 percent of the market and the Gillette Mach 3 Turbo controls 28 percent of the market.
- Razor sales are extremely important to Gillette: 40 percent of Gillette's sales revenue and 70 percent of Gillette's operating profit are generated from razor and blade sales.
- Gillette is a resourceful company; its key strengths are in technology, product innovation, and marketing.
- The Gillette brand name has an enviable image and reputation among males. It is a well-known, male heritage brand.
- Gillette invests significant sums of money in marketing activity and appears to be getting a better return for its investment.

COMPETITOR ACTIVITY ASSESSMENT

Both the Sensor 3 and Mach 3 Turbo are marketed by similar means. Both brands receive considerable marketing support as Gillette's goal is to build and protect market share.

Product   Gillette promises a clean, close, and comfortable shave. The Mach 3 Turbo offers a closer shave with fewer strokes and less irritation. Technological advancements keep Gillette in the forefront of razor product development. Male consumers perceive Gillette brands to be reliable.

Price   Sensor 3 is competitively priced; Mach 3 Turbo is premium priced (about 15 percent more). The additional benefits offered by the Mach 3 Turbo justify the higher price.

Distribution   Both the Sensor 3 and Mach 3 Turbo have extensive retail distribution in drug, grocery, and mass merchandise stores. Gillette's financial resources allow for significant spending with channel customers to ensure that distribution is maintained.

Marketing Communications   Both brands have significant media advertising support to create awareness and interest. As well, sales promotions are implemented annually across all company brands to generate seasonal interest and to stimulate purchasing patterns. Trial coupons, product sampling, and contests are important elements of Gillette's marketing communications mix. Gillette summarizes its positioning strategy in all of its marketing communications with the famous slogan: "The Best a Man Can Get."

New Products   Gillette will be launching the new M3 Power battery-operated razor in May 2004. M3 Power is a more sophisticated version of its Mach 3 Turbo. The battery power delivers a pulse that makes hair stand away from the skin. M3 Power is Gillette's immediate response to the Schick Quattro.

Marketing Plan

MARKETING OBJECTIVES

1. To achieve a market share of 5 percent for Schick Quattro the end of the first year (2004). This will increase overall market share to 19 percent.
2. To generate sales revenue of $9 500 000 for Schick Quattro (at point of manufacture) by the end of the first year (2004).
3. To position Schick Quattro as a razor that provides a superior shave to any competing product on the market, particularly the Gillette Mach 3 Turbo.

TARGET MARKET PROFILE

Razor products appeal to all males, but since older males exhibit a high degree of brand loyalty (Gillette's dominant position in the market) Quattro will give priority to younger males whose loyalties are yet to be established.

Primary Target Market   Since brand loyalty is an issue in this market, priority will be given to younger males who are in the process of forming brand relationships. However, all males between the ages of 16 and 49 years are potential targets due to attitude and lifestyle considerations. Across all ages, the penchant for good grooming has increased significantly in recent years.

Demographics

- Primary: Males 16 to 29 years old
- Secondary and post-secondary education
- Students; newly employed graduates, and career-minded
- Income is not that important

Psychographics

- Time-pressed daily routines
- Socially active; friends and significant others
- Recreational orientation with an interest in sports viewing and participation
- Very concerned with appearance and health; a strong desire to look and feel good

Geographics

- Across Canada but metropolitan markets will be given priority

Behaviour Response

- These males are looking for products that are reliable, easy to use, and offer superior performance. Price is not a significant issue in the purchase decision.

Secondary Target A secondary target comprising males between the ages of 30 and 49 years will also be targeted. While this age group tends to be more loyal and have an established regimen for purchasing shaving products, they are nonetheless interested in innovative products that will improve their self-image. Their psychographic and geographic profile is similar to that of the primary target.

PRODUCT STRATEGY

Schick Quattro has numerous unique selling points; hence there are numerous benefits for potential users.

- **Blades and Head** Four precisely synchronized blades and head allow for optimal contact over the contours of a man's face. There are two conditioning strips containing aloe and Vitamin E.
- **Handle Design** An ergonomic design with a comfortable, slip-resistant handle (textured rubber grips) offers enhanced precision and control.
- **Blade Changing** When the blade "clicks" in, a successful blade change has been made.
- **Convertible Stand** With a futuristic look, the stand allows the razor to air-dry upright, or store securely for travel.
- **Packaging** A highly advanced (futuristic-looking) package design will draw attention to the revolutionary nature of the Quattro. Blade refills will be available in packages of four or eight.

PRICE STRATEGY

The Schick Quattro will be competitively priced with the Gillette Mach 3 model at $11.99. The advantage of Quattro's four-blade system will be communicated by advertising and other forms of marketing communications. The goal is to generate high perceived value for the Quattro. The price strategy complements the competitive positioning strategy that Quattro is adopting.

DISTRIBUTION STRATEGY

Through significant investments in trade promotion programs the Schick Quattro will be available in leading drug, grocery, and mass merchandise stores across Canada. Introductory trade offers will secure listings and ongoing trade discounts will help secure merchandising support among channel customers. Key targets are leading national and regional chains such as Shoppers Drug Mart, Jean Coutu, Loblaws and its various other store banners, A&P/Dominion, Safeway, Wal-Mart, and Zellers.

POSITIONING STRATEGY

Schick Quattro will be positioned as a distinctive and competitive alternative to the Gillette Mach 3 razor. Schick offers a technologically advanced four-blade system that provides optimal contact over the contours of the face, resulting in the best possible shave.

Marketing Communications Strategy

BUDGET

For the launch year, a budget of $2.6 million has been allocated for advertising and other marketing communications expenditure. The budget represents 27.4 percent of forecast revenues for the year.

ADVERTISING OBJECTIVES

1. To create a 70 percent awareness level among the primary target market, described as males 16 to 29 years old.
2. To position Schick Quattro as a product that offers customers equal or better performance than the Gillette Mach 3 Turbo.
3. To achieve a trial purchase rate of 25 percent among the primary target market.

Creative Plan

CREATIVE OBJECTIVES

1. To communicate that Schick Quattro offers a close, comfortable, and smooth shave
2. To communicate that the four-blade system (precisely synchronized blades with two conditioning strips) provides enhanced performance compared to any other razor

KEY BENEFIT STATEMENT

The Schick Quattro razor offers an incredibly close, smooth shave.

SUPPORT CLAIMS STATEMENT

Numerous tests have been conducted using proper marketing research methods to evaluate and determine the performance level of the Schick Quattro. Tests confirm the Quattro offers men the best shave possible. As well, the four-blade synchronized system offers technology that goes beyond what any other competitor offers.

CREATIVE STRATEGY

Since this is almost a David-versus-Goliath battle, advertising will not incorporate direct comparisons with the Gillette Mach 3. Since the Schick Quattro offers equal or better performance, clear, direct, and precise claims will be made in all forms of advertising. The ads will tempt males to compare the Schick Quattro with the Gillette Sensor 3 or Mach 3 Turbo.

Image   By showing how effectively the product performs, the consumer will see how easy the product is to use and how reliable it is at providing the key benefit: a close, comfortable shave. The goal is to communicate in such a manner that Schick Quattro is quickly perceived as a serious alternative to the Gillette Mach 3 and Mach 3 Turbo.

Theme   The four-blade synchronized system separates Schick Quattro from all other brands. Therefore, advertising messages will focus on blade technology and the benefits it offers.

Tone and Style   All messages will be straightforward, positive, and easy to understand. By showing the razor in action and the satisfaction of the user after shaving, the choice will be obvious to the consumer.

Appeal Techniques   Since the four-blade system is a step ahead of Gillette's Mach 3 Turbo's three-blade system, comparisons will be implied rather than made directly. The benefits offered by Schick Quattro stand alone: a superior shaving experience will be communicated positively and convincingly in order to stimulate interest and to invite comparison.

Slogan   Considering the positioning strategy and creative strategy, the essence of Schick Quattro's message will be captured in a clearly stated tagline: "Schick Quattro. The power of 4."

CREATIVE EXECUTION

All advertising and other forms of marketing communications will deliver the same style of message. It is anticipated that the campaign will embrace 30-second television spots, four-colour magazine advertisements, black and white newspaper advertisements, outdoor posters, and a website. Promotional aspects of the introductory campaign will include trial coupons and a product-seeding initiative. Creating high levels of awareness for the brand name and the slogan will be given priority in the early stages of the campaign.

Media Plan

BUDGET

A budget of $2.0 million has been allocated for media advertising to cover a one year period from January 1, 2004 to December 31, 2004.

MEDIA OBJECTIVES

Who   The primary target market is males, 16 to 29 years old, interested in appearance and health (a desire to look and feel good), living in metropolitan markets across Canada. A secondary target market embraces males, 30 to 49 years old.

What   The message for the Schick Quattro will focus on the benefits offered by the four-blade synchronized shaving system. Such innovation offers males an incredibly close, comfortable shave.

When   The initial launch period (January to March) will be given heavier support than other times of the year. A pulsing strategy will be employed for the balance of the year with a slightly heavier spending in the back-to-school season (high school, college, and university).

Where   The campaign will be national in scope with additional emphasis on key urban markets. The budget available will determine the extent of key market coverage.

How   Since awareness is the primary objective initially, both reach and frequency will be given equal attention in the launch phase of the campaign. A multimedia campaign in the launch phase will effectively reach the intended target audience. In the latter stages of the campaign, more attention will be given to continuity.

MEDIA STRATEGY

Target Market Strategy   A shotgun approach will be used initially to announce the arrival of the Schick Quattro. Media choices that reach beyond the primary target will be employed during the blitz portion of the launch. As the campaign progresses there will be a shift to a profile-matching media strategy. The profile of the target market is fairly precise and allows for a certain amount of selectivity when making media choices. Targeted media options are available in print media and television.

Market Coverage   Schick Quattro will be launched nationally, so there is a need to use media that reach a national audience. Key urban markets such as Toronto, Montreal, Vancouver, Ottawa-Hull, Edmonton, Calgary, and Winnipeg will receive additional coverage. Reaching young urban males is a priority of this campaign. The degree of key market coverage will depend on how far the budget can be stretched while still generating the desired impact on the target audience.

Timing   The strategy is to enter the market with a bang. Since the benefits offered by the four-blade technology are very newsworthy a heavy spending pattern in the first three months of the launch is recommended. Coming out of nowhere, Schick Quattro will make an immediate impact in the marketplace. Following the launch period (January to March) advertising will taper off considerably. Advertising will rebound again between September and December, a period when students return to school and routines are back to normal.

Reach/Frequency/Continuity   Since brand awareness and trial purchases are the immediate objectives, both reach and frequency will be a priority in the launch phase of the campaign. Reach will be stressed throughout the entire year with various media being employed at different times to reach the same target market in different ways. Flights of advertising will be planned to ensure message continuity and maximum impact regardless of the media being employed at any given time.

Media Selection Rationale   A combination of television, magazines, newspaper, outdoor posters, and online communications is recommended.

a) *Television*   The quickest and most dramatic way to demonstrate the tangible benefits of the Schick Quattro is through television. Since television is a multisense medium, the demonstration can be that more dramatic. While television is a mass medium and males in this age category are watching less television than they used to, television is still the best medium for reaching a large audience. A combination of conventional networks (to reach the mass audience) and cable networks (to reach a more targeted audience) will be employed. Further, our primary competitor is a heavy user of television, so there must be an attempt to mute the impact of their message in this medium.

b) *Magazines*   Magazines are a targeted medium that will provide Schick Quattro certain efficiencies when reaching the primary target market. For the younger half of the primary target, titles such as *Maxim* and its clones offer potential, as do sports and outdoor magazines. For the older half of the target market, men's magazines and general interest magazines offer effective reach.

c) *Outdoor Posters*   The target market is time-pressed and on-the-go. Therefore, outdoor posters are an ideal medium for reaching the target while they are travelling around town. The habitual nature of one's travel patterns, either to and from school or to and from work, means the Schick Quattro message will be seen repeatedly through the course of a week. Outdoor posters offer effective reach and frequency among males in the target market and are an ideal medium for emphasizing the brand name and showing what the package looks like.

d) *Newspapers*   Daily newspapers are recommended since they deliver high reach in major urban markets across Canada. Since the primary target has a sports orientation, placing the ad on sports pages is important but not mandatory. Newspapers will be used only in the launch phase and will carry a trial purchase incentive.

e) *Online Communications*   Web-based communications via a website and banner advertising and sponsorships on third-party sites provide a means of communicating detailed information about Schick Quattro. A more complete story about Schick Quattro can be communicated at the website (the story behind the story!). All other forms of advertising will include the website address. The domain name address is **www.schickquattro.com**. Banner advertising and sponsorships will be pursued on sites that the primary target visits frequently. Such sites include TSN and Sports Net.

Media Rejection Rationale   Radio was not recommended because the product and package would not be visible. The futuristic looking design of the product and package are essential elements for achieving the awareness and brand recognition objectives.

MEDIA EXECUTION

For a summary of the media expenditures by medium and time of year refer to the Exhibits Section at the end of this plan. The budget has been effectively allocated between media advertising and various sales promotion activities.

Sales Promotion Plan

CONSUMER PROMOTION OBJECTIVES

1. To generate awareness and interest for the new Schick Quattro among the primary target market
2. To encourage first time purchases of the Quattro shaving system

TRADE PROMOTION OBJECTIVES

1. To secure listings in key retail accounts across Canada
2. To stimulate merchandising support (retail product advertising, special prices, and display activity) during the launch phase of the campaign

PROMOTION STRATEGY

Since this is a new product launch, equal attention must be given to pull and push strategies. To encourage trial purchases, coupons will be distributed through daily newspapers in the initial launch phase of the campaign. To generate interest among the younger portion of the target market a product sampling (product seeding) campaign will be implemented. Putting product in the hands of influencers will help generate some buzz among younger target members.

To secure product listing and encourage merchandising support, adequate funds will be allocated to trade promotions. Funds will also be allocated for the production of point-of-purchase materials that can be used at shelf locations or on displays.

PROMOTION EXECUTION

Coupons   A trial coupon ($1.50 value) will be issued in the newspaper launch advertisement. The launch ad and coupon will appear in newspapers in Canada's Top 10 urban markets.

Product Seeding (Sampling)   To generate some buzz about the Schick Quattro, a seeding campaign will be implemented among all major Junior A hockey teams across Canada. Junior teams consist of players between the ages of 16 and 20 years. A shaving kit comprising a case, Schick Quattro shaving system, and two sets of replacement blades will be given to each player on all junior teams. In the longer term Schick plans on developing a stronger relationship with major junior hockey across Canada. This is simply the start of a long-term sponsorship program that will be implemented in future years.

The cost of the initial seeding promotion is estimated to be $48 300. See the Exhibits section for details.

Trade Allowances   Sufficient funds will be allocated to secure listings in key accounts and to secure periodic merchandising support throughout the year. A sum of $425 000 is earmarked for listing allowances and trade allowances for the year. Key accounts that will be targeted include all major supermarket chains, major pharmacy chains, and the pharmacy sections of various discount department stores.

Point-of-Purchase Material   Funds will be allocated for posters and sundry other point-of-purchase materials that are appropriate for in-store product displays. A budget of $25 000 will be established for this activity.

For a summary of all sales promotion activities, their timing, and costs, refer to the Exhibits section of this plan.

Exhibits

EXHIBIT 1   **Television advertising**
All spots are 30 seconds in length.

Network	# of Spots	Cost/Spot	Total Cost
CBC—HNIC	24	$20 000	$480 000
CTV—Prime Time	24	12 000	288 000
TSN—Prime Time	48	3 000	144 000
RDS—Prime Time	48	1 000	48 000
Total	**144**		**$960 000**

EXHIBIT 2   **Outdoor advertising**

Outdoor ads are horizontal posters (Viacom or Pattison Outdoor).

Market	GRPs	Weeks	Total Cost
Toronto	50	4	$178 968
Montreal	50	4	118 936
Vancouver	50	4	71 225
Ottawa-Hull	25	4	33 920
Edmonton	25	4	18 332
Calgary	25	4	20 608
Quebec City	25	4	19 512
Winnipeg	25	4	9 869
London	25	4	9 387
Halifax	25	4	6 440
St. John's	25	4	4 200
Total			**$491 397**

EXHIBIT 3   **Magazine advertising**

All magazine ads are four-colour.

Magazine	# Insertions	Cost/Insertion	Total Cost
Maclean's	5	$31 300	$156 500
Maxim	5	26 600	133 000
UMM	2	8 200	16 400
Toro	3	16 200	48 600
Total	**15**		**$354 500**

EXHIBIT 4   **Newspaper advertising**

All newspaper ads are 900 lines black and white. Launch ad will run once in each newspaper.

Market/Newspaper	Line Cost	Total Cost	Circulation
Toronto Star	19.16	$17 244	463 840
Toronto Sun	7.91	7 119	201 612
Montreal Gazette	6.13	5 517	140 503
Montreal Journal de Montreal	9.31	8 379	262 160
Vancouver Sun	10.15	9 135	183 171
Vancouver Province	10.15	9 135	160 681
Ottawa Citizen	7.01	6 309	130 431
Ottawa Sun	3.58	3 222	50 766
Calgary Herald	5.49	4 941	110 236
Calgary Sun	4.28	3 852	65 279
Edmonton Journal	7.55	6 795	128 204
Edmonton Sun	4.28	3 852	69 346
Quebec Journal de Quebec	5.00	4 500	97 178
Winnipeg Free Press	5.81	5 229	117 625
Winnipeg Sun	2.64	2 376	43 770
Hamilton Spectator	5.79	5 211	104 037
London Free Press	4.99	4 491	94 097
Total		**$107 307**	**2 422 936**

EXHIBIT 5   **Online advertising**

Banner ads on the TSN website will be linked to the Schick Quattro site.

Site	Impressions/Month	CPM	Cost	# of Months	Total Cost
TSN.ca	1 000 000	$40.00	$40 000	4	$160 000

EXHIBIT 6 **Media expenditures by market**

National media comprises network television, national magazines, and online advertising. Key market media comprises outdoor posters and daily newspapers.

Market	$ Expenditure	% of Total	% of Key Markets
National Media	1 474 500	71.1	
Key Market Media	598 704	28.9	
Total	**2 073 204**	**100.0**	
Key Markets			
Toronto	203 331		34.0
Montreal	132 832		22.2
Vancouver	89 495		5.0
Ottawa-Hull	43 451		7.2
Calgary	29 401		4.9
Edmonton	28 979		4.8
Quebec City	24 012		4.0
Winnipeg	17 474		3.0
London	13 878		2.4
Hamilton	5 211		0.8
Halifax	6 440		1.0
St. John's	4 200		0.7
Total	**598 704**	**100.0**	**100.0**

EXHIBIT 7   **Expenditures by medium**

Medium	Expenditure	% of Total
Television	$ 960 000	46.3
Outdoor	491 397	23.7
Magazines	354 500	17.1
Internet	160 000	7.7
Newspapers	107 307	5.2
Total	**$2 073 204**	**100.0**

EXHIBIT 8 **Media expenditures by month**

Approximately half of the budget (49.6 percent) will be spent during the launch period January to March.

Month	Expenditure	% of Total
January	$ 517 997	25.0
February	298 807	14.4
March	210 600	10.2
April	186 600	9.0
May	191 300	9.2
June	48 200	2.3
July	31 300	1.5
August	42 800	2.0
September	87 500	4.2
October	152 200	7.3
November	137 900	6.7
December	168 000	8.2
Total	**$2 073 204**	**100.0**

EXHIBIT 9 **Coupon promotion expenditures**

An on-page coupon with a face value of $1.50 will accompany the launch newspaper ad in all key markets.

Coupon Value	$1.50
Circulation (All daily newspapers)	2 425 000
Redemption Rate (Estimate)	1.5%
Handling Charges	$0.15
Cost of Coupon Offer	**$60 020**

Note:

Circulation × redemption rate × face value and handling fees = cost of coupon offer
2 425 000 ×.015 × $1.65 = **$60 020**

EXHIBIT 10 **Total sales promotion expenditures**

Activity	Cost
Coupon Offer	$ 60 020
Product Seeding—Junior A Hockey 46 teams × 30 units × $35.00	48 300
Trade Promotions—Listing Allowances and Trade Allowances	425 000
Point-of-Purchase Material	25 000
Total	**$558 320**

EXHIBIT 11   **Total marketing communications budget**

Activity	Cost
Media Advertising	$2 073 204
Sales Promotion	558 320
Total	**$2 631 524**

EXHIBIT 12   **Plan budget vs. actual budget**

Actual Budget (Based on Activities)	$2 631 524
Plan Budget	2 600 000
Expenditure Over Budget	**(31 524)**

Sales and marketing communications budgets will be reviewed quarterly. Adjustments to the budget will be made when necessary.

EXHIBIT 13   **Blocking Chart**

Activity	Jan	Feb	Mar	Apr	May	Jun	Jul	Aug	Sep	Oct	Nov	Dec
Television												
CBC – HNIC (Sat.)				8	8						4	4
CTV Network – Prime		8	8							8		
TSN		12	12						12			12
RDS		12	12						12			12
Outdoor												
11 Key Markets	←→											
Magazines												
Maclean's		1			1		1		1		1	
Maxim	1		1	1				1			1	
UMM						1			1			
Toro		1						1				
Internet												
TSN.ca			←→			←→				←→		←→
Quattro website	←——————————————————————————————————→											
Newspaper												
10 Key Markets		←→										

Notes:

Television—Figures indicate the number of spots on *CBC Hockey Night in Canada* and other networks each month (prime time).

Outdoor—4-week flight in Toronto, Montreal, Vancouver, Ottawa-Hull, Edmonton, Calgary, Quebec City, Winnipeg, London, Halifax, and St. John's.

Magazines—Figures indicate one insertion in each month scheduled (*Maclean's* is a weekly magazine; others are monthly).

Internet—Ads will stop running when 1 000 000 impressions is reached during the months the ads are scheduled.

Newspapers—Key markets are Toronto, Montreal, Vancouver, Ottawa, Calgary, Edmonton, Quebec City, Winnipeg, Hamilton, and London.

The Schick Quattro website (**schickquattro.com**) will commence January 1, 2004. A separate budget has been established for website development and maintenance.

This marketing communications plan was compiled for illustration purposes. It is designed to show the relationship between various components of marketing communications and how they interact with each other to achieve marketing and marketing communications objectives. The plan also shows the direct relationships between objectives, strategies, and execution for the various sub-plans within. The actual plan for Schick Quattro had a budget of approximately $2 million and embraced television, radio, online advertising, and a website. A consumer sampling program tied to a contest was also part of the first year plan.

The following is a summary of relevant advertising regulations and information about the Advertising Standards Council, an organization responsible for administering regulations in Canada.

Advertising Standards Canada

Advertising Standards Canada is a national industry association committed to ensuring the integrity and viability of advertising through self-regulation. Membership in the organization consists of advertisers, advertising agencies, media organizations, and suppliers to the advertising industry.

ASC administers the *Canadian Code of Advertising Standards*, the principal instrument of self-regulation. Through regional councils, consumer complaints about advertising are accepted, reviewed, and adjudicated. ASC is also responsible for some other self-regulating codes and provides commercial clearance services for food, non-alcoholic beverages, cosmetics, and tobacco products. It also administers guidelines for advertising directed to children.

The primary Codes and Guidelines administered by ASC include the *Canadian Code of Advertising Standards, Gender Portrayal Guidelines*, and *The Broadcast Code for Advertising to Children*.

The Complaint Process

Consumers who witness advertising that is contrary to the Canadian Code of Advertising Standards must lodge a complaint in writing (emailed complaints are accepted) to one of the Advertising Standards Council offices. Complaints can be submitted by letter or by filling in a form that is available at the ASC website. All written complaints are acknowledged and reviewed, and if there appears to be a violation the advertiser will be contacted.

The critical factor in determining whether an advertisement should be reviewed is not the number of complaints received. The fundamental issue is only whether an advertisement appears to contravene the Code.

If there is an infraction of the Code the advertiser in question is notified. The advertiser can respond to the complaint. If a violation has occurred, the advertiser is asked to amend the advertisement or withdraw it. Once the advertiser has taken either of these steps, the complaint is closed and the complainant is informed in writing of the corrective action. If the complaint is not sustained, the ASC will explain why to the complainant. Occasionally, an advertiser refuses to take corrective action. In this case, the ASC will advise broadcasters and publishers carrying the ad. Usually, the media drop the ad in question.

Canadian Code of Advertising Standards

The Code was first published in 1963. It is periodically reviewed and updated when necessary. The Code sets the criteria for acceptable advertising and forms the basis upon which advertising is evaluated in response to consumer or trade complaints. It is endorsed by all members of the ASC.

For the purpose of the Code:

Advertising is defined as any message (the content of which is controlled directly or indirectly by the advertiser) expressed in any language and communicated in any medium to Canadians with the intent to influence their choice, opinion, or behaviour.

Advertising also includes advocacy advertising, political advertising, and election advertising. **Advocacy advertising** is advertising that represents information or a point of view bearing on a publicly recognized controversial issue. **Political advertising** is advertising by any part of local, provincial, or federal governments, or concerning policies, practices, or programs of such governments, as distinct from election advertising. **Election advertising** refers to advertising by political parties, a political or government policy or issue, an electoral candidate, or any other matter before the electorate.

Scope of the Code

Authority applies only to the content of advertisements and does not prohibit the promotion of legal products or services or their portrayal in circumstances of normal use. The context and content of the advertisement and the audience actually, or likely to be, or intended to be, reached by the advertisement and the medium/media used to deliver the advertisement are relevant factors in assessing its conformity with the Code.

The provisions of the Code should be adhered to both in letter and in spirit. Advertisers and their representatives must substantiate their advertised claims promptly when requested to do so by any one or more of the Councils. Key elements of the Code deal with:

- Accuracy and Clarity
- Disguised Advertising Techniques
- Price Claims
- Bait and Switch
- Guarantees
- Comparative Advertising
- Testimonials

- Professional or Scientific Claims
- Imitation
- Safety
- Superstition and Fears
- Advertising to Children
- Advertising to Minors
- Unacceptable Depictions or Portrayals

For complete text of the Code visit the Advertising Standards Canada website at **www.adstandards.com**.

Gender Portrayal Guidelines

Gender portrayal guidelines include a list of do's and don'ts for advertisers. The key elements of gender portrayals are as follows:

- That men and women be portrayed equally as decision-makers regarding purchases and that men and women are shown as equal participants in joint decision-making in the workplace and at home.
- To avoid inappropriate use or exploitation of sexuality (e.g., people must not be portrayed as primarily sexual or defined by their sexuality, boys and girls under 16 must not be portrayed as displaying adult sexual characteristics, and a woman's sexuality must not be used or displayed to sell a product that has no relation to sexuality).
- To avoid the use of violence or domination of one sex over the other, either with overt or implied threats or actual force.
- To portray women and men in diverse roles and in a manner that shows them as being equally competent in a wide range of activities.
- To avoid language that misrepresents, offends, or excludes women or men.

The Broadcast Code for Advertising to Children

Children's advertising is defined as paid commercial messages directed to persons less than 12 years of age. Key elements of the Code are as follows:

- Messages cannot be subliminal (e.g., they cannot be below the threshold of normal awareness).
- Characteristics such as performance, speed, and size cannot be exaggerated.
- Ads should not encourage children to buy, or ask their parents to buy, a product or service.
- The use of puppets, persons, and characters well known to children as endorsers to promote products is to be avoided.
- Prices must be clear and complete. Accessories that seem to be part of the product but must be purchased at extra cost must be clearly stated and shown.
- There will be no portrayal of unsafe situations except for specific safety messages (e.g., using flames or fire or showing extreme recreational activities).
- Advertising cannot imply that owning or using a product makes the child superior, or that without it a child will be open to ridicule or contempt.

For more complete details of gender portrayal guidelines, the broadcast code for advertising to children, and other industry regulations visit the ASC website at **www.adstandards.com**.

Other Codes and Guidelines

The following are other codes and guidelines administered by Advertising Standards Canada.

- Guide to Food Labelling and Advertising
- Advertising Code of Standards for Cosmetics, Toiletries, and Fragrances
- Guidelines for the Use of Comparative Advertising in Food Commercials
- Guidelines for the Use of Research and Survey Data in Comparative Food Commercials
- Guiding Principles for Environmental Labelling and Advertising
- Trade Dispute Procedure

Where to Write

You may obtain a free copy of the Code of Advertising Standards by writing ASC in either Toronto or Montreal:

Standards Division
Advertising Standards Canada

175 Bloor Street East
South Tower, Suite 1801
Toronto ON M4W 3R8
Tel: (416) 961-6311
Fax: (416) 961-7904
Email: **info@adstandards.com**

La division des normes
Les normes canadiennes de la publicité

4823 rue Sherbrooke ouest, Bureau 130
Montreal QC H3Z 1G7
Tel: (514) 931-8060
Fax: (514) 931-2797
Email: **info@normespub.cpm**

REGIONAL COUNCILS

British Columbia Consumer Response Council

P.O. Box 3005
Vancouver BC V6B 3X5
Fax: (604) 983-3558
Alberta Consumer Response Council
P.O. Box 2400, Station M
Calgary AB T2P 0W8
Fax: (403) 932-7008

Atlantic Consumer Response Council
P.O. Box 701 Central
Halifax NS B3J 2T3

Account director   The senior member of the account management group in an advertising agency, responsible for the agency's performance in handling client accounts.

Account executive   The liaison between the agency and client; coordinates the agency's services for the benefit of the client and represents the agency's point of view to the client.

Account shifting   Moving an advertising account from one agency to another.

Account supervisor   A mid-manager in an agency who manages the activities of a group of account executives; generally takes a longer-term perspective on product advertising assignments.

Ad network   A specialist company that represents a host of websites and serves as a sales force for participating publishers. This term could apply to other media as well.

Ad-tiles   Ad messages affixed to the floor of retail stores. Also called *floor advertising*.

Advertising   A paid form of marketing communication designed to stimulate a positive response from a defined target market.

Advertising manager   Generally, the individual in the client organization responsible for advertising planning and implementation.

Advertising plan   An annual planning document that outlines the advertising activities (creative and media) for the forthcoming year. The plan includes discussion of objectives, strategies, and tactics for both creative and media plans.

Advertising research   Any form of research providing information useful in the preparation or evaluation of creative, of media alternatives, and of media usage.

Advertising share   A brand's media expenditure, expressed as a percentage of total product-category media expenditures.

Advocacy advertising   Advertising that communicates a company's stand on a particular issue (usually one that will affect a company's operations).

Affiliates   Independent stations that carry network programming.

Agate line   A non-standardized unit of space measurement in a newspaper equal to one column wide and one-quarter-inch deep.

Agency commission   Compensation that a medium pays an agency for placing advertising with the medium. Agencies use a commission system, a fee system, or a combination of both.

Agency of record (AOR)   A central agency, often used by multiple-product advertisers that use more than one advertising agency, responsible for media negotiation and placement.

Aided recall   A research situation where respondents are provided with certain information to stimulate thought.

AM (amplitude modulation)   Refers to the height at which radio waves are transmitted.

Ambush marketing   A promotional strategy used by non-sponsors to capitalize on the status and prestige of an event by giving a false impression that they are the sponsors.

Animated banners   An internet banner ad that spins or has some form of action.

Animated commercials   A commercial technique involving the use of hand-drawn cartoons or stylized figures and settings.

Answerprint   Final post-production stage of a television commercial, where film, sound, special effects, and opticals are combined and printed (final copy of an advertisement for distribution to television stations).

Appeal   The creative angle taken to motivate a consumer to purchase a particular product or service.

Approach   The initial contact with a prospect in a personal-selling situation.

Art director   The individual responsible for the visuals in an advertisement (illustrations in a print ad and storyboards in a broadcast ad).

Attitude   An individual's feelings, favourable or unfavourable, toward an advertised product.

Audience flow   In radio, the change in audience demographics based on the time of day.

Backlit poster   A luminous sign containing advertising graphics printed on translucent polyvinyl material.

Balance   The relationship between the left side and the right side of a print advertisement. Equal weight (left versus right) refers to *formal balance*, and unequal weight is *informal balance*.

Banner   On the internet, an ad that stretches across the page in a narrow band. The viewer clicks on the ad for more information. Banner ads are now available in a variety of shapes and sizes.

Banners   In outdoor advertising, large-size vinyl-painted ads that are framed and mounted on the outside of a building.

Behaviour-response segmentation   Dividing buyers into groups according to their occasions for using the product, the benefits they require in a product, the frequency with which they use it, and their degree of brand loyalty.

Billboard   (1) A common name associated with outdoor poster advertising. (2) In television, a sponsoring announcement at the beginning, end, or break of a television program.

Bleed (bleed page or bleed ad)   A situation where the coloured background of an advertisement extends to the edge of the page so that there is no margin.

Blitz schedule   A schedule characterized by heavy media spending in a short space of time (saturation), with spending tapering off over an extended period of time.

Blocking chart   A visual document usually one or two pages in length that outlines all of the details of a media execution.

Body copy   Informative or persuasive prose that elaborates on the central theme of an advertisement.

Bounce back   Advertisements and offers distributed in monthly charge account statements or with the delivery of goods purchased by direct mail.

Brand manager   An individual assigned responsibility for the development and implementation of marketing programs for a specific brand or group of brands.

Branded content   The visible placement of branded merchandise in television shows, films, and video games.

Build-up schedule   A schedule characterized by low initial media weight that gradually builds to an intensive campaign.

Bus murals   Painted advertising on the side of a bus or the tail of a bus.

Business-to-business advertising   Advertising of finished products and services that is directed at other business-es that can use the advertised items to advantage.

Button(s)   On the internet, an ad in the shape of a small square or circle.

Call centre   A central operation from which a company operates its inbound and outbound telemarketing programs.

Car cards   Print ads in racks above the windows in buses and subway cars. Also called *interior overhead cards*.

Cash refund   A predetermined amount of money returned directly to a consumer by a manufacturer after a purchase has been made.

Catalogues   Reference publications, usually annual, distributed by large retail chains and other direct-marketing organizations.

Category manager   An individual who is assigned responsibility for developing and implementing marketing programs for products grouped into the category (e.g., all laundry detergent products).

CD-ROM   A computer-based multimedia sales presentation platform.

Circulation   The average number of copies of a publication sold by subscription, through retail outlets, or distributed free to predetermined recipients.

Circulation list   A magazine subscription list that targets potential customers by interest or activity.

Clicks   A form of advertising measurement on the internet. It is a count of every time a visitor clicks on a banner ad.

Clickthrough rate   A ratio that indicates the success of an advertiser in attracting visitors to click on its ad. The formula is clicks divided by ad impressions.

Closing   In a personal-selling situation, asking for the order. If the buyer says no, the close is referred to as a *trial close*.

Cluster   The grouping of commercials in a block of time during a program break or between programs.

Clutter   (1) In broadcast advertising, the clustering of commercials together in a short space of time. (2) In print advertising, the extent to which a publication's pages are fragmented into small blocks of advertising.

CNU (Canadian newspaper unit)   A standardized newspaper format that divides a 13-inch-wide broadsheet into six columns and a $10\frac{1}{4}$-inch-wide tabloid into five columns.

Each unit has a depth of 30 modular agate lines. A broadsheet contains 60 CNUs; a tabloid has 30 CNUs.

Combination rates   Rates used for selling advertising time on independent radio stations controlled by one owner.

Comparative advertising   A form of advertising where a brand is compared with a competitive brand on the basis of similar attributes that are judged to be important to the target market.

Compiled list   A direct-mail list that is prepared from government, census, telephone, warranty, and other publication information.

Comprehensive   A mechanical art layout that has all copy and illustrations pasted precisely into place (often referred to as *camera-ready artwork*).

Concentrated media strategy   A media strategy in which a majority of media dollars are allocated to one primary medium.

Concept shop   A store-within-a-store that allows a company to showcase its full range of products in a certain area.

Consumer advertising   Persuasive communications designed to elicit a purchase response from consumers.

Consumer behaviour   The acts of individuals in obtaining and using goods and services; the decision processes that precede and determine these acts.

Consumer promotion   Promotion activity directed at consumers and designed to encourage quicker purchase response.

Content analysis   A process of recording exposure actually received as a result of public relations activities.

Contest   A consumer promotion technique that involves the awarding of cash or merchandise prizes to consumers when they purchase a specified product.

Continuity   The length of time required to ensure impact on a target market through a particular medium.

Continuity discount   A discount based on the purchase of a minimum number of designated spots over an extended period of time (usually 52 weeks).

Controlled circulation   Publications that are distributed free to individuals who fall within a specific demographic segment or geographic area.

Cookie   An electronic identification tag sent from a web server to a browser to track a person's browsing patterns.

Co-operative advertising   The sharing of advertising costs and materials by suppliers and retailers or by several retailers.

Co-operative direct mail   Mailings containing specific offers from non-competing products (e.g., coupons, samples, subscription offers).

Copywriter   The individual responsible for developing the headline, body copy, and signature in a print advertisement, or the script in a broadcast ad.

Corporate advertising   Advertising designed to convey a favourable image of a company to its various publics.

Coupons   Price-off incentives offered to consumers to stimulate quicker purchase of a designated product (coupons are usually product-delivered or media-delivered).

Coverage   The percentage of individuals reached by a publication in a specific geographic area.

CPM (cost per thousand)   Cost of delivering a message to 1000 individuals.

Creative boutique   An advertising agency that specializes in the development of creative concepts and executions.

Creative brief   A document prepared by the client for the agency that outlines all relevant information pertaining to a new creative development assignment.

Creative concept   The central theme, or basic sales message, that an advertisement communicates through verbal and visual devices.

Creative department   The department in an advertising agency that provides creative services such as copy and art.

Creative execution   A more precise definition of creative strategy (i.e., tactical considerations regarding the best way to present products for maximum impact, such as celebrity spokespersons, dramatizations, and use of colour).

Creative objectives   Clearly worded statements that outline the basic content of an advertising message (i.e., brand name and benefits that are of high interest to potential buyers).

Creative research   Evaluating and measuring the impact of an advertising message on a target market.

Creative strategy   Clearly worded statements that provide direction regarding how the message will be presented. Such statements usually consider appeal techniques, tone, style, and theme.

Cross coupon (cross-ruff)   One product carrying a coupon offer for another product (often done by complementary products, such as coffee and biscuits).

Cross sampling   One product carrying a free sample of another product.

Cross-marketing   A strategy in which two independent organizations share facilities and/or resources to market their goods to similar customers.

Custom-designed research   Primary research that focuses on resolving a specific problem or obtaining specific information.

Customer relationship management   A practice designed to attract, cultivate, and maximize the return from each customer a company does business with.

DAR (day-after recall)   Research conducted the day following the respondent's exposure to a commercial message to determine the degree of recognition and recall of the advertisement, the brand, and the selling message.

Data mining   The analysis of information that establishes relationships between pieces of information so that more effective marketing and communications strategies can be identified and implemented.

Database marketing   A system for analyzing data contained in a database concerning customers and prospects, for the purpose of identifying new target markets and opportunities and preparing marketing and communications plans targeted to the customers most likely to buy.

Daypart   A block of time during the day, in a station or network's daily programming schedule, used to distinguish viewing and listening patterns.

Dealer premium   An additional incentive (usually merchandise) offered to a distributor by a manufacturer to encourage special purchase or to secure additional merchandising support from a retailer.

Delayed payment incentive   The granting of a grace period during which no interest or principal is paid on a purchased item.

Demographic segmentation   The process of dividing a large market into smaller segments on the basis of various combinations of age, sex, income, occupation, education, race, and religion.

Department maker (POP)   An elaborate, often permanent merchandise display unit (store-within-a-store concept).

Dialogue copy   Messages delivered from someone's point of view.

Direct advertising   A form of media advertising that communicates messages directly to marketing prospects.

Direct mail   A form of direct advertising that uses the postal service as the vehicle for delivering the message.

Direct marketing   A marketing system, controlled by the marketer, whereby products are developed, then promoted to a variety of end users through a variety of media options, and then distributed to the customer.

Direct-response advertising   Advertising through any medium (mail, television, telephone, or fax) designed to generate a response that is measurable.

Direct-response print   A response-oriented message delivered to prospects by magazine or newspaper advertisements.

Direct-response television (DRTV)   Television advertising that has two distinct formats: the 30-, 60-, or 120-second spot and the 30-minute infomercial.

Direct segmentation   Targeting customers on an individual basis.

Display advertising   Advertising that appears anywhere in a newspaper, excluding the classified section.

Display cards (POP)   Small advertisements located at the point of purchase (shelf talkers, tear-off ad pads, counter posters) that are designed to encourage impulse purchases.

Double truck   In newspaper advertising, an ad that covers an entire double page spread.

Display shipper (POP)   A shipping carton containing a predetermined amount of merchandise that, when assembled, will form a temporary display at the point of purchase.

Door cards   In subway cars, ads positioned on both sides of the exit doors.

Double targeting   Devising a single marketing strategy for both genders or an individual strategy for each of the genders.

Efficiency   The relative cost effectiveness of a particular medium, based on CPM.

Electronic coupons   Discounts offered at point-of-purchase after a transaction has been made.

Email   A means of communication on the internet. It is a cost-effective way for companies to communicate with customers and prospects.

Endorsement   A form of advertising that uses a celebrity (e.g., rock star, television personality, sports star) to present the product message.

End-product advertising   Advertising by a firm that makes part of a finished product (e.g., Kodak advertises the benefits of processing film on Kodak paper).

Even schedule   The purchase of media time and space in a uniform manner over an extended period of time.

Event marketing   The process, planned by a sponsoring organization, of integrating a variety of communication elements behind an event theme.

Event sponsorship   The financial support of an event by a sponsor in return for advertising privileges associated with the event.

Event-oriented advertising   Retail advertising that revolves around a central theme that a target market will find appealing, such as an annual midnight-madness sale.

Execution (tactics)   Action plans that outline specific details of implementation.

Exterior bus poster   A poster-type advertisement appended to the side or rear section of a bus.

Eye-camera test   A test whereby a hidden camera records eye movement to gauge the point of immediate contact in an advertisement, how a reader scans the ad, and the amount of time spent reading.

Fade   An optical effect in a television commercial, whereby one scene gradually disappears and another gradually appears.

Family life cycle   The stages an individual progresses through during a lifetime (bachelor stage to solitary survivor).

Feature sheet   A sheet, commonly used in radio personality announcements, that provides the station with the key benefit and the slogan for the product advertised. The DJ develops the specific message wording from the sheet.

Flexform advertising   An advertisement that does not conform to normal shapes (an odd-shaped ad designed to stand out from traditional square advertising spaces in a newspaper).

Flexibility   The ability to modify media spending plans throughout the media spending (planning) period.

Flights (or flighting)   Refers to the purchase of media time in periodic waves of advertising, separated by periods of total inactivity.

Flow   The reader's eye movement (e.g., from left to right and from top to bottom) when reading an advertisement.

FM (frequency modulation)   The speed at which waves travel, in thousands of cycles per second (kilohertz).

Format   A term that, in the context of radio, describes the nature of the programming done by an individual station.

Fragmentation   A situation where a television or radio station audience has numerous stations to choose from.

Freelancer   A self-employed, independent creative specialist (e.g., a graphic artist, a copywriter, or an art director).

Free-standing insert (FSI)   Preprinted ads that are inserted loose into newspapers.

Frequency   The average number of times an audience is exposed to an advertising message over a period of time, usually a week. Also called *average frequency*.

Frequency discount   A discount based on a minimum number of spots purchased over a specified period of time.

Frequent-buyer program   A promotion strategy that provides consumers with a small bonus, such as points or play money, when a purchase is made. These incentives are intended to encourage loyalty toward a product or company.

Fulfillment costs   The costs to receive and fill orders received by direct-marketing techniques.

Full-service agency   An advertising agency that provides a complete range of services to the client (i.e., creative and media planning, marketing research, sales promotion, and, possibly, public relations).

Game (instant win)   A promotion that includes a number of predetermined, pre-seeded winning tickets.

Gatefold   A printed magazine advertisement that consists of a series of folded pages, with the folded pages conforming to the publication's page size.

Geographic segmentation   The process of dividing a large geographic market into geographic units (e.g., Canada is divided into the Maritimes, Quebec, Ontario, the Prairies, and British Columbia).

Grid card   A broadcasting price schedule that quotes different price levels, depending on certain criteria such as demand for time, frequency of advertising, volume of advertising, and time of year.

Grocery cart advertising   Advertising (small posters) appended to the ends of shopping carts, which are visible to approaching shoppers in supermarkets.

Group head (or associate media director)   The member of the media department who carries an administrative workload and is responsible for the management of the department.

GRP (gross rating points)   An aggregate of total ratings in a schedule, as determined by reach times frequency, usually in a weekly period, against a target audience.

Guaranteed position   A specific position for an advertisement, with a premium rate charged for such positioning.

Gutter   The blank space on the inside page margins in a bound publication, or the blank space between two facing pages in a newspaper.

Hiatus   The period of time between advertising flights.

Hierarchy-of-effects model   Various theories concerning how advertising influences the behavioural stages an individual passes through prior to making a purchase decision.

Hit   Any connection to an internet site.

Home page   The initial page of an advertiser's website on the internet. A viewer who clicks on certain buttons on the home page will get more detailed information about that website.

Hooker (or tag)   The local dealer's name added to national advertisements in newspapers.

Horizontal co-operative advertising   The sharing of advertising costs by a group of retailers.

Horizontal publications   Publications appealing to people who occupy the same level of responsibility in a business.

Horizontal rotation   The placement of radio commercials based on the day of the week.

Horizontal split   A situation in the layout of a print advertisement where the page is divided across the middle, with an illustration in one half and copy in the other.

House list   An internal customer list.

House organ   A document that outlines news and events about an organization and its employees.

Impressions   In online advertising, the number of times a banner image is downloaded to a page being viewed by a visitor.

Impressions   The total audience reached by a media plan. Often referred to as "total exposures," impressions are calculated by multiplying the number of people who receive a message (reach) by the number of times they receive it (frequency).

Inbound telemarketing   The reception of calls by the order desk, or customer inquiry and direct-response calls generated from toll-free telephone numbers.

Industrial advertising   Advertising of products that are used to produce and distribute other products.

Infomercial   A long commercial (e.g., 10 to 30 minutes in length) that presents in detail the benefits of a product or service.

In-house agency   An organizational structure used in a manufacturer's or retailer's operation that handles its own advertising function; creative is developed by staff copywriters and artists; media time and space are purchased by in-house specialists; external agencies are used only as needed.

Insert   A preprinted advertisement (e.g., a leaflet, a reply card) that is specially placed in a newspaper or magazine.

Insert layout   The inclusion of a secondary visual (an insert) in a print layout.

Insertion order   A statement of specifications for an advertisement sent by an advertising agency to print media, including insertion dates, size, position, and rates.

Institutional advertising   Advertising designed to create a favourable image of a store or product in the minds of potential and current customers.

Integrated marketing communications (IMC)   The coordination of all forms of marketing communications into a unified program that maximizes the impact on consumers and other types of customers.

Interlock   The synchronizing of sound and picture for a television commercial through the use of a special editor's projector.

Internet   A network of computers linked together to act as one.

Interstitial   An ad that pops onto a computer screen during a browsing period. Often referred to as a *pop-up*.

Key-benefit statement   A statement of the basic selling idea, service, or benefit that an advertiser promises a consumer.

Key-market media plan   Purchasing media time on the basis of market priorities (i.e., on a market-by-market basis).

Kiosks   Interactive computers in stand-alone cabinets usually located in stores. The kiosk is interactive and communicates information about company products.

Layout   The design and orderly formation of the various elements of an advertisement, within specified dimensions. A layout integrates all copy elements with the illustration to create a complete message.

Lifestyle advertising   A form of advertising that attempts to associate a product with the lifestyle of a certain market segment.

Line rate   The newspaper advertising rate charged for one modular agate line.

List broker   A company specializing in finding or developing lists for direct-marketing purposes. They find prospects based on descriptions provided by marketing organizations.

Live-action commercials   Advertisements that use real-life situations with real people.

Lobbying   Activities and practices designed to influence policy decisions of governments.

Local-spot advertising   Purchase of advertising time on a station by local market advertisers.

Long copy   A copy-dominant advertisement that makes little or no use of illustration.

Long list   In the agency selection process, a listing of the advertising agencies that could potentially meet the advertising needs of a client.

Make good   A rerun of an advertisement at the publisher's expense, to compensate for an error in or substandard printing of the original insertion.

MAL (modular agate line)   A standardized unit of space equal to one column wide and one-quarter-inch deep. Broadsheet column widths are $2\frac{1}{16}$ inches; tabloids $1\frac{15}{16}$ inch.

Market discount (transit)   A discount based on the purchase of a predetermined list of markets.

Market segmentation   The process of dividing a large market into smaller homogeneous markets (segments) according to common needs and/or similar lifestyles.

Marketing communications plan   A single document that provides details for all of the components of a communications plan (e.g., advertising, sales promotion, events, public relations, internet, and so on).

Marketing control   The process of measuring and evaluating the results of marketing strategies and plans, and taking corrective action to ensure objectives are achieved.

Marketing objectives   Statements identifying what a product will accomplish over a one-year period of time.

Marketing plan   An annual planning document for a product, service, or company that includes background analysis (of the market, the product, and the competition) and objectives, strategies, and tactics for the forthcoming year.

Marketing planning   Planning activities that relate to the achievement of marketing objectives.

Marketing research   The systematic gathering, recording, and analyzing of data to resolve a marketing problem.

Marketing strategies   The process of identifying target markets and satisfying those targets with a blend of marketing-mix elements.

Marketing tactics   Detailed activity plans that contribute to the achievement of marketing objectives.

Media billings   The total dollar-volume of advertising handled by an agency in one year.

Media brief   A document prepared by a client for an agency that outlines relevant background information pertaining to the development of a new media strategy and plan.

Media buyer   A media specialist who is familiar with the competitive claims of the various media alternatives. The media buyer's primary function is to purchase media time and space for clients as efficiently as possible.

Media-buying service   An advertising agency that specializes in media planning and placement.

Media convergence   The consolidation of ownership of a variety of media outlets by relatively few companies.

Media delivery   A method of coupon distribution using various print media alternatives, including newspapers, magazines, and co-operative direct mail.

Media director   The most senior media position in an advertising agency; responsible for the management of the media department and accountable for media planning and placement for all clients.

Media mix   The combination of media used in a media schedule.

Media objectives   Clearly worded statements that outline exactly what a media plan should accomplish (e.g., who, what, when, where, and how).

Media placement   The actual purchase of media time and space once a media plan has been approved.

Media planner   A media specialist who assesses the strengths, weaknesses, costs, and communications potential of various media in order to develop a media plan.

Media planning   Preparation of a plan that documents how the client's money will be spent to achieve advertising objectives.

Media relations   In public relations, a company's ability to develop a good relationship with the media that cover their particular industry.

Media strategy   Strategic recommendations showing how media objectives will be achieved.

Media supervisor   A senior-level media specialist who supervises the activities of media planners and buyers.

Merge/purge   The process of purchasing lists, combining them, and then stripping them of duplicate names.

Mission statement   A statement of purpose for an organization that usually reflects the organization's operating philosophy.

Mixed interlock   The addition of sound effects and music to the interlock.

Mixed tape   The finished radio commercial tape containing the spoken words, music, and special effects.

Modular agate line (MAL)   A standardized unit of space measurement in a newspaper equal to one column wide and one-quarter-inch deep. A modular agate line is wider than an agate line.

Modular display rack (POP)   A permanent display unit, provided by a manufacturer, to display a certain line of merchandise.

Motives   Conditions that prompt action to satisfy a need (the action elicited by marketing and advertising activity).

Multiple illustration   In a print advertisement layout, the use of many individual illustrations in sequence.

Narrative copy   Messages presented in the third person.

Narrowcasting   Specialized programming designed to attract a narrowly defined target market (a special age or interest group).

National advertising (or general advertising)   Advertising of a trademarked product or service wherever that product or service is available.

Needs   A state of deprivation—the absence of something useful.

Network advertising   Advertising that comes from one central source and is broadcast across the entire network of stations.

Noise   Competitive advertising messages aimed at a specific target market.

Objection(s)   An obstacle that a salesperson must confront and resolve if a sales transaction is to be completed.

Objectives   Statements outlining what is to be accomplished in a plan (corporate, marketing, or advertising plan).

Omnibus study (syndicated service)   Research data collected by, or available to, participants in a common study (the Print Measurement Bureau databank, for example, provides such studies).

Online advertising   The placement of electronic communication on a website, in email, or over personal communications devices connected to the internet.

Opinion-measure testing   A form of research yielding information about the effect of a commercial message on consumers' brand-name recall, their interest in a brand, and their purchase intentions.

Optimizer   A software program that searches a media database(s) to identify media combinations that increase target reach or reduce the cost of buying it.

Outbound telemarketing   Telephone and telefax calls a company makes to a customer to develop new accounts, generate sales leads, and even close a sale.

Outdoor advertising   Advertising that is directed at vehicular or pedestrian traffic (e.g., posters or billboards, backlit posters, transit-shelter advertising, and mall posters).

Pace (television)   Designing message content so that it falls within the time parameters of the commercial—usually 15, 30, or 60 seconds.

Package plans   Discounted rate plans that combine prime-time spots with fringe time and daytime spots.

Pass-along reader (secondary reader)   A person who reads a magazine after having received it secondhand.

Perception   How individuals receive and interpret messages (three levels have been defined: selective exposure, selective perception, and selective retention).

Performance allowance   An additional trade discount (beyond a trade allowance) used to encourage retailers to perform a specific merchandising function.

Permission-based email   A situation where an individual agrees to accept email advertising and marketing offers.

Personal selling   A personalized form of communication that involves a seller presenting the features and benefits of a product or service to a buyer for the purpose of making a sale.

Personality announcement   In radio, a situation where the disc jockey presents a commercial message in his or her own style.

Planning   The process of anticipating the future business environment and determining the courses of action to take in that environment.

Point-of-purchase (POP) advertising   Advertising or display materials located in a retail environment to build traffic, advertise a product, and encourage impulse purchasing.

Pop-up coupon   A coupon printed on heavier paper stock and stitched into a popular consumer magazine (it is usually positioned directly before an advertisement for the couponed product).

Portal page When an internet banner ad is clicked on, the visitor is linked to the advertiser's website or special webpage that gives more information about the company or product.

Position charge An additional cost for requesting a particular location in a medium.

Positioning The place a brand occupies in the minds of consumers; in other words, the selling concept that motivates purchase.

Poster A picture-dominant advertisement that uses a minimum of copy.

Post-testing The evaluation and measurement of a message's effectiveness during or after the message has run.

Pre-approach An information-gathering exercise to qualify customers.

Pre-emption A situation in which a special program replaces regular programming. Advertisers of the regularly scheduled programs are rescheduled for comparable time slots at a later date.

Preferred position Requesting a specific position in a medium.

Premium An item offered free, or at a low price, to encourage consumers to buy a specific product (offered to consumers in four different forms).

Premium rates In radio, an extra charge the advertiser pays for sponsoring a special program.

Press conference The gathering of news reporters invited to witness the release of important information about a company or product.

Press release A document containing all essential elements of a story (who, what, when, where, and why).

Pre-testing Evaluating commercial messages or advertisements, prior to final production, to determine the strengths and weaknesses of the communications.

Primary reader A person qualifying as a reader who receives the publication initially.

Primary research Refers to data observed, recorded, and collected on a first-time basis with a view to resolving a specific problem.

Prime/fringe/daytime (television) In television, the basic dayparts sold—*prime time* normally runs from 7:00 p.m. to 11:00 p.m.; *fringe time* usually from 4:30 p.m. to 6:30 p.m. and 11:00 p.m. to sign-off; *daytime* from sign-on until 4:30 p.m.

Product advertising Advertising that informs customers about the benefits of a particular brand.

Product delivery A method of coupon distribution using coupons inside or on a package.

Product life cycle The path a product follows from its introduction to its eventual withdrawal from the market (a four-stage process).

Product manager (brand manager) A manager in the client organization who is assigned responsibility for carrying out the marketing planning (four Ps) for a product or a group of products.

Product placement The visible placement of branded products in television shows and commercial movies.

Profile-matching strategy Matching the demographic profile of a product's target market with a specific medium that has a compatible profile.

Promotional advertising Advertising designed to accomplish a single task—to get consumers to take action immediately.

Prospecting A systematic procedure for developing sales leads.

Psychographic segmentation Market segmentation based on the activities, interests, and opinions (the lifestyles) of consumers.

Public affairs In public relations, the development of programs and strategies to deal with governments.

Public relations The firm's communications with its various publics (shareholders, employees, suppliers, governments).

Publicity The communication of newsworthy information about a product, service, or idea.

Publisher's statement A statement of circulation data issued by a publisher to the Audit Bureau of Circulations. The statement, used in ABC's compilation of circulation data, is unaudited at the time of issue but is subject to audit by the ABC.

Pull strategy Creating demand for a product by directing promotional efforts at consumers or final users of the product.

Pulsing (or pulse media schedule) Refers to the grouping of advertisements in flights over a predetermined period of time.

Pupillometer A device that measures the pupil dilation (enlargement) of a person's eye when the person is reading.

Push strategy Creating demand for a product by directing promotional efforts at intermediaries, who in turn promote the product among consumers.

Qualitative research Data collected from a small sample size; usually the initial step in assessing target-market feedback for an idea or concept.

Quantitative research   Data collected from a much larger sample size that quantifies respondents' feelings, attitudes, and opinions.

Ratings   Audience estimates expressed as a percentage of a population in a defined geographic area.

Reach   The total audience (number of people reached) potentially exposed, one or more times, to an advertiser's message over a period of time (a week).

Reach plan (total audience plan)   A plan that involves rotating a radio commercial through the various dayparts so that the same message can reach different groups of people.

Readers per copy   The average number of people who read a single issue of a publication.

Recall testing   A test that measures an advertisement's impact by asking respondents to recall specific elements (e.g., the selling message) of the advertisement.

Recency   A media advertising model that suggests advertising works best by reminding consumers of a product when they are ready to buy.

Recognition tests   Tests that measure a target audience's awareness of a brand, of its copy points, or of the advertisement itself after the audience has been exposed to the message.

Redemption rate   Refers to the number of coupons actually redeemed. The rate of redemption for a specific coupon offer equals the number of coupons redeemed divided by the number of coupons distributed.

Reference group (or peer groups)   A group of people with a common interest who have an influence on the individual member's attitudes and behaviour. It is a group to which a person thinks they belong.

Refund (rebate)   A predetermined amount of money returned directly to a consumer by a manufacturer after specified purchases have been made.

Related recall   The percentage of a test commercial audience who claim to remember a test commercial and can provide, as verification, some description of the commercial.

Relationship marketing   Marketing strategies designed to reach customers on a one-to-one basis. These strategies are based on the collection of useful information from internal and external databases.

Reply card (business reply card)   A type of mail that enables the recipient of direct-mail advertising to respond without paying postage (encourages response).

Repositioning   Changing the place a product occupies, relative to competitive products, in the consumer's mind.

Residual   The additional payments granted to actors or models for appearing in a commercial over an extended period of time. Individuals are paid for each time the advertisement appears onscreen (during a 13-week cycle).

Response list   A list of proven mail-order buyers.

Retail advertising   Advertising by a retail store (the advertising of a store name, image, and location, and the re-advertising of branded merchandise carried by the retailer).

Retail in-ad coupon   A coupon printed in a retailer's weekly advertising, either via run of press or supplements inserted in a newspaper.

Rich media   Internet media that allow for greater use of interaction with animation, audio and video, and advanced tracking and measurement capabilities.

Rich-media banners   Banner ads that engage a viewer by means of a contest, game, or request for information.

Rifle strategy   A strategy that involves using a specific medium that effectively reaches a target market defined by a common characteristic.

Roadblocking   Buying up space at the same time on many stations and programs so that the viewers can barely avoid seeing the commercial.

ROP (run of paper or run of press)   The placing of advertisements anywhere within the regular printed pages of a newspaper.

ROP colour   A colour process printed in a newspaper during the regular press run.

ROS (run of schedule)   A discount offered to advertisers who allow the television or radio station to schedule the commercial at its own discretion.

Rotation plan   A selection of radio time slots, specified by the advertiser and based on time of day (vertical rotation) and day of week (horizontal rotation).

Rough art   The drawing of an advertisement, done to actual size and with the various elements (i.e., headline, copy, illustration, and signature) included to show relative size and position.

Rough cut   The best film takes (as shot on location or in a studio) spliced together to form the video portion of a television commercial.

Sales presentation   A persuasive delivery and demonstration of a product's benefits in a personal-selling situation.

Sales promotion Activity designed to generate prompt response from consumers, distributors, and the field sales force.

Sample Free distribution of a product to potential new users.

Satellite paper A publication whose typesetting signal is sent to distant printing facilities via satellite for regional or expanded national distribution.

Script A document used in the production of television and radio commercials. In the case of television, the script describes the video presentation on one side, the audio on the other. In the case of radio, the audio presentation, sound effects, and music are described in the script.

Seasonal discounts (television) Discounts offered to advertisers in traditionally slow seasons (television viewership drops in the summer, so additional summer discounts are offered).

Seasonal schedule A schedule whereby media spending is heavier in the preseason (to create awareness) and tapers off during the season of usage.

Secondary research The compiling and publishing of data by disinterested sources; the data are used by companies for purposes other than resolving a specific problem.

Selective media plan (rifle strategy) A plan for reaching a specific target market via a specific interest medium.

Selective-spot advertising During a network show, some commercial time is not allocated and is left to regional or local stations to sell. Advertisers can purchase this time on a station-by-station basis.

Self-concept An individual's understanding of him- or herself. (In advertising, four categories of consumer self-concept are significant: real self, self-image, looking-glass self, and ideal self.)

Shortlist A brief list of the advertising agencies that a prospective client is interested in hiring; the agencies are invited to make a business presentation to the client (to win an account).

Short rate A charge incurred by an advertiser who does not meet a contractual estimate of advertising time or space.

Shotgun strategy A strategy involving the use of mass media to reach a more loosely defined (i.e., more general) target market.

Showing In outdoor advertising, the purchase of multiple panels in a geographic market to maximize reach.

Signature The part of an ad that closes the selling message. It usually contains the brand name, logo, and slogan. It is often called a *tagline*.

Simulcasting A situation in which an episode of a U.S. network program is scheduled to appear on a Canadian station at the same time. Cable companies must carry the Canadian signal, and, therefore, viewers are exposed to Canadian advertising.

Situation analysis The compilation of internal and external data to assist in resolving a problem.

Skip schedule The purchase of media time and space on an alternating basis (every other week, month, etc.); use of alternate media types.

Skyscrapers Tall, skinny, oblong ads that appear on the side of a webpage.

Slippage When a consumer collects proofs of purchase for a refund offer but neglects to follow through and submit a request for the refund.

Social classes Hierarchically ordered groups whose members share similar values, interests, and beliefs.

Social responsibility marketing In conducting business, a firm considers the best interests of consumers and society.

Solo direct mail Individually prepared and distributed direct-mail offers. Also called *selective direct mail*.

Spam Inappropriate use of a mailing list or other communications facility as if it were a broadcast medium. Also referred to as *junk email*.

Specialty advertising A form of advertising that uses items, often clothing or small gifts, to communicate an advertiser's name, logo, and brief message.

Spectacular A non-standardized outdoor advertising unit constructed according to the customized specifications of the advertiser (often with protruding components, to attract attention).

Split 30s Two 15-second commercials for the same product, one appearing at the start and one at the end of a commercial cluster.

Split run A situation in which an advertiser splits the full circulation of a newspaper to test two different advertisements—half the circulation contains one ad; the other half contains another ad. It is commonly used to test the effectiveness of different advertising layouts.

Spot television The purchase of local broadcast time on a station-by-station basis (sometimes called *selective spot*).

Stair risers Ads that appear on the sides of steps in subways.

Starch readership test   A post-test recognition procedure that measures readers' recall of an advertisement (noted), their ability to identify the sponsor (associated), and whether they read more than half of the written material (read most).

Statement stuffers (bounce backs)   Advertisements that are distributed by monthly charge account statements.

Station posters   Advertisements located on platforms and entrance and exit areas of subway and light rail transit systems.

Storyboard   A set of graphic renderings in a television-frame format, accompanied by appropriate copy, depicting what a finished commercial will look like.

Strategic alliance   A relationship between two or more companies who decide to work co-operatively to achieve common goals.

Strategic planning   The process of determining objectives and identifying strategies and tactics that will contribute to the achievement of objectives.

Strategies   Statements that outline how objectives will be achieved.

Subculture   Subgroups of a larger culture that have distinctive lifestyles, yet maintain important features of the dominant culture.

Subheadline (subhead)   A smaller headline that amplifies the main point of a headline.

Super   A print message superimposed on a television frame.

Superboard (bigboard)   In outdoor advertising, a much larger outdoor poster that is more expensive to produce.

Superbus   A bus completely painted so that it displays an advertising message.

Supplements   Prepaid and preprinted advertisements inserted into the folds of newspapers (commonly used by large department store chains).

Support-claims statement   A statement describing the principal characteristics of a product or service that substantiate the promises made about the product in the key-benefit statement.

Sweepstakes   A chance promotion involving a giveaway of products or services of value to randomly selected participants.

SWOT analysis   An evaluation of a brand's (company's) strengths, weaknesses, opportunities, and threats.

Tagline   An alternative expression for the signature portion of an advertisement. Usually includes the brand name, a distinctive logo, and a slogan.

Target market (or target audience)   A specific group of individuals at whom an advertising message is directed.

Tear sheet   A page supplied to an advertiser by a newspaper that carries the advertiser's insertion; the tear sheet verifies that the advertisement ran as scheduled.

Telemarketing (and telefaxing)   Advertising that uses telecommunications to promote the products and services of a business.

Testimonial   A form of advertising in which a credible source, usually a typical consumer, presents the product message.

Text messaging   The transmission of text-only messages on wireless devices such as cell phones and personal digital assistants.

Thumbnail sketches   Small, experimental sketches of a variety of design concepts.

Tipping   Gluing items into the seam (gutter) of a magazine (e.g., recipe pamphlets or small catalogues).

Torture test   An advertising technique whereby a product is exposed to extremely harsh punishment in a commercial to substantiate a claim.

Total paid circulation   In print, the total of all classes of a publication's distribution for which the ultimate purchasers have paid (single-copy sales plus subscription sales).

Total-paint buses   Buses whose exteriors have been totally painted to carry an advertising message. Also called a *superbus*.

Trade advertising   Advertising by manufacturers directed at channel members to secure distribution of the advertised product.

Trade allowance   A temporary price reduction intended to encourage larger purchases by distributors.

Trade promotions   Promotion activity directed at distributors and designed to encourage volume purchases and merchandising support for a manufacturer's product.

Trade show   An event that allows a company to showcase its products to a captive audience. Buyers visit trade shows to seek new information; hence, the show is a means for a company to generate leads.

Transient rate The base rate, or open rate, charged to casual advertisers in a newspaper; it is the maximum rate charged.

Transit cards (or car cards) Print advertisements contained in racks above the windows of public-transit vehicles.

Trial close A failed attempt at closing a sale.

Triples Three transit shelter ads placed side-by-side, giving advertisers more impact capability.

Unaided recall A research situation where respondents are provided no information to encourage thought.

Unity (print) The blending of all elements in a print advertisement to create a complete impression.

Unity (television) The visual and aural flow of a broadcast commercial, from the customer's perspective.

USP The unique selling points of a particular brand.

Vertical co-operative advertising The sharing of advertising costs between a supplier and a retailer.

Vertical publications Publications that reach people with different jobs in the same industry.

Vertical rotation The placement of radio commercials based on the time of day.

Vertical split A type of print advertisement layout in which copy dominates one side and illustration the other—left and right sides are divided by an imaginary line down the middle of the page.

Virtual advertising The insertion of electronic images such as signs, logos, and packages into live or taped programs.

Visit A sequence of hits made by one user at an internet site.

Voice-over Spoken copy or dialogue delivered by an announcer who is heard but not seen.

Volume discount A discount that is based on the dollar volume purchased over a 52-week period.

Web browser A software program that allows the user to navigate the World Wide Web.

Website A company's location on the internet. A website provides a company the opportunity to communicate information about itself, including words, graphics, video clips, and audio clips.

White space The part of an advertisement that is not occupied by any elements.

Wild postings Ads that appear on the sides of hoardings at construction sites (often in downtown areas).

Wipe An optical effect in a television commercial that involves one scene pushing the other away.

World Wide Web The collection of websites on the internet.

Zapping The practice of switching channels by means of a remote control device to avoid commercial messages.

Zipping A method of reducing commercial viewing that involves using the fast-forward device on a VCR while watching a prerecorded program.

Index